NOCTURNAL SEEING

Cultural Memory in the *Present*

Hent de Vries, Editor

NOCTURNAL SEEING

Hopelessness of Hope and Philosophical Gnosis in Susan Taubes, Gillian Rose, and Edith Wyschogrod

Elliot R. Wolfson

STANFORD UNIVERSITY PRESS
Stanford, California

Stanford University Press
Stanford, California

©2025 by Elliot R. Wolfson. All rights reserved.

Printed in the United States of America on acid-free, archival-quality paper.

Library of Congress Cataloging-in-Publication Data
Names: Wolfson, Elliot R., author.
Title: Nocturnal seeing : hopelessness of hope and philosophical gnosis in Susan Taubes, Gillian Rose, and Edith Wyschogrod / Elliot R. Wolfson.
Other titles: Cultural memory in the present.
Description: Stanford, California : Stanford University Press, 2024. | Series: Cultural memory in the present | Includes bibliographical references and index.
Identifiers: LCCN 2024012304 (print) | LCCN 2024012305 (ebook) | ISBN 9781503640665 (cloth) | ISBN 9781503640962 (paperback) | ISBN 9781503640979 (epub)
Subjects: LCSH: Melancholy (Philosophy) | Ethics, Modern—20th century. | Philosophy, Modern—20th century. | Jewish philosophy—20th century.
Classification: LCC B825.4 .W65 2024 (print) | LCC B825.4 (ebook) | DDC 121—dc23/eng/20240603
LC record available at https://lccn.loc.gov/2024012304
LC ebook record available at https://lccn.loc.gov/2024012305

Cover design: Lindy Kasler
Cover painting: Ellliot R. Wolfson, *Chiaroscuro*, oil, 36 x 36 in.

in memory of genevieve

    moonlight
    descending
    on clouds
    indissoluble
    thwarting
    deathshadow
    ominously
    luminescent

Just don't overestimate what I've written, in that way
I make what is to be written unattainable.
—Franz Kafka, *Diaries* (March 26, 1912)

When I say something it immediately and definitively loses its importance,
when I write it down it always loses it too, but sometimes gains a new one.
—Franz Kafka, *Diaries* (July 3, 1913)

In the genius, God speaks and listens for the contradictions of language.
—Walter Benjamin, "The Metaphysics of Youth"

To understand a thing is a bridge and possibility of returning to
the path. But to explain a matter is arbitrary and sometimes even
murder. Have you counted the murderers among the scholars?
—Carl G. Jung, *The Red Book: Liber Novus*

Contents

INTRODUCTION
Together Apart 1
Melancholia and the Solitude of Philosophic Meditation

1. Brokenness of Being and Errancy of Ontological Untruth ... 19
   Susan Taubes's Joyful Suffering

2. Between Athens and Jerusalem 67
   The Dubious Certainty of Gillian Rose's Broken Middle

3. Death and the Infinitization of Finitude 116
   Edith Wyschogrod's Heterological Hermeneutic

4. Melancholic Redemption and the Hopelessness of Hope ... 158

Notes 199
Bibliography 321
Index 357

NOCTURNAL SEEING

INTRODUCTION

Together Apart
Melancholia and the Solitude of Philosophic Meditation

I am light; oh that I were night! But this is my loneliness, that I am girded by light.
—Friedrich Nietzsche, *Thus Spoke Zarathustra*

The mystery of pain remains veiled.
—Martin Heidegger, "What Are Poets For?"

In this monograph, I will investigate the theme of philosophical gnosis in the writings of Susan Taubes (1928–1969), Gillian Rose (1947–1995), and Edith Wyschogrod (1930–2009). To the best of my knowledge, this is the first scholarly analysis that triangulates these individuals. Lest there be any misunderstanding, let me state unequivocally at the outset that the methodology I employ in the following pages should not be construed as a comparative analysis of these three extraordinary Jewish philosophers. It is rather a juxtaposition of their thought in an effort to provide a medium through which to scrutinize the interplay of ethics, politics, and theology. Beyond the detailed examination of the literary corpora of these figures, a main objective of this book is to offer a platform to contemplate a host of theoretical issues that still have pressing practical relevance in today's perilously divisive environment, a milieu threatened, as it is, by the disintegration of claims to truth and the consequent collapse of the integrity and rectitude indispensable to securing the interdependence of individual and community.

All too often, as we have seen in public debate and various forms of social media, frequently cloaked under the cover of anonymity or pseudonymity, the deterioration of political discourse has brought about the dissolution of the inexorable need of the self to respond empathetically to the other and the collateral devolution of civility into reckless violence in word and in deed. Additionally, from an ecological perspective, the disregard of the nonhuman other is epitomized in the exploitation of natural resources that has led to the increasingly ominous premonition that our time is one in which time is running out. The indisputable decline in the ecosystem has triggered the trepidation that we are living not only in anticipation of but already in confrontation with a future when humans may be without the universe we presently inhabit and the universe may be without humans as we are currently constituted.[1] To make matters worse, the process of dehumanization has been exponentially augmented by the bifurcation of human intelligence and artificial intelligence even though the latter is patently the technological invention of the former.[2]

The bond that ties together the diverse and multifaceted worldviews promulgated by Taubes, Rose, and Wyschogrod is the mutual recognition of the need to enunciate a philosophical response to the calamities of the twentieth century, a response rendered all the more urgent by the vexing fact that in the twenty-first century, an age that extols difference and tolerance, invariably there is a difference that is tolerated only as intolerable, reinforced by an obsession with heterodox diversity that has menacingly evolved into an orthodox uniformity and an allegiance to liberalism that has too often fostered an illiberalism to dissenting voices. The complex musings of the women discussed in this book steadfastly resist simplification and popularization, but it is nonetheless striking that their respective philosophies have the potential to enhance our moral sensitivity in the present and to encourage participation in the ongoing struggle for meaning and decency, alerting us to the hazard of the homogeneous commitment to a heterogeneity that engenders the marginalization of anyone who stubbornly defies integration into the body that professes to exclude none but those who do not wish to be included. Moreover, in the writings of these philosophers, one can unearth an incontrovertible acknowledgment of the decadence and malevolence of human beings, without, however, succumbing to acrimony and disconsolateness.

Although the theorizing of each of these philosophers on melancholia and the tragicomedy of being is unquestionably intricate—exhibiting a plethora of nuances, subtle variations, and idiosyncrasies—we can identify a common denominator in their attempt to find the midpoint positioned between hope and hopelessness. In this regard, Taubes and Wyschogrod would have surely been sympathetic to Rose's surmise in *Love's Work: A Reckoning with Life*, the riveting account of her fatal illness, that the only viable counsel against sorrow is buttressed by Staretz Silouan's maxim "Keep your mind in hell, and despair not."[3] Ironically, to keep the mind out of hell, one must keep the mind in hell. Not only is success in life to be gauged by failure, but disappointment is the catalyst that exhorts one to forgive both oneself and the other in an endless cycle of reprimand and exoneration. In a religious register, as Julia Kristeva has suggested, the aforecited axiom points to the experience of *metanoia*, the process of "deep transformation," "change of spirit," or "repentance," a descent into the "memory of death," which has been compared to depressive acts related to the existentialist experience of the absurd that pervades Sartre's *Nausea*.[4] The characterization of the turning of intellect or heart to repent, which perforce is instigated by an awareness of the downfall of the spirit separated from God, goes well with Rose's evocation of the proverb of Silouan the Athonite to explain the acceptance of suffering as integral to happiness. Estrangement not only procures the possibility of reconciliation, but it is the mandatory first step in the process.

The speculative wisdom appropriated by Rose, and which I am applying to Taubes and Wyschogrod, pragmatically requires occupying the chiasm between the hope of hopelessness and the hopelessness of hope. The acquiescence that such an occupation necessitates is to be differentiated both from Thucydides's renowned declaration about the incurable human propensity for hope that unvaryingly ends in disaster and ruin,[5] and from the acerbic resignation that life is not worth living, as we find in Schopenhauer's conjecture that the human will is an aimless striving that can never be wholly satisfied, and therefore existence is an unfaltering cause of torment from which there is no emancipation.[6] Notwithstanding Taubes's eventual suicide—and the understandable inference that she finally succumbed to the judgment that the horrors of life outweigh the horrors of death, as Schopenhauer opined on an individual's decision to opt for self-destruction[7]—we should not lose sight of her impassioned proclamation that what is wrong with our existence is at once what is most precious:[8] a philosophical adage that provides the psychological antidote to the renunciation of despondency by endorsing a tragic optimism,[9] or perhaps what might be referred to as an optimistic pessimism that is concurrently a pessimistic optimism.[10] Empathizing with the suffering that her psychoanalyst father, Sándor Feldman, bore in the world, Taubes granted that "human passions are dark dark things,"[11] but in the end, to paraphrase a passage from *Lament for Julia*, one must ride both horses: the tragic and the comic.[12]

The shared agenda to face the inevitability of misfortune and to eschew promoting the cultivation of eunoia was inspired by the exigencies of the historical moment in which the three thinkers discussed in this book lived and philosophized, the second half of the twentieth century, a moment that called for reaction to the nihilism that arose in the aftermath of the cataclysm of the Holocaust, the actual deployment and continued menace of nuclear power, the lingering dominance of totalitarian ideologies, and the escalating suppression of human liberties. In one way or another, Taubes, Rose, and Wyschogrod conceived of their philosophical undertaking in light of Nietzsche's utilization in *Human, All Too Human* of the expression *times of darkness* (*Dunkel-Zeiten*) to name the situation of "all thinkers for whom the sun of humanity's future has for a time disappeared."[13] If we attend carefully to these words, we can infer that the mission summoned by such times to counterbalance the darkness is not to dispel the clouds blocking the sunlight but to peer through the obstructions so that the disappearance disappears in the dissipation of its disappearance.

Despite the many differences that distinguish these three figures, they exemplify the larger point that the philosophical sensibility is informed by a *nocturnal seeing*, which is not merely a seeing in the night—an act of visualization associated with dreams[14]—but rather a seeing of the night. But how does one see the night? Can one envision darkness as one would envision light? The task, I propose, implies the ability to fathom the unfathomable as the epistemic sine qua non of what is fathomable, to sense the sensation of limit at the limit of sensation. Alternatively, to use the language of Derrida, we can say that the philosophical ponderings of Taubes, Rose, and Wyschogrod were anchored in perceiving the nocturnal luminosity as the *"originary light, the very invisibility of visibility.*"¹⁵ The seeing of this light, which divulges the nature of nocturnality—the nonphenomenal that makes all phenomena visible by eluding visibility, the supplement that "introduces the incalculable at the heart of the calculable"¹⁶—can be viewed as a protracted critical engagement with Heidegger's supposition that history is a fallacy that of necessity emerges from the forgetfulness of being, an obliviousness that is not provoked by human negligence but belongs rather to the essential destiny of being that is concealed in the very beings in which it is revealed.¹⁷ Departing from Heidegger, as we may adduce from the three philosophers discussed in this book, it is not remembering the forgetfulness of being that is crucial to extracting significance from history, but rather commemorating the beings who have been forgotten and thereby bestowing a voice on those who have been silenced. The rejoinder to Heidegger is connected to what I have called *nocturnal seeing*, which, in contrast to the oxymoron "darkness visible"—Milton's celebrated depiction in the first book of *Paradise Lost* of the flames emitted by the furnace of hell¹⁸—is a mode of being that champions the possibility of hope in the face of an unassailable hopelessness, a beam of light that permeates the murkiness of human existence, without, however, appealing to the nostalgia for origins and the purity of self-presence or to the affirmation of the play of becoming and the world of signs entangled in a web of interpretation that has no recourse to definitive truth,¹⁹ no unmasking that does not unmask another mask to be unmasked.²⁰

Here it is apropos to recall Foucault's comment on Nietzsche's condemnation of the philosophical search for the paradigmatic depth of truth. The hermeneutical act may seem like a descent to excavate an interiority of meaning buried in the covering of a "glittering exteriority," but "the movement of interpretation is, on the contrary, that of a projection [*surplomb*], of a more and more elevated projection, which always leaves depth above it to be displayed in a more and more visible fashion; and depth is now restored as an absolutely superficial secret."²¹ The verticality of the ascent is verily a plummeting to the discovery that depth is "only a game and a surface fold. To the extent that the world becomes deeper under our gaze, we perceive that everything which elicited man's depth was only child's play."²² The infinite task of interpretation, which is propelled by the discernment that beneath the surface there is only more surface, delineates the experience that Foucault considered critical to modern hermeneutics:

The farther one goes in interpretation, the closer one comes at the same time to an absolutely dangerous region where interpretation not only will find its point of return but where it will disappear as interpretation, perhaps involving the disappearance of the interpreter himself. The existence that always approached the absolute point of interpretation would be at the same time that of a point of rupture.... What is in question in the point of rupture of interpretation, in this convergence of interpretation on a point that renders it impossible, could well be something like the experience of madness.... This experience of madness would be the sanction of a movement of interpretation that approaches its center at infinity and that collapses, charred.[23]

The nocturnal seeing of which I speak is to be sought exactly at this spot of madness where the absolute point of interpretation intersects with the point of the rupture of interpretation, and hence the interpretation of the interpretive gesture is indexical of the very impossibility of interpretation that makes interpretation possible.

The analyses of Taubes, Rose, and Wyschogrod that I offer in this book will shed light on the mandate to see darkness elucidated continuously by its own obscuration. For Taubes, night vision facilitates the wisdom to detect that perfection rests on the ability to accept imperfection unqualifyingly. The most suitable means to express this perspicacity is through the cessation of speech, albeit a cessation that is effectuated by speech attaining its own limit, as we find quintessentially in works of poetry. For Rose, the beholding of darkness entails positing an ecclesiological love situated in the broken middle between a radical universalism that effaces the particular and a radical particularism that effaces the universal. The antiutopian spirit of this middle is marked by the infiltration of the singular that mitigates against the setting in opposition of the law of the collective and the ethics of the individual. For Wyschogrod, cognizance of the gloomy depravity of the past prompts a reply that is principally ethical in nature, a form of witnessing on behalf of the deceased. Although everyone has a share in bearing witness, it is especially the responsibility of the historian to bestow a name on those who would otherwise have remained nameless and to speak of the inherently unspeakable atrocities.

Relatedly, a central concern of Taubes, Rose, and Wyschogrod—each from her own perspective—is an evaluation of the challenge that Gnosticism as world-denial presents to postmodern philosophy in its assessment of the relation of law and ethics in the sociopolitical domain, the respective merit assigned to truth and untruth in theopolitical discourse, and the viability of a secular religion centered on a radical sense of finitude and the rejection of a transcendence traditionally conceived as an eternity outside time. All three thinkers acknowledged that thinking in the time of darkness demands rejecting the misguided endeavor to envisage the fractured world as an undivided whole. The bolder and undoubtedly more risky response is to concede that there is no wholeness of which to speak but in the breach of the disjointed aggregate. The onus, then, is to accept the inchoate nature of the completeness of the incompleteness that inscribes the bookends of every individual's lifetime. A final obliteration of suffering is not possible as it would occasion the eradication of the ontogenetic pattern of gestation and corruption to which every sentient organism is subject. To be healed, accordingly, the brokenness must be broken, but the brokenness cannot be broken except by allowing the brokenness to be unbroken. We are impelled to arrogate the perfection of the imperfection that is part and parcel of the imperfection of the perfection of our indubitably flawed deportment in an impoverished world. As Nietzsche sagaciously mused, "What ultimately are the truths of humanity?—They are the *irrefutable* errors of humanity."[24]

The trialogue between Taubes, Rose, and Wyschogrod serves as a prelude to the concluding chapter, which casts their cogitations on the shattered nature of the world and the inescapable deferment of an eschatological future in the larger context of the melancholic jouissance and the diremptive temporality of Jewish messianism. The assiduous waiting for a redeemer who is coming has yielded historically the impasse of waiting for a redeemer who can come only by not coming. Translated phenomenologically, the belief in a future that is always to be realized is equivalent to the lack of belief in a future that can ever be realized. The collocation of belief and unbelief is emblematic of the composition of melancholia in which the expectation of the future is foiled repeatedly by the apprehension that the future is the duplication of the past. More broadly, we can speak of Jewish messianic speculation as proffering the elemental conception of the cadence of every moment of time as the reiteration of the novel or the replication of the disparate, the tomorrow that is presumptively today because today is proleptically tomorrow. Apocalyptic hope resides in the interval between no longer and not yet, the temporal location subject to the constant unsettling of the linear alignment of past, present, and future, and the possibility of one modality being transposed into another.[25] In spite of the disillusionment that might arise from the apparently permanent postponement of the materialization of the soteriological promise in history, its melancholic nature signifies the surplus of time that surmounts the foreboding linked to our finitude and the ubiquitous fear of the fragmentariness to which we all unavoidably capitulate. From the vantage point of this temporal deficiency, death itself is apprehended as the expiration that cannot expire whence we further extrapolate that life is the brokenness of the broken middle that cannot be mended and endure as the bearer of the existence whose contingency is necessarily dependent on that brokenness remaining intact.

Many have opined on the nexus between the philosophical disposition and the psychological-emotional condition of melancholia.[26] Needless to say, melancholy, as any and every form of malaise, cannot be abstracted from the language in which it is expressed, a language that is embedded in historically and culturally specific ways of understanding and interpreting human experience. Hence, what may appear as immediacy is in fact rhetorical construction.[27] It is likely that this is the intent of Walter Benjamin's quip, "On the melancholic's Via Dolorosa, allegories are the stations."[28] I accept the legitimacy of this hermeneutical truism, but I still accord validity to the hypothetical appraisal of the melancholic nature of philosophic reflection and the philosophic nature of melancholic rumination. Tellingly, in a letter dated May 27, 1810, to Karl Joseph Hieronymus Windischmann, Hegel confessed to having suffered from a "hypochondria," which he further described as the nocturnal point of the contraction of one's essence.[29] The two characteristics mentioned by Hegel—nocturnality and contraction—are worthy of further consideration. Melancholia belongs essentially to the dim-sightedness we associate with nighttime and the constriction of breath that calls to mind the disquiet related to the sensation—whether imagined or real—of being in a state of danger and vulnerability. But what can these qualities tell us about the vocation of the philosopher? One would assume that the lover of wisdom more typically seeks illumination and amplification of spirit, the antitheses of the properties noted by Hegel. Upon closer inspection, however, one could argue that the attainment of these qualities is only possible from experiencing their opposite. From darkness one sees light, from constraint one feels expansiveness.

The ostensible banality of this platitude can be deceiving. If the reader decodes the directive to see darkness from light and to feel expansiveness from constraint in a rectilinear progression such that one thing unilaterally replaces its opposite, the cogency of the message I am trying to communicate is obfuscated. The affliction of melancholia should be compared figuratively to the crossing of a threshold, a crossing that dictates that passing from one side to the other transpires in such a manner that the side wherefrom the peripatetic has passed cannot be totally obliterated but rather must be persistently recrossed. The threshold, on this score, is the magical locus[30] where opposites converge in their divergence and diverge in their convergence. The movement of crossing, therefore, is predicated on the seemingly illogical assumption that a thing both is and is not its opposite. The coalescence of opposites should not be understood dialectically but rather dialetheically. That is, the sameness of the antinomies consists of the preservation of their difference as opposed to the sublation of that difference in the identity of identity and nonidentity. Opposites are the same in the opposition of their sameness, and hence α and $\neg \alpha$ are discriminated with reference to the same α only insofar as they are distinguished in their indistinguishability.

Melancholia has been classified as "a deviance from the ideal of a homeostatic balance of humors in the body."[31] This may very well be the case but perhaps, when specularized through the philosophical prism, the inability to sustain an internal stability while adjusting to changing external circumstances should be related to the fact that the melancholic temperament induces a repudiation of the law of noncontradiction and thereby reclaims the middle excluded by the logic of the excluded middle wherein opposites are identical in the identity of their opposition. This way of experiencing the world gives way to an irresolvable contradiction as any statement of truth doggedly presumes the paradoxical form α and $\neg \alpha$, which translates into the disjunctive syllogism "if it is the case that α, then it is not the case that α," a direct reproach of the more prevalent logic that for every proposition either α or $\neg \alpha$ is true, but both cannot be true at the same time and in the same relation. The standard logic persists as the primary way we structure our empirical reality as it readily accommodates a sense of stability and order and allows for the postulating of the laws of physics that impose a degree of predictability on the unpredictable and enable the determination of the indeterminate and the quantification of the unquantifiable. To deny the rudimentary principle of identity—α is α and not ¬α—is demonstrably disorienting and destabilizing. And yet, one afflicted with melancholia is acclimated precisely to the impediment implied in the belief that a statement can be simultaneously true and untrue.

The assault on a binary logic seems apposite to the physiological dearth of homeostasis in one diagnosed with melancholia and the psychological oscillation that leads to the blurring of the distinction between joy and grief, elation and dejection. And here it is pertinent to recall that in the pseudo-Aristotelian *Problemata*, we are told that the fluctuation of moods associated with the melancholic humor—the black bile present in human beings—is a mixture of heat and cold: when the cold predominates, one is dull and stupid, but when the heat predominates, one is frenzied and clever, erotic and easily moved to anger and desire, and in some cases more loquacious.[32] The two ingredients of the mixture are separate, and hence the element of the black bile that is in the more extreme state prevails. Prima facie, it appears that no middle is established as an alternative to the extremes.[33] However, the vacillation from one state to its opposite must be logically grounded in the positing of an intermediate where there is a conjunction of heat and cold. Indeed, the text explicitly asserts that the black bile becomes both very hot and very cold because "the same thing naturally admits both heat and cold, like water, which, though cold, yet when it is sufficiently heated (for example, when it boils) is hotter than the actual flame which heats it, and similarly a stone or a piece of iron when thoroughly heated becomes hotter than charcoal, though they are naturally cold."[34] The melancholic condition is marked by this coincidence. To borrow the locution of Kristeva, melancholy is a mood disorder of extreme sadness described as the *black sun*,[35] an image that conveys metaphorically the regulating principle of the *mesótēs*, the middle of "the controlled interaction of opposites."[36] In this concurrence, dimness does not eclipse but rather illumines the radiance more brightly. Analogously, the philosopher—in kinship to the poet[37]—discerns darkness coiled in light and munificence enfolded in compression.

The attentiveness to the underlying unity of opposites may explain the connection between the atrabilious persona and individuals eminent in philosophy, politics, poetry, and the arts that are attested in the *Problemata*,[38] an idea reiterated in a variety of ways in the course of subsequent centuries including notably in the Renaissance philosophy of Marsilio Ficino, who highlighted the propensity of learned people to be driven by the bad effects of black bile to depression and folly.[39] Related to this motif is the delineation of the melancholic proclivity as exemplary of lucid thinking. It is worth recalling the comment made by Freud in his study "Mourning and Melancholia," completed on May 4, 1915, but not published until 1917:

> He also seems to us justified in certain other self-accusations; it is merely that he has a keener eye for the truth than other people who are not melancholic. When in his heightened self-criticism he describes himself as petty, egoistic, dishonest, lacking in independence, one whose sole aim has been to hide the weaknesses of his own nature, it may be, so far as we know, that he has come pretty near to his understanding himself; we only wonder why a man has to be ill before he can be accessible to a truth of this kind.[40]

I would add to the Freudian insight that the keener eye of the melancholic is sensitized to the gnostic myth of the fallen self who experiences truth as a dark light that cannot be extricated from untruth. Thus, commenting on Heidegger's notion of the ontological difference, rendered as *the oblivion of being is oblivion to the difference between being and the being*, Taubes wrote:

> Because the self is lost to the world and has forgotten that it belongs to Being, forgotten the difference between the world and Being, the self is in error. Since the self is essentially fallen prey to the world (*wesenhaft verfallend*), the self *is* in untruth. The untruth is the veiling of the Being. This cover is not only a darkness; it has its own light, its own presence, a "dark" light, as the gnostic myth would say.[41]

It is incumbent to stress, however, that the correlativity of truth and untruth is to be differentiated from the cynical view that there is no truth or that all truths amount to a lie. The astuteness germane to melancholia is the upholding of the premise that truth can only be disclosed through the veil of untruth and untruth through the veil of truth. The melancholic dispenses with the fiction that there can be naked truth divested of every garment, that it is possible to behold the face without any mask. Even more profound is the apperception that there is no face that is not itself a mask of the face, the upshot of which may be the acute sense of being cut off from life in its quotidian minutiae.[42] The appearance of truth is naught but the truth of appearance, which is to say, the illusion of reality debunked as the reality of illusion. Insofar as the distortion of truth is constituent of the truth, there can be no truth that is not itself grounded in the truth of distortion.⁴³ To maintain the truthfulness of there being no truth that is not concomitantly untruth is certainly prone to render problematic the more conventional forms of societal commerce and may even guide us to the point of translucence wherein the distinction between sanity and insanity is indefensible on phenomenological grounds.⁴⁴

It comes as no surprise, therefore, that loneliness and introversion have been long identified as clinical indicators of those afflicted with melancholy. As Jung succinctly noted, "Melancholics sink down into a sort of embryonic condition, therefore you find that accumulation of peculiar physical symptoms."⁴⁵ While the philosopher may not suffer the same physical agony, on the emotional scale the life of contemplation warrants a comparable severance from intersocial affairs. One is reminded of the passage in Nietzsche's *Thus Spoke Zarathustra*:

"Where is—*my* home?" I asked, and I search and searched for it, but I have not found it. Oh eternal everywhere, oh eternal nowhere, oh eternal—in vain!⁴⁶

For the thinker, the homecoming (*Heimkehr*) is a return to the home that is one's solitude (*Du meine Heimat Einsamkeit*), a home that beckons a sense of forsakenness and homelessness in the world.⁴⁷ The melancholic nature of the solitude of the philosopher was developed further by Heidegger. In the lecture course "The Fundamental Concepts of Metaphysics," given at the University of Freiburg in the winter semester of 1929–1930, building on Novalis's dictum "Philosophy is really a homesickness, an urge to be at home everywhere [*Die Philosophie ist eigentlich Heimweh, ein Trieb überall zu Hause zu sein*],"⁴⁸ Heidegger set out to explicate how homesickness is the fundamental attunement (*Grundstimmung*) of philosophizing through which we can expound the questions concerning world, finitude, and individuation, which taken together circumscribe the metaphysical dilemma of human existence, that is, the fundamental predicament that defines being human.⁴⁹ Commenting on the aforementioned definition of Novalis, Heidegger wrote:

Philosophy can only be such an urge if we who philosophize are *not* at home everywhere [*wenn wir, die philosophieren, überall nicht zu Hause sind*].... To be at home everywhere—what does that mean? Not merely here or there, nor even simply in every place, in all places taken together one after the other. Rather, to be at home everywhere means to be at once and at all times within the whole [*im Ganzen sein*]. We name this *"within the whole"* ["im Ganzen"] and its character of wholeness the *world*. We are, and to the extent that we are, we are always waiting for something. We are always called upon by something as whole. This "as a whole" is the world.... *What is that—world*? This is where we are driven [*getrieben*] in our homesickness: to being as a whole. Our very being is this restlessness [*Getriebenheit*].[50]

From Novalis Heidegger found confirmation of the idea that the philosophical comportment—whence he deduced the more general status of humankind—is one of congenital restlessness. The philosopher is perpetually adrift, and hence the urge to be at home everywhere results from the fact that he, she, or they is at home nowhere. Heidegger adds that to be at home everywhere would mean to be within the whole, which is to say, the world. However, since to be human is to be in a never-ending condition of longing, to be as a whole is experienced as the melancholic nostalgia to return home.[51]

We are driven to the world as an imaginary confabulation of wholeness, but this only underscores the insufficiency of our being, what Heidegger called in *Being and Time* the fundamental mood (*Grundbefindlichkeit*) of anxiety (*Angst*) that leaves one disoriented as the tranquility and self-assurance of "being-at-home" (*Zuhause-sein*) in the everyday world slip away and one enters the existential "uncanniness" (*Unheimlichkeit*), the sense of "not-being-at-home" (*Nicht-zuhause-sein*), an ontological conditionality in which the familiar unfailingly is experienced as unfamiliar.[52] The nature of human finitude (*Endlichkeit*) is not solely that we perish, that we come to an end, which is the fate of everything that is alive, but rather that we are incessantly underway (*Unterwegs*) or in transition (*Übergang*) such that we are continually "neither the one nor the other," relentlessly wavering to and fro. This unrest of the not (*Unruhe des Nicht*) is *our fundamental way of being* (die Grundart unseres Seins), that is, the uncertainty that marks our innermost way of "being finite" (*Verendlichung*). In becoming finite, there occurs the individuation (*Vereinzelung*) of Dasein, the solitariness (*Vereinsamung*) through which each human being "enters into a nearness to what is essential in all things, a nearness to world."[53]

Novalis's description of the urge to be at home everywhere signals the method of comprehension (*Begreifen*) by which we are gripped (*ergriffen*) in the attunement (*Stimmung*) that is the ground of Dasein. Philosophy happens in the space of this fundamental attunement.⁵⁴ Heidegger thus referred to philosophizing as the "ultimate pronouncement" in which the human being is "individuated" in relation to Dasein, a process that must be carried out in solitude in contrast to the teacher who seeks to address the masses and thus runs around "in the marketplace as a professor in public."⁵⁵ From the exceptional calling of the philosopher we learn about humanity more generally. The homesickness, the being-lonely, reveals our sense of uniqueness, the solitude of our finitude, which sheds light as well on the nature of the world whose poverty and deprivation—when viewed from the human perspective—even "belongs to the animal's being" such that pain and suffering "permeate the whole animal realm and the realm of life in general."⁵⁶ Consistent with Heidegger's earlier analysis of Dasein in *Being and Time*, the authenticity of being human is related to the submission to one's mortality, the being-toward-death, but in this later account what is accentuated is that through finitude we draw closer to the world.

Assuredly, the individuation of self by which every human being can be considered unique (*Einziger*) is accomplished in solitude (*Einsamkeit*), for, as the poet William Cowper incisively put it, "We perish'd, each alone."⁵⁷ However, as Heidegger recurrently emphasized, solitude is the means by which commonality (*Gemeinsamkeit*) can be achieved. Thus, touching on this theme in his notebooks, Heidegger wrote, "Only if and only as long as this originary *aloneness* [Alleinheit] of Dasein is experienced can true community [*Gemeinschaft*] grow indigenously; only thus is to be overcome all publicness of those who have come together and are driven together."⁵⁸ Or, as he put it another passage, "The meeting of the solitary ones [*Einsamen*] can happen only in solitude."⁵⁹ There is no question that Heidegger was committed to the conviction that "the highest discipline of knowledge-stimulated questioning" commands a great measure of sequestration,⁶⁰ and thus he recommended that when thinking and the act of meditation fall into the superficiality of the everyday, it is necessary for recollection to come as a call "by which the thoughtful mode of Dasein is withdrawn into the most extreme solitude."⁶¹ Nevertheless, the withdrawal ultimately is for the purpose of inaugurating the "site of the opening up and founding of being [*die Stätte des stiftenden Eröffnens des Seins*] and thereby also of the ground of the creative affiliation [*des Grundes der schaffenden Zugehörigkeit*]."⁶²

The criticism of Heidegger leveled by Susan Taubes—in a way anticipating the reprimand of Levinas—that he treated the self in isolation without realizing that the topics essential to his analysis of the human being, such as language, freedom, guilt, and dread, are all categories of the community that describe relations to others[63] is itself subject to critique. Taubes's rebuke of Heidegger turns on his argument that the individualizing nature of death discloses that the own-most possibility of Dasein is nonrelational (*unbezügliche*).[64] Despite the veracity of this claim, I submit that Taubes downplayed Heidegger's notion of being-with (*Mitsein*): that is, the existential structure that undergirds the capacity for relationality in his understanding of the selfhood of Dasein as the subject of everydayness (*Alltäglichkeit*), the "they" of *das Man*, which is equiprimordial with being-in-the-world (*In-der-Welt-sein*) that is shaped ineludibly by being with other Daseins (*Mitdasein*).[65]

Given the tendency to misread Heidegger on this decisive point, it is worth paying attention to his precise language in *Being and Time*:

The Dasein-with of others is disclosed only within the world, and so too for beings who are Daseins with us, because Dasein in itself is essentially being-with. The phenomenological statement that Dasein is essentially being-with has an existential-ontological meaning. It does not intend to ascertain ontically that I am factically not objectively present alone, rather that others of my kind also are [*vorkommen*]. If the statement that the being-in-the-world of Dasein is essentially constituted by being-with meant something like this, being-with would not be an existential attribute that belongs to Dasein of itself on the basis of its kind of being, but something which occurs at times on the basis of the existence of others. Being-with existentially determines Dasein even when an other is not factically present and perceived. The being-alone [*Alleinsein*] of Dasein, too, is being-with in the world. The other can be *lacking* only *in* and *for* a being-with. Being-alone is a deficient mode of being-with, its possibility is a proof of the latter.[66]

The discerning ear will hear in the assertion that Dasein-with is existentially constitutive for being-in-the-world, and thus the essential structure of being-with must be construed as an attribute of one's own Dasein[67]—encapsulated in the statement "The being-alone of Dasein, too, is being-with in the world" (*Auch das Alleinsein des Daseins ist Mitsein in der Welt*)—a foreshadowing of the idea later expressed by Heidegger that the sense of aloneness is rooted in the belief that an authentic community can only be formed on the basis of individuals resolutely fixated on their inimitable individuality. We might even go so far as to say that the Heideggerian ideas of uniqueness (*Einmaligkeit*) and singularity (*Einzigkeit*)—two terms that he often juxtaposed to demarcate the nonrepeatable univocity of being[68]—are expressive of an ontological pluralism;[69] this is not to be understood in the traditional metaphysical sense of imagining one reality that can appear in multiple guises but rather in the decidedly nonmetaphysical sense of presuming that the one is intrinsically not one inasmuch as it is configured by the polyontological difference[70] of an infinitely systemic nondifferentiation that undulates between an absolute minimum of everything dissimilar by virtue of being similar and an absolute maximum of everything similar by virtue of being dissimilar.[71] Be that as it may, the charge for the "creative ones" (*Schaffenden*) to abandon metaphysics and to arrive at beings out of the truth of beyng, or to bring beings into arrival out of that truth, can only take place in solitude,[72] but the recoil of thinking is the thread from which the web of interconnectivity is woven. The desolation of solitude, consequently, is the womb that harbors the possibility of meaningful belonging-together (*Zugehörigkeit*). Heidegger's position strikes me as parallel to what Hegel expressed in a letter to Christian Gotthold Zellman written on January 23, 1807: "philosophy has something solitary about it. It does not, to be sure, belong in alleys and marketplaces, but neither is it held aloof from the activity of men, from that in which they place their interest, nor from the [sort of] knowing to which they attach their vanity."[73] Philosophical meditation requires retreat from society not because it is detached from social concerns but because those concerns are best served by seclusion.

The desynchronizing capability of depression aligns itself with the philosopher's involvement with the natural world through the endless resolve of questioning its intelligibility. Philosophical inquiry is fueled by a skepticism that is tied to the obdurateness of our mortality and the heightened sense that the only intransient dimension of time is its transience. In the notorious words that Plato ascribed to Socrates, "true philosophers make dying their profession," and thus, since they have trained themselves throughout their lives to live in a state as close as possible to death, "to them of all men death is least alarming."[74] Death is not the mystery of the eventual inability to be but rather the aporia of the irrevocable ability to be. But how is the impossibility of the possible not impossible in light of the possibility of the impossible? At the core of these reflections is a thinking about time that seems to mark the distinctiveness of the human being on this planet. Obviously, the ravages of time affect every living entity, and thus it would be foolhardy to adopt an overtly anthropocentric view. And yet, the compulsion to impose a narrative framework on our temporal experience and the unremitting awareness of the looming demise do impart something unique about our species. Undeniably, we pass away like all other finite creatures, but the occurrence of the nonoccurrence of death is fundamentally different for human beings. The lifespan of each person is recounted from the perspective of an interminable termination—from the beginning we are moving toward the end, the moment of generation comprises the kernel of degeneration, and hence, as Hegel observed, the hour of birth is the hour of death.[75]

Paradoxically, a corollary of the permanent impermanence of our contingent existence, and the attendant realization that depreciation is not antithetical to but is rather an integral component of maturation, is that the prospect of dying does not die. The evanescence of time evinces phenomenological affinity with the melancholic susceptibility to suffer intensely the autumnal nature of the ephemerality of being and to abide fervently in the sadness that proceeds from the anguish of yearning for the presence of an absence that has never been present and thus can only be represented as nonrepresentable. The luminal bleakness of the philosophical penchant for a hermeneutics of suspicion—the duplicitous ambiguity "always suspended between an excess and a deficiency of interpretation"[76]—can be delineated, to invoke Derrida once more,[77] as the form of play that disrupts presence insofar as it exists before the alternative of presence and absence, the joyful avowal of an engrained joylessness that *determines the noncenter otherwise than as the loss of the center*, the unveiling of nothing that reveals there is nothing to reveal. It is in this sense that the veil of night becomes, in the words of Novalis, "the mighty womb of revelations."[78]

ONE

Brokenness of Being and Errancy of Ontological Untruth

Susan Taubes's Joyful Suffering

life is more true than reason will deceive
(more secret or than madness did reveal)
deeper is life than lose: higher than have
—but beauty is more each than living's all

—e. e. cummings

In a previous publication, I examined in great detail the philosophical ruminations of Susan Taubes on a variety of topics,[1] including her critical engagement with Heidegger's thought that can be elicited from the epistolic exchanges with Jacob Taubes between 1950–1952,[2] and from the essay that was published in 1954, the *urzelle* of the doctoral thesis that she eventually abandoned.[3] Building on that analysis, I will explore in this chapter Susan's astute criticism of Heidegger's *Seinsdenken* that pivots around her contention that he absolutized the nothingness of being in a manner that is analogous to but yet significantly different than the role assigned to the Godhead on the part of many mystical visionaries. The common denominator is in Heidegger's dogged concern with being to the neglect of fully engaging the patterns of life manifest in the plethora of beings that make up the world. As Susan wrote to Jacob on March 6, 1952, reflecting on the interest and sympathy for primitive myths and the rites of sacred societies:

This sounds a little like the old Heidegger (or the "new"—time runs both ways, the oldest is the youngest) except that H. sees the descent and the transtemporal moment of union when the poet names the holy as a contemplative act, as a moment in the process of "Seinsdenken". All the worse for Heidegger that the contemplative act is not merely "objective" but initiated by the Being so that everything is caught in a thinking process, everything is signification; but if there is no chaos (not just a formal "nothing") no sheer unsignificative energy, there is no genuine signification. And H.'s Seinsdenken and naming of the holy remains an empty form on paper. Let him come out dancing from his cubiculum and then I'll believe him.[4]

Susan was ahead of her time in questioning the chronoscopic temporalizing of Heidegger's work and challenging the distinction between the old and the new based on the supposition that the timeline is reversible.[5] But what is most important for our analysis is Susan's insight that Heidegger's *Seinsdenken* implicates him in a thinking process whereby everything becomes signification, the descent into the transtemporal moment of union wherein the poet names the holy as a contemplative act. As a consequence, there is no purchase on the chaotic, which falls outside the purview of what can be signified, and in the absence of the unsignifiable, there can be no signification. Reminiscent of Nietzsche,[6] Susan invoked the bodily image of dance as the marker of a trustworthy form of cogitating about being.

Skeptical Faith and Estrangement from the World

It is incontestably the case that after years of reading Heidegger intensively—even writing her honors thesis at Bryn Mawr, under the direction of Isabel Stearns, on the topic "Myth and Logos in Heidegger's Philosophy"[7]—Susan began to distance herself from both Heideggerian thought and Gnosticism; she ultimately decided to dispose of her plan to work on Heidegger for her dissertation because, as she expressed it in a letter to Jacob written on April 20, 1952, she harbored doubts about the credibility of her thesis and her competence "to show the 'gnostic' elements in Heidegger in their total historical setting."[8] As she put it in an undated letter to Jacob, presumably also written sometime in April 1952:

But the "Heideg. Categories" are certainly a re-interpretation of theological categories whether this re-interpretation can be called "gnostic" is disputable + rather a question of choice. It's certainly not the old visionary gnosis* [*and I think the gnosis is essentially visionary rather than "nihilistic" (the nihilism comes after the vision evaporates like a soap-bubble) therefore "atheistic theology" doesn't work—nor is it gnostic + the gnosis is not the key to the atheistic re-interpretation of theological categories in Sein und Zeit.]⁹

The operative, and perhaps simplistic or reductionist, understanding of Gnosticism from which Susan dissociated herself can be gleaned from another letter she wrote to Jacob on April 21, 1952:

Gnosis is after all a judgement on reality, + it is as a judgement on reality that it must be questioned + tested.... But the gnosis says "the world is bad" "the world is worth nothing". But discontent with the world contains an implicit affirmation of strictly worldly values; in the case of Christianity most common values: a world without want, work, worry, without sickness + death; a world which is all "good". The otherworldlyness [sic] of the gnosis is false only insofar [as] it is a cry against the harshness of the world + thus a secret yearning for a less harsh world—even an infantile yearning for a paradisic world.... Otherworldlyness is an ambivalent nihilism.¹⁰

Undeniably, as Jerry Z. Muller noted, in the first years of their marriage, Susan shared Jacob's "Gnostic view of the world as fundamentally evil, not to speak of banal,"¹¹ and sought to interpret Heidegger's ontological hermeneutics through that prism. However, by 1952, as the aforecited letters attest, she became "increasingly disillusioned with Heidegger and skeptical of the fruitfulness of tracing Gnostic motifs in his work."¹²

Thus, despite a longstanding battle with melancholia and the sense of dislodgment that badgered her throughout life—the psychological component that doubtlessly fed her intellectual interest in modern nihilism and "the loss of a coherent metaphysical world picture and man's growing sense of alienation and homelessness in the universe"¹³—coupled with the gnawing sensitivity to the mendacity, ignorance, adversity, and meaninglessness of life, Susan did not embrace Jacob's acceptance of the gnostic view of the world as fundamentally evil or the echoes of that conception in the Heideggerian analysis of the modalities of inauthenticity—curiosity, ambiguity, and idle talk—that prevent human beings from confronting their temporal finitude and the inevitability of death.¹⁴ As she put it in a letter to Jacob written on February 12, 1952:

But if there has been a rupture in my thinking is not so much a rupture with "gnosis" as with a certain kind of "radical" thinking in general. The experience is true; and its mythological expression in the "stranger" is authentic insofar as a human being understands his life in the image of this myth; the intellectualization of the experience leads nowhere (or anywhere) not even to suicide; it is a statement of paralysis. Insofar as the gnosis is by its nature a radical intellectualization of experience in general it is a statement of death. . . . The self revolts against the evil, the suffering, the senselessness of the world; but goodness, joy and meaning are to be found only in the world, the good is the relative, the limited par excellence. If the gnostic revolt is absolute it must in order to remain consistent negate the world as world, absolutely without reference to judgement; i.e. negate good as well as evil, meaning as well as absurdity, purpose as well as senselessness; in other words it must negate salvation and eschatology. But then it is no longer "gnosis".[15]

The displeasure with the worldview that promulgates an unqualified negation of good and evil and the indiscriminate condemnation of rational and irrational is exemplified in her comment to Jacob that she was becoming "anti-gnostic."[16] Rather than recoiling from a world deemed to be irredeemably evil, human nobility requires acquiescence to evil and good, chaos and order, torment and jubilation. Even the feeling of desperate strangeness in this world was perceived early on by Susan to serve as the catalyst to convene communion with other human beings and perhaps with all creatures in the universe.[17]

And yet, it seems to me equally indisputable that the years she was immersed in reading Heidegger through a gnostic lens, largely informed by the early work of Hans Jonas,[18] left an indelible mark. One of the areas wherein this impact is discernible is in what Susan identified as the gnostic bedrock of Heidegger's nihilism, that is, the world-negating posture that she related to his idea of *Geworfenheit*, the thrownness that marks the nullity (*Nichtigkeit*) that is the not (*Nicht*) that constitutes the being of Dasein. "The quality of this not as a not," wrote Heidegger, "is determined existentially. Being a *self* [Selbst *seiend*], Dasein, *as* self, is the thrown being [*geworfene Seiende*]. *Not through* itself, but *released* [entlassen] to itself from the ground in order to be *as the ground*."[19] In being the ground, however, Dasein "itself *is* a nullity of itself" (*Grund-seiend* ist *es selbst eine Nichtigkeit seiner selbst*).[20] Paradoxically, the existential meaning of thrownness is that Dasein is not itself the ground of its being, but it is the being whose being has to take over being-the-ground (*Grundsein*) by existing, which is to say, by understanding itself as a potentiality-of-being that stands in one possibility by relinquishing other possibilities in its existentiell project. As the thrown being, the project of Dasein is determined by the nullity of being-the-ground, and therefore it is itself "essentially *null* [*wesenhaft* nichtig]."[21] The historical era notoriously tagged by Heidegger as the "overcoming of metaphysics" signals that we stand as "thrown into the abandonment by being [*geworfen in die Seinsverlassenheit*]."[22] This abandonment by being, or the forgetting of being, is experienced as "*Estrangement* from the word the *violence* of the '*actual*' [*Die Entfremdung gegen das Wort, die* Gewalt *des* 'Wirklichen']."[23] In Susan's interpretation of this Heideggerian trope, indebted to Jonas's application of some of his teacher's anthropological thoughts to Gnosticism, thrownness bespeaks a form of alienation in the spatiotemporal realm, the dislocation of the homelessness of being at home. As she put it in the essay "The Gnostic Foundations of Heidegger's Nihilism" (1954), "Both for Heidegger and for the gnosis, thrownness expresses, beyond the manner of the self's entrance into the world, the essential violence of the self's being-in-the-world."[24]

Susan exerted much of her philosophical effort—and later her literary endeavors—to overcome the pessimism implied by this estrangement and the inherently tragic nature of being. In part, this was facilitated by her turn to the mystical atheism of Simone Weil.[25] Although highly critical of the sociopolitical underpinnings of Weil's negative theology, Susan was attracted to the assumption that experiencing the world as deprived of the divine is the religious experience par excellence, and hence the sole experience of God's presence accessible to us is the awfulness of his absence.[26] Susan was openly suspicious about Weil's attempt to reconcile gnosticism and agnosticism, but she gave her credit for delving into the depths of the finitude of our being and fighting "for the reality which is contained in the most negative situations, and which we would throw away for illusions. Thus the real pain of any grief is better than an act of violence or an imaginary revolt into which we would like to transform it in order to get rid of it."[27] Recapitulating the atheistic tenet underlying Weil's spiritual pathos, Susan wrote:

He who, seeking God, does not find him in the world, he who suffers the utter silence and nothingness of God, still lives in a religious universe: a universe whose essential meaning is God, though that meaning be torn in contradiction and the most agonizing paradoxes. He lives in a universe that is absurd, but whose absurdity is significant, and its significance is God. God, however negatively conceived, explains the world, explains the nothingness of God in the world. The thesis of religious atheism has been most boldly formulated by Simone Weil: the existence of God may be denied without denying God's reality.[28]

The roots for Weil's theology are to be uncovered in the atheistic ground that "God can be present to us only under the form of absence."[29] Even though the cross "remains the symbol of redemptive suffering it loses its specifically Christian content" and becomes "the point where gnostic revolt against the world and stoic resignation converged."[30] Effectively, according to Susan's reading of Weil, the elevation of hardship as liberating excludes the element of hope and by extension any credibility to a messianic religion based on the expectation for salvation in history and the improvement of society is undermined.[31]

In emulation of the "figure of the crucified Jesus, abandoned by God and dying without hope of resurrection,"[32] we must bear the cross of misery, confronting the absence of presence as the presence of absence. According to Susan, for Weil, as for Naḥman of Bratslav, there is no resolution to human affliction but through entreating the divine in the space from which the divine has withdrawn.[33] I submit that the paradoxical implication of this theological quandary helped shape Susan's belief that the pledge that life must go on, despite the futility of living, is the deceit that tragedy and mysticism share.[34] Tragedy so conceived is the dissolution of structure that endows the human with structure insofar as it is an assault on the very possibility of meaning that nevertheless imparts a "total interpretation of life" by concentrating "on a single action, which develops complete and self-enclosed from its own inner causality," and thus it "may be considered as an *alternative* to the mythical, philosophical or religious interpretation."[35] Precisely in the bleak negativity of the tragic, we discover pathways of positivity. Thus, in spite of many misgivings with Weil's idea of redemptive suffering,[36] Susan concurred that envisaging the spiritual destiny of humankind in terms of the idea of anguish is a worthy substitute for the Heideggerian philosophy of death.

The atheism sanctioned by Weil—the supreme pious devotion anchored in the keen awareness of the death of God—is no longer a charge leveled against skeptics insofar as it has become itself the foundation of what may be designated fittingly as *skeptical faith*, that is, belief abetted by doubt. Although Susan did not use the words "skepticism" or "skeptic" frequently, it seems to me legitimate to claim these words to name her eccentric perspective. Corroboration may be elicited from Susan's comment in a letter to Jacob written on March 11, 1952, inspired by the argument of Éric Weil that the positive must be prior to the negative because we cannot have an idea of error without an idea of truth or an idea of imperfection without an idea of perfection. Furthermore, according to Weil, the Heideggerian predicament, which comes out of a theory of knowledge that remains unexamined and therefore resistant to reason, has its source in a commitment to the ideal of revelation that is deficient insofar as it continues to presume that there is something affirmative that is revealed:

> Because the world as it is ultimately does not make sense, we hope one day to enter into the divine truth whereby the truth of everything (from which we are excluded while we live) will be revealed to us. Heidegger begins with the experience of the exclusion from the truth and rejecting positive revelation remains excluded.... The conversation brought me a little closer to myself because I see that I am not a philosopher because I neither believe in reason nor disbelieving in reason am I content to remain a sceptic; the truth I demand is "not of this world"—insofar as I demand truth. And if not the truth that is redemption then better no truth and no redemption and then Camus is right . . . and everything is ultimately absurd and we must learn to live without hope and meaning.[37]

The intention of this chapter is to plumb deeper into Susan's orientation that was fashioned as a response to the secular atheology of Heidegger and to the religious atheism of Weil, a vision that sets its sights on the truth of redemption wavering between the light of darkness and the darkness of light.

Truth and the Hope of Hopelessness

Let me initiate the discussion with Susan's comment in a letter written to Jacob on March 4, 1952:

Ontologically, I wonder if one can go further than Heidegger, namely, to say that "truth" is the openness of error; it is of the essence of the realm of error, of brokenness, of disequilibrium to be open to truth, atonement, equilibrium. If the absolute would "exist" nothing else could exist. However, the "wrong" of our existence is at once what is most precious, it is all that we have. That is why I object to mysticism. The separation from the absolute is our condition which must not so much be "overcome" as lived. Finally the "Seinsdenken" is as much an evasion of our condition as a blind enchainment in the profane. There are ways of "breaking bounds", but this not "contemplatively" where there is no resistance but orgiastically where we concretely experience the limit by breaking it.[38]

In what sense is marking truth as the openness of error a venturing beyond Heidegger? I gather that Susan is here referring to Heidegger's reflections in "On the Essence of Truth" (1930) on the un-truth (*Un-wahrheit*) of errancy (*Irre*) as "the essential counteressence to the originary essence of truth" (*das wesentliche Gegenwesen zum anfänglichen Wesen der Wahrheit*).[39] Summarizing this basic precept of thinking about the history of being, Heidegger wrote: "In the simultaneity [*Zugleich*] of disclosure and concealing, errancy holds sway. Errancy and the concealing of what is concealed belong to the originary essence of truth."[40] Inasmuch as truth is the unveiling of what remains veiled, it cannot be disentangled from untruth. Indeed, for Heidegger, the term *alētheia* implies that the un-disclosedness (*Un-entborgenheit*) of the concealment discloses the truth that *untruth is most proper to the essence of truth*,[41] and hence the concealing of the concealed can be manifest only in the concealment of the manifestation. The full essence of truth (*Wahrheitwesen*) as unconcealment includes the concealment of errancy as its nonessence (*Unwesen*). From the proposition that "the non-essence remains in its own way essential to the essence and never becomes unessential in the sense of irrelevant,"[42] we may infer that the insistent ek-sistence of the human being is molded invariably by a perpetual turning to and fro, the incessant oscillating between truth and untruth.[43] It is apropos to recall that already in *Being and Time* (1927), Heidegger wrote in his explication of the premise that falling prey (*Verfallen*) belongs to the constitution of Dasein's being,[44] "The full existential and ontological meaning of the statement, 'Dasein is in the truth,' also says equiprimordially that 'Dasein is in untruth.' But only insofar as Dasein is disclosed is it also closed off."[45]

In a letter to Jacob written on January 4, 1951, Susan summarized Heidegger's position as it was articulated in the 1946 study "Anaximander's Saying,"[46] the focus of which is the saying "From what things existing objects come to be, into them too does their destruction take place, according to what must be: for they give recompense and pay restitution to each other for their injustice according to the ordering of time" (ἐξ ὧν δὲ ἡ γένεσίς ἐστι τοῖς οὖσι καὶ τὴν φθορὰν εἰς ταῦτα γίνεσθαι κατὰ τὸ χρεών διδόναι γὰρ αὐτὰ δίκην καὶ τίσιν ἀλλήλοις τῆς ἀδικίας κατὰ τὴν τοῦ χρόνου τάξιν).⁴⁷ Heidegger offered two German translations.⁴⁸ The first is from Nietzsche's *Philosophy in the Tragic Age of the Greeks* (1873): "Woher die Dinge ihre Entstehung haben, dahin müssen sie auch zu Grunde gehen, nach der Notwendigkeit; denn sie müssen Buße zahlen und für ihre Ungerechtigkeiten gerichtet werden, gemäß der Ordnung der Zeit." The second is from Diels' *The Fragments of the Presocratics* (1903): "Woraus aber die Dinge das Entstehen haben, dahin geht auch ihr Vergehen nach der Notwendigkeit; denn sie zahlen einander Strafe und Buße für ihre Ruchlosigkeit nach der festgesetzten Zeit." The former is rendered in the English translation of Heidegger's text as "Whence things have their coming into being there they must also perish according to necessity; for they must pay a penalty and be judged for their injustice, according to the ordinance of time." And the second as "But where things derive their coming into being, there their passing away also occurs according to necessity; for they pay each other punishment and penalty for their dastardliness according to firmly established time."⁴⁹

With this philological and textual background, we can turn to Susan's comment about Heidegger's essay:

I understand nothing—I only smell "madness". I try to understand it "mythologically" (and I may be on the wrong track) i.e.: any advance through "thinking" beyond the sheer, awe-full reception of the present (—as "now" and as a "gift")—just this sky this grass at all—is going into "Errdom": but we cannot "chose" "therefore" not to make this step because we are expelled every moment from the "ineffable". We are thus every moment living the expulsion from Paradise. (Those who live "as if" all is all-right, i.e. who do not think that they are expelled only feast on the error.) Then H. would say that the "expulsion" happens already in the heart of Being, i.e. the "Seiende" is expelled from the "Sein". Then the beginning of history is the casting out of the Seiende—the burying-it-out-from the "Sein" (where it "ought" to be buried?)—the ἐποχή the "Ansichhalten" the remaining in itself, the not-appearing of the Sein.⁵⁰

The madness that Susan detected in the concluding part of Heidegger's study relates to his idiosyncratic interpretation that associates the dictum attributed to Anaximander with the ontological difference occluded by Western metaphysics: *"The oblivion of being is oblivion to the difference be-*

tween being and the being [Die Seinsvergessenheit ist die Vergessenheit des Unterschiedes des Seins zum Seienden]."[51] The obliviousness to being, which results from the occlusion of the ontological difference, belongs to the essence of the being that it itself conceals; this is the import of Anaximander's contention that things simultaneously come into being and perish in accord with the law of necessity determined by the temporal order. Susan rephrased the Heideggerian formulation in the traditional idiom of being expelled from Paradise. The expulsion occurs in the heart of being insofar as beings are flung from being at the beginning of history or what Heidegger called the dawn (*Frühe*) of the destiny of being (*Geschick des Seins*),[52] that is, the beginning marked by the appearance of the being that appears by not-appearing. The making apparent of the inapparent—the emission outward of what remains held in reserve within—is the movement of *Sein* "that expels man so that man is the being whose being is at stake on the truth (ἀ-λήθεια) of Being: who thus 'seems' as the center of the problem, ie. [*sic*] as the one who 'rapes'. What Augustinian Gnosticism!"[53] The intriguing hybridity of the expression coined by Susan is meant to convey that, for Heidegger, to live in error is an inescapable effect of our relation to being, since human history is regulated by the tossing out of beings from being, an ontological banishment that can be translated theologically as the continual eviction from Paradise or theopoetically as the dismissal from the ineffable. Heidegger's end-vision is thus regarded as intrinsically catastrophic insofar as nature (φύσις) becomes identical with the eschatological *Sein* that is determined by the identity of the history of metaphysics as the history of nihilism.[54]

Returning to this theme in "The Gnostic Foundations of Heidegger's Nihilism," Susan wrote:

Following Heraclitus, Heidegger interprets truth and error as "dis-covery" (*Unverborgenheit*) and "covery" (*Verborgenheit*). Heidegger opens the privative mode in the Greek term for truth, ἀ-λήθεια. The first syllable of *aletheia* is an alpha privative; truth means to lift out of oblivion (*lethe*). . . . The analysis of the fragment of Anaximander reveals the relation between *Verborgenheit* and *Unverborgenheit* as the cosmogonic drama between *Sein* and *Seiendes*. "Die Seinsvergessenheit ist die Vergessenheit des Unterschiedes des Seins zum Seienden."[55] Because the self is lost to the world and has forgotten that it belongs to Being, forgotten the difference between the world and Being, the self is in error. Since the self is essentially fallen prey to the world (*wesenhaft verfallend*), the self *is* in untruth. The untruth is the veiling of the Being.[56]

Oblivion to being, which ensues from the oblivion to the difference between being and the being, allows the coming to be of beings just as concealment (*Verborgenheit*) is the condition that makes unconcealment (*Unverborgenheit*) possible. By exposing the ontological difference between being and the being, the former would be recovered, but the metaphysical errancy,[57] which is the obfuscation of this difference, can never be fully amended, since being (*Sein*) can appear only by not appearing and hence it is persistently not the being (*das Seiende*) that it appears to be.[58] "The unconcealment of the being, the brightness granted it, darkens the light of being. By revealing itself in the being, being withdraws."[59] Metaphysics, as Heidegger understood it, is "the destruction of ἀλήθεια; but thus, it is the obliteration of the differentiation between being and beings in its capacity to be grounded; and herein lies the abandonment of beings by being and the forgottenness of being."[60] Insofar as being must be veiled so that there can be beings, we can say that nature is the nonphenomenalizable ground of phenomenality, the foundation of all visible phenomena that of necessity absconds from visuality. Susan judiciously drew the logical upshot of Heidegger's meontology: "The world that in its very apparentness covers the ground of the nothing is in errdom: its erring coalesces with its openness."[61] The forgetfulness of the truth of being allows beings to be in their untruthfulness, and hence error must be accorded a positive and not merely a negative valence. Indeed, the human self is in a state of untruth to the extent that it has fallen prey to or has been thrown into the domain that is thoroughly determined by the mode of erring caused by the covering of being by the beings that disclose that being. Conversely, discovery of truth is an awakening that is "the first step toward redemption from the world of error."[62]

Discerning the world as the self-dissimulation of being is not the consequence of ignorance; on the contrary, it is the spirit of gnosis procured by the few who are cognizant of the connotation of the Heraclitean axiom that nature loves to hide, *physis kryptesthai philei*, that is, the giving of being is concomitantly a withholding.[63] As Heidegger put it in one of the entries in his notebooks, attunement to the errant and the uncanny is the comportment of the philosopher because only by actually going into errancy can one strike up against the truth.[64] Expanding this idea in a second entry, Heidegger wrote:

Errancy is the most concealed gift of truth—for in it is bestowed the essence of truth as the stewardship of the self-refusal and as the purest preservation of beyng in the unrecognizable protection of what always is. To be sure: errancy is here not "error," an established mistake, the failure of truth as correctness—but instead is that which belongs to the "there"—of Da-*sein*.[65]

The errancy affirmed by Heidegger is not an error that issues from the neglect to mark the correct truth, nor is it the untruth that stems from a double negation, the coupling of two errors that gives way to a third error, but rather from "the *semblance* of a truth [*der* Anschein *einer Wahrheit*] . . . which cannot be surpassed with respect to self-evidence."[66] In Susan's language, Heidegger's conjecture that history is a fallacy (*Irrtum*) that of necessity issues from the forgetfulness of being (*Seinsvergessenheit*)—an obliviousness that is not provoked by human negligence but rather "belongs to that essence of being which it itself conceals . . . the destiny of being that the dawn of this destiny begins as the unveiling of what presences in its presence"[67]—is grounded in a gnostic-nihilistic experience.[68] Bracketing the question of nomenclature and the viability of linking Heidegger's thinking to Gnosticism,[69] it is unquestionable that by rejecting the metaphysical binary of reality and appearance, Heidegger was led to postulate that there is no semblance of truth apart from the truth of semblance and thus unconcealment is perforce a disclosure of the concealment that is both a refusal (*Versagen*) and a dissembling (*Verstellen*). The opening of the clearing (*Lichtung*) is a twofold concealment (*zwiefache Verbergen*), a concealment that conceals and thereby reveals itself whence it follows that, in its essence, truth is untruth.[70] On this score, we can apply to the Heideggerian *Lichtung* the Latin pun *lucus a non lucendo*, literally, "a grove from not shining,"[71] which is to say, the lighting up of the clearing is akin to a small orchard of trees illumined ironically by the absence of light.

This epistemological oxymoron undergirds Heidegger's declaration, "*Wer groß denkt, muß groß irren*," "He who thinks greatly must err greatly."[72] Dasein's being, its sense of freedom, is made possible by the inexorability of the wayward, "the errancy-fugue of the clearing," which commences from and is sustained by the interplay of concealment and unconcealment in the guise of truth as the concealing of the concealment.[73] The clearing wherein thinking occurs is always also an obscuration, the "placelessness of error, a landscape of placelessness, an a-topography, which appears as a 'fugue' or 'conjuncture' [*Fuge*]."[74] As the *Lichtung* concomitantly opens and closes, so the conjuncture unifies and divides, thereby enabling the materialization of the conjoined structure within which the appropriative event of truth eventuates as the straying of thought into the place of error, the placeless place, the place from which one is relentlessly displaced, the place that can be possessed only by dispossession.

Prima facie, it seems that Susan was capitulating to Heidegger when she wrote that "truth" is the essence of the realm of error and thus any sense of equilibrium can be attained only by being open to the brokenness of the disequilibrium. Curiously, however, she opposed Heidegger's view because ostensibly he did not acknowledge that what is most fallacious and disagreeable with our existence is what is most endearing. Echoing this perspective in a letter to Jacob from November 3, 1950, Susan reported that she was working on the chapter of her honors thesis at Bryn Mawr dedicated to the topic of the "lie in myth," which was glossed as "the real ontological untruth—every attempt to reconstruct the broken world into a totality has an ontological 'flaw' which is most important for the understanding of the meaning of that attempt."[75] A peculiar phrase indeed, the *real ontological untruth*—that is, a truth that is untrue insofar as it comes forth from the ill-advised effort to envisage the fractured world as an undivided whole, a mistaken way to view reality that, as was noted above,[76] she attributed as well to the phenomenon of mysticism and its exclusive concern with the absolute. The paramount spiritual obligation rather is to accept the brokenness of our being in the completeness of our incompleteness. As Susan put it in the poem "Post Apocalypse," "After the spell has been broken how shall we not break / every other thing?"[77] To be healed, the brokenness must be broken, but the breaking of brokenness can come about only by appropriating the perfection of the imperfection that is part and parcel of the imperfection of the perfection of existence.

Susan found support for her perspective in what she referred to in a letter to Jacob, written on April 21, 1952, as the "utterly sober" character of "Buddhist nihilism" in contradistinction to the "sentimentality" of the "gnostic (pseudo)-nihilism."[78] Forgoing the opposition of heavenly to earthly life, Buddhism posits the antinomy of nonexistence to existence. From this distinction Susan deduced the following conclusion:

A world in which there is life without death, splendor without squalor, pleasure without pain is idle nonsense: To long for it seriously is to reveal the lack of the least conception of human life, joy + dignity.... The "eschatologischer Geist" in all its forms is a sickness of the spirit, a puerility a not-coming-to-terms with human life such as it is. It has almost achieved the impossible: to glut + spoil the limitless thirst.[79]

The advantage of Buddhist nihilism—a somewhat dubious locution but one that Susan may have appropriated from Nietzsche[80]—to gnostic nihilism is that the former, unlike the latter, especially when it is circumscribed within the axiological scaffold of Christianity, is not dependent on a distinction between this world and the other world. Perceptively, Susan grasped that the gnostic judgment about the evil nature of reality comprises an implicit veneration of the world it negates, albeit projected onto the imaginary otherworld of transcendence. The mythic postulation of another world of spirit—the pleroma of divine aeons—can be decoded psychoanalytically as an infantile desire for a utopian escape from the severity of this world. To the extent that otherworldliness is predicated on the repudiation of this world coupled with an avowal of the values operative in that world, it can be classified as a form of ambivalent nihilism.[81] By contrast, the opposition of being and nonbeing upon which Buddhist nihilism is predicated does not presume the possibility of a world in which there is no polarity of life and death, splendor and squalor, pleasure and pain.

To imagine such a scenario is to aspire for what Susan considered "idle nonsense," that is, the state of consciousness that reveals a profound paucity of understanding about the human condition, the glory and dignity of which depend on knowing cerebrally and somatically the correlative truth that there cannot be one opposite without the other. Hence, the eschatological spirit, which envisions a world that is all good, signifies the sickness of spirit, an inability to come to terms with the rudimentary nature of our being in the world. Even philosophy is labeled by Susan in a letter written to Jacob on January 4, 1952, as a "highly dubious occupation" insofar as it is governed by "the will to conquer 'non-being': death, 'le temps perdu' + strangeness, the quality of otherness of being."[82] The occupation of the philosopher may be preparation for death, but the will to conquer nonbeing cannot be extricated from the scientific will to conquer beings in the world. To pursue death through philosophical speculation, therefore, is a form of eviscerating our corporal existence. Denouncing Heidegger's idea of the angst that arises from *Sein zum Tode*, the being-toward-death, referred to variously as the strangeness, the otherness of being, or the lost time—tellingly annotated by Jacob as *aber das "perdu" bleibt*,[83] that is, what is lost even so remains—Susan suggested that death testifies to the painfully negative relation to the nontemporal. What is intended by the latter is clarified in the comment that the dread before the constant and ultimate annihilation is the fear that one experiences in relation to the divine. This is the source of the uncanniness that Heidegger failed to name, the question of why there is anxiety, a question that beckons not an answer in positing the terminus of death but rather the need to abide humbly in the question in the course of one's lifetime.

It comes as no surprise, therefore, that Susan approved of the criticism of Heidegger offered by Paul-Louis Landsberg in *Essai sur l'expérience de la mort suivi de le problème moral du suicide* (1951): "the anguish before death … would be incomprehensible if man did not feel himself related to a Beyond—i.e. death would not even be a problem unless we understand ourselves as trans-natural—as having some relation to a 'beyond'."[84] Against the Heideggerian neutralization of the experience of angst by discounting the element of protest contained therein, we must speak of a "hope beyond hope," which is "not hope for anything in particular, not 'worldly' hope, a hope whose contents is the person itself; who has a 'home' if not a 'continuation' beyond time, perishing, death."[85] Resonating with Susan's personal outlook that the psychic welfare of the individual depends on the willingness to vacillate between the nadir of sorrow and the summit of glee is Landsberg's conclusion passionately voiced in the following passage:

The acceptance of death transforms death, but this acceptance presupposes a resistance. The human person is not, in its true essence, an *existence toward death*. Like every other existence, after its own fashion, it is a movement towards self-realisation and towards eternity. It tends towards its own perfection, even if this means passing through the strait and narrow gate of death. It can only change its outer ontological aspect by turning death into the means of its own fulfilment. Metaphysics do not originate in the nothingness revealed by anguish but in the being which by its very nature participates in the philosophic Eros. Thus the ontological character of the person is not derived from a negative which the person can only *accept*. The special decision through which the person may, in fact, become existence towards death, is an intermediate state between this primary exteriority of death, and the hope of the spirit, which transcends death itself.[86]

Hope, and not death, continuously gives shape and structure to the inimitable being of the human person, determined above all by the confidence one exudes in the possibility of reaching the future when the aspirations of the self will be fulfilled.[87]

Piety of Impiety and the Dark Night of Illumination

In a letter to Jacob from January 11, 1952, Susan distinguished the biblical emphasis on trust in God and the pessimism of the gnostic intuition in terms that are jarring in light of how her life ended:

> The gnosis tries to resolve the agony of mistrust and distrust by relieving God of all responsibility for the world, for fate and for history. But we who have chosen to live on earth eating the bread, suffering and enjoying and struggling to sanctify the bonds of human love, we long to be reconciled with the God of the wor[l]d, the God of fate and history. The other way is no reconciliation, it is pure negation, whose only legitimate form of expression is suicide.[88]

The optimal task before us is diametrically opposed to world negation. What is necessary is to extol the this-worldliness of the reality of our experience in all of its illusive nature. As Susan mused in a letter to Jacob written one year earlier on January 11, 1951:

> I suspect and fear at times that the gnosis is sick at heart with the sickness of Christianity. Now I am not interested in an "other-world" all I care about is this world with the sky and the earth and Jacob and Susan, all the "worlds" <u>and</u> "non-worlds" must find "place" right here under the stars and if they cannot find their place within the "ideal unity of Reason" we must abandon Reason: Kant was not firm enough in attacking "dialectic"—all the dialectical play with unity—duality etc. is a "magic" to coerce the God. But shall we gain anything by "coercing"—is it not better to pray or to curse—unless we love these exquisite dark flowers of thought, unless perhaps this strange rose is as pleasant to God as his "earthly" flowers—for both are as the Indians would say "maya".[89]

Gnosticism, as the Christianity it rejects, posits the otherworldliness as a way to negotiate the rejection of this world. Enlightenment consists rather of discerning that the dark flowers of thought and the earthly flowers of touch are equally part of the illusion that is the sensory world. To invoke the Hindu philosophical identification of the phenomenal world as māyā does not mean that our universe is pitted against some metaphysically real world. There is no ideal of transcendence that renders the illusion of the illusion illusory; to know the illusion is to be acclimated to the reality of the appearance that is apparently real because it is really apparent.[90] It follows, moreover, as was emphasized particularly in the Advaita school of Vedānta, within the contours of the cosmic illusion there is no duality—since there is nothing but the force of the illusion that makes phenomena appear to be real, there is no ontological ground to verify the autonomous being of the antinomies that structure our ontic experience of the world—and hence evil is to be adjudicated phenomenologically as an aspect of good, just as darkness is a modification and not a privation of light, and impurity is a variation of and not a deviation from purity.

In a letter written to Jacob on October 13, 1950, Susan offered the advice, "listen to the Old Man (: all is ultimately mechanism; beyond that there is only illusion). And the Muses sleep in the darkness of my unilluminated body."[91] The emotional sensibility is developed philosophically in a rather lengthy exposition of Kantian thought in a letter to Jacob from January 9–10, 1951. Focusing on the distinction between noumenal reality and phenomenal appearance, Susan astutely noted that by identifying the transcendental subject as the noumenon, Kant left the self as something that "can never become an object to itself, any attempt issues in dialectical illusion, a mirror play without a mirror (Balthasar)[92] the paralogisms of the soul."[93] Aligned with post-Kantian idealists, Susan understood that despite positing the thing-in-itself, metaphysical truths are inaccessible not because they are epistemically unattainable but because they are ontically illusory.[94] Philosophy begins and ends with the discernment that there is no truth to access but the truth of illusion that is the illusion of truth. Thus, in a letter to Jacob written on March 4, 1952, Susan contested Descartes's grounding the certainty of belief in the quality of perfection by proffering that if there is "an irrefutable proof of the reality of something by our having an idea of it, it might be the reality of 'wrong', of imperfection.... For the 'wrong' always wins: if my idea of wrongness 'doesn't correspond to external reality'—is an 'illusion' than there is something that nevertheless remains wrong in the world."[95] Faith, on this account, is not the antinomy of doubt but rather "a euphemism for profound trembling in uncertainty—an ultimate abandon to uncertainty: Angst."[96] Religion, consequently, is most advantageous when it discloses and covers the emptiness of our being. And here Susan conceded that the path of her thinking winds back to Heidegger's determination in *Being and Time* to approach the sacred by speaking out of the dimension of the profane, to focus on the finitude of our temporality, the senseless nothingness of a lost existence, the damnation that marks our authenticity.[97]

In the "Review of *Tragedy and the Paradox of the Fortunate* by Herbert Weisinger" (1954), Susan, availing herself of Gershom Scholem's "gnostical heretical" idea of redemption through sin found in Judaism and Christianity,[98] extrapolated that sin is

> a necessary phase in redemption, of which the paradox of the fortunate fall is the orthodox and somewhat compromised version. The orthodox version focuses our attention on the single, idealized instance of Adam's fall and its paradoxically fortunate repercussions for mankind in general; and only beyond the pale of circumscribed orthodoxy do we meet with an interpretation that develops the concept to its radical consequences.[99]

In the continuation, Susan specified the nature of that interpretation: "Thus in certain gnostic doctrines saint and sinner coincide, and the drama of redemption of the individual soul involves acts of transgression against the natural order."[100] What is most relevant to our analysis is the inference that Susan made from this premise:

> In the drama of redemption, the cosmic powers of darkness play a double role: even while they seduce man to the ways of darkness and blind him to evil and falsehood, they drive him to the very brink of violence where the "noise of the world"—the gnostic image for the active aspect of evil—startles him into awakening and sets him on the path of salvation. Once the cup of sin is drained to the dregs, evil works dialectically to its own exposure and destruction.[101]

The gnostic myth destabilizes the dualism upon which it is established insofar as evil becomes a mechanism to stimulate the good and bring about redemption. From that vantage point, the holy most fully expresses its potentiality as holy at the point when it exceeds the limits of its holiness; compliance with the sacrosanct is substantiated in the negation of its propensity to negate. On these grounds, Susan vehemently opposed the very notion of sin, arguing that the only sin is the Christian creed decrying the inherent sinfulness of human agency. In truth, however, what is iniquitous is not disobedience but rather the wrongs perpetrated against living creatures. The Pauline concern with the incapacity of the law to absolve one's guilt is a false problem because the issue is the intractable enforcement of the law. In Kafkaesque irony, a law that is not enforced does not have the status of a law that is real and therefore it cannot be a menace or a source of conflict.[102] From the perspective of the hypernomian surpassing of the nomos, insubordination is a facet of subservience.[103]

Although obviously not a scholar of Jewish mysticism, lacking the requisite philological and textual skills to grapple with the primary material independently, Susan unwittingly validated one of the deeper insights in the kabbalistic tradition about the potential of the law to exceed its limits and the relationship of the blemish (*pegam*) and the rectification (*tiqqun*). It is likely that Susan acquired knowledge of Jewish mystical ideas through conversations with Jacob and reading figures like Scholem and Buber. However, in spite of her limited access to the original sources, what is striking is that there are indeed deep connections between some aspects of her thought and ideas that may be culled from kabbalistic literature. I would go so far as to say that the kabbalah can serve as a mirror through which to view Susan's thinking just as the latter can serve as a mirror through which to view the former. Admittedly, this is not a methodology customarily adopted by intellectual historians, but it can be justified philosophically on hermeneutical grounds and therefore it is worthwhile pursuing this matter more extensively.

Common sense would dictate that blemish and rectification are polar opposites, the latter coming to remedy the former, but the mystical gnosis subverts this perspective by advocating for the identity of opposites in the opposition of their identity, a paradoxical truth that retrieves the middle excluded by the Aristotelian logic of the excluded middle.[104] Of the many sources that could be cited to demonstrate this principle, I will mention the following comment in a passage from the *Zohar*, the major repository of kabbalistic lore that began to be composed piecemeal in the late thirteenth and early fourteenth centuries but whose redaction and anthologizing took several centuries until it was published in the sixteenth century.[105] When two members of the imaginary fraternity central to the narrative of this anthology, Ḥiyya and Yose, entered into the heavenly academy to see the master Simeon ben Yoḥai and his son Eleazar, an angelic voice called out "Who among you can turn darkness to light, and taste bitterness as sweetness before you arrived here?"[106] Inverting the prophetic admonition against those who would call evil good and good evil, and who would present darkness as light and light as darkness, or bitter as sweet and sweet as bitter (Isaiah 5:20), the zoharic prerequisite for a soul to gain access to the celestial realm is to have transmogrified darkness into light and bitterness into sweetness when it resided in a fleshly body on earth. Such a transposition is possible because darkness is a residue that issues from the spark of light and bitterness a subsidiary that is discharged from the superfluity of sweetness, whence we can deduce that darkness is the opposite of light by virtue of the sameness of their difference, and sweetness is the opposite of bitterness by virtue of the sameness of their difference.[107]

Implied in the words of the *Zohar* is the cornerstone of the secret enunciated by later kabbalists that hinges on the identification of antinomies, which in turn prompts the paradoxical discernment that the blemish is itself an aspect of the rectification. Consider the following passage of the nineteenth-century Lithuanian kabbalist Yiṣḥaq Eizik Ḥaver Wildmann, "Rectification is appropriate only in the place where the impairment is appropriate" (*ein shayyakh tiqqun ella be-maqom she-shayyakh qilqul*).[108] On the exoteric level, the import of this statement is that it is not relevant to speak of rectification where it is prohibited to speak of defect. The principle is thus invoked to explain why the word *tiqqun* is not applicable to the highest aspect of the Godhead, the head that is not known (*reisha de-lo ityyeda*), according to the zoharic terminology,[109] because there is no *pegam* in relation to it. However, on the esoteric level, the deeper intent that may be educed eisegetically from this adage is that impairment is part of the repair, and thus it is germane to speak of repair only where we can speak of impairment. The more intricate wisdom insinuates that the blemish is not antithetical to but is itself an obligatory part of the recuperation.[110]

Perhaps the best known instantiation of this principle is the practice of uplifting the strange or alien thoughts (*maḥashavot zarot*) to God, especially during prayer and Torah study, disseminated by the fountainhead of modern East European Ḥasidism, Israel ben Eliezer, the Baʿal Shem Ṭov, and his two major disciples, Jacob Joseph of Polonnoye and Dov Ber, the Maggid of Mezhirech.[111] Instead of ascetically suppressing these precarious thoughts—often of a sexually seductive nature—the Ḥasidic teaching recommended transubstantiating those thoughts and restoring them to their divine source, and in so doing, the soul itself is elevated from a state of diminution (*qaṭnut*) to a state of aggrandizement (*gadlut*). That lustful desires can be transmuted into the love of God rests on another rudimentary belief of Beshṭian Ḥasidism: there is nothing that is not holy, since God is "all in all,"¹¹² a monistic mindset often buttressed by the zoharic apothegm *leit atar panuy minneih*, "there is no place bereft of him."¹¹³ Rather than simply signifying the omnipresence of God in all things, this pronouncement, according to the Ḥasidic rendering, leads to the panentheistic-acosmic assumption that everything is godliness, which is to say, the substance of all that appears in the sentient world of space and time is the manifestation of the light of infinity, the *or ein sof*.¹¹⁴ When specularized through the medium of this mystical temperament, those who possess the gnosis (*anshei daʿat*) recognize that the strange thoughts are not only garments (*levushin*) and coverings (*kissuyyin*) that temporarily conceal the divine presence but are themselves made of the same essence as his blessed essence (*eṣem me-aṣmuto yitbarakh*). The alleged concealments (*hastarot*) are thus naught but an optical delusion, *aḥizat einayim*—literally, the clutching of the eyes, the technical rabbinic term for the magical act of conjuration¹¹⁵—because "everything essentially is the essence of his blessed essence [*be-eṣem ha-kol hu eṣem me-aṣmuto yitbarakh*]."¹¹⁶ On the face of it, the pietistic duty is to unshackle the sparks of divinity from their entrapment in the demonic shells. The enlightened ones know, however, that the demonic shells themselves are divine, an idea that can be traced to the kabbalistic teaching transmitted by Isaac Luria that the vessel (*keli*) itself is constituted by the light (*or*) that remains in the space (*ḥalal*) from which the light was withdrawn.¹¹⁷ Attentiveness to this paradox precludes the possibility of positing an ontological dualism as a viable typology to analyze kabbalistic sources.

The breakdown of these binaries is indicative of the messianic consciousness developed and propagated by Ḥasidic masters, the realization that revolves around unveiling the veil as veil as opposed to discarding the veil, that is, beholding the disclosure of the essence of the unknowable being of infinity in the finite beings wherein it is hidden to the point that the infinite and the finite are differently the same in the sameness of their difference. This insight was stated lucidly by Kalonymus Kalman Shapira, the Piaseczno rebbe, in his *Mevo ha-Sheʿarim*. The revelation of the *Zohar* is compared to the revelation of the soul before it is garbed entirely in the body, whereas the revelation of Ḥasidism at the hands of the Baʿal Shem Ṭov and his disciples, which is designated as the disclosure of the messianic beginning (*hitgallut reʾshit ha-meshiḥit*), consisted not only of the fact that the vessels no longer concealed the soul within them but that through the essence of the vessels the light was manifest, and as a consequence many zoharic passages were elucidated in more detail.[118] Worthy of accentuation is that the messianic character of Ḥasidism is related to the gnosis that the vessel itself is purified and sanctified to the point that it is no longer distinguishable from the light, and hence the metaphysical polarity of the unholiness of matter and the holiness of spirit is upended as the corporeality of the world is transfigured into the letters of the luminous body of the divine name. The knowledge apposite to the eschaton illumines the mystery of the origin: the vessel—the ultimate semiotic mark of alterity in the Lurianic lexicon—is itself made of the light, and therefore the ability to sustain a genuine sense of the otherness of the vessel vis-à-vis the light is severely compromised. Difference of identity, accordingly, is subsumed under the identity of difference.

Against the backdrop of this nondualism, transgression itself must be reconsidered insofar as there is no justification for a sharp distinction between pure and impure, sacred and profane. Moreover, the ontological monism enjoins a more drastic interpretation that dissipates the dyad of damage and reparation, that is, the damage itself would be exposed as a feature of the reparation. To cite one striking example where this construal is stated explicitly: commenting on the talmudic ruling that one who tears a fabric on Sabbath in order to sew two stitches, *ha-qoreʿa al menat litpor shetei tefirot*, an act that would make such a person legally responsible for desecrating the holiness of the day,[119] Samuel of Sieniawa, the personal secretary of Simḥah Bunem of Przysucha,[120] wrote in his *Ramatayim Ṣofim*, first published in Warsaw in 1881:

> However, the manner in which something is called labor concerning which one is liable is when it is done in order to rectify [*al menat letaqqen*] as one who tears in order to sew, for there can be no rectification and upholding [*tiqqun we-qiyyum*] as is appropriate if not by means of tearing [*al yedei qeriʿah*].... Consequently, the tearing is verily the rectification and not in the category of that which destroys [*ha-qeriʿah hu tiqqun mammash we-eino bi-khelal meqalqel*].[121]

To assert so unambiguously that tearing is an act of restoration and not destruction clearly has far-reaching consequences.

For her part, Susan articulated a similar point of view in her maintaining that wholeness is configured by rupturing—and not by rectifying—the dissolution of the fragmented whole. In a letter to Jacob, written on November 24, 1950, pondering the sense of exile and the skewed nature of place and time that governed her way of being in the world, Susan wrote that in Israel—represented by the image of the Jewish star, the *magen david*—she "experienced a positive hopelessness because hope stood there only raped at every turn," whereas in her "dark night hours of illuminations," she sensed that "there is a sheer hope-less-ness, hope cannot even form itself."[122] The tragic play of being, which hovers between hope and nihilism,[123] partakes of the former as opposed to the latter; hope may be violently assaulted at every turn, but it still lingers as a source of hopefulness. Thus, even "the house of knowledge when it is the House of Hades" is no good, for the only knowledge that is profitable is the knowledge that affirms unequivocally that "god is the god of the living."[124] Along congruent lines, Susan wrote in the novella *Lament for Julia*, "At times I succumbed to utter hopelessness, cursed God, the canvas, myself. And I would have ripped it to shreds, but how could I lay my hands on that intangible entity the canvas of her life! I would have to wrest it from God's own hands."[125] Leaving aside the use of traditional theistic rhetoric, what is laudable is the prominence that Susan ascribed to that which cannot be extinguished by feelings of forlornness and desolation, the vital impetus of existence, depicted metaphorically as the inviolable canvas of Julia's life as opposed to a canvas that contains a pictorial representation of that life, that is, the virtually real set in contrast to the really virtual. The stimulus of that virtual reality, which pulsates with the vivacity of visceral ipseity and factual solidity,[126] is the wellspring that engenders hope from the womb of hopelessness. Susan believed that this melancholic sanguinity—the longing for light issuing from the darkness of night[127]—was patently missing in the Heideggerian notion of errancy and in the pseudo-nihilism of Gnosticism.

All Is Presence: Immortality of Death and the Nothingness of the Moment

Susan's rejection of Heidegger's perspective is on a par with her denunciation of the phenomenon of mysticism more generally insofar as in both cases there is a failure to endorse the separation from the absolute that is the benchmark of our finitude. In a response to George Bataille's lecture on "the teaching of death" (*l'enseignement de la mort*), Susan deduced the following insight from György Lukács's taxonomy of tragedy as the negation of going on in the world and affirming the continuation of life: "It is in the sense in which life 'stops' in a tragedy or in a mystical vision that we must think of death. And yet the lie in tragedy + mysticism is that life <u>does</u> go on."[128] The tragic and the mystic worldviews respectively fail to accommodate the tenacious challenge to death posed by the perseverance of life, not as a sign of immortality beyond the grave but as the deepest inflection of our mortality. The blurring of the line separating life and death is in accord with Hölderlin's line *Leben ist Tod, und Tod ist auch ein Leben*, "Life is death, and death is also a life."[129] Commenting on this verse, Heidegger wrote, "Insofar as death comes, it vanishes. The mortals die the death in life. In death the mortals become *im*-mortal [un-*sterblich*]."[130]

It is notable that the view of Heidegger denounced by Susan was anticipated in Walter Benjamin's essay "The Metaphysics of Youth," written in 1913–1914. An analysis of Benjamin will provide a clearer sense of Susan's quarrel with Heidegger's understanding of death, time, and the nihility of the present. In the section called "The Diary," Benjamin mulled over the existential question, "In what time does man live?" Thinkers, he went on to write, "have always known that he does not live in any time at all. The immortality of thoughts and deeds banishes him to a timeless realm at whose heart an inscrutable death lies in wait."[131] On the basis of this sweeping and somewhat oversimplified statement, Benjamin distinguished two types of time. First, there is the everyday time of finitude—designated as calendar time, clock time, and stock-exchange time—that is suffused with the "countless demands of the moment," an empty time that is beset with the menacing possibility of death. Second, in addition to this quotidian time, there is the modulation of immortal time, a time that is timeless, the "pure time" in which the self can experience its own time.[132] At first glance, it might seem that Benjamin reified the traditional dichotomy between time and timelessness, the temporality of this-worldliness and the eternality of otherworldliness.[133] However, a more circumspect reading demonstrates that this is not the case. Quite to the contrary, as Benjamin remarked, the immortality of timelessness (*Zeitlosigkeit*) "is *time* after all. In this self, to which events occur and which encounters human beings—friends, enemies, and lovers—in this self courses immortal time [*unsterbliche Zeit*]. The time of its greatness runs out in it; it is the glow that radiates from time and nothing else."¹³⁴ Through the act of writing the diary—a book *of* time (*ein Buch von der Zeit*)—the self can experience the silence of the temporal interval (*Abstand*) that "does not occur in developmental time [*der Zeit der Entwicklung*], for that has been abrogated [*aufgehoben*]. It does not occur *in* time at all, for time has vanished."¹³⁵ Pointedly, the disappearance of time corresponds to silence that is identified by Benjamin as "the internal frontier of conversation" (*die innere Grenze des Gespräches*), the hearing of "the rhythm of one's own words in the empty space."¹³⁶

Despite the language of abrogation and vanishing, the overcoming of the linearity of mundane time and the heeding of the eternal silence that is subsequent to speech achieved by the writer are in fact illustrative of a deeper undergoing of time:

> Instead time is overcome, and overcome, too, is the self that acts in time: I am entirely transposed into time; it irradiates me [*Sondern die Zeit ist aufgehoben und aufgehoben ein Ich, das in ihr handelt; ich bin ganz und gar in Zeit versetzt, sie strahlt mich aus*]. Nothing further can happen to this self, this creation of time.... But time no longer impinges on this self, which is now the birth of immortal time. The self experiences timelessness, all things are assembled in it.... Time, which shines forth as the self that we are, impinges on all things around us as they become our fate. That time, our essence, is the immortality in which others die. What kills them lets us feel our essential nature in death (the final interval).¹³⁷

Years before Heidegger professed that in death the life of mortals becomes immortal, Benjamin proffered that the final interval—the interval that cannot be written—reveals that the experience of timelessness, the time that is not in time, portends that the immortality of self encompasses the mortality of others. Resurrection, accordingly, is not a postmortem phenomenon; it is rather the experience of being restored to life by means of a more enrapturing appreciation of the destiny of what happens in the depth of the landscape of the ever-widening waves of time:

> As landscape all events surround us, for we, the time of things, know no time [*denn wir, die Zeit der Dinge, kennen keine Zeit*]. Nothing but the leaning of the trees, the horizon, the silhouetted mountain ridges, which suddenly awake full of meaning because they placed us in their midst.... Are we time? Arrogance tempts us to answer yes—and then the landscape would vanish.... The only answer is that

we set out on a path. As we advance, the same surroundings sanctify us. Knowing no answers but forming the center, we define things with the movement of our bodies [*mit der Bewegung unseres Leibes die Dinge bestimmen*]. By drawing nigh and distancing ourselves once again on our wanderings, we single out trees and fields from their like and flood them with the time of our existence [*der Zeit unseres Daseins*]. We give firm definition to fields and mountains in their arbitrariness: they are our past existence [*sie sind unser vergangenes Sein*]—that was the prophecy of childhood. We are their future [*Wir sind zukünftig sie*]. Naked in this futurity, the landscape welcomes us, the grownups. Exposed, it responds to the shudder of temporality [*die Schauer der Zeitlichkeit*] with which we assault the landscape.[138]

In this remarkably dense passage, Benjamin anticipated Heidegger's view that the constitution of Dasein is grounded in temporality and the constitution of temporality is grounded in Dasein. Temporality is the horizon from which humans understand the beings of the world, but it is also the perimeter that makes the existential analytic of being human possible.[139] This, I presume, is the import of Benjamin's remark that we are the time of things. He added, however, that we know no time to communicate that in order to be the measure of temporality, we must be timeless. What confers immortality on the human being, in contrast to all other mortal beings, is the ability to write the story of life in the diary from the vantage point of death.

The androcentrism here is obvious: not only are we the one species that experiences the nonexperience of death whereas all other species simply expire,[140] but we are placed in the center from which all objects are defined by the movement of our bodies. Permeated by the time of human embodiment, the landscape breathes before us. Benjamin described this relation metaphorically in amorous terms—the I is the male lover and the landscape the female beloved. Safe in each other's care, the external terrain of the world and the internal mindscape of the self mutually plunge from nakedness to nakedness; in being gathered together, we come to ourselves (*Wir stürzen von Nacktheit in Nacktheit. Wir erreichen uns gesammelt*).[141] Physical entities are accorded the status of the past, corresponding to childhood, whereas human beings are accorded the status of the future, corresponding to adulthood. Through the time of the self, there is an inversion of these temporal delineations: "The past of things is the future of the 'I'-time. But past things have futurity."[142] When the world is exposed to the bareness of the futurity disclosed through the embodied consciousness of human beings, the landscape is assaulted with the shudder of temporality, and the time of objects is overcome by the time of subjectivity. "With us things sink toward the center, with us they await the new radiance. For immortality can be found only in death, and time rises up at the end of time [*Denn Unsterblichkeit ist nur im Sterben und Zeit erhebt sich am Ende der Zeiten*]."[143] Contained here are the seeds of Benjamin's later articulation of the eschatological reversal of time and the construal of the scholarly reconstruction of history as an act of recollecting (*Eingedenken*) that has the capacity to redeem the past, not by describing how the past really was in actuality but by refashioning it and thereby imputing to it meaning that it only had potentially[144] in the same manner that citation acquires new meaning from a text and tears it from its original context through an unceasing process of rereading and revision in the now-time (*Jetztzeit*) of the present directed toward the future.[145] For Benjamin, as Hannah Arendt correctly noted, transmissibility of the past on the part of the historian is replaced by its citability.[146]

In contradistinction to the confounding of life and death, upheld in particular by the writer in the case of Benjamin and by the poet in the case of Heidegger as the bearer of the fate of humanity at large, the mystic, epitomized by Simone Weil, is plagued by the problem of the irreconcilability of time and death, and thus the soul must become a void so that God can enter into it. Susan vigorously objected:

But god is not something other than the void; god is the void, god tastes like nothing in the mouth of mortals. But is it necessary then to speak of god? I think it is rather an abuse of the word.[147]

Contemplation of the pleromatic nihilation of the moment led Susan to criticize Weil's stance that God enters the soul that negates itself by becoming a void. More appropriately, one should speak of the divine as the void, that is, the nothing that nothings, the nihil that is not the deprivation of an ontological plentitude, the negative relative to a positive, but rather the nothingness, the absence of some potentially present presence that is presently absent, the absence that presents itself as nonpresent, the absence that can never be present except as the absence of any possible presence, the chiasm of being that resists the reification of nothing as something or of something as nothing.[148] It is not only unnecessary to speak of God—either theistically or atheistically—but it is a misuse of the word to name the unnameable in its unnameability.

Needless to say, there is a critical difference between the mystical piety of

Weil and the path of Heidegger's thinking. In the case of the former, there is a presumed exaltation of the sacred, whereas the latter—despite the vestige of theological speculation in his philosophical cogitations[149]—is entrapped by a *blind enchainment in the profane*.[150] Noteworthy in this regard is another passing comment of Susan in a letter written to Jacob on January 31, 1952,

> Heid. is right in one thing, the remnants of Christianity must be exorcized from Philosophy. Only he does not do it, (does he?). The evil is not "eternal truths" but an eschatological notion of truth which reaches its ridiculous sublimity in Hegel.[151]

Christina Pareigis[152] surmised that Susan was alluding here to the following passage in *Being and Time*: "The claim that there are 'eternal truths,' as well as the confusion of the phenomenally based 'ideality' of Dasein with an idealized absolute subject, belong to the remnants of Christian theology within the philosophical problematic that have not yet been radically eliminated."[153] Susan located the Christological residual in the eschatological truth affirmed by Hegel as part and parcel of his systematic thought, but she confessed that Hegel proved to be impossible to comprehend, an impossibility that she tied to his penchant to view everything in history as equitable and justifiable. She went so far as to state explicitly that she was flabbergasted by this teleological predilection. No explanation is given but it is reasonable to assume, and it can be supported by other texts, that Susan was of the opinion that not everything that transpires in history is satisfactory and auspicious. For our immediate purposes, it is telling that she questioned if Heidegger was able to exorcize Christian dogma from philosophy.[154]

To complicate the picture, I will mention one example from Heidegger that seems to not only express a position that resembles Weil's mystical atheism but that will enhance our understanding of Susan's divergence from his views on the temporal calculus of the nothingness of being. As a counterargument to those who portrayed Hölderlin's apparent running away from Greece as a turning toward the homeland and as a return to Christendom, Heidegger proffered the following lines from the poem "Der Einzige" ("The Only One"):

> Es hänget aber an Einem
> Die Liebe. Diesesmal
> Ist mir vom eigenen Herzen

> Zu sehr gegangen der Gesang,
> Gut will ich aber machen
> Den Fehl, mit nächstem
> Wenn ich noch andere singe.
> Nie treff ich, wie ich wünsche,
> Das Mass.
>
> Yet love clings
> To One alone. This time
> Too much from my own heart
> The song has come,
> Yet I want to make good
> The lack, with what lies nearest
> When others still I sing.
> Never do I hit, as I wish,
> The measure.[155]

According to Heidegger's reading, these words suggest that to speak only of the Christian God—the only One—amounts to a lack "in the sense of not hitting the measure, due to excess and excess of will."[156] To illumine further the nature of this dearth that arises from a surplus, Heidegger made reference to the demeanor of the poet offered in Hölderlin's "Dichterberuf" ("Poet's Calling"):

> Furchtlos bleibt aber, so er es muss, der Mann
> Einsam vor Gott, es schüzet die Enfalt ihn,
> Und keiner Waffen braucht's und keiner
> Listen, so lange, bis Gottes Fehl hilft.
>
> Fearless, however, as he must be, the man remains
> Solitary before God, simplicity protects him,
> And no weapons are needed, and no
> Cunning, until God's lack is of help.[157]

The lack, as Heidegger perspicaciously underscored, which is attributed as well to God, does not signify shortcoming or inefficiency.[158]

48   Chapter One

But what is meant by an insufficiency that is viewed as a benefit rather than a liability? Heidegger elaborated as follows:

> What is to be emphasized is not God's *lack*, but *God's* lack [*Zu betonen ist nicht: Gottes* Fehl, *sondern* Gottes Fehl]. That is to say, insofar as the lack is a lack of the God [*als der Fehl ein Fehl des Gottes ist*]. With this, it becomes clear what "God's lack" means here. Not absence of the God, but presence—the fact that the vocation [*Bestimmung*] imposed by the God is not suspended. Such vocation is, in its being taken up, always lack and missing the mark—not out of weakness [*Schwäche*], but out of having to bear the overpowering [*Übermächtigen*]. Yet precisely "until"— that is, insofar as—the lack is one coming from the God, the fidelity to this calling persists, even if it falls short in the work.[159]

Admittedly, in this passage, Heidegger is explicating Hölderlin, but it is not unreasonable to propose that his exposition supplies a window through which we can glimpse at his own depiction of the divine epiphany—perhaps most conspicuous in the image of the last god whose trace unfailingly is found nowhere—as the paradoxical confluence of the manifest and the unmanifest, the showing of the nonshowing.[160] In the clash between the visibility of the invisible and the invisibility of the visible, we can discern an atheological reverberation of the idea that the lack attributed to God signifies a presence accessible through absence, a diminution occasioned by the profusion of power, a deficit fostered by the surfeit of will.

For Susan, both Weil and Heidegger, whatever the differences that separate them, represented an inability to demarcate the periphery of the vacuum by violating its limit. Fracturing the fracture is innate to, and not derivative from, the continuous coming to be of the multitudinous oneness that is the "nothingness of the moment that is and shall never be again,"[161] that is, the resolute emptiness impervious to duplication except as the recurrence of what cannot recur, the repetition of the "again" that is "altogether otherwise."[162] The replication of difference, which characterizes the sacredness of the void, defies the linear conception of time whereby the expectation of what will be in the future is dependent on the reminiscence of what was in the past. Religious experience, in Susan's thinking, involves encountering an object subsisting in the momentousness of the present just as the vibrancy of love cannot be conserved only by recollection and anticipation but necessitates seizing the erotic exuberance of the elusive nothingness of the momentariness of the moment. Accordingly, the absence that is apprehended tactilely in the instantaneous presence of time is naught but a transitory stage between the nothing that is no more and the nothing that is not yet, a blink of the eye, the portal that opens the "almost vanishing space of the present filled with the shadows of past and future."[163] Rebuffing the theological proclivity to posit a sense of totality as bombastic and irrelevant, Susan emphasized that the holy "shines not from an 'All-' but from the mystery of the 'this' and better than praising the 'Allmighty' is to praise a leaf or any moment of grace. Again, no presence: all either was or will be done."[164]

Susan's view is in accord with the contention of Reiner Schürmann that the pure now is not surrounded by other instants that form a line, but it is a now that is fissured. That is, there is no now "without a singularizing withdrawal dispersing us toward that which was, nor without the universalizing attraction toward that which always is (posited as being). There is a double tug where an infrangible *discordance of times* is declared."[165] The singularity of the moment—the henological difference of the temporalizing event[166]—is not to be conceived as a discrete presence, an objective now,[167] since the present itself is nothing but a bridge between the absence of the past and the absence of the future. Alluding to this quality of time, Susan wrote in a letter to Jacob from April 20, 1952, to which I have already referred towards the beginning of this chapter:

Retreat from the world is necessary not because there is no salvation or truth, except in retreat, but because only in the hour of quietness, of love, understanding + prayer are we freed from the bondage of the demons of the day and given a vision of ages, + experience past + future as presence.[168]

Implicit in these words is Susan's turning away from the gnostic insistence that redemption is reliant on escaping from the spatiotemporal world conditioned by the laws of physics. Deliverance is possible within the sphere of history, but what is mandatory is the fortitude and the tranquility to receive the presence through love, understanding, and prayer when the demons of the day are dispelled. However, to face the daemonic numen of the holy, one must be able to attend to the gracious bestowal of the moment without conceding to the metaphysical enticement to ontologize the sense of thisness as a rigid presence.[169]

Inspired by the representation of the Hindu deity Śiva as articulated in

Joseph Campbell's *The Hero with a Thousand Faces* (1949), Susan wrote the following in a letter to Jacob dated October 19, 1950:

> All is presence + present. If the Torah were consequential it would condemn the dependence on the divine name (word magic) as well as the dependence on the divine picture (picture magic)—but it seems that the antithesis was not between a "magical" and a "spiritual" relation to God but rather between two different symbolic expression[s]—but the decision of the Name rather than the physical presence may have been a step to "spiritualization" which is also a step toward dividing male and female, worship of the abstract father turn out of the trinity of eternal present, revulsion at the mother, nature and all its powers and mysteries.[170]

The Torah falls short of its own iconoclasm inasmuch as it does not rebuke the power of either the name or the picture attributed to the divine. The antithesis that we may obtain from Hebrew scripture is not between the magical and the spiritual relationship to God but rather between two alternate systems of symbolic mediation. By apportioning potency to the linguistic and the graphic portrayals of the nonportrayable—thereby according value to both word magic and picture magic—there is a spiritualization of the concrete religiosity of ancient Israel, which was reinforced by the immediacy of the indwelling of the luminous glory. Intriguingly, Susan opined that this process resulted in the gender division of male and female, the adulation of the father and the revulsion of the mother, the former personified in the threefold compresence of the eternal present and the latter in the diversified powers and mysteries of nature. Moreover, idolatry is rooted pneumatically in the susceptibility to flee from the phenomenological sine qua non that *all is presence and present*; that is, there is nothing but the presence—the potent nonentity of time[171]—that resists presentification even as it is constellated by the intertwining of past, present, and future in a manner that tallies with what Heidegger called in *Being and Time* the equiprimordiality (*Gleichursprünglichkeit*) of the three temporal ecstasies,[172] or what he later referred to as the simultaneity of time (*Gleich-Zeitige der Zeit*), which entails the oneness (*Einzigkeit*) of the has-been (*Gewesenheit*), the presence (*Anwesenheit*), and the present (*Gegenwart*) that we are awaiting as the future (*Zukunft*).[173]

Based on a comparable conception of time, Susan argued that in the epoch succeeding the Shoah and the establishment of the modern state of Israel, it is necessary for Jewish praxis to disrupt the fascination with nostalgia, the hankering for homecoming fraught by pain.[174] The onus is to live sacramentally in the present wherein the remembrance of the past is projected and the projection of the future is remembered. As Susan wrote to Hugo Bergmann on September 18, 1950, religion cannot be "essentially allegorical" or "essentially historical," but it should ideally prescribe "that there must be a divine present and that when this divine present is broken so that there is only the divine past—a remembering—and a divine future—a hoping and believing—we lose the very ground and soil of sacrament."[175] Applied specifically to Judaism, the repossession of the ground to augment allegiance to its teachings and rituals cannot be based exclusively on remembering the past or believing and hoping in the future; it is contingent rather upon the existence of a sustainable present, albeit a present shaped by a past that continues to resound into the future but that nonetheless shoulders the gravitas of the onticity of the moment. If the allegorical approach to religion is questionable insofar as it casts doubt on the criterion of demonstrable facticity, the historical approach is fatally misguided insofar as it divides the divine presence into a past and a future and thereby shatters the ground of the possibility of a consecrated life. The sacramental and the nihilistic are commensurately legitimate and irrefutable possibilities; the secular is identified as the state of limbo between these two worlds: one marked by the power of mystery and the other by the power of death.[176]

Translated hermeneutically, in the case of Judaism, the inviolability of revelation is predicated on the supposition that the letter of the holy book "is not fixed but open to the exploration of new meanings."[177] In these words, Susan confirmed the venerable rabbinic belief in the chain of oral interpretation that complements and expands the revelation of written scripture. The ancient text must be read continually, albeit always from a new perspective calibrated to the impending of the future in the theophanous moment at hand. Reprimanding those who would adamantly impose a literal reading on the Bible, such as Camus, Weil, and the worst of the Zionist zealots, Susan wrote, "If there can be any understanding, not to say judgement, of Judaism it must be in its historical totality."[178] However, inasmuch as history by nature is always emerging, the notion of historical totality likewise must be construed as that which is ceaselessly in the process of coming to be. Petitioning this form of totality, therefore, is in effect acknowledging that there is no form of totality that can be petitioned.

The tensiveness of time implied in the ever-evolving tradition, inspired by the never-ending revelation, consists of the simultaneity of past, present, and future. The future repeatedly interrupts the present, but interruption does not signal an unmitigated rupture of the past. The timeswerve of circular linearity intimates that without continuity we could not detect discontinuity. The synchronic and diachronic elements thus coincide in the coalescence of the three temporal modes in the interminable termination of the momentary becoming. The dual deportment of tradition as malleable and durable—malleable in its durability and durable in its malleability—rests on the assumption that each moment instantiates the concurrence of the recollection of the past, the palpability of the present, and the anticipation of the future. What is actual about the moment is the inversion of the rectilinearity that promotes the memory of what will be and the expectancy of what was. Accordingly, the injunction to remember, which legitimately can be called a central pillar of Jewish self-understanding both individualistically and communally, comprises not the nostalgic reclamation of a past sealed in its factical obstinance, but an auspicious proclamation of a future foreseen in its evental unforseeability.

It strikes me that Susan's understanding of time bears similarity to the diremptive conception according to which our temporal experience is anchored always in the present on account of which meaning is both imparted to and rescinded from past and future. However, in contrast to the theory of presentism, that is, the conviction that everything is present or that only that which is present exists,[179] the phenomenological chronology I derive from Susan's intermittent musings about our experience of time presumes that what ensures presence in the present is the absence of any presence being present insofar as every now is a single and transient event that is concurrently homogenous in its heterogeneity and heterogenous in its homogeneity. Our experience of temporal passage, consequently, is minimally real exactly because the time that speciously passes therein is maximally unreal.[180] I presume that this is the philosophical import of Susan's demarcation of time in the letter written on December 5, 1950, as the "openness toward the divine—that possibility of a 'space' where our fleeting existence becomes coincident with an 'always'."[181]

Expounding further on the meeting of the ephemeral and the permanent in a letter from March 6, 1952, Susan wrote that the "notion of definitiveness" implied by various forms of the "eschatological Weltanschauung" close our eyes to both of the essential poles of the eternal, its double instantenaity [*sic*] whereby each instant is in eternity and all instants are in eternity; neither a "now" nor an absolute point of beginning or end can be fixed in time. Or to be heideggerien [*sic*]: "eternity" is the very timeliness of time. Whereby time running around and around, going nowhere, continually generates itself and continually defeats itself.[182]

Susan was negatively predisposed to the Heideggerian idea of eternity, which is essentially the elongation of time forged by the recurrent cycles of generation and degeneration. In her mind, this is conceptually on a par with the Christian sense of time that is "a monster made on the model of the finite human will, taken as 'infinite'."[183] In my view, however, in spite of Susan's criticism, it is possible to unearth from Heidegger a perspective on time that is more compatible with the position that she herself espoused; that is, a notion of time centered on the indeterminacy of each moment that is always in the process of being delimited by the determinacy of what was and what will be apperceived in their discontinuous continuum through the channel of the continuous discontinuum of the present.[184] The time-consciousness of duration is dependent on the simultaneity of the three tenses in the empirical effervescence of the instant—in the present there is no presence because all either was or will be done—but in that instant there is no definitive sequence that delineates what is anterior and what is posterior. Notably, in a diary entry written on September 10, 1969, occasioned by returning to Budapest "after thirty years of disembodied rootless wandering," and standing before her childhood home, Susan wrote of how the "frozen memory now thaws suddenly into live, raging, devouring monster of time."[185] Memory collapses the gulf that separates past and present and thereby impedes the all-consuming monstrosity that is time. Only by commandeering the unexpected expectancy of the expected unexpectancy of the moment—a temporal exclusivity that is experienced with equal inclusivity in love and in death—can one concretely experience the limit by breaking it.[186]

Breaking the Brokenness and the Disjointedness of the Holy

In some measure indebted to Heidegger's claim that there is no truth that is not at the same time untruth, Susan identified the measure of truth as the real ontological untruth. Indeed, at the heart of Susan's skeptical faith, as we noted above, is the commitment to this proposition and the attendant wisdom that mending the brokenness of being turns on the acknowledgement that to break the brokenness, the brokenness must be left unbroken. Moreover, breaking the brokenness is related to Susan's acceptance of the hypernomian principle of preserving the boundary by breaching it. The prospect of exceeding the margin is stated in the letter Susan wrote to Jacob on April 4, 1952:

> If as you say "inwardness" needs no philosophy—nor, for that matter religion—then all genuine "spiritual" problems must find their formulation in the mundane, social sphere. If there is something to be healed, the brokenness is within the world. To ask for the eradication of brokenness as such is to wish the annihilation of the world. To heal the broken relations within the world, requires first that we acknowledge the reality of these relations (instead of fleeing into the imaginary) + then drawing from the tree of life, science, art, wisdom, cultivate + transform them. The powers of creation, of life are also the powers of destruction; every transformation passes through chaos.[187]

There is no appeal in the aforecited passage to an external transcendence; what needs to be rectified is the brokenness that is within the world without beseeching a *deus ex machina*. The urge to destroy that brokenness would be tantamount to exterminating the world. Therein lies the crux of Susan's irritation with the word "mysticism" to name an ideology that posits truth beyond the reality of the mundane: "The term 'mysticism' annoys me a little. In any case if I am a mystic it is only in protest against the vulgar discourse of the world: there is nothing 'beyond' the 'reality', but there is a truth and many shades of truth that remain unsaid in 'positive' discourse, and that today are even denied."[188]

In her categorical denial of any transcendent being, Susan is in agreement with the radical finitude of Heidegger's thinking. And yet, astonishingly she was of the opinion that Heidegger fell short of embracing the disjointed nature of our existence, an ineptitude in thinking that prevented him from realizing that the power of creation is inextricably bound to the power of destruction and that chaos is the vehicle of transformation. Heidegger may have well recognized that creation—or, in his language, the history of being—is constitutionally violent, but he did not, in Susan's mind, appreciate that the holy itself comprises order and disorder.[189] In the letter to Jacob from March 17, 1952, Susan expressed a similar criticism but in that context framed the matter in relation to the exposition of the technique of Heidegger's word-mysticism in "Les Philosophes et leur Langage" by Yvon Belaval:

> Let's grow up and stop this "thumb-sucking" there is no mystical shortcut to creating anything of value, whether a house, a poem or a philosophy. Constructing a philosophy or a poem should take more work and should entail more difficulties than building a house or the poets and philosophers are really loafers and escapists. I am speaking for both of us. There is some wisdom in the Church in considering despair the greatest sin; despair always tempts the soul to embrace an aim for which it does not have to work. The "truth" that is revealed once and for all is the truth of death of nought and not the truth of life. For the truth of life we have to sweat and toil.[190]

The reproof of Heidegger implied in this remark is uncompromising, alluding to his notion of the poetic dwelling of Dasein as an infantile thumb-sucking that is akin to a mystical shortcut to fabricate value. Despair may be the greatest transgression, as Christian authorities have taught through the centuries, but the danger in thinking this way is that the soul might be deceived into believing it can achieve a goal for which it does not have to labor. The solemn reality, however, is that truth does not ensue from the submission to the nothingness divulged in the Heideggerian being-toward-death but rather from the truth of life for which we must sweat and toil.

Susan revisited this idea in the following deliberation in *Lament for Julia*, although without mentioning Heidegger:

> I was on the path celebrated by mystics as the dark night of the soul, or on the road to extinction described by eastern sages.... But no. My tracks wound inward like a burrowing worm's. The point around which I circled was not deliverance but uttermost bondage. Not God, but I. With each turn I was more hopelessly walled in. The sense of my existence, far from diminishing, grew more acute, and at last became excruciating. I was seized by the terror of my indestructability. Nothing that I was, nothing could annihilate me.[191]

It is not death that demarcates the contours of selfhood—à la St. John of the Cross's mystical dark night of the soul or the Buddhist anātman, the nonself, attained in the nonattainment of nirvāṇa—but rather the imperishability of the I, the horrifying realization that all that one has been precludes the abolition of self. Not death but the indestructible sense of one's existence is insufferable.

The criticism leveled against Heidegger's signature idea is found as well in the letter that Susan wrote to Jacob on March 12–13, 1952, responding to a lecture given by Jean Wahl on the romantic spirit of poetry typified by Rimbaud, Hölderlin, Keats, Shelley, and Wordsworth. After criticizing the classification of poetry as a "religion" or as a path to "religious salvation"—a viewpoint ascribed especially to Rimbaud and Heidegger—on the grounds that poetry, as other forms of art, is "born out of a revolt against the sacred society," and hence the poet could not "set out to find the way to the sacred except through the renunciation of his art,"[192] Susan offered the following meditation on time, life, and death, which is worthy of full citation:

> One must descend, one must surrender one's delicate complexities or else live one's complexity; the lamentation of the romantics is not a descent to the source but only another element another twist in the complexity. Let the complexity reach its limit and then it will break down by itself. Into what? Is there any other possibility than madness? Are we doomed to descend alone, each in his private furies? The cult was at the beginning but is it at the end? We were born together but perhaps we must die alone. Time may be a reality and the child in the cradle and man on his deathbed are not identical. But ultimately only the present is our business. What does it mean "Sein zum Tode"? Would a wise man knowing that tomorrow he might die, knowing even that tomorrow he shall surely die live his day any differently than otherwise? A day is a day and death scares only people who think they have something terribly important to do—something somehow more important than the day, than the present. We must think in terms of life in terms of the day, knowing that life and its categories are not the ultimate reality. Whether knowledge is stronger than death, death and not knowledge decides. And love in order to be love must play into the hands of death.[193]

There is much to unpack in this comment, but for our purposes I will concentrate on the main points of Susan's disagreement with Heidegger. Implicitly pushing against the latter's depiction in *Being and Time* of death as the "most extreme not-yet" (*äußersten Noch-nicht*), the "being-toward-the-end" (*Sein zum Ende*), that bequeaths to Dasein its "*ownmost* potentiality-of-being" (*eigensten Seinkönnen*),[194] Susan proposed that it is not death that is the orienting endpoint but the complexity of life itself that reaches the limit of its own accord and then degenerates into madness. However, seemingly acceding to Heidegger's emphasis on the ontological sense of mineness (*Jemeinigkeit*) that is distinctive to Dasein's being as it is disclosed in death,[195] Susan averred that while we may be born together, it is likely that we must die alone, an aloneness that denotes the distinctiveness of the person on the deathbed, who is emphatically not the same as the infant in the cradle. Time may be circuitous in its linearity, but the end is not a palindromic retrieval of the beginning; what will be manifest at the expiration of a life journey is distinctively different from what is manifest at the inception.

One might contend that this line of argument bolsters Heidegger's privileging of the future as the primary phenomenon of the primordial and authentic temporality that determines the horizon of Dasein's being,[196] since it is through the nonoccurrence of the occurrence of dying that one is fully individuated. Susan insists nonetheless that ultimately it is only the present that matters to a living human being, and hence she questioned the pertinence of Heidegger's being-toward-death. In fairness to Heidegger, Susan ignored a crucial part of his understanding of the future that emerges from what he called the "temporalization of temporality" (*Zeitigung der Zeitlichkeit*). This process decidedly does not involve a succession of the ecstasies such that the future necessarily would be later than the past or the past necessarily earlier than the present. Rather, in Heidegger's typically convoluted jargon, temporality is said to temporalize itself "as a future that makes present, in the process of having been."[197] The futural status of Dasein, therefore, is favored because it makes present what has authentically been.[198] Heidegger has applied the principle of hermeneutical circularity to the structure of temporality: Dasein projects to the future to the extent that Dasein is thrown back to the past, but Dasein is thrown back to the past only to the extent that it projects to the future.[199] From that standpoint, the future imbibes the copresence of the three ecstasies as opposed to the accumulation and sequence of allegedly disconnected atomized units, a representation that ratifies the reciprocal spatialization of time and the temporalization of space.

Be that as it may, Susan blatantly opposed the prioritizing of the future that is implied in Heidegger's being-toward-death. The moment of death, although predictable in its unpredictability, is inconsequential to a person propelled to live life in the present. Paraphrasing the acclaimed verse "For love is as strong as death" (Song of Songs 8:6), Susan suggested that in the end death decides whether it is stronger than knowledge. Irrespective of the outcome of that confrontation, we can be certain that love must play into the hands of death; that is, the metrics of the immortality pledged by love is to be gauged from the mortality guaranteed by death. It is in the constant coming to be after passing away that the impermanence of love is rendered permanent just as it is through death itself, and not some eternal state in an afterlife or the promise of bodily resurrection, that mortals become immortal.[200] As Susan wrote to Jacob on February 22, 1952, in a wide-ranging letter theorizing about apocalyptic hope and the feasibility of redemption:

We cannot bring about the apocalypse and yet we must go on living; suicide is not consequential, my life and my death are equally meaningless without total redemption. What are we to do? We are in the midst of an ocean dying of thirst, the saltwater only increases our thirst; but we must drink the saltwater and die of it and that's all there is to do; sometimes there is a little rain from heaven which relieves for a while the nausea and suffocation. Or make peace with the earth, a suffering peace, not without some sadness and reproach and in the knowledge that the craving is always greater than the fulfillment and that perhaps this is the eternity of love.[201]

Returning to this sentiment in a letter dated April 21, 1952, Susan noted that human life is beguiled by a thirst that all the waters of the world cannot quench, that is, a divine thirst, which she explained as "a thirst not so much <u>for</u> truth or God as <u>from</u> the true + the divine. Man drinks at a source that makes him thirst."[202] What is true, and what may be considered divine, is the human inclination to seek to satisfy a desire that cannot be satisfied except as the desire that continues to ignite one's desire, to drink at the source that makes one thirsty, a hunger that feeds upon itself.[203] Alas, whether the focus is the extravagance of carnal passion or the abstemiousness of saintly adoration, the "rawness of the wound of longing makes life both unendurable and endurable."[204]

For Susan, it is an act of hybris on the part of philosophers to believe that thought can "seek its own salvation in the truth. There is no salvation beyond love and there is no technique, nor 'gnosis' of love."[205] Loyalty, therefore, is "the virtue by which the soul lives" and "betrayal is its own death." However, "in this torn world loyalty is hardly possible except at the expense of an equal betrayal. The past is swept away in a chaos, in the present everything is futuric, everything is only temptation."[206] Infidelity disturbs the temporal flow by hurling the past into chaos and denying the present by making it into the allure of the future. "Time, change, and death," Susan wrote to Jacob on January 12, 1952, "work for oblivion; we fear to forget and to be forgotten; truth, (as Heid. says somewhere) is rooted in being true . . .

oblivion is a monster who devours truth. In the kingdom of oblivion those who were lovers, pass without recognizing each other."[207] The dismal assessment notwithstanding, in more optimistic moments, Susan championed that true love can reclaim the present in the infinity of its finitude, and thus it is truly as strong as death[208] insofar as it mimics the unveiling of the face that facilitates the face-to-face encounter with the faceless.[209] In facing that which has no face, one confronts the tragedy of being, but contra Heidegger, this tragedy is mitigated by the openness to the error of untruth exposed as an integral component of the intricacy of life, the threshold of integration that disintegrates after reaching its limit.[210]

In the final analysis, it is the victory of chaos and death that makes synthesis and love eternally possible, but that synthesis should not be construed in Hegelian terms:

> The ideal is to attain the coincidence of the "ideal" and the "real" of heaven and earth, of the natural and the transnatural in the acts of eating, loving, fighting, building, cultivating and producing. Because the "authentic life" the authentic reality and authentic ideality is neither the real nor the ideal but their coincidence. This sounds "hegelian"; but again whereas Hegel thinks that by thinking these things we arrive at them I do not think that the synthesis is rational it is not the synthesis of reason. Nor is the irrational "integrated" (aufgehoben) in the rational; chaos and form are not eschatologically reconciled "in the end", do not tend toward any such reconciliation, but are eternal and eternally antinomical. The victory of form in synthesis is not final but momentary, chaos reasserts itself and breaks the bonds of forms. The final victory is to chaos and death in order that synthesis and love should be eternally possible.[211]

From Susan's perspective, neither Hegel nor Heidegger appreciated that authentic life presumes the coincidence of the ideal and the real that does not entail the eschatological reconciliation of chaos and order. On the contrary, these forces are everlastingly oppositional. Formlessness is periodically overcome by form, but the rhythm of life is that form will always be subject to the disarray of formlessness. In this sense, victory is allocated to chaos and death because they make possible—dialetheically as opposed to dialectically—order and synthesis.

Poetic Speech, Parabolic Dissimulation, and Saying the Unsayable

Despite Susan's disapproval of Heidegger's position on the nature of error, his gnostic disavowal of history, and his tempocentric devaluation of our temporal circumstances, there is a fundamental affinity between her view of poetry and his poiēsis. For Susan, poetry is a way to speak silently, not the silence of not speaking but the silence of speaking-not, an apophatic gesture that spawns a never-ending attempt to express the inexpressible. Concerning what cannot be spoken, we can, and indeed must, speak endlessly. Apophaticism, as Schürmann shrewdly observed, has "traditionally served the interests of maximization."[212] Poetic speech, on this accord, is the language that is the crossing of language, in Heidegger's expression, the "telling silence"[213] or, quite literally, the "saying not-saying" (*sagenden Nichtsagens*).[214] To understand the full force of this paradoxical elocution, we should recall Heidegger's assertion in *Being and Time* that authentic silence is possible only in genuine discourse, and hence to be silent one must have something to say.[215] The focus of Heidegger's aside in this early work is the speech of Dasein that will amount to "an authentic and rich disclosedness [*Erschlossenheit*] of itself." To that end, what is indispensable is reticence (*Verschwiegenheit*), as opposed to idle talk (*Gerede*), which is described as a form of discourse that "articulates the intelligibility of Dasein so primordially that it gives rise to a genuine potentiality for hearing and to a being-with-one-another that is transparent."[216] What Heidegger intended is made clear in a second passage where he noted that the call to conscience "is lacking any kind of utterance. It does not even come to words, and yet it is not at all obscure and indefinite. *Conscience speaks solely and constantly in the mode of silence.*"[217]

In his diary from 1931, Heidegger offered the following directive, "First thoroughly fathom the silence, in order to learn *what* may be said and *must* be said."[218] Reversing the relationship in another entry, Heidegger wrote, "Now the sayable word found, behind which the proper fruitful silence can unfold."[219] The path of this apperception regarding the autumnal nature of silence as a new time of waking to the unfolding (*Entfaltung*) and to the bursting forth (*Ausbruch*) of the inexhaustible greatness of being,[220] the essence of which is branded as the ineluctability of the *taciturnity that conceals* (verbergende Schweigsamkeit),[221] led Heidegger to the following startling observation in the section "The Ability to Keep Silent as the Origin and Ground of Language" in the lecture "On the Essence of Truth," delivered in the winter semester of 1933–1934:

> In order to further clarify our conception of the essence of language we should now characterize the ability to keep silent. Here we come again to that philosophical situation that we have already encountered: circularity [*Kreisbewegung*]. This circularity makes itself known now in that we are supposed to speak about keeping silent—and this is highly problematic. For whoever discourses about keeping silent is in danger of proving in the most immediate way that he neither knows nor understands keeping silent.[222]

Developing further the presumption regarding the wordless origin of language in the *Contributions to Philosophy (Of the Event)*, composed between 1936–1938, Heidegger noted that we can never say the event of beyng immediately, and thus what is ownmost to language is itself expropriated in the *sigetic*, the term coined to convey the sense of bearing silence (*Erschweigung*).[223] Elaborating on the theme elsewhere in this composition, Heidegger wrote: "Every saying already speaks *out of* the truth of beyng and can never immediately leap over itself to beyng itself. . . . Bearing silence arises out of the essentially occurring origin of language itself."[224]

The unspoken dimension of the word thus yields the unspoken dimension of language. The latter, however, "is not the consequence and result of silence, rather it is the bequest (overcoming and destiny) of stillness."[225] For Heidegger, stillness is not equated with soundlessness,[226] and what is unspoken is not preserved by not speaking but rather by speaking that which cannot be spoken. To capture our thoughts, then, words must be mindful of the "remembrance of the unsaid and the unsayable [*das Andenken an das Ungesagte und Unsägliche*]. How would the unsaid ever be able to remain within what it is if the saying does not bear what it has said as if it were on an offering plate?"[227] The final image imparts the idea that the efficacy of speech in communicating our thoughts and in establishing the relation of word to thing—enacted especially by the poet—demands the renunciation (*Verzicht*) of self-denial (*Entsagung*) or releasement (*Gelassenheit*) that compels one to defend the silent treasure of the unspoken that is the source of all that is spoken.[228] From the poet's abdication of the "representational rule of the word," we learn about the higher nature of language that Heidegger named "bethinging" (*die Bedingnis*), that is, letting a thing be as thing.[229] Here it is beneficial to recall that in "The Thing" (1950), Heidegger utilized the image of the jug as vessel to advance a conception of thingness as the void that holds the gift of the outpouring in the twofold manner of taking and keeping.[230] In Buddhist terms, the suchness of the container is constituted by its emptiness. Applying this conception of thingliness as the vacuity of the clearing, the free space of the opening, we can say that for language to execute the bethinging of the thing—the decisive experience (*eigentliche Erfahrung*) of the poet by which the word makes the thing appear as the thing it is and thus accords it presence in the world,[231] what Heidegger elsewhere called the "fundamental attunement" (*Grundstimmung*) of the poet's "telling projection" (*sagenden Entwurf*) that opens up beings as a whole to the province that prevails as the unity of a world, thereby transporting us to the truth of the earth and of the homeland, and entrusting Dasein to the taking up, configuring, and sustaining of beyng[232]—it is necessary that one commit oneself to the mystery of the originary silence that begets the word.

The ramifications of this perspective were explicated in the lecture "The Way to Language" included in the collection *On the Way to Language* (1959):

> To say and to speak are not identical [*Sagen und Sprechen sind nicht das gleiche*]. A man may speak, speak endlessly, and all the time say nothing. Another man may remain silent, not speak at all and yet, without speaking, say a great deal.[233]

What does Heidegger mean by saying a great deal while remaining silent? How are we to construe the nature of that silence? Is it the muteness of not speaking or the restraint of speaking-not? The answer may be adduced from the continuation of the aforecited passage:

> What is unspoken [*Ungesprochene*] is not merely something that lacks voice, it is what remains unsaid [*Ungesagte*], what is not yet shown [*Gezeigte*], what has not yet reached its appearance. That which must remain wholly unspoken is held back in the unsaid, abides in concealment as unshowable [*verweilt als Unzeigbares im Verborgenen*], is mystery [*Geheimnis*].[234]

The unspoken is not simply what is not vocalized as in the severe condition of dysfluency or in the more ubiquitous experience of not being able to summon the right word to express an idea or a feeling in a given moment.[235] It is rather what is unremittingly withheld as the unsaid, the mystery of all mysteries of the thoughtful saying (*das Geheimnis aller Geheimnisse des denkenden Sagens*) through which everything named on the way returns to what the names steadfastly leave unspoken,[236] the unnameable hiddenness of being revealed as hidden by Dasein's comportment (*Verhalten*) in the bearing (*Verhältnis*) toward beings and their disclosure that lets the forgottenness of the mystery (*Vergessenheit des Geheimnisses*) take precedence such that it disappears in the forgottenness of what has been forgotten.[237] The concealment thus persists as concealed in the disclosure of the concealment disclosed in the concealment of disclosure, the appearance of what can appear only as inapparent. If the essential being of language may be deduced from the assertion that saying (*Sage*) is showing (*Zeige*),[238] it is necessary nevertheless to emphasize that what is shown in that showing is the unshowable, for every unconcealment of truth is ineludibly a concealment of untruth. Illustrating the proposition that saying is showing, Heidegger made this very point:

> Language speaks by saying, this is, by showing. What it says wells up from the formerly spoken and so far still unspoken Saying which pervades the design of language.... In everything that speaks to us, in everything that touches us by being spoken and spoken about, in everything that gives itself to us in speaking, or waits for us unspoken, but also in the speaking that we do *ourselves*, there prevails Showing which causes to appear what is present, and to fade from appearance what is absent.[239]

Poetic discourse is endowed with the distinctive charge of speaking about and therewith safeguarding what cannot be spoken.[240] Thus, as Heidegger ardently decreed, "Poetry's spoken words shelter the poetic statement as that which by its essential nature remains unspoken."[241] Insofar as the poem is a speaking about the unspoken, the genre of speech proper to the undertaking of poiēsis is "to say after [*nach-sagen*]—to say again the music of the spirit of apartness [*Abgeschiedenheit*] that has been spoken to the poet."[242]

The linear circularity of the temporal path is such that the anterior is subsequent to the posterior, and thus the saying-after (*Nachsagen*) of poetic speech—depicted by the Eckhartian notion of detachment[243]—transposes speaking into a pious form of listening (*Hören*) that becomes "more pliable to the promptings of the path on which the stranger walks ahead, out of the dark of childhood into the stiller, brighter earliness."[244] The reversibility of time's curvature indicates that posteriority must be thought from the vantage point of the anteriority of the before that always comes after, the effect that precedes the cause,[245] the no longer that is continually not yet,[246] in Derrida's lingo, the mark of writing the postscriptum that "takes place after taking place."[247] But how can something take place after having taken place unless what takes place is perpetually in a state of what is still to take place? Apophatic discourse brings to light that every interpretive performance rests on a preunderstanding, which is

> the fact from which we should indeed start, in relation to which we would be placed-after [*post-posés*]. We come *after the fact* [après le fait]: and the discursive possibilities of the *via negativa* are doubtless exhausted, that is what remains for us to think.[248]

Only by advancing forward to take hold of what lies ahead does one retrieve what lies behind. Since novelty is the effect of replication, disparity the corollary of resemblance, the hermeneutical enterprise is to repeat the unrepeatable.[249]

In the letter to Jacob written on November 28, 1950, Susan expressed her desire to live in holiness and to heed the silence, believing that speaking about important things was a form of desecration. Castigating the especially egregious defilement on the part of professional academicians, who speak about matters that should be kept silent, Susan noted that

> the wise men of the past, the gnostics, + kabalists had to disguise their thought in fantastic garments to protect them, because to utter these things nakedly is to kill them and ourselves too. We must guard the truth in silence + in "disguise".[250]

From the practice of the wise men of old—the gnostics and the kabbalists—to hide their thoughts in garments in order to shield them, we can extract the hermeneutical truism that uttering secrets nakedly, that is, stripped of their imaginal encasements, has lethal consequences for both the truths laid bare and for the recipients of those truths. Emulating these sages, it is necessary to secure the truth in silence; however, this is accomplished not by refusing to speak—in accord with Wittgenstein's aphorism at the conclusion of the *Tractatus Logico-Philosophicus* that one must be silent about that of which one cannot speak[251]—but rather by speaking in such a way that the unspeakable is adorned symbolically and thereby preserved in its unspeakability.

As Susan wrote to Jacob in a letter dated December 26, 1950, "The 'hidden' realms do not allow straight forward description—and about that what cannot be spoken one should be silent or speak in a 'silent' way i.e. using words that point to the silences between the words."[252] She goes on to write that the term "allegory" is not sufficient to capture the correlation between the earthly and the heavenly insofar as it "destroys meaning" and thereby undercuts the manner in which the two realms are divergent in their congruence. "What we must think and speak is how the one is and is not the other, how their relation is the ultimate category of being, and meaning—and this can be thought or said only 'negatively' in the parable."[253] The contrast between parable and allegory corresponds more or less to the distinction Scholem famously made between symbol and allegory.[254] Just as Scholem, implementing in his interpretation of the kabbalah the Romantic understanding of the symbol as a linguistic mode of communicating the incommunicable, forged an analogical pairing of the incomparable spheres of divinity and nature,[255] so Susan understood parable as a way to speak silently or negatively about indescribable hidden realms, to speak about the silences between words.[256] To paraphrase a passage in the *Gospel of Philip* that lends support to Susan's generalization, truth cannot come into the world denuded but only in "types" and "images" that are homologous to the world. Devoid of all metaphoric embellishments, truth in and of itself is rendered metaphorically as a being that is unclothed. To appear phenomenally, however, truth had to be arrayed in the symbolic alignments that could be received by the inhabitants of the world.[257]

Susan's poetics share with Heidegger and the kabbalists the presupposition that unconcealment is not a disrobing of the naked truth but rather the disposing of the garment in which truth is attired for the sake of donning another garment in its place. Insofar as the nameless is declaimed by way of the name that both reveals and conceals its namelessness, and the formless is envisaged by way of the form that both reveals and conceals its formlessness, gnosis is inseparably bound to agnosia; that is, one cannot know the unveiling of the veil of truth but through unknowing the truth veiled in the veil of untruth. From kabbalistic material one may elicit the maxim that, in my opinion, is expressed in other mystical traditions as well: *the removal of the veil inevitably results in the unfurling of another veil*. The enlightened visionary, therefore, comprehends that the apocalyptic notion of the final veil to lift implies that the final veil to lift is the veil of thinking there is a final veil to lift. We can speak of the removal of all barriers once we realize that the greatest of barriers is to speak of the removal of all barriers. Only when it is understood that we cannot see without a veil may the veil of seeing without a veil be discarded. Nudity itself is thus an acclamation of the imagistic representation against which it purportedly revolts.[258]

This, I surmise, is the import of Susan's comment cited toward the beginning of this chapter: "The separation from the absolute is our condition which must not so much be 'overcome' as lived."[259] To live in the space of that separation is to be attuned to the unbridgeable chasm that can only be bridged through the language of parable that is based on a logic that impugns the principle of noncontradiction and the law of the excluded middle insofar as it affirms the dialetheic paradox of the sameness of two things that persist in their difference—*the one is and is not the other*. The innately disparate nature of the worlds juxtaposed in their irreducible otherness fortifies Susan's hypothesis that every attempt to reconstruct the broken world into a totality contains the flaw of an ontological untruth.[260] The effort at totalization is not only the methodological weakness of tragedy and mysticism, but it is also the nihilistic basis of the role accorded to the nothingness of being in Heidegger's *Seinsdenken*.[261] The erroneous nature of the world is not denied by Susan, but she struggled to uphold the ontological untruth that *what is most wrong in our existence is what is most precious*. The paradoxical retrieval of the truth of this untruth affords the poetic soul the opportunity to confront the limit by breaking it, an infringement of boundary that is redolent equally with the enduring transience of love and the transient endurance of death.

TWO

Between Athens and Jerusalem
The Dubious Certainty of Gillian Rose's Broken Middle

There's metaphysics enough in not thinking about anything. . . .
The only mystery is that there are people who think about mystery. . . .
The only inner meaning of things
Is that they have no inner meaning at all.
—Fernando Pessoa, *The Complete Works of Alberto Caeiro*

I initiate my discussion of Gillan Rose with her insight that the entanglement of aporia with itself is marked by the coalescence of the difficulty of beginning with the beginning of difficulty.[1] In *The Broken Middle: Out of Our Ancient Society*, Rose lucidly laid out the logical provocation of this gridlock:

The beginning can no longer be made by presupposing the concept any more than it can be made by denigrating the System, even ironically. We are now—and have been—beginning by coming to recognize the occlusions and stumbling blocks lying across the beginning. Every beginning so far encountered, whether contra or pro the System, appears as a mask: contra-masks of new-born beginning, *restitutio in prisinum*, yet wrested from the System's authority; pro-masks, drawn from hypostatized representations of the System itself, yet intended, perversely, to re-enter its inner process: the latter—illusory mask, the former—masked illusion.[2]

The penetrating explication of the puzzle of the beginning was occasioned by Rose's consideration of the play of system and fragment in Adorno's

Minima Moralia, but she remarked that this "philosophical wit" can be elicited as well from Hegel's *Phenomenology of Spirit*.[3] Without entering into the thicket of that discussion, what is important to highlight at this juncture is that we launch the analysis of Rose's thought with the acknowledgment that she coherently marked the quandary of how to begin a beginning that cannot begin and therefore cannot be a beginning except in the paradoxical mode of being the beginning before the beginning.[4]

Anxiety of Beginning, Beginning of Anxiety, and Equivocation of the Middle

From Kierkegaard's ruminations over the contradiction between immortality and mortality, Rose identified the "origin of anxiety" as the "anxiety of beginning" prompted by the assessment that the stages of life are simultaneous even though the humdrum of everyday existence forces us to concentrate sequentially on one or the other.[5] Seeing through that perceptual sleight of hand, we come to appreciate that it is not only the middle that is Janus-faced but the beginning, too, insofar as it looks "both to the anxiety of beginning and to the beginning of anxiety."[6] The difficulty of beginning a deliberation about the beginning brings us to the point where the anxiety of beginning meets the beginning of anxiety.[7] Tantalizingly, Rose coupled Kierkegaard and Freud around their mutual positioning the identification of the anxiety of beginning as the beginning of anxiety in the equivocation of the middle.[8]

> The beginning of anxiety is . . . returned to or restated at its middle, immersed in its multiple dangers—internal and external: "real", neurotic and moral. This middle—the conflicting words of command—is equally the anxiety of beginning—not only an account of "the compulsion to repeat", but an inducement of repetition forwards which cannot take place as the result of any authorial authority.[9]

From the conflation of the anxiety of beginning and the beginning of anxiety in the elusiveness of the middle, we discern that every beginning is an illusory mask of the masked illusion that there can be a beginning that is an absolute novum causally severed from the now that came before and the now that comes after. In the curvature of time, there is no before that is not after an after that is before it was after. The linear circularity of the timeswerve thus presumes a beginning that cannot begin and an ending that cannot end.

Between Athens and Jerusalem   69

Notwithstanding the intractable nature of this paradox, I will commence my explication of Rose's thought by recalling the sparse inscription engraved on her tombstone:

> In loving memory of
> Gillian Rose
> Philosopher
> September 20th 1947
> December 9th 1995

Strikingly, a lifetime undoubtedly multifaceted and complex reduced to one seemingly simple epithet "philosopher." What are we to make of this laconic and somewhat stoical description that does not even bother to offer more details about the nature of her philosophical disposition and most assuredly overlooks so many other aspects of the rich tapestry of her biography? Can the plethora of embodied experiences—the desires and the disappointments, the pains and the pleasures, the triumphs and the failures, the dreams and the disenchantments—all be reduced to this diminutive identification? A hint is given by Rose herself in the opening paragraph of the introduction to *The Broken Middle*, subtitled the *Diremption of Spirit*. The reader is told that the Owl of Minerva has spread her wings, and thus

> we may now be prepared and readied for philosophy's grey in grey; not for the colour on colour of post-modernity, with its premature celebration of a new epoch for the coming millennium, even if incipient in the old. For our antiquity has yet to see the soaring of the soft-plumaged Minerva in her nocturnal figuration.[10]

As philosopher, Rose's life was inundated with the craving to behold the grayness of night in all of its grayness, that is, in the distinctiveness of the indistinctness that lays forth the trajectory of flight that always brings the thinker back to the ground of the past where one has already never been.

Nocturnality and the Tragicomic Seeing the Dark

In the final decade of the twentieth century, Rose audaciously pushed back on what she considered the false promise of postmodernism and in its place attributed to philosophy the task of bringing into view her nocturnal figuration. At the heart of Rose's criticism of postmodern thought is her contention that it constitutes a tradition that understands itself to have no tradition.[11] Alternatively expressed, the postmodern turn represents the most unscientific critique that scientifically affronts systematic thinking, exemplified by Hegel, without allowing that the totalizing nature of that system is such that if nothing can be removed from the system, then the lack of system perforce must itself be included as part of the system, an aspect of Hegelian philosophy that Rose called concomitantly the seriousness and the facetiousness of irony.[12] Pragmatically speaking, the search for a new ethics without ground, principle, transcendence, or utopia on the part of the neo-nihilism and the antinomianism of postmodernism, which took shape in the wake of the perceived demise of Marxism and the disgrace of Heidegger's Nazism, fails to accommodate the fact that Hegel viewed *the movement of the Absolute as comedy*.[13] It is worth citing in full the relevant words of Hegel upon which the exposition of Rose is based:

A truly tragic suffering... is only inflicted on the individual agents as a consequence of their own deed which is both legitimate and, owing to the resulting collision, blameworthy, and for which their whole self is answerable.... In tragedy the eternal substance of things emerges victorious in a reconciling way, because it strips away from the conflicting individuals only their false one-sidedness, while the positive elements in what they willed it displays as what is to be retained, without discord but affirmatively harmonized. In comedy, conversely, it is subjectivity, or personality, which in its infinite assurance retains the upper hand.... In tragedy the individuals destroy themselves through the one-sidedness of their otherwise solid will and character, or they must resignedly accept what they had opposed even in a serious way. In comedy there comes before our contemplation, in the laughter in which the characters dissolve everything, including themselves, the victory of their own subjective personality which nevertheless persists self-assured. The general ground for comedy is therefore a world in which man as subject or person has made himself completely master of everything that counts to him otherwise as the essence of what he wills and accomplishes, a world whose aims are therefore self-destructive because they are unsubstantial.... But it does not follow at all that every unsubstantial action is comical on account of this nullity. In this matter the laughable is often confused with the comical. Every contrast between something substantive and its appearance, between an end and the means may be laughable; this is a contradiction in which the appearance cancels itself and the realization of an end is at the same time the end's own destruction.... On the other hand, the comical as such implies an infinite light-heartedness and confidence felt by someone raised altogether above his own inner contradiction and not bitter or miserable in it at all: this is the bliss and ease of a man who, being sure of himself, can bear the frustration of his aims and achievements.[14]

The comical must be distinguished from the laughable. Epistemically, the latter entails the contrast between subjective caprice and insubstantial action, whereas the former implies an infinite lightheartedness and confidence felt by someone elevated above contradiction, the bliss of self-assurance that breeds an enjoyment impermeable to the thwarting of one's ambitions. The ruling principle of the comical is "the contingency and caprice of subjective life"[15] to the point that the "nullity and self-destructive folly displays the abused actuality of substantial life."[16] In contradistinction to tragedy wherein the powers that oppose one another as pathos in the person are hostile, in comedy, they are revealed inwardly as self-dissolving insofar as

the comical rests as such throughout on contradictory contrasts both between aims in themselves and also between their objects and the accidents of character and external circumstances, and therefore the comic action requires a solution almost more stringently than a tragic one does. In a comic action the contradiction between what is absolutely true and its realization in individuals is posed more profoundly.[17]

We are told, moreover, that comedy, as much as tragedy, is always *divine comedy*; that is, the comical revolves around the assumption that the absolute and infinite substance is brought into existence as something concrete and finite.[18] Here we must heed the distinction drawn by Hegel between irony and comedy. The divine is portrayed as essentially ironical as opposed to comical. This reflects Hegel's depiction of the irony of the individual genius as that which "lies in the self-destruction of the noble, great, and excellent; and so the objective art-formations too will have to display only the principle of absolute subjectivity, by showing forth what has worth and dignity for mankind as null in its self-destruction."[19] Not only does such a conception question the seriousness about law, morals, and truth, but it vilifies the valorization of the lofty and the best, "since, in its appearance in individuals, characters, and actions, it contradicts and destroys itself and so is ironical about itself."[20] Thus, irony may be compared to the knife by means of which one cuts oneself to the point that one is entirely eviscerated. With regard to this loss of character there is kinship between the ironic and the comic, but the latter "must be restricted to showing that what destroys itself is something inherently null, a false and contradictory phenomenon, a whim, e.g., an oddity, a particular caprice in comparison with a mighty passion, or even a *supposedly* tenable principle with a firm maxim." By contrast, the ironic necessitates that "what is in fact moral and true, any inherently substantial content, displays itself in an individual, and by his agency, as null. . . . Therefore in this difference between the ironic and the comic what is essentially at issue is the content of what is destroyed."[21]

From the delineation of irony as the keynote of aesthetic representation, we may deduce that "the most inartistic of all principles is taken to be the principle of the work of art."[22] This, in turn, yields the metaphysical axiom that the limited is an inextricable part of the limitless, and thus the wholeness of the system contains the cracks that paradoxically will not fit into the system except as the exceptions to the system. Needless to say, there can be no absolute exception because every exception comprises an exception to the exception, and thus the very notion of exception suspends our pretense to know the totality in relation to which the exception is made.[23] Cast in a different ideational register, which Rose elicited from both Kierkegaard and Hegel, the expression or the negotiation of immediacy always involves the mediation of ideality, and hence the "resulting duplexity inside and outside language demands a countervailing duplicity to overcome the doubt engendered by the remove of ideality."[24] Insofar as the general must always be assessed from the perspective of the unassimilability of the particular, we might do well to adopt the taxonomy of an open system, a systemless system, a system that has renounced the comprehensiveness of the system, a system whose consistency of necessity will be its inconsistency, or in the language of cybernetics, a hypersystem in which the properties are not explained by the unilateral interaction of the component elements and in which compartmentalization of the parts cannot be reductively subsumed under the aggregation of the whole nor the aggregation of the whole under the compartmentalization of the parts.[25] Algorithmically, incoherence of the nonsystematic is the metric of the coherence of the systematic whence it follows that the limitless complexity of the plurivocality of the singular delimits the parameters of the limited simplicity of the univocity of the whole. The irrational should thus be regarded as the supplementary constituent of the rational[26] in the same manner that the nonconceptual is conceptualized unfailingly as an aspect of the conceptual.[27]

With respect to this matter, Adorno served as a model for Rose about whom she wrote: "On the one hand, he was opposed to all philosophical and sociological systems, yet on the other, he wanted his fragments to be read as if they were systematic."[28] To cite Adorno's own language,

> the *telos* of philosophy, its open and unshielded part, is as anti-systematic as its freedom to interpret the phenomena with which it joins unarmed issue. Philosophy retains respect for systems to the extent to which things heterogeneous to it face it in the form of a system.[29]

The philosophical system is antinomical from the outset insofar as each system is ordained to elimination with the materialization of the next system. Hence, all systems are marred by an a priori inescapable failure: to prevail as a system, the ratio of the system comes into an irreconcilable conflict with the objectivity it necessarily violates by pretending to grasp it.[30] "The slightest remnant of nonidentity," therefore, "sufficed to deny an identity conceived as total. The excrescences of the systems ... show the untruth, the mania, of the systems themselves."[31] To think against thinking requires positing a negativity at the ground of reason—the nonidentity comprised within the principle of identity as the other to thinking that can be thought only as what cannot be thought—that leads to a limitation to thinking that makes thinking against thinking possible because impossible. Rose credited Blanchot for recognizing the fragment as that which signals to the system that it ceaselessly demands even as it is being dismissed:

> Then, since nothing escapes it because of its omnipresent unity and the perfect cohesion of everything, there remains no place for fragmentary writing unless it come into focus as the impossible necessary: as that which is written in the time outside time, in the sheer suspense which without restraint breaks the seal of unity by, precisely, not breaking it, but by leaving it aside without this abandon's ever being able to be known.[32]

The fragment set in contrast to the totality is the *impossible necessary*, necessary because it is part of the whole but impossible because the fragmentary ipso facto cannot be defined as being part of the whole. Hence, the oxymoron denotes that the fragment breaks the seal of unity by not breaking it, and, from a temporal standpoint, it is written in time that is outside time, that is, an atemporal time, a time that cannot be measured by the quantitative metrics of a chronological succession stretched between an atomized now that is no more and an atomized now that is not yet. However, the time outside time should not be understood as timeless perpetuity or even as the *nunc stans*, the immobile moment of an interminable eternity.[33] Rather, it is conceptually contiguous with Giorgio Agamben's notion of "dys-chrony," the noncoincidence that one feels with the contemporary time to which one irrevocably coincides, a relationship to the present to which one adheres by keeping a distance through the twin gestures of disjunction and anachronism.[34] What is outside time, therefore, is the untimely incorporated inside time, the too soon that is always too late, the already that is not yet.[35] Analogously, the antisystem is inevitably encompassed in the system in the same manner that finitude must be comprised potentially within infinity and inclusivity that is exclusive must include what is excluded by an exclusivity that is inclusive. Heterogeneity, on this score, is an indispensable property of homogeneity.[36]

But what is meant by the aforementioned reference to the nocturnal figuration of philosophy? How are we to understand this turn of phrase? What does it tell us about the path Rose walked in this world? Here it is well to call attention to the following comment in her autobiography *Love's Work: A Reckoning with Life*:

Night time is psyche time: the accumulation of excess emotion, aroused but unattended during the day; it must have its say—in dream or in prayer, in love making and taking. Neglected or unrehearsed, these residues exact their revenge: they trouble my sleep or keep me awake with an acuity unknown to the day. Morning is holy terror: awakening, a naked dawning with no consolation of the work of mourning. Grief has been expended during the night; curiosity for the day is still held at bay. . . . Eros passion is fled: its twin, the passion of faith, is taunting my head.[37]

Nocturnality is demarcated as the psychic time of excessive emotion, the time of erotic passion, which is intriguingly correlated with perspicacity and sorrow. Wisdom belongs to the nighttime—a time of prayer, dreams, and sexual intimacy—whose intonation is modulated by gloom and not elation. By contrast, diurnality, the time of awakening and the passion of faith, is correlated with curiosity that lacks the consolation of the work of mourning.

The nocturnal is most often linked to the sensation of blackness, but in Rose's understanding, as we saw in the passage from *The Broken Middle* cited above,[38] the darkness of night conjures a sense of grayness, the color that is intermediate between black and white,[39] the achromatic color—the color without color—that conveys contemplative quiescence, servility, and resignation. Perhaps Rose's emphasis on gray in part reflects the following comment of Adorno:

> Grayness could not fill us with despair if our minds did not harbor the concept of different colors, scattered traces of which are not absent from the negative whole. The traces always come from the past, and our hopes come from their counterpart, from that which was or is doomed; such an interpretation may very well fit the last line of Benjamin's text on *Elective Affinities*: "For the sake of the hopeless only are we given hope."[40] And yet it is tempting to look for the sense, not in life at large, but in the fulfilled moments—in the moments of present existence that make up for its refusal to tolerate anything outside it.[41]

The grayness of night is not so much the absence of color as it is the fullness of many colors that are scattered traces contained in a nondescript way within the negative whole. Just as these traces come from that which was rebuked in the past, so hope can spring only from the hopeless as is implied in the statement of Benjamin cited by Adorno. If hopelessness were totally annihilated, we would not be capable of experiencing hopefulness in the present moment at hand. The pessimism undergirding the optimism is heightened by Rose's formulation "*grey in grey*," a doubling that is meant to turn "hubris" into "motile configuration" and to warn against philosophy's pride of *Sollen*, the infinite and unrealizable ought of the stipulation to promulgate proscriptions or prescriptions and to impose ideals, imaginary communities, and progressive narratives.[42] On the contrary, the idealizations of philosophy act as the third element that occupies the middle positioned "between the potentiality and actuality of the world and engaging at the point where the two come into a changed relation: not *ex post facto* justification, even less *a priori* rejuvenation, but reconfiguration, oppositional yet vital—*something understood*."[43]

Much can be gleaned from these words, but for our immediate purpose I want to focus on the location of philosophy in the middle betwixt the potentiality and the actuality of the world, as this is surely an important clue to decode the meaning of the description of Rose on her tombstone as philosopher. Although indebted to the Hegelian quest to articulate a form of knowing that makes the absolute thinkable.[44] Rose was cognizant of the fact that there can be no unqualified statements about the absolute even in Hegel, and thus we are cognitively condemned to an indisposable degree of vagueness.[45] If the whole is still presumed to exist, it must be visualized without capitulating to the forces of totalization or reductionism.[46] Rose's speculations are both conspicuously unsystematic and unambiguous in divulging that her mission was not to offer decisive and irrefutable statements on philosophical issues or debates.[47] A perusal of her work intimates that she was closer in spirit to Adorno's understanding of philosophy as a critical intervention that ensues from the conceptual space that she denominated as *the broken middle*, that is, the middle whose brokenness cannot be broken.[48] To assert otherwise would be to undermine the *middleness* of the middle.

Rationalism Without Reason and the Agnosticism of Gnosis

Fidelity to self-limiting reason[49] as the diremptive means to destabilize and to strengthen previous theories is the underpinning of the role that Rose assigns to the philosopher as social critic:

Neither politics nor reason unify or "totalize": they arise out of diremption—out of the diversity of peoples who come together under the aporetic law of the city, and who know that their law is different from the law of other cities—what Rousseau called "power", and which we now call "nation". Philosophy issues, too, out of this diremption and its provisional overcoming in the culture of an era—without "disowning" that "edifice", it (philosophy) steps away to inspect its limitations, especially when the diremptions fixated in the edifice have lost their living connections. We should be renewing our thinking on the invention and production of edifices, that is, cities, apparently civilized within yet dominating without—not sublimating those equivocations into holy cities.[50]

In *Love's Work*, Rose explicitly related that she was attracted by the ethical impulse of Adorno's thought as well as by the difficulty of his literary style and vocabulary replete with foreign words (*Fremdwörter*), an embarkation that oddly brought to fruition an inner need to experience her dyslexia in daily intercourse with the signs and syntax of the forbidding universe of this German polymath.[51] Here it is relevant to recall that in *The Melancholy Science: An Introduction to the Thought of Theodor W. Adorno*, Rose noted:

Two of the three parts of Adorno's book on Hegel are concerned with how to read Hegel's texts, especially the *Phenomenology of Mind* and the (greater) *Logic*. One of these parts is entitled *Skoteinos oder Wie zu lesen sei*. *Skoteinos* is a Greek word which means "dark, dusky, obscure or blind". *Oder wie zu lesen sei* means "or how to read".[52]

To know how to read Hegel one must acquiesce to the austere truth that there is no light but in darkness, no transparency but in obscurity, no vision but in blindness. I suspect no one would quarrel over the ascription of this hermeneutical precept to Rose's own writings.

In lieu of categorical and authoritative pronouncements, Rose aspired to offer oppositional arguments that might lead to something being understood, that is, achieving the motile reconfiguration of how one might think and behave. Rose's critical method is clarified succinctly in her comments on Judith Plaskow's feminist revision of Jewish ritual:

> This simultaneous abuse and use of prophetic reason might suggest a dialectic and equivocation, but instead it founds a new certainty—the innocence and immediacy of "women's experience". But all and any experience, however long abused and recently uncovered, will be *actual* and not simply *alter* (Other): the discrepant outcome of idea and act will be traceable to meanings which transcend the boundaries of idea and act—to norm, imperative, commandment and inhibition, that is, to the law and its commotion. To promise anything else, any new righteousness which will not be subject of and subject to the difficulty of actuality, which will never become unjust, is to disempower. Reason that is actual is ready for all kinds of surprises, for what cannot be anticipated, precisely because of the interference of meanings which are structured and reconstructable.[53]

Rose's objective was not to enunciate clear and indubitable truths à la the deductive epistemology of Descartes. In her post-postmodern thought, clarity is at best the elucidation of an opacity that incontrovertibly affirms an equivocality that bespeaks the capricious nature of the actual. Again, following Adorno, Rose maintained that meaning or conceptuality is a property of social structure—determined in Marxist ideology by the production and exchange of commodities—which is not only mutable and capricious in nature but also illusory to the extent that reality is presented in such a way that citizens of a given society may be prevented from becoming conscious of the actual conditions under which they live. The process thus insists on the systematic formation of social reality according to a principle which can be specified without any reference to the meaning conferred on that reality by individuals, and yet this principle produces illusions which need to be interpreted at the level of meaning. "Meaning" refers to the ways in which the social structure seems intelligible when it is not, and unintelligible when it is.[54]

Insofar as meaning is not predicated on the intentional actions of individuals or even based on the negotiation of shared meanings by social actors but is rather the result of a whimsical process by which social structures appear to be intelligible when unintelligible and unintelligible when intelligible, one must be suspicious of reified positions—even if they profess to overturn the status quo by advocating for an eminently liberal agenda as in the case of Plaskow's feminism[55]—since they will prove to be inadequate to deal with the mutability of reality. Declarations of certainty are fundamentally uncertain by virtue of the certainty they proclaim, and thus the petition for simplification of complexity is obfuscation disguised as lucidity.

Pointedly, in a radio interview with Andy O'Mahony, broadcast on November 4, 1995, and edited by Vincent Lloyd for publication in 2008, after confessing that she believed in something outside the spatiotemporal continuum, Rose confirmed the need to be agnostic:

> But I think one has to preserve an agnosticism about it. I love what Simone Weil said, that agnosticism is the most truly religious position. You must be able to say you don't know. Agnosticism is the only true religion because to have faith is not to give up knowledge, but to know where the limit of knowledge is.[56]

Relying on Weil's mystical avowal that skepticism and agnosticism are preferable to idolatry, and hence atheism paradoxically portends the purification of theism by bolstering the conviction that denial of God is the most earnest belief in God,[57] Rose maintained that faith is not the antithesis of knowledge but rather the delimitation of its limit. The true possessor of gnosis, therefore, is the agnostic, the one who knows that knowledge consists of knowing that one cannot know. I suspect that it is for this reason that Rose declared that the only criterion to determine if one deserves to be called a philosopher is if that person falls in love with Socrates.[58] She even went so far as to write about Socrates that he was almost her Christ figure.[59] This agnosticism is consistent with Rose's insistence that reason deals with the actual that is typically unreasonable, and consequently, it must be flexible, expecting the unexpectable, entertaining the prospect of intervention that constantly subjects structures of meaning to periodic deconstruction and reconstruction.

The method adopted by Rose, which she eventually named *Mourning Becomes the Law*,

> affirms that the reassessment of reason, gradually rediscovering its own moveable boundaries as it explores the boundaries of the soul, the city, and the sacred, can complete its mourning. Completed mourning acknowledges the creative involvement of action in the configurations of power and law: it does not find itself unequivocally in a closed circuit which exclusively confers logic and power.[60]

It follows—whether fastidiously or erratically—that we claim ownership of the very conventions and beliefs that we disown, and thus we must be sensitive to the likelihood that we are oblivious to the replication of traditions that are to be gauged from the standpoint of their capacity for regeneration through the articulation of the novel in the guise of the ancient. In the introduction to *Dialectic of Nihilism: Post-Structuralism and Law*, tellingly subtitled *Legalism Without Law*, Rose commented:

> The newly vaunted demise of metaphysics has been cast as a theoretical jurisprudence which, nevertheless, leaves law as unknowable as it finds it. The "deconstruction" of metaphysics involves a reconstruction of the history of law which blinds us to the very tradition which it disowns and repeats. . . . This destruction of knowledge is justified by its perpetrators as the only way to escape the utopian projections and historicist assumptions of dialectic; "eternal repetition of the same" is said to be a harder truth than the false and discredited promise of reconciliation. Yet neither the form of this hard truth nor the terms in which it is expressed are neutral: they are always borrowed from some historically identifiable epoch of juridical experience.[61]

The proper analytical orientation must take stock of the connection between the history of philosophy and the philosophy of history. This is the criterion that can help establish an independent perspective from which to evaluate "the intrinsically historical claims that metaphysics, dialectics and structuralism have been overcome."[62]

The various claims that metaphysics has been surpassed are merely rhetorical in concurrence with the original meaning of this term to serve as guard and guide to the law:

> Metaphysics, pre-critical and post-critical, pre-Nietzschean and post-Nietzschean, has not been overturned by its transmogrification into positive science, nor by the

return to its archaic beginning, nor by the timeless and tireless reception of our disowned and projected powers. For these glimpses into the metajuridical vault are still purchased with those Aristotelian categories we were just using: science (*episteme*); principle or beginning (*arche*); timeless (*apeiron*); power (*dynamis*). The invariable reversal of such attempts to cashier metaphysics reveals in each case a speculative jurisprudence: a story of the identity and non-identity of law and metaphysics retold by the rhetor in the mask of the *histor*.[63]

In the end, postmodernism and deconstruction fail to uphold the tenet that there is no overcoming that is not an undergoing, or in Heideggerian language, that every *Überwindung* is a *Verwindung*, a surpassing through meandering.[64]

Rose's criticism of contemporary philosophical trends repeating the very patterns of thought that they sought to undermine is reminiscent of her explanation of Adorno's critical method:

> The *Dialectic of Enlightenment* reveals the paradox of the late eighteenth-century concept of reason: instead of bringing emancipation as it promised, it turned out to be a new form of domination. Adorno, however, reveals more persistently the paradoxes of new philosophical and theoretical movements of the twentieth century which promise emancipation, "the dialectic of humanism". Adorno and many other German writers of the inter-war period were attracted to an anti-humanist stance. They rejected the humanist legacy of historicism, philosophical anthropology, "realism" in art, and epistemology, for these were seen as bankrupt, incapable of providing any analysis of a much-changed historical reality. Adorno held that these varieties of "anti-humanism" were enslaving rather than liberating because they recreated the very evils which they sought to define and eschew. He thus recognised a "dialectic of humanism" and showed how the "new" philosophy, sociology, and literary theory relapsed into the assumptions which they deplored.[65]

The postmodern and deconstructive repudiation of what Adorno identified as the "old ambition of philosophy to establish indubitable grounds for its own endeavour"[66] is dubious insofar as the claims that strive to undercut certitude are proffered as certain. The proposition that there are no unconditional truths is self-contradictory as it is proposed unconditionally as truth. By concentrating on the middle, Rose did not pursue a dialectical resolution of this antinomy but rather identified the conceptual space where the uncertainty of truth and the certainty of untruth enduringly coexist in the dialetheic antagonism of the truth of uncertainty and the untruth of certainty.

Misrecognition and Recognizing the Singularity of the Middle

In political terms, as Rose remarked in *The Broken Middle*, the risk of coming to know depends on accepting the tension between subjective freedom and objective unfreedom, an opposition that instigates the two axes of process and pain that intersect in the middle.[67] Fleshing out the implication of this insight and noting that the attempts of postmodernism to restore the middle have had the effect of undermining it by the projection of social utopianism and the insinuated sense of the holy that must be reconfigured by the very brokenness it seeks to heal, Rose observed:

> The more the illusory independence of the individual and "the community" is figured in a middle—architecture—the more vulnerable that *topos* will become to the animus of social dystopia; while the reconfiguration of individual and state proceeds apace without recognition in its imbricated legal space.[68]

Rose thus expanded on the nature of her displeasure with the postmodern leanings of contemporary philosophy:

> Postmodernism is submodern: these holy middles of ecstatic divine milieu, irenic other city, holy community—face to face or halachic—and the unholy one of the perpetual carnival market, bear the marks of their unexplored precondition: the diremption between the moral discourse of rights and the systematic actuality of power, within and between modern states. And therefore they will destroy what they would propagate, for once substance is presented, even if it is not "represented", however "continuous" with practice, it becomes procedural, formal, and its meaning will be configured and corrupted within the prevailing diremptions of morality and legality, autonomy and heteronomy, civil society and state. Mended middles and improvised middles betray their broken middle: antinomian yet dependent on renounced law; holy yet having renounced "ideals"; yearning for nomadic freedom, yet having renounced nature and freedom. This thinking concurs in representing its tradition—reason and institutions—as monolithic domination, as totalitarian. It overlooks the *pre*dominance of form, abstract legal form, as the unfreedom *and* freedom of modern states, thereby falling into the trap, not of positing another totalitarian ideal, but of presenting a holy middle which arises out of and will be reconfigured in the prevalent broken middle.[69]

Lingering in the interval between contraries equipped with no possibility of dialectical resolution but only the tendency to dismantle what is promoted, this is the import of the aforementioned subtitle of the introduction to *The Broken Middle*: "*Diremption of Spirit.*" The disjunction of consciousness evolves primarily from the philosophical examination of the split between law and ethics as it appears within the conceptuality of Hegel and Kierkegaard.[70] It is through that diremption—identified by Rose as modernity's ancient predicament[71]—that philosophy "is always and hence currently being revalued."[72] Precisely by admitting this task, philosophy assumes the mantle of social theory as a way of reclaiming the ethical immediacy disturbed by the dichotomization of the particularity and the universality converging in the divergence of the middle.[73]

The historical event that was the catalyst that helped give shape to Rose's conception of philosophy was the revolution of 1989, an upheaval that did not destroy Marxism as an ideology but rather dismantled the socioeconomic institutions of postwar state socialism. The fall of communism occasioned the potential to scrutinize the connection between liberalism and fascism. However, writ larger, the insurgency presented Rose with the opportunity to mount a rigorous appraisal of postmodernity for its turn against philosophy and its implementation of sophistry expressed in the replacement of genuine knowledge with the oratorical emphasis on discourse, the substitution of meticulous critique with the contrived appeal to plurality, and exchange of conscientious conceptuality with the grandiose aggrandizement of the notion of the other.[74] Although the skeptical conceit of philosophers more generally has been to "affect disaffection from philosophy," postmodern thinkers in particular must be deemed to be deadly unironic in their claim that philosophy "is revenge for the unbridgeable distance between thought or language and concrete being; metaphysics is spleen at the diversity and difference of beings; ethics is the violent domination of the troubling otherness of the other."[75]

This is the crux of Rose's criticism of postmodernism's disingenuous depiction of reason as totalitarian, imperialistic, and monolithic, and its dissembling denial of itself as a rational critique of rationality. Rose thus labeled postmodernism as a "despairing rationalism without reason," that is, a rationalism predicated not on the devastation of reason but on the utilization of reason to ratify unreason as an inexorable component of reason.[76] Postmodernity celebrates the overcoming of Western metaphysics, but it falls short of achieving its objective inasmuch as it disallows any means for investigating the implications of its own confabulations within the broken middle. To plumb the depths of that middle, what is required is the sagacity to apprehend that the fissures of the "still straining contraries" persist in that space as they are "neither disbanded nor rendered disarmable by such intellectual velleities."[77] Based on a letter of Franz Kafka to Max Brod proffering a talmudic interpretation of a passage from Kierkegaard, Rose referred to the *anxiety of the middle* where angels and demons are engaged in an altercation. Only by undertaking the gamble to venture out into the world are these forces of good and evil opened to a person and only then can one join the battle to the end so that the oppositions may be provisionally overpowered albeit never conclusively overcome.[78] Notionally, postmodernity remains dualistic insofar as it pits itself as the particular against its alleged others chiefly garbed in the machinating and universalizing guise of political-legal autocracy. By contrast, the broken middle is triune in its structure, comprising the universal, the particular, and the singular.

The nature of the broken middle reflects Rose's presentation of the originality of Hegelian philosophy as a move beyond the dualistic structure of the critical philosophy of Kant to the triadic structure of recognition in both form and content, a shift in logic that heralds a transition from *Anschauen*, seeing-into, to *Anerkennen*, recognizing. The emergence of recognition and the identity construction associated with it depends on the analysis of social and historical patterns of misrecognition or lack of identity. By definition, recognition is the re-cognizing of the identity of nonidentity in the nonidentity of identity, and hence recognition and misrecognition are inseparably interwoven.[79] Rose elaborated on the Hegelian concept that is at the center of her philosophy:

> "Recognition" refers to the lack of identity or relation which the initial dichotomy between concept and intuition, or consciousness and its objects, represents. But it also implies a unity which includes the relation or lack of identity. This unity mediates between the poles of the opposition and is hence triune. "Recognition", "concept" and "spirit" all have this triune structure. They all refer initially to lack of identity, relation, or domination. They all yield speculative propositions, and eschew the propositions of identity based on the primacy of the concept of pure practical reason. Miscognition implies, but does not pre-judge, real recognition.[80]

Ostensibly, it is reasonable to presume the imprint of the Hegelian dialectic and the threefold structure of recognition on Rose's depiction of the broken middle, and thus the singular would be construed as the sublation (*Aufhe-*

bung) of the antipathy between the universal and the particular. For Rose, however, the singular is not the mitigation of this dissonance, but it is rather the concretization of the dialetheic paradox that defies both the indexicality of the universal as particular and the indexicality of the particular as universal. The singularity of the middle mitigates equably against an absolute universalism that subsumes the particular and an absolute particularity that disregards the universal. I would submit that this conception of the singular is indebted to Adorno's interpretation of Kierkegaard's idea of faith as the "repetition or plenitude without possession or presence," the state wherein there are positions but no oppositions, and thus contraries "can be suffered simultaneously." Appreciably, it is in silence alone that we can hear that the "realization or lack of realization is not only not the same as redemption but not even its opposite." The denial of language—the "nots" of *de silentio*—implies "no negative theology but sacramental passion."[81] From within the reticence of this passion one unearths the truism that of the unspeakable one must speak endlessly in the gesticulation of speaking-not rather than in the moderation of not speaking.

Accentuating this understanding of singularity in the introduction to *The Broken Middle*, Rose proposed that

> the tension between the contraries of subjective freedom and objective unfreedom appears as unconceptualized aporia—Event of Being, Incursion of the Singular—as a singularity without its contraries of universal and particular. This . . . for all its anti-Utopia and anarchy, will turn into triumphant ecclesiology, as the sociology of the over-controlled secular is inverted into the sociality of saints.[82]

Even though the brokenness of the middle is never fully remedied, the benefit of situating oneself therein is the possibility of overcoming the scission between law and ethics by accepting that the singularity of one's being presumes the particularity of the universal manifest as the universality of the particular. Rose granted that recompositions of the threefold structure, whether applied to individuals or to institutions, continue to pervade our commonsense as binary oppositions "between inner morality and outer legality, individual autonomy and general heteronomy, active cognition and imposed norm. Made anxious by such inscrutable disjunctions, we invariably attempt to mend them . . . with *love*, forced or fantasized into the state."[83] The goal, however, is to move beyond the dyad and to lay claim to the indefinite third, the midpoint of ethics, mediating between the two definite cultural paradigms, the reason of Athens and the unreason of Jerusalem,[84] in an effort to ameliorate the contradiction that derives from the clash of the universal and the particular, the tension that is apposite to the void of the broken middle.[85] As Rose put it in *Judaism and Modernity*,

> Having renounced teleological philosophy of history, general philosophy produces in its place the newly purified polarity of reason and ethics, which Jewish philosophy, scared of the charge of Pharisaical legalism, intensifies with its purified polarity of law and love. Philosophy and Judaism want to proclaim *a New Testament* which will dispose of the broken promises of modernity.[86]

Rose may have considered the longstanding polarization of love and law simplistic, fallacious, and precarious, but this judgment did not stop her from privileging love as is attested in the sobering words in her memoir:

> However satisfying writing is—that the mix of discipline and miracle, which leaves you in control, even when what appears on the page has emerged from regions beyond your control—it is a very poor substitute indeed for the joy and agony of loving. Of there being someone who loves *and* desires you, and he glories in his love and desire, and you glory in his ever-strange being, which comes up against you, and disappears, again and again, surprising you with difficulties and with bounty. To lose this is the greatest loss, a loss for which there is no consolation. There can only be that twin passion—the passion of faith.[87]

Although there is no explicit mention of Christianity, it is prudent to assume that the invocation of the passion of faith at the end of the passage, portrayed as the twin passion to love, is an allusion to this religious tradition set in contrast to the personal relationships with which it bears affinity. The Song of Songs serves as the scriptural basis to justify the juxtaposition of the carnal and the spiritual and the articulation of a mystical theology that is "inseparable from attention to divine and human law, to the workings of the world."[88] As Rose put it in the O'Mahony interview, "*Eros* ranges from sexual desire to intellectual curiosity. It's just hunger, I think that's a good way to put it, because a hunger acknowledges a lack, but knows also that it can be filled."[89]

Both somatic and noetic eros are subject to the vacillation between desire and lack, a central theme in the Song of Songs encapsulated in the refrain couched as an oath taken by the maiden in the name of her female companions, the daughters of Jerusalem, "Do not arouse love until it desire" (Song of Songs 2:7, 3:5, 5:8, 8:4). The exhortation that love should not be stimulated until the pertinent time attests not only to the fact that there is no desire without lack, but that, more profoundly, the lack itself constitutes the temporal reflexivity of the desire to desire.[90] The deficiency of contemporary philosophy, especially deconstruction, is the myopic focus on lack to the point of seeing the whole of intellectual life as founded on an absence that we illegitimately try to represent as something that can be made to be present. In Freudian terms, this posture leaves the psyche in a state of melancholia insofar as it fails to complete the work of mourning, which would occasion the return to the fullness of being.[91] The crucial insight of Rose is that spiritual eros and carnal sexuality conjointly attest to the fact that love is the submission of power, but whereas love in the intersubjective sphere exhibits the dialectic of mercifulness and mercilessness, in the divine sphere, the dialectic is undone as there is only mercy.[92]

It should come as no surprise that on December 9, 1995, Rose was baptized into the Anglican Church on her deathbed.[93] According to the sermon delivered on Christmas Day 1996 by George Carey, at the time the Archbishop of Canterbury, Rose reportedly told friends that she was "too Jewish to be Christian and too Christian to be Jewish."[94] Lloyd suggested that this statement was applicable to Rose until her final day in spite of the parting conversion to Christianity.[95] I accept that Rose likely grappled with indecision regarding personal religious commitments and thus lived with an ambivalence of identity throughout her life. The choice to convert, however, did entail a repudiation of Judaism on the social and the theological planes. Lamentably, she did not live very long after her conversion so we have no way of knowing how she would have negotiated the Marrano identity of being simultaneously a Jewish Christian and a Christian Jew. It is safe to assume that it is unlikely that she would have relinquished her ethno-cultural Jewishness, which she identified as the primary emphasis of her childhood and perhaps responsible for the open-mindedness and intellectual promiscuity that she developed.[96] Be that as it may, despite her efforts to correct the prejudicial rivalry of love versus law that has colored centuries of Jewish and Christian polemics, Rose's baptism commemorated the triumph of love over law. Hence, at the culmination of her life she reinscribed the very dichotomy she sought to depose, thereby fortifying her depiction of the end as the middle where "form and actuality can arise out of the observable inversion of meaning in configuration."[97] The characterization of this decision as curious is grossly misleading.[98] By taking this final step, Rose addressed the dilemma that inspired her to write *The Broken Middle*, the reexamination of "the original moment of the modern opposition between holistic comprehension and existential, ethical, Christian Revelation."[99] I concur with Andrew Shanks, who surmised that, in contrast to Weil's refusal to be baptized in order "to underline her freedom of flamboyant prophetic utterance," Rose "understood baptism, in principle, as entry into a community of good, honest listening, the special gift of the 'knight of faith'."[100] Even if some of Rose's secular-minded friends may have been astounded by her baptism, Shanks concluded, "there is no reason to suppose that it signified any recantation of her published philosophic views.... Rather, she represents faith at its most authentically philosophic. That is to say: faith understood, in essence, as a sheer *intensification* of true philosophic questioning."[101] The further conjecture that Rose's baptism was a celebration of her faith in the God of the broken middle[102] is incontestably defensible, but it must be said that in receiving Christ at the end of her life, the opposition between the holistic comprehension of reason and the Christian revelation of faith was attenuated palpably with her flesh and not abstractly through philosophical discourse.

Moreover, the monumental decision settled a second conceptual problem that plagued her—namely, the idealization of jurisprudence in contemporary Jewish philosophers and theologians, who failed to concede that the

> exclusive emphasis on subjective freedom insists on remaining ignorant of the inversion of intention, while exclusive defence of legal procedure as self-perficient casuistry insists on remaining ignorant of inversion of form in configuration. Once again, within *halachic* Judaism, as within philosophical presentation of Judaism from Rosenzweig to Levinas, there is *no comprehension to complement commandment*: no recognition of freedom and unfreedom. And there is also the further irony that the unresolvable, intra-normative diremption of Judaism between ethics and *halacha* should become the model, the aspiration for new political theologies winged between singularity and holiness, that would mend their broken middles at the furthest remove from the conflict of the laws.[103]

Revisiting this point in the essay "Is There a Jewish Philosophy?," Rose noted:

> The idea of Halachic contestation has recently found favour with general philosophy because it does not posit an end to law within or beyond history, and does not resolve or aim to resolve law and ethics. This interest on the part of philosophy utterly overlooks the dispute within Judaism over law and ethics.... Judaism and philosophy idealize the *potentialities* of each other and fail to locate their own uncertainties and fate in the *actual* discordances of modern political and intellectual life. This rediscovery of Judaism at the end of the end of philosophy can be witnessed therefore as a convergent aspiration *without a third—tertium quid—*on which to converge.[104]

Christianity arose as this third in which the convergent aspiration of Judaism is fulfilled, and positive meaning is concocted within the prevailing division of morality and legality, the autonomy of the individual and the heteronomy required by allegiance to civil society and the state.[105] It appears that Rose finally decided that to become Christian assuaged the schism between ethics and law insofar as that leap of faith was predicated on discriminating that the former is neither grounded in nor dependent on the latter. Love, above all else, performs the reconfiguring inversion of form and thus has the potential to amend the broken middle at the furthest remove of the conflict between communal ritual and individual conscience.

Angelus Dubiosus *and the Facetious Irony Beyond Irony*

Instructively, Rose informed her readership that she wrote "out of the violence infecting these philosophical purifications which ignore their own preconditions and outcomes."[106] Subsequently, she offered the following *apologia pro vita sua*: the only way she could approach her life story was to explore how the difficulties she confronted might articulate the vagaries and the whimsicalities of that life. There is no fleeing from the adversities that one encounters on the path. On the contrary, the philosophical narrativization of an individual's lifespan necessitates a frontal engagement with those complications. By extension, the diagnostic method necessary to yield the structuring of the unrecognized third of the new philosophical purifications likewise "involves deployment of the resources of reason and of its crisis, of identity and lack of identity." Notably, Rose called this method *"the face-*

tious style—the mix of severity and irony, with many facets and forms, which presents the discipline of the difficulty."[107] In accord with her description of Hegelian philosophy, which I noted above, her own method combines the serious and the ironic in an effort to present the *disciple of what is difficult*. Expounding this point in more detail, Rose opined, "The discovery of the difficult, dangerous and irrational impulses and actualities of individual and social life can only be *the work of faceted and facetious reason*, which—like Socratic irony equally beyond irony—is at the same time beyond its facetiousness."[108]

Rose invoked Paul Klee's *Angelus Dubiosus* to represent pictorially the facetiousness of the dubious angel that "is contrary to the ethos of the so-called 'ironic liberalism,' with its cynical display of indifference towards 'the plurality' of the Other."[109] The image of the doubtful and doubting angel is suitable to emblematize the work of the facetious reason inasmuch as it

continues to try to do good, to run the risk of idealization, of abstract intentions, to stake itself for ideas and for others. Experience will only accrue if the angel discovers the violence in its initial idea, when that idea comes up against the actuality of others and the unanticipated meanings between them. . . . The dubious angel constantly changes its self-identity and its relation to others. Yet it appears commonplace, pedestrian, bulky and grounded—even though, *mirabile dictu*, there are no grounds and no ground.[110]

Contrary to Benjamin's use of Klee's *Angelus Novus* to symbolize the faculty of memory and the redemptive potency of writing history by looking back into the past,[111] Rose chose the *Angelus Dubiosus* to be her guardian angel as it "spoils the opposition between Athens and Jerusalem" that has been reinvented by the new ethics of postmodernism, especially as it has been cultivated by Levinas and Weil. This angelic phantasm, a "hybrid of hubris and humility," allegorically epitomizes the skepticism essential to the facetiousness of reason that "takes issue with the claim that Judaism provides the refuge for thought which has finished with the jaded rationalism of the philosophical tradition."[112] Far from being beyond reason, Judaism is faced with the identical trauma of reason that has inflicted philosophy from time immemorial, and in that sense, it partakes of the Socratic irony that transports thinking beyond irony, enacting the facetiousness beyond facetiousness.

Pushing against the postmodernist dismissal of metaphysics and the discrediting of the major concerns of philosophy through the centuries, Rose sought to reclaim these resources to establish the basis for ethics even as she readily admitted that *there are no grounds and no ground*. From Kierkegaard we can deduce the foundation of Rose's social theory in response to postmodernism and deconstructionism:

> The challenge is to cease this abolition of the ethical and to restore the political history of ethical life: without the cynicism of violence, without the facetiousness of myth, but not without authorial irony—not without the anxiety of beginning and the equivocation of the middle. This irony has been learnt from the pseudonymous one: it is the lesson that the most existential moment of ethical suspension is the most consistent witnessing of the history of ethical and political actuality.[113]

It is precisely the "low tolerance of equivocation" that has resulted in "the reproduction of dualistic ways of thinking and of formulating public policy. In philosophy 'truth' or 'reason', in their perennial or in their modern meanings, are charged with legitimising forms of domination which have destroyed or suppressed their 'others' in the name of the universal interest."[114] Equivocation of the middle, which is "manifest in the manifold *failing towards form*,"[115] a failing that is Janus-faced, makes us flee to the beginning whether pagan or erotic, spiritual or religious.[116] But the anxiety of beginning, whence we apprehend the beginning of anxiety, is such that the beginning is not attainable, and thus we find ourselves destined to weather a movement of repetition backwards and forwards that pivots around the equivocal middle and tenaciously yields an ethical reflection.[117] The ambiguousness attached to our being embedded in the middle is essential to theoretical and practical wisdom as both develop "when the different outcomes of ideas and policies are related to the predictable modifications and to the unpredictable contingencies affecting their meaning and employment."[118] The scrutiny of principle and practice alike circumnavigate about the discovery of limitation "so that the strengths and shortcomings of ideas and policies may be revised or modified in the light of experience."[119] From Adorno's interpretation of Kierkegaard's doctrine of the dialectic of the hopelessness of hope, instituted by Christ's sacrificial death and the ensuing melancholic gnosis related to God's being devoured by nature in the antinatural spiritualism implied in his mournfulness over humanity,[120] Rose elicited that the proposition that "Christ came into the world to suffer" is paradoxical inasmuch as "the idea of abolishing suffering amounts to a mythical extirpation of nature. Not only the ethical but life, too, disappears in the abyss of the natural: expiated by the sacrifice of Christ in the moment."[121]

The purging of suffering is not possible because it would entail the eradication of nature and hence the cessation of the very condition of life that makes suffering viable. Along these lines, Rose emphasized that the ethical character of *agapē*, experienced by lovers who spend the night together, is a "shared journey" that entails "honesty embracing dishonesty."[122] It would be foolhardy and naïve to think that even unselfish and charitable love could be sustained by sincerity without an admixture of mendacity. The navigation of these antithetical forces is the means by which the sacramental act of love helps the lovers to achieve the sense of routine and habit by which they return to the considerations of the finite world, "to be present to each other, both at the point of difficult ecstasy and at the point of abyssal infinity."[123] Proving herself to be a faithful disciple of Adorno's meditations on the credibility of metaphysics after Auschwitz,[124] Rose argued that there is no scaling the ecstatic height but through plummeting to the boundless abyss, no experiencing eternity but in the finitude of time, no perceiving the specter of transcendence that is not radical immanence.[125]

Transmuting the philosophical insight into a code of how to withstand the hardships and vicissitudes of life, in *Love's Work*, Rose offered the following *counsel of despair to keep the mind out of hell*:

A crisis of illness, bereavement, separation, natural disaster, could be the opportunity to make contact with deeper levels of the terrors of the soul, to loose and to bind, to bind and to loose.... To grow in love-ability is to accept the boundaries of oneself and others, while remaining vulnerable, woundable, around the bounds. Acknowledgement of conditionality is the only unconditionality of human love.[126]

The counsel of despair to keep the mind out of hell rests on the directive to keep the mind in hell and despair not, a maxim reported as a teaching communicated by Jesus to the Eastern Orthodox monk of Russian origin Staretz Silouan, born as Simeon Ivanovich Antonov (1866–1938). Significantly, not only did Rose choose the proverb of Staretz Silouan as the epigraph of *Love's Work*, but she utilized it to find a way to describe her mother's "unresolved suffering" and her "all-jovial unhappiness," that is, "the unhappiness of one who refuses to dwell in hell, and who lives, therefore, in the most static despair."¹²⁷ In another passage, her own unhappiness and acceptance of her pain and grief is rendered by partially citing this very dictum: "Now I am not dissociated from my ululation.... Keep your mind in hell and ... I want to sob and sob and sob ... until the prolonged skrieking becomes a shout of joy."¹²⁸ Loss may mean that the "original gift and salvation of love have been degraded," that "love's arrow" has been "poisoned and sent swiftly back into the heart," but the only remedy is "to pluck the arrow and to prove the wound" so that one "may desire again."¹²⁹

Highlighting the monk's teaching, Rose remarked that the person who lives a "normally unhappy life" is "predestined to eternal damnation." Such a person is instructed as follows:

> This is the counsel of despair which would keep the mind out of hell. The tradition is far kinder in its understanding that to live, to love, is to be failed, to forgive, to have failed, to be forgiven, for ever and ever. Keep your mind in hell, and despair not.¹³⁰

By welcoming the fortune of misfortune, one is empowered to overcome the misfortune of fortune. To keep the mind in hell amounts to refusing to surrender to despair and therefore to perceiving that hopelessness itself is the womb whence hope is born.¹³¹ We recall that Rose argued that the anxiety of beginning, which we can extract from Freud, is manifest in the elaboration of the psychology of despair. While facetiousness may imply the movement from anxiety to sin, from sin to despair, and from despair to grace, the need to destroy the possibility of despair implies its very opposite, that is, the never-ending predicament of multifarious forms of despair.¹³² This is experienced acutely in relationship, since love mandates respecting the boundaries that separate self and other no matter how much those boundaries are traversed in moments of intimacy. Thus, it is around those boundaries that lovers remain vulnerable and woundable. There is nothing unassailable about human relationships except their unconditional conditionality. In the O'Mahony interview, Rose forthrightly affirmed that she was able to bring the strands of the intellectual and the emotional together through suffering, growing, failing, and illness.¹³³ Admittedly, Rose's vision is not fatalistic, but it does expose a somber susceptibility as the travails of affliction, disease, and defeat are pinpointed as the means by which one succeeds.

Corroboration of this deep-seated devotion to the inescapability of suffering and the clear-cut acceptance of the inevitability of mortality is found in another exchange in the aforementioned interview wherein Rose's responded to the question of whether she believed in eternity:

Definitely. It's the only thing I believe in. . . . If there is eternity, then it's now, and it's at all time. So it's the only thing you can believe in, because, after all, time is devastation. You can't believe in time. Time is going to destroy you. You can't believe in time, you have to believe in eternity.[134]

Prima facie, it would seem that Rose was expressing belief in something outside the spatiotemporal continuum as she explicitly stated in the continuation of the interview. However, that belief was immediately qualified by her suggestion that we need to preserve an agnosticism, supported by summoning Weil as I noted above.[135] The caveat elucidates her previous comment about time and eternity. She fervently responded that she believed in eternity because time represents destruction and thus is unworthy of one's belief. But the eternity she accepted is *now* and *at all time* and not in the future or the hereafter. The only flight from the desolation of time is to take hold of the eternity that is omnipresent in and not transcendent to time. There is no eternal realm that obliterates the temporal obliteration of our evanescent existence.[136]

Rose offered no pledge of an indisputable release from suffering, no way to sever the shadow completely from the light, no means to render the liabilities of living advantageous, no program to allay the brokenness of the middle definitively. If we persist in speaking about a utopian stimulus, we must heed Rose's warning that it "always has a relation in the real world to things that are difficult."[137] We may not be able to abandon the idea of paradise but when projecting it onto actual social communities, we should be mindful that there is no paradise without an impediment.[138] "The only paradises cannot be those that are lost, but those that are unlocked as a result of coercion, reluctance, cajolery and humiliation, their thresholds crossed without calm prescience, or any preliminary perspicacity."[139] Utilizing the medieval tale of the implacable unhappiness endured by King Arthur as a result of his enforcement of the law that brought about the sentencing to death of his wife Guinevere, the banishment of her lover Lancelot, and the forfeiture of his vision of Camelot,[140] Rose inferred that philosophy, ancient and modern, is born of necessity out of a condition of sadness. This is the import as well of Aristotle's understanding of metaphysics as the *perplexity* or *aporia* that arises from the attempt

> to find the path from the law of the concept to the peculiarity of each instance.... If metaphysics is the *aporia*, the perception of the difficulty of the law, the difficult way, then ethics is the development of it, the *diaporia*, being at a loss yet exploring various routes, different ways towards the good enough justice, which recognizes the intrinsic and the contingent limitations in its exercise.[141]

The philosophical temperament is ineludibly framed by this earthly sense of human sadness, which is identified concurrently as the countenance of divine comedy, the melancholy that transpires from "the ineluctable discrepancy between our worthy intentions and the ever-surprising outcome of our actions. This comic condition is *euporia*: the always missing, yet prodigiously imaginable, easy way."[142] We see again how tragedy and comedy are patently intertwined. The abundance and ease of the comic condition, signified by the word *euporia*, is opposed to the impoverished standstill of the tragic condition, signified by the word *aporia*. The easy way must be avoided in favor of taking the difficult way to confront the actual in all of its indeterminacy and volatility. However, we should not lose sight of the fact that the euphoric implications of *euporia* cannot be surgically disentangled from the forlorn implications of *aporia*. Philosophical reflection is consolation for the discontent that can be dissipated temporarily but never surmounted permanently. Rose's vision of aporetic universalism stipulates an arduous process towards the reciprocal recognition of the self and the other fostered by social and political institutions, but, following Hegel,[143] this recognition only reinforces the possibility of future misrecognition.[144] Comparing Levinas's claim that philosophy is inseparable from skepticism to Rose's insistence on the indissoluble relationship between recognition and misrecognition, Martin Kavka concluded,

> Skepticism is philosophy's sidekick, its comic foil which always exposes the ephemerality of the validity of our acts, and reveals revision as the absolute in human action. Skepticism and misrecognition show that the revelation we experience in the Other's disrobing is instantaneously lost, that transcendence is so majestic as to hide from us and cause us to search for it always and everywhere in the midst of the public sphere.[145]

Once more, we note the intermingling of the tragic and the comic, an insatiable hankering for what can be envisioned only as invisible.[146]

Suggestively, in *Paradiso*, the final and unfinished book that Rose composed, she wrote that the model for Edna, the nun whom she had befriended, was the life of Augustine of Hippo, not because he led a dissolute lifestyle until he converted, but because of "the continuities—the integrity and the brokenness—of the whole life which is relevant."[147] Thus, Augustine is credited for introducing the abyss, the dark night of the soul, into the Latin Christian tradition, and for effectuating the movement from the light of the Transfiguration to the solitude and abandonment of the night of Gethsemane. Rose designated these aspects of Augustine's thought as the "Gnostic remnant," which "has re-emerged, as it always does in the modern—including the post-modern—world."[148] I shall have the occasion to discuss the place of Gnosticism in Rose's thinking in the final section of this chapter, but for our immediate purposes what needs to be underscored is that the *Gnostic remnant* that persisted in Augustine's life, and this despite his eventual writing of polemical treatises against the Gnostics, denotes the estrangement from this world based on the Manichean dualism of the cosmological combat between good and evil.[149]

Christologically, Rose detects a residual of Augustine's Manichean period in the contrast in *De Trinitate* between the great evocations of the Father and the Son and the insipid treatment of the Holy Spirit. Mystically conceived, the third member of the divine family is the mediator of holiness whose hiddenness enables humans to perceive the changes engendered by the Transfiguration and to communicate the appropriate knowledge made available to them. From this discrepancy, Rose concluded, "To put it in literary terms, *the lack of irony* in St Augustine's *oeuvre* indicates a troubled contrast between his appearance and his hiddenness, his power and his powerlessness."[150] The relative weakness of the Holy Spirit translates into a binary between the invisible Father and the visible Son. And this, in turn, yields the paradox exploited in the Kierkegaardian irony of hiddenness and erotic self-revelation camouflaged in the appearance of the disappearance of its appearance. This is not only the true meaning of the *Confessions,* but it is the hallmark of his writings more generally wherein he concealed his soul so well that even the best scholars attribute to him "the carefully crafted views communicated by his aesthetic, philosophical, psychological and edifying pseudonyms."[151] The gnostic heresy, as Adorno observed, is posited by Kierkegaard's doctrine of the imprisonment of God in his own "incognito," just as this imprisonment follows rationally for Kierkegaard from the paradox of the immediate unity of divine and human nature.... Kierkegaard's theology cannot escape this entanglement because the conception of the paradoxy and absolute difference of God is itself bound to the autonomous spirit as God's systematic negation, an autonomous spirit that ultimately cancels divine transcendence by construing God dialectically out of itself and its own necessity.[152]

According to Adorno's reading of Kierkegaard, the mythical dialectic of the Passion leads to the unsettling conclusion that God is occluded in the manifestation of nature that is the locus of human spirituality. Suffering, on this account, assumes the nature of paradox, which is "the sum of all possible reconciliations and annihilations."[153]

Rose has undeniably offered a key to the reader about her own identity in her recounting the deportment of Sister Edna. Just as Augustine's conversion was not an unmitigated break with the depravity of his past, and the entirety of his biography, which encompasses periods of integration and disintegration, is significant in the evaluation of his life, so too in the case of Rose, her thought and her life sanctioned the coinciding embrace of darkness and luminosity, totality and fragmentation, rectitude and fraudulence. Furthermore, the mystery of Edna's hiddenness can be explained in view of Bernard of Clairvaux's description in his *De Laudibus Virginis Matris* of the sacramental relation of the visible to the invisible world.[154] Bernard's combination of political power and spiritual humbleness, the clerical pride of preaching and the solitary devastation of prayer, and Edna's amalgamation of a keen intellectual presence and unfathomable piety[155] can be applied to Rose's philosophical desire to conjoin the contemplative and the practical, the mystical and the ethical.[156] Note that *Love's Work* was designated by the author as a "profoundly Kierkegaardian work" insofar as "it allows one to pass unnoticed. It deploys sensual, intellectual and literary eros, companions of pain, passion and plain curiosity, in order to pass beyond the preoccupation with endless loss to the silence of grace."[157] The exemplar of personhood is the knight of faith who lets go of the loss of the past and

turns her attention to the astonishing nature of what is normally expected until she becomes both invisible, hidden, and quite ordinarily visible. As the sublime in the pedestrian, the knight of faith simply appears as whatever she is: she returns to her vocation beyond the endless anxiety of the test of salvation.[158]

The ostensible lack of irony insinuates the most profound irony: exposure through concealment, appearing through nonappearing, veiling that can be unveiled only through the awareness that with every veil lifted another veil is unfurled.[159] The pairing of visibility and invisibility should not be conceived in Hegelian terms as "mutually reproducing dialectical contraries."[160] The opposites are dialetheically juxtaposed such that they are similar in virtue of their dissimilarity, and thus the mystery of the hiddenness of the disclosure in the disclosure of the hiddenness is never alleviated by assimilation into a higher synthesis that would unravel the knot of the paradox. In contrast to the dialectical negation of negation, dialetheic logic posits the negation of the negation of negation, a triple negativity that resists resolution of the incongruity implied by the double negative.

The position I attribute to Rose, the deconstructing and reconstructing of the antinomies of modernity to keep the ethical-political apprehensions of the middle open, is redolent with her report of Adorno's debate with Benjamin's idea of the now-time (*Jetztzeit*) that is shot through with splinters of messianic time.[161]

For to Adorno, "universal history must be construed and denied".[162] Instead of crystallizing "the configuration pregnant with tensions" into a Messianic monad, Adorno would unravel the antinomies of realization before staking everything on the flash of redemption—which could leave everything as it is; restore the old regime; or inaugurate a greater violence.[163]

I surmise that Rose's position is inadvertently proximate to Heidegger's circumscribing the matter of thought as thinking the same (*das Selbe*) as opposed to the identical (*das Gleiche*)[164]—the former adheres to the ontological difference between being and beings and thus should be considered as the modality that beckons the thinking of difference as difference—in contradistinction to Hegel's idea of thought as thinking the concept of being with respect to the beings that have been thought in and as absolute thinking.[165] This is not to deny that Rose is critical of Heidegger's metapolitical transcription of the history of being into the historical present that is experienced recurrently as the variable that is invariable:

Yet Heidegger's apparent enlarging of rationality so that it includes the oppositions which seem otherwise to establish and limit it, becomes a characterless, empty infinity in its own way. The *Gestell*, the framework, which holds the disowned op-

98   Chapter Two

positions of consciousness, is offered as a new way to think of presence without the *vor* or "re" of *Vorstell(ung)*, "re-present(ation)", and the *da* of *Darstell(ung)*, "present(ation)". The *ge* in *Gestell*, the particle which forms the past tense, indicates an event, something which has happened and is present or occurring in what happens, which is not re-presented or presented.[166]

Particularly relevant to Rose's overall philosophical enterprise is her contention that Heidegger's use of *Gestell* in place of *Gesetz*—a conceptual affinity anchored philologically in the comparison of *ge-stell*, which is from *stellen*, to put or to place, and *ge-setz*, which is from *setzen*, to fix or to posit—indicates the dominance of modern technology through an unknowable law. Even more remarkable is Rose's suggestion that Heidegger's notion of *es gibt*, the "it gives," and the event (*Ereignis*) of being that is withdrawn from beings, and therefore concealed in its revelation, "seems to give us *Yahweh* without *Torah*: the event seems to include advent and redemption, presence and owning, but not the giving of the law on Mount Sinai, and its repeated disowning."[167]

I will bracket a longer conversation about the comparison drawn by Rose between Heidegger and the rabbinic-kabbalistic delineation of the Tetragrammaton as the predicative signifier of the generative ground of being; that is, *Yahweh* names the eventfulness of being—to be understood as a process rather than a substance—comprised in the compresence of the three temporal ecstasies, past (*hayah*), present (*howeh*), and future (*yihyeh*).[168] What is more pertinent to our immediate interest is that despite Rose's overall disapproval of Heidegger's philosophical method, which she called by the Schleiermachian expression "grammatical hermeneutics," that is, the verbplay that "opens out the critical court so that it reveals the syntax and semantics of a different time,"[169] there is affinity between her own philosophical understanding of tradition as an incessant wavering between possessing and dispossessing and the Heideggerian idea of *Ereignis*, the event of appropriation, which includes two ways of being present, *Vereignen* and *Zueignen*, disowning and owning.[170] I would contend, moreover, that the disowning that must be owned in this event wherein subject and object are delivered to one another[171]—or what Heidegger also refers to as the refusal (*Verweigerung*) in which the event bestows itself on the human being,[172] the ungivenness that is integral to every act of giving just as every manifestation is a nonmanifestation, every disclosure is a concealment, every truth is an untruth[173]—is

Between Athens and Jerusalem 99

the dynamic that substantiates Heidegger's temporalization of time as the reverberation of the same that is always unique, the reiteration of the again that is altogether otherwise.[174]

Despite Rose's stated displeasure with what she considered to be Heidegger's following Husserl in his phenomenology of consciousness by bequeathing a central role to the *apeiron*, the infinite, or literally the "without-goal" (*a-peiron*), which led him to affirm a form of light that blinds one from seeing anything and to posit a law without legalism, a natural law, that is, a law of nature, which eternally repeats itself,[175] Rose's emphasis on the open-ended praxis of rational inquiry imparts an analogous sense of purposelessness that fuels the limitless fluctuation between appropriation and disappropriation, the counterplay that provides the justification for an ethics based on the law beyond law, or in the technical lexicon of Judaism, the halakhah beyond halakhah.[176] The complementarity of comprehension to the diremption of spirit, which she sought to disseminate, does not bring closure but rather "involves reflection on what may be ventured—without mending diremption in heaven or on earth."[177] There is no repairing the breach, only the healing that comes through diagnosing the malady. In consonance with the perspective of Susan Taubes discussed in the previous chapter, we can ascribe to Rose as well the kabbalistic adage that tearing itself is integral to rectification, and hence recuperation may consist of nothing more or less than identifying the blemish. Emphatically rejecting the antinomies of monistic uniformity and dualistic dissension, Rose endorsed the "speculative negotiation of the middle between truncated mourning and endless melancholy, abstract equality and absolute alterity, tragic resignation and messianic utopianism."[178] In this middle lies the rationale for espousing a hopeless hopefulness—to be contrasted with the hope of messianicity commended by the Derridean counsel of hopelessness[179]—that is, adhering to the hope beyond and without hope in the chiasm wherein *euporia* and *aporia* crisscross. We should speak, therefore, of a continual teetering between the easy way and the difficult way rather than the replacement of the former by the latter or of the latter by the former.[180]

It would not be hyperbolic to say that the calling of the philosopher immortalized on Rose's tombstone is intricately and indissolubly connected to the reclamation of this agnostic middle, an appropriation based on accepting the brokenness unreservedly, for only by acknowledging the rupture can the task of refurbishing through love unfold, a restoration that intermittently placates but does not imperishably extinguish the heartbreak. Rose's philosophical ambition most certainly was to navigate between modernist absolutism and postmodern relativism, to contribute to the reparation of the disjunction between the universal and the particular through a painstaking phenomenological renovation of the ideological deconceptualizations and practicable displacements that governments have levied on their citizens through acts of violence. This is the import of her assertion that "post-modern antinomianism completes itself as political theology, a new ecclesiology, mending the diremption of law and ethics."[181] However, her own thinking similarly secured the possibility for an articulation of a new ecclesiology that would palliate this diremption without succumbing to the defects of postmodernism in its promulgation of exclusive thought that falls short of promoting an inclusivity and partial action that cannot mollify its exclusive impartiality.[182] Rejecting the epistemological skepticism of postmodernism, Rose steadfastly argued that truth and meaning are not arbitrary. Nevertheless, as Joshua B. Davis duly noted, she was not interested in

> the absence or instability of truth, but the fact that unpredictability and even failure are essential aspects of all truth worthy of the name. For Rose, every act of communication or meaningful understanding entails a fundamental risk—of failure, falsehood, misunderstanding, devastation, loss.[183]

The discernment that disillusionment is intrinsic to the sense of accomplishment—in agreement with Taubes's adherence to the proposition that the wrong of our existence is what is most precious[184]—allows philosophy to adjudicate the eternal conflict between guilt and innocence and to arbitrate the endless wrangle between lawfulness and lawlessness.

This sentiment and the harboring of hope in a state of hopelessness echo the words of Adorno:

> The slightest difference between nothingness and coming to rest would be the haven of hope, the no man's land between the border posts of being and nothingness. Rather than overcome that zone, consciousness would have to extricate from it what is not in the power of the alternative. The true nihilists are the ones who oppose nihilism with their more and more faded positivities, the ones who are thus conspiring with all extant malice, and eventually with the destructive principle itself. Thought honors itself by defending what is damned as nihilism.[185]

Rose can be called a true nihilist to the extent that she opposed nihilism by imploring the positivities that would conspire against—although not annihilate—the destructive principle. The critical theory that informed Rose's thinking, indebted to but venturing beyond Adorno, hinges on the belief that the path beyond nihilism is through nihilism, an undertaking that is to be distinguished from her diatribe against the disengagement of the nihilistic utopianism of poststructuralism and postmodernism, which she considered a deliberately mendacious attempt to coverup the goallessness by pursuit of goals that are goalless.[186] To be sure, the mourning she affirmed exceeds melancholia, whose denial of the efficacy of law results in sheer violence and the incapacity to explore the legacy of ambivalence and the working through of the contradictory emotions aroused by bereavement.[187] However, in my estimation, her sense of the mournful does not elude the clasp of nihilism if the latter is understood principally as the recognition of the lack of goals and the consequent renunciation of a teleological view of history.[188]

Breaking the Broken Middle and the Spectral Truth of Untruth

Rose posited two responses to the relation to the Hegelian dialectic that have been tendered anew for our time. The first is the postmodern consciousness that "restricts its operation to *the dialectical oppositions of the Understanding*, and proceeds dualistically and deconstructively." The second, which she claimed as her own, "comprehends the dualisms and deconstructions of the first response as the dynamic movement of a political history which can be expounded speculatively out of the broken middle." Whereas the former may be classified as "tragic in the sense of the baroque mourning play, *aberrated* mourning," the latter is "the comedy of absolute spirit, *inaugurated* mourning."[189] But what is the comportment of this comedy that is an inaugurated mourning? How are we to envision an absolute spirit synchronously elated in its gleefulness and downcast in its despondency?

The comic is contrasted with the tragic insofar as it is resistant to a dialectic that proceeds dualistically and deconstructively. Invoking the discrepancy between Athens and Jerusalem mentioned previously, we could say that the former represents the rational philosophy that culminates in modernism and the latter represents the postmodern abandonment of reason in favor of love and community, the veneration of the alienated and the marginal. The injunction proffered by Rose is to situate oneself between these two poles such that any presumed certainty in one's philosophical truth would be undermined by the skeptical solicitation of what is contrary to that truth. Indeed, the possibility of Athenian truth can be entertained only in light of the Jerusalemite untruth, which is to say, conceding the hazard of theoretical error and the practical violence it might unleash. Judaism stands as a reminder that we are not only impure, but we are also perpetually implicated in the power struggle between law and ethics, a squabble that necessitates not only an imperative or a commandment but also the macabre recognition that it is solely from the vantage point of what is untrue that we can fathom what is true. This epistemological ploy is implied in what Rose names the "equivocation of the ethical," which provokes the "inversion of intentions" that is "not relieved by any danger which is not double."[190] The unmasking of the mask of this doubling is vital to understanding Rose's philosophy of the broken middle:

> Theory, therefore, does not present, as post-modernism argues, "grand narratives"—fictions which have the "function" of legitimizing spurious universality by conferring on it an arcadian beginning and a utopian end. "Fictions", theoretical and literary, are themselves facetious forms which configure the double danger as it changes historically: *aporia* of the universal and *agape* of the singular. They configure the aporia, the difficulty, of the relation between universal, particular and singular. This difficulty is *the* political difficulty *par excellence*: the opposition between particular and general will, to use Rousseau's terms; or the struggle between particular and universal class, to use Marx's terms; and the difficulty of representing this relation in terms of political institutions and aesthetic values. While arcadian and utopian universalism would reconcile and posit the unity of particular and universal, aporetic universalism explores and experiments with the disunity of singular and universal. Fiction and facetiousness maintain this tension, this aporia of the universal, and prevent it, even when personified and characterized, from succumbing to the contrary danger: from representing the agape of the singular, the inwardly piteous, outwardly pitiless individual, or the clockwork love-community set in an authoritarian locality.[191]

In place of the postmodern obsession with debunking the postulation of grand narratives, Rose hypothesized about the need to sustain the double competition of authorship, the dramatic conflict that centers around the

Janus-face of fiction and facetiousness. The idea of struggle formulated by Rose has the advantage of politically examining authority without arrogating it and suspending the ethical without discarding it. In the final analysis, however, we are left with an aporetic universalism that explores and experiments the disunity of the singular and the universal.[192] Thus, Rose concluded, "attention to the agon of the middle where individuals confront themselves and each other as particular and as universal yields the dynamics always at stake in any comprehension of diremption—the articulation and reconfiguration of activity and passivity, norm and cognition, morality and heteronomy."[193]

Rose buttressed the idea of the twofold nature of truth by invoking one of the Zürau Aphorisms composed by Kafka from September 1917 to April 1918: "Truth is indivisible, hence it cannot recognize itself; anyone who wants to recognize it has to be a lie" (*Wahrheit ist unteilbar, kann sich also selbst nicht erkennen; wer sie erkennen will, muss Lüge sein*).[194] In the entry from Kafka's notebooks dated January 14, 1918, whence this aphorism was extracted, Kafka began by writing that there are two disparate things, truth and lies,[195] but he ends up subverting this disparity by declaring that to discern the truth one must be a lie. The point here is not only that one who claims to recognize the truth must be lying, since the indivisibility of truth renders it effectively unrecognizable,[196] but rather to recognize the truth, to know the unknowable,[197] one must be a lie, as is made clear in the original German, *wer sie erkennen will, muss Lüge sein*.

Perhaps the best analogy to grasp this statement is the situation of the writer, who does not lie in the conventional sense but must embody the lie to bear witness to the veracity of the confabulated fiction. The destiny of the writer is to be distinguished from the challenge presented to the more general human population, for as Kafka remarked in another aphorism, the opportunity to lie is always available, and thus the way to lie as little as possible is only by lying as little as possible.[198] By contrast, the writer has no choice but to lie insofar as fictional truth is a truthful fiction that can be fabricated only by one who has become the very untruth that one seeks to propagate as the truth.[199] The writer—as the poet described by Nietzsche as one who seeks to make the unreal appear as real[200]—is thus ensnared in the double bind of veritable deceit, the truth that is true insofar as it is untrue and untrue insofar as it is true. The point I am making can be clarified from the following entry in Nietzsche's notebooks written between the summer of 1872 and the beginning of 1873:

> We too easily confuse *Kant's* thing-in-itself and the *Buddhists'* true essence of things: i.e. reality shows either a complete *illusion* or an *appearance that is quite adequate* to the *truth*. Illusion as non-being is confused with the appearance of being.[201]

In the world of sentient experience, the noumenal truth is not attainable; all we have access to is the phenomenal appearance that Kant believed was adequate to the truth, since he maintained that the appearance is shaped by universal categories of reason. From Nietzsche's perspective, the antithesis of the thing-in-itself and the appearance is untenable because the thing-in-itself at bottom is the subject-in-itself, and we know that the subject is fictitious; it follows, therefore, that the concept of appearance also disappears.[202]

Creative writers function in a sphere beyond the distinction of the noumenon and the phenomenon, an imaginal realm that resonates more with the Buddhist wisdom that the essence of being is its nonbeing, that the discriminate suchness (*tathātā*) of all that exists consists of its indiscriminate emptiness (*śūnyatā*). As in a dream, so in the work of fiction, deceit dissimulates as truth as opposed to covering the truth. The only truth we can ascertain is the truth veiled in the veil of untruth, that is, the truth manifest in the dissimilitude of its nonmanifestation, the doubling of illusion implied in the depiction of the dream as the irreal appearance of the appearance to which we assign the status of reality.[203] As Nietzsche put it in *Human, All Too Human*,

> usually the dream is a bungled product—chains of symbolic scenes and images in place of the language of poetic narration; they paraphrase our experiences or expectations or circumstances with such poetic boldness and definiteness that in the morning we are always astonished at ourselves when we recall our dreams. In dreaming we use up too much of our artistic capacity—and therefore often have too little of it during the day.[204]

Bearing in mind Nietzsche's insight, we would do well to consider Kafka's sixty-third aphorism: "Our art is a way of being dazzled by truth: the light on the grotesquely grimacing retreating face is true, and nothing else" (*Unsere Kunst ist ein von der Wahrheit Geblendet-Sein: Das Licht auf dem zurückweichenden Fratzengesicht ist wahr, sonst nichts*).[205] Apart from being blinded by the truth of the light that strikes the recoiling and contorted grimace on the face of the artist, there is nothing more to execute. This does not imply that there is no truth but rather that truth can be seen only from the disjointed viewpoint of the aporetic withdrawal of truth. As Kafka wrote in his notebooks on January 22, 1918:

> Art flies around truth, but with the definite intention of not getting burnt. Its capacity lies in finding in the dark void a place where the beam of light can be intensely caught, without this having been perceptible before.[206]

Attending to Kafka's words, art hovers about truth, but it is specifically in the vacuum that the artist catches a glimpse of that truth because light can be seen only in darkness, which is not the privation or absence of light but rather the spectral incandescence of the invisible that illumines the phenomenally visible, just as neurophysiologically the dark that we perceive accrues not from the lack of stimuli external to the brain but from the depolarization of the photoreceptors of the retina and the increase of their release of the neurotransmitter glutamate, which provide signals to the off bipolar cells.[207] Seeing the dark, accordingly, is not akin to the nonvision of blindness but is rather an internal vision, the perceiving of nothing from without impelled by a complex neuroretinal process from within. This ocular phenomenon may be applied to Kafka's assertion that the artist finds in the dark void a place where the beam of light can be apperceived; that is, the artist is beholden to an inner envisaging of the luminal darkness by which he or she incarnates the lie that sheds light on the truth expressed in the fifty-fifth aphorism: "Everything is deception: seeking the minimum of illusion, keeping within the ordinary limitations, seeking the maximum" (*Alles ist Betrug: das Mindestmass der Täuschungen suchen, im üblichen bleiben, das Höchstmass suchen*).[208] One cannot fail to note the logical conundrum implicit in the premise that everything is deception: this truth can be true only if it is false, but it can be false only if it is true. Attunement to the liar's paradox facilitates the enowning of the middle excluded by the logic of the excluded middle.

Translating this insight back into the typological division between Athens and Jerusalem, Rose averred that *the end of the end of philosophy*, which began in the former, is to be sought in the latter. The end of the end, however, is located in the middle, the *tertium quid*, which is identified with ethics. Thus, the commencement and termination of philosophy is in the middle, the locus whence we can examine the social and historical conditions that are marred by tension and contradiction:

And then renouncing knowledge as power, too, to demand total expiation for domination without investigation into the dynamics of configuration, of the triune relation which is our predicament—and which, either resolutely or unwittingly, we fix in some form, or with which we struggle, to know, and still to misknow and yet to grow. Because the middle is broken—because these institutions are systematically flawed—does not mean it should be eliminated or mended.[209]

The brokenness of the middle cannot be jettisoned or overhauled, and harmony between the polar opposites cannot be achieved—this is the specious anticipation tied to the image of the New Jerusalem.[210] Philosophically, we are indefatigably situated *in medias res*, in the middle of the plot, whence we hypothetically construct the beginning and the end, the open termini of the linear circle of time. Politically, the efficacy of the concrete universal that our social and religious laws seek to embody must be reckoned from the standpoint of the middle that is everlastingly broken, the middle that is divided between a beginning that cannot begin and an end that cannot end.[211]

The hermeneutic underlying Rose's philosophico-historical schematization was stated cogently by Hans-Georg Gadamer,

the circumstances of the end are similar to the circumstances of the beginning. There is no first word as there is no last word. In so far as thinking and language accompany one another, we always stand in the middle of a conversation.[212]

To stand in the middle of a conversation disparages the cogency of postulating an initial word or a final word; hermeneutically, there is always more to say especially about that of which there is nothing more that can be said. As the end of the end, Judaism represents the missing middle that lays claim to the ethical obligation and the religious ordinance. Moreover, since we are forever entrenched in the middle, the quintessential end, the terminus of the terminus, must bear the condition of the anxiety of the beginning triggered by the consciousness that the law is in the status of that which has "always already begun."[213]

Judaism can be seen as a response to the Greek quest for the beginning, the *archē*. Hence, the rediscovery of Judaism at this terminal point of history occurs at the deepest difficulty of both philosophy and Judaism, where they are equally cast into crisis over the conceiving of law and ethics, ethics and *halacha*. This convergence on ethics turns out to be a mutual aspiration *without* a third, a middle, on which to converge. Yet the converging proceeds apace in the form of holy middle, loveful polity—beyond nature and freedom, freedom and unfreedom—but also without law and therefore without grace.[214]

Evocatively, the title of the section in which the above extract appears is *New Jerusalem Old Athens: The Holy Middle*. The former expression is well known from the apocalyptic vision in Revelation 21:2, where the holy city of the new Jerusalem is described as coming down from heaven, prepared as a bride adorned for her husband. Surely, in a somewhat incendiary tone, Rose chose to refer to the transformation of Judaism by a term that named the heavenly Jerusalem with the clear intention of supplanting the eschatological belief in the rebuilding of the mundane Temple and the restoration of the earthly Jerusalem. As far as I know, the locution Old Athens is an innovation.[215] Rose harnessed the two city names without a conjunction or a hyphen. The seemingly trivial grammatical anomaly signals that the bringing together of the New Jerusalem and the Old Athens transpires— indeed constitutes—the holy middle, the third in which there is the desired merging of law and ethics. Moreover, the middle can be characterized as the loveful polity beyond the polarity of freedom and unfreedom, and since there is no law, there is also no grace. Hence, theopolitically, the apposition of New Jerusalem and Old Athens signifies the overcoming of the polemical divide that has afflicted the relationship between Judaism and Christianity through the centuries:

> For law in Judaism itself offers precisely the experience claimed exclusively for the cancelling of "anxious possibility" by the actuality of sin. Always already within the law, the commandment in Judaism is known both in its existence and in its content which is negotiable and negotiated. There is therefore no anxiety of beginning or beginning of anxiety: the "guilt" of being able is not an anxiety of possibility but always the actuality of the individual, because the law is "actual"—collective, inclusive, contentful; on the one hand, 613 commands, on the other, perpetual negotiation of their meaning.... The Jew is inside the law, the Christian outside: for the Jew, within the command, atonement is actual and annually renewable; for the Christian, within the anxiety of uncomprehended prohibition, the law is external, salvation only posited with sin.[216]

Refocusing the time-honored dichotomization of deed and faith, Rose noted that anxiety for Judaism occurs when the law within meets the law without, the potential enmity between the halakhah and the dictates of the pagan Roman or Christian state.[217] Expressed in the typology adopted by Benjamin in his 1921 essay "Critique of Violence,"[218] from the Jewish perspective, we can speak of a clash between the law-making and law-preserving violence of the state and the law-abolishing violence of divine sovereignty, mirrored in the inalienable right of the proletariat to organize general strikes against management; but there is no justification to presume the Pauline opposition between the intransigence exacted by the commandments and the suppleness stipulated by agapeic love, an erroneous caricature that arises from the mistranslation of the word "*Torah*" as law rather than as teaching or instruction.[219] Additionally, there is the contrast between the Judaism of Jerusalem and the philosophy of Athens. The convergence of the two seems untenable from the perspective of the middle, but this is duplicitous insofar as the middle reinscribes the subservience of one to the other. In Rose's own words:

> For, in spite of the inversion of their previous meliorist intentions into contrary configuration, they introduce no reflection on that repetition; but, claiming such unconstrued inversion to be the "totalized" and "totalizing" domination of Western metaphysics, and its cognates, they would enthrone the equally "total" expiation of holy jurisprudence, refusing any recognition of their own implication in the *rearticulation* of domination.[220]

Criticizing both John Milbank's postmodern theology and Mark Taylor's postmodern atheology, Rose argued that despite the obvious disparities between them, they both

> reinstate the *age-old* oppositions between law and grace, knowledge and faith, while intentionally but, it will turn out, only apparently, working without the *modern* duality of nature and freedom. This replacing of old Athens by new Jerusalem consigns the opposition between nature and freedom to one of any number of arbitrary, binary, metaphysical conceits—instead of recognizing it as index and indicator of freedom and unfreedom—and then proceeds to complete such "deconstruction" in holiness.[221]

The opposition of the new ethics to the old city, Jerusalem to Athens, the replacement of modernity's emphasis on law with a postmodern emphasis on the moral nature of the community established on the basis of responsibility for the other, is a false dichotomy as both are ultimately indebted conceptually to a Kantian dualism that neglects the middle.²²² In neglecting this middle, we are overtaken by a perennial melancholy and constrained by a refusal to mourn that would permit us to negotiate and to contest the inner and outer boundaries of the soul and of the city.

To oppose new ethics to the old city, Jerusalem and Athens, is to succumb to loss, to refuse to mourn, to cover persisting anxiety with the violence of a New Jerusalem masquerading as love. The possibility of structural analysis and of political action are equally undermined by the evasion of the anxiety and ambivalence inherent in power and knowledge.²²³

The duty before us is to transition from melancholic disquiet to a state where mourning becomes law. In this state, mourning will draw "on transcendent but representable justice, which makes the suffering of immediate experience visible and speakable. When completed, mourning returns the soul to the city, renewed and reinvigorated for participation, ready to take on the difficulties and injustices of the existing city."²²⁴

The suffering is made visible and speakable, but there is no guarantee that it will be exterminated once and for all; participation entails preparedness to take on the difficulties and injustices, not the assurance that they can be decimated. Poignantly, in *Paradiso*, Rose wrote that her terminal illness brought her to the point not of resignation in the face of adversity but to the point of the intensified awareness of existence, a moment of *doxological terror*, which she described as a weighty lightness brought on by the confrontation with the impending emptiness of death and the forfeiture of her quotidian moorings:

The withdrawal of the abyss, the overwhelming plenitude of every moment, leaves me more vulnerable than the busy tumult of distress: I have nothing to clutch, nothing to point to as my burden, nothing from which to beg alleviation. My soul is naked: it has lost its scaffolding of regret and remorse or even repentance: it is turned: and the unexpected result is the sensation and the envelope of invisible and visible beauty. This does not make me ecstatic, unreal, unworldly: it returns me to the vocation of the everyday ... but it needed some response, some way of singing its mystery so that I can concentrate as ever on any fellowship or fickleness which presents itself.²²⁵

110   *Chapter Two*

In encountering death and the suspension of all the structures that provided some degree of security, what is called for is not an ecstatic departure from but rather a prosaic return to the world. There is no Pollyannaish delusion, no irrepressible optimism in a this-worldly or an otherworldly existence devoid of bickering, disagreement, and obstacles. The laudable choice is to seek the middle that dispassionately affirms the light of darkness and the darkness of light, the fracture of the whole and the whole of the fracture.

Only by positioning ourselves in the brokenness of the middle can we avoid the pitfall of bifurcating law and grace, which amplifies the hyperemphasis on an autonomous self and the infatuation with the alterity of the other. What is necessary is not the ecclesiological vow of a shimmering New Jerusalem to replace the Old Athens either in the guise of a post-rational rationalism or a post-theological theology, but rather commitment to establish *the third city*, whose architectural composition reflects the middle, the *tertium quid*, "the city in which we all live and with which we are too familiar."[226] In the time when Rose's philosophical path was forged, the opposition of Athens and Jerusalem was overshadowed by the imponderable and immeasurable magnitude of the Second World War. With her characteristic intellectual courage, Rose shed a spotlight on the idealization of Auschwitz as the satanic anti-city, the embodiment of the collapse of modernity, which called for the ethical decree to erect a New Jerusalem. From her role as consultant for the Polish Commission on the Future of Auschwitz, which began in 1990, Rose elicited the "deeply equivocal nomenclature"[227] that the salient question still goading us is "the relation between knowledge and power."[228] Critical reflection on her mission brought her to the following consequential and intrepid conclusion that I will cite in full:

Working at Auschwitz has, however, convinced me that the apparently unnegotiable and expiatory opposition between reason and witness, between knowledge/power and new ethics, or between relativising explanation and prayer, protects us from confronting something even more painful, which is our persistent and persisting dilemma, and not something we can project onto a one-dimensional, demonic rationality, which we think we have disowned. New Jerusalem, the second city, is to arise out of Auschwitz, the fourth city, which is seen as the burning cousin—not the pale—of the first city, Athens. Might not this drama of colliding cities cover a deeper evasion—fear of a different kind of continuity between *the third city* and Auschwitz, which itself gives rise to the ill-fated twins of the devastation of reason and the phantasmagoric ethics of the community? For the perfection of the idealism of the political community is at the same time the perfection of the devastation of theoretical reason and of political action.[229]

The architectonic constructed by Rose extends the polarity of Athens and Jerusalem to a fourfold: Athens, New Jerusalem, the third city, and Auschwitz.[230] Reversing the expected numerical sequence, we can approach the third city only by reconsidering the fourth city; that is, to ponder the third city, which is the middle, the actual city that we presently populate that is expressive of neither the immaculate law of Old Athens nor the uncompromising love of New Jerusalem,[231] we must penetrate the impenetrable reality of Auschwitz, the paragon of irrationality, that counters the rationality of Athens, epitomized in the Enlightenment, the anti-reason that supplants the arch-reason as the measure of history and truth.[232] The reductionist proposing of an unmistakable and unnegotiable meaning for Auschwitz "prevents any acknowledgement of our implication as agents and as actors, as flexibly rational as well as abjectly irrational, as ambivalent—capable of succumbing to the promise of a violent overcoming but also of resisting and taking on the difficulty of living politically."[233] The way to circumvent the futility of such reductionism is by occupying the middle, the third city "that separates each individual into a private, autonomous, competitive person, a bounded ego, and a phantasy life of community, a life of unbounded mutuality, a life without separation and its inevitable anxieties."[234] By affirming opposites without any dialectical sublation, one can find the sociopolitical option beyond the extremes of rationally extolling the universal and irrationally lionizing the particular, the tyranny of rational order and the despotism of irrational chaos, the lawful calculus of the compulsory canon of the collective and the lawless frenzy of the redeeming love of the individual. The gathering of the ashes of Auschwitz "is a protest against arbitrary power; it is not a protest against power and law as such. To oppose anarchic, individual love or good to civil or public ill is to deny the third which gives meaning to both—this is the other meaning of *the third city*—the just city and just act, the just man and the just woman."[235]

Gnosticism, Melancholia, and the Mournful Dawning of the Future Morning

As we noted previously, Rose viewed Gnosticism not only as the feeling of abandonment in and estrangement from this world but also as the donning of the mask of irony that performatively gestures toward the friction between appearance and disappearance, manifestation and nonmanifestation, power and powerlessness. In virtue of this ability to conceal the hidden matter that is disclosed, Rose identified Gnosticism as "our normal spiritual condition: pre-modern, modern, post-modern. It is the spiritual condition of those who do not consider that they have any spiritual condition."[236] *The spiritual condition of those who do not consider that they have any spiritual condition*—this marks the twofold gnostic alienation, the double concealment of being alienated from being alienated. In accord with Hans Jonas,[237] Rose described Gnosticism as offering "a catastrophic cosmogony: creation is not the work of a loving God, for the Godhead is infinitely removed. Primal man is deposited by maleficent demiurgic Aeons, epochs or ages, who dominate myriad realms of cosmic disorder in space."[238] Rather than seeing evil as the privation of good, *privatio boni*, the gnostic myth treats evil as *sui generis*, "an independent principle belonging to material reality, to eternal, autonomous material substance. Gnosticism is founded on dualisms: of matter and reason, of body and soul."[239] The gate to salvation, therefore, is the illumination of knowledge that liberates the soul from the love of neighbor that would keep it fettered to the inherently and irredeemably evil world, a gnosis that frees the divine spark dwelling in each imprisoned being.[240] What is noteworthy is that Rose viewed the myth of Gnosticism as the subtext—or the counterhistory—of Western philosophy. She even considered the Enlightenment and the reaction against it as "deeply Gnostic," an alternative to Protestantism categorized as a form of "Gnosticism's humanism," while the exoteric, psychological soteriological humanism was depicted as an "anti-Gnostic anti-humanism" offered in the place of grace.[241]

Despite her criticism of modern Gnostics, who preserve their detachment from any ecclesiastical or political institutions, Rose granted that as a spiritual phenomenon, Gnosticism is "insidiously compelling, whether we harbour it unselfconsciously as our commonsense, or whether we embrace it in one of its doctrinal forms."²⁴² The allure of Gnosticism—as she tried to prove especially from Thomas Mann's *Joseph and His Brothers*²⁴³—is rooted in the Greek motto inscribed on the Temple of Apollo in the precinct of Delphi, *gnōthi sauton*, "Know thyself," which "still provides the call for the exercise of reason to fathom the irrational, for the emphasis on the isolated self separate from community and corporation, for the dualisms, which modernity has reinvented, between the body and the soul, matter and spirit, nature and culture."²⁴⁴ In contradistinction to the dominant narrative of both Judaism and Christianity, the myth of Gnosticism emphasized that we need to overcome ignorance and not transgression, that knowledge is empowering whereas love is disempowering, that evil is intrinsic to the nature of the world and not a result of misguided human agency. "Gnosticism exalts its mysticism of knowledge against the background of the disordered polis and the disordered cosmos: the disaster—*disaster* means the tearing out of the stars—is opposed to the harmonious music of the spheres."²⁴⁵

Even though Rose admitted in her final work that Gnosticism is as captivating today as it was in Late Antiquity insofar as it alerts us to the calamitous tragedy of being projected globally on the social and political disarray of our nation-states to the point that "the world-order displays an anarchic infinity of internecine forces,"²⁴⁶ she held fast to her view that the resurgence of Gnosticism in modern times failed to engage the existential brokenness of the middle. I would propose nevertheless that in her criticism of Gnosticism, Rose is decidedly gnostic in her dogged insistence that the foundation of the ethical law is in the commendation that each person realize the Delphic edict to know oneself. We might say, ironically, that Rose's social theory offers an anti-gnostic Gnosticism. On the one hand, she did not waver from the condemnation of the belief that redemption is achievable by negating the world and escaping to the transcendental realm of spirit, liberating and restoring the light from its imprisonment in the material cosmos. Hence, one must be sobered from the "Gnostic laughter" incited by the inebriating mirage of the "would-be redeemer."²⁴⁷ On the other hand, in her thought, we can discern the gnostic-inflected view that redemption consists of being redeemed from the need to be redeemed by accepting the ongoing nature of the struggle, acceding to the path that is abidingly difficult, dwelling in the brokenness of the middle whose brokenness can be broken only by being unbroken.

The finale of Adorno's *Minima Moralia* serves as a terse summary of the abstaining from avowing or disavowing the ubiquity of dejection that governed Rose's understanding of the exigencies of human life:

> The only philosophy which can be responsibly practised in face of despair is the attempt to contemplate all things as they would present themselves from the standpoint of redemption. Knowledge has no light but that shed on the world by redemption: all else is reconstruction, mere technique. Perspectives must be fashioned that displace and estrange the world, reveal it to be, with its rifts and crevices, as indigent and distorted as it will appear one day in the messianic light. To gain such perspectives without velleity or violence, entirely from felt contact with its objects—this alone is the task of thought.[248]

The philosophically responsible way to deal with despair is to envisage everything from the standpoint of redemption. But to see things redemptively means to apprehend the fallibility of the infallible. Salvation consists of arrogating the world in all its rifts and crevices. The task of thought, accordingly, is to advance contact with the objects of reality to the point of ascertaining that perfection itself entails assenting to imperfection. As Adorno went on to note, this is the simplest of all things because "the situation calls imperatively for such knowledge," but it is also impossible because

> it presupposes a standpoint removed . . . from the scope of existence, whereas we well know that any possible knowledge must not only be first wrested from what is, if it shall hold good, but is also marked, for this very reason, by the same distortion and indigence which it seeks to escape. The more passionately thought denies its conditionality for the sake of the unconditional, the more unconsciously, and so calamitously, it is delivered up to the world.[249]

The view articulated by Adorno corresponds to Rose's belief that the only possession of absolute truth of which we are capable is the dispossession of possessing a truth that is absolute. From the inconclusive conclusivity of the middle, we come to know with the certainty of uncertainty that every truth is represented by its configural misrepresentation as the image of appearance cloaked in the appearance of image. This gnosis translates politically into the appropriation of the ethical life (*Sittlichkeit*) that we can never experience directly but to which we must constantly strive by being attentive to the incumbrances of the law and its sociocultural repercussions as we strategize communally and individually to deal with the infinite ambiguity of our finite being in the incorrigible world that we inhabit. In taking hold of the mourning of our shared destiny, the dawn of the new morning breaks unremittingly on the horizon and momentarily disrupts the darkness. In this disruption, the seeing of night—the nocturnal figuration of messianic mystification—is the enlightenment that is feasible for one entrapped in the endless beginning and the beginningless ending of the chasm of the broken middle.

THREE

Death and the Infinitization of Finitude
Edith Wyschogrod's Heterological Hermeneutic

The heart asks Pleasure—first—
And then—Excuse from Pain—
And then—those little Anodynes
That deaden suffering—

And then—to go to sleep—
And then—if it should be
The will of its Inquisitor
The privilege to die—

—Emily Dickinson

In this chapter, I will explore the crisis of modernity in the thought of Edith Wyschogrod as it pertains to what she labeled the death event, that is, the unprecedented phenomenon of mass murders, which attests to the fact that "the *means* of annihilation are the result of systematic rational calculation, and scale is reckoned in terms of the compression of time in which destruction is delivered."[1] The technological capability of bringing death to vast numbers of people represents the "ever-present danger of the irreversible null point," the inconceivable and impracticable yearning to eradicate all human life.[2] Intriguingly, Wyschogrod related the logic undergirding the objective of the total destruction to be delivered through the compression of time, or what she called the sorting myth of the death event, to the infracalculative structure of Zeno's paradoxes that emerge from the presumed infinite divisibility of the finite qualities of space that lead to the conundrum that the very possibility of motion is denied.[3] Analogously, the final solution proffered by the Nazis rested hypothetically on the premise that the execution of a finite number of individuals constituted a seemingly infinite reserve even though the goal to exterminate the non-Aryan population entirely, fostered by the phantasmic desire to achieve ideological purity,[4] inevitably would be thwarted by the realization that "all division must come to an end when the null point is reached."[5] The sadistic impulse of those who sought to implement the death-world revolved around the demand that "every individual destined for extermination is to be eliminated." A proclamation of this nature imposed an "obsession with numerability" on both the executors and the executed, but

the unconscious underlying assumption is that the null point—at which not a single individual in the group to be eliminated is left—functions as a *regulative ideal* which cannot be attained. Although these persons will be eliminated, still others will come who will continue to bear the symbolic significance of their predecessors.[6]

Thus, just as the paradox enunciated by Zeno "is a radical negation of motion and an eating away of space, so the death world sorts and sorts but produces nothing."[7]

From the standpoint of the death event, the human cannot be considered, in Heidegger's technical language,[8] a "standing reserve" that "belongs to a reservoir of interchangeable units."[9] The appalling degradation of humanity at the hands of Nazi inhumanity notwithstanding, the stamina of the victims—displayed especially in their merciless massacre—disrupts the mathematical denunciation of the exceptionality of each person. In Heideggerian terms, the Nazi extermination of human beings was a form of sacrificing the particularity of each person to an abstract universal.[10] The issue, however, is not just quantitative in scope; indeed, pondering the matter from a quantitative perspective reinforces the deleterious objectification of humanity that arose in the twentieth century, an anthropological decline that has only been magnified with the onslaught of the digital revolution and the ascendency of computationally engaged research in the humanities and the social sciences in the twenty-first century, including most ominously the ever-increasing roles assumed by the simulated forms of artificial intelligence. The crisis of the death event goes to the core of how the finitude of human life is to be evaluated, which is to say, how we comprehend the inexorability of our exorability, the predictability of our unpredictability.

It is worthwhile citing the language of Hegel invoked by Wyschogrod to describe the character of finite beings as the demarcation of finitude is critical to her philosophical ruminations on the nature of humankind:

> They *are*, but the truth of this being is their *end*. The finite not only alters, like something in general, but it *ceases to be* [*es* vergeht]; and its ceasing to be is not merely a possibility, so that it could be without ceasing to be [*ohne zu vergehen*], but the being as such of finite things is to have the germ of decease [*Keim des Vergehens*] as their Being-within-self [*Insichsein*]: the hour of their birth is the hour of their death.[11]

The quality of a finite being's perishing is not merely a possibility such that we could imagine this being without the property of perishing. On the contrary, the in-itselfness (*Insichsein*) of that which is finite entails the inevitability of its not being in itself. What it is for such a being to be is that unfailingly it will not be, and hence this being can only refer to itself negatively. From that point of view, the passing of time is the offense—the German word used by Hegel *Vergehen* has both denotations[12]—that informs the constitution of our finitude or what Wyschogrod designated as the "ontological mark."[13] But, as she perceptively noted, insofar as "Hegel's analysis of finitude is subject to dialectical reversal," the finite must become its other, "not by way of an external cause but by virtue of what is already inherent in its own nature."[14] According to this logic, finiteness would be driven into its opposite, which is to say, finitude of necessity incorporates the quality of infinitude, or as Hegel himself expressed it, in their self-reference, finite beings "propel themselves beyond themselves, beyond their being" (*eben in dieser Beziehung auf sich selbst sich über sich, über ihr Sein, hinauszuschicken*).[15] The sorrow of finitude—standing in perpetual opposition to the infinite—is overcome by the fact that the passing away itself passes away and the determination of the nothing is negated in the termination of the imperishable and absolute nonbeing.[16]

On this basis, Wyschogrod distinguished Hegel's analysis of finitude and Heidegger's view of death in *Being and Time*. Even though the finite disappears for Hegel, he does not, in the end, affirm the infinite transiency of finite beings to the extent that he posited the overpowering of being over nonbeing, whereas for Heidegger, the human being is decidedly and resolutely the being whose truth consists of its finitude, and thus the angst of living in anticipation of coming to an end precludes the possibility of the negation of the negative.[17] I will return later to this crucial Heideggerian motif, but what is apposite to underscore at this juncture is that despite the differences between Hegel and Heidegger, they both serve as proof of Wyschogrod's allegation that even though there have been varied articulations of the significance of human mortality in Western thought, the understanding of death "has been dominated by a single pattern which depends upon interpreting the self as a cognition monad and the process of dying as requiring behavior appropriate to a rational subject."[18] It is only now, she averred, in light of the multiple forms of mass death, that "the limitations of the model make themselves existentially felt. For when we hold the classical paradigm of both the self and the demeanor appropriate to its dying before the light of atomic conflagration and death camps the paradigm can only appear as a tour de force."[19]

Demythologizing the Death Event and Reconstructing the Life-World

This insight is crucial to the attempt—as feeble as all such attempts are in the final analysis—to fathom the unfathomable, to discern that the concrete reality of the concentration camps surfaced as a consequence of a systematic effort to deconstruct the life-world. For Wyschogrod, the latter term denotes the horizon of experience from which the meanings of human existence originate, the whole of our pre-reflective experiential field, the point of intersection between what is constructed noetically in consciousness and what is given noematically to consciousness.[20] Drawing on previous phenomenological literature, Wyschogrod categorized the life-world as a three-tiered field of experience: the inanimate world given in primary sensation; the vital world given to us as living beings; and the axiological or ethical dimension in which other persons are apprehended as centers of value. Reflecting a postmodern aversion to essentialize or to posit a grand explanatory narrative, Wyschogrod maintained that there is no specific pattern of culture that is endemic to the life-world as such. Rather, the structure of experience, which enables cultural forms to transpire, involves the pedagogical ordering of these three levels as concentric circles. From that vantage point, the inanimate and the vital are classified as the ontological ground of the ethical,[21] and hence it follows that the corrosion of the former instigates the weakening of the latter.

National Socialist ideology occasioned not only a reconsideration of the existential import of the permanence of our impermanence, but it triggered a fundamental shift in the way we calibrate the merit of safeguarding the prolongation of our species. Prior to the appearance of concentration camps, it may have been possible to imagine the extirpation of human life, but it was not possible to imagine the paradox that *life perdures even as the life-world ceases to exist*.[22] But what is the value of protecting and promoting life in the absence of a life-world? In what way can this be accounted as a mode of preserving the propriety of self-esteem? Wyschogrod insisted that the phenomena of atomic conflagration and death camps—and I am fairly confident she would have assented to adding to the list the potential ecological genocide we are presently combatting[23]—requires a shift in orientation away from the monadic conception of self that has overwhelmed the modernist construal of individual and communal identities.

To rectify this situation, Wyschogrod proposed a new transcendental framework by which she did not mean something eternal and unchangeable—a retrieval of an ontotheological hyperessentiality to secure a postmetaphysical religion after religion—but rather a "new historically conditioned a priori by considering the logical and ontological structures exhibited by man-made mass death" in the twentieth century.[24] The purported rectification is commensurate with the surmise that even though the myths of the death event are derived from earlier gnostic and apocalyptic myths of purity granted to a given section of the human population, the former are self-contained inasmuch as they are not organized around a God who brings history to an end. Accordingly, the myths of the death event advanced by the Nazis are not "an assault upon transcendence," but on "the creation of a new wholly immanent totality."[25] The latter expression, I submit, refers implicitly to the Christological underpinning of Hegel's idea of Spirit, a totalization of the identity of the absolute that conceals difference in the subsumption of the other under the stamp of the same.[26] The antidote to the attack on viewing history through the trajectory of the wholly immanent totality, and the ensuing reclamation of a heteromorphic sense of plurivocality, are tied to postulating a Deleuzian plane of immanence that is concomitantly "that which must be thought and that which cannot be thought. It is the nonthought within thought.... It is the most intimate within thought and yet the absolute outside—an outside more distant than any external world because it is an inside deeper than any internal world."[27]

Pushing against the Hegelian dialectic whereby even what cannot be thought is sublated within the contours of what can be thought, and hence the nonthought is itself relegated to an object of thought within the parameters of thinking, Wyschogrod appealed to Deleuze to support the theorizing of a hypernoetic margin at the center of noēsis, or in Foucauldian terms, the unthought that lies at the heart of thought, the "impossibility of thinking which doubles or hollows out the outside," the finitude of the interior that comprises the fold of the exterior of infinity.[28] Notably, in explicating the Deleuzian idea of the plane of immanence as the image of thought that "gives itself of what it means to think," that is, the movement "that can be carried to infinity," the "infinite movement or the movement of the infinite,"[29] Wyschogrod detected, paraphrasing Genesis 27:22, the hand of Deleuze but the voice of Heidegger.[30] A signature idea of the latter was his conviction that the *un*-thought (*Un*-Gedachte), which in each case is only the un-*thought* (Un-*gedachte*), is "the greatest gift that thinking can bestow" insofar as it marks the unique element in a thinker's thought that must be rethought constantly from new perspectives to the point that the "more original the thinking, the richer will be what is unthought in it."[31]

Since the unthought is always what is yet to be thought, it is prevented from ever being objectified as a thing that is no longer on the way to being thought, and hence we can speak of the kinesis of thought as the infinite movement or the movement of the infinite. However, as Wyschogrod astutely noted, the reference to the movement to infinity suggests "a left-handed Heideggerian swipe by Deleuze against Levinas in that the infinite is now subject to thought rather than the converse."[32] Without denying this possibility, it must be emphasized that even if the infinite is subject to thought, it is the image of thought, which is the unthought, that delimits the asymptotic progress to infinity, and thus it is not entirely clear to me that speaking of the unthought as that which is concurrently outside and inside thought—the remoteness that is contiguous and the contiguity that is remote—is a betrayal of Levinas. Leaving that aside, taking the full measure of Wyschogrod's own thinking, appeal should be made to Levinas for whom "the infinite is an outside that maintains its exteriority, even when inwardized, in that glory persists in the internalized infinite as disrupting thematization and 'giving sign' to the other.... But if glory is Saying, substituting oneself for another, taking responsibility for the other, proclaiming peace or proscribing violence, and if infinition is this process... then glory is the dynamism of the infinite."[33]

Somewhat implausibly, Wyschogrod argued that the irrational and unspeakable upheaval of the death event enabled opening the discursive space to this infinite, the nonconceptual within the purview of the conceptual,[34] the utterance of the unutterable,[35] an externality that is most internal in virtue of being an internality that is most external. Contra to Hegel's insistence that the truth of space is to be assessed from the quality of punctiformity, which is "the negation of continuity," and that time as the form of the ideality of space is "the negation of the negation,"[36] Wyschogrod argued that temporal duration provides the key to ascertain the truth of space. Insofar as the extended beings that become in space are made of time, we can delineate the latter as the template through which the exteriority is internalized and the interiority externalized. Time is not simply the destructive power of negation in things—the intransigent contingency marked by the incessant coming to be and passing away—such that the nonbeing of past and future assure the primacy of the present characterized by the fullness of being, but it is rather the radical becoming of the discontinuous continuity that challenges the portrayal of eternity as an absolute timelessness that is altogether different from time.[37] It is in and through the *dark diachronicity* of time— the now that is always the same because it is always different, a quandary already noted by Aristotle[38] and articulated more explicitly in Merleau-Ponty's depiction of the present as that which is simultaneously *toujours neuf* and *toujours la même*[39]—that eternity is instantiated as a profounder and a more lasting reverberation of the diremptive heterogeneity of lived time that overcomes the punctiform homogeneity of clock time.[40]

Consonant with the promise of the impossible implied by the Derridean notion of messianicity—that is, the possibility that is in no way possible but as impossible, an unconditional opening to a future that is determinately indeterminate and expeditiously deferrable, a future that issues from the negative infinity of time[41]—Wyschogrod tendered a conception of hope and the redemptive potential of remembering and retrieving the past in the ever-postponed not yet of the "messianic now",[42] a pining for a presence that can never be represented as present[43] through the writing of history:

> Hope then is the hope for presence. Although the historian may already be persuaded of the impossibility of getting hold of the present, this impossibility continually vitiates itself. . . . It is this inextinguishable longing for the present and the impossibility of laying hold of it that constitutes hope. Hope relates to a future that is always yet to come but may never arrive. To remain hope, hope must desire the possible, yet it wants what escapes the domain of possibility, the plenitude of a presence that cannot be appropriated.[44]

Wyschogrod's statement that the hope related to a future that is always yet to come *but may never arrive* may be tweaked to a more definitive conclusion that such hope *can never arrive* precisely because of its permanent impending status. It is reasonable to conclude, therefore, that hopelessness lies coiled in the heart of the hope that Wyschogrod affirmed.

The messianic significance of the historian's task is underscored by the fact that what is experienced phenomenologically as temporal continuity in reaching backward through memory and extending forward through anticipation is constructed hermeneutically in the moment that cuts the timeline by looping pastness, presentness, and futurity in the eternal continuity of a threefold bond of temporal discontinuity. Time's passing is not overcome by the dissolution of temporal transience in an ocean of eternity, but by persisting in the persistent demise of what has never been but what is ever to come, the eternal cycle of recurring difference wherein being becomes interminably in the terminable becoming of being. As Blanchot expressed it, "We must always, with respect to each moment, conduct ourselves as if it were eternal and relied on us to become ephemeral again."[45] In the ephemerality of time's ebb and flow lies its endurance; the one thing constant in the inconstancy of our transitory existence is change.[46] Inspired by several prominent twentieth-century Jewish thinkers, including Rosenzweig and Heschel, Wyschogrod identified the Sabbath as the ritual that exemplifies this temporalization of eternity in the eternalization of temporality, that is, "the turning of space into time, the respite from creation as the temporal self-articulation of identity-in-difference."[47]

Implicit here is Wyschogrod's innovative reading of the Lurianic account of divine emanation as self-exile—the condensation of the expanse of infinity into the infinitesimal point of singularity—through a Hegelian lens. The kabbalists, she argued, speculatively interpreted creation "as spatial continuity and divine self-contraction within the pleroma.... This theology presages Hegel's and becomes fully clarified in Hegel's interpretation of the relation of time to space."[48] Underlying this comment is the Hegelian distinction between two aspects of space, the "existence of an uninterrupted continuity" and the "existence of things in their separateness." The differentiation of separate entities is related to the property of punctiformity, the "dot-quality" that "gives rise to lines and planes." This attribute, however, cannot be expressed spatially; it can exist only as time.[49] Wyschogrod's intent is clarified from her analysis of Hegel's assertion regarding the "punctiformity of space as the truth of space" to which I alluded above: "From the standpoint of space, punctiformity is the negation of continuity, and time the negation of the negation.... Time is what it is not, space, in the form of its ideality."[50] The existence of discrete objects requires that space be both an uninterrupted continuity and the negation of this continuity, a negation that is negated by means of the affirmation that time is what time is not. To identify time as the truth of space means that the extended beings that become in space retreat to the inwardness of their temporal enfolding whence they unfold not in the immanent nothingness of an absolute transcendence but in the transcendental nothingness of nature.

In line with the soteriological characterization of the Sabbath enunciated in rabbinic dicta and exploited by the kabbalists,[51] Wyschogrod remarked that the Sabbath is "conceived as outside time within time," and hence it proleptically portends a "redeemed temporality" that "opens out the possibility of an eternally recurring time of mercy and grace."[52] The subversive reading of the kabbalistic mythology does not posit a final rectification (*tiqqun*) as the repetition of the original contraction (*ṣimṣum*) but rather highlights that there is an endless diffusion of time that is continuous in its discontinuity and discontinuous in its continuity.[53] In this manner, the temporalization of space liberates the spatialization of time. This does not imply that there is an end of time in which time triumphs in such a way that time is sublated in a dialectical return to the self-alienation of the divine in the beginning. The endtime signifies rather that there is no end to time as the end of time cannot end and persist as the time of the end. In a decidedly anti-Hegelian move, Wyschogrod attributed the triumph of time to the cosmic Sabbath, which, as we have already noted, is the "respite from creation as the temporal self-articulation of identity-in-difference." Respite does not imply retrieval of the beginning and the amalgamation of difference under the synchronizing force of identity; on the contrary, it conveys the releasement of time from spatial subjugation and the declaration of difference of identity as opposed to identity of difference. There is no decisive *tiqqun* unless it is understood that this term decisively signifies the want of a decisive *tiqqun*.

As a corrective to the dominance of technology that helped expedite the downfall of the life-world through the dawn of the death event and the violent suppression of diversity, the Jewish Sabbath endures as the possibility of retrieving the time that is within time as what is outside time, thereby inhabiting the place of the nonplace, the respite from identity-in-difference—characterized by Wyschogrod as the "always already a nomadic identity"[54]—that stands in diametric opposition to the logical ramifications of the Hegelian absorption of difference in the identity of the nonidentity of the particular and the universal as well as in the sociopolitical corollary in the autochthony promulgated by the ethnonationalism of the Nazis; that is, the valorization of the other whose otherness is grounded in the deficiency of a signifier that consummately signifies the signifier of deficiency. The Lacanian influence of the sense of the other on Wyschogrod's thinking is made explicit in the following passage:

This Other, the place of truth and of "the treasure of the signifier," is nonetheless grounded in lack, a nonplace, as it were, whose signifier is a signifier of lack that Lacan calls the signifier of the barred other [$S(\emptyset)$]. Yet this Other, unable to come into plenary presence and still remain Other, cannot fail to respond to the value of the treasure.[55]

The sense of lack, the signified of the other that cannot be reified as a plenary presence, is embodied historically by the Jewish people and particularly by the observance of Sabbath, which enacts the nonspatiality of space and the nontemporality of time. Elsewhere Wyschogrod universalized the idiomatic marker of Jewish specificity by avowing that the dispersion of the Jews amongst the nations bestowed upon them the rank of the saint, for they are "neither inside nor outside." Moreover, as a consequence of the itinerancy of the Jews in the world, all the nations are endowed with a nomadic status.[56]

The spatial displacement translates into the surmounting of the temporal evanescence insofar as the penchant to wander effectuates the "overcoming of death," which is the "boundary that separates interior from exterior, absence from presence." The conquest of mortality is expressed in the vision of Isaianic peace, the eventual end to violence, and thus the ideal of identity-in-difference is realized through the "nomadic crossing over of nations."[57] Far from being an impediment, the homelessness of the Jew serves as the utopian antithesis to the toxic enrootedness of Nazi ethnocentrism.

Technology and the Quantification of the Unquantifiable

Insofar as the geopolitical ideology of National Socialism availed itself of industrial machinations to carry out its homicidal intentions, technological society—understood by Wyschogrod in Heideggerian terms as the instrumentality through which the truth of being is clandestinely disclosed in the present age as the will to produce, which is described in terms of enframing (*Gestell*) or the standing reserve (*Bestand*), the bringing-forth that has the character of setting-upon (*Stellen*) or challenging-forth (*Herausforderung*), the art of revealing, *technē*, that is the essence of technology,[58] and the service of that will by means of the ratiocination of calculative thinking[59]—can be branded as the precondition for the death-world. Indeed, the pretext for the appearance of the death-world is the

> movement toward a single homogeneous culture, global in scale, whose functions are transparent to everyone [who] has emerged along with technique, but no overarching system of meaning has accompanied it, because such meaning cannot derive from the language of utility and quantification. The death-world makes its appearance upon this already demythologized ground as an effort to sacralize a world of impoverished symbolic meanings by creating a totalizing structure to express what is irreducible even in technological society: the binary opposition of life and death.[60]

Technological society is to be distinguished from the death-world, since the aim of the former is to increase technique whereas the aim of the latter is to inculcate the terror that brings about the demise of the inhabitants deemed unworthy to remain in the life-world.[61] The distinction notwithstanding, the nexus between the augmented depletion of the death-world and the constricted expansion of the technological society casts a dark shadow on the utilitarian dehumanization and disavowal of the willfulness of the self that ensued from the negativity imposed on the world by Nazism. Disconcertingly, Hitler's agenda is coincident with Heidegger's assumption that the ferocity of the self-will that belongs to the essence of technology gives way to the renunciation of the self-will that allows the human being to gather into his or her own mortality to fulfill the exceptional duty allocated to Dasein, in contradistinction to all other nonhuman animals, not just to be but to *become* mortal.[62] This is the implication of Heidegger's statement that the animal perishes and the human dies; that is, the latter alone is capable of the expropriative appropriation of death as

> that which in every respect is never something that merely exists, but which nevertheless presences, even as the mystery of Being itself. As the shrine of Nothing, death harbors within itself the presencing of Being. As the shrine of Nothing, death is the shelter of Being.[63]

Mortality does not signify the obvious factical reality that our earthly life—as the life of every being that exists on the planet—invariably comes to an end but that of all sentient beings we are capable of foreseeing death as death, which is to say, foredisclosing death in the sheltering of the nothingness of being as the beingness of nothing. "To be able to die means: to be capable of death as death. Only man dies—and indeed continually, so long as he stays on this earth, so long as he dwells."[64] Death is not the terminus, the nonevent at the end of a lifetime; it is rather lived continually as the possible impossibility that makes tenable the impossible possibility of an ethical rejoinder to human immorality.[65]

The distinctive capacity of humanity to die is closely connected to the prospect of attaining the world as world whence what is conjoined out of this world becomes a thing,[66] the ontological clue through which Heidegger pondered the coming-to-presence of being and thereby restored the meaningful relationship of thingliness and the deportment of being human. We can refer to this hermeneutically as the ontopoetic tenet of bethinging by which the word makes the thing into a thing,[67] "the granting saying in which the being of language speaks as the language of being."[68] The primary task of language, for Heidegger, is the act of naming through which the things named are called into their thinging and thereby unfold the world wherein those things abide as the abiding ones without being objectified in their thinghood,⁶⁹ a remedy to the technological bedrock of nihilism, the "blindness to the destining of Being which shows itself as technique."⁷⁰ The world so conceived—depicted mythopoetically by Heidegger as the unitary world play of the fourfold of sky, earth, mortals, and divinities by which time-space is enacted⁷¹—is "no longer used in the metaphysical sense. It designates neither the universe of nature and history in its secular representation nor the theologically conceived creation (*mundus*), nor does it mean simply the whole of entities present (*kosmos*)."⁷² For Heidegger, world designates the deed of worlding (*Welten*), the term coined to name the intimacy of world and thing present in the dif-ference (*Unter-Scheid*) of the between, the middle in and through which the two are at one with each other in their disclosingly appropriated separateness,⁷³ the space of divergence in which language as the peal of stillness (*das Geläut der Stille*) takes place and calls world and thing into the simple onefold of their disparate propinquity.⁷⁴

In contrast to Heidegger, who spoke of technological calculation as a mode of thinking that "could blast everything to nothingness,"⁷⁵ Wyschogrod argued that the dwelling that is the death event can be considered the unworlding that demarcates the characteristic that is genuinely new in the age of technique: what is living and what is dead cannot be easily disentangled.⁷⁶ Here it is well to recall the tacit criticism of Heidegger offered by Levinas in his effort to question the dominant interpretation of death as either a transition from being to nothingness or to another existence:

> The movement of annihilation in murder is therefore a purely relative annihilation, a passage to the limit of a negation attempted within the world. In fact it leads us toward an order of which we can say nothing, not even being, antithesis of the impossible nothingness.⁷⁷

Against Heidegger, Levinas affirmed that death, the source of all myths, "is *present* only in the Other, and only in him does it summon me urgently to my final essence, to my responsibility."⁷⁸ Thus, speculating on the nature of his own death brings Levinas to the deduction that death need not be explained by the alternative between being and nonbeing. The unforeseeable character of death bespeaks that it cannot be contained in any spatiotemporal horizon, and therefore it cannot be grasped phenomenologically. From this supposition Levinas further extrapolated,

In death I am exposed to absolute violence, to murder in the night. But in fact already in struggle I contend with the invisible.... The Other, inseparable from the very event of transcendence, is situated in the region from which death, possibly murder, comes.[79]

This Levinasian conjecture is crucial for Wyschogrod. The variation between death and murder is inconsequential insofar as the former, as the latter, exposes one to absolute violence, which is understood as the struggle with the invisible. But it is from that struggle that a path is opened to the other and the event of transcendence. Eliciting a similar conclusion from Lacan, albeit expressed inversely, Wyschogrod wrote, "The 'I' comes to stand in the place where neither life nor death can be said to exist and from which the voice of the Other is heard. The 'I' is a defect in this pure nonplace just as, Lacan insists,[80] 'the universe is a defect in pure non-being.' "[81] The pure nothing of the death-world is the silent void of pure being,[82] the place wherein living and dead cannot be separated, since neither life nor death exist in that nonplace. From the negation of the world, and the attendant reduction of alterity to the same, the nonself of the self materializes as the locus of the other.

Negating the Negation of Negation

By her own admission, Wyschogrod's thinking sways between efforts to overcome manifestations of the negative and claims about its irrevocability and that an especially important influence haunting her project is Hegel's grappling with the negative as "the possibility of the nonexistence of the totality of all that is currently seen as world or as the maximal intensity of disvalue that can be attributed to the world."[83] In the Hegelian dialectic, history culminates with the "emergence of an all-encompassing Absolute ... an ontological and logical vacuum that has sucked into itself all that is and sees itself as having brought to completion the work of historical and philosophical negation, thereby obviating the need for further inquiry into the labor of the negative."[84] Sublation of the negative in its ultimate overcoming is thus intrinsic to each moment of the World-Spirit's history. The latter, in Hegel's own words, wins its truth "by looking the negative in the face and tarrying with it,"[85] which is to say, Spirit's unfolding is "contingent upon a continual undoing."[86] But if the labor of the negative is this continual undoing, can the undoing ever be undone? Would this undoing of the undoing not be equivalent to a double negative that yields a positive, the negation that is no longer subject to negation because its own negativity would have been positively negated? As Wyschogrod reminded the reader:

For Hegel negation is never merely the contrary of what has been affirmed, since negation always brings something new into the world. How is this new work of the negative to be achieved? It can ... appear, become manifest in a work, by virtue of difference—the difference between what has been sublated and what comes into being. The negation of the Absolute, therefore, must itself be absolute, and the difference generated by this negation must itself be an absolute difference. Hegel all too quickly passes over the uniqueness of the negation when what is negated is the Absolute itself.[87]

The negation to which Wyschogrod referred is "without voice; it can only be interpreted as silence and therefore mystery."[88] From the Hegelian perspective, since nothing of the history of Spirit lies outside of intelligibility, the unsurpassable negation of the Absolute, the negation of negation, "can only be thought of as transconceptual, transymbolic, and translinguistic." If the unimaginable can be imagined at all, it is in the "annihilation of man" implied in the death event.[89] Philosophically speaking, the crisis of modernity is to be located in the extinction of the human being that is a consequence of the negation of Hegel's immanent Absolute—the trinitarian circle of history whereby the transcendence of the Father, the hidden *Abgrund*, is incarnated in the Son revealed through the Holy Spirit in the life of the Christian[90]—such that revelation is no longer possible, or at least the revelation of anything but the revelation that there is nothing to be revealed.

Hegel's dialectic necessitates that every presence becomes what it is by negating what it is not, and hence every negation brings some affirmation in its wake. The idea of negativity in Hegel, therefore, "is harnessed to the logic of presence so that the idea of the negative as reserve, pure loss, silence—that which is irrecoverable—is foreign to Hegel. Instead, the negative is brought into plenary presence carried forward by the dialectical activity of Spirit."[91] What is unthinkable for Hegel, and consequently unsayable, is the dialectical overcoming of the dialectic that results in the negation of the Absolute, a negation so extreme that it generates an absolute difference—the Derridean *différance*[92]—in which all difference is demolished, the pure void, the emptiness that is neither something that is nothing nor nothing that is something, the absence in which all presence is abolished. The ultimatum set for postmodern thought is to persist in tarrying with the negative à la Hegel while still seeking to erect temporary conduits in the vein of Nietzsche's vision of the between, that is, to set a bridge by which one crosses over through undergoing. The moments of negation to be affirmed in the affirmation of what is negated are these crossings.

Theologically, the negation of negation entails the obliteration of transcendence foreshadowed in the Nietzschean slaying of God, and anthropologically, the annihilation of human beings attested most brazenly by the Nazi death camps. It follows that the negation wrought by the horror of the Holocaust

> is manifest as unique and ultimate silence—not the awesome quiet of cosmic space to which Pascal alludes but a historical absence of speech, the silence that supervenes upon speech. The traces of this silence are to be found in language, in the speech of the death-world and its survivors where death attaches to every signifier.[93]

The *mysterium tremendum* of the Holocaust, to use the formulation of Arthur Cohen referenced by Wyschogrod, is to be gauged by the silence that has transformed language to the extent that death as the limit of experience has become the ultimate signifier of meaning.[94] Note that the silence of which Wyschogrod speaks is not muteness but rather the fact that speech is beleaguered by the inhibition of its ability to affirm anything that is not a gesticulation of our inability to affirm anything but the nothingness of our finitude.

> *But, at the same time the signified is also and always death.* The signifier "collapses" into the signified which is now no longer more extensive in range than the signifier. For each and every signifier the full range of obsolete meanings is retained together with their negation, the new signified, death.[95]

Psychologically, we are prone to think of death as the terminus beyond which there is no experience of which to speak, but a deeper philosophical propulsion impels us to reflect on the ontological root of the silence concerning that of which we cannot properly say anything factual. When viewed from this perspective, death repels a hermeneutical homogeneity by providing the standpoint in terms of which the commonsensical understanding of the events of human life may be radically reinterpreted.[96] Applying this upending of the more general platitude to the analysis of the death event, the power of taciturn speaking is tied specifically to the role of the survivors to carry the burden of being witnesses to the intent of the Nazis to degrade the inmates of the camps to the single signification of death whereby the signifier collapses into the signified, robbing them of the capacity to see themselves or others as centers of value.[97] However, this goal was ultimately foiled, since the modes of significance systematically destroyed by the executioners were restricted to the vital level of existence, and thus the dissolution of meaning they intended did not affect the ethical level. "Once survival in order to bear witness was conceived as a value, living for others, for the destroyed sociocultural community, came to the fore.... Even with the virtual destruction of the vital level, the apprehension of the other as a node of values was sustained."[98]

As it happens, the darkness of the Shoah spotlights the shortcoming of Heidegger's analysis of death in *Being and Time*, which not only ignored the body as the essential psychosomatic datum but also did not break with the primacy of things over persons. From the vantage point of the nonevent of the death event, "space is not grasped primordially by way of equipmental being but is intersubjectively constituted as that which lies between persons separating them or drawing them together. Human beings or selves are encountered as the ultimate referents of moral acts."[99] Hence, in the context of the death event, corporeality "carries complex symbolic meaning in the absence of a rich equipmental nexus. The dead are not only human existents whose lives have come to an end; they are also symbols of contemporary violence and of the possible death of the entire human world."[100]

In Heidegger's early work, the nullity of death—examined phenomenologically through the structure of care and anxiety—confers individuality on Dasein, for in the case of each person, it is only death that one can truly appropriate as one's own.[101] The Heideggerian perspective is captured succinctly by Reiner Schürmann: "Life has to do with the general, with the common, with the species. Death, on the other hand, arrives unexpectedly in the form of a 'this,' and every non-subsumed 'this' harbors it."[102] The peculiarity of each individual, which grounds the idea of death as evil, distinguishes humans from gods and animals. Needless to say, Schürmann's view corresponds especially to Heidegger's position in *Being and Time* regarding the distinctiveness of human existence as being-toward-death (*Sein zum Tode*), that is, the anticipatory resoluteness of the end that compels one to confront the "nonrelational ownmost potentiality" (*eigenste, unbezügliche Möglichkeit*), which is defined as "the possibility of the absolute impossibility of Dasein" (*die Möglichkeit der schlechthinnigen Daseinsunmöglichkeit*).[103] But even in Heidegger's later work, the lingering grip of his focus on the individualizing nature of death is conspicuous. It comes as no surprise, therefore, that he scarcely mentioned the creation of death and slave labor camps as the institutional forms that resulted in the aggregation of the unnumbered corpses of the two world wars.[104] Similarly, the slaughter propagated by the Nazis—albeit in a grotesque magnitude not envisioned or embraced by Heidegger[105]—construed the man-made mass death as the intervention that imparts a sense of mineness that sublates the social character of the human being. However, when our finitude is considered from the standpoint of the death event, "what comes to an end is a being constituted by its social relations. More, this being is equiprimordially a body. But the body too carries social significance.... The existent who dies is both an I and a we."[106]

Wyschogrod's position can be clarified further if we recall the conclusion of Derrida's lecture "Force of Law: The 'Mystical Foundations of Authority.'" In the summation of his analysis of the essay "Critique of Violence," Derrida accentuated the affinity between Benjamin's *Zerstörung* and Heidegger's *Destruktion*, on the one hand, and the difference between them both and his own method of deconstruction, on the other hand:

> It is at that point that this text, despite all its polysemic mobility and all its resources for reversal, seems to me finally to resemble too closely, to the point of specular fascination and vertigo, the very thing against which one must act and think, do and speak, that with which one must break (perhaps, perhaps). This text, like many others by Benjamin, is still too Heideggerian, too messianico-marxist or archeo-eschatological for me. I do not know whether from this nameless thing called the final solution one can draw something which still deserves the name of a lesson. But if there were a lesson to be drawn, a unique lesson among the always singular lessons of murder, from even a single murder, from all the collective exterminations of history (because each individual murder and each collective murder is singular, thus infinite and incommensurable) the lesson that we can draw today—and if we can do so then we must—is that we must think, know, represent for ourselves, formalize, judge the possible complicity between all these discourses and the worst (here

the final solution). In my view, this defines a task and a responsibility the theme of which (yes, the theme) I have not been able to read in either Benjaminian "destruction" or Heideggerian "*Destruktion.*" It is the thought of difference between these destructions on the one hand and a deconstructive affirmation on the other that has guided me tonight in this reading. It is this thought that the memory of the final solution seems to me to dictate.[107]

Wyschogrod would have concurred with Derrida's assertion that the unique lesson to be drawn from the final solution is the extolling of the eccentricity of each death and not the collective exterminations because the worth of each individual is indeed infinite and incommensurable. Extending this rationale of upholding the unparalleled merit of each perished soul against the irrationality of the mass murderers, Wyschogrod maintained that the self-sacrificial act of witnessing—the feat of remaining alive under odious conditions more difficult than suicide[108]—is what protracted the virtue of living for others, an axiological principle indicative of the fact that the semiosis of language is to be measured by the metrics of the ultimate mystery we now must confront at the periphery of hopelessness, the mystery that there is no mystery but the repudiation of mystery in the absolute disbanding of any absolute induced by the omnipresence of the nonpresence that plagues the death-world.

Heidegger notoriously argued that to be underway (*Unterwegs*) on the way of thinking, one must walk the way by means of thoughtful questioning, the movement by which thinking clears its way in projecting forward from the clearing of the past.[109] To think originarily—that is, to think from the root in the search for the ground of the foundation in the foundation of the ground—is to question,[110] or as he pithily put it, "questioning is the piety of thought" (*das Fragen ist die Frömmigkeit des Denkens*).[111] However, the elemental questioning that comes forth from the cataclysms of the twentieth century "points to the impossibility of the possibility of the question," and thus, journeying beyond the border to which the path of Heidegger's thought reaches and adopting the argument of Blanchot in *The Writing of Disaster*, Wyschogrod declared that questioning the question "circumvents thinking negation as unfolding in Being itself."[112] The weight of the calamity may be felt epistemically "as annulling the question of self so that both question and self disappear,"[113] but the universality of the death event, its inclusivity, is always determined by the incomparability of each individual, and this despite the aspiration of the Nazis to depersonalize the victims with the unanimous verdict that all were going to die. The quelling of the primordial modes of vital being notwithstanding, death did not rob the martyrs of their selfhood.

The ignoble sense of sameness imposed by the diminution of everyone to nothing but a potential or an actual cadaver did not vitiate the magnanimous sense of difference stipulated by the dignity of personhood. To the contrary, the birth of the death event opened up "a new phantasmatic meaning borne by the speaker, one that accompanies all discourse. This is the self's demand that it be permitted to persevere in its existence."[114] The will to endure on the part of the transactional self is an expression of the living being's essence and carries no teleological resolve or axiological weight. Yet, the impact of man-made death upon the social self is such that there is a "transition from a psychological to an axiological or moral conception of the I pole."[115] Facing what Wyschogrod presciently called the "pandemic humanly contrived death," the dilemmas of the depleted self will "be posed within the ambit of this radically altered intersubjective space."[116] A salient outcome of the death event was the fragmentation of the two components of the transactional self, "an I which is a nondiscursive spontaneity and a me which is integrated through time into a relational field. . . . By stressing the me and thus collapsing the self's spontaneity—its I pole—the self requires increasing effort to maintain itself."[117] The perseverance of those marked to be exterminated conveys the ineluctable truism that the ontic experience of being human was fundamentally altered by the atrocities of the camps. This discernment led Wyschogrod to conclude, "*Once the death-world has existed it continues to exist, in the mode of eternity, as it were, for it becomes part of the sediment that is the irrevocable past.*"[118]

Heterological Epiphany: Seeing Nothing to Be Seen

Cast in the language of Blanchot, the disaster's mode of self-temporalization is such that it "recurs in perpetuity not as something positive but as a 'nonevent' that never did and never will happen in any straightforward sense. The time of the disaster is a time that always already was and a time that will be in the mode of not being it."[119] Poignantly, envisaging the Holocaust as the event of the nonevent accentuates that the tenacity of the transience of time somatically demonstrated by the denizens of the death camps—heralding the inescapability of the ephemeral comportment of the human condition as such—signified the tangible embodiment of the abstract idealization of the negation of negation. In some respect, Wyschogrod follows Hegel's contention that the truth of the present must preserve the past and that this preservation can only be achieved through memory.[120] The calculus by which the past is computed is the difference between the content of the in-itself and that content as it effects and is commemorated by our consciousness in the present.[121] The philosophical postulate corresponds to Wyschogrod's contention that in each of the religious traditions—she specifies Judaism, Christianity, Islam, Hinduism, and Buddhism—"the past must be repatterned and in some way neutralized before a change in moral practices is possible."[122] But remembering the nameless condemned not to be remembered presents an inimitable problem that coerces the memory of forgetfulness, a thinking of nothing that has no recourse to being—to think the "not" even more primordially than the *Nichts* of Heidegger[123]—and hence remembering the past on the part of the historian requires hearkening to the unsayability that breaks into language in light of the disaster. Ineffability does not betoken some content that eludes language but rather the saying that escapes so that the unsaid can burst into speech, the alterity of what is held back by the other who deters linguistic captivity.[124]

The historian is thus compared by Wyschogrod to a time traveler who wishes to enter the material and conceptual world of the past but can do so only from the vantage point of the idiom that is comprehensible in terms of the culture of specularity and information available in the present.[125] The ethical obligation to bring back the past—as a presence of absence that is neither present nor absent[126]—is perforce a reiteration (*Wiederholung*) colored by the dual idealization of time as a stretched fluctuation of mobile individual events ordered in the volatility of their pastness, presentness, and futurity, and a punctiform sequence of mensurable and disarticulated now points that succeed one another disjointedly; but in either case, the past is an alterity that can never be spoken or visualized by the historian except as a nostalgic hypostatization in the present, a return to where one has unrelentingly never been, that is, the hyperreal past that is always already awaiting the technological instantiation it receives anew in each recurrence of the now that is differently the same.[127]

The past is disclosed by the "not" that is imprinted, in Derrida's phrase, *sous rature* in what is actually imaged and told. The no, not, never is not merely a mode of time's disclosure, one of time's ec-stases, but *is* time as the break thrown open by the world between itself and itself in the mode of "it was before but cannot be again." *The only way in which that which was can return is through its volatilization in images.*[128]

Contrary to the chronoscopic alignment of time as moving irreversibly from "it was" to "not yet," the vocation of the historian rests on the reversibility of the timeline, and thus the historical narrative is created on the basis of the act of remembering that involves grasping occurrences of the past not only as that which was but as that which could have been. It is this *double disclosiveness of memory* that places the possibility of including paths not taken within the conspectus of the past,[129] a temporal bilocation that negates the negative grounding of historical narrativization in the absolute insistence that what came to pass in the causal chain of events could not have been otherwise.[130]

Wyschogrod rejected the "everyday belief" that "history is a recounting of the remembered events of a community's past" such that "the narrated material history aims at a truth that is understood as a matching of event and narration."[131] Historical statements are not to be adjudicated from the standard of veracity predicated on the presumption that what is alleged to have happened did actually happen, a presumption that further presumes that the truthfulness of the retelling of events is proportionate to one's proximity to the occurrence of those events. Upon reflection, however, it can be shown that this commonplace assumption is dubious as we repeatedly discern that ambiguity and ambivalence are coterminous with the eventality of what has transpired and not a feature of the temporal deferral that slants the retention or the recitation of the event. The analysis of historians is inexorably circumscribed within the paradox of the simultaneity of the nonsimultaneous, and this is so irrespective of the closeness or the distance of the one doing the analysis and the incident being analyzed. Having accepted the need to break with the historicist view of historical writing as "the representation of factlike events," Wyschogrod insisted nonetheless that it is necessary "to thematize the structure of time and memory generally presupposed by narrative form."[132] And by so doing, we become accustomed to the fact that forgetfulness is as much a rudimentary component of the task of history as is memory: "Is human existence not torn between the impetus to get on with it, to be rid of the ball and chain of *Nachträglichkeit*, of what comes later, as

Nietzsche advises, on the one hand and, on the other, the desire to speak for the dead, who cannot speak for themselves?"[133]

Historical events may be shaped by narratives that are independent of those events, but this shaping itself takes place within the scissions in the structure of those narratives, blank spaces that are "the placeholders of revelation" precisely because they cannot become "the focus of visibility."[134] The crevices constitute the discursive space of authorization, the *hors texte*, history's outside that is exterior to what is recorded in the narrative exegeses of the historian that enjoins his or her rememoration, the barren intermezzo that points to the governance of events,[135] whence the break with the past is thrown open by the elision of the no longer into the not yet of the future. Rather than being determined uniformly by the irrecoverability of what has taken place, the past is "a fissure in the world as a spatially organized assemblage."[136] Wyschogrod credited Heidegger for being

> right to insist that the everyday view of time is blind to its grounding in existence as a giving oneself over to time, right to conclude that nonbeing is encountered in death. But what has been passed over in his thought is the primacy of the past in determining the structure of time.[137]

While it is undoubtedly the case that Heidegger privileged the future, for, as I noted above, advancing toward death is signaled out as the distinctive property of human existence, one could nevertheless challenge Wyschogrod on the grounds that she did not sufficiently take into account his notion of equiprimordiality based on the inseparability of the three temporal ecstasies that is opposed to the more conventional spatialization of time predicated on the accumulation and sequencing of allegedly disjointed atomized units.[138]

When this central idea is accorded the attention it deserves, we can appreciate that the future is privileged in Heidegger's tempocentrism because it makes present that which has been.[139] According to the vulgar conception of time, which rests on the irreversibility of time and its assimilation into space expressed as the homogenization into now-points, the past is the irretrievable no-longer-present and the future is the indeterminate not-yet-present.[140] By contrast, authentic time is lived in the present from the perspective of the prospective retrieval of the past in the future. This act, which constitutes the nature of Dasein as historicity (*Geschichtlichkeit*),[141] is predicated on privileging futuricity (*Zukünftigkeit*) as the fundamental phenomenon of time:

Running ahead to the past is Dasein's running up against its most extreme possibility; and in so far as this "running up against" is serious, Dasein in this running is thrown back upon itself as still Dasein. . . . In so far as it holds before Dasein its most extreme possibility, running ahead is the fundamental way in which the interpretation of Dasein is carried through. . . . *This running ahead is* nothing other than *the authentic and singular future of one's own Dasein*. In running ahead Dasein *is* its future, in such a way that in this being futural [*Zukünftigsein*] it comes back to its past and present. Dasein, conceived in its most extreme possibility of Being, *is time itself*, not *in* time. Being futural as we have characterized it is, as the authentic "how" of being temporal, that way of Being of Dasein in which and out of which it gives itself its time. . . . Being futural gives time [*Zukünftigsein gibt Zeit*], cultivates the present and allows the past to be repeated in how it is lived. With regard to time, this means that *the fundamental phenomenon of time is the future* [das Grundphänomen der Zeit ist die Zukunft].[142]

From the vantage point of the everydayness (*Alltäglichkeit*) of clock time (*Uhrzeit*), the past is irretrievable and thus it remains closed off from any present; from the vantage point of authentic time (*eigentliche Zeit*), however, the past is retrievable as it is experienced repeatedly from new hermeneutical perspectives.

Dasein, however is in itself historical [*geschichtlich*] in so far as it is its possibility [*Möglichkeit*]. In being futural Dasein is its past [*Im Zukünftigsein ist das Dasein seine Vergangenheit*]. . . . The past—experienced as authentic historicity [*eigentliche Geschichtlichkeit*]—is anything but what is past. It is something to which I can return again and again.[143]

The ability to return repeatedly to the past as what is still to come in the future yields the *"first principle of all hermeneutics,"* according to Heidegger, which is based on access to history, as opposed to the mistaken method of historicism, *"grounded in the possibility according to which any specific present understands how to be futural."*[144] The historicity of Dasein is thus centered on the capability of altering the past in the present through the future whence it follows that the future epitomizes the compresence of the three ecstasies such that there is a coincidence of preserving what will be and anticipating what has been in the present. Hermeneutically, this concurrence substantiates the paradox later expressed by Heidegger as repetition depicted as the iteration of the same that in each occurrence is entirely different,[145] the "again" that is "altogether otherwise."[146] In contrast to the linear succession of one moment sequentially following another, the time-space affirmed by Heidegger entails the circularity of going back to retrieve where one has never been as the authentic mode of going forward, and consequently, the past need not be comprehended as coming before the future nor the future as coming after the past.[147]

This construal of Heidegger, which has affinity to Benjamin's idea of the dialectical image and the calibration of the past as an act of futural remembering that dispels the semblance of sameness and repetition in history[148]—the codification of the past as a still unrealized messianic promise of a revolutionary act as opposed to a fixed point within the continuum of an evolutionist historicism[149]—brings him much closer to Wyschogrod's own insistence that to portray the past on the part of the historian is not meant to verify the way it really was but rather to cultivate a remembrance that alters what is retained in the breach within time imprinted in image and word. The historical narrative assumes the prestige of a revelatory text inasmuch as the historian serves as a narrator for the dead others who belong to an ostensibly irrecoverable past and therefore cannot be made present except through the metonymic ambiguity of reminiscence.[150] Memory, on this score, "is not something apart from the ongoing experience of retrieval but is the process of bringing back what was previously encoded."[151] To be sure, not only is there an "unsurpassable difference" that separates the original and the replication, but it is meaningless to speak of an original because "access to the past is constituted after the fact. Firstness is conferred in the very act of remembering. . . . Upon analysis, language about the past is second-order discourse but without any first-order level to which definitive appeal can be made."[152] As disconcerting as this might seem, this disjuncture empowers the ability of memory to recall not only what actually was but what potentially could have been. The historian, according to Wyschogrod, is bound by this "negative grounding of historical narrative,"[153] and to the extent that this is so, it is incumbent to obey "the command of dead others that transcends narrative intention," the surfeit that cannot be integrated into any interpretive framework or into any system of signs, the superfluity of meaning that "opens the dimension of the more, of an unincorporable infinite. . . . The invisible dead undo or unwrite the predicative and iterative historical narrative in the blank space that is the placeholder, in historical writing, of an infinite transcendence."[154]

In this foray into the impossible task of speaking for the deceased, "the historian must make the dead other re-member, speak through the literary and artifactual remains that constitute the historical record or, in their absence, through the burial places which encrypt the memories of the dead others."[155] The heterology of the historical narrative must evade the totalization of a metanarrative by confronting the cataclysm from the nonspace of ethics[156] and providing the language to frame prosecution and the defense of a juridical discourse about the past that prevails terminably in its interminable passing.[157] Wyschogrod rejected Hegel's idea of history as a rational process progressing toward an end marked by the immanent and self-reflective Absolute, but she did find useful his belief that we can look back at the images of history. This looking backward—which is enhanced considerably in the age of virtuality—"initiates a responsibility to dead others. We cannot say for sure 'Thus it was,' but we remain responsible for the dead others."[158] The pain and suffering of the aggrieved do not disappear but remain the limiting condition of the semiological memory of the volatilized hyperreality.[159] Correspondingly, the apocalyptic notion of the endtime is transformed hyperliterally by the victims and survivors of the death camps into the time of the end that is not the end of time but the anticipatory victory of eternity over temporal becoming, a deeper oscillation of time through discerning that time is immutable in its mutability, abiding in its nonabiding.[160] The historical recollection of those judged worthy of being disregarded and erased from the book of our collective memory establishes the cognitive apparatus necessary to negate the negation affirming the affirmation of nothing to affirm.

The twofold negativity is tagged by Wyschogrod as the "non-negotiable negative" implied by the event of Auschwitz, in the language elicited from Lyotard's reflections on Adorno's thinking about the Hegelian dialectic in the aftermath of the Holocaust, "the negation of a negative that would eventuate in a new moment of Spirit's development."[161] Wyschogrod agreed with Adorno's critique of Hegel's "positive negation," that the "nonidentical" cannot be obtained as "something positive" or by "a negation of the negative," for equating the "negation of negation with positivity" is the "quintessence of identification."[162] The conclusion reached by Adorno can well serve as a summary of Wyschogrod's own view:

To negate a negation does not bring about its reversal; it proves, rather, that the negation was not negative enough.... The thesis that the negation of a negation is something positive can only be upheld by one who presupposes positivity—as all-conceptuality—from the beginning.¹⁶³

The Hegelian system depends on the dialectical principle that "to negate negation is positive," but the "empirical substance of dialectics," endorsed by Adorno, "is not the principle but the resistance which otherness offers to identity."¹⁶⁴ If one speaks of the nothing as nothing, one negates the negation and thereby transposes the negative into a positive. What is necessary, therefore, is to negate the negation of the negative, to reclaim a negativity that no longer contains its own other within the identity of the same.

Analogously, from Wyschogrod's perspective, the unprecedented possibility of the total abolition of human subjectivity necessitates that the ultimate negation can no longer be sublated by the movement of Spirit in history.¹⁶⁵ The undoing of the undoing begets a negative that is no longer subject to negation, since its own negativity would have been positively negated, whence it follows that the antinomy of being and nonbeing is dismantled and primacy no longer given to the positive or to the negative. The nihilatory inferences to be elicited from the Holocaust are not meant to reinstate a "discursive negation" to express the inexpressible along the lines of traditional negative theology; their intent rather is "to bring to the fore the problem of unsayability" by raising questions concerning the plausibility of the descriptive and analytic functions of language routinely postulated by historical consciousness.¹⁶⁶ The language of the death-world may have been attenuated by the fact that it lacked a "rich referential structure," but it was nonetheless "dense with psychological reference and metalinguistic irony. Personal names, even if they embody incompatible characteristics, resist the rule of cynical doubling which otherwise governs language in the death-world."¹⁶⁷ The irenic occupation of language, expressed in naming the other in terms of kinship and in the use of proper names, endured even in the death-world.¹⁶⁸ Hence, in spite of the effort to quash the individual identity of the victims, their personal names persist—if only through rituals of mourning that annihilate the annihilation of the deceased and defuse the endeavor to foist upon them eternal oblivion—as the means to open up the possibility of the self's answering for itself. "In actual discourse," observed Wyschogrod, "the I is always present, even when unuttered, as the nonreferential null point showing that discourse does not float in linguistic space but belongs to a speaker, for whom this null point crystallizes in the pronoun 'I.' "¹⁶⁹

Excluded Middle and the Nonplace of Diachronic Transcendence

The deployment here of the image of the null point is telling. From the perspective of the sinister fantasy of the death-world, the null point signals the unattainable goal of total eradication. At a deeper register, however, what Wyschogrod seemed to be suggesting is that the negation implied in this idea is negated by the nonreferential null point at the edge of language, the pronominal axis upon which to anchor the response to every other person equally addressed as a self who answers as an I. The negation of death becomes not something negative, "the altogether inconstant and null," as in Heidegger's reading of Rilke,[170] but rather something positive, the negation of negation, the gravitational intensity of zero between two subjects, the womb of apophatic discourse—the speaking-not that is the sign that precedes the constitution of any system of signs, the essence of language that is prior to every particular language[171]—that contains the infinite fecundity of speech that is dialogical rather than monological in nature.[172] Thus, implicitly polemicizing against Heidegger's view of language and its theopolitical undertones, Levinas expounded the difference between the said (*le dire*) and the saying (*le dit*):

Is not the inescapable fate in which being immediately includes the statement of being's *other* [*l'énoncé de l'autre de l'être*] not due to the hold the *said* has over the *saying*, to the *oracle* in which the said is immobilized? Then would not the bankruptcy of transcendence be but that of a theology that thematizes the *transcending* in the logos, assigns a term to the passing of transcendence, congeals it into a "world behind the scenes," and installs what it says in war and in matter, which are the inevitable modalities of the fate woven by being in its interest? . . . Saying is not a game. Antecedent to the verbal signs it conjugates, to the linguistic systems and the semantic glimmerings, a foreword preceding languages, it is the proximity of one to the other, the commitment of an approach, the one for the other, the very signifyingness of signification.[173]

The assertion of another being presumes the proximity of one to the other, but that proximity, in turn, presumes the distance between one and the other. Levinas named this gap between approach and approached the nullsite (*non-lieu*),[174] literally, the "nonplace." Alluding to the colloquial connotation of this expression as "dismissal," the term is said to denote more technically the "extraction from essence" (*l'arrachement à l'essence*) that uproots the topographical bias of seeking an ontological plane.[175]

The place that is no place, which can be equated with the excluded middle wherein the signification beyond essence and before identity is to be sought,[176] is the ground of the Levinasian ethical metaphysics:

> The responsibility for the other is the locus in which is situated the null-site of subjectivity, where the privilege of the question "Where?" no longer holds. The time of the *said* and *of essence* there lets the pre-original saying be heard, answers to transcendence, to a dia-chrony, to the irreducible divergency that opens here between the non-present and every representable divergency, which in its own way ... makes a sign to the responsible one.[177]

The exorbitance of the null-site (*la démesure du non-lieu*) in the matter of subjectivity—the "excess" of tangency (*la "surenchère" de la tangence*) that we can adduce carnally from the phenomenon of the sexual caress—is akin to the superlative that is more than the negation of categories and thus interrupts the application of the dialectic of formal logic to philosophical propositions by the structures of what is beyond being.[178] Rendering the nonspatiality in temporal terms, albeit a temporality that is "completely cut off from adventure and reminiscence," that is, the anticipation of a future and the recollection of a past, Levinas described the null-site—the "strange sort of nature," utilizing Plato's description of the instant situated between motion and rest,[179] which is "on the hither side, without any reference to thematization"—as the interval that is "between time or against time (or misfortune) [*entre-temps ou contre-temps (ou malheur)*]," the nontemporal interlude that "is on the hither side of being and the hither side of nothingness, which is thematizable like being [*en deçà de l'être et en deçà du néant thématisable comme l'être*]."[180]

Language hyperbolically expresses the superlative of the supreme being, which surpasses the ontological dyad of something and nothing, by retaining

> the trace of a beyond-being where day and night do not divide the time that can make them coexist in the dusk of evening, the trace of a beyond borne by a time different from that in which the overflowings of the present flow back to this present across memory and hope.... This would produce a diachrony which maddens the subject but channels transcendence.[181]

The precipice of the meontological that is spatially beyond the division of somewhere and nowhere and temporally beyond the disparity of daytime and nighttime—the nonbeing that is otherwise than being—demarcates the perimeter of discourse that facilitates the crystallization of the null point into the nominative case of the first-person pronoun. Wyschogrod's summation of the Levinasian unsaying of the Heideggerian saying determined by the event of appropriation (*Ereignis*) could surely be applied to her own postmodern moral philosophy: "the Other's existence reduces the individual's rights to what there is to the null point, including the right to one's own life, which must be placed at the Other's disposal."[182] Along these lines, the liquidation of selfhood envisioned by Wyschogrod points to the "nameless subject of ethics" that "must be deterritorialized so that she or he emanates from a null site."[183] In these words, we hear an echo of Levinas's rejection of the egoity of the I—in the technical terms of Husserlian phenomenology, the intentional subject constituted by the unity of transcendental apperception—described by the "unjustifiable identity of ipseity," and his advocating instead for understanding the notion of self that is proper to consciousness as the "non-quiddity" of the "nameless singularity" (*singularité sans nom*) upon which is conferred the function of a personal pronoun.[184] The subjectivity beyond representation is the inimitable unicity of self that withdraws from essence and thus is without the identity of an ego coinciding with itself.[185]

The withdrawal from essence is what allows the ability to draw near to one's neighbor, the ethical gesture that is the tissue of the self, the means by which one becomes a subject.

As a subject that approaches, I am not in the approach called to play the role of a perceiver that reflects or welcomes, animated with intentionality, the light of the open and the grace and mystery of the world. Proximity is not a state, a repose, but, precisely a restlessness [*inquiétude*], nullsite, outside of the place of rest.... Proximity is the subject that approaches and consequently constitutes a relationship in which I participate as a term, but where I am more, or less, than a term. This surplus or this lack throws me outside of the objectivity of relationship.... One can no longer say what is the me or the I. From now on one has to speak in the first person. I am a term irreducible to the relation, and yet in a recurrence which empties me of all consistency.[186]

One can speak in the first person (*la première personne*) only when it is no longer possible to speak objectively of the ego or subjectively of the I (*On ne peut plus dire ce qu'est le Moi ou le Je*).[187] The subjectivity of the subject—the "pre-originary susceptibility, before all freedom and outside of every present"[188]—is to be appraised from the vantage point of this "null-place in which inspiration by the other is also expiation for the other, the psyche by which consciousness itself would come to signify."[189] To be in-oneself, therefore, means to

> be backed up against oneself, to the extent of substituting oneself for all that pushes one into this null-place [*non-Lieu*], it is precisely this to be in oneself [*c'est précisément cela être en-soi*], lying in itself beyond essence. The reclusion of the ego in itself, on the hither side of its identity, in the other, the expiation supporting the weight of the non-ego, is neither a triumph nor a failure.... The self as an expiation is prior to activity and passivity.[190]

The proximity of the chasm—labeled as the "interval of difference" (*l'intervalle de la différence*) and as the "meanwhile" (*l'entretemps*) of the "non-indifference of responsibility" (*la non-indifférence de la responsabilité*) in which the self comes close to the other by being separated from the other—repudiates the reification and the synchrony of structure linked to the ego and the I.[191] To approach the other is likened, therefore, to the tactile sensation of caressing insofar as the caress is "the unity of approach and proximity," that is, the immediacy of the caress, like the contact of saying,[192] presupposes the remoteness of a presence that is always also an absence.[193]

In a caress, what is there is sought as though it were not there, as though the skin were the trace of its own withdrawal, a languor still seeking, like an absence which, however, could not be more there. The caress is the not coinciding proper to contact, a denuding never naked enough [*une dénudation jamais assez nue*].[194]

A denuding never naked enough—an arresting image indeed! What is it to be not naked enough? Is there a laying bare through which consciousness attains a nudity that is more nude than nudity? The undressing of the undressing is demanded by the exposedness of oneself to the other, a stripping of all layers, even the layer of I-ness, that only enhances the pursuit of the other as the other is not an object that can be possessed.

In the neighbor's presence there then rises an absence by virtue of which proximity is not a simple coexistence and rest, but non-repose itself, restlessness. Not an intentional movement tending to fulfillment, and which is in this sense always *less* than the plenitude of this fulfillment. . . . But is it an absence? Is it not the presence of infinity? Infinity cannot be concretized in a term; it contests its own presence. In its unequalable superlative, it is an absence, on the verge of nothingness. It always flees. But it leaves void, a night, a trace, in which its visible invisibility is the face of the neighbor. Thus the neighbor is not a phenomenon, and his presence is not resolvable into presentation and appearing. It is ordered out of *the absence in which the infinite approaches*, out of its *null site [Non-Lieu]*, ordered *in the trace of its own departure*; it is ordered to my responsibility and my love, beyond consciousness, which it obsesses.[195]

The hiatus is not a state of rest but rather restlessness, the disquietude of the null-site wherein the profusion of privation lifts one beyond the circumference of objectivity. In a manner somewhat reminiscent of Gillian Rose,[196] Levinas deployed the expression *divine comedy* to name the depiction of the idea of the infinite, or the infinite in thought, as the negation of the finite. More specifically, the negation relates to "the subjectivity of the subject, which is behind intentionality. . . . The difference between the Infinite and the finite is a non-indifference of the Infinite to the finite, and is the secret of subjectivity."[197] Just as the presence of infinity must be an absence, since infinity is the unequalable superlative on the verge of nothingness that cannot be concretized, the "other with an alterity prior to the alterity of the other,"[198] so the presence of another human being is not a phenomenon subject to the dynamics of intentionality, presentation, and appearing in accord with Husserlian phenomenology. The inimitability of the neighbor imbibes the very absence in which the infinite approaches, the null-site of the nondifferential difference, which occasions the paradox of the trace that can come forth only through its own retreat. In facing the other, *one manifests oneself by undoing one's manifestation* (se manifester en défaisant la manifestation), and thus the face is "the point at which an epiphany becomes a proximity."[199]

The infinition of infinity—the mode of being that is the idea of infinity—is produced as revelation,[200] but that revelation is determined by the metaphysical desire for the invisible transcendence that is impervious to vision.[201] Invisibility, for Levinas, does not denote the relinquishment of relation, but it implies rather relations with what is not given to consciousness. If vision is the adequation of idea with thing, beholding the invisible is the nonadequation that is "beyond the light and the night, beyond the knowledge measuring beings—the inordinateness of Desire. Desire is desire for the absolutely other."[202] The exteriority of the relationship to the other breaks the interiority of the self by the incommensurability that reveals

an insufficiency full of this very insufficiency and not of hopes, a distance more precious than contact, a non-possession more precious than possession, a hunger that nourishes itself not with bread but with hunger itself.... Desire does not coincide with an unsatisfied need; it is situated beyond satisfaction and nonsatisfaction.[203]

The "manifestation of the invisible," accordingly, averts

the passage of the invisible to the status of the visible.... For the invisible is not the "provisionally invisible," nor what remains invisible for a superficial and rapid glance, and which a more attentive and scrupulous investigation would render visible, nor what remains unexpressed as hidden movements of the soul, nor what, gratuitously and lazily, is affirmed to be a mystery.[204]

What, then, is the invisible? It is "the offense that inevitably results from the judgment of visible history," that is, the judgment that issues from the universal principles of reason that inflict harm on the singularity of the subject that cannot be subsumed in a totality.[205]

Every revelation of the infinite is concomitantly a concealment, the giving of what is ungiven. Levinas's thinking on this matter is bolstered by his appropriation of the aniconism associated with the Jewish tradition to shape his linkage of the personhood of God to the quality of invisibility. The invisible and indescribable God, however, is accessible to justice, and hence ethics is taxonomized as a spiritual optics.[206] Expanding the philosophical footing of the showing of nonshowing as it pertains to the simultaneous revelation and concealment of infinity, Levinas wrote:

Once come into a correlation, the divinity of God dissipates, like the clouds that served to describe his presence. All that could have attested to his holiness, that is, to his transcendence, in the light of experience would immediately belie its own witness already by its very presence and intelligibility, by its chain of significations, which constitute the world. To appear, to seem, is forthwith to resemble terms of an already familiar order, to compromise oneself with them, to be assimilated to them. Does not the invisibility of God belong to another game, to an approach which does not polarize into a subject-object correlation but is deployed as a drama of several personages?... Let us fix the point of departure: the nonmanifestation, the invisibility which language sets forth.[207]

In the manifestation of the nonmanifestation, the "thematization of a face undoes the face and undoes the approach. The mode in which a face indicates its own absence in my responsibility requires a description that can be formed only in ethical language."[208]

Wyschogrod extended Levinas's nonintentional phenomenology and his delineation of ethics as an elevation beyond being to the historiological task of preserving the memory of those who were savagely subject to the death event. The murderous ambition that fueled the null point of Nazi aggression is inverted by the Levinasian *non-lieu*, the nonplace that is the atopographical foundation of the diachronic transcendence. The moral mandate for the historian is to bear witness to the faces of those who were defaced. The face shows itself resiliently as a refusal to show itself, and thus it cannot be rendered faceless as it always speaks contrariwise to the objectification of self and thereby contests the sovereignty of the subject. In Levinasian terms, the death event epitomizes the violence perpetrated as a result of the collapse of attentiveness to the command that ensues from the inundation of sociality embodied in the face that reveals itself as what cannot be revealed.[209] However, there is one crucial incongruity between Levinas and Wyschogrod: according to the former, the trace of illeity attests to a past that can never be made present, whereas according to the latter, the trace is indexical of the past that can never be past because it must constantly be made present.

Replying to the observation of Carl Raschke that in contrast to thinkers such as Derrida, Taylor, and Levinas, who maintained that the trace is an unrecoverable presence, Wyschogrod seemed to argue that the ethical demands of historiography lead us toward a new understanding of "heterology," she elucidated her position as follows:

Your question raises fundamental issues of absent presence. I argue that the past itself is inscrutable and thus always already an unsurpassable negation. It would seem that only an apophatics of history would be possible. Yet here the model—I invoke it with fear and trembling—of a broken natural theology may help. Just as Levinasian ethics is contingent upon the face not in its phenomenological *Leibhaftigkeit* but as trace, so that there both is and is not flesh, so too the artifacts and images of the past both are and are not signifiers.... In what sense are we to construe alterity, the subject of the heterological historian? Whose alterity? What narrative? Two directions occur to me. First, there is the character of the past itself. I claim that the past is "an unsurpassable negation" that can never be brought back materially, so that there is an apophasis belonging to the past that cannot be overcome. Yet second, the past is transmitted via language and image. So the past is a secret in the Derridean sense. But this secret begs to be revealed.[210]

Building on but deviating from Levinas, Wyschogrod affirmed the paradoxical nature of the trace as the signifier of an absent presence. From one perspective, the materiality of the past is irrecoverable, and thus it is an unsurpassable negation. And yet, from another perspective, the apophasis belonging to the past can be overcome insofar as it is transmissible through language and image, albeit a language that succumbs to the inadequacy of language to communicate and an image that capitulates to the inability of the image to divulge.

Wyschogrod emphasized the importance of the trace so understood to theological discourse:

What has theology to gain from the depiction of an artwork as a system of traces, of images that are nested inside one another? Theologically understood, the trace is the mark of the sacred that has disrupted or passed through the beautiful. One must know how to read or, rather, not to read traces, how to remain attentive to them. There is in the trace the suggestion of a "more," of something uncontainable in language.[211]

Taking the apophatic nature of the trace into account, we can say that the past is akin to the Derridean double bind of secrecy; that is, the secret must be revealed as a secret that is concealed if it is the secret that is revealed. Hence, the secret can be spoken of *ad infinitum* because there is no end to speak of that which cannot be spoken. "No more secrecy," Derrida infamously wrote, "means more secrecy: that is another secret of secrecy."[212] The secret implicates one in the vicious circle that the unavowable speech is the only speech that may be avowed, and thus the secret is most hidden when it is most exposed.[213] For Wyschogrod, interpreting the trace in light of this duplicitous sense of the secret buttresses the argument that it is because the aniconic face transcends all imagistic representation that it has the capacity to fabricate an ethical imperative that is a distillation of faciality.

Poetic Stuttering and the Polysemic Language of the Brokenhearted

In conformity with Derrida's analysis of the logic of the supplement as the moment of *différance*, Wyschogrod accepted the following modification of Hegel's idea of the negation necessary to secure the actuality of finite existents:

> If the idea of difference yields deeper insight into negation itself, difference acquires meaning only because we become aware of negation through the *play* of differences which leaves tracks or traces in that which is present.... But a negation so profound that all presence would be snuffed out would annihilate difference as well. Difference and presence alike depend upon continuity of the world. Without it, alterity would be reduced to the same.[214]

It is the charge of thinking the nonbeing that cannot be thought that forges an intrinsic connection between the radical annihilation of the Holocaust and the postmodern sensibility.[215] The unmasking of rationality, which is indispensable to the ethos of postmodernity, is personified by the depersonalizing event of the Shoah, which prototypically illustrates the inversion of the Husserlian conception of the life-world (*Lebenswelt*) in the death-world.[216] Ironically, the questioning of reason that evolves from indisputably one of the most wretched chapters of human history sheds light on what Wyschogrod pinpointed as the Jewish predilection for multivocality and the constant interrogation of texts to derive novel meaning. Following this time-honored tradition, Wyschogrod placed a premium on the conspicuous tolerance for a plurality of opinions. Moreover, when read through the Lacanian psychoanalytic lens, the sources of Judaism, as theological texts more generally, can be viewed as "manifesting multiple strands of meaning, which become intelligible through the analytic process."[217] Using this criterion, the manifold meanings are entertained as credible so long as it is recognized that all of them are true. "As a religion of the text," wrote Wyschogrod, "Judaism is compatible with the intertextuality of hermeneutical and poststructuralist interpretation."[218] Jewish exegesis, accordingly, would allow in Derridean terms for a "textual dissemination," which, in contrast to "discursive polysemy," implies an "implacable difference," that is, a "textual stream whose interpretations cannot be brought to closure."[219] Ideationally, the iconoclastic proclivity of Jewish aniconism is isomorphic with the demise of the absolute prompted by the negation of negation.

The "logic of the text" is altered hermeneutically by an absence of any presence of a transcendental signifier—even an absence that presents itself as nonpresent—and thus it "opens previously unthinkable configurations, an errancy, wandering or leaching of meaning that is irrecoverable as that which is fully present."[220] As Wyschogrod put it in another context, the mark of postmodernism "is not sheer ineffability, but a negation that deconstructs language so that, to borrow a metaphor from the Hasidic master Nahman of Bratslav, language itself stutters."[221] To stutter, as we know, is not to remain silent; it is to speak, albeit in such a way that what is verbally spoken is never what is audibly said, an "apophatics of denial," in Derrida's locution, a "self-deconstructing speech."[222] Since the term "transcendence" signifies an infinite that cannot be an object of signification, the "ambiguity of an event situated at the limit of immanence and transcendence,"[223] that is, the transcendence that transcends transcendence in immanence and immanence in transcendence, presumably we must speak of this infinite as a consciousness of being that exceeds the being of consciousness. Wyschogrod thus charted the transition from the Derridean *erotics of transcendence* to the Levinasian *ethics of transcendence*:

> But a transcendent Absolute that is beyond consciousness necessitates an apophatic theology that may be disclosed as an unremitting yearning *for* an absent Other or as a divestiture of self *on behalf of* an Other who, as Other, never appears. I shall maintain that, in his questioning of the primacy of the transcendental subject and in his description of the desire *for* God, Derrida's account of naming and negative theology is essentially transgressive, an *erotics* of transcendence. When the sheer contingency of fact leads neither to an eidetic science, to the certainty of an eidos that remains invariant through all of an object's variations, nor to an erotic desire for the Other, but rather to an alterity that is beyond consciousness, the way is open for a Levinasian *ethics* of transcendence.[224]

To imagine the desire of God, which would imply both the human desire for God and God's desire for the human, we must posit a transcendence that cannot be desired except as what cannot be desired. But could a desire for what cannot be desired be anything but the cessation of desire that paradoxically inflames the desire not to desire? If so, the translation of the erotics of transcendence into the ethics of transcendence would necessarily entail an *ascetic renunciation*, a disowning of self in relation to the other that facilitates the possibility of the self that confronts the other in the overabundance of its otherness, a becoming less that makes possible the always more, the inexhaustible ultramateriality that

> does not designate a simple absence of the human in the piles of rocks and sands of a lunar landscape, nor the materiality that outdoes itself, gaping under its rent forms, in ruins and wounds; it designates the exhibitionist nudity of an exorbitant presence coming as though from farther than the frankness of the face, already profaning and wholly profaned, as if it had forced the interdiction of a secret. *The essentially hidden throws itself toward the light, without becoming signification.*[225]

To be thrown toward the light, without becoming signification, indicates that the light on the way to being seen is incapable of ever having been seen. Expressed temporally, the light, which "manifests itself at the limit of being and non-being,"[226] is not nothingness (*le néant*) but what is not yet (*ce qui n'est pas encore*), the unreality (*irréalité*) at the threshold of the real, the essence of the nonessence.[227] This light, the radiance of the beyond that "has meaning only negatively, by its non-sense,"[228] is the glory of the infinite, the "trace of a withdrawal which no actuality had preceded" and whose "essence is undone in signification, in saying beyond being and its time, in the diachrony of transcendence." This transcendence is not capable of being converted into immanence because it is "beyond reminiscence, separated by the night of an interval from every present . . . a time that does not enter into the unity of transcendental apperception."[229] It is at this spatiotemporal "*no man's land* between being and not-yet-being"[230] that the inessential essence of the secret, which is "not a hidden existent or a possibility for an existent" but "what is not yet and what consequently lacks quiddity totally,"[231] is displayed, an appearance of nonappearance that translates into an inherent and incontrovertible dissemblance. The secret, if it is to persist as secret, can be revealed only as what is hidden and hidden only as what is revealed, the simultaneity of the clandestine and the exposed, which defines profanation and the immodesty it incites.[232]

The exorbitant *ultramatérialité*—the materiality that is more material than all matter (*une matérialité plus matérielle que toute matière*)[233]—precipitates the secret that appears without appearing, a paradox that, in turn, exhorts an abjuration of self that is symmetrical to the constraint on language. Wyschogrod highlighted the ethical repercussion of the halting nature of speech: "Language is not only communication but always already inter-diction, the no-saying of a speech that prohibits, even if such prohibition is on behalf of the other."[234] The language of negation—the no-saying of the stutterer as opposed to the reticence of the mute—can be expressed in ocular terms as the negative epiphany, a seeing of nothing to be seen, the invisible that is beyond the opposition of visible and nonvisible,[235] the nonphenomenalizable that shapes the phenomenalizability of the phenomenal world of human experience. Beholding the unseen and heeding the unsaying are the consequences of mounting the heights of joy and plumbing the depths of despair. In the heterological nonspace of *différance*, there is no discrepancy between the sacred and the cataclysmic: one, as the other, directs the mind to the void that is not amenable to linguistification, conceptualization, or confabulation.[236]

The task of poiēsis is critical, for the "proper subject" of the poem is the death event, and hence it has the potential to open "a discursive space for remembering the lost or dead other."[237] As an invocation of the forgotten remembered other, poetry is the path by which "space is intersubjectively constituted within the ambit of the death event."[238] The poet is thus bequeathed with the mission that Wyschogrod assigned to "the sphere of ethics to be a holding open of a discursive and ontic space for becoming, specifically the becoming of moral change."[239] Utilizing the taxonomy offered by Jean Genet that "poetry is the break (or rather the meeting at the breaking point) between the visible and the invisible,"[240] Wyschogrod extracts the moral claim that appearances must be unmasked not because they hide a noumenal truth but because they mask the absence of the justification for such a truth. As the art that brings nonbeing into view, poetry is "inscribed as a negative ethics on the aesthetic surface of the text."[241] Further support for the ethical understanding of poetry is elicited by Wyschogrod from her reading of Levinas's depiction of aesthetic experience as "a kind of shamanistic seizure of consciousness by being prior to being's assumption of form. But if being as disclosed in art is formless and ethics (for Levinas, bound up with and often indistinguishable from the religious) is also beyond form, then common strategies for grasping this immediacy may be developed."[242]

Art and ethics are two fields marked by the disclosure of formlessness.

In this capacity to illustrate the tenability of positing a singularizing individuality phenomenologically that does not belong to the domain of phenomenality—in Blanchot's terms, the invalidating of pure negation that is extraontological[243]—art in general, and poetry in particular, stand as correctives to what Wyschogrod identified as the malady of the postmodern culture of images:

> In a world of semblances, people die by violence, but their deaths are and are not understood as being real. Violence is envisaged as simultaneously actualizing and derealizing death. If all is semblance, a game, death's finality is fictive, undecidable.[244]

Poetry undoes the spell of virtuality by offering a way of visualizing the invisible through an aniconic iconicity and saying the unsayable through a language that is "a self-questioning that opens the possibility of its own unmaking."[245] Divested of its referential function, poetic language "signals to us, without the sign's bearing a meaning by giving up meaning."[246] Following Levinas's summation of Blanchot, Wyschogrod accepted that poetry

> transforms words—indices of a manifold, moments of a totality—into signs set free, that break through the walls of immanence, disrupting order.... To introduce a meaning into Being is to move from Same to the Other, from *I* to the other person; it is to give a sign, to undo the structures of language.[247]

The poetic word thus

> preserves that movement that is located between seeing and saying, that language of pure transcendence without correlation—like the waiting that nothing awaited yet destroys[248]—noesis without noema—pure extra-vagance, a language going from one singularity to another without their having anything in common ... a language without words that beckons before signifying anything, a language of pure complicity, but of a purposeless complicity.[249]

The interweaving of aesthetics and ethics, exemplified by poetry, pivots around the fact that both "exhibit totality as the plane of the always already broken and incomplete infiltration by alterity."[250] Positioned like the infinite between vision that has been abandoned in the act of seeing and speech that has been discarded in the act of speaking, poetry "refers back to [*en appelle à*] a saying *properly so-called*, a saying that thematizes, even if it may be obliged to unsay itself in order to avoid disfiguring the secret it exposes."[251] The disfiguration of the figuration, however, is unavoidable insofar as the saying renders every said unsaid, and thus the secret can be uncovered only to the extent that it is obscured. It is in this sense that we should speak of poetry as an apophatic materialization of the ethical.

Adorno famously proffered in the 1949 essay "Cultural Criticism and Society" that to write poetry after Auschwitz is barbaric.[252] In *Negative Dialectics*, published in 1966, Adorno revised his earlier view, but in so doing posed an even more agonizing question:

Perennial suffering has as much right to expression as a tortured man has to scream; hence it may have been wrong to say that after Auschwitz you could no longer write poems. But it is not wrong to raise the less cultural question whether after Auschwitz you can go on living—especially whether one who escaped by accident, one who by rights should have been killed, may go on living. His mere survival calls for the coldness, the basic principle of bourgeois subjectivity, without which there could have been no Auschwitz; this is the drastic guilt of him who was spared.[253]

Heidegger, as is well known, argued that in the wake of the catastrophic failures of the technologically driven ideologies of the twentieth century—Nazism, communism, and capitalism—poiēsis as a metapolitical gesture[254] is the sole ratification of life and the only way to paint a world-picture (*Weltbild*) based on the truth of the measure-taking[255] that provokes the freedom to let *the veil appear as what veils*,[256] that is, the unconcealment that reveals nothing but the concealing of the unconcealed revealed as the nothing that is concealed.

Following, but significantly deviating from Heidegger, Wyschogrod likewise regarded poetry—typified by Rilke's insistence that we must prepare an abode for those who have perished and thus reach into the abyss to find "a counterlogos able to encompass the scale of what is moving toward extinction as well as the speed of this passing"[257]—as the viable route to accommodate "the possibility of thinking not only my death but also the numberless dead."[258] Specularized through the prism of the death event, the one who survived shoulders no drastic guilt, as Adorno suggested, nor is there a primary blame tied to Dasein's finitude, as Heidegger argued; the culpability rather "belongs to every Dasein," which leads to the conclusion that "the guilt of victim and agent are equalized."[259] There is, however, one crucial way in which the guilt of the victim is not equal to the guilt of the agent: the former singularly embodies the poetic directive to live as the witness to the death event; such agency is denied the agent who committed horrific crimes against humanity. As the survivors suffer the obdurate fate of tackling their own mortality, those who retell the story must assume the responsibility of being witnesses to teach each and every human being how to die both as I and as we, acceding to the aporia of a death that defies the perpetrators of the death-world by proffering an endtime that timelessly engenders the infinitization of finitude.

FOUR

Melancholic Redemption and the Hopelessness of Hope

Where there is much light, there the shadow is strongest.
—Johann Wolfgang von Goethe, *Götz von Berlichingen*

True sadness is in harmony with what is most joyful—but in this way, that the greatest joy withdraws, halts in its withdrawal, and holds itself in reserve. By learning that renunciation, the poet undergoes his experience with the word's lofty sway.... The poet could never go through the experience he undergoes with the word if the experience were not attuned to sadness, to the mood of releasement into the nearness of what is withdrawn but at the same time held in reserve for an originary advent.
—Martin Heidegger, "The Nature of Language"

I commence the final chapter with the brief but evocative exchange between Max Brod and Franz Kafka from February 28, 1920.[1] Two versions of this conversation were offered by Brod. The first was recorded in 1921.[2] I will cite the text as it is transmitted by Walter Benjamin:

I remember a conversation with Kafka which began with present-day Europe and the decline of the human race.
"We are nihilistic thoughts, suicidal thoughts, that come into God's head," Kafka said. This reminded me at first of the Gnostic view of life: God as the evil demiurge, the world as his Fall.

"Oh no," said Kafka, "our world is only a bad mood of God, a bad day of his."
"Then there is hope outside this manifestation of the world that we know."
He smiled. "Oh, plenty of hope, an infinite amount of hope—but not for us."³

For the sake of comparison, I will quote the second version of the dialogue found in Brod's biography of Kafka:

He: "We are nihilistic thoughts that came into God's head." I quoted in support the doctrine of the Gnostics concerning the Demiurge, the evil creator of the world, the doctrine of the world as a sin of God's. "No," said Kafka, "I believe we are not such a radical relapse of God's, only one of his bad moods. He had a bad day." "So there would be hope outside our world?" He smiled, "Plenty of hope—for God—no end of hope—only not for us."⁴

There are some interesting discrepancies between the two versions. Insofar as the first was written in closer proximity to the actual conversation, there is an understandable tendency to view it as more trustworthy. I will analyze the text by combining the two versions.

Duplicitous Truth Unmasking Truthful Duplicity

With his characteristic penchant for paradox, Kafka equates the possibility of boundless hope with a state of hopelessness, thereby reversing the old adage that less is more by postulating that more is less, indeed infinitely so, as the infinite expanse is reduced to the infinitesimal point. The irony casts a stark light on the intractable darkness of this world. Pushing against Brod's suggestion that his pessimism was reminiscent of the gnostic view that the world arose as a consequence of the fall of the evil demiurge, Kafka protested that the misery and misfortune of this world can be explained simply as a result of a bad day or a bad mood on the part of God and not due to some radical relapse.⁵ The distinction, however, is undermined by Kafka's concluding presumption that even if there is an infinity of hope, it does not mean there will be hope specifically for Brod or for himself but only perhaps for God according to Brod's second version of the exchange.⁶ Precisely the limitlessness of hope in general delimits the limit of the hopelessness of any individual in particular. Kafka's admonition reads like an inversion of the concluding statement of Benjamin's essay "Goethe's Elective Affinities" that we have been given hope only for the sake of the hopeless.⁷ From Kafka's perspective, one can be hopeful only in the recognition that the fulfillment of the hope one espouses will never come to pass except as the hope that hopelessly defies fulfillment.[8]

It is difficult to see how Kafka's final assurance to Brod averts the peril of nihilism. Brod recorded in both versions that Kafka smiled when uttering the pronouncement that the infinity of hope precluded the possibility that it was applicable to their individuated circumstances. This may very well attest to the comic undercurrent of the tragic abdication of any sense of positivity for the future. As Levinas elicited from Tolstoy's tale about the requisition for the supply of twenty-five years of boots sent to one sentenced to die that very evening, "through this image one sees that the comical is also tragic, and that it belongs to the same man to be a tragic and a comical personage."[9] Analogously, Wittgenstein argued that tragedy and comedy should not be viewed in opposition but rather as the intersection of two nodes traversing the same plane of dramatic space.[10] In the spirit of Gillian Rose's depiction of irony as the pathos of the middle that she elicited from Thomas Mann's analysis of Goethe, we can say that Kafka's statement that there is "an infinite amount of hope—but not for us" points to the infinite irony of the harmony of eternal contraries that endure in their contrariety even beyond the state of tension without resolution.[11] Admittedly, it seems inappropriate to assign to Kafka the pathos of the middle as yielding the playful reserve of politics that relates to an ethics of a national and a universal nature. Nevertheless, the insight of Rose does capture the melancholic cynicism imparted by Kafka's concluding remark, a facetiousness that does not feast but that dissembles its dirge.[12]

In the second chapter, I referred to the stark and uncompromising misgiving about human nature articulated in the fifty-fifth of Kafka's Zürau aphorisms: insofar as everything is deception, there is no difference between those who seek the minimum of deceptions and those who seek the maximum, for in the end, there is nothing but duplicity.[13] The gnostic underpinning of this sentiment is made clear in the fifty-fourth aphorism: "There is nothing besides a spiritual world; what we call the world of the senses is the Evil in the spiritual world, and what we call Evil is only the necessity of a moment in our eternal evolution" (*Es gibt nichts anderes als eine geistige Welt; was wir sinnliche Welt nennen ist das Böse in der geistigen und was wir böse nennen ist nur eine Notwendigkeit eines Augenblicks unserer ewigen Entwicklung*).[14]

Kafka artfully reinterprets the dualistic posture of ancient Gnosticism by locating the material world of the senses in the spiritual world. With this shift in focus, evil is not set in opposition to good but is seen rather as a moment in our eternal evolution. The modicum of hope implied in this shift is still tied to a hopelessness of harboring any sense of hopefulness, a consequence of the assumption regarding the inherently evil nature of the world even if that sense of evilness is viewed as an inherent aspect of the realm of spirit.

Further support for my conjecture can be drawn from Rose's own reflections on the exchange between Brod and Kafka.[15] This "remorseless account," which was "delivered with the smile of the ironist," confirmed Brod's assertion that peculiar to Kafka were "his dream-poetical and his paradox-humoristic turns of expression."[16] Elaborating Brod's characterization of Kafka's literary style and mode of thinking, Rose commented:

> More precisely, the meaning of this exchange depends on both the ironic-smile *and* the humour-paradox: irony, the incognito at the aesthetic border of the ethical; humour-paradox, the incognito at the ethical border of the religious. . . . Here, the idea of God with His transient moodiness, with the arbitrariness of the finite, set against the infinite ethical requirement, in such a way that the ethical passion of the ironist is both accentuated and passes unnoticed into the cultural infinity, here human hopelessness, accentuated at the same time. The smile is all that remains of this contradiction which seems otherwise flatly to deny the ethical by insisting on human hopelessness, and which brings finiteness into God himself.[17]

Rose appreciably augmented Brod's interpretation by connecting the musing of Kafka to Kierkegaard's distinction between three spheres of existence—the aesthetic, the ethical, and the religious—and the respective boundary zone (*confinium*) to which they correspond: irony is the boundary between the aesthetic and the ethical, whereas humor is the boundary between the ethical and the religious.[18]

To grasp Kierkegaard's point, we must recall that he defined religiosity as "the task of the individual to understand that he is nothing before God, or to become wholly nothing and to exist thus before God," an impotence that of necessity is at odds with the youthful exuberance for power exemplified by immediate consciousness and manifest through the sense of comicality that is ubiquitously found in the world.[19] Even though the religious individual does not become comical in relation to himself, since inwardly he must surrender to the earnestness required to maintain a sense of nothingness before God, an abnegation of selfhood described as the essential persistence of the dying away from immediacy,[20] the comical nonetheless presents itself when it appears to the outer world that such an individual is emboldened to execute many things.[21] When the religious individual, the "knight of the secret inwardness," leaves the confines of the monastic withdrawal and is set down in the medium of existence, a contradiction will emerge when he relates to his environment:

> The contradiction does not consist in his being different from all others ... but the contradiction is, that with all this inwardness hidden within him, with this pregnancy of suffering and blessing in his soul, his appearance is precisely like that of other men—whereby his inwardness is concealed, by the fact that he looks like other men. Something comical is here present, for there is a contradiction here, and where there is a contradiction, there the comical is also present.[22]

From the fact that the farcical ploy exists exclusively for the religious individual, who uniquely experiences the contradiction between overtly appearing identical to everyone else and covertly concealing an inwardness that distinguishes and removes him from the sociality of human affairs, humor is designated as his incognito.[23] In the final analysis, however, the goal is to protect the interior passion by repudiating the allure of the exterior stimulated by intersubjective interactions. "Religiosity with humor as its incognito is therefore a synthesis of absolute religious passion (the inwardness being dialectically produced) with a maturity of spirit, which withdraws the religiosity away from all externality back into inwardness, where again it is absolute religious passion."[24] Extrapolating from this particular example, Kierkegaard generalized that the outward gaze of others signals the concern of a person to be something, whereas turning inward gestures toward obeisance to the look of the absolute and the resultant obliteration of the sense of personhood molded by a distinct sense of ownness.[25] The holy jest consists of the friction between the external appearance of power vis-à-vis other human beings and the internal reality of powerlessness vis-à-vis the divine.[26]

Delving more deeply into this matter, the irony implicit in Kierkegaard's analysis of irony is that the religious individual is acclimatized to the comical in the largest measure precisely because such a person does not regard either that the comical is the highest of human emotions or that religiosity is the purest pathos. The dissimilitude, however, is to be distinguished from self-deception,[27] since the knight of faith is well aware that being enmeshed in the world demands a playfulness that conceals the true nature of being detached from the world. Moreover, insofar as the comical must always lie in contradiction, it makes its showing most visibly in the one who does not consider the comical supreme; by contrast, the comic consciousness of the individual who considers the comical as highest is in fact lower, since it is lacking the contradiction in and through which the comical consists.[28] This is the paradox that buttresses Kierkegaard's aforecited assertion that just as irony is the boundary between the aesthetic and the ethical, so humor is the boundary between the ethical and the religious. The common denominator is that irony

> arises from the constant placing of the particularities of the finite together with the infinite ethical requirement, thus permitting the contradiction to come into being. . . . Irony is a synthesis of ethical passion which infinitely accentuates inwardly the person of the individual in relation to the ethical requirement—and of culture, which infinitely abstracts externally from the personal ego, as one finitude among all other finitudes and particularities.[29]

Perspicaciously, Rose utilized this Kierkegaardian insight to explain Kafka's sardonic retort about the infinity of hope set against the hopelessness of the finite human being. The smile with which Kafka reportedly prefaced his melancholic acquiescence is the token of irony based on the contradiction between infinite hopefulness and finite hopelessness. The preservation of that contradiction facilitates the bridging—as opposed to collapsing—of the gap that brings finiteness into the infinite and infiniteness into the finite. Reading Kafka through the lens of Kierkegaard lead Rose to conclude: "God's bad humour coupled with human hopelessness—dispassionately delivered—conceal and reveal, ironically, the passionate good humour of the utterer and the utterance, beyond hope or hopelessness."[30] The dialetheic truth that occupies the middle excluded by the syllogistic logic of the excluded middle is the implication of Kafka's seemingly preposterous contention that the only plausible safeguarding of hope is through the relinquishment of hope.

Veil of Nature and the Ground of Luminescent Darkness

By way of amplification and not disagreement, I would add that Kafka's words convey a deep structure of thought amply instantiated in the concrete experience of countless Jews through the course of history.[31] To be sure, the particular case of the Jews is indexical of the metaphysics of melancholy attributable more universally to humankind,[32] that is, a melancholic state kindled by the existential displacement in the world and the wistful yearning for transcendence. Consider the formulation in the discussion on the possibility of positing a force of evil within God in Friedrich Wilhelm Joseph Schelling's *Philosophical Investigations into the Essence of Human Freedom* (1809). After asserting that personality cannot be ascribed to what exists without a condition (*Bedingung*) that facilitates it becoming real, Schelling noted that this applies as well to the divine existence, but in that case, the condition is internal and not external. This crucial distinction notwithstanding, like any other existent being, God cannot abolish the condition without abolishing himself, and thus, at best, God must "come to terms with the condition only through love and subordinate it to himself for his glorification [*Verherrlichung*]. There would also be a ground of darkness [*ein Grund der Dunkelheit*] in God, if he had not made the condition into *his own*, bound himself to it as one and for the sake of absolute personality [*absoluten Persönlichkeit*]."[33]

In a manner consonant with the theosophical ruminations of Jacob Böhme, which in turn resonate with kabbalistic speculation on the polarity of good and evil in the Godhead,[34] Schelling proposed that there is a force of darkness within the divine, but that its autonomy is ameliorated by the fact that God appropriates what is potentially other and makes it part of himself, an othering of otherness that is necessary for the glorification of the absolute personality. Schelling's insight that the nature of the light of the absolute can appear only through darkness is suggestive of Hölderlin's assertion that the significance of tragedy is grasped on the basis of the paradox that

> inasmuch as all abundance is justly and equally apportioned, no original appears as actual in its original strength; rather, it genuinely appears in its debility alone, so that quite properly the light of life and the appearance of debility pertain to every whole. . . . For the original can appear in a genuine way only in its debility.[35]

With respect to the tragic, the sign is meaningless, and hence it is equal to zero, but it is only in the weakest gift of this nothingness that the original, the concealed ground of every nature, can present itself as the strongest gift.

Burning the candle at both ends, as the proverbial expression goes, Schelling argued that evil is necessary for the personal existence of God even though we cannot say that evil comes from the ground or that the will of the ground is the originator of evil.[36] For Schelling, as for Böhme and the kabbalists, since there cannot be a genuine ontological dualism within the infinite, we must say of the darkness that it both is and is not divine; that is, evil is subordinate to the good in the manner that what is other than God is in God as that which is not of God.

We recognize rather that the concept of becoming is the only one appropriate to the nature of things. But they cannot become in God, considered in an absolute manner, since they are different from him *toto genere* or infinitely, to speak more correctly. In order to be divided from God, they must become in a ground different from God. Since, however, nothing indeed can be outside of God, this contradiction can only be resolved by things having their ground in that which in God himself is not *He Himself* [*was in Gott selbst nicht* Er Selbst *ist*], that is, in that which is the ground of his existence. If we want to bring this way of being closer to us in human terms, we can say: it is the yearning [*Sehnsucht*] the eternal One feels to give birth to itself [*sich selbst zu gebären*]. The yearning is not the One itself but is after all co-eternal [*gleich ewig*] with it.[37]

Alternatively expressed, the delimiting condition is incorporated into the limitlessness of the one in relationship to which there is nothing demarcated as outside the one. By contrast, insofar as a human being can never gain control over the constraining condition, which remains autonomous and is not subject to absorption, one's personality and selfhood never rise to full actuality.

This is the sadness [*Traurigkeit*] that clings to all finite life: and, even if there is in God at least a relatively independent condition, there is a source of sadness in him that can, however, never come into actuality, but rather serves only the eternal joy of overcoming [*Überwindung*]. Hence, the veil of dejection [*der Schleier der Schwermut*] that is spread over all nature, the deep indestructible melancholy of all life [*die tiefe unzerstörliche Melancholie alles Lebens*]. Joy must have suffering, suffering must be transfigured in joy.[38]

Just as the sadness within the divine does not denote an intrinsic imperfection but rather the impetus that stimulates the eternal joy of overcoming, so in the case of the human being, the mandate is to transfigure suffering into joy, to take hold of the deep and indestructible melancholy of life by peering through—rather than by discarding—the veil of gloom spread over nature. The veil, in other words, cannot be lifted, and melancholia is not a pathological condition that can be remedied by the unveiling of some primeval desire or instinct—some naked truth—that has been repressed and obstructed. The essence of human freedom is to move from the darkness to light, but this can only be achieved by one who discerns that darkness itself is an inflection and not a privation of light.

The lachrymose view of finite reality is reiterated by Schelling in the reflection on the demeanor of the temperament (*Gemüth*)—which together with spirit (*Geist*) and soul (*Seele*) comprise the three pneumatic powers of the human being—in his *Stuttgart Seminars* (1810):

> The most obscure and thus the deepest aspect of human nature is that of nostalgia [*Sehnsucht*], which is the inner gravity of the temperament, so to speak; in its most profound manifestation it appears as *melancholy* [*Schwermuth*]. It is by means of the latter that man feels a sympathetic relation to nature. What is most profound in nature is also melancholy; for it, too, mourns a lost good, and likewise such an indestructible melancholy inheres in all forms of life because all life is *founded* upon something independent from itself (whereas what is *above* it elevates while that which is *below* pulls it down).[39]

Schelling identified melancholia as the most profound dimension in nature, the inextinguishable force that resides in all forms of life, insofar as it bemoans a sense of a lost good that is presumed to be independent. However, if we are to apprehend the melancholic state as a form of mourning for a lost possession, then it is a possession that is irrecoverably lost, since it was lost from the beginning; what is absent, therefore, was never present except as absence.[40]

The melancholic nature of life revolves around this sense of irretrievable loss for which there is no reparation or consolation, only the nostalgic longing—conveyed by the German *Sehnsucht*—and the illimitable mourning that propagates, in Derrida's felicitous formulation, the "law of mourning" that is "always in mourning," a law that "would have to fail in order to succeed. In order to succeed, it would well have to *fail*, to fail *well*."⁴¹ The paradox of success that can only be measured as failure, and failure that can only be measured as success, is exemplified above all in the aporia that becomes clear when considering the language that might be suitable to speaking about mourning:

> There is thus no metalanguage for the language in which a work of mourning is at work. This is also why one should not be able to say anything about the work of mourning, anything about this subject, since it cannot become a theme, only another experience of mourning that comes to work over the one who intends to speak.... And that is why whoever thus works *at* the work of mourning learns the impossible—and that mourning is interminable. Inconsolable. Irreconcilable.⁴²

The concession that there is no expiration of suffering that would not initiate further suffering—the Derridean interminability of mourning—is the tragic provision that undergirds Schelling's unsettling conjecture that

> evil itself proves perhaps the most spiritual [phenomenon] yet, for it wages the most vehement war against all *Being*; indeed, it wishes to destroy the very ground of all creation. Whoever is somewhat acquainted with the mysteries of evil (and we ought to ignore evil only with our heart, yet not with our mind) will know that the most intense corruption is precisely the most spiritual one, and that under its sway everything natural, and consequently also our sensibility and even the most base pleasure, will disappear; such corruption will turn into cruelty, and a character of demonic-devilish evil is a far more of a stranger to pleasure than a good one. Hence, if error and evil are both spiritual in kind and origin, the spirit itself cannot possibly be the highest form.⁴³

The proclivity to view nature as inherently melancholic underlies Kafka's excruciating intuition that even if—or rather just because—there is the prospect of hope external to the world, we will be denied access to it.

Awaiting Nothing More to Await and the Appearing of Nonappearing

Here it is germane to evoke the insight of Levinas regarding the melancholic rapture essential to the plight of one facing the "anonymous rustling of existence," the "bare fact of presence" that "arises behind nothingness... neither *a being*, nor consciousness functioning in a void, but the universal fact of the *there is*, which encompasses things and consciousness."⁴⁴ In the ecstatic encounter with the brute factuality of *il y a*, the ego "is swept away by the fatality of being," and hence there "is no longer any outside or any inside."⁴⁵ The complete exposure to being in the vigilance of night results in the depersonalization of the persona—or, in Levinas's language, the impersonal event of *il y a*, the wakefulness in which consciousness participates⁴⁶— the expansion of self through self-contraction. "Insomnia thus puts us in a situation where the disruption of the category of the substantive designates not only the disappearance of every object, but the extinction of the subject."⁴⁷

Levinas elicits support for this notion of nocturnality and the oblivion of self from Maurice Blanchot's observation in *Awaiting Oblivion*: "Waiting is always a wait for waiting, wherein the beginning is withheld, the end suspended, and the interval of another wait thus opened. The night in which nothing is awaited represents this moment of waiting."⁴⁸ Levinas elaborated on this nexus of themes:

> A nocturnal time.... But primordial forgetting is forgetfulness of self. Is not *ipseity* both absolute origin and an insatiable turning back upon oneself, an imprisoning of self by self just as language is?... Forgetting restores diachrony to time. A diachrony without protension or retention. To wait for nothing and to forget everything, the opposite of subjectivity.... A relaxing of the Self, and its tension in upon itself.⁴⁹

In another passage from the aforementioned work of Blanchot, also cited by Levinas,⁵⁰ the attenuation of self is related explicitly to the state of despondency: "With what melancholy and yet with what calm certainty he felt that he would never again be able to say 'I.' "⁵¹ The solitary waiting, therefore, is a "waiting for ourselves without ourselves, forcing us to wait outside our own waiting, leaving us nothing more to await."⁵² To proclaim that the waiting consists of having nothing more to await validates William S. Allen's conclusion that Blanchot's aporetic logic of the noncoincidence of language and the world "extinguishes any scope for redemption and leaves a melancholy without relief, which entirely reconfigures what we might understand by hope for change."⁵³

In the subjectivity without a subject, the distinction between exteriority and interiority dissolves, an experience that Levinas related phenomenologically to insomnia:

In insomnia one can and one cannot say that there is an "I" which cannot manage to fall asleep. The impossibility of escaping wakefulness is something "objective," independent of my initiative. This impersonality absorbs my consciousness; consciousness is depersonalized. I do not stay awake: "it" stays awake. Perhaps death is an absolute negation wherein "the music ends" (however, one knows nothing about it). But in the maddening "experience" of the "there is," one has the impression of a total impossibility of escaping it, of "stopping the music."[54]

Death as the absolute negation, depicted metaphorically as the cessation of music, is contrasted with the mindfulness—or perhaps mindlessness would be more appropriate—that comes forth from the *il y a*, the inassimilable otherness of being, whose impenetrable force is exhibited as the inability to stop the music. Touching on this theme in slightly different terminology in the essay "On Escape," published in 1935, Levinas wrote:

The experience of pure being is at the same time the experience of its internal antagonism and of the escape that foists itself on us. Nevertheless, death is not the exit toward which escape thrusts us. Death can only appear to it if escape reflects upon itself. As such, nausea discovers only the nakedness of being in its plenitude and in its utterly binding presence.[55]

The term *"melancholia"* is not used in this passage, but it is reasonable to surmise that the description of the nausea one experiences in the face of the nakedness of being corresponds to what is described elsewhere as the melancholic engagement with the ferocity of the *il y a*.[56]

Levinas's view on the melancholy of death is in accord with the critique of Heidegger that he extracts from Ernst Bloch's utopian speculation on the constant deferral of the future and the collateral incompleteness of the present:

For Bloch, the anxiety of death comes from the fact of dying without finishing one's work [*œuvre*], one's being. It is in an unfinished world that we have the impression of not finishing our work.... The work of man is historical, but it is not proportionate to utopia. There is failure in every life, and the melancholy of this failure is its way of abiding in unfinished being. This is a melancholy that does not derive from anxiety. On the contrary, the anxiety of death would be a mode of this melancholy of the unfulfilled (which is not a wounding of one's pride). The fear of dying is the fear of leaving a work unfinished, and thus of not having lived.... The subject, in the darkness of the pure fact of being, works for a world to come and for a better world. His work is therefore historical. In the immediate future, the utopia succeeds only partially; it is therefore always a failure, and the melancholy resulting from this failure is the way in which man reconciles himself with his historical evolution [*son devenir historique*]. This is a melancholy that does not derive from anxiety, as in Heidegger's case. On the contrary, for Bloch, it is the anxiety of death that would be a modality of melancholy. The fear of dying is the fear of leaving a work unfinished.[57]

According to Heidegger's being-toward-death, as may be gleaned from *Being and Time*, the anxiety that pertains to death is signaled in the consciousness of the end of one's being, whereas Bloch unearths in the anxiety over dying a threat that is concerned with "what is higher or better than being."[58] Heidegger's discussion of the anxiety of death caused by the consideration of the inevitability of one's nonbeing presumes that the ultimate event is the event of being.[59] However, as Levinas argued, in the case of Bloch,

the event of being is subordinated to a completion in which man finds his home. Being, in a certain sense, contains more or better or something other than being; for Bloch, this is the completion of the world, its quality as a home, which is attained in the perfected world.[60]

The messianic drive is to the future that is always coming, the "future never future enough, more remote than the possible."[61] For Levinas, this betokens the diachronic surfeit of time, the not yet that surmounts the anxiety of death linked to the melancholic dread of the work being left uncompleted.

What counts above all for Bloch, and what must be kept in mind here, is that such an emotion could dominate the ineluctability of death, that death might not be marked solely by the threat that weighs upon my being, and that death does not exhaust its meaning in being the sign of nothingness.... What we call, by a somewhat corrupted term, love, is *par excellence* the fact that the death of the other affects me more than my own. The love of the other is the emotion of the other's death. It is my receiving the other—and not the anxiety of death awaiting me—that is the reference to death. We encounter death in the face of the other.[62]

That sleep should serve figuratively as a modulation of the absolute negation of death is not surprising. More interesting is the fact that Levinas highlighted the disquietude of insomnia—encountering the destitution of the other as a fecundity that disrupts and disaggregates the self in its resisting rest[63]—as that which engenders the "absolute impossibility to slip away and

Melancholic Redemption and the Hopelessness of Hope 171

distract oneself."[64] The very structure of consciousness as consciousness of the other, a gathering into being or into presence whose luminosity permits no shadow, is a

> modality or modification of *insomnia*. . . . Insomnia, wakefulness or vigilance, far from being definable as the simple negation of the natural phenomenon of sleep, belongs to the categorical, antecedent to all anthropological attention and stupor. . . . Insomnia—the wakefulness in awakening—is disturbed in the core of its formal or categorical *sameness* by the *other*, which tears away at whatever forms a nucleus, a substance of the same, identity, a rest, a presence, a sleep. Insomnia is disturbed by the other who breaks this rest, breaks it from this side of the state in which equality tends to establish itself. . . . The other is in the same, and does not alienate the same but awakens it.[65]

The lucidity of this confrontation shares with lunacy the stark clarity and profound obscurity of acquiescing to the inability to escape from the inability to escape, the unavoidability of being condemned to stand before the exit from which there is no exit.[66] Like the figure in Kafka's parable "Before the Law," only by being consummately outside does one imagine that one is inside; that is, there is no way to be embedded internally but from the vantage point of being positioned externally.[67]

It is well to recall that Levinas began the pivotal chapter on substitution in *Otherwise Than Being or Beyond Essence* with an epigraph from Celan's poem "Lob der Ferne" ("Praise of Distance"),[68] *Ich bin du, wenn ich ich bin*, "I am you, when I am I."[69] Ostensibly, Levinas's analysis of the dependence of self-consciousness on the consciousness of the other is an exegesis of this comment. In his own words,

> It is as though subjective life in the form of consciousness consisted in being itself losing itself and finding itself again so as to *possess itself* by showing itself, proposing itself as a theme, exposing itself in truth. This identification is not the *counterpart* of any image; it is a claim of the mind, proclamation, saying, kerygma.[70]

In some measure still indebted to Husserlian phenomenology, consciousness signifies the relationship with beings; however, deviating significantly from his mentor, Levinas maintained that this relationship is not to be construed as the adequation or correspondence between the thought of the knower and the object that is known. Moreover, in contrast to Heidegger, Levinas rejected the idea that the relationship of consciousness to being is determined primarily as the potential of Dasein's being-in-the-world to disclose poetically the being that is veiled in its unveiling, a vision "where the relation of the subject with the object is subordinated to the relation of the object with light, which is not an object. The understanding of a being will thus consist in going beyond that being (*l'étant*) into the *openness* and in perceiving it *upon the horizon of being*."[71]

As Levinas correctly noted, Heidegger unwittingly reaffirmed the tradition that has prominently informed Western philosophy: "to comprehend the particular being is already to place oneself beyond the particular. To comprehend is to be related to the particular that only exists through knowledge, which is always knowledge of the universal."[72] Despite Heidegger's concerted effort to overcome the idealist correlation of thinking and being, epitomized by the Parmenidean dictum *to gar auto noein estin te kai einai*, "For it is the same thing to think and to be,"[73] he succumbed to the supposition that our relation to being cannot be anything but the comprehension of that being unless the latter is the absolute other whose invocation of necessity—by virtue of its unassimilable alterity as the other that is other vis-à-vis every other, the other that is perforce otherwise—overflows comprehension. If we assume that is the case, then the truth of being is implemented as the nonintentional simultaneity enunciated in the response of sympathy or love,[74] *the resistance of what has no resistance—the ethical resistance*.[75] Ethical resistance—facing the face of the other that cannot be subsumed under the stamp of the same and thereby effaced—portends the presence of infinity,[76] whence it follows that the ethical condition, which is the essence of language, is "prior to all disclosure of being and its cold splendor."[77] Regarding the "presentation of the face," it would seem that we cannot say categorically that it is true, "for the true refers to the nontrue, its eternal contemporary, and ineluctably meets with the smile and silence of the skeptic. The presentation of being in the face does not leave any logical place for its contradictory."[78] Hence, the "true universality of reason" is grounded in the irrecusable duty that results from the opening of the face to another human being, the epiphany that occasions the "discourse that obliges the entering into discourse.... Preexisting the disclosure of being in general taken as basis of knowledge and as meaning of being is the relation with the existent that expresses himself; preexisting the plane of ontology is the ethical plane."[79] The attentive ear will assuredly hear the criticism of Heidegger in these statements: the indisputable truth disclosed through love in the visage of the other—the truth that does not logically allow for anything contradictory—is not subject to the Heideggerian contention that truth as *alētheia*, the unconcealment of the concealment in the concealment of the unconcealment, necessitates that untruth belongs inextricably to truth.[80]

The human subject becomes conscious of a particular being when it grasps that being across an unbridgeable chasm of ideality that disrupts the immanence of the said; indeed, insofar as an interlocutor can at all times break through and impede the said, discourse qua discourse belies the claim to totalize, even in the case of the ultimate discourse that alleges to thematize and to envelop all things. The said "remains an insurmountable equivocation, where meaning refuses simultaneity, does not enter into being, does not compose a whole."[81] To the extent that the saying proceeds from and heralds the relationship of one-for-the-other, it is repeatedly a "subversion of essence that begins to signify before being, the disinterestedness of essence."[82] Levinas thus compared the verbal act of saying to the writing of a book. Prima facie, we might think that "writing the saying" results in the "pure said," that is, the "simultaneousness of the saying and of its conditions." However, Levinas insisted—perhaps reflecting the plurivocality of the rabbinic hermeneutic[83]—that the book displays the nature of an interrupted discourse, calling for other books and being subject to a process of interpretation—a process that continues potentially ad infinitum—whereby the saying will be rendered distinct from the said.[84]

Traditionally, saying is the act of making signs to communicate with the other, the sign that signifies the giving of signs. But the saying to which Levinas referred is an excess of words that

> opens me to the other before saying what is said, before the said uttered in this sincerity forms a screen between me and the other. This saying without a said is thus like silence.... If silence speaks, it is not through some inward mystery or some sort of ecstasy of intentionality, but through the hyperbolic passivity of giving, which is prior to all willing and thematization. Saying bears witness to the other of the Infinite which rends me, which in the saying awakens me.[85]

Undermining the longstanding correlation in Western philosophy between thought and being, Levinas put the emphasis on language as the saying that is prior to the said, a saying that is without words, a silence that is not to be conceived in mystical or ecstatic terms but as the passivity of giving that bears ethical witness to the other. We revert again to the issue of sleep or the lack thereof, the arousal or the awakening that ensues from the testimony of the saying that is a way of signifying that precedes the said, the testimony of the responsibility that I have toward the other, a "pure testimony" that is not dependent on the disclosure of a prior religious experience, an obedience that precedes the hearing of any order, a testimony that attests "to the Infinite which is not accessible to the unity of apperception, non-appearing and disproportionate to the present."[86]

By gesturing toward the proximity of the absolutely other, the other that cannot be conceived noetically or visualized imagistically,[87] the saying divulges the trace of infinity configured in its disfiguration as the *imageless image of the possible*,[88] the appearance of the inapparent,[89] the invisible manifest as the nonmanifest in the face of the stranger for whom I am unconditionally responsible,[90] a responsibility that "does not derive from any commitment, project or antecedent disclosure, in which the subject would be posited for itself before being-in-debt."[91] The devotion to the other is a form of passivity in the extreme that Levinas most often characterizes by the image of exposedness to the face of the other, the awakening to the "shudder of incarnation through which *giving* takes on meaning, as the primordial dative of the *for another*."[92]

A face does not function in proximity as a sign of a hidden God who would impose the neighbor on me. It is a trace of itself, a trace in the trace of an abandon, where the equivocation is never dissipated. It obsesses the subject without staying in correlation with him, without equalling me in a consciousness, ordering me before appearing, in the glorious increase of obligation. . . . A face as a trace, trace of itself, trace expelled in a trace, does not signify an indeterminate phenomenon; its ambiguity is not an indetermination of a noema, but an invitation to the fine risk of approach qua approach, to the exposure of one to the other, to the exposure of this exposedness, the expression of exposure, saying. In the approach of a face the flesh becomes word [*la chair se fait verbe*], the caress a saying. The thematization of a face undoes the face and undoes the approach. The mode in which a face indicates its own absence in my responsibility requires a description that can be formed only in ethical language.[93]

Polemicizing against the foundational myth of Christianity,[94] Levinas emphasized that the word does not become flesh through the hypostatic presencing of the father in the body of the son—the theological dogma that is the philosophical corollary to the thematization of the face as a result of which the equivocation between transcendent and immanent is dissipated—but rather the flesh becomes word through the saying of the other, the face of the trace expelled in the trace, the trace that perseveres in the absence of being present, the evocation that fosters the "primordial discourse whose first word is obligation."[95]

In facing the face, the breach is not eliminated; the tender beauty of the face preserves

> the very gap between approach and approached, a disparity, a non-intentionality, a non-teleology. . . . Proximity, immediacy, is to enjoy and to suffer by the other. But I can enjoy and suffer by the other because I-am-for-the-other, am signification, because the contact with skin is still a proximity of a face, a responsibility, an obsession with the other, being-one-for-the-other, which is the very birth of *signification* beyond *being*.[96]

Levinas effectively inverted the premise and the conclusion of Celan's poetic syllogism: the subjectivity implied in the tautological statement "I am I" is realized only to the extent that one gauges that "I am you," which is not to say that the difference between self and other is overcome, but rather that the interiority of being-for-oneself is constituted by the exteriority of being-for-the-other, the exterior that one absolutely can neither take in nor possess.[97] Freedom consists of renouncing the imperialism proper to the ego[98] by fathoming that the obligation with regard to the other is to be placed before the obligation to oneself, that justice enduringly demands that the other takes priority to the same.[99] "The relation with the Other as a relation with his transcendence—the relation with the Other who puts into question the brutal spontaneity of one's immanent destiny—introduces into me what was not in me."[100]

The I that says I is thus

> not that which singularizes or individuates a concept or a genus. It is I, unique in its genus, who speaks to you in the first person. That is, unless one could maintain that it is in the individuation of the genus or the concept of the ego that I myself awaken and expose myself to others, that is, begin to speak.[101]

The profoundly personal nature of the encounter with the face is predicated, therefore, on a depersonalization, the infinite task of liberation, as opposed to nihilation, which consists of the solitude of the I drawing back from its object and from itself[102]—the consciousness of self that is depleted of the self of consciousness,[103] a depletion that Levinas demarcates as the incessant reception of the teaching of infinity, an incessant overflowing of self, which he further presumes is commensurate with the nature of time.[104] Bearing this in mind, Rose spoke of "Levinas's *Buddhist* Judaism,"[105] which she further explained: "The self, according to this new ethics, cannot experience truly transforming loss, but plunders the world for the booty of its self-seeking interest. To become ethical, this self is to be devastated, traumatised, unthroned, by the commandment to substitute *the other* for itself."[106] The altruistic foundation of the ethics promulgated by Levinas comes with the sacrificial price of the self-divestiture and self-negation before the infinite other that the ego identifies as the transcendence against which it must constantly struggle.[107]

Levinas further depicted the anonymity of this nocturnal experience as "the very return of presence into the void left by absence—not the return of *some thing*, but of a presence," a presence, that is, with nothing present, the "reawakening of the *there is* in the heart of negation."[108] This can be compared profitably to mourning without an object to be mourned, the melancholic feeling of bereavement determined by the intransience of there being nothing that can be lost and therefore nothing that can be found.[109] Levinas's pairing of mourning and melancholia can be clarified if we contrast it with Freud's classic study "Mourning and Melancholia."[110] Whereas Levinas delineated the melancholic state as a mourning without an object to be mourned—congruent with his description of the trace as the anarchy of what has never been present rather than the absence of a yet non-revealed presence[111]—Freud maintained that both mourning and melancholia are psychic strategies to deal with a sense of libidinal deprivation, the former a reaction to the loss of a person or to the loss of some abstraction that has taken the place of a person, and the latter a turning inward predicated on the loss of the capacity to love, which leads to a diminution of one's self-regard and an inhibition of all activity. For Levinas, the disenchantment of melancholia on the psychological plane corresponds on the more communal-historical plane to the disillusionment of Jewish messianism and its propagating an overflowing of sense by the nonsense of the disequilibrium wrought as a consequence of the disconnect between expectation and denial, the pure evacuation of the prospect of repair beyond the acceptance of the nonreparative character of repair.

In Levinas's own turn of phrase, the messianic resolve of *awaiting without an awaited* is disclosive of the diachronic nature of time as inadequation, the "*always* of noncoincidence, but also the *always* of the *relationship*, an aspiration and an awaiting, a thread finer than an ideal line that diachrony does not cut."[112] The insatiable desire peculiar to Jewish messianism reveals more universally the timbre of temporal transcendence that comports paradoxically as the distance that is distant by being proximate and proximate by being distant. Expressing a concordant attitude, Gershom Scholem mused in the essay he wrote to honor Bloch, "The water that separates us is too shallow to provide the necessary depth for the development of a true encounter."[113] In Levinasian terms, I can approach the other only if the infinite breadth of the fissure between us is preserved. Furthermore, as I have argued with respect to the phenomenological landscape of the dream,[114] the hope imparted by the messianic creed renews itself sporadically as the hope deferred perpetually. Neither pessimism nor optimism seems apposite to categorize the bequeathing of hope through its adjournment, a pure futurity that would be compromised if the future were ever to abandon its status as that which is present only by being absent and absent only by being present. Hope can be envisioned as the unremitting projection of an elementally calibrated retrospection, to foretell what has been in the recollection of what is to come. Every undertaking entails a relapse of what never was, divulging thereby the deportment of time as the recurrence of the same difference that is differently the same, the loop of the double negative that yields the positivity of our becoming the being we are not, a predilection well understood through the centuries by mystic visionaries.

Abyss of Nothingness and the Anarchy of Theopolitical Resignation

The philosophic import of the melancholic nature of the asymptotic curvature of messianic time, and by extension of the finitude of temporality more generally, that we educed from Levinas strikingly parallels the despondent implications of Scholem's theopolitical Zionism.[115] We would do well to draw attention to the beginning of the poem "Traurige Erlösung" ("Melancholy Redemption"), composed by Scholem in 1926, three years after his arrival in Jerusalem:

> Der Glanz aus Zion scheint vergangen
> das Wirkliche hat sich gewehrt.
> Wird nun sein Strahl, noch unversehrt
> ins Innere der Welt gelangen?
>
> The light of Zion is seen no more,
> the real now has won the day.
> Will its still untarnished ray
> attain the world's inmost core?[116]

Remarkably, at this early stage, Scholem was already expressing doubt about the potential of Zionism to transform the world materially.[117] The poem ends with an ostensible glimmer of hope:

> Nie konnte Gott dir näher sein,
> als wo Verzweiflung auch zerbirst:
> in Zions selbstversunkenem Licht.
>
> God never comes more close
> than when despair bursts into shards:
> in Zion's self-engulfing light.[118]

To my ear, the image of God coming close when despair bursts into shards likely reflects the cosmological myth of Lurianic kabbalah according to which the light of infinity is dispersed into the world through the cataclysmic shattering of the vessels. From Scholem's perspective, the image is ambiguous insofar as hope is framed in apocalyptic terms whence he adduced in a manner compatible with Levinas that the most proximate is the most distant: the divine presence is most palpable in the place from which that presence has absconded; the God most exposed is the God who is hiding.[119] The light that engulfs Zion can emerge only from a rupture just as Luria taught that the light that sustains reality is manifest in the sparks attached to the fragments of the vessels that have been broken. Extrapolating further we can postulate that the juxtaposition of redemption and melancholy in the poem's title amply underscores the unassailable sense of the tragic and catastrophic nature of reality, on the one hand, and the saturnine distrust[120] in the prospect of rectification of the world's blemish, on the other hand. The point is accentuated as well in the concluding stanza of Scholem's poem "Begegnung mit Zion und der Welt" ("Encounter with Zion and the World"), dated June 23, 1930, and significantly subtitled *"Der Untergang" ("The Decline")*:

> Was innen war, ist nach Außen
> verwandelt, der Traum in Gewalt,
> und wieder sind wir draußen
> und Zion hat keine Gestalt.
>
> What was within is now without,
> the dream twists into violence,
> and once again we stand outside
> and Zion is without form or sense.[121]

Striking a similar note in the opening stanzas of the poem "Media in Vita," composed between 1930–1933, Scholem wrote:

> Ich habe den Glauben verloren
> der mich hierher gebracht.
> Doch seit ich abgeschworen,
> ist es um mich Nacht.
>
> Das Dunkel der Niederlage
> zieht mich unheimlich an;
> seit ich keine Fahne mehr trage,
> bin ich ein ehrlicher Mann.
>
> I have lost the faith
> that brought me to this place.
> And in the wake of this forsaking,
> night is my surrounding space.

> I am uncannily attracted
> by the darkness of this defeat;
> since I no longer carry any banners,
> I'm as honest a man you'll ever meet.[122]

Despite—or perhaps on account of—his allegiance to Zionist ideology, Scholem's faith turned, as it did for Kafka, on the bleakness that hope inescapably galvanizes. There is a sense of pride in the honest acknowledgment that he is attracted to the darkness of defeat, having lost the fervor that motivated his emigration to Palestine. Scholem's melancholy is brought to the fore in his candidly admitting that he can no longer carry any banners for the ideology that failed to be actualized historically. In the concluding part of another poem composed in 1933 on the occasion of the wedding of Kitty Marx and Karl Steinschneider, "Mit Einem Exemplar von Walter Benjamins 'Einbahnstraße'" ("With a Copy of Walter Benjamin's 'One-Way Street'"), Scholem reiterated the primacy accorded to melancholy in the religious outlook of Benjamin and in his own worldview:

> In alten Zeiten führten alle Bahnen
> zu Gott und seinem Namen irgendwie.
> Wir sind nicht fromm. Wir bleiben im Profanen,
> und wo einst "Gott" stand, steht Melancholie.
>
> In days of old all roads somehow led
> to God and to his name.
> We are not devout. Our domain is the profane,
> and where "God" once stood, Melancholy takes his place.[123]

An arresting intonation of the disconsolate disposition that shaped Scholem's spiritual susceptibility to the piety of hopelessness: the sacred has given way to the profane and melancholia takes the place of the divine. Reality is described in the last stanza of the poem "Media in Vita" as *der Abgrund des Nichts, / in dem die Welt erscheint*, "that abyss of nothingness / in which the world appears."[124] It is probable that this language is indebted to the kabbalistic axiom that all existents are manifest in the concealment of *Ein Sof*, the nihilating nonground of being.[125] For Scholem, however, this abyss of nothingness is not an infinite being—the supreme gradation on the ontological ladder, the *hyperousios* of the Neoplatonic tradition, the being beyond being, the being otherwise than being, the essence not properly called essence, in the locution of John Scotus Eriugena, the essence above essence (*superessentialis essentia*)[126]—but the aggregate of finite beings that constitute the infinitude in the very absence of such a being. The metaphysical distinction between real and apparent is no longer viable because there is no reality behind or beyond the appearance; what is real is the vacuum of spacetime wherein the really apparent is apparently real and the apparently real is really apparent.

Scholem's use of the image of the abyss of nothingness brings to mind Benjamin's comment in the "Theological-Political Fragment" that humanity's quest for happiness, which is the foundation of the secular world or the profane order, "runs counter to the messianic direction," and thus it is inevitable that the "immediate messianic intensity of the heart, of the inner man in isolation [*des innern einzelnen Menschen*], passes through misfortune, as suffering."[127] The messianic is inexorably intertwined with torment since it provokes not happiness (*Glück*) but misfortune (*Unglück*). Insofar as the "worldly restitution," which corresponds to the spiritual *restitutio in integrum*, leads to an "eternity of downfall"—the agonizing awareness that the only thing permanent is impermanence—the method appropriate to the "task of world politics" (*Aufgabe der Weltpolitik*) is nihilism.[128] I concur with Rose's educing from this passage—following the reading proffered by Jacob Taubes—that the political agenda envisaged by Benjamin

> presupposes the inner man in isolation, able to bear a suffering that promises neither realization nor redemption. *E contrario*, it implies misfortune which is unable to bear this suffering, a thirst for the realization of entreated redemption, for the politics of the world, and total perdition.[129]

As Rose astutely added,

> The object, style and mood of Benjamin's philosophy converge, not in the Christian mournfulness or melancholy, discerned from the Baroque *Trauerspiel* to Baudelaire, but in the Judaic state of desertion—in Hebrew, *agunah*—the stasis which his *agon* with the law dictates. . . . Benjamin is the *taxonomist of sadness*, and he adds figures of melancholy to the philosophical repertoire of modern experience . . . stoicism, scepticism, the unhappy consciousness, resignation and *ressentiment*.[130]

In a second passage, Rose expanded on this dimension of Benajmin's melancholic messianism:

Agunah, the deserted wife, is the Judaic category and Messianic image of this forsakenness, which I have suggested by analogy with the Christian, baroque image of melancholy. In Judaic terms, I would argue that, in spite of his emphasis on creating new holy days, Benjamin knew no Day of Atonement, no Yom Kippur, although this date is already in the liturgical calendar. In his work, the hard heart of judgment does melt into grief, into forgiveness, or into atonement. In philosophical terms, I would argue, Benjamin only knew the dialectical image as a lightning flash, "the Then . . . held fast", in the Now of recognizability.[131] . . . It is this unequivocal refusal of any dynamic of mutual recognition and struggle which keeps Benjamin's thinking restricted to the stasis of desertion, *aberrated mourning*, and the yearning for invisible, divine violence.[132]

Benjamin's melancholia is not a hankering for paradise lost—whether otherworldly or mundane—but it is rather the recognition that there is no justification for such misplaced wistfulness.[133] As he elicited from Baudelaire, "The awareness of time's empty passage and the *taedium vitae* are the two weights that keep the wheels of melancholy going."[134] Benjamin's view is in accord with the criticism of the concept of progress in Hermann Lotze's *Mikrokosmos* that he cites:

In opposition to the readily accepted doctrine that the progress of humanity is ever onward and upward, more cautious reflection has been forced to make the discovery that the course of history takes the form of spirals—some prefer to say epicycloids. In short, there has never been a dearth of thoughtful but veiled acknowledgments that the impression produced by history on the whole, far from being one of unalloyed exultation, is preponderantly melancholy. Unprejudiced consideration will always lament and wonder to see how many advantages of civilization and special charms of life are lost, never to reappear in their integrity.[135]

The dark luminosity of Benjamin's suspicion about the human condition is captured perfectly by the words *history on the whole, far from being one of unalloyed exultation, is preponderantly melancholy*.

Benjamin, together with Bloch, as Scholem judiciously noted, shared what he deemed to be the innately impossible goal of superimposing mystical experience, understood as an anarchistic turning toward messianism, upon the coordinates of a Marxist system.[136] The hybridity, in no small touch of irony, led the two atheist metaphysicians to reclaim the melancholic temperament of

Jewish utopianism predicated on the obdurate impossibility and noneschatological nature of the future. History does not progress toward any end nor is the anguish of time alleviated by a divine fiat. And just as there is no teleological advance to a utopia at the end, so there is no nostalgic return to a paradise at the beginning. The psychogenic structure of melancholia, consequently, does not entail the retrieval of a lost object à la Freud's taxonomy of the abandoned object-cathexis, that is, the response to a loss that redirects the allocation of psychic energy from the external entity to the internal space of the ego.[137] Particularly pertinent is the following comment of Judith Butler:

> The internal topography by which melancholia is partially explained is itself the effect of that melancholia. Walter Benjamin remarks that melancholia spatializes, and that its effort to reverse or suspend time produces "landscapes" as its signature effect. One might profitably read the Freudian topography that melancholy occasions as precisely such a spatialized landscape of the mind.[138]

Melancholia, I would counter, is the absence of such an absence and the consequent discovery that there is nothing to discover and hence nothing to recover. Lacan seems to be alluding to this dimension of melancholia when he observed,

> The melancholiac never tells you that he looks bad, that his face is at its worst, or that it is contorted; instead he tells you that he is the lowest of the low, that he brings on one catastrophe after another for his entire family, and so on. In his self-accusations he remains entirely within the realm of the symbolic.[139]

Diverging from Freud's connection between mourning and melancholia, Lacan goes on to say that the place where these two meet

> is a question of what I will call, not mourning, nor depression owing to the loss of an object, but remorse of a certain type triggered by a dénouement that involves something along the lines of suicide on the part of the object. Remorse, thus, regarding an object that has entered in some way into the field of desire and that, owing to its own actions or some risk it took in a venture, has disappeared.[140]

Muteness of Nature and the Aphasic Naming the Unnameable

Typically, the melancholiac is encumbered with an inability to speak because there is nothing of which to speak, not even the unspeakable, insofar as every object of regretfulness is not merely lost but eradicated from consciousness in the manner of someone who has been subject to defenestration.[141] The depiction of melancholia as an indescribable language of invisible angst incited by the love of a lost identity of attachment and situated at the juncture of the biological and the symbolic is central to the analysis in Julia Kristeva.[142] Melancholia is thus defined by her as "a noncommunicable grief that at times, and often on a long-term basis, lays claim upon us to the extent of having us lose all interest in words, actions, and even life itself."[143] In a second passage, she elaborated:

> Naming suffering, exalting it, dissecting it into its smallest components—that is doubtless a way to curb mourning. To revel in it at times, but also to go beyond it, moving on to another form, not so scorching, more and more perfunctory... Nevertheless, art seems to point to a few devices that bypass complacency and, without simply turning mourning into mania, secure for the artist and the connoisseur a sublimatory hold over the lost Thing. First, by means of prosody, the language beyond language that inserts into the sign the rhythm and alliterations of semiotic processes. Also by means of the polyvalence of sign and symbol, which unsettles naming and, by building up a plurality of connotations around the sign, affords the subject a chance to imagine the nonmeaning, or the true meaning, of the Thing.[144]

The psychic process of attenuating melancholic devalorization of self through the aesthetic production of allegory is described in more detail as follows:

> Sublimation's dynamics, by summoning up primary processes and idealization, weaves a *hypersign* around and with the depressive void. This is *allegory*, as lavishness of that which *no longer is*, but which regains for myself a higher meaning because I am able to remake nothingness, better than it was and within an unchanging harmony, here and now and forever, for the sake of someone else. Artifice, as sublime meaning for and on behalf of the underlying, implicit nonbeing, replaces the ephemeral. Beauty is consubstantial with it. Like feminine finery concealing stubborn depressions, beauty emerges as the admirable face of loss, transforming it in order to make it live.[145]

Kristeva makes clear that her explication is based, in part, on Benjamin's view expressed in the *Trauerspiel* that allegory

> best achieves melancholy tension. By shifting back and forth from the *disowned meaning*, still present just the same, of the remnants of antiquity for instance ... to the *literal meaning* that the Christian spiritualist context attributes to all things, allegory is a tenseness of meanings between their depression/depreciation and their

signifying exaltation.... It endows the lost signifier with a signifying pleasure, a resurrectional jubilation even to the stone and corpse, by asserting itself as coextensive with the subjective experience of a named melancholia—of melancholy jouissance.[146]

However, the experience of a *nameable melancholia*

opens up the space of a necessarily heterogeneous subjectivity, torn between the two co-necessary and co-present centers of opacity and ideal. The opacity of things, like that of the body untenanted by meaning—a depressed body, bent on suicide—is conveyed to the work's meaning, which asserts itself as at the same time absolute and corrupt, untenable, impossible, to be done all over again. A subtle alchemy of signs then compels recognition—musicalization of signifiers, polyphony of lexemes, dislocation of lexical, syntactic, and narrative units—and this is *immediately* experienced as a psychic transformation of the speaking being between the two limits of nonmeaning and meaning, Satan and God, Fall and Resurrection.[147]

Expressing a similar viewpoint in her analysis of Freud, Butler wrote,

What cannot be declared by the melancholic is nevertheless what governs melancholic speech—an unspeakability that organizes the field of the speakable.... What the melancholic does declare, namely, his own worthlessness, identifies the loss at the sight of the ego and, hence, continues to fail to identify the loss. Self-beratement takes the place of abandonment, and becomes the token of its refusal.[148]

This inability to speak, welling from the depth of detachment and loneliness, bears affinity to mystical anarchists who have worn the melancholic reprimand of self as a badge of honor; on the path of discontentment and condemnation of the world, abstention is the currency of indulgence.

Mention should be made of Benjamin's "On Language as Such and on the Language of Man," written in 1916 but not published in his lifetime. According to Benjamin's reading of the Genesis narrative, originally, there was a clear-cut distinction between the blissful life of the human in the "pure spirit of language" and the mute constitution of nature, which becomes somewhat blissful when it is named by Adam.[149] The *Sprachgeist* initially entailed the "immediacy in the communication of the concrete," that is, the name that Adam gave to all beings, but, as a consequence of his transgression in the Garden of Eden—referred to in the overtly Christian inflected term *Sündenfall*—the "immediacy in the communication of abstraction came into being as judgment," the "abyss of the mediateness" symbolized by the Tree of Knowledge, which does not "dispense information on good and evil" but is rather "an emblem of judgment" over the one who would question about good and evil, an irony that "marks the mythic origin of law."[150] After the fall, God cursed the earth, and the appearance of nature was "deeply changed" from an aboriginal speechlessness (*Sprachlosigkeit*) to a muteness (*Stummheit*) that bespeaks a melancholic mourning far more profound than the need to be named that arises from the incapacity to name:

> Now begins its other muteness, which is what we mean by the "deep sadness of nature" [*der tiefen Traurigkeit der Natur*]. It is a metaphysical truth that all nature would begin to lament if it were endowed with language (though "to endow with language" is more than "to make able to speak"). This proposition has a double meaning. It means, first, that she would lament language itself [*sie würde über die Sprache selbst klagen*]. Speechlessness: that is the great sorrow of nature [*das große Leid der Natur*] (and for the sake of her redemption the life and language of *man*—not only, as is supposed, of the poet—are in nature). This proposition means, second, that she would lament [*sie würde klagen*]. Lament, however, is the most undifferentiated, impotent expression of language [*der undifferenzierteste, ohnmächtige Ausdruck der Sprache*].... Because she is mute, nature mourns. Yet the inversion of this proposition leads even further into the essence of nature: the sadness of nature makes her mute. In all mourning there is the deepest inclination to speechlessness, which is infinitely more than the inability or disinclination to communicate.[151]

Reflecting on this passage, Derrida noted that, according to Benjamin, "the sadness, mourning, and melancholy (*Traurigkeit*) of nature and of animality are born out of this muteness (*Stummheit, Sprachlosigkeit*), but they are also born out of and by means of the wound without a name: that of having *been given a name*. Finding oneself deprived of language, one loses the power to name, to name oneself, indeed to answer [*répondre*] for one's name."[152]

It is exactly the deprivation of language—the inability to name that commences with being stripped of the name that once had been given—that constitutes the great sorrow of nature, the deeper sadness expressed disconcertingly by Benjamin as nature's lamentation, an undifferentiated and impotent expression of language, a speech without speech, the speechlessness of mourning and melancholia.

What is already more interesting is that this putative sadness doesn't just derive from the inability to speak ... and from muteness, from a stupefied or aphasic privation of words. If this putative sadness also gives rise to a lament, if nature laments, expressing a mute but audible lament through sensuous sighing and even the rustling of plants, it is perhaps because the terms have to be inverted.... There must be a reversal, an *Umkehrung* in the essence of nature. According to the hypothesis of this reversing reversal, nature (and animality within it) isn't sad because it is mute (*weil sie stumm ist*). On the contrary, it is nature's sadness of mourning that renders it mute and aphasic, that leaves it without words. (*Die Traurigkeit der Natur macht sie verstummen*).¹⁵³

For Benjamin, the suffering of nature is alleviated redemptively by human language that finds expression in nature that has no language but the no more of language that is more than language, that is, the naming of the named that cannot name itself. The speechlessness of nature consists of this redemptive gesticulation, the language of lament that laments language by speaking aphasically. Melancholia mimics this desolate longing to utter the unutterable.

One can discern the impact of Benjamin on Scholem's attempt in "On Lament and Lamentation" (1917) to translate a series of Hebrew lamentations into German out of the conviction that the genre of lament conveys the essence of "language on the border, language of the border itself. Everything it says is infinite, but just and only infinite with regard to the symbol. In lament, nothing is expressed and everything is implied."¹⁵⁴ For Scholem, lament is a language that both reveals nothing because the being it reveals has no content and conceals nothing because its entire existence is based on a revolution of silence through which there is a restoration (*Zurückführung*) of the symbolic to the revelation that induces mourning's self-overturning (*Sichselbst-überschlagen*) and the consequent reversal (*Umkehrung*) that "allows for the course toward language to emerge as *expression* [Ausdruck]."¹⁵⁵ The expression that emerges from this revolution, however, is an expression of the inexpressible, the language of silence, a kataphatic avowal of the apophatic disavowal.

Messianic Deferment and the Temporal Suspension of Temporality

These dimensions of Scholem's youthful dismay became critical to his more mature understanding of the messianic element in Judaism and to his use of the term "gnostic" as a tool of historical and phenomenological inquiry of kabbalistic sources, especially the depiction of the cosmic drama as a crisis within the inner workings of the Godhead according to the Lurianic teaching and its elaboration in the heretical myth of Sabbatian theology.[156] Scholem's celebrated remark that the messianic idea in Judaism "compelled a *life lived in deferment*, in which nothing can be done definitively, nothing can be irrevocably accomplished"[157] is indicative of a pessimistic utopianism that rejects the possibility of a lasting sociopolitical redemption.[158] Scholem remained beleaguered by a sense of disjointedness in the world that was askew with his ethnonationalist politics, a melancholic dislocation that led him to feel like a *stranger in a strange land*,[159] even when entrenched in the soil of what he demonstrably considered to be the Jewish homeland. Parenthetically, I note Rosenzweig's remark about Scholem in a letter to Rudolf Hallo, written on May 12, 1921: "He may be the only one who has actually returned home. But he came home *alone*" (*Er ist vielleicht der einzige schon wirklich Heimgekehrte, den es gibt. Aber er ist* allein *heimgekehrt*).[160] I gather that what Rosenzweig meant is that Scholem's Zionist ambition was devoid of fidelity to the traditional sense of community.

In light of Rosenzweig's comment, it is of interest to consider the perspective on Zionism affirmed by Scholem in "Farewell," an open letter to Dr. Siegfried Bernfeld and against the readers of the journal *Jerubbaal, Eine Zeitschrift der jüdischen Jugend*, published in 1918–1919.[161]

The great demand of Zionism, which is eternally one, to be a holy people, has a presupposition the misunderstanding of which is in a real sense the chimerical basis for that objective mendacity against which witness is to be given here. Community demands solitude: not the possibility of together desiring the same, but only that of common solitude establishes community. Zion, the source of our nationhood, is the common, indeed in an uncanny sense, the identical solitude of all Jews, and the religious assertion of Zionism is nothing other than this: the midst of solitude happens at the same time to be where all gather together, and there can be no other place for such a gathering together.... There is only one place from which Zion can be reached and youth restituted: solitude. And there is only one medium, brought to radiance by labor, that will be the source of renewal: the existence that must be the argument against a youth that has desecrated words.[162]

Scholem's epistle was a targeted critique of what he referred to as the "pseudo-Zionist lie of community" promulgated by the German Zionist youth movement,[163] but his view is related to an idea proffered by a number of thinkers in the early part of the twentieth century, including Landauer and Buber, to the effect that true individuality is expressive of community, that the latter can only proceed from an originary aloneness, that the solitude of the contemplative is what generates the possibility of genuine sociality.[164] Perhaps even more astonishingly is the resonance of Scholem's view with Heidegger's contention that true community can only grow out of Dasein's sense of aloneness.[165]

Curiously, despite their obvious differences regarding the prognosis of the future of German Jewry versus the renewal and rebirth of Jewry in the land of Israel,[166] Scholem and Rosenzweig shared anxieties about the secularization of the holy language expedited by Zionism and the quest to become a nation-state governed by the dictates of geopolitics. For both thinkers, the essence of Hebrew lies in a holiness that cannot be rendered mundane or limited territorially without distortion or destruction.[167] Ironically, a sense of uncanniness (*Unheimlichkeit*) results from the updating and actualization (*Aktualisierung*) of Hebrew in the Jewish homeland as a vernacular of everyday life and the ensuing transition from linguistic sacrality to profanity.[168] Early on, as is attested in the 1926 letter written to celebrate Rosenzweig's fortieth birthday, Scholem predicted that the secularization of Hebrew would ultimately fail because, like an abyss, the language is "pregnant with catastrophe," and the latent power therein, which consists of the divine names comprised within the ineffable name, will one day surface and assume new form.[169] The sanguinity expressed by Scholem in all likelihood was never realized, or at least there is no indication that he thought that the calamitous eruption he foretold ever came to fruition. It seems rather that the particular unease he detected as a young man with respect to the desecration of Hebrew mirrored his larger concern about the inability of the utopian ideal to be realized in space and time.

Scholem's understanding of the messianic as continual deferral has deep roots in Jewish sources, but his particular formulation is in accord with another passage from the "Theological-Political Fragment" where Benjamin wrote that since the Messiah alone can redeem and complete history, nothing

historical can relate itself, from its own ground, to anything messianic [*Darum kann nichts Historisches von sich aus sich auf Messianisches beziehen wollen*]. Therefore, the Kingdom of God is not the telos of the historical dynamic; it cannot be established as a goal [*Ziel*]. From the standpoint of history, it is not the goal but the terminus [*Ende*].[170]

Benjamin distinguishes sharply between the profane and the sacred, the political notion of a secular order and the theocratic idea of the divine kingdom. If we are to think of nature as messianic, it is only "by reason of its eternal and total passing away. To strive for such a passing away—even the passing away of those stages of man that are nature—is the task of world politics, whose method must be called nihilism."[171] Scholem's interpretation of Jewish messianism, especially as it overlaps with Lurianic kabbalah and its aftermath in the Sabbatian and Frankist movements, is faithful to Benjamin's insight that messianic redemption is not the goal of history but its end, and hence the method most appropriate to *Weltpolitik* is the nihilistic passing away of nature. The messianic objective, on this account, is not an enduring ideal to be attained at the cessation of history but rather the relentless disintegration that is indicative of the eternal transience of historical events,[172] a notion that is anchored in the temporal paradox of the present that is always the same in virtue of never being the same.[173]

In the essay "Toward an Understanding of the Messianic Idea in Judaism," Scholem insists that the constant postponement of messianic redemption—what he calls the "anti-existentialist idea"—accounts for both the greatness and the constitutional weakness of Jewish messianism: whenever the tension between the expectation and the delay has been alleviated by an actual messianic movement, when the abyss that separates the internal-symbolic and the external-historical has been crossed, it has been decried or unmasked as pseudo-messianism.[174] In the continuation of the aforementioned essay, written in 1959, fourteen years after the end of the Second World War and eleven years after the establishment of the modern state of Israel, Scholem bluntly acknowledged that the implementation of the Zionist dream may have been born out of horror and destruction, but it jeopardizes the metahistorical and antipolitical nature of traditional Jewish eschatology, thereby compromising its anarchic and antinomian lifeblood. Scholem went so far as to pose the question if Jewish history "will be able to endure this entry into the concrete realm without perishing in the crisis of the Messianic claim."[175] The apocalyptic propensity incarnates the infinite negativity of time, the impossible possibility that makes it incontrovertibly possible—indeed necessary—that the future that is coming will not be the future that has been anticipated.[176] In this space of time wherein nothing is certain but the certainty of uncertainty, belief and disbelief are no longer viably distinguishable—the messianic spectacle must be enacted, to quote Blanchot again, in the "extreme point of waiting where for a long time what is awaited has served only to maintain the waiting.... Waiting, waiting that is the refusal to wait for anything, a calm expanse unfurled by steps.... The impossibility of waiting belongs essentially to waiting."[177] Building on this paradox, we might say that the hope of the hopelessness of hope evolves from the fact that the future we are awaiting can never transpire in time, and the homeland we are coveting can never materialize in space.

It is feasible to construe the emphasis on open-endedness optimistically in the spirit of Bloch's ontology of not-yet.[178] The end can be imagined only as the terminus that can never be terminated, and hence belief in the future that never comes because it is continuously coming may seem to be an unending source for the possibility of change, renewal, resurrection. A more recent articulation of this perspective can be detected in Claude Romano's phenomenological account of the feeling of surprise and the power of the revelation of the evential that subverts any computable expectancy with respect to the future:

> The event is, instead, that which *by principle* eludes every intentionality of expectation, that of which an expectation would amount, by itself, to an absurdity.... Consequently, what surprise reveals is the availability according to which the advenant is turned toward the future as the vista conditioning the occurring of *events*. Availability is this exposition to the impossible of ourselves, to the event in its pure meaning. If it indeed implies an "expectation," this expectation bears quite singular features: it is directed toward no fact to come, it is turned toward nothing, except the nothing of the future itself, and it is only to this extent that it can be related to the event in its bursting forth from nothing, that it can be opened to the eventuality of the arrival of that which happens only against all expectations, in its irreducible novelty—of that which, with regard to every foreseen possibility, is the im-possible, as well.[179]

The apocalyptic secret comprises this element of surprise insofar as it orients one to the decisive interlude in time, the impossible possibility of the future foreseeable in its unforseeability, the limitless limit, the limit that is the limit by exceeding any limit, the end close at hand impersistently persisting in the distance.

Unpacking the words "dark patience of the end" (*dunkle Geduld des Endes*) at the conclusion of Georg Trakl's poem "Jahr" ("Year"),[180] Heidegger noted, "Patience bears hidden things toward their truth. Its forbearance bears everything toward its descent down into the blue of the ghostly night."[181] Inadvertently, we are handed a key to unlock the door of the concomitant buoyancy and tentativeness of messianic faith: the golden ray of the impending light seems always to be submerged unvaryingly in the darkness of the ghostly night. Inasmuch as the end qua end can never be ascertained, to foresee the dawning of the end demands the fortitude to abide dutifully in the state of detachment (*Abgeschiedenheit*),[182] to dwell patiently "in the blissfilled blueness of night" (*der beseelten Bläue der Nacht*),[183] to subsist in the resounding clarity of the ghostliness of dusk whence the holy shines through veiling itself and bestowing in its withholding withdrawal.[184] The notion of the unending end—the end that can have no ending to being the end—facilitates the inculcation of the wisdom that liberation consists of being liberated from the need to be liberated; that is, if the ending can never end, and still remain as the end, then it can never actualize its potential to come as the end. Ingrained in the texture of Jewish apocalypticism is the double structure of secrecy: the mystery of the past that conceals the concealment of the future revealed in the present as not being present. What is yet to be, accordingly, reverts to what has already been, but what has already been issues from what is yet to be. To remember, on this score, is to retrieve the past that awaits its futural unfolding.

The melancholic jouissance[185] of the apocalyptic passion stems from the linear circularity implied in this sense of *Nachträglichkeit*.[186] As Scholem perceptively opined in the concluding stanza of the poem "Paraphrase, aus der Prosa des 'Tagebuchs'" ("Paraphrase of the Prose of 'The Diary'"), inspired by reading Benjamin's "The Metaphysics of Youth" and written on May 12, 1918:

> Die Zukunft war. Vergangenheit wird sein
> Die Gegenwart wird uns vor Gott entzwein
> In der Entfremdung werden wir befreit.

> The future was. The past shall be
> The present will disunite us before God
> In this estrangement we shall be free.[187]

We can perceive here an intricate nexus between the reversibility of time and the quest for liberation: the future was, the past shall be, and the freedom we experience is the alienation of the present that segregates us from God. Counterintuitively, it is not union but disunion that constitutes our emancipation, which is keyed to the present, the moment of decision[188] that cuts the timeline.[189] As Benjamin would later express the matter, "It is the present that polarizes the event into fore- and after-history."[190]

The messianic underpinnings of the diremptive temporality alluded to in Scholem's words can be understood better if we recall his diary entry from June 17, 1918:

> As a religious category, Time becomes the eternal present.... The notion of God correlates to the idea of the messianic realm. God is 'ehje asher 'ehje—"I will be who I will be."... In Hebrew 'ehje means both the present ("I am") and the future. For God, Time is always future. Hebrew has no other means to express the concept of the eternal present than by making the future permanent. Cohen writes, "In the future when the meaning of the present is given, the difference between present and future will also be reduced. Existence will not be fixed in the present but will float above it. Present and future will be bound together in God's being."[191] ... God's true name is thus the Self of Time [*Gottes wahrer Name ist also das Ich der Zeit*].... The contemporary moment expresses this central point better than the future because the true unreality [*Unwirklichkeit*] of the present—because the present only has existence [*Sein*] as a *source* [Ursprung] ... whose nothingness [*Nichts*] gives birth to the eternal Time as the empirical future—makes it suitable to express what we intend to say here. This notion of Time corresponds to the messianic realm.... The messianic realm is the present of history [*die Gegenwart der Geschichte*]. The prophets could speak about the idea only hypothetically in the image of the future [*im Bilde der Zukunft*].... The kingdom of God is the *present*, for the present moment is the beginning and the end. It has no metaphysical future. The God who "will be" demands from Time that it "will be" [*Der Gott, der "sein wird", fordert die Zeit, die "sein wird"*]. But just as God *is*, so also *is* Time.... God has no Existence; he has only Being [*Gott hat kein Dasein, nur Sein*].[192] Being represents itself. Why does Rambam deny that God has life? Because by saying he's alive contradicts the thought of the eternal present.... *Time is transformed through fusion* [In der Verbindung verwandeln sich die Zeiten]: the past is in the future and the future is in the past [*Vergangenheit in Zukunft und Zukunft in Vergangenheit*]. How does this happen? Through the vehicle of the present [*Im Medium der Gegenwart*]. The Time of the *waw ha-hippukh* is the messianic Time.[193]

Messianic hope hinges on the dialectical intertwining and transposability of the restorative and utopian poles, the past and the future that meet in the present. The convergence of the two temporal modes is signified in the name revealed by God to Moses at the burning bush, *ehyeh asher ehyeh*, "I will be what I will be," a future that is actualized in the unreality of the present, the nothingness that gives birth to the eternal future of the end that is recollected and the eternal past of the beginning that is anticipated. Hebrew, we are told, has the rhetorical peculiarity of not being able to express the concept of the eternal present except by making the future permanent. This is the nature of biblical prophecy as well: seemingly predicting the future, the prophet is actually speaking about the eternal present that is the time of the kingdom of God.[194] Scholem illustrates the point by referring to the *waw ha-hippukh*, that is, the consecutive or conversive *waw*, the prefix that converts the perfect tense of the predicate into the imperfect tense, as in the case of *we-hayah*, which can mean "and it was" in the past or "and it shall be" in the future.[195] If the *waw* of reversal is placed before a verb in the past, the word gets a futuristic meaning, but if it is placed before a verb in the future, the meaning changes into the past. From the comparatively simple grammatical rule, Scholem deduces an intricate theoretical assumption about the nature of messianic time as the crevice of the present wherein there is a reciprocal transmutation of past into future and future into past.

Cast even more broadly, we can speak of Jewish messianism—not definitively or unequivocally but with respect to one conspicuous trajectory—as a nonteleological teleology, an agency that is comparable to the quietude of acting without a specific purpose to act, exemplified in the Taoist idea of *wuwei*,[196] or in the Heideggerian *Gelassenheit* as the will that wills with a willfulness outside the distinction between activity and passivity,[197] the will of nonwilling that is not merely the renunciation of the will but the nonwilling of the will that does not pertain at all to the will.[198] The spontaneity of calculating the incalculable—the elusiveness of conceptualizing truth and the falling silent of every effort to verbalize it in speech or in writing, the too much that is always too little, the surplus of meaning that resounds as inadequate and insufficient—is a facet of the melancholia that is the wellspring of human creativity.[199] The very same sensation, however, is prone to yield a desperation in the realization that the future one is expecting is ceaselessly arriving and therefore can never have arrived. To believe in a future that can never be realized is phenomenologically on a par with the lack of belief in a future wherein there is a possibility of change, a tendency that is typical of melancholia in which hope in a future is consistently thwarted by the trepidation that things will not improve. The point was articulated poignantly by Martin Wyllie:

Temporality is produced by the activity of the body-subject in the world. One would not be passing something (past) if one were not going somewhere (future). Nor would the body-subject be doing anything or going anywhere (and thereby sensing the passage of time) unless one could track one's experience. It is the changing experience that produces our sense of lived-time in terms of either noticing the passage of lived-time or of being oblivious to the passage of lived-time. This is important when considering melancholia because every situation normally (non-pathologically) contains the possibility of change. The possibility of change is denied the melancholic, as there is no possibility of change without a future in which to make that change. The future gets blocked in melancholia by the conviction that things will not get any better. This conviction dominates the melancholic's outlook rendering it deterministic. Chance and contingency no longer play a role in the melancholic's life. Without activity, temporality stops because it is that activity which produces lived-time.[200]

Expressed somewhat more prosaically and pointedly by Bob Dylan: "Night after night . . . You look for salvation, you find none / Just another broken heart."[201] In the nocturnality of exile, one rummages for redemption but comes up emptyhanded except for enduring more heartbreak. However, in this brokenness, we remain unbroken; in the inability to find deliverance, we are delivered.

We find a similar capitulation to the futility of hoping for redemption that adamantly refuses to come in the second stanza of the searing elegy of Leonard Cohen:

> Magnified and sanctified
> Be Thy Holy Name
> Vilified and crucified
> In the human frame
> A million candles burning
> For the help that never came
> You want it darker
> We kill the flame[202]

On display here is the syncretistic transconfessionalism of Cohen—evident in his novels, poems, and lyrics—combining the opening line of *qaddish*, the mourner's prayer for the deceased, wherein the name of God is magnified and sanctified, and the incarnational dogma of Christianity, the vilification and crucifixion of the divine son who has lowered himself and assumed the form of the corruptible body. Even more revealing is the intent of the latter invocation, which is made clear in the image of a million candles burning for the help that never came. The palpable sadness and resignation is amplified by the likelihood that performatively Cohen was saying *qaddish* for himself in the face of his imminent demise. From the degradation of the holy name in the human frame, Cohen constructed a *lullaby for suffering* that extols the inescapable and irredeemable agony of our melancholic condition in emulation of the kenotic travail of Christ, the stranger to death who nevertheless descended into a world of death to rescue humanity from the abyss of death.[203] Turning the Christian hopefulness on its head, Cohen bewailed that the help never came because the savior could not be saved from the infliction he was destined to withstand for the sake of saving others. Each person must similarly bear the cross in facing the transitoriness of being. A million candles could not suffice to depose the desire of God that it be darker. Repeating this line in the penultimate stanza of the song, Cohen evocatively changed one word: "A million candles burning / For the love that never came."[204] The image is devouring in its desolation. Not even a million candles could suffice to conjure the love necessary to annul the demand to make it darker. To this plea, the poet can only utter the scriptural refrain "*Hineni Hineni / I'm ready, my Lord.*"[205] There is nothing more to see, nothing more to say. The obstinance of the quietistic feebleness issues from and reinforces the melancholic spirit of dejection.

Melancholia, as Butler noted, is related to what cannot be directly spoken or what is occluded from sight, absent from the visual field, "an absorption by something that cannot be accommodated by vision, that resists being brought into the open, neither seen nor declared."[206] Appropriating this insight, I would say that the messianic impulse acquires its vitality from the melancholic spectrality of the nonspectral—the savior is a ghost that arrives by not arriving, that appears by not appearing. Drawing out the implications of this coming of a beyond coming, Werner Hamacher writes:

If the future is to be thought in its pure movement, if it is to be thought as itself, and thus as mere coming without the arrival (*Ankunft*) of any sort of present, and thus thought without any determination through this present, then it must be thought as come-able—as the mere possibility of coming or as the possibility that is itself nothing other than coming, the coming of the coming without term or determination. If, however, the coming itself is merely coming, then it is in no sense already there; it is not an actual, in some way empirical or sensory coming, nor does it accord with a transcendental schema that would constitute its coming-to-be. It rather voids the sense of its every being present and dissolves the structure that grants the actuality of its being coming; indeed, it can never—so long as it, as coming, is referred to as coming—and at no time (namely, in no coming), *be* a coming. It is not we who wait; the coming itself waits for the coming. It is the already-there of the still-never-having-been-there and of the never-ever-being-there.[207]

What hope we can muster springs from this phantasmic deficiency, the inconsummate suspension of consummation, the resolute incursion that propagates the abundance of time, the futurity of the past recollected in the pastness of the future as the pastness of the future anticipated in the futurity of the past, a temporal displacement from every emplacement, the homecoming of exile, the voyage that returns indefatigably to the place whence one feels out of place. The melancholy of Jewish messianism procures this certitude of endless doubt, the questioning of the questioning that prompts no response but another question seeking a response.

Notes

Introduction

1. See Julia Grillmayr and Christine Hentschel, "World Without Humans, Humans Without World: Apocalyptic Passions in the Anthropocene," in *Worlds Ending, Ending Worlds: Understanding Apocalyptic Transformation*, edited by Jenny Stümer, Michael Dunn, and David Eisler (Berlin: Walter de Gruyter, 2024), pp. 209–225.

2. See the comment of Wittgenstein cited in ch. 3 n. 76.

3. Gillian Rose, *Love's Work: A Reckoning with Life*, introduction by Michael Wood (New York: New York Review of Books, 2011), p. 105. See ch. 2 at n. 126, and compare Einat Avrahami, "'Keep Your Mind in Hell and Despair Not': Illness as Life Affair in Gillian Rose's *Love's Work*," *Narrative* 9 (2001): 305–321.

4. Julia Kristeva, *Dostoyevsky in the Face of Death or Language Haunted by Sex*, translated by Armine Kotin Mortimer (New York: Columbia University Press, 2024), pp. 189–190. The maxim of Staretz Silouan, rendered here as "Keep your wits in hell and do not despair," is cited without attribution. Kristeva mentions parenthetically Olivier Clément, evidently alluding to the references to *metanoia* in Olivier Clément, *The Roots of Christian Mysticism: Text and Commentary*, translated by Theodore Berkeley and Jeremy Hummerstone (Hyde Park, NY: New City Press, 1995), pp. 16, 126–127, 155, 339, 354. For discussion of the role of *metanoia* in Clément's religious journey and philosophy of personal transcendence, see Stefanie Hugh-Donovan, "Olivier Clément: French Thinker and Theologian of the Eastern Orthodox Church in Dialogue with Western Catholic Thought on Ecclesiology, Theology and the Identity of Europe," PhD dissertation, Heythrop College, University of London, 2015, pp. 34, 38, 114, 203, 205, 211, 232, 234. Finally, it is noteworthy that Clément's spiritual mentor was Father Sophrony, a monk who eventually

settled in the Monastery of Saint Panteleimon in Mount Athos where he became a disciple of Staretz Silouan.

5. See Joel Alden Schlosser, "'Hope, Danger's Comforter': Thucydides, Hope, Politics," *Journal of Politics* 75 (2013): 169–182; Natalia Tsoumpra, "The Politics of Hopelessness: Thucydides and Aristophanes' *Knights*," in *Hope in Ancient Literature, History, and Art*, edited by George Kazantzidis and Dimos Spatharas (Berlin: Walter de Gruyter, 2018), pp. 111–129.

6. See Arthur Schopenhauer, *Parerga and Paralipomena: Short Philosophical Essays*, vol. 2, translated and edited by Adrian del Caro and Christopher Janaway, with an introduction by Christopher Janaway (Cambridge: Cambridge University Press, 2015), p. 262:

> If suffering is not the closest and most immediate goal of our life, then our existence is the most inexpedient thing in the world. For it is absurd to assume that endless pain, which springs from the distress that is essential to life and of which the world is everywhere full, should be pointless and purely accidental. Our sensitivity for pain is almost infinite, while that for pleasure has narrow limits. Each individual misfortune appears to be an exception, to be sure, but misfortune is the rule.

For discussion of pessimism in the *Zeitgeist* of German thought in the eighteenth and nineteenth centuries, see Andrew Cooper, *The Tragedy of Philosophy: Kant's Critique of Judgment and the Project of Aesthetics* (Albany: State University of New York Press, 2016); Frederick C. Beiser, *Weltschmerz: Pessimism in German Philosophy, 1860–1900* (Oxford: Oxford University Press, 2016), pp. 1–12; idem, "Schiller and Pessimism," in *Aesthetic Reason and Imaginative Freedom: Friedrich Schiller and Philosophy*, edited by María del Rosario Acosta López and Jeffrey L. Powell (Albany: State University of New York Press, 2018), pp. 83–97. Both Cooper, *Tragedy* (pp. 136–140, 145–148, 151, 154–155), and Beiser, *Weltschmerz* (pp. 13–66), discuss the legacy of Schopenhauer as it pertains to the adoption of a pessimistic worldview and the castigating of any possibility of alleviating misery as nothing but illusion. See also Jordi Fernández, "Schopenhauer's Pessimism," *Philosophy and Phenomenological Research* 73 (2006): 646–694; Dennis Vanden Auweele, *The Kantian Foundation of Schopenhauer's Pessimism* (London: Routledge, 2017).

7. Schopenhauer, *Parerga*, p. 279.

8. Susan Taubes, *Die Korrespondenz mit Jacob Taubes 1952*, edited by Christina Pareigis (Munich: Fink, 2014), §191, p. 123. The full passage is cited in ch. 1 at n. 38. Compare Susan's comments on suicide cited in ch. 1 at nn. 15, 88, and 201.

9. This is the expression coined by Steven S. Schwarzschild, *The Tragedy of Optimism: Writings on Hermann Cohen*, edited by George Y. Kohler (Albany: State University of New York Press, 2018), pp. 102–103, to describe Cohen's acceptance of the neo-Kantian ethical ideal of regulative progress in spite of acknowledging

the irrationality of history and rejecting Hegelian utopianism. Schwarzschild also designated this tragic optimism—or what he calls, following Antonio Gramsci, the Italian Marxist philosopher, a pessimism of intellect and an optimism of will—an act of heroism.

10. See Mara van der Lugt, *Dark Matters: Pessimism and the Problem of Suffering* (Princeton: Princeton University Press, 2021), pp. 152, 172–178.

11. Susan Taubes, *Die Korrespondenz mit Jacob Taubes 1950–1951*, edited by Christina Pareigis (Munich: Fink, 2011), §24, p. 71.

12. Susan Taubes, *Lament for Julia*, introduction by Francesca Wade (New York: New York Review of Books, 2023), p. 13. See Elliot R. Wolfson, *The Philosophical Pathos of Susan Taubes: Between Nihilism and Hope* (Stanford: Stanford University Press, 2023), pp. 201–202, and compare the additional comments of Susan and the passage of Nietzsche cited on p. 387 n. 84. See the language of Susan regarding her joyous and gloomy moods in a letter to her father cited in ch. 1 n. 184.

13. Friedrich Nietzsche, *Menschliches, Allzumenschliches I–II*, edited by Giorgio Colli and Mazzini Montinari (Munich: Walter de Gruyter, 1999), p. 638; idem, *Human, All Too Human: A Book for Free Spirits*, translated by R. J. Hollingdale, with an introduction by Richard Schacht (Cambridge: Cambridge University Press, 1996), p. 358. It is of interest to recall the title of the work by Jacqueline Rose, *Women in Dark Times* (London: Bloomsbury, 2014), a feminist study that explores the lives of Rosa Luxemburg, Charlotte Salomon, Marilyn Monroe, Shafilea Ahmed, Heshu Yones, Fadime Sahindal, Esther Shalev-Gerz, Yael Bartana, and Thérèse Oulton.

14. This is attested scripturally in Genesis 46:2, Job 33:15, Daniel 2:19, 7:2, and Acts 16:9, 18:9. For the use of this motif in a contemporary work, compare Bert O. States, *Seeing in the Dark: Reflections on Dreams and Dreaming* (New Haven: Yale University Press, 1997).

15. Jacques Derrida, *Acts of Religion*, edited and with an introduction by Gil Anidjar (New York: Routledge, 2002), p. 55 (emphasis in original).

16. Ibid., p. 100.

17. Although Susan Taubes, Gillian Rose, and Edith Wyschogrod are not discussed in Daniel M. Herskowitz, *Heidegger and His Jewish Reception* (Cambridge: Cambridge University Press, 2021), my argument resonates with his hypothesis that the confrontation with Heidegger on the part of Jewish thinkers in the twentieth century was a reaction to two major crises: the breakdown of faith in progress and reason that emerged from the First World War and the catastrophe of the Second World War and the Holocaust. See ibid., p. 291: "From this perspective, the encounter with Heidegger is placed in the context of two major intersections of twentieth-century European and Jewish history—and appropriately so, for he is personally and philosophically tied to both." My analyses differ from those of Herskowitz, but I concur with this assumption.

18. John Milton, *Complete Poems and Major Prose*, edited and with notes and introduction by Merritt Y. Hughes (Indianapolis: Hackett, 2003), p. 213.

19. Jacques Derrida, *Writing and Difference*, translated and with an introduction and additional notes by Alan Bass (Chicago: University of Chicago Press, 1978), p. 292. To be precise, Derrida contrasted two interpretations of interpretation: an ethics of nostalgia for origins associated with Lévi-Stauss and an affirmation of the play of the world associated with Nietzsche.

20. See the discussion of Foucault and Derrida in the section "The Limits of Unmasking" in Maurizio Ferraris, "The Aging of the 'School of Suspicion,'" in *Weak Thought*, edited by Gianni Vattimo and Pier Aldo Rovatti, translated and with an introduction by Peter Carravetta (Albany: State University of New York Press, 2012), pp. 140–143.

21. Michel Foucault, "Nietzsche, Freud, Marx," in *Essential Works of Foucault, 1954–1984*, vol. 2: *Aesthetics, Method, and Epistemology*, edited by James D. Faubion (New York: New Press, 1998), p. 273.

22. Ibid.

23. Ibid., pp. 274–275.

24. Friedrich Nietzsche, *Morgenröte, Idyllen aus Messina, Die fröhliche Wissenschaft*, edited by Giorgio Colli and Mazzino Montinari (Munich: Walter de Gruyter, 1999), p. 518; idem, *The Joyful Science, Idylls from Messina, Unpublished Fragments from the Period of* The Joyful Science *(Spring 1881–Summer 1882)*, translated and with an afterword by Adrian Del Caro (Stanford: Stanford University Press, 2023), p. 160 (emphasis in original).

25. I have benefited from the analysis in Sanem Yazicioğlu, "Identity or Identities? The In-Between of 'No Longer and Not Yet,'" in *Phenomenological Perspectives on Plurality*, edited by Gert-Jan van der Heiden (Leiden: Brill, 2015), pp. 75–87.

26. See the discussion of this theme in eighteenth- and nineteenth-century German philosophy in Wolf Lepenies, *Melancholy and Society*, translated by Jeremy Gaines and Doris Jones, with a foreword by Judith N. Shklar (Cambridge, MA: Harvard University Press, 1992), pp. 75–86. Particularly instructive is the wide-ranging analysis of Alina N. Feld, *Melancholy and the Otherness of God: A Study of the Hermeneutics of Depression* (Lanham: Lexington Books, 2011), and the more recent analysis of and challenge to the pessimistic proclivity of philosophers in Brian Treanor, *Melancholic Joy: On Life Worth Living* (London: Bloomsbury Academic, 2021). See additional sources cited in ch. 4 n. 38.

27. Elizabeth S. Goodstein, *Experience Without Qualities: Boredom and Modernity* (Stanford: Stanford University Press, 2005), p. 4.

28. Walter Benjamin, *Gesammelte Schriften*, 1.2, edited by Rolf Tiedemann and Herman Schweppenhäuser (Frankfurt am Main: Suhrkamp, 1991), p. 663; idem, *Selected Writings*, vol. 4: *1938–1940*, edited by Howard Eiland and Michael W. Jennings, translated by Edmund Jephcott and others (Cambridge, MA: Harvard University Press, 2003), p. 167.

29. Georg Wilhelm Friedrich Hegel, *Hegel: The Letters*, translated by Clark Butler and Christiane Seiler, with a commentary by Clark Butler (Bloomington: Indiana University Press, 1984), p. 561, cited in Francesca Brencio, "'The Nocturnal Point of the Contraction': Hegel and Melancholia," in *Melancholia: The Disease of the Soul*, edited by Dariusz Skórczewski and Andrzej Wierciński (Lublin: Wydawnictwo KUL, 2014), p. 152.

30. The image was suggested to me by Benjamin's use of the expression *dem Zauber der Schwelle* in *Das Passagen-Werken*. See Walter Benjamin, *Gesammelte Schriften*, 5.1, edited by Rolf Tiedemann (Frankfurt am Main: Suhrkamp, 1991), p. 141. For the English rendering "the magic of the threshold," see Walter Benjamin, *The Arcades Project*, translated by Howard Eiland and Kevin McLaughlin (Cambridge, MA: Harvard University Press, 1999), p. 88.

31. Goodstein, *Experience*, p. 4.

32. *Problemata* 30.1, 954^{a}1, 12–35, in Aristotle, *The Complete Works of Aristotle: The Revised Oxford Translation*, edited by Jonathan Barnes (Princeton: Princeton University Press, 1984), pp. 1500–1501. See William W. Fortenbaugh, "On *Problemata* 3: Wine-Drinking and Drunkenness," in *The Aristotelian Problemata Physica: Philosophical and Scientific Investigations*, edited by Robert Mayhew (Leiden: Brill, 2015), p. 120; Eckart Schütrumpf, "Black Bile as the Cause of Human Accomplishments and Behaviors in *Pr*. 30.1: Is the Concept Aristotelian?" op. cit., pp. 362–363.

33. Schütrumpf, "Black Bile," pp. 367–368.

34. *Problemata* 30.1, 954^{a}1, 15–20, in *Complete Works of Aristotle*, p. 1500.

35. Julia Kristeva, *Black Sun: Depression and Melancholia*, translated by Leon S. Roudiez (New York: Columbia University Press, 1992).

36. Ibid., p. 7.

37. Compare the view attributed to Baudelaire that melancholy is the source of all sincere poetry cited by Benjamin, *Gesammelte Schriften*, 5.1, p. 315; idem, *Arcades Project*, p. 243. Also relevant is the comment of Baudelaire in a letter to Jules Janin that melancholy is always inseparable from the feeling for beauty, cited by Benjamin, *Gesammelte Schriften*, 5.1, p. 365; idem, *Arcades Project*, p. 286. On Baudelaire and melancholy, see Benjamin, *Gesammelte Schriften*, 5.1, pp. 414, 421, 437, 1231, 1232; idem, *Arcades Project*, pp. 328, 334, 346, 894, 895, 896.

38. *Problemata* 30.1, 953^{a}1, 10–30, in *Complete Works of Aristotle*, pp. 1498–1499. See Elliot R. Wolfson, *The Duplicity of Philosophy's Shadow: Heidegger, Nazism, and the Jewish Other* (New York: Columbia University Press, 2018), pp. 128, 250 n. 104. See also Feld, *Melancholy*, pp. 7–11; Schütrumpf, "Black Bile," pp. 364–367; and the more extensive exploration in László F. Földényi, *Melancholy = Melankólia*, translated by Tim Wilkinson, with a foreword by Alberto Manguel (New Haven: Yale University Press, 2016), pp. 7–48. Kristeva, *Black Sun*, p. 7, surmised that the treatment of melancholia, counterbalanced by genius, in the pseudo-Aristotelian *Problemata* "is coextensive with man's anxiety in Being," and it can thus "be seen as the forerunner of Heidegger's anguish as the *Stimmung* of thought. Schelling found

in it, in similar fashion, the 'essence of human freedom,' an indication of 'man's affinity with nature.'"

39. Marsilio Ficino, *Three Books on Life: A Critical Edition and Translation*, introduction and notes by Carol V. Kaske and John R. Clark (Tempe: Renaissance Society of America, 1998), pp. 112–123.

40. Sigmund Freud, *The Standard Edition of the Complete Psychological Works of Sigmund Freud*, vol. 14: *On the History of the Psycho-Analytic Movement, Papers on Meta-Psychology and Other Works (1914–1916)*, translated under the general editorship of James Strachey in collaboration with Anna Freud, assisted by Alix Strachey and Alan Tyson (London: Hogarth Press, 1957), p. 246.

41. See Susan Anima Taubes, "The Gnostic Foundations of Heidegger's Nihilism," *Journal of Religion* 34 (1954): 169–170 (emphasis in original). For previous analysis, see Wolfson, *Philosophical Pathos*, p. 166. As I noted there, the image of the dark light is also reminiscent of Hölderlin's memorable catchword *das dunkle Licht*, which conveys that illumination does not dispel darkness but rather is its innermost inflection, appearing in the nonappearing of appearance, manifesting in the refusal to manifest but as the nonmanifestation. See Martin Heidegger, *Hölderlins Hymne "Andenken"* [GA 52] (Frankfurt am Main: Vittorio Klostermann, 1992), p. 149; idem, *Hölderlin's Hymn "Remembrance,"* translated by William McNeill and Julia Ireland (Bloomington: Indiana University Press, 2018), p. 127; Wolfson, *Philosophical Pathos*, pp. 258 and 427 n. 181, where I mentioned the monograph of Herbert Leerink, *Das dunkle Licht: Gnosis, Irrsinn und Genialität im Werk Friedrich Hölderlins* (Varik: De Betuwsche Morgen, 2019).

42. Carl G. Jung, *Psychological Types*, a revision by R. F. C. Hull of the translation by H. G. Baynes [CW 6] (Princeton: Princeton University Press, 1971), pp. 279–280. Perhaps the subversion of the distinction between face and mask underlies Wittgenstein's aside in *Moments of Thought: Ludwig Wittgenstein's Diary, 1930–1932 and 1936–1937*, translated by Alfred Nordmann, edited by James C. Klagge and Alfred Nordman, with an introduction by Ray Monk (Lanham: Rowman & Littlefield, 2023), p. 47: "And on the whole the theater of masks, as I mean it, is of a spiritualist character. Therefore it is perhaps (also) that only Jews will tend toward this theater." For the continuation of this passage, see ch. 4 n. 10. Also of relevance is the remark about self-knowledge in Wittgenstein, *Moments*, p. 50: "When a certain number of veils is left upon me, I still see clearly, namely the veils. But if they are removed so that my gaze could penetrate closer to my self [*mein ich*], my image begins to blur for me."

43. My formulation here is indebted to Slavoj Žižek, *The Fragile Absolute or, Why Is the Christian Legacy Worth Fighting For?* (London: Verso, 2000), p. 86:

> Perhaps this is how one can understand Heidegger's notion that metaphysics is unable fully to endorse this interplay of truth and the monstrous concealed

kernel at its very heart: the 'illusion' of metaphysics is that this monstrous foreign body is ultimately accidental, affecting not the truth itself but only our access to it—that is, metaphysics is not ready to admit that our distortion of truth is grounded in an inherent distortion constitutive of the truth itself.

44. Elliot R. Wolfson, *A Dream Interpreted Within a Dream: Oneiropoiesis and the Prism of Imagination* (New York: Zone Books, 2011), p. 64.

45. Carl G. Jung, *The Symbolic Life: Miscellaneous Writings*, translated by R. F. C. Hull [CW 18] (Princeton: Princeton University Press, 1950), p. 32.

46. Friedrich Nietzsche, *Also Sprach Zarathustra I–IV*, edited by Giorgio Colli and Mazzino Montinari (Berlin: Walter de Gruyter, 1999), p. 341; idem, *Thus Spoke Zarathustra: A Book for All and None*, edited by Adrian Del Caro and Robert B. Pippin, translated by Adrian Del Caro (Cambridge: Cambridge University Press, 2006), p. 222 (emphasis in original).

47. Nietzsche, *Also Sprach Zarathustra*, pp. 231, 232; idem, *Thus Spoke Zarathustra*, pp. 146, 147. On the affinities between melancholia and solitude, see Lepenies, *Melancholy*, pp. 62–66.

48. Novalis, *Novalis: Philosophical Writings*, translated by Margaret Mahony Stoljar (Albany: State University of New York Press, 1997), p. 135.

49. Martin Heidegger, *Die Grundbegriffe der Metaphysik: Welt—Endlichkeit—Einsamkeit* [GA 29/30] (Frankfurt am main: Vittorio Klostermann, 1983), p. 7; idem, *The Fundamental Concepts of Metaphysics: World, Finitude, Solitude*, translated by William McNeill and Nicholas Walker (Bloomington: Indiana University Press, 1995), p. 5.

50. Heidegger, *Grundbegriffe*, pp. 7–8; idem, *Fundamental Concepts*, p. 5 (emphasis in original). For an analysis of this passage, see Jacques Derrida, *The Beast & the Sovereign*, vol. 2, edited by Michel Lisse, Marie-Louise Mallet, and Ginette Michaud, translated by Geoffrey Bennington (Chicago: University of Chicago Press, 2011), pp. 29–30, 32–33, 37, 94–98; and my previous discussion in Wolfson, *Duplicity*, pp. 67–68.

51. Goodstein, *Experience*, pp. 299–300; Barbara Cassin, *Nostalgia: When Are We Ever at Home?*, translated by Pascale-Anne Brault (New York: Fordham University Press, 2016), p. 51.

52. Martin Heidegger, *Sein und Zeit* (Tübingen: Max Niemeyer, 1993), §40, pp. 188–189; idem, *Being and Time*, translated by Joan Stambaugh, revised and with a foreword by Dennis J. Schmidt (Albany: State University of New York Press, 2010), pp. 182–183. For an extensive discussion of this theme, see Katherine Withy, *Heidegger on Being Uncanny* (Cambridge, MA: Harvard University Press, 2015), pp. 48–101.

53. Heidegger, *Grundbegriffe*, p. 8; idem, *Fundamental Concepts*, p. 6.

54. Heidegger, *Grundbegriffe*, pp. 9–10; idem, *Fundamental Concepts*, p. 7.

55. Heidegger, *Grundbegriffe*, pp. 18–19; idem, *Fundamental Concepts*, p. 13.

56. Heidegger, *Grundbegriffe*, p. 393; idem, *Fundamental Concepts*, p. 271. Žižek, *Fragile Absolute*, p. 87, detects in this Heideggerian text an influence of Schelling's idea of the infinite melancholy that covers living nature like a veil. See the text cited in ch. 4 at n. 38, and compare the analysis in Joseph Carew, *Ontological Catastrophe: Žižek and the Paradoxical Metaphysics of German Idealism* (Ann Arbor: Open Humanities Press, 2014), pp. 174–175. On Heidegger's sharp contrast of the human and the animal in relation to death, see the passage cited in ch. 3 at n. 63.

57. The line is from the poem "The Castaway" (March 20, 1799) in William Cowper, *The Poetical Works of William Cowper: Complete Edition* (New York: John Wurtele Lovell, 1881), p. 511. It was referenced several times in Virginia Woolf, *To the Lighthouse* (New York: Harcourt, Brace & Company, 1927), pp. 219, 220, 247, 249, 284, 308.

58. Martin Heidegger, *Überlegungen II–VI (Schwarze Hefte 1931–1938)* [GA 94] (Frankfurt am Main: Vittorio Klostermann, 2014), p. 59; idem, *Ponderings II–VI: Black Notebooks 1931–1938*, translated by Richard Rojcewicz (Bloomington: Indiana University Press, 2016), p. 45 (emphasis in original). The passage is previously cited in Elliot R. Wolfson, *Heidegger and Kabbalah: Hidden Gnosis and the Path of Poiēsis* (Bloomington: Indiana University Press, 2019), p. 326 n. 126. Note the comment of Gershom Scholem mentioned there that the renewal of Zionism should be based on the principle that the community will be established by the common solitude of the Jewish people. The text is quoted in ch. 4 at n. 162.

59. Heidegger, *Überlegungen II–VI*, p. 112; idem, *Ponderings II–VI*, p. 82.

60. Heidegger, *Überlegungen II–VI*, p. 304; idem, *Ponderings II–VI*, p. 222.

61. Heidegger, *Überlegungen II–VI*, p. 251; idem, *Ponderings II–VI*, p. 184. See also Heidegger, *Überlegungen II–VI*, p. 71; idem, *Ponderings II–VI*, p. 54, cited in Wolfson, *Heidegger and Kabbalah*, p. 313.

62. Heidegger, *Überlegungen II–VI*, p. 285; idem, *Ponderings II–VI*, p. 209. On the link between *Einsamkeit* and *Zugehörigkeit*, see also Heidegger, *Überlegungen II–VI*, p. 288; idem, *Ponderings II–VI*, p. 211. And consider the portrayal of the intensification of Hölderlin's solitude in the application of his poetry to "cultural politics" (*Kulturpolitik*) noted by Heidegger, *Überlegungen II–VI*, p. 340; idem, *Ponderings II–VI*, p. 247.

63. Taubes, *Die Korrespondenz mit Jacob Taubes 1952*, §187, p. 115.

64. Heidegger, *Sein und Zeit*, §53, p. 263; idem, *Being and Time*, p. 252. Susan's criticism of Heidegger resounds with the comments of Paul-Louis Landsberg, *The Experience of Death: The Moral Problem of Suicide*, translated by Cynthia Rowland (New York: Philosophical Library, 1953), p. 19:

> The possibility of a change in our own being, considered as "being towards Death" (*Sein zum Tode*) which may follow on the experience of the death of a

fellow-creature, is based on the possibility of personal love. No one would claim that the experience of the death of one's neighbor is the same as an experience of one's own death, which one has to meet: but its personal significance is so profound that it is an essential part of oneself, and not of the impersonal "one."

In the accompanying note, Landsberg added, "Heidegger does not seem to grasp the importance of this distinction. His *'Mitsein'* is always a highly formalised concept. His philosophy does not include love, just as it includes neither faith nor hope." On Susan's reference to Landsberg's study and her endorsement of his denunciation of Heidegger, see ch. 1 at n. 84.

65. Heidegger, *Sein und Zeit*, p. 114; idem, *Being and Time*, p. 111. See Wolfson, *Philosophical Pathos*, p. 191, and references to other scholars cited on p. 383 n. 34.

66. Heidegger, *Sein und Zeit*, §26, p. 120; idem, *Being and Time*, p. 117 (emphasis in original).

67. Heidegger, *Sein und Zeit*, §26, p. 121: "Mitsein ist eine Bestimmtheit des je eigenen Daseins. . . . Das eigene Dasein ist nur, sofern es die Wesensstruktur des Mitseins hat, als für Andere begegnend Mitdasein." English translation in idem, *Being and Time*, pp. 117–118 : "Being-with is an attribute of one's own Dasein. . . . Only because it has the essential structure of being-with, is one's own Dasein encounterable by others as Dasein-with." Compare Heidegger, *Sein und Zeit*, §26, p. 118; idem, *Being and Time*, p. 115–116. Rather than understanding the encountering of others as a transition from an isolated subject to others, Heidegger argued that "others" signifies

> those from whom one mostly does *not* distinguish oneself, those among whom one also is. . . . The "with" is of the character of Dasein, the "also" means the sameness of being [*die Gleichheit des Seins*] as circumspect, heedful being-in-the-world. "With" and "also" are to be understood *existentially* [existenzial] not categorially. On the basis of this *with-bound* [mithaften] being-in-the-world, the world is always already the one that I share with others. The world of Dasein is a *with-world* [Mitwelt]. Being-in is *being-with* others [*Das In-sein ist* Mitsein *mit Anderen*]. The innerworldly being-in-itself [*Ansichsein*] of others is *Dasein-with* [Mitdasein] (emphasis in original).

And see *Sein und Zeit*, §26, pp. 124–125; idem, *Being and Time*, p. 121. Although Heidegger rejected the presupposition that Dasein's being towards the other should be identified with its being toward itself, maintaining that the being-with, or the being towards others, is an autonomous and irreducible relationship of being, he did not deny that

> a lively mutual acquaintanceship on the basis of being-with often depends upon how far one's own Dasein has actually understood itself, but this only means that it depends upon how far it has made one's essential being with others transpar-

ent and not disguised it. This is possible only if Dasein as being-in-the-world is always already with others. "Empathy" does not first constitute being-with, but is first possible on its basis, and is motivated by the prevailing deficient modes of being-with in their inevitability.

68. See Wolfson, *Heidegger and Kabbalah*, pp. 80 and 93 n. 169.

69. This term has been discussed by a variety of philosophers from different methodological perspectives. See Jason Turner, "Ontological Pluralism," *Journal of Philosophy* 107 (2010): 5–34; idem, "Logic and Ontological Pluralism," *Journal of Philosophical Logic* 41 (2012): 419–448; Sara Bernstein, "Ontological Pluralism About Non-Being," in *Non-Being: New Essays on the Metaphysics of Non-Existence*, edited by Sara Bernstein and Tyron Goldschmidt (Oxford: Oxford University Press, 2021), pp. 1–16; Byron Simmons, "Ontological Pluralism and the Generic Conception of Being," *Erkenntnis* 87 (2022): 1275–1293. My own use of the expression has benefited from the analysis in Matthew David Segall, *Crossing the Threshold: Etheric Imagination in the Post-Kantian Process Philosophy of Schelling and Whitehead* (Olympia: Integral Imprint, 2023), pp. 145–147.

70. My use of this terminology is beholden to the thought of David G. Leahy. See Wolfson, *Heidegger and Kabbalah*, pp. 94–95 n. 173; idem, "Heeding the Law Beyond the Law: Transgendering Alterity and the Hypernomian Perimeter of the Ethical," *European Journal of Jewish Studies* 14 (2020): 220 n. 11.

71. See Wolfson, *Heidegger and Kabbalah*, pp. 80–82, 93–94 n. 170, 94 n. 173, 140, 222, 225–226. For a different approach that emphasizes Heidegger's "organic monadism which renders thinking about the plural and the different difficult," see Nicholas Davey, "Towards a Community of the Plural: Philosophical Pluralism, Hermeneutics, and Practice," in *Phenomenological Perspectives on Plurality*, p. 94. In my opinion, Davey has imposed a problematic binary on Heidegger by failing to grasp that his sense of singularity encompasses plurality, and hence there is a hermeneutical possibility to achieve a reciprocal understanding between historical communities individuated by different orientations to their past and future.

72. Heidegger, *Überlegungen II–VI*, pp. 449–450; idem, *Ponderings II–VI*, p. 326. On the precarious repercussions of this solitude, see Heidegger, *Überlegungen II–VI*, p. 481: "*Großen Denker* können nicht geliebt werden—die eisige Einsamkeit, die um sie sein muß und in die nur der fragende Kampf mit ihnen einbricht, versagt jeden ausruhenden und behüteten Bezug" (emphasis in original). English translation in idem, *Ponderings II–VI*, p. 349: "*Great thinkers* cannot be loved—the icy solitude which must surround them, and which can be penetrated only by an interrogative battle with them, repudiates any restful and protected relation" (emphasis in original).

73. *Hegel: The Letters*, p. 122. The remark of Hegel was referenced by Hannah Arendt, "Martin Heidegger at Eighty," in *Heidegger and Modern Philosophy: Critical Essays*, edited by Michael Murray (New Haven: Yale University Press, 1978), p.

298. According to Arendt's interpretation, the solitariness of the philosophical life is related to the unsayable and the incommunicable element of thought, an idea that she traced back to Plato. The Heideggerian position is implicit in the distinction that Arendt made between the solitude that is the philosopher's authentic way of life and the more general experience of loneliness. See Hannah Arendt, *The Human Condition*, second edition, introduction by Margaret Canovan (Chicago: University of Chicago Press, 1996), p. 76. Both passages are cited and discussed in Wolfson, *Duplicity*, pp. 114–115.

74. Plato, *Phaedo* 67e, in *The Collected Dialogues of Plato Including the Letters*, edited by Edith Hamilton and Huntington Cairns, with introduction and prefatory notes (Princeton: Princeton University Press, 1961), p. 50.

75. The relevant passage of Hegel is cited in ch. 3 at n. 11, and see discussion in Elliot R. Wolfson, *Suffering Time: Philosophical, Kabbalistic, and Ḥasidic Reflections on Temporality* (Leiden: Brill, 2021), pp. 8–9. It goes without saying that this insight is hardly unique to Western philosophy. Consider, for instance, the poetic reflection of Chandrakīrti in his *Cathuḥśatakaṭīkā*, cited in Tsongkhapa, *The Middle-Length Treatise on the Stages of the Path to Enlightenment*, translated by Philip Quarcoo (Somerville: Wisdom Publications, 2021), p. 84: "Hero of humanity, beginning from that first night / of entering a womb in this world— / one starts to proceed day by day, / without pausing a step, toward the Lord of Death." This precept is applied more broadly by Tenzin Gyatso, the fourteenth Dalai Lama, to the fundamental Buddhist maxim that all conditioned phenomena are impermanent and the further conjecture that impermanence signifies the insubstantial momentariness of the present. See Tenzin Gyatso and Thubten Chodron, *The Foundation of Buddhist Practice* (Somerville: Wisdom Publications, 2018), p. 8:

> All the main Buddhist philosophical tenet schools (except for Vaibhāṣika, which has a slightly different understanding of the process of change and cessation), accept that the moment a thing comes into being, it contains the seed of its own cessation simply by the fact that it is produced by causes and conditions.... From the very first moment of a thing's existence, it has the nature of coming to an end. The very nature of conditioned phenomena is that they do not last from one moment to the next.

Ostensibly, the positivity of coming into being and the negativity of ceasing to be might seem incompatible and contradictory, but "if we reflect on the deeper meaning of impermanence, we see that its very definition—momentary change—applies to both the arising and ceasing of a thing. Nothing, whether it is in the process of arising or the process of ending, lasts into the next moment."

76. Ferraris, "Aging," p. 141.

77. Derrida, *Writing and Difference*, p. 292.

78. Novalis, *Hymns to the Night*, third edition, translated by Dick Higgins (Kingston: McPherson & Company, 1988), p. 29.

Chapter 1

1. Elliot R. Wolfson, *The Philosophical Pathos of Susan Taubes: Between Nihilism and Hope* (Stanford: Stanford University Press, 2023). For a meticulous and well-documented intellectual biography, see Christina Pareigis, *Susan Taubes: Eine intellektuelle Biographie* (Göttingen: Wallstein, 2020), and the more concise account of the early years of the relationship between Susan and Jacob in Jerry Z. Muller, *Professor of Apocalypse: The Many Lives of Jacob Taubes* (Princeton: Princeton University Press, 2022), pp. 134–140.

2. The correspondence was published in two volumes: Susan Taubes, *Die Korrespondenz mit Jacob Taubes 1950–1951*, edited by Christina Pareigis (Munich: Fink, 2011); idem, *Die Korrespondenz mit Jacob Taubes 1952*, edited by Christina Pareigis (Munich: Fink, 2014).

3. Susan Anima Taubes, "The Gnostic Foundations of Heidegger's Nihilism," *Journal of Religion* 34 (1954): 155–172. See my extensive analysis in Elliot R. Wolfson, "Gnosis and the Covert Theology of Antitheology: Heidegger, Apocalypticism, and Gnosticism in Susan and Jacob Taubes," in *Depeche Mode: Jacob Taubes Between Politics, Philosophy, and Religion*, edited by Herbert Kopp-Oberstebrink and Hartmut von Sass (Leiden: Brill, 2022), pp. 151–202, revised version in Wolfson, *Philosophical Pathos*, pp. 128–185. Susan added the name "Anima" during her graduate student years at Radcliffe, and it appears in several of her publications. Pareigis, *Susan Taubes*, p. 274, suggests it may have been inspired by Jung's counterconcept to Persona, whereas Muller, *Professor*, p. 182, writes that it has "vaguely mythic or Gnostic connotations."

4. Taubes, *Die Korrespondenz mit Jacob Taubes 1952*, §193, p. 129. For previous citation and discussion of this passage, see Wolfson, *Philosophical Pathos*, pp. 245–246.

5. For discussion of the periodization of Heidegger's thought and references to other scholars, see Elliot R. Wolfson, *Heidegger and Kabbalah: Hidden Gnosis and the Path of Poiēsis* (Bloomington: Indiana University Press, 2019), p. 55 n. 102. This is not the place to elaborate, but even though Susan Taubes did not write a distinct exposition on the subject of temporality, we can extract from her writings that she affirmed both a nonlinear conception and the reversibility of time. Although she does not mention quantum physics, to the best of my knowledge, her thinking about time is not incompatible with some contemporary scientific views. For a comprehensive overview of this complex subject, see Mike Sandbothe, *The Temporalization of Time: Basic Tendencies in Modern Debate on Time in Philosophy and Science*, translated by Andrew Inkpin (Lanham: Rowman & Littlefield, 2001), pp. 7–62.

6. On the importance of the motif of dance in Susan's thought and her likely indebtedness to Nietzsche, see Wolfson, *Philosophical Pathos*, p. 163, and references cited on pp. 369–370 n. 176.

7. See Wolfson, *Philosophical Pathos*, p. 2 and references cited on p. 282 n. 8.

8. Taubes, *Die Korrespondenz mit Jacob Taubes 1952*, §230, pp. 199–200.

9. Ibid., §233, p. 206 (emphasis in original). See Wolfson, *Philosophical Pathos*, pp. 130–131. Oddly, despite these unmistakable reservations, Susan allowed her study on Heidegger to be published in 1954.

10. Taubes, *Die Korrespondenz mit Jacob Taubes 1952*, §232, p. 204.

11. Muller, *Professor*, p. 136. For the record, I note the difference between my approach and Muller's characterization of "Susan's decidedly non-Jewish, and increasingly anti-Jewish, propensities." See ibid., p. 144, and the fuller discussion of Susan's paganism versus Jacob's heresy on pp. 164–171, especially pp. 169–170, where the conflict between the two with respect to religious affiliation and Jewish practice is duly noted. I concur that there were tensions between Jacob and Susan around the issue of her commitment to halakhah, or as Jacob put it in a letter to Hugo Bergmann from March 25, 1952, her attitude to the very matter of "Jewish existence" (*jüdischen Existenz*) was a source of contention, but I think her struggle with Jewishness was far more complex as I tried to demonstrate in *Philosophical Pathos*, pp. 31–100. I cited the aforementioned remark of Jacob on p. 31 and gave the reference on p. 302 n. 2. In fairness, I should add that Muller seems to have followed Jacob's own characterization of Susan's "antijudaism" (*Antijudaismus*). See Wolfson, *Philosophical Pathos*, pp. 86, 157–158, 301 n. 1, and 330 n. 206.

12. Muller, *Professor*, p. 168. See ibid., p. 160, where Muller surmised that "Jacob's growing disenchantment with Heidegger betrayed the influence of Susan upon his intellectual development."

13. These words are from Susan's announced dissertation project in the application for doctoral studies at Radcliffe College from February 1953, cited from the Schlesinger Library/Radcliffe Institute for Advanced Study, Harvard University, Student Record Susan Taubes, in Pareigis, *Susan Taubes*, p. 274.

14. Muller, *Professor*, p. 165.

15. Taubes, *Die Korrespondenz mit Jacob Taubes 1952*, §172, p. 91. A portion of the passage was previously cited and discussed in Wolfson, *Philosophical Pathos*, p. 142.

16. Taubes, *Die Korrespondenz mit Jacob Taubes 1952*, §162, p. 72.

17. See the text of Susan Taubes, *Briefe an Susan Taubes, diverse Absender hauptsächlich zweite Hälfte 1940er*, Archiv 172, *Zentrum für Literatur- und Kulturforschung Berlin*, cited in Pareigis, *Susan Taubes*, p. 156, and compare Wolfson, *Philosophical Pathos*, p. 190.

18. See Wolfson, *Philosophical Pathos*, pp. 130, 136, 183–184, and references to other scholars cited on pp. 346–347 n. 14. I will not repeat the litany of sources mentioned in my previous publication with the exception of Daniel M. Herskowitz, "Reading Heidegger Against the Grain: Hans Jonas on Existentialism, Gnosticism, and Modern Science," *Modern Intellectual History* 19 (2022): 527–550, esp. 547–548. Herskowitz cites Jonas's evaluation of Susan's essay wherein he expressed skepticism regarding her thesis concerning the gnostic foundation of Heidegger's ontology, even as he noted

that she relied heavily on his own work for her understanding of Gnosticism. The influence of Jonas on the doctoral dissertation of Jacob Taubes and his larger intellectual world is documented by Muller, *Professor*, pp. 67–70, 76. For Jacob's efforts to encourage Jonas to publish *The Gnostic Religion* in 1958, see ibid., p. 217.

19. Martin Heidegger, *Sein und Zeit* (Tübingen: Max Niemeyer, 1993), §58, pp. 284–285; idem, *Being and Time*, translated by Joan Stambaugh, revised and with a foreword by Dennis J. Schmidt (Albany: State University of New York Press, 2010), p. 273 (emphasis in original).

20. Heidegger, *Sein und Zeit*, §58, p. 284; idem, *Being and Time*, p. 273 (emphasis in original).

21. Heidegger, *Sein und Zeit*, §58, p. 285; idem, *Being and Time*, p. 273 (emphasis in original).

22. Martin Heidegger, *Metaphysik und Nihilismus: 1. Die Überwindung der Metaphysik 2. Das Wesen der Nihilismus* [GA 67] (Frankfurt am Main: Vittorio Klostermann, 1999), p. 56; idem, *Metaphysics and Nihilism: 1. The Overcoming of Metaphysics 2. The Essence of Nihilism*, edited by Hans-Joachim Friedrich, translated by Arun Iyer (Cambridge: Polity Press, 2022), p. 49. Compare the analysis of Heidegger's account of nihilism in Gianni Vattimo, *The End of Modernity: Nihilism and Hermeneutics in Postmodern Culture*, translated and with an introduction by Jon R. Snyder (Baltimore: Johns Hopkins University Press, 1991), pp. 19–30.

23. Martin Heidegger, *Zum Wesen der Sprache und Zur Frage nach der Kunst* [GA 74] (Frankfurt am Main: Vittorio Klostermann, 2010), p. 63; idem, *On the Essence of Language and the Question of Art*, edited by Thomas Regehly, translated by Adam Knowles (Cambridge: Polity Press, 2022), p. 54 (emphasis in original).

24. Taubes, "Gnostic Foundations," p. 163. See Wolfson, *Philosophical Pathos*, p. 132.

25. For a fuller analysis, see Wolfson, *Philosophical Pathos*, pp. 186–225.

26. Taubes, *Die Korrespondenz mit Jacob Taubes 1952*, §149, p. 50.

27. Ibid., §184, p. 110.

28. Susan Anima Taubes, "The Absent God," *Journal of Religion* 35 (1955): 6.

29. Ibid. The point is repeated in Susan Taubes, "The Absent God: A Study of Simone Weil," PhD dissertation, Radcliffe College, 1956, p. 2.

30. Taubes, "Absent God: A Study," p. 36. See ibid., p. 35, where Susan reports that Marcel Moré

> in a warning to Christian followers, exposes Simone Weil's mysticism as a "gnosis in decomposition" impregnated by demonic Manichaeism and the aesthetic intellectualism of the Pythagorean and Platonic tradition. Moré's attack is not altogether unjustified from a Catholic point of view, and shows a deeper understanding of Simone Weil than the kind of enthusiastic appraisal that would put her writings on the shelf of mystical literature for devotional reading.

See, however, the more attenuated assessment in Susan's letter to Jacob, written on January 26, 1952, in Taubes, *Die Korrespondenz mit Jacob Taubes 1952*, §157, p. 67: "About S. Weil. Since on the most important points we have only haphazard notes of a highly contradictory nature—[it] might really be good to talk to people who knew her to find out her 'point of departure'. I suspect she is not a Christian + even a gnostic au fond."

31. Taubes, "Absent God: A Study," pp. 289–290.

32. Taubes, "Absent God," p. 12.

33. Taubes, *Die Korrespondenz mit Jacob Taubes 1952*, §149, p. 51. In the concluding part of the letter, Susan speculated about Weil's "real affinity to Jewish mysticism" and the "secret bridge between jewish + christian gnostic mysticism." Susan admitted, however, that the proper explication of this matter would depend on her knowing more about Jewish mysticism. We can presume that Jacob introduced Susan to the thought of Naḥman of Braslav. On Jacob's interest in Naḥman, see Muller, *Professor*, p. 161, and see especially p. 165: "In the early years of their marriage, both Jacob and Susan were attracted to thinkers who suggested—paradoxically, and perhaps absurdly—that recognizing the absence of God from the world was a step toward faith (as in the case of Simone Weil), or that doubt was at the heart of faith (as in the case of Nachman of Breslov)."

34. Taubes, *Die Korrespondenz mit Jacob Taubes 1952*, §241, p. 219. The passage is cited below at n. 128. See Wolfson, *Philosophical Pathos*, pp. 188 and 317 n. 117.

35. Susan Taubes, "The Nature of Tragedy," *Review of Metaphysics* 7 (1953): 193 (emphasis in original).

36. See Wolfson, *Philosophical Pathos*, pp. 218–225.

37. Taubes, *Die Korrespondenz mit Jacob Taubes 1952*, § 196, pp. 136–137. See below, n. 88.

38. Ibid., §191, p. 123.

39. Martin Heidegger, *Wegmarken* [GA 9] (Frankfurt am Main: Vittorio Klostermann, 1996), p. 197; idem, *Pathmarks*, edited by William McNeill (Cambridge: Cambridge University Press, 1998), p. 150. See my previous discussion of the errancy of untruth as the counteressence to truth in Elliot R. Wolfson, *The Duplicity of Philosophy's Shadow: Heidegger, Nazism, and the Jewish Other* (New York: Columbia University Press, 2018), pp. 6–7.

40. Heidegger, *Wegmarken*, p. 198; idem, *Pathmarks*, p. 151.

41. Heidegger, *Wegmarken*, p. 193; idem, *Pathmarks*, p. 148.

42. Heidegger, *Wegmarken*, p. 194; idem, *Pathmarks*, p. 148.

43. Heidegger, *Wegmarken*, p. 197; idem, *Pathmarks*, p. 151. On the essential belonging-together of truth and untruth, see also Martin Heidegger, *Vom Wesen der Wahrheit: Zu Platons Höhlengleichnis und Theätet* [GA 34] (Frankfurt am Main: Vittorio Klostermann, 1988), pp. 91–92; idem, *The Essence of Truth: On Plato's Cave Allegory and Theaetetus*, translated by Ted Sadler (New York: Continuum,

2002), p. 66. See Elliot R. Wolfson, *Giving Beyond the Gift: Apophasis and Overcoming Theomania* (New York: Fordham University Press, 2014), pp. 48–52, 130–131; idem, *Duplicity*, pp. 6, 131–145; idem, *Heidegger and Kabbalah*, pp. 4, 17 n. 31, 20 n. 61, 39, 94 n. 170, 120, 158, 266, 304–305, 324 nn. 66 and 72. For previous studies on Heidegger's notion of truth, see the sources cited in Wolfson, *Giving*, pp. 314–315 n. 106, 316 n. 128, 347 n. 339; idem, *Duplicity*, pp. 251–252 n. 1; idem, *Heidegger and Kabbalah*, p. 17 n. 29; to which may be added Rudolf Bernet, "Phenomenological Concepts of Untruth in Husserl and Heidegger," in *Husserl: German Perspectives*, edited by John J. Drummond and Otfried Höffe, translated by Hayden Kee, Patrick Eldridge, and Robin Litscher Wilkins (New York: Fordham University Press, 2019), pp. 239–262.

44. Heidegger, *Sein und Zeit*, §44, p. 221; idem, *Being and Time*, p. 213.

45. Heidegger, *Sein und Zeit*, §44, p. 222; idem, *Being and Time*, p. 213. For citation and analysis of this passage, see Wolfson, *Giving*, pp. 49–50; idem, *Philosophical Pathos*, p. 161.

46. Martin Heidegger, *Holzwege* [GA 5] (Frankfurt am Main: Vittorio Klostermann, 2003), p. 364; idem, *Off the Beaten Track*, edited and translated by Julian Young and Kenneth Haynes (Cambridge: Cambridge University Press, 2002), p. 275.

47. I have availed myself of the Greek text and the English translation in *The Texts of Early Greek Philosophy: The Complete Fragments and Selected Testimonies of the Major Presocratics*, part 1, edited and translated by Daniel W. Graham (Cambridge: Cambridge University Press, 2010), pp. 50–51.

48. Heidegger, *Holzwege*, pp. 321–322.

49. Heidegger, *Off the Beaten Track*, p. 242.

50. Taubes, *Die Korrespondenz mit Jacob Taubes 1950–1951*, §77, p. 182. For previous citation and analysis of this passage, see Wolfson, *Philosophical Pathos*, pp. 132–133. I have taken the liberty to repeat some of my discussion here.

51. Heidegger, *Holzwege*, p. 364; idem, *Off the Beaten Track*, p. 275 (emphasis in original).

52. Heidegger, *Holzwege*, p. 364; idem, *Off the Beaten Track*, p. 275. See below, n. 67.

53. Taubes, *Die Korrespondenz mit Jacob Taubes 1950–1951*, §77, p. 182. Compare Gillian Rose's reference to the "Gnostic remnant" in Augustine's thought in the passage cited in ch. 2 at n. 148.

54. Taubes, *Die Korrespondenz mit Jacob Taubes 1952*, §230, p. 200.

55. I have corrected the slight mistake in Susan's transcription of the German text based on the original in Heidegger, *Holzwege*, p. 364.

56. Taubes, "Gnostic Foundations," pp. 169–170 (emphasis in original).

57. Compare Heidegger, *Metaphysik und Nihilismus*, pp. 52–53; idem, *Metaphysics and Nihilism*, p. 46. The errancy of metaphysics consists of its fleeing from

the empty universal into the positivism of the particular and the concrete, whether in the dominion of natural or human sciences, and thereby "keeps the opening of beings into beingness [*Seiendheit*] open in the jointure [*Gefüge*]." But in this errancy lies hidden the direction that guides us into "the question concerning beyng." Thus, the further that "the thinking of beingness loses itself in and seemingly flees into what is the most universal, the closer this not yet unfolded thinking of being comes to the nearest, the most singular and purest, the truth of beyng itself, without being able to know it." Noteworthy is the distinction that Heidegger draws between the "most singular and purest" (*Einzigste und Gediegenste*) and "the particular and the concrete" (*Besondere und Konkrete*). The latter terms signify the flip side of the universal abstraction and hence they have the capacity to open the way to the singular, which is the truth of beyng. The effort of metaphysics to derive its legitimacy from what is construed as the most universal is related to the "ungrounding of the truth of beyng" (*der Ungründung der Wahrheit des Seyns*), that is,

> the inceptual self-gathering in the permanence of presence, which for its part is the appearing and, at the same time, the concealing of being as φύσις. The unconcealment of being (in ἕν and καθόλου) still takes its departure from the uniqueness and fullness of the overtly close proximity to being over all beings. Yet, precisely this interpretation of being becomes a misinterpretation of it as beingness, as the emptiest and most general, against which beings in their particularity will acquire primacy and come to be anchored in a first cause.

On the depiction of the event and the inception of the "truth of beyng" as the "singular essential realm of the most singular [*einzigen Wesensbereich des Einzigen*]," see Martin Heidegger, *Über den Anfang* [GA 70] (Frankfurt am Main: Vittorio Klostermann, 2005), p. 9; idem, *On Inception*, translated by Peter Hanly (Bloomington: Indiana University Press, 2023), p. 3. See also Heidegger, *Zum Wesen*, pp. 12–13; idem, *On the Essence*, pp. 9–10. And compare Heidegger, *Holzwege*, p. 345:

> Die archaische Sprache und so auch Parmenides und Heraklit gebrauchen stets ἐόν und ἐόντα. Aber ἐόν, "seiend", ist nicht nur der Singular des Participiums ἐόντα, "Seiendes", sondern ἐόν nennt das schlechthin Singuläre, das in seiner Einzahl einzig das einzig einende Eine vor aller Zahl ist.

English translation in Heidegger, *Off the Beaten Track*, pp. 259–260:

> Archaic Greek, and so, too, Parmenides and Heraclitus, use ἐόν and ἐόντα all the time. But ἐόν, "being [*seiend*]," is not only the singular of the participle ἐόντα, "the being [*Seiendes*]," but also names the singular as such, which, as one in its singleness, is uniquely the uniquely unifying One that precedes all number.

Heidegger goes on to write, admitting the exaggerated nature of his words but nevertheless touching on the truth, "the destiny of the West rests on the translation of the word ἐόν, given that the translation [*Über*setzung] is a crossing over [Übersetzung] to the truth of what comes to language in the ἐόν." Putting aside the question of the accuracy of Heidegger's philology, it should be apparent that reflected here is the central concern of his philosophical thinking on the nature of language and being, and the claim that the latter names the singular and the unique one that is before mathematical enumeration. See the discussion of the singular simplicity of the event in Jussi Backman, *Complicated Presence: Heidegger and the Postmetaphysical Unity of Being* (Albany: State University of New York Press, 2015), pp. 155–186, and compare the chapter on the Heideggerian event of being in François Raffoul, *Thinking the Event* (Bloomington: Indiana University Press, 2020), pp. 186–232. For an instructive utilization of the Heideggerian topos as a key to understand the negative henology of the Plotinian doctrine of the nonbeing of the one that comes to presence in the being of all that is, see Reiner Schürmann, *Broken Hegemonies*, translated by Reginald Lilly (Bloomington: Indiana University Press, 2003), pp. 143–151, and especially p. 149:

> "Singularity" does not signify dispersion, nor does "event" signify an incident. Which will the good singularity be, here? . . . The one is the *self-configuring* by virtue of which—but without virtue or force—there are figures. . . . The one is the factor with which all things are coordinated and in the absence of which they would disintegrate. . . . The good singularization answers to the "each time" in the following quasi-tautology (which is a figure that is as apophatic as are the negations): "Union happens each time that there is an entering into presence" (emphasis in original).

58. Heidegger, *Wegmarken*, p. 334; idem, *Pathmarks*, p. 255. Compare the poetic encapsulation of the ontological difference in Heidegger, *Zum Wesen*, p. 22: "Das Seyn ist das Seiendste; / aber das Seiendste ist kein Seiendes, / sondern das Seyn als Er-eignis. / Das Seyn ist das Seyn." English translation in Heidegger, *On the Essence*, p. 18: "Beyng is what is most in being; / but what is most in being is not a being, / rather beyng as appropriating event. / Beyng is beyng." See also Heidegger, *Über den Anfang*, p. 9: "Das Verstehen von 'Sein' ist wesentlich entfernt von einem Wissen des Seyns. Denn jenes Verstehen neigt stets dazu, das Sein aus dem Seienden zu erklären. Das Wissen des Seyns kann nur in einem Absprung aus dem Verstehen des Seins vorbereitet, jedoch auch dann nicht geradehin erlangt werden." English version in Heidegger, *On Inception*, p. 3: "The understanding of 'being' is essentially far removed from a knowing of beyng. That understanding always tends to explain being from out of beings, whereas the knowing of beyng can only be prepared for in a leap beyond the understanding of being and, even then, is not arrived at directly." The tautology "Das Seyn ist das Seyn" exemplifies the circular logic that Heidegger deemed most felicitous for the path of thinking. See, for example, Martin Heidegger, *Seminare* [GA 15] (Frankfurt am Main: Vittorio Klostermann, 2005), pp. 397–

399; idem, *Four Seminars: Le Thor 1966, 1968, 1969, Zähringen 1973*, translated by Andrew Mitchell and François Raffoul (Bloomington: Indiana University Press, 2003), pp. 79–80; and discussion in Wolfson, *Heidegger and Kabbalah*, pp. 37–38, 308.

59. Heidegger, *Off the Beaten Track*, p. 253. German text in idem, *Holzwege*, p. 337: "Die Unverborgenheit des Seienden, die ihm gewährte Helle, verdunkelt das Licht des Seins. Das Sein entzieht sich, indem es sich in das Seiende entbirgt." The passage is cited by Taubes, "Gnostic Foundations," p. 170. See ibid., p. 171, where Susan remarked that "Heidegger's concept of the self-withdrawal of Being recalls the idea of divine retraction in gnostic mysticism which infused German idealism through Schelling's philosophy of freedom." In Wolfson, *Philosophical Pathos*, p. 165, I observed that it is curious that Susan did not mention in this context the kabbalistic doctrine of *ṣimṣum*, the primal contraction and withdrawal of *Ein Sof* to create a vacuum within the plenum, a mythopoeic idea that may have influenced Schelling and, by extension, Heidegger. For fuller documentation of the evidence of kabbalistic motifs, especially the doctrine of *ṣimṣum*, discernible in Schelling, see Wolfson, *Heidegger and Kabbalah*, pp. 8, 18–19 n. 40, 170–171, 193–194 n. 279, 209–211, and for the trace of the myth of *ṣimṣum* in Heidegger's *Lichtung* and the bestowing refusal of being, see ibid., pp. 137–196. At the time that Susan wrote her essay on Heidegger, she was well aware of the kabbalistic idea from discussions with Jacob Taubes and from reading Gershom Scholem. See Wolfson, *Philosophical Pathos*, p. 372 n. 187.

60. Heidegger, *Metaphysik und Nihilismus*, p. 55; idem, *Metaphysics and Nihilism*, p. 48.

61. Taubes, "Gnostic Foundations," p. 170.

62. Ibid.

63. See Wolfson, *Giving*, pp. 51–52; idem, *Heidegger and Kabbalah*, pp. 5 and 328 n. 148.

64. Martin Heidegger, *Überlegungen II–VI (Schwarze Hefte 1931–1938)* [GA 94] (Frankfurt am Main: Vittorio Klostermann, 2014), p. 13: "Nur wenn wir wirklich irren—in den Irre *gehen*, können wir auf 'Wahrheit' stoßen. Die tiefe, unheimliche und d. h. zugleich große Stimmung des Irrgängers im Ganzen: *der Philosoph*" (emphasis in original). English rendering in idem, *Ponderings II–VI: Black Notebooks 1931–1938*, translated by Richard Rojcewicz (Bloomington: Indiana University Press, 2016), p. 11: "Only if we are actually errant—actually *go* into errancy, can we strike up against 'truth.' The deep, uncanny and thus at the same time great attunement of the errant ones as a whole: *the philosopher*" (emphasis in original).

65. Martin Heidegger, *Ponderings VII–XI: Black Notebooks 1938–1939*, translated by Richard Rojcewicz (Bloomington: Indiana University Press, 2017), p. 11 (emphasis in original). German text in Martin Heidegger, *Überlegungen VII–XI (Schwarze Hefte 1938/39)* [GA 95] (Frankfurt am Main: Vittorio Klostermann,

2014), p. 14: "Die *Irre* ist das verborgenste Geschenk der Wahrheit—denn in ihr verschenkt sich das Wesen der Wahrheit als die Wächterschaft der Verweigerung und als die reinste Verwahrung des Seyns im unkenntlichen Schutz des Immerseienden. Freilich: die Irre—ist hier nicht der 'Irrtum', der festgestellte Fehler, das Fehlen der Wahrheit als Richtigkeit—sondern jenes, was zum Da—des Da-*seins* gehört" (emphasis in original).

66. Heidegger, *Überlegungen II–VI*, pp. 472–473; idem, *Ponderings II–VI*, p. 343 (emphasis in original).

67. Heidegger, *Off the Beaten Track*, p. 275. German text in Heidegger, *Holzwege*, p. 364: "Die Vergessenheit des Seins gehört in das durch sie selbst verhüllte Wesen des Seins. Sie gehört so wesentlich in das Geschick des Seins, daß die Frühe dieses Geschickes als die Enthüllung des Anwesenden in seinem Anwesen beginnt." Part of the passage is cited by Taubes, "Gnostic Foundations," p. 171.

68. Taubes, "Gnostic Foundations," p. 171. For my brief comments on Susan's gnostic interpretation of Heidegger, see Wolfson, *Heidegger and Kabbalah*, pp. 143–144, and the expanded discussion in idem, *Philosophical Pathos*, pp. 128–185.

69. On the possible gnostic resonances in Heidegger's thought, see Wolfson, *Duplicity*, p. 181 n. 35; idem, *Heidegger and Kabbalah*, pp. 9, 69, and references to other scholars cited on pp. 25–26 n. 97, 178–179 n. 61.

70. Heidegger, *Holzwege*, p. 41; idem, *Off the Beaten Track*, pp. 30–31. See Wolfson, *Heidegger and Kabbalah*, p. 4. It goes without saying that numerous scholars and thinkers have written about the interface of revealing and concealing implied in Heidegger's insistence that the concealment of untruth belongs to the essence of truth as unconcealment. For an enumeration of some of the relevant studies, see Wolfson, *Heidegger and Kabbalah*, p. 17 n. 29. To the sources mentioned there, one might add Katherine Withy, "Concealing and Concealment in Heidegger," *European Journal of Philosophy* 25 (2017): 1496–1513, and idem, *Heidegger on Being Self-Concealing* (Oxford: Oxford University Press, 2022). My contribution to this topic was to suggest that the paradox of the concurrent concealment and disclosure in Heidegger may be due to the influence of the kabbalah on Schelling. See Wolfson, *Heidegger and Kabbalah*, pp. 202–211.

71. Heidegger used the Latin expression to describe the word "humanism" in his "Letter on 'Humanism'." See Heidegger, *Wegmarken*, p. 345; idem, *Pathmarks*, p. 263. See also Martin Heidegger, *The Concept of Time*, translated by William McNeill (Oxford: Blackwell, 1992), p. 20: "The present generation thinks it has found history, it thinks it is even overburdened with history. It moans about historicism—*lucus a non lucendo*. Something is called history which is not history at all." For a philological and conceptual analysis of this motif, see Leonardo Amoroso, "Heidegger's *Lichtung* as *lucus a (non) lucendo*," in *Weak Thought*, edited by Gianni Vattimo and Pier Aldo Rovatti, translated and with an introduction by Peter Carravetta (Albany: State University of New York Press, 2012), pp. 155–179.

72. Martin Heidegger, *Aus der Erfahrung des Denkens 1910–1976* [GA 13] (Frankfurt am Main: Vittorio Klostermann, 2002), p. 81; idem, *Poetry, Language, Thought*, translations and introduction by Albert Hofstadter (New York: Harper & Row, 1971), p. 9.

73. Peter Trawny, *Freedom to Fail: Heidegger's Anarchy*, translated by Ian Alexander Moore and Christopher Turner (Cambridge: Polity Press, 2015), pp. 28–29.

74. Ibid., p. 5.

75. Taubes, *Die Korrespondenz mit Jacob Taubes 1950–1951*, §28, p. 79.

76. See the passage cited at n. 38. See also the passage cited below at n. 187.

77. Taubes, *Die Korrespondenz mit Jacob Taubes 1952*, §266, p. 255, n. 2.

78. Ibid., §232, p. 204.

79. Ibid., §232, pp. 204–205.

80. For instance, see Friedrich Nietzsche, *The Will to Power*, translated by Walter Kaufmann and R. J. Hollingdale, edited and with commentary by Walter Kaufmann (New York: Random House, 1967), p. 7: "Buddhistic tendency, yearning for Nothing. (Indian Buddhism is *not* the culmination of a thoroughly moralistic development; its nihilism is therefore full of morality that is not overcome: existence as punishment, existence construed as error, error thus as a punishment—a moral valuation)" (emphasis in original). Ibid., p. 16: "Every purely moral value system (that of Buddhism, for example) ends in nihilism." Ibid., p. 18: "Its opposite: the weary nihilism that no longer attacks; its most famous form, Buddhism; a passive nihilism, a sign of weakness." Ibid., p. 36: "This is the most extreme form of nihilism: the nothing (the 'meaningless'), eternally! The European form of Buddhism: the energy of knowledge and strength compels this belief. It is the most *scientific* of all possible hypotheses. We deny end goals: if existence had one it would have to have been reached" (emphasis in original). Ibid., p. 37: "Nihilism as a symptom that the underprivileged have no comfort left; that they destroy in order to be destroyed; that without morality they no longer have any reason to 'resign themselves'—that they place themselves on the plain of the opposite principle and also want power by *compelling* the powerful to become their hangmen. This is the European form of Buddhism—*doing* No after all existence has lost its 'meaning'" (emphasis in original). Ibid., p. 43: "The second Buddhism. The nihilistic catastrophe that finishes Indian culture.—Early signs of it: The immense increase of pity. Spiritual weariness." Ibid., p. 128: "The two great nihilistic movements: (a) Buddhism, (b) Christianity. The latter has only now attained to approximately the state of culture in which it can fulfill its original vocation—a level to which it belongs—in which it can show itself pure." Most relevant to understanding Susan's invocation of Buddhist nihilism is Nietzsche's lengthy discourse in ibid., pp. 95–97:

> *Buddha against the "Crucified."* Among the nihilistic religions, one may always clearly distinguish the Christian from the Buddhist. The Buddhist religion is

the expression of a fine evening, a perfect sweetness and mildness—it is gratitude toward all that lies behind, and also for what is lacking: bitterness, disillusionment, rancor; finally, a lofty spiritual love; the subtleties of philosophical contradiction are behind it, even from these it is resting: but from these it still derives its spiritual glory and sunset glow.... Emancipation even from good and evil appears to be of the essence of the Buddhist ideal: a refined state beyond morality is conceived that is identical with the state of perfection, in the presupposition that one needs to perform even good actions only for the time being, merely as a means—namely, as a means to emancipation from *all* actions (emphasis in original).

On the possibility that Susan similarly intuited from the identity of nirvāṇa and saṃsāra in the Mahāyāna tradition the wisdom that emancipation consists of overcoming all binaries, including the binary of attainment and nonattainment, and of unveiling the veil of illusion as the illusion of the veil, see Taubes, *Die Korrespondenz mit Jacob Taubes 1952*, §164, p. 76, cited and analyzed in Wolfson, *Philosophical Pathos*, pp. 38–39, and note the reference there to another pertinent passage from Nietzsche. Many have discussed Nietzsche's characterization of Buddhism as a form of nihilism, and here I mention a few salient examples: Benjamin A. Elman, "Nietzsche and Buddhism," *Journal of the History of Ideas* 44 (1983): 671–686; Robert G. Morrison, *Nietzsche and Buddhism: A Study in Nihilism and Ironic Affinities* (Oxford: Oxford University Press, 1997); Brian Schroeder, "Dancing Through Nothing: Nietzsche, the Kyoto School, and Transcendence," *Journal of Nietzsche Studies* 37 (2009): 44–65; Antoine Panaïoti, *Nietzsche and Buddhist Philosophy* (Cambridge: Cambridge University Press, 2013), pp. 17–26, 66, 212–229. Compare the text of Nietzsche cited in ch. 2 at n. 201.

81. See the text of Susan cited above at n. 10, and compare Wolfson, *Philosophical Pathos*, p. 134.

82. Taubes, *Die Korrespondenz mit Jacob Taubes 1952*, §136, p. 21. For previous citation and analysis of this passage, see Wolfson, *Philosophical Pathos*, pp. 154–155.

83. Taubes, *Die Korrespondenz mit Jacob Taubes 1952*, §136, p. 21.

84. Ibid., §148, p. 48. Pareigis, op. cit., p. 49 n. 9, identified as the source for Susan's comment the following passage from Paul-Louis Landsberg, *Essai sur l'expérience de la mort suivi de le problème moral du suicide* (Paris: Éditions du Seuil, 1951), p. 50: "L'angoisse de la mort, et pas seulement des douleurs du mourir, serait incompréhensible si la structure fondamentale de notre être ne contenait pas le postulat existentiel d'un 'au- delà.'" English translation in Paul-Louis Landsberg, *The Experience of Death: The Moral Problem of Suicide*, translated by Cynthia Rowland (New York: Philosophical Library, 1953), p. 24: "The anguish of death, and not only the pain of dying, would be incomprehensible if the fundamental structure of our being did not include the existential postulate of something beyond."

85. Taubes, *Die Korrespondenz mit Jacob Taubes 1952*, §148, p. 48.
86. Landsberg, *Experience of Death*, pp. 22–23 (emphasis in original).
87. Ibid., pp. 25–26.
88. Taubes, *Die Korrespondenz mit Jacob Taubes 1952*, §142, pp. 37–38. Also relevant is the passage from Camus's *L'homme révolté* cited in ibid., §149, p. 51: "Au temps de la négation, il pouvait être utile de s'interroger sur le problème du suicide. Au temps des idéologies, il faut se mettre en règle avec le meurtre." Compare Susan's remarks cited below at n. 201. Also germane is the discussion on absurdity and suicide placed at the beginning of Albert Camus, *The Myth of Sisyphus*, translated by Justin O'Brien (New York: Alfred A. Knopf, 1955), pp. 3–10. Camus initiated his book with the contention that suicide is the "one truly serious philosophical problem," and thus to judge "whether life is or is not worth living amounts to answering the fundamental question of philosophy." Despite her passionate debates with Camus, and her efforts early on to reject suicide as a credible yardstick to assess the meaningfulness of life, I suspect that Susan would have concurred with the claim that the question of the cogency of taking one's own life is the quintessential philosophical conundrum.
89. Taubes, *Die Korrespondenz mit Jacob Taubes 1950–1951*, §85, pp. 198–199 (emphasis in original). For previous citation and analysis of this passage, see Wolfson, *Philosophical Pathos*, p. 135. I have taken the liberty to repeat some of my discussion here.
90. On the breakdown of the distinction between reality and appearance, see the passages from *Lament for Julia* discussed in Wolson, *Philosophical Pathos*, pp. 314–316 n. 109.
91. Taubes, *Die Korrespondenz mit Jacob Taubes 1950–1951*, §14, p. 49.
92. See ibid., p. 196 n. 4, where Pareigis identified the passage paraphrased by Susan from the first volume of Hans Urs von Balthasar, *Apokalypse der deutschen Seele. Studien zu einer Lehre von letzten Haltungen. I: Der deutsche Idealismus* (Salzburg-Leipzig, Pustet, 1937), pp. 93–94:

> Als Verstand geht der Geist restlos darin auf, Erfahrung zu synthetisieren. Er erblickt sich also im Spiegel der Natur und nur darin. Aber das Zueinander selber, in welchem der Geist sich selbst als endlicher erkennt und kritisiert, weist auf einen Einheitsgrund, von dem aus allein solche Kritik und Erkenntnis möglich ist: die Unendlichkeit der Vernunft. Gegenständlich wird diese Einheit nicht, weil sie keinen Spiegel hat, sich zu sehen. Wo sie es versucht, ist "dialektischer Schein" das Ergebnis, eine Spiegelfechterei ohne Spiegel.

93. Taubes, *Die Korrespondenz mit Jacob Taubes 1950–1951*, §83, p. 192.
94. For an extended discourse based on this reading, see Markus Gabriel and Slavoj Žižek, *Mythology, Madness and Laughter: Subjectivity in German Idealism* (London: Continuum, 2009).

95. Taubes, *Die Korrespondenz mit Jacob Taubes 1952*, §191, pp. 121–122.
96. Ibid., p. 122.
97. Ibid. See Wolfson, *Philosophical Pathos*, pp. 358–359 n. 95.
98. Gershom Scholem, *The Messianic Idea in Judaism and Other Essays on Jewish Spirituality* (New York: Schocken Books, 1971), pp. 78–141. Susan does not mention this essay of Scholem, but in the "Review of *Tragedy and the Paradox of the Fortunate* by Herbert Weisinger," *Ethics* 64 (1954): 324 n. 2, she does refer to his *Major Trends in Jewish Mysticism*, which contains a chapter on Sabbatianism in which Scholem discussed this idea under the rubric of the holiness of sin and religious nihilism. See Gershom Scholem, *Major Trends in Jewish Mysticism* (New York: Schocken Books, 1954), pp. 315–320. Compare the discussion in Wolfson, *Philosophical Pathos*, pp. 361–362 n. 118. As I noted, the expression "redemption through sin" appears in Susan Taubes, *Divorcing*, introduction by David Rieff (New York: New York Review of Books, 2020), p. 139. The passage was noted as well by Muller, *Professor*, p. 357. It is plausible that Susan learned of the contents of Scholem's essay from discussions with Jacob. See Muller, op. cit., pp. 94–96. Jacob likely would have known the Hebrew version published in *Kenesset* 2 (1937): 347–392 with the title "Miṣwah ha-ba'ah ba-aveirah," literally, the pious act that comes through transgression, later included in Gershom Scholem, *Studies and Texts Concerning the History of Sabbetianism and Its Metamorphoses* (Jerusalem: Bialik Institute, 1982), pp. 9–67 (Hebrew). For a history of the various redactions and editions of this essay, see Gershom Scholem, *Erlösung durch Sünde*, edited by Jonatan Meir (Jerusalem: Blima Books, 2023), pp. 9–22. Meir printed the manuscript version that Scholem sent to Fischel Lachover in July or August 1936 in preparation for its printing in December. Many have written on this motif in Scholem's scholarship, but I note, in particular, Steven M. Wasserstrom, "Defeating Evil from Within: Comparative Perspectives on 'Redemption Through Sin,'" *Journal of Jewish Thought and Philosophy* 6 (1997): 37–57; idem, *Religion After Religion: Gershom Scholem, Mircea Eliade, and Henry Corbin at Eranos* (Princeton: Princeton University Press, 1999), pp. 62, 130, 136 (Wasserstrom theorized that Scholem's essay "Redemption Through Sin" bears the influence of Jonas's Heideggerian study of Gnosticism as well as correspondence with Corbin), 188, 215–224. The influence of Scholem on Susan is attested as well by the fact that he repeatedly applied the terms "gnostic" and "heretical" to what he identified as the antinomianism that informed the Sabbatian messianic movement. See also Scholem, *Major Trends*, p. 359 n. 24: "Of the existence of a heretical Gnosis of a dualistic and antinomian character on the outskirts of Judaism there cannot be any doubt, to my mind." This aspect of Scholem's oeuvre has also been discussed by many scholars, but this is not the place to elaborate.
99. Taubes, "Review," p. 324.
100. Ibid.
101. Ibid., pp. 324–325. See Pareigis, *Susan Taubes*, p. 273.

102. Taubes, *Die Korrespondenz mit Jacob Taubes 1952*, §181, pp. 104–105. In that context, to support her contention that wrongdoing relates not to breaking the law but mistreating living creatures, Susan invoked the maxim attributed to Jesus in Mark 2:27, which has a parallel in rabbinic literature, to the effect that Sabbath was created for man and not man for the Sabbath. Compare Taubes, *Die Korrespondenz mit Jacob Taubes 1952*, §193, p. 128, and discussion in Wolfson, *Philosophical Pathos*, p. 55. On Susan's disparaging attitude toward Paul, see the evidence adduced in Wolfson, *Philosophical Pathos*, pp. 53–56, 311 n. 85, 355 n. 57; Muller, *Professor*, p. 171.

103. On the hypernomian excess of the nomos in Susan's thinking, see Wolfson, *Philosophical Pathos*, pp. 58–71.

104. In many of my publications, I have emphasized that the logic most pertinent to grasp the kabbalistic approach to truth is one that regains the middle wherein opposites are the same in virtue of their difference. I have also expressed this in terms of the tetralemic logic of the middle way (*madhyamaka*) in the Mahāyāna Buddhist tradition: S is P; S is ¬P; S is both P and ¬P; S is neither P nor ¬P. See Elliot R. Wolfson, *Open Secret: Postmessianic Messianism and the Mystical Revision of Menaḥem Mendel Schneerson* (New York: Columbia University Press, 2009), pp. 109–114; idem, *A Dream Interpreted Within a Dream: Oneiropoiesis and the Prism of Imagination* (New York: Zone Books, 2011), pp. 110, 212–213; idem, *Heidegger and Kabbalah*, pp. 106–108. It is of interest to compare my position with the remark in Joseph B. Soloveichik, "Rabbi Joseph B. Soloveichik's Lectures on 'Concepts in Halakha as Elaborated Upon by the Aggada and Kabbala,'" transcribed and edited by Yaakov Homnick, with contributions by Daniel Rynhold, Jeffrey Saks, and Shlomo Zuckier, *Tradition: Special Digital Issue* (2023): 10–11: "The religious mentality can be investigated on various planes. The outcome, however, would be contradictory. The philosophy of nature speaks of multiple-valued logic. It wants the exclusion and the elimination of the Aristotelian excluded middle. In religion, the excluded middle is wrong; A and B and at times, B and A together. The naïve quest for uniformity is bound to share the disappointment of a desert mirage." For an alternative version, see Joseph B. Soloveitchik, "Lectures of Rabbi Dr. Joseph B. Soloveitchik: The Relationship Between Halakhah, Aggadah, and Kabbalah," transcribed by Robert Blau, edited and footnotes by Eliyahu Krakowski, Heshey Zelcer, and Mark Zelcer, *Ḥakirah: The Flatbush Journal of Jewish Law and Thought* 33 (2023): 23–24: "The religious mentality may be investigated on various planes. This would produce many paradoxes. Philosophy speaks of multi-valued logic. The same with religious experience. A and B cannot be both A and B. But religious experience is sometimes A, B, or A and B."

105. For an exhaustive discussion of the compositional and redactional issues surrounding the zoharic compilation, see Daniel Abrams, *Kabbalistic Manuscripts and Textual Theory: Methodologies of Textual Scholarship and Editorial Practice in the Study of Jewish Mysticism*, foreword by David Greetham (Los Angeles: Cherub Press, 2010), pp. 17–117, and 224–428.

106. *Zohar* 1:4a. The analysis of this motif was the subject of one of my earliest academic essays. See Elliot R. Wolfson, "Light Through Darkness: The Ideal of Human Perfection in the Zohar," *Harvard Theological Review* 81 (1988): 73–95.

107. Compare the interpretation of the zoharic passage in Naftali Bacharach, *Emeq ha-Melekh* (Jerusalem: Yerid ha-Sefarim, 2003), 14:126, p. 713:

> For there are palaces and dwellings that are dark, and through good deeds they are transformed into light. And the judgments as well, which are called "the one that is dark," because it is the spark from which the darkness emerged in the margin of the vessel, which is called the lamp of darkness [*boṣina de-qardinuta*], and if they are worthy, the good deeds make purity from the shell.

In my scholarly publications, I have translated *boṣina de-qardinuta* as "hardened spark," but it is obvious that in this context "lamp of darkness" makes more sense. Philologically, the latter expression better translates the variant *boṣina de-qadrinuta*. See Elliot R. Wolfson, *Circle in the Square: Studies in the Use of Gender in Kabbalistic Symbolism* (Albany: State University of New York Press, 1995), pp. 174–175 n. 93. As it happens, the expression *boṣina de-qadrinuta* appears several times in Bacharach's *Emeq ha-Melekh*. See 6:7, p. 187; 6:38, p. 224; 6:41, p. 228; 6:51, p. 262; 6:53, p. 271; 6:68, p. 310. For other references to this zoharic symbol, see Wolfson, *Circle*, pp. 60–69; idem, *Through a Speculum That Shines: Vision and Imagination in Medieval Jewish Mysticism* (Princeton: Princeton University Press, 1994), pp. 382 n. 204, 389 n. 236; idem, *Language, Eros, Being: Kabbalistic Hermeneutics and the Poetic Imagination* (New York: Fordham University Press, 2005), pp. 137, 321, 487 n. 198, 571–572 n. 200.

108. Yiṣḥaq Eizik Ḥaver Wildmann, *Beit Olamim* (Warsaw: Meir Yeḥiel Halter, 1889), 16b.

109. *Zohar* 3:288b, 289a-b (*Idra Zuṭa*). See the discussion of this symbol in Elliot R. Wolfson, "Heeding the Law Beyond the Law: Transgendering Alterity and the Hypernomian Perimeter of the Ethical," *European Journal of Jewish Studies* 14 (2020): 233–243.

110. See the more extended discussion of this motif, connected to the use of the image of sacramental rape, in Wolfson, *Philosophical Pathos*, pp. 63–68.

111. The topic has been discussed by numerous scholars of which I will mention a few of the more prominent examples wherein one can find ample references to primary sources: Joseph Weiss, "Beginnings of Hasidim," *Zion* 16 (1951): 80–82, 88–103 (Hebrew); Louis Jacobs, *Hasidic Prayer* (New York: Schocken Books, 1973), pp. 104–120; Moshe Idel, *Hasidim: Between Ecstasy and Magic* (Albany: State University of New York Press, 1995), pp. 149–150, 162–163, 181, 350 n. 123 (Idel proposed an Abulafian source for the expression *maḥashavot zarot*); idem, "Prayer, Ecstasy, and 'Alien Thoughts' in the Religious Experience of the Besht," in *Let the Old Make Way for the New: Studies in the Social and Cultural History of Eastern Eu-*

ropean Jewry Presented to Immanuel Etkes, vol. 1: *Hasidism and the Musar Movement*, edited by David Assaf and Ada Rapoport-Albert (Jerusalem: Zalman Shazar Center, 2009), pp. 57–120 (Hebrew); Yehuda Yifrach, "The Elevation of Foreign Thoughts in the Traditions of R. Israel Baal Shem Tov as Transmitted in the Works of His Students," MA thesis, Bar-Ilan University, 2008 (Hebrew); Tsippi Kaufman, *In All Your Ways Know Him: The Concept of God and Avodah be-Gashmiyut in the Early Stages of Hasidism* (Ramat-Gan: Bar-Ilan University Press, 2009), pp. 107–108, 110–111, 123–125, 141–142, 528 (Hebrew); Ariel Evan Mayse, *Speaking Infinities: God and Language in the Teachings of Rabbi Dov Ber of Mezritsh* (Philadelphia: University of Pennsylvania Press, 2020), pp. 219–222.

112. The expression is used to describe the Ḥasidic perspective by Scholem, *Major Trends*, p. 341. On the Beshṭian teaching concerning the presence of divinity in all that exists, see Rachel Elior, *Israel Ba'al Shem Tov and His Contemporaries: Kabbalists, Sabbatians, Hasidim and Mitnaggedim*, vol. 1 (Jerusalem: Karmel, 2014), pp. 418–426, 623–624, 667–668, 676–678 (Hebrew).

113. *Tiqqunei Zohar*, edited by Reuven Margaliot (Jerusalem: Mosad ha-Rav Kook, 1978), sec. 70, 122b.

114. In the works of the Ḥabad-Lubavitch dynasty, this teaching received a particularly significant emphasis to the point that all of reality is perceived as the manifestation of the essence (*aṣmut*) that names the unnameable nihility at the core of the plurality of existence, the invisibly visible transcendence of infinity underlying the visibly invisible immanence of the finite multiverse, the one that is continuously reconfigured by the manifold in which it is both incarnate and disincarnate, the nonbeing that is present in all beings by withdrawing from those beings. Hence, the frequent appeal to the wordplay between *ha-olam*, the world, and *he'lem*, concealment, to communicate the paradox that the world hides the light of the infinite that is disclosed therein to the extent that it is hidden. Messianic awareness consists of exposing the concealment of the concealment so that the dissimilitude of self-concealing will become fully transparent, and we become sensitized to the fact that "nature is divinity" (*ha-ṭeva hu elohut*) or that "divinity and the world are one and the same thing" (*elohus un olam in die zelbe zakh; olam we-elohut hu kolla ḥad*), to cite two of the formulations of the seventh master of this lineage, Menaḥem Mendel Schneerson. For references, see Wolfson, *Open Secret*, pp. 92, 150. On the aforementioned wordplay of *ha-olam* and *he'lem*, see ibid., pp. 26, 52, 93, 103–114. The Ḥabad view should be contrasted with Spinoza's *Deus sive Natura*, according to which divinity and nature are so completely identified that any sense of difference between them is obliterated. The Ḥabad identification of nature and divinity is based on preserving the identity of their nonidentity in the nonidentity of their identity. That the world is God, therefore, does not mean that there is no ontically independent universe but rather that ontologically everything in the universe is the concealed manifestation of the essence of *Ein Sof*. This insight is often conveyed

by the slogan *ein od milvado* from Deuteronomy 4:35, the monotheistic belief that there is only one God rendered monistically as there is nothing but the infinite, or in the zoharic formulation regularly utilized by these masters, *kolla qameih ke-la ḥashivin*, "everything before him is considered as naught" (*Zohar* 1:11b).

115. See Philip S. Alexander, "The Talmudic Concept of Conjuring (*'Aḥizat 'Einayim*) and the Problem of the Definition of Magic (*Kishuf*)," in *Creation and Re-Creation in Jewish Thought: Festschrift in Honor of Joseph Dan*, edited by Rachel Elior and Peter Schäfer (Tübingen: Mohr Siebeck, 2005), pp. 7–26.

116. Jacob Joseph of Polonnoye, *Ben Porat Yosef* (Korzec: Avraham Dov of Melnyk, 1781), 88a. The passage of Jacob Joseph and the parable reported in the name of the Besht have been discussed by many scholars, but this is not the place to elaborate.

117. See the textual evidence adduced in Wolfson, *Heidegger and Kabbalah*, pp. 214–216, 243–244 n. 134, 244 n. 138, 363; idem, "Phenomenology, Theosophic Topography and the Structures of Being: Unveiling the Seventh of Scholem's Ten Unhistorical Aphorisms on the Kabbalah," *Kabbalah: Journal for the Study of Jewish Mystical Texts* 55 (2023): 59–61 n. 128.

118. Kalonymus Kalman Shapira, *Hakhsharat ha-Avrekhim—Mevo ha-She'arim* (Jerusalem: Ḥasidei Piaseczno, 2001), p. 254.

119. Babylonian Talmud, Shabbat 73a.

120. See Glenn Dynner, "The Hasidic Tale as a Historical Source: Historiography and Methodology," *Religion Compass* 3–4 (2009): 660.

121. *Tanna de-vei Eliyahu im ha-Perush Ramatayim Ṣofim* (Jerusalem: Meqor ha-Sefarim, 2012), pp. 317–318.

122. Taubes, *Die Korrespondenz mit Jacob Taubes 1950–1951*, §41, p. 114. For previous citation and discussion, see Wolfson, *Philosophical Pathos*, pp. 113–114, 157, 200.

123. Taubes, "Nature of Tragedy," p. 195.

124. Taubes, *Die Korrespondenz mit Jacob Taubes 1950–1951*, §41, p. 114. See Christina Pareigis, "The Connecting Paths of Nomads, Wanderers, Exiles. Stationen Einer Korrespondenz," op. cit., p. 284.

125. Susan Taubes, *Lament for Julia*, introduction by Francesca Wade (New York: New York Review of Books, 2023), p. 36.

126. See ibid., p. 63:

> Unlike Descartes I did not presume to doubt everything. Far from it. I never doubted that the sun shone, if not on me, on the wheatfields. Nor was the existence of my desk or my chair a problem. The world I have always found to be all too solidly there. It was only my own existence I doubted. To say then, that here is something beyond doubt, namely, that I doubt, does not advance me a step further, if anything it enjoins upon me a step back: an endless series of certainties

regarding the existence of a doubt. As to the leap from *I think* to *I am*, it takes such an effort and in the end I discover I've been hopping on the same spot, without, perhaps, touching ground (emphasis in original).

127. Wolfson, *Philosophical Pathos*, pp. 201–202.

128. Taubes, *Die Korrespondenz mit Jacob Taubes 1952*, §241, p. 219 (emphasis in original).

129. Friedrich Hölderlin, *Poems and Fragments*, translated by Michael Hamburger (Cambridge: Cambridge University Press, 1980), pp. 604–605 (translation slightly modified).

130. Martin Heidegger, *Erläuterungen zu Hölderlins Dichtung* [GA 4] (Frankfurt am Main: Vittorio Klostermann, 1981), p. 165; idem, *Elucidation of Hölderlin's Poetry*, translated by Keith Hoeller (Amherst, NY: Humanity Books, 2000), p. 190 (emphasis in original). I have previously cited this passage in Elliot R. Wolfson, *Suffering Time: Philosophical, Kabbalistic, and Ḥasidic Reflections on Temporality* (Leiden: Brill, 2021), pp. 580–581, and in idem, *Philosophical Pathos*, p. 234, where I emphasized the affinities between Heidegger's interpretation of Hölderlin and the blurring between life and death expressed by Susan Taubes.

131. Walter Benjamin, *Gesammelte Schriften*, 2.1, edited by Rolf Tiedemann and Hermann Schweppenhäuser (Frankfurt am Main: Suhrkamp, 1991), pp. 96–97; idem, *Selected Writings*, vol. 1: *1913–1926*, edited by Marcus Bullock and Michael W. Jennings (Cambridge, MA: Harvard University Press, 1996), pp. 10–11.

132. Benjamin, *Gesammelte Schriften*, 2.1, pp. 97–98; idem, *Selected Writings*, vol. 1, pp. 11–12.

133. In his interpretation of Benjamin's text, Yotam Hotam, *Critiques of Theology: German-Jewish Intellectuals and the Religious Sources of Secular Thought* (Albany: State University of New York Press, 2023), pp. 69–70, emphasized the "stark distinction" between the eternal and the timeless, on the one hand, and the linear and the worldly, on the other hand.

134. Benjamin, *Gesammelte Schriften*, 2.1, pp. 97–98; idem, *Selected Writings*, vol. 1, p. 11 (emphasis in original).

135. Benjamin, *Gesammelte Schriften*, 2.1, p. 98; idem, *Selected Writings*, vol. 1, p. 11 (emphasis in original).

136. Benjamin, *Gesammelte Schriften*, 2.1, pp. 92–93; idem, *Selected Writings*, vol. 1, p. 7.

137. Benjamin, *Gesammelte Schriften*, 2.1, p. 98; idem, *Selected Writings*, vol. 1, p. 12.

138. Benjamin, *Gesammelte Schriften*, 2.1, p. 99; idem, *Selected Writings*, vol. 1, pp. 12–13.

139. See Martin Heidegger, *Die Grundprobleme der Phänomenologie* [GA 24] (Frankfurt am Main: Vittorio Klostermann, 1997), pp. 323–324; idem, *The Basic*

Problems of Phenomenology, translation, introduction, and lexicon by Albert Hofstadter (Bloomington: Indiana University Press, 1982), p. 228.

140. This would mark another similarity between Benjamin and Heidegger. Regarding the latter's distinction between the mortality of the animal and the death of the human, see ch. 3 at n. 63.

141. Benjamin, *Gesammelte Schriften*, 2.1, p. 100; idem, *Selected Writings*, vol. 1, p. 13.

142. Benjamin, *Gesammelte Schriften*, 2.1, p. 102; idem, *Selected Writings*, vol. 1, p. 15.

143. Benjamin, *Gesammelte Schriften*, 2.1, p. 103; idem, *Selected Writings*, vol. 1, pp. 15–16.

144. Walter Benjamin, *Gesammelte Schriften*, 1.2, edited by Rolf Tiedemann and Herman Schweppenhäuser (Frankfurt am Main: Suhrkamp, 1991), p. 694; idem, *Selected Writings*, vol. 4: *1938–1940*, edited by Howard Eiland and Michael W. Jennings, translated by Edmund Jephcott and others (Cambridge, MA: Harvard University Press, 2003), p. 390: "Of course only a redeemed mankind is granted the fullness of its past—which is to say, only for a redeemed mankind has its past become citable in all its moments. Each moment it has lived becomes a *citation à l'ordre du jour*. And that day is Judgment Day." An especially evocative passage is found in Walter Benjamin, *Gesammelte Schriften*, 5.1, edited by Rolf Tiedemann (Frankfurt am Main: Suhrkamp, 1991), pp. 588–589; idem, *The Arcades Project*, translated by Howard Eiland and Kevin McLaughlin (Cambridge, MA: Harvard University Press, 1999), p. 471. In response to the question of the incompleteness of history raised in Horkheimer's letter of March 16, 1937, Benjamin wrote:

> The corrective to this line of thinking may be found in the consideration that history is not simply a science [*Wissenschaft*] but also and not least a form of remembrance [*Eingedenken*]. What science has "determined," remembrance can modify. Such mindfulness can make the incomplete (happiness) into something complete, and the complete (suffering) into something incomplete. That is theology; but in remembrance we have an experience that forbids us to conceive of history as fundamentally atheological, little as it may be granted us to try to write it with immediately theological concepts.

I previously cited a portion of this passage in Wolfson, *Suffering Time*, p. 613. For additional references to Benjamin's notion of historical writing as an act of futural remembering, see ch. 3 n. 148. On Benjamin's philosophy of memory, shaped in part by the nonlinearity and noncausality of Proust's pattern of literary weaving, see Nathan Ross, *Walter Benjamin's First Philosophy: Experience, Ephemerality and Truth* (New York: Routledge, 2021), pp. 50–54.

145. See Benjamin, *Gesammelte Schriften*, 5.1, pp. 595; idem, *Arcades Project*, p. 476:

The events surrounding the historian, and in which he himself takes part, will underlie his presentation in the form of a text written in invisible ink. The history which he lays before the reader comprises, as it were, the citations occurring in this text, and it is only these citations that occur in a manner legible to all. To write history thus means to *cite* history. It belongs to the concept of citation, however, that the historical object in each case is torn from its context (emphasis in original).

Compare Benjamin E. Sax, *Winged Words: Benjamin, Rosenzweig, and the Life of Quotation* (Leiden: Brill, 2023), p. 111:

Quotations in the writing of philosophy enter into history and into experience (*Erlebnis*) by continually being in the process of *being read, being interpreted, being reinterpreted, and being revised*. For Benjamin, this process should not be confused with an aesthetic one, which takes place in the realm of empirical experience (*Erfahrung*). In other words, the act of writing is never actually *seen*, but rather, as stated above, is in the process of *being read, being interpreted, being reinterpreted, and being revised*, and the *Jetztzeit* remains pointed to a future rather than committed to a present (emphasis in original).

146. Hannah Arendt, "Introduction—Walter Benjamin: 1892–1940," in Walter Benjamin, *Illuminations*, edited and with an introduction by Hannah Arendt, translated by Harry Zohn (New York: Schocken Books, 1969), p. 38:

Insofar as the past has been transmitted as tradition, it possesses authority; insofar as authority presents itself historically, it becomes tradition. Walter Benjamin knew that the break in tradition and the loss of authority which occurred in his lifetimes were irreparable, and he concluded that he had to discover new ways of dealing with the past. In this he became a master when he discovered that the transmissibility of the past had been replaced by its citability and that in place of its authority there had arisen a strange power to settle down, piecemeal, in the present and to deprive it of "peace of mind," the mindless peace of complacency.

See the more recent analysis in Sax, *Winged Words*, pp. 58–59, 177–178, 190–198.

147. Taubes, *Die Korrespondenz mit Jacob Taubes 1952*, §164, p. 76.

148. The description of God as the plenitudinal void has resonance with some of the insights of quantum physics. For a clear exposition of this very thorny topic, see James Owen Weatherall, *Void: The Strange Physics of Nothing* (New Haven: Yale University Press, 2016). And compare the blunt remark offered by Quentin Smith, "The Uncaused Beginning of the Universe," in *Theism, Atheism, and Big Bang Cosmology*, edited by William Lane Craig and Quentin Smith (Oxford: Clarendon Press, 1993), p. 135:

The fact of the matter is that the most reasonable belief is that we came from nothing, by nothing and for nothing. With some exceptions, such as Stephen

Hawking, thinkers are too often adversely affected by Heidegger's dread of "the nothing". We should instead acknowledge our foundation in nothingness and feel awe at the marvellous fact that we have a chance to participate briefly in this incredible sunburst that interrupts without reason the reign of non-being.

Bracketing the woefully inadequate presentation of Heidegger's speculation on the nothing, I accept Smith's summary of the repercussions of the big bang cosmology. In some of my previous publications, I have taken small steps to put the kabbalistic speculation on the nothingness of infinity in conversation with notions of the void and the nothingness of matter proclaimed by quantum physicists as well as the Buddhist teaching of nonduality and the indiscriminate emptiness (*śūnyatā*) that is the discriminated thusness (*tathātā*) of all that exists. See Wolfson, *A Dream*, pp. 287–288 n. 30; idem, *Heidegger and Kabbalah*, p. 166; idem, *Suffering Time*, pp. 220–221 n. 435. I have discussed other features of quantum physics that are germane to the study of Jewish mysticism, but this is not the place to elaborate.

149. Many have opined on this topic. See, for instance, Benjamin D. Crowe, *Heidegger's Religious Origins: Destruction and Authenticity* (Bloomington: Indiana University Press, 2006); idem, *Heidegger's Phenomenology of Religion: Realism and Cultural Criticism* (Bloomington: Indiana University Press, 2008); Ben Vedder, *Heidegger's Philosophy of Religion: From God to the Gods* (Pittsburgh: Duquesne University Press, 2007). See below n. 154.

150. See reference above in n. 38. Susan's nascent comments on Heidegger's atheology anticipated the views developed at greater length by a number of scholars. See Robert S. Gall, *Beyond Theism and Atheism: Heidegger's Significance for Religious Thinking* (Dordrecht: Kluwer Academic, 1987); George Kovacs, *The Question of God in Heidegger's Phenomenology* (Evanston: Northwestern University Press, 1990), pp. 47–53, 201–216; Laurence Paul Hemming, *Heidegger's Atheism: The Refusal of a Theological Voice* (Notre Dame: University of Notre Dame Press, 2002).

151. Taubes, *Die Korrespondenz mit Jacob Taubes 1952*, §162, p. 72.

152. Ibid., p. 73 n. 2.

153. Heidegger, *Being and Time*, §44, p. 220. Original German in idem, *Sein und Zeit*, p. 229: "Die Behauptung 'ewiger Wahrheiten', ebenso wie die Vermengung der phänomenal gegründeten 'Idealität' des Daseins mit einem idealisierten absoluten Subjekt gehören zu den längst noch nicht radikal ausgetriebenen Resten von christlicher Theologie innerhalb der philosophischen Problematik."

154. Many interpreters of Heidegger have emphasized the impact of Christian theological training on his thought. For select references, see Wolfson, *Giving*, pp. 309 n. 57, 310–311 n. 58, 352–353 n. 391, 437 nn. 29, 31; idem, *Duplicity*, p. 225 n. 256; idem, *Philosophical Pathos*, pp. 351–352 n. 45.

155. I have cited the German text as it is transcribed in Martin Heidegger, *Hölderlins Hymnen "Germanien" und "Der Rhein"* [GA 39] (Frankfurt am Main:

Vittorio Klostermann, 1999), pp. 209–210, and the English translation as it appears in Martin Heidegger, *Hölderlin's Hymns "Germania" and "The Rhine,"* translated by William McNeill and Julia Ireland (Bloomington: Indiana University Press, 2014), p. 191. For a variant version and translation, see Hölderlin, *Poems and Fragments*, pp. 450–451.

156. Heidegger, *Hölderlins Hymnen*, p. 210; idem, *Hölderlin's Hymns*, p. 192.

157. German text in Heidegger, *Hölderlins Hymnen*, p. 211; and English translation in idem, *Hölderlin's Hymns*, p. 192. For an alternative translation, see Hölderlin, *Poems and Fragments*, p. 177. The critical expression "Gottes Fehl" is rendered by Hamburger as "God's being missed."

158. Heidegger, *Hölderlins Hymnen*, p. 211; idem, *Hölderlin's Hymns*, p. 192.

159. Heidegger, *Hölderlins Hymnen*, p. 232; idem, *Hölderlin's Hymns*, p. 212 (emphasis in original)

160. Elliot R. Wolfson, "*Gottwesen* and the De-Divinization of the Last God: Heidegger's Meditation on the Strange and Incalculable," in *Heidegger's Black Notebooks and the Future of Theology*, edited by Mårten Björk and Jayne Svenungsson (New York: Palgrave Macmillan, 2017), pp. 211–255, esp. 215, 223–224.

161. Taubes, *Die Korrespondenz mit Jacob Taubes 1952*, §164, p. 76.

162. On this Heideggerian motif and citation of primary sources, see Wolfson, *Giving*, pp. 243–244; idem, *Heidegger and Kabbalah*, pp. 35–40; idem, *Suffering Time*, pp. 61–62, 70, 357–358, 569 n. 160, 593. See ch. 3 n. 146.

163. Taubes, *Die Korrespondenz mit Jacob Taubes 1950–1951*, §12, p. 44.

164. Ibid., §21, p. 64 (emphasis in original). The comment appears as part of Susan's description of Romano Guardini's *Theologische Gebete* (1944) in a letter to Jacob written on October 24, 1950.

165. Schürmann, *Broken Hegemonies*, p. 231 (emphasis in original).

166. Ibid., pp. 145–151. See the passage from Schürmann cited above in n. 57.

167. Compare Mary Jeanne Larrabee, "There's No Time Like the Present: How to Mind the Now," in *The Many Faces of Time*, edited by John B. Brough and Lester Embree (Dordrecht: Kluwer Academic, 2000), pp. 85–111.

168. Taubes, *Die Korrespondenz mit Jacob Taubes 1952*, §230, p. 200.

169. On Susan's understanding of the holy and the role of the religious symbol, see Wolfson, *Philosophical Pathos*, pp. 50–51.

170. Taubes, *Die Korrespondenz mit Jacob Taubes 1950–1951*, §17, pp. 57–58. I am here repeating part of my analysis of this passage in Wolfson, *Philosophical Pathos*, pp. 74–75.

171. The formulation is appropriated from Eva Brann, *What, Then, Is Time?* (Lanham: Rowman & Littlefield, 1999), pp. 189–216.

172. Heidegger, *Sein und Zeit*, §65, pp. 328–329; idem, *Being and Time*, p. 314. See Wolfson, *Duplicity*, pp. 90–91; idem, *Heidegger and Kabbalah*, pp. 45–46, 60 n. 136, 263–265; idem, *Suffering Time*, pp. 14–17.

173. Martin Heidegger, *Unterwegs zur Sprache* [GA 12] (Frankfurt am Main: Vittorio Klostermann, 1985), pp. 201–202; idem, *On the Way to Language*, translated by Peter D. Hertz (New York: Harper & Row, 1971), p. 106. It is of interest to compare Heidegger's perspective with the following account of the experience of time engendered in the relationship between habitus and the social world, that is, between the dispositions to be and to do and the regularities of the natural and social cosmos, offered by Pierre Bourdieu, *Pascalian Meditations*, translated by Richard Nice (Stanford: Stanford University Press, 2000), p. 210:

> The present is the set of those things to which one is present, in other words, in which one is interested. . . . It therefore cannot be reduced to a momentary instant . . . it encompasses the practical anticipations and retrospections that are inscribed as objective potentialities or traces in the immediate given. Habitus is that presence of the past in the present which makes possible the presence in the present of the forth-coming. . . . The autonomy with respect to the immediate event, a trigger rather than a determinant, that is given by habitus . . . is correlative with the dependence on the past that it introduces and which orients one towards a certain forth-coming: habitus combines in a single aim a past and a forth-coming neither of which posited is as such. The already-present-forth-coming can be read in the present only on the basis of a past that is itself never aimed at as such (habitus as incorporated acquisition being a presence of the past—or to the past—and not a memory of the past).

174. Susan's understanding of nostalgia is based on the etymological combination of returning home (*nostos*) and the personification of pain (*algos*). See Taubes, *Die Korrespondenz mit Jacob Taubes 1950–1951*, §75, p. 179, and discussion in Wolfson, *Philosophical Pathos*, pp. 84–85.

175. Taubes, *Die Korrespondenz mit Jacob Taubes 1950–1951*, §13, p. 47 (emphasis in original). The passage appears as well in ibid., §127, p. 255.

176. Ibid., §4, p. 21.

177. Taubes, *Die Korrespondenz mit Jacob Taubes 1952*, §156, p. 64.

178. Ibid. For the critique of the Zionism implied in this letter, see my previous citation and analysis in Wolfson, *Philosophical Pathos*, pp. 125–126.

179. See the survey by M. Joshua Mozersky, "Presentism," in *The Oxford Handbook of Philosophy of Time*, edited by Craig Callender (Oxford: Oxford University Press, 2011), pp. 122–144, and the detailed study by Dean Zimmerman, "Presentism and the Space-Time Manifold," op. cit., pp. 163–244.

180. For an extended discussion of this phenomenological chronology, see Wolfson, *Suffering Time*, pp. 9–26.

181. Taubes, *Die Korrespondenz mit Jacob Taubes 1950–1951*, §193, pp. 134–135.

182. Taubes, *Die Korrespondenz mit Jacob Taubes 1952*, §193, p. 130 (emphasis in original).

183. Ibid.

184. Consider Susan's language in a letter to her father, cited in Pareigis, *Susan Taubes*, p. 132, from *Briefe an Sandor S. Feldman 1945–1952*, Susan Taubes Archiv 125, *Zentrum für Literatur- und Kulturforschung Berlin*:

> Forget about the whole thing don't write me to be "average" that's a nonexistent abstraction. I am what I am, live, full of interest + spontaneity—I am one thing today + another tomorrow, + so are you. I dislike some things, try to remove disturbances when there is a possibility of removing them. I get annoyed at groups of people who lower the level of our existence physically or spiritually. I have many moods both joyous + gloomy. What do you want. Don't analyze me.

185. The text is cited in Pareigis, *Susan Taubes*, p. 9, from *Budapest Journal. Reise-Tagebuch September-Oktober 1969*, Susan Taubes Archiv 103, *Zentrum für Literatur- und Kulturforschung Berlin*.

186. See above at n. 38.

187. Taubes, *Die Korrespondenz mit Jacob Taubes 1952*, §217, pp. 171–172.

188. Ibid., §164, p. 76.

189. See Wolfson, *Philosophical Pathos*, pp. 42–43.

190. Taubes, *Die Korrespondenz mit Jacob Taubes 1952*, §202, p. 146.

191. Taubes, *Lament for Julia*, p. 61.

192. Taubes, *Die Korrespondenz mit Jacob Taubes 1952*, §198, p. 140.

193. Ibid., pp. 140–141.

194. Heidegger, *Sein und Zeit*, §50, pp. 250–251; idem, *Being and Time*, pp. 240–241.

195. Heidegger, *Sein und Zeit*, §47, p. 240; idem, *Being and Time*, p. 231.

196. Heidegger, *Sein und Zeit*, §65, p. 329; idem, *Being and Time*, p. 314.

197. Heidegger, *Sein und Zeit*, §69, p. 350; idem, *Being and Time*, p. 334. Compare Heidegger, *Zum Wesen*, p. 40: "Die Zeitigung der Zeit ist nicht ein bloßer Ablauf, ein Fluß und Ab-fluß des Nacheinander, kein unbestimmter 'Prozeß', sondern durch und durch ekstatisch—*über*greifend und *zurück*haltend und nur aus dem Ereignungswesen des Ereignisses und der Ab-gründigkeit des Seyns zu denken" (emphasis in original). English translation in Heidegger, *On the Essence*, p. 34: "The temporalization of time is not a mere sequence, current, effluent of succession, nor an indeterminate 'process,' rather it is ecstatic through and through—encroaching *beyond* and yet holding *back* and it can only be thought from the essence of the essential prevailing of the event and the abyssal aspect of beyng" (emphasis in original). See Joan Stambaugh's presentation of Heidegger's perspective cited in ch. 3 n. 147, and compare references to my own work cited above in n. 172. On the psychological implications of a temporality oriented toward the past in Heidegger's analysis of anxiety in *Being and Time*, see Petr Kouba, *The Phenomenon of Mental*

Disorder: Perspectives of Heidegger's Thought in Psychopathology (Cham: Springer, 2006), pp. 76–89. See the discussion in ch. 3 at nn. 139–142.

198. Compare Heidegger, *Sein und Zeit*, § 65, pp. 325–326; idem, *Being and Time*, p. 311: "Only because Dasein in general *is* as I *am*-having-been, can it come futurally toward itself in such a way that it comes-*back*. Authentically futural, Dasein is authentically *having-been*. . . . Dasein can *be* authentically having-been only because it is futural" (emphasis in original). And see Heidegger, *Sein und Zeit*, § 74, p. 385; idem, *Being and Time*, p. 366: "*Only a being that is essentially futural in its being so that it can let itself be thrown back upon its factical there, free for its death and shattering itself on it, that is, only a being that, as futural, is equiprimordially having been, can hand down to itself its inherited possibility, take over its own thrownness and be* **in the Moment** *for 'its time.' Only authentic temporality that is at the time finite makes something like fate, that is, authentic historicity, possible*" (emphasis in original).

199. See Wolfson, *Heidegger and Kabbalah*, pp. 38–39.

200. See above at nn. 129–130.

201. Taubes, *Die Korrespondenz mit Jacob Taubes 1952*, §181, p. 103. For my previous citation and analysis of this passage, see Wolfson, *Philosophical Pathos*, pp. 173–174.

202. Taubes, *Die Korrespondenz mit Jacob Taubes 1952*, §232, p. 204 (emphasis in original).

203. See the text of Levinas cited in ch. 3 at n. 203 and the reference to Edith Wyschogrod mentioned in the accompanying note.

204. Taubes, *Die Korrespondenz mit Jacob Taubes 1950–1951*, §24, p. 71.

205. Taubes, *Die Korrespondenz mit Jacob Taubes 1952*, §156, p. 62.

206. Ibid., p. 64. See my previous citation and analysis of this passage in Wolfson, *Philosophical Pathos*, pp. 270–271.

207. Taubes, *Die Korrespondenz mit Jacob Taubes 1952*, §142, p. 38.

208. Ibid., §148, p. 48: "It is strange to be without you, it is on the one hand 'illegitimate' to enjoy the freedom of solitude and the security of belonging to you at the same time; + sometimes, unbearable to experience at the same time, the anguish of solitude and the anguish of togetherness, of love which at the very best is <u>as</u> strong <u>as</u> death but no more—and where are we then?"

209. Compare the lines from the poem "Post Apocalypse" in ibid., §266, p. 255 n. 2: "After we have tasted death how shall we taste / any other thing? // A great shudder we felt at the instant of unveiling / Our faces peeled off, face to face with the faceless."

210. For a more extended discussion, see the chapter "Facing the Faceless: Poetic Truth, Temporal Oblivion, and the Silence of Death," in Wolfson, *Philosophical Pathos*, pp. 226–280.

211. Taubes, *Die Korrespondenz mit Jacob Taubes 1952*, §193, p. 130. For previous citation and analysis of this passage, see Wolfson, *Philosophical Pathos*, pp. 193–194.

212. Schürmann, *Broken Hegemonies*, p. 149.

213. Martin Heidegger, *Identity and Difference*, translated and with an introduction by Joan Stambaugh (New York: Harper & Row, 1969), p. 73.

214. Ibid., p. 142.

215. Heidegger, *Sein und Zeit*, §34, p. 165; idem, *Being and Time*, p. 159. Congruent with my approach is the attempt to view Heidegger's later reflections on language as having roots in the notion of the world he enunciated in *Being and Time* offered by Gianni Vattimo, *Beyond the Subject: Nietzsche, Heidegger, and Hermeneutics*, translated, edited, and with an introduction by Peter Carravetta (Albany: State University of New York Press, 2019), pp. 35–48.

216. Heidegger, *Sein und Zeit*, §34, p. 165; idem, *Being and Time*, p. 159.

217. Heidegger, *Sein und Zeit*, §56, p. 273; idem, *Being and Time*, p. 263 (emphasis in original).

218. Heidegger, *Überlegungen II–VI*, p. 16; idem, *Ponderings II–VI*, p. 13 (emphasis in original).

219. Heidegger, *Überlegungen II–VI*, p. 68; idem, *Ponderings II–VI*, p. 52.

220. Heidegger, *Überlegungen II–VI*, p. 34; idem, *Ponderings II–VI*, p. 26.

221. Heidegger, *Überlegungen II–VI*, p. 52; idem, *Ponderings II–VI*, p. 40 (emphasis in original).

222. Martin Heidegger, *Sein und Wahrheit* [GA 36/37] (Frankfurt am Main: Vittorio Klostermann, 2001), p. 107; idem, *Being and Truth*, translated by Gregory Fried and Richard Polt (Bloomington: Indiana University Press, 2001), pp. 84–85.

223. Martin Heidegger, *Beiträge zur Philosophie (Vom Ereignis)* [GA 65] (Frankfurt am Main: Vittorio Klostermann, 1989), §37, p. 79; idem, *Contributions to Philosophy (Of the Event)*, translated by Richard Rojcewicz and Daniela Vallega-Neu (Bloomington: Indiana University Press, 2012), p. 63. For previous discussions of this dimension of Heidegger's thought, see Niall Keane, "The Silence of the Origin: Philosophy in Transition and the Essence of Thinking," *Research in Phenomenology* 43 (2013): 27–48; Richard Polt, "The Secret Homeland of Speech: Heidegger on Language, 1933–1934," in *Heidegger and Language*, edited by Jeffrey Powell (Bloomington: Indiana University Press, 2013), pp. 63–85, esp. 65–70; idem, *Time and Trauma: Thinking Through Heidegger in the Thirties* (London: Rowman & Littlefield, 2019), pp. 92–103; Elliot R. Wolfson, "Heidegger's Apophaticism: Unsaying the Said and the Silence of the Last God," in *Contemporary Debates in Negative Theology and Philosophy*, edited by Nahum Brown and J. Aaron Simmons (New York: Palgrave, 2017), pp. 185–216; idem, *Duplicity*, pp. 109–130, and references cited on pp. 243 n. 25 and 245 n. 42; idem, *Heidegger and Kabbalah*, pp. 299–302, 307–311, and references cited on p. 322 nn. 13 and 17; Wanda Torres Gregory, *Speaking of Silence in Heidegger* (Lanham: Lexington Books, 2021).

224. Heidegger, *Beiträge*, §38, p. 79; idem, *Contributions*, p. 63 (emphasis in original). On the identification of the stillness of silence as the origin or fore-word (*Vor-*

wort) of language, see Heidegger, *Zum Wesen*, pp. 58–59; idem, *On the Essence*, pp. 49–50.

225. Heidegger, *Zum Wesen*, pp. 60–61; idem, *On the Essence*, p. 52.
226. Heidegger, *Unterwegs*, p. 26; idem, *Poetry*, p. 206.
227. Heidegger, *Zum Wesen*, p. 73; idem, *On the Essence*, p. 59.
228. See Heidegger, *Unterwegs*, pp. 158–159, 162–163; idem, *On the Way*, pp. 65–66, 69. On the Heideggerian *Gelassenheit*, see ch. 4 n. 197.
229. Heidegger, *Unterwegs*, p. 220; idem, *On the Way*, p. 151. The poet's repudiation of the representational role of language—a semantic objectivism predicated on the presumed correlation between the words we use to name objects and the objects that exist in the world outside consciousness (Claude Romano, *At the Heart of Reason*, translated by Michael B. Smith and Claude Romano [Evanston: Northwestern University Press, 2015], pp. 90–91)—parallels Heidegger's criticism of understanding thinking primarily as a mode of conceptual and systematic apprehension. See Martin Heidegger, *Was Heißt Denken?* [GA 8] (Frankfurt am Main: Vittorio Klostermann, 2002), p. 215:

> Das Denken ist demnach kein Greifen, weder ein Zugriff auf das Vorliegende, noch ein Angriff dagegen. Das Vorliegende wird im λέγειν und νοεῖν nicht mit Griffen be-arbeitet. Das Denken ist kein Be-greifen. In der hohen Frühe seiner Wesensentfaltung kennt das Denken nicht den Begriff. . . . Aber das gesamte große Denken der griechischen Denker, Aristoteles eingeschlossen, denkt begrifflos.

English version in idem, *What Is Called Thinking?*, translated by Fred W. Wieck and J. Glenn Gray, with an introduction by J. Glenn Gray (New York: Harper & Row, 1968), pp. 211–212:

> Thinking, then, is not a grasping, neither the grasp of what lies before us, nor an attack upon it. In λέγειν and νοεῖν, what lies before us is not manipulated by means of grasping. Thinking is not grasping or prehending. In the high youth of its unfolding essence, thinking knows nothing of the grasping concept. . . . But all of the great thinking of the Greek thinkers, including Aristotle, thinks non-conceptually.

See Rudolf Bernet, "The Limits of Conceptual Thinking," *Journal of Speculative Philosophy* 28 (2014): 219–241, esp. 234–235. On the role of the nonconceptual in Adorno, see ch. 2 n. 27.

230. Martin Heidegger, *Vorträge und Aufsätze* [GA 7] (Frankfurt am Main: Vittorio Klostermann, 2000), pp. 167–187; idem, *Poetry*, pp. 165–186. See Wolfson, *Heidegger and Kabbalah*, p. 139, and references cited on p. 175 n. 18.
231. Heidegger, *Unterwegs*, p. 158; idem, *On the Way*, p. 65.
232. Heidegger, *Hölderlins Hymnen*, p. 223; idem, *Hölderlin's Hymns*, p. 203.

233. Heidegger, *Unterwegs*, p. 241; idem, *On the Way*, p. 122.

234. Heidegger, *Unterwegs*, pp. 241–242; idem, *On the Way*, p. 122.

235. On occasion, Heidegger does advocate for understanding the unspoken in this manner as we can see in the following passage from "Das Wesen der Sprache" in Heidegger, *Unterwegs*, p. 151, translated in idem, *On the Way*, p. 59:

> But when does language speak itself as language? Curiously enough, when we cannot find the right word for something that concerns us, carries us away, oppresses or encourages us. Then we leave unspoken what we have in mind and, without rightly giving it thought, undergo moments in which language itself has distantly and fleetingly touched us with its essential being.

The widespread experience described by Heidegger is something that puts us in touch with the unspoken, which is the essential being of language, but the unspoken itself names the mystery of the unsaid that is withheld in every act of saying and not only in the instance of a person who is not able to conjure the right words to express what he or she is thinking or feeling. The two connotations are brought together in the following passage from "Der Weg zur Sprache" in Heidegger, *Unterwegs*, p. 240, translated in idem, *On the Way*, p. 120: "Everything spoken stems in a variety of ways from the unspoken, whether this be something not yet spoken, or whether it be what must remain unspoken in the sense that it is beyond the reach of speaking." Even though Heidegger is not always consistent, overall it is accurate to conclude that these two options merge in the insight that the unspoken is what endures as the not yet spoken that is beyond the parameter of speech just as the unthought is what endures as the not yet thought that is beyond the horizon of thinking.

236. Heidegger, *Unterwegs*, p. 187; idem, *On the Way*, p. 92. In that context, Heidegger utilizes the symbol of the Tao in Laotse's poetic thinking to illumine the nature of the mystery of mysteries whereby what is spoken preserves the unspoken. On Heidegger's engagement with Taoism, see sources cited in Wolfson, *Heidegger and Kabbalah*, pp. 82 n. 1 and 232–233 n. 10, to which we can now add the collection of essays *Daoist Resonances in Heidegger: Exploring a Forgotten Debt*, edited by David Chai (London: Bloomsbury Academic, 2022), and Eric S. Nelson, *Heidegger and Dao: Things, Nothingness, Freedom* (London: Bloomsbury Academic, 2024).

237. Heidegger, *Wegmarken*, pp. 194–195; idem, *Pathmarks*, p. 149. On the interpretation of *Geheimnis* in Heidegger as a way of thinking the *Einkehr in das Ereignis*, the return to the event, which is a *Heimkehr*, a returning home or a homecoming, see David Michael Kleinberg-Levin, *Critical Studies on Heidegger: The Emerging Body of Understanding* (Albany: State University of New York Press, 2023), pp. 164–168.

238. Heidegger, *Unterwegs*, pp. 242, 246; idem, *On the Way*, pp. 123, 126.

239. Heidegger, *Unterwegs*, pp. 243, 246; idem, *On the Way*, pp. 124, 126 (emphasis in original).

240. Heidegger, *Unterwegs*, pp. 151–152; idem, *On the Way*, p. 59. Regarding the assertion that the "single poem" (*einzige Gedicht*) to which the "great poet" (*große Dichter*) gives expression sustains that which remains unspoken (*ungesprochen*), see Heidegger, *Unterwegs*, p. 33; idem, *On the Way*, p. 160. See also the comment about our mission with respect to Hölderlin's poetry in "Wozu Dichter?" (1946) in Heidegger, *Holzwege*, pp. 273–274; idem, *Poetry*, p. 96: "But there would be, and there is, the sole necessity, by thinking our way soberly into what his poetry says, to come to learn what is unspoken. That is the course of the history of Being. If we reach and enter that course, it will lead thinking into a dialogue with poetry, a dialogue that is of the history of Being [*dann bringt sie das Denken in eine seinsgeschichtliche Zwiesprache mit dem Dichten*]."

241. Heidegger, *Unterwegs*, p. 67; idem, *On the Way*, p. 188.

242. Heidegger, *Unterwegs*, p. 66; idem, *On the Way*, p. 188.

243. On the Eckhartian *abegescheidenheit*, see Markus Vinzent, *The Art of Detachment* (Leuven: Peeters, 2011), and references to other scholars cited in Elliot R. Wolfson, "Patriarchy and the Motherhood of God in Zoharic Kabbalah and Meister Eckhart," in *Envisioning Judaism: Studies in Honor of Peter Schäfer on the Occasion of His Seventieth Birthday*, edited by Ra'anan S. Boustan, Klaus Hermann, Reimund Leicht, Annette Yoshiko Reed, and Giuseppe Veltri, with the collaboration of Alex Ramos (Tübingen: Mohr Siebeck, 2013), p. 1063 n. 52. On detachment and the inculcation of the eternal within the temporal, see ibid., p. 1070 and references to other scholars cited in n. 88. For the traces of the ideal of *Abgeschiedenheit* in Heidegger, see John D. Caputo, *The Mystical Element in Heidegger's Thought* (Athens: Ohio State University Press, 1978), pp. 28–29, 144–145, 177–178; Sonya Sikka, *Forms of Transcendence: Heidegger and Medieval Mystical Theology* (Albany: State University of New York Press, 1997), pp. 133–134; Sean J. McGrath, *The Early Heidegger and Medieval Philosophy: Phenomenology for the Godforsaken* (Washington, DC: Catholic University Press, 2006), pp. 134, 136–138, 141–142; Ian Alexander Moore, *Eckhart, Heidegger, and the Imperative of Releasement* (Albany: State University of New York Press, 2019), pp. 6–7, 62–67, 75–79, 121, 142–143, 187, 258–259 n. 5, 259–260 n. 3. See the additional sources mentioned in ch. 4 n. 197.

244. Heidegger, *Unterwegs*, p. 67; idem, *On the Way*, p. 188.

245. For analysis of the philosophical feasibility of the effect preceding its cause and the corollary proposition of the possibility of bringing about the past, see Michael Dummett, *Truth and Other Enigmas* (Cambridge, MA: Harvard University Press, 1978), pp. 319–350. The reversal of the timeswerve of which I speak, predicated on a circle that is open at both ends and thus inducing a return to where one has never been, is to be distinguished from the ancient Greek view that since events repeat themselves in the form of a closed circle, what is before from the present standpoint can be considered as after from a future standpoint. Compare Henri-Charles Puech, "Gnosis and Time," in *Man and Time: Papers from the Eranos Year-*

books (New York: Bollingen Foundation, 1957), pp. 40–44. As Puech noted, p. 42, this perspective was stated explicitly in the pseudo-Aristotelian *Problemata* 17.2, 916 ᵃ1, 18–38. See *The Complete Works of Aristotle: The Revised Oxford Translation*, edited by Jonathan Barnes (Princeton: Princeton University Press, 1984), p. 1426:

> In what sense must we understand the terms "prior" and "posterior"? As those who lived in the time of Troy are prior to us, so are those who lived before them prior to them and so on *ad infinitum*? Or since there is a beginning and a middle and an end of the universe, and when a man, as he becomes old, reaches the limit and turns again towards the beginning, that which is nearer to the beginning is earlier, what prevents our being nearer to the beginning than to the end, in which case we should be prior? Just as the course of the firmament and of each of the stars is a circle, why should not also the coming into being and the decay of perishable things be of such a kind that these things again come into being and decay? This agrees with the saying that "human life is a circle". To demand that those who are coming into being should always be numerically identical is foolish, but one would more readily accept that they were identical in kind. And so we should ourselves be prior, and one might suppose the arrangement of the series to be such that it returns back in a circle to the point from which it began and thus secures continuity and identity of composition. For Alcmaeon declares that men perish because they cannot link together the beginning to the end—a clever saying, if one supposes that he uses it metaphorically and the literal meaning is not insisted upon. If then human life is a circle, and a circle has neither beginning nor end, we should not be prior to those who lived in the time of Troy nor they prior to us by being nearer to the beginning.

246. Compare the reference to Mark Taylor's depiction of the "pretext of the text" in Jacques Derrida, *On the Name*, edited by Thomas Dutoit (Stanford: Stanford University Press, 1995), p. 58.

247. Ibid., p. 61.

248. Ibid., p. 49 (emphasis in original).

249. For an innovative discussion of this motif applied to the discourse of graphology and forensic analysis, see Michaela Fišerová, *Event of Signature: Jacques Derrida and Repeating the Unrepeatable* (Albany: State University of New York Press, 2022).

250. Taubes, *Die Korrespondenz mit Jacob Taubes 1950–1951*, §45, p. 122. I am here taking the liberty to repeat my argument in Wolfson, *Philosophical Pathos*, pp. 259–260.

251. Ludwig Wittgenstein, *Tractatus Logico-Philosophicus*, translated by Charles K. Ogden, with an introduction by Bertrand Russell (London: Routledge, 1995), §7, pp. 188–189: "Whereof one cannot speak, thereof one must be silent [*Wovon man nicht sprechen kann, darüber muss man schweigen*]." In the Preface, ibid., pp. 26–27,

Wittgenstein wrote that the whole meaning of the book could be summed up as follows: "What can be said at all can be said clearly; and whereof one cannot speak thereof one must be silent [*Was sich überhaupt sagen lässt, lässt sich klar sagen; und wovon man nicht reden kann, darüber muss man schweigen*]."

252. Taubes, *Die Korrespondenz mit Jacob Taubes 1950–1951*, §66, p. 164. Susan's comment was occasioned by her reading the essay by Alexander Altmann, "Symbol and Myth," *Philosophy* 20 (1945): 162–171. See Wolfson, *Philosophical Pathos*, p. 431 n. 223.

253. Taubes, *Die Korrespondenz mit Jacob Taubes 1950–1951*, §66, p. 164.

254. For references to Scholem's understanding of the symbol, see Wolfson, *Language*, pp. 402–403 n. 57, 407 n. 88.

255. See ibid., pp. 31–42.

256. I am here modifying my interpretation of Susan's comments in her letter from December 26, 1950, which served as the basis for my discussion in Wolfson, *Philosophical Pathos*, pp. 258–259. I did not attend sufficiently to the distinction that she made between allegory and parable in this letter. I was misled by another letter in Taubes, *Die Korrespondenz mit Jacob Taubes 1950–1951*, §40, p. 110. In the context of discussing Schelling's distinction between allegorical and tautogorical meaning, on the one hand, and Heidegger's contrast between the word in its metaphorical and authentic meaning and its allegorical and everyday meaning, on the other hand, Susan wrote,

> Is not there something quite "Kabalistic" (or as least mystic) in conceiving of the empirical as mere "allegory"[?] So that to speak of the "arm" of God is no crude anthropomorphic "projection" but rather the "animal" arm in all its forms is only an echo, a reminiscence, a symbol of the "divine" arm—that is not merely a form, or idea, but more substantial than its physical "copy".

For discussion of this passage, see Wolfson, *Philosophical Pathos*, pp. 247–248. The distinction that Susan attributed to Heidegger and to which she allotted kabbalistic or mystical significance was triggered by the following comment in "Brief über den 'Humanismus,'" in Heidegger, *Wegmarken*, p. 358: "Die Rede vom Haus des Seins ist keine Übertragung des Bildes vom 'Haus' auf das Sein, sondern aus dem sachgemäß gedachten Wesen des Seins werden wir eines Tages eher denken können, was 'Haus' und 'wohnen' sind." English translation in Heidegger, *Pathmarks*, p. 272: "The talk about the house of being is not the transfer of the image 'house' onto being. But one day we will, by thinking the essence of being in a way appropriate to its matter, more readily be able to think what 'house' and 'dwelling' are." I am not certain of the validity of utilizing the words "metaphorical" and "allegorical" to mark the contrast between authentic and everyday meaning, but I take the point that Heidegger seemed to be saying that when we properly think the essence of being, the language that we use to speak about being will be more suitable and disclosive. Finally, mention should be made of Susan's expression "Heidegerian Kabbala." See Taubes, *Die Korrespondenz mit Jacob Taubes 1952*, §141, p. 34, and Wolfson, *Philosophical Pathos*, pp. 7, 427 n. 185.

257. Elliot R. Wolfson, "Becoming Invisible: Rending the Veil and the Hermeneutic of Secrecy in the *Gospel of Philip*," in *Practicing Gnosis: Ritual, Magic, Theurgy and Liturgy in Nag Hammadi, Manichean and Other Ancient Literature: Essays in Honor of Birger A. Pearson*, edited by April D. DeConick, Gregory Shaw, and John D. Turner (Leiden: Brill, 2013), pp. 125–126.

258. See Maurice-Jean Lefebve, "The Nude as Symbol," in *Facets of Eros: Phenomenological Essays*, edited by F. Joseph Smith and Erling Eng (The Hague: Martinus Nijhoff, 1972), pp. 101–115.

259. See above at n. 38.

260. See above at n. 75.

261. On the identification of beyng and nothing, see Heidegger, *Zum Wesen*, pp. 23–24; idem, *On the Essence*, pp. 19–20. For discussion of this theme and citation of other relevant passages, see Wolfson, *Heidegger and Kabbalah*, pp. 97–99, 123 n. 8, 130 n. 130, 137–138, 149, 265; idem, *Philosophical Pathos*, pp. 165, 372 n. 185. Compare the correlation of the event (*Ereignis*) and the nothing (*Nichts*), and the critique of Hegel's dialectical negativity, in Heidegger, *Über den Anfang*, p. 50; idem, *On Inception*, p. 37.

Chapter 2

1. Gillian Rose, *The Broken Middle: Out of Our Ancient Society* (Oxford: Blackwell, 1992), p. 30.

2. Ibid., p. 10.

3. Ibid. For a comprehensive discussion of Rose's Hegelianism, see Andrew Brower Latz, *The Social Philosophy of Gillian Rose* (Eugene: Cascade Books, 2018), pp. 11–95.

4. Regarding this theme, see Paul Ashton, "The Beginning Before the Beginning: Hegel and the Activation of Philosophy," *Cosmos and History: The Journal of Natural and Social Philosophy* 3 (2007): 328–356. Although the work of Rose is not mentioned in this study, the analysis of Hegel resounds with much of her thought, and especially the surmise that Hegel's need to activate philosophy should be evaluated in light of the historical event of the French Revolution and the corollary claim that his speculative thought is the consequence of the relation between philosophy and the freedom procured by political revolution.

5. Rose, *Broken Middle*, p. 56.

6. Ibid., p. 85.

7. Ibid., p. 90.

8. Ibid., pp, 85, 101. On the triangulation of Kierkegaard, Kafka, and Freud, see Andrew Shanks, *Against Innocence: Gillian Rose's Reception and Gift of Faith*, foreword by Giles Fraser (London: SCM Press, 2008), pp. 56–71.

9. Rose, *Broken Middle*, p. 105.
10. Ibid., p. xi.
11. Ibid., p. 3.
12. Ibid., pp. 3–4.
13. Gillian Rose, *Mourning Becomes the Law: Philosophy and Representation* (Cambridge: Cambridge University Press, 1996), p. 64. On the development of Rose's recovery of the theological and political ramifications of the Hegelian analysis of the role of the comic, see Marcus Pound, "Political Theology and Comedy: Žižek Through Rose Tinted Glasses," *Crisis and Critique* 2 (2015): 179–191; idem, "Rose *Contra* Girard: Kenotic Comedy and Social Theory (Or, Žižek as a Reader of Rose)," in *Misrecognitions: Gillian Rose and the Task of Political Theology*, edited by Joshua B. Davis (Eugene: Cascade Books, 2018), pp. 67–86.
14. Georg Wilhelm Friedrich Hegel, *Aesthetics: Lectures on Fine Art*, vol. 2, translated by Thomas Malcom Knox (Oxford: Oxford University Press, 1975), pp. 1198–1200.
15. Ibid., p. 1180.
16. Rose, *Mourning*, p. 64. The passage paraphrased by Rose is in Hegel, *Aesthetics*, p. 1202:

> The comic subjective personality has become the overlord of whatever appears in the real world. From that world the adequate objective presence of fundamental principle has disappeared. When what has no substance in itself has destroyed its show of existence by its own agency, the individual makes himself master of this dissolution too and remains undisturbed in himself and at ease.

17. Hegel, *Aesthetics*, p. 1201.
18. Rose, *Mourning*, p. 64. See the passage of Levinas cited in ch. 3 at n. 197.
19. Georg Wilhelm Friedrich Hegel, *Aesthetics: Lectures on Fine Art*, vol. 1, translated by Thomas Malcom Knox (Oxford: Oxford University Press, 1975), p. 67.
20. Ibid.
21. Ibid. (emphasis in original).
22. Ibid., p. 68.
23. My position can be profitably compared to Vincent Lloyd, *Law and Transcendence: On the Unfinished Project of Gillian Rose* (Hampshire: Palgrave Macmillan, 2009), p. 155:

> The purity of the pure exception results from its unaccountability. Yet the unaccountability of the exception is distinct from the unaccountability that defines transcendence. The exception would only be transcendent if it were a total exception, if every law were suspended at the same moment. But to make the specific claim that, at a particular moment, there are no laws at all, in other words that not only is every possible model in error but no model is better than an-

other, does not slip into transcendence. It acknowledges that the world is made of normative grooves; it just represents a pause from the attempt to match those grooves in our world. The exception does not really suspend the law; it suspends our pretensions to know the law.

See ibid., p. 166:

> Just as there is no total exception, there is never a total revolution. For there to be either, there would have to be a total break between two laws; there would be no chain of accountability whatsoever between them, and there would be transcendence. The significance of this chain of accountability, with its opaque link between regimes, is that the components of the revolutionary law are not totally foreign. They may be quite familiar, but it is their arrangement in a cohesive but non-standard form which is novel.

24. Rose, *Broken Middle*, p. 30.

25. I am here repeating my formulation in Elliot R. Wolfson, *Heidegger and Kabbalah: Hidden Gnosis and the Path of Poiēsis* (Bloomington: Indiana University Press, 2019), p. 63. For an elaboration of this theme and reference to some of the philosophical sources that have influenced my own thinking, see op. cit., pp. 31, 48 n. 8, 62–63, 68–69, 75–82, 87–88 n. 80, 91 n. 119, 93 n. 160, 164, 220–224, 225–228, 256.

26. Compare Schelling's criticism of Hegel briefly referenced in Wolfson, *Heidegger and Kabbalah*, p. 237 n. 74.

27. Theodor W. Adorno, *Negative Dialektik* [GS 6] (Frankfurt am Main: Suhrkamp, 1966), pp. 22, 24, 27; idem, *Negative Dialectics*, translated by E. B. Ashton (New York: Seabury Press, 1973), pp. 10, 12, 15. For citation and analysis of these passages, see Elliot R. Wolfson, *Suffering Time: Philosophical, Kabbalistic, and Ḥasidic Reflections on Temporality* (Leiden: Brill, 2021), pp. 642–644. Compare the text from Heidegger's *Was Heißt Denken?* cited in ch. 1 n. 229.

28. Gillian Rose, *The Melancholy Science: An Introduction to the Thought of Theodor W. Adorno* (London: Macmillan, 1978), p. 8.

29. Adorno, *Negative Dialektik*, p. 31; idem, *Negative Dialectics*, p. 20.

30. Adorno, *Negative Dialektik*, pp. 32–33; idem, *Negative Dialectics*, p. 21.

31. Adorno, *Negative Dialektik*, p. 33; idem, *Negative Dialectics*, p. 22.

32. Maurice Blanchot, *The Writing of Disaster*, translated by Ann Smock (Lincoln: University of Nebraska Press, 1986), p. 61, cited with slight modifications in Rose, *Broken Middle*, pp. 4–5.

33. A concise definition is offered by Franz Rosenzweig, *The Star of Redemption*, translated by Barbara Galli (Madison: University of Wisconsin Press, 2005), p. 308: "In the hour, the moment is therefore turned into that which, when it should have perished, always newly begins again and thus into the imperishable, the *nunc*

stans, eternity." Note that according to this articulation eternity is not antithetical to time but it is rather the iteration of the fullness of time—what Rosenzweig calls the "hour"—as the constant renewal of the moment. This notion of the eternal thus leads to the paradox of novel repetition, that is, each moment is the same because different and different because the same. See Elliot R. Wolfson, *Giving Beyond the Gift: Apophasis and Overcoming Theomania* (New York: Fordham University Press, 2014), pp. 57, 63–64. Concerning this paradox, as expressed particularly by Merleau-Ponty, see Wolfson, *Suffering Time*, pp. 32, 385 n. 27, 573 n. 172.

34. Giorgio Agamben, *What Is an Apparatus? and Other Essays*, translated by David Kishik and Stefan Pedatella (Stanford: Stanford University Press, 2009), p. 41.

35. Ibid., p. 47.

36. See the section "Homogeneity and the Heterogeneous Fluctuation," in Wolfson, *Heidegger and Kabbalah*, pp. 30–32. Also germane to this topic is Agamben's notion of dishomogeneity—the caesura in which the continuous discontinuity of the discontinuous continuity of time is inscribed so that there is an unremitting encounter between past and present—that he elicits from Foucault's interpretation of the Nietzschean idea of genealogy. See Giorgio Agamben, "Philosophical Anthropology," *Law and Critique* 20 (2009): 213, reprinted in idem, *The Signature of All Things: On Method*, translated by Luca D'Isanto with Kevin Attell (New York: Zone Books, 2009), pp. 82–83. See also Giorgio Agamben, *The Use of Bodies*, translated by Adam Kotsko (Stanford: Stanford University Press, 2016), p. 112: "every historical study inevitably runs up against a constitutive dishomogeneity: that between the ensemble of facts and documents on which it labors and a level that we can define as archeological, which though not transcending it, remains irreducible to it and permits its comprehension." Compare Agamben, *What Is an Apparatus?*, p. 52:

> Those who have tried to think about contemporariness have been able to do so only by splitting it up into several times, by introducing into time an essential dishomogeneity. Those who say "*my* time" actually divide time—they inscribe into it a caesura and a discontinuity. But precisely by means of this caesura, this interpolation of the present into the inert homogeneity of linear time, the contemporary puts to work a special relationship between the different times (emphasis in original).

In the continuation of this passage, Agamben links the caesura of the dishomogeneous with the messianic time proclaimed by Paul as the "time of the now" (*ho nyn kairos*), the time of the *parousia* that is chronologically indeterminate, that is, the end that is unquestionably near but whose coming is not calculable. See my previous discussion of this dimension of Agamben's thought in Wolfson, *Suffering Time*, pp. 602–603, and references to other scholars cited on p. 603 n. 98. For various analyses of dishomogeneity in Agamben, see Anke Snoek, "Agamben's Foucault: An Overview," *Foucault Studies* 10 (2010): 62; Ido Govrin, *Philosophical Archaeology: With and Beyond Agamben on Philosophy, History, and Art* (Albany: State University of New York Press, 2023), pp. 5–6, 11–12, 26–27, 33, 78.

37. Gillian Rose, *Love's Work: A Reckoning with Life*, introduction by Michael Wood (New York: New York Review of Books, 2011), p. 70.

38. See above, n. 10.

39. Compare Martin Heidegger, *Vorträge und Aufsätze* [GA 7] (Frankfurt am Main: Vittorio Klostermann, 2000), p. 205. Commenting on Hölderlin's language "der Schatten der Nacht," Heidegger noted, "die Nacht selber ist der Schatten, jenes Dunkle, das nie bloße Finsternis werden kann, weil es als Schatten dem Licht zugetraut, von ihm geworfen bleibt." English translation in Martin Heidegger, *Poetry, Language, Thought*, translations and introduction by Albert Hofstadter (New York: Harper & Row, 1971), p. 226: "the night itself is the shade, that darkness which can never become a mere blackness because as shade it is wedded to light and remains cast by it." See ch. 4 n. 184.

40. The citation is from the final line in the essay "Goethes Wahlverwandtschaften." See Walter Benjamin, *Gesammelte Schriften*, 1.1, edited by Rolf Tiedemann and Herman Schweppenhäuser (Frankfurt am Main: Suhrkamp, 1991), p. 201: "Nur um der Hoffnungslosen willen ist uns die Hoffnung gegeben." English translation "Goethe's Elective Affinities" in Walter Benjamin, *Selected Writings*, vol. 1: *1913–1926*, edited by Marcus Bullock and Michael W. Jennings (Cambridge, MA: Harvard University Press, 1996), p. 356: "Only for the sake of the hopeless ones have we been given hope."

41. Adorno, *Negative Dialektik*, pp. 370–371; idem, *Negative Dialectics*, pp. 377–378. See my previous discussion of this passage in Wolfson, *Suffering Time*, pp. 632–633.

42. Compare Gillian Rose, *Hegel Contra Sociology* (London: Verso, 2009), p. 201. See ibid., pp. 12–13, where Rose offers a more detailed account of the epistemological and the axiological validity of the transcendence of *Sollen* in the thought of Heinrich Rickert:

> Unlike Lotze and Cohen, however, Rickert argued that a judgement is not valid because it affirms or posits what is true, but, on the contrary, it is the prescriptive force of the judgement which confers validity on what we call truth. This prescription which we acknowledge when we make a judgement is "an ought" (*ein Sollen*) or "a value", and the moral connotations of *Sollen* and "value" are retained in this account of judging. In other terms, a judgement does not have a value because it is true, but it acquires truth by force of its value. Value confers both meaning and authority on the judgement, its validity. Rickert claimed that this explication of validity was no more circular than the one it replaced. Validity is thus in no sense derived from the relation of the judgement to empirical

reality, but originates in the validity of the *Sollen*. This validity does not depend on the judging subject or consciousness. For it belongs to the very meaning of affirming a judgement that the prescription which is thereby acknowledged has a validity independent of the act of acknowledgement.... Rickert calls values or *Sollen* both the *criterion* of cognition and the *object* of cognition. This paradox arises because, from the point of view of the judging consciousness, the *Sollen* or value is a criterion, a prescriptive force which confers validity. But judging consciousness is itself only possible because value or *Sollen* is valid independent of the act of judgement. In this sense value or *Sollen* is the object of knowledge (emphasis in original).

On the unjustifiable and unacknowledged *Sollen* in Hegel's thought, see ibid., pp. 84 and 213–217, and see p. 196, where Rose proffered that the role of *Sollen* has informed both right-wing and left-wing Hegelianism.

43. Rose, *Broken Middle*, p. xi (emphasis in original).

44. Tony Gorman, "Gillian Rose and the Project of a Critical Marxism," *Radical Philosophy* 105 (2001): 28–31; Shanks, *Against Innocence*, pp. 41–97. See also Howard Caygill, "The Broken Hegel: Gillian Rose's Retrieval of Speculative Philosophy," *Women: A Cultural Review* 9 (1998): 19–27. For a different approach to the middle as a commitment to unity and tension between the religious ideal and the state, see Clare Greer, "A Critical Conversation Between Gillian Rose and John Milbank and Its Implications for an Aporetic Political Theology," PhD dissertation, University of Manchester, 2011, pp. 121–143.

45. Latz, *Social Philosophy*, pp. 87–93.

46. Ibid., p. 93.

47. Ibid. Latz generously concludes that Rose's "work leans toward therapy rather than solution though it is not without substantive commitments."

48. Many have discussed the signature idea of the broken middle in Rose's later thought. Here I mention only a few representative examples: Rowan D. Williams, "Between Politics and Metaphysics: Reflections in the Wake of Gillian Rose," *Modern Theology* 11 (1995): 3–22; Isobel Armstrong, "Writing from the Broken Middle: The Post-Aesthetic," *Women: A Cultural Review* 9 (1998): 62–96; Anthony Gorman, "Whither the Broken Middle? Rose and Fackenheim on Mourning, Modernity and the Holocaust," in *Social Theory After the Holocaust*, edited by Robert Fine and Charles Turner (Liverpool: Liverpool University Press, 2000), pp. 47–70; Shanks, *Against Innocence*, pp. 36–38, 45–46, 71–72, 77, 90–91, 96–99, 108–110, 140, 141–143, 162–163, 170, 172–174; Latz, *Social Philosophy*, pp. 158–209.

49. Latz, *Social Philosophy*, pp. 100–105.

50. Rose, *Broken Middle*, p. 286.

51. Rose, *Love's Work*, p. 58.

52. Rose, *Melancholy Science*, pp. 56–57.

53. Gillian Rose, *Judaism and Modernity: Philosophical Essays* (Oxford: Blackwell, 1993), p. 5 (emphasis in original).

54. Rose, *Melancholy Science*, p. 139. On pp. 141–142, Rose criticizes Adorno for neglecting to consider more carefully the role of social forms in understanding political organization and the relations of power in capitalist society. Adorno thus finds himself in the same predicament as the voluntarism that he ascribed to Heidegger, that is, the belief that the fulfillment and realization of the human being depends on an act of personal choice, ignoring the power of social and political institutions that circumscribe any possibility of self-determination or autonomy on society. It is beyond the scope of this note to assess Rose's criticism of Adorno or the latter's criticism of Heidegger.

55. This is not the place to discuss in detail Rose's attitude towards feminism. A brief statement on this topic can be found in the radio interview she did with Andy O'Mahony. See Vincent Lloyd, "Interview with Gillian Rose," *Theory, Culture & Society* 25, 7–8 (2008): 215:

> One tends, to think, first of all, that things are happening to you. What you have to discover from unhappy love affairs is your own agency and your own ambivalence. I think some forms of feminism detract from women being able to do that. They teach women that they're oppressed, and they don't encourage women to see their own active involvement in situations where they may indeed be unequal. But you need to see your own involvement in that, commitment in that, in order to move beyond it.

See also Rose, *Love's Work*, pp. 140–141:

> There is one sense in which I do not want to rewrite my history. Even in the earlier version of that history, feminism never offered me any help. For it fails to address the power of women as well as their powerlessness, and the response of both women and men to that power.... Feminism does not discern the beauty of the limitation of such a love in which each is equally teacher and taught, Lover and Beloved.... Feminism does not speak of the woman with the gift and power of Active Intelligence—to speak in terms of Avicenna's angelology—who gives love and draws it to her, enabling and difficult.

The utilization of the Avicennean idea in the context of criticizing feminist thought is fascinating, but I cannot elaborate here. A number of scholars have discussed the criticism of feminism in Rose's thought. For instance, see Liz Stanley, "Mourning Becomes...: The Work of Feminism in the Spaces Between Lives Lived and Lives Written," *Women's Studies International Forum* 25 (2002): 1–17; Vincent Lloyd, "Gillian Rose, Race, and Identity," *Telos* 173 (2015): 109–110, 119; Asaf Angermann, "The Diremption of Love: Gillian Rose on Agency, Mortality, and Hegelian Feminism," *Hypatia* 34 (2019): 309–328.

56. Lloyd, "Interview," p. 217.

57. See Wolfson, *Giving*, p. xx and references to primary and secondary sources cited on pp. 266–267 n. 38, to which I would add Lissa McCullough, *The Religious Philosophy of Simone Weil: An Introduction* (London: I. B. Tauris, 2014), pp. 3–6. See the discussion in ch. 1 at nn. 25–31.

58. Lloyd, "Interview," p. 207.

59. Ibid., p. 211.

60. Rose, *Mourning*, pp. 11–12.

61. Gillian Rose, *Dialectic of Nihilism: Post-Structuralism and Law* (Oxford: Basil Blackwell, 1984), p. 1.

62. Ibid., p. 2.

63. Ibid., p. 208.

64. Gianni Vattimo, *The End of Modernity: Nihilism and Hermeneutics in Postmodern Culture*, translated and with an introduction by Jon R. Snyder (Baltimore: Johns Hopkins University Press, 1991), pp. 164–181; Wolfson, *Giving*, pp. 100, 361 n. 77, 385–386 n. 289; idem, *Heidegger and Kabbalah*, pp. 72, 78 n. 89.

65. Rose, *Melancholy Science*, p. 138.

66. Ibid.

67. Rose, *Broken Middle*, p. xiii. See ibid., p. 25, where Rose thus describes the fourth stage of freedom and repetition in Hegel's *Phenomenology of Spirit*, "repetition is readiness for anxiety; phenomenologically, knowledge and risk continue colliding at the individual and at the world-historical level." These words could be applied to Rose herself.

68. Ibid., p. 297. See Kate Schick, "Gillian Rose and Vulnerable Judgement," in *The Vulnerable Subject: Beyond Rationalism in International Relations*, edited by Amanda Russell Beattie and Kate Schick (Hampshire: Palgrave Macmillan, 2013), pp. 43–61.

69. Gillian Rose, "Diremption of Spirit," in *Shadow of Spirit: Postmodernism and Religion*, edited by Philippa Berry and Andrew Wernick (London: Routledge, 1992), p. 52 (emphasis in original). The text appears as well in Rose, *Judaism and Modernity*, pp. 47–48. For an earlier version with some variations, see Rose, *Broken Middle*, pp. 284–285.

70. Rose, *Broken Middle*, p. xiv.

71. It seems that Rose anticipated the relationship between the archaic and the modern articulated more fully by Agamben, *What Is an Apparatus?*, pp. 50–51:

> Contemporariness inscribes itself in the present by marking it above all as archaic. Only he who perceives the indices and signatures of the archaic in the most modern and recent can be contemporary. "Archaic" means close to the *arkhē*, that is to say, the origin. But the origin is not only situated in a chronological past: it is contemporary with historical becoming and does not cease to operate

within it, just as the embryo continues to be active in the tissues of the mature organism, and the child in the psychic life of the adult. Both this distancing and nearness, which define contemporariness, have their foundation in this proximity to the origin that nowhere pulses with more force than in the present.... It is in this sense that one can say that the entry point to the present necessarily takes the form of an archaeology; an archaeology that does not, however, regress to a historical past, but returns to that part within the present that we are absolutely incapable of living. What remains unlived therefore is incessantly sucked back toward the origin, without ever being able to reach it. The present is nothing other than this unlived element in everything that is lived.

72. Rose, *Broken Middle*, p. xii.
73. Ibid., pp. xiii, 307.
74. Ibid., p. xii.
75. Rose, *Love's Work*, p. 125.
76. Rose, *Mourning*, p. 11; Lloyd, "Interview," p. 209. Rose's position seems to reflect or bear affinity to the words of Theodor Adorno, *Minima Moralia: Reflexionen aus dem beschädigten Leben* [GS 4] (Frankfurt am Main: Suhrkamp, 1951), p. 81: "Die dialektische Vernunft ist gegen die herrschende die Unvernunft: erst indem sie jene überführt und aufhebt, wird sie selber vernünftig." English translation in idem, *Minima Moralia: Reflections from a Damaged Life*, translated by E. F. N. Jephcott (London: Verso, 1974), pp. 72–73: "Dialectical reason is, when set against the dominant mode of reason, unreason: only in encompassing and cancelling this mode does it become itself reasonable."
77. Rose, *Broken Middle*, p. xii.
78. Ibid., p. 77.
79. Rose, *Hegel Contra Sociology*, p. 64.
80. Ibid., pp. 76–77. See Schick, "Gillian Rose," pp. 48–49; idem, *Gillian Rose: A Good Enough Justice* (Edinburgh: Edinburgh University Press, 2012), pp. 3–4, 7, 17–18.
81. Rose, *Broken Middle*, p. 15.
82. Ibid., p. xiii.
83. Ibid., p. xii (emphasis in original).
84. Ibid., p. 277.
85. For an extensive analysis of this theme, see Gregory David Parry, "The 'Void' in Simone Weil and the 'Broken Middle' in Gillian Rose: The Genesis of the Search for Salvation," PhD dissertation, University of Durham, 2006.
86. Rose, *Judaism and Modernity*, p. x (emphasis in original).
87. Rose, *Love's Work*, pp. 59–60 (emphasis in original).
88. This is the perspective that Rose attributes to Sister Edna in Gillian Rose, *Paradiso* (Bristol: Shearsman Books, 2015), p. 19. I have taken the liberty to apply it

to her own view on the relationship of spiritual eros and carnal sexuality. Especially pertinent is Rose's observation that "Edna's passion for the *Song of Songs* was inseparable from her insight into *Talmud Torah*, the learning of the law." It is warranted to argue that Rose herself affirmed an intrinsic connection between eros and the textual investigation of the law.

89. Lloyd, "Interview," p. 208.

90. Elliot R. Wolfson, "Do Not Wake or Arouse Love: Erotics of Time and the Dream of Messianic Waiting," in *The Song of Songs Through the Ages: Studies on the Song's Reception History in Different Epochs, Contexts, and Genres*, edited by Annette Schellenberg (Berlin: Walter de Gruyter, 2023), p. 140.

91. Lloyd, "Interview," p. 208.

92. Rose, *Love's Work*, p. 55.

93. See Shanks, *Against Innocence*, pp. 1–13.

94. Cited in ibid., p. 1.

95. Lloyd, "Interview," p. 202. For other assessments of Rose's conversion and the nature of her faith, see Martin Jay, "The Conversion of the Rose," *Salmagundi* 113 (1997): 41–52; Martin Kavka, "Saying Kaddish for Gillian Rose, or on Levinas and *Geltungsphilosophie*," in *Secular Theology: American Radical Theological Thought*, edited by Clayton Crockett (London: Routledge, 2001), pp. 104–107; Vincent Lloyd, "The Secular Faith of Gillian Rose," *Journal of Religious Ethics* 36 (2008): 683–705. A succinct account of Rose's complex relationship to Judaism is offered by Vincent Lloyd, "Law All the Way Down: Gillian Rose and Robert Cover as Jewish Philosophers," in *Misrecognitions*, pp. 204–206.

96. Lloyd, "Interview," p. 211. In response to the question of the nature of her Jewish upbringing, Rose said,

> It was a Judaism as a culture rather than a religion. My grandparents were Orthodox Jews. My mother was culturally a Jew, not religiously a Jew, which again was rather liberating because it meant that I could explore what it meant to be a Jew religiously.... It's made me very open-minded. I'm very intellectually promiscuous, but I'd like to think that it doesn't make me superficial, because I'm always reading at the heart of matters.

97. Rose, *Broken Middle*, p. 276.

98. See Elliot Ashley Ratzman, "At the Common Altar: Political Messianism, Practical Ethics and Post-War Jewish Thought," PhD dissertation, Princeton University, 2009, p. 162. The author writes the following about Rose: "Curiously, she also purportedly underwent a deathbed conversion to Anglicanism."

99. Rose, *Broken Middle*, p. xiii.

100. Shanks, *Against Innocence*, pp. 123–124.

101. Ibid., p. 170 (emphasis in original).

102. Ibid.

103. Rose, *Broken Middle*, p. 277 (emphasis in original).
104. Rose, *Judaism and Modernity*, pp. 21–22 (emphasis in original). Compare the criticism of Strauss and Levinas in idem, "Diremption," pp. 49–50.
105. Rose, *Judaism and Modernity*, p. 22.
106. Ibid., p. x.
107. Ibid., p. xi (emphasis in original).
108. Ibid., p. 9 (emphasis in original).
109. Ibid., pp. 9–10. Compare ibid., p. 209: "I prefer another angel of Klee's, *Angelus Dubiosus*. With voluminous, blue, billowing and enfolded wings in which square eyeholes are cut for the expanse of rotund, taupe flesh to gaze through, this molelike angel appears unguarded rather than intent, grounded and slack rather than backing up and away in rigid horror. To me, this dubious angel suggests the humorous witness who must endure." On the role of Klee's *Angelus Dubiosus* for Rose, see Schick, *Gillian Rose*, pp. 47, 129–130.
110. Rose, *Judaism and Modernity*, p. 10.
111. Wolfson, *Suffering Time*, pp. 628 n. 177, 631–632. See ch. 1 n. 144 and ch. 3 n.148.
112. Rose, *Judaism and Modernity*, p. 10.
113. Rose, *Broken Middle*, p. 152.
114. Rose, *Mourning*, p. 2.
115. Rose, *Broken Middle*, p. 55 (emphasis in original).
116. Ibid., p. 85.
117. Ibid.
118. Rose, *Mourning*, pp. 2–3.
119. Ibid., p. 2.
120. Theodor W. Adorno, *Kierkegaard: Konstruktion des Ästhetischen* [GS 2] (Frankfurt am Main: Suhrkamp, 1962), pp. 153–161; idem, *Kierkegaard: Construction of the Aesthetic*, translated, edited, and with a foreword by Robert Hullot-Kentor (Minneapolis: University of Minnesota Press, 1989), pp. 108–113.
121. Rose, *Broken Middle*, p. 14. The critical passage on the sacrificial annihilation of Christ appears in Adorno, *Kierkegaard: Konstruktion*, pp. 157–158; English translation in idem, *Kierkegaard: Construction*, p. 111:

> Moral requirements are properly promulgated only in a life for which reconciliation is a continuous possibility; if life is sacrificed, ethos disappears with it in the abyss of the natural. The distinction of good and evil no longer holds under the domination of death.... Sacrifice is that point in the system where the tangent of an abstract and unreachable "meaning" touches the closed circle of life, and his doctrine insists on this "point" without progressing along the circumference; if, according to the paradox, it is only here that he can participate in "meaning," he must pay for it according to a graceless mythical calculus with the loss of the

living person.... Through sacrifice, the difference between Christ and man is abolished. If Christ, as sacrifice, falls to the mercy of the natural, in sacrifice the individual raises himself up, sacrificially, as a follower.... The mythical content of suffering is hardly mastered by Christology and by being a follower; occasionally this mythical content breaks through, autonomously, and sacrifice is presented in its true natural form: as expiation, performed for the sinful corps of the present "generation."

122. Rose, *Love's Work*, p. 70.
123. Ibid., p. 71.
124. Adorno, *Negative Dialektik*, p. 354; English translation in idem, *Negative Dialectics*, p. 361:

We cannot say any more that the immutable is truth, and that the mobile, transitory is appearance. The mutual indifference of temporality and eternal ideas is no longer tenable even with the bold Hegelian explanation that temporal existence, by virtue of the destruction inherent in its concept, serves the eternal represented by the eternity of destruction. One of the mystical impulses secularized in dialectics was the doctrine that the intramundane and historic is relevant to what traditional metaphysics distinguished as transcendence—or at least, less gnostically and radically put, that it is relevant to the position taken by human consciousness on the questions which the canon of philosophy assigned to metaphysics. After Auschwitz, our feelings resist any claim of the positivity of existence as sanctimonious, as wronging the victims; they balk at squeezing any kind of sense, however bleached, out of the victims' fate. And these feelings do have an objective side after events that make a mockery of the construction of immanence as endowed with a meaning radiated by an affirmatively posited transcendence.

125. On this point I see another similarity between Rose's thinking and Heidegger. See Rose, *Dialectic of Nihilism*, p. 83. Rose's rejection of transcendence understood as a location outside the law that would offer immunity from the necessary contagion of law is discussed by Lloyd, *Law and Transcendence*, pp. 28–32, 64, 174, 188, 189, and compare the passage cited above in n. 23.
126. Rose, *Love's Work*, p. 105.
127. Ibid., p. 19.
128. Ibid., p. 74.
129. Ibid., pp. 74–75.
130. Ibid., p. 105.
131. My interpretation of Rose's use of the maxim of Staretz Silouan has benefited from the discussion of Michael Wood in his introduction to *Love's Work* pp. xiii–xiv.
132. Rose, *Broken Middle*, p 110.

133. Lloyd, "Interview," p. 212.

134. Ibid., p. 217.

135. See above at n. 56.

136. My reading of Rose should be compared to the hypothesis that, for Hegel, eternity is a structure of time rather than a realm outside of time offered by Tereza Matějčková, "Eternity's Death in Modernity: A Case of Murder? Of Resurrection?" *International Journal of Philosophical Studies* 28 (2020): 452–469.

137. Lloyd, "Interview," p. 209.

138. Ibid.

139. Rose, *Love's Work*, p. 40.

140. Ibid., pp. 121–124. See the letter to Rose from Tom and Barbara Goodfellow, dated February 5, 1995, reproduced in Rose, *Paradiso*, p. 13, which makes reference to her "eloquent analysis of King Arthur's dream of Camelot with its tragic and inevitable outcome of sadness, no matter what choice he makes. The law that he has sworn to uphold will always rebound against his human weakness, whether or not he fulfils or ignores its requirements."

141. Rose, *Love's Work*, p. 124.

142. Ibid., pp. 124–125.

143. See above at nn. 79–80.

144. Schick, *Gillian Rose*, p. 128; Kavka, "Saying Kaddish," pp. 107–108.

145. Kavka, "Saying Kaddish," p. 125.

146. On the coalescing of the comical and the tragic, see the passage of Levinas cited in ch. 4 at n. 9 and the passage of Wittgenstein cited in ch. 4 n. 10.

147. Rose, *Paradiso*, p. 23.

148. Ibid., p. 24. Compare Susan Taubes's reference to "Augustinian Gnosticism" in the passage cited in ch. 1 at n. 53.

149. Rose, *Paradiso*, p. 28.

150. Ibid., p. 24 (emphasis in original).

151. Ibid., p. 25. Adorno, *Kierkegaard: Konstruktion*, p. 159 (idem, *Kierkegaard: Construction*, p. 112), suggested that Kierkegaard's gnostic doctrines are presented as literary works and fantasies in order to mask the heterodox nature of those doctrines.

152. Adorno, *Kierkegaard: Konstruktion*, pp. 160–161; idem, *Kierkegaard: Construction*, pp. 112–113.

153. Rose, *Broken Middle*, p. 14.

154. Rose, *Paradiso*, p. 16.

155. Ibid., p. 17.

156. I have no reason to question that the combination of the contemplative and the practical was Rose's ambition. One can question, however, if this ideal was realized, and if we should not apply to her what she concluded with respect to Horkheimer and Adorno in *Melancholy Science*, p. 8:

They created an academy precisely to criticise traditions which the academic community abused or ignored. Yet neither men, Adorno least of all, was a "public" man. They were not suited for responsibility in the sense of providing any platform. Hence they seemed to recreate the evils of the old academic community—indulging in intense, idiosyncratic cultural criticism deeply imbedded in the scholarly and institutional constraints which they were committed to transcend.

157. Rose, *Paradiso*, p. 18.
158. Ibid., pp. 18–19.
159. The dynamic I have described seems to be implied in the discussion of the tradition of irony in Rose, *Melancholy Science*, pp. 18–26, and esp. p. 19:

Yet both Nietzsche and Adorno undercut and contradict even their most sacred assertions and provide instructions for interpreting their strongly-voiced claims. The works of both must be read from a methodological point of view and not literally. In both cases too, their work was designed to resist popularisation, but in effect encouraged it. They tried, in very different ways, to make their style esoteric in order to defy the norms which they opposed, and they wrote in essays or in fragments to avoid the appearance and presuppositions of the traditional philosophical system. Yet fragments and aphorisms are easily detachable and equally easily misunderstood, since their significance can only be appreciated on the basis of an understanding of the whole of which they are the fragments—hence the paradoxes that such idiosyncratic and radical thinkers can be so widely and quickly assimilated but so often misunderstood.

160. Rose, *Paradiso*, p. 17.
161. Walter Benjamin, *Gesammelte Schriften*, 1.2, edited by Rolf Tiedemann and Herman Schweppenhäuser (Frankfurt am Main: Suhrkamp, 1991), p. 704; idem, *Selected Writings*, vol. 4: *1938–1940*, edited by Howard Eiland and Michael W. Jennings, translated by Edmund Jephcott and others (Cambridge, MA: Harvard University Press, 2003), p. 397. The comparison of Rose's own view of the middle and Adorno's criticism of Benjamin was already noted by Anthony Gorman, "Gillian Rose's Critique of Violence," *Radical Philosophy* 197 (2016): 32.

162. Adorno, *Negative Dialectics*, p. 320. To understand Adorno's critique of the Hegelian idea of universal history, it is useful to cite from the paragraph that precedes the one from which Rose extracted the quotation. See ibid., pp. 319–320:

Hegel himself had conceived universal history as unified merely on account of its contradictions. The materialistic turnabout in dialectics cast the weightiest accent on insight into the discontinuity of what is not comfortably held together by any unity of spirit and concept. Yet discontinuity and universal history must be conceived together. To strike out the latter as a relic of metaphysical superstition would spiritually consolidate pure facticity as the only thing to be known and therefore to be accepted; it would do this exactly in the manner in which sovereignty, aligning facts in the order of the total march of One Spirit, used to confirm them as the utterances of that spirit.

163. Rose, *Judaism and Modernity*, p. 207.

164. For citation and analysis of some of the relevant texts wherein this distinction is made, see Wolfson, *Heidegger and Kabbalah*, pp. 11–13, 40, 55 n. 102, 265.

165. Rose, *Dialectic of Nihilism*, pp. 80–81. The passage cited and analyzed by Rose is from Martin Heidegger, *Identity and Difference*, translated and with an introduction by Joan Stambaugh (New York: Harper & Row, 1969), p. 47; German text, pp. 112–113.

166. Rose, *Dialectic of Nihilism*, pp. 82–83. On Heidegger's metapolitics, see ch. 3 n. 254.

167. Rose, *Dialectic of Nihilism*, p. 80. Compare ibid., p. 84, where it is said of Heidegger, "For he shows us 'I am who I am' but keeps the commandments of the *Torah* from us." Rose's comment about Heidegger's offering the idea of Yahweh divorced from the Torah is mentioned briefly by Lloyd, "Law All the Way Down," p. 208.

168. In my own work, I have compared the rabbinic-kabbalistic notion of the Tetragrammaton as the compresence of past, present, and future to the Heideggerian idea of the equiprimordiality (*Gleichursprünglichkeit*) of the three temporal ecstasies. See Wolfson, *Heidegger and Kabbalah*, pp. 45, 223, 259, 264, 272, 275–276, and references to the studies of Gabriel Motzkin and Michael Fagenblat cited respectively on p. 294 nn. 170 and 172. I regret not mentioning the astute comment of Rose referenced in the previous note. The affinity that Rose drew between Heidegger and kabbalah is parallel to Susan Taubes's notion of Heideggerian kabbalah. See ch. 1 n. 256.

169. Rose, *Dialectic of Nihilism*, p. 57.

170. Ibid., p. 59. Rose's comments are an explication of Heidegger, *Identity and Difference*, p. 100: "Das Zusammen*gehören* von Mensch und Sein in der Weise der wechselseitigen Herausforderung bringt uns bestürzend näher, daß und wie der Mensch dem Sein vereignet, das Sein aber dem Menschenwesen zugeeignet ist. Im Ge-Stell waltet ein seltsames Vereignen und Zueignen" (emphasis in original). English translation, op. cit., p. 36: "The *belonging* together of man and Being in the manner of mutual challenge drives home to us with startling force that and how man is delivered over to the ownership of Being and Being is appropriate to the essence of man. Within the framework there prevails a strange ownership and a strange appropriation" (emphasis in original). Rose, *Dialectic of Nihilism*, p. 59, translates the final sentence, "Within what has been placed there prevails a strange disowning and owning." In light of Rose's philological intervention, it is of interest

256 Notes to Chapter 2

to compare Heidegger, *Beiträge zur Philosophie (Vom Ereignis)* [GA 65] (Frankfurt am Main: Vittorio Klostermann, 1989), §191, p. 311:

> *Das Dasein* ist der Wendungspunkt in der Kehre des Ereignisses, die sich öffnende Mitte des Widerspiels von Zuruf und Zugehörigkeit, das *Eigentum*, verstanden wie Fürsten-tum, die herrschaftliche Mitte der Er-eignung als Zueignung des Zu-gehörigen zum Ereignis, zugleich zu *ihm:* Selbstwerdung (emphasis in original).

English translation in idem, *Contributions to Philosophy (Of the Event)*, translated by Richard Rojcewicz and Daniela Vallega-Neu (Bloomington: Indiana University Press, 2012), pp. 246–247:

> *Da-sein* is the axis in the turning of the event, the self-opening center of the counterplay between call and belonging. Da-sein is the "domain of what is proper" [*Eigen-tum*, "property"], understood in analogy with "domain of a prince" [*Fürsten-tum*, "principality"], the sovereign center of the appropriating eventuation as the assignment, of the ones who belong, to the event and at the same time to *themselves*: becoming a self (emphasis in original).

And see the further explication of Dasein, the domain of what is proper, and selfhood in Heidegger, *Beiträge*, §197, pp. 319–320:

> Selbstheit entspringt als Wesung des Da-seins aus dem Ursprung des Da-seins. Und der Ursprung des Selbst ist das *Eigen-tum*. Dieses Wort hier genommen wie Fürsten-tum. Die Herrschaft der Eignung im Ereignis. Die Eignung ist zumal Zueignung und Übereignung. Sofern das Da-sein *sich* zu-geeignet wird als zugehörig zum Ereignis, kommt es zu sich *selbst*, aber nie so, als wäre das Selbst schon ein vorhandener, nur bisher nicht erreichter Bestand. Vielmehr zu sich selbst kommt das Da-sein erst, indem die Zu-eignung in die Zugehörigkeit zugleich Über-eignung wird in das Ereignis (emphasis in original).

English translation in Heidegger, *Contributions*, p. 253:

> Selfhood, as the essential occurrence of Da-sein, arises out of the origin of Da-sein. And the origin of the self is the *domain of what is proper*. This term taken in analogy with "domain of a prince." The reigning of appropriation in the event. Appropriation [*Eignung*] is at once assignment [*Zu-eignung*] and consignment [*Übereignung*]. Inasmuch as Da-sein is assigned to *itself* as belonging to the event, Da-sein does come to its *self*, but never as if the self were already an objectively present item that simply had not previously been reached. Rather, Da-sein comes to itself first precisely when the assignment to the belonging becomes at once a consignment into the event (emphasis in original).

It appears to me that the import of Heidegger's insistence that *Ereignis* comprises both *Zueignung* and *Übereignung* may be the same as the connotation that Rose derived from the distinction between *Zueignen* and *Vereignen*, rendered respectively as owning and disowning.

171. Rose, *Dialectic of Nihilism*, p. 69.

172. Heidegger, *Beiträge*, §116, p. 228; idem, *Contributions*, p. 180.

173. See Elliot R. Wolfson, "Imagination, Theolatry, and the Compulsion to Worship the Invisible," in *Religion in Reason: Metaphysics, Ethics, and Politics in Hent de Vries*, edited by Tarek R. Dika and Martin Shuster (London: Routledge, 2023), pp. 55–56 and references to primary and secondary sources cited there in nn. 21–25.

174. See ch. 1 n. 162 and ch. 3 n. 146.

175. Rose, *Dialectic of Nihilism*, p. 83.

176. Rose, *Judaism and Modernity*, p. 26. See Lloyd, "Law All the Way Down," pp. 207–216.

177. Rose, *Broken Middle*, p. xv.

178. Schick, *Gillian Rose*, p. 12.

179. Rose, *Mourning*, p. 70.

180. Schick, *Gillian Rose*, p. 125.

181. Rose, *Broken Middle*, p. xv.

182. Rose, *Broken Middle*, pp. xii–xiii. For a critical analysis, focused especially on *Love's Work*, see Gorman, "Gillian Rose's Critique of Violence."

183. Joshua B. Davis, "Introduction: By Way of the Valley of Roses," in *Misrecognitions*, p. 3.

184. See Introduction at n. 8 and ch. 1 at n. 38.

185. Adorno, *Negative Dialektik*, p. 374; idem, *Negative Dialectics*, p. 381.

186. See Heidegger, *Beiträge*, §72, p. 139; idem, *Contributions*, p. 109. The "greatest nihilism" resides in the "noisy intoxication" (*Trunkenboldigkeit*) to lived experience (*Erlebnis*), "the deliberate turning of a blind eye to human goal-lessness" (*der Ziel-losigkeit des Menschen*), which results in the "avoidance of any goal-setting decision, the dread of all decisive domains and of their opening." In this matter, I detect a closer affinity between Rose and Heidegger than she was willing to admit. The Heideggerian approach informed the provocative analysis of David Michael Levin, *The Opening of Vision: Nihilism and the Postmodern Situation* (New York: Routledge, 1988). For instance, see Levin's summation on p. 5 of what inspired the writing of his book and his call to chart a new vision:

> The modern epoch brought into being a world in which the effects of nihilism are spreading. Now, we can see, today, if we look with care and thought, that nihilism is a rage against Being: "nihilism" means the destruction of Being: the Being of all beings, including that way of being which we call "human" and consider to be our own. Thus, in the postmodern situation, we need to achieve, both individually and collectively, a recollection of Being, of its dimensionality. This is possible, however, only if the question of Being can become, for us, a question of character—a question that questions the historical character of our vision.

187. Rose, *Mourning*, p. 70.
188. For a different approach, see Tony Gorman, "Nihilism and Faith: Rose, Bernstein and the Future of Critical Theory," *Radical Philosophy* 134 (2005): 18–30.
189. Rose, *Mourning*, p. 71 (emphasis in original).
190. Rose, *Broken Middle*, p. 164.
191. Ibid. (emphasis in original).
192. The concept of aporetic universalism is explored in detail by Schick, *Gillian Rose*, pp. 11, 43, 81–104.
193. Rose, *Broken Middle*, p. 303.
194. Ibid., p. 79. The author cites aphorism 80 as it appears in Franz Kafka, *Wedding Preparations in the Country and Other Posthumous Prose Writings*, notes by Max Brod, translated by Ernst Kaiser and Eithne Wilkins (London: Secker and Warburg, 1973), p. 47. The aphorisms are published in that edition under the title "Reflections on Sin, Suffering, Hope, and the True Way" as they were in Franz Kafka, *Dearest Father: Stories and Other Writings*, translated by Ernst Kaiser and Eithne Wilkins (New York: Schocken Books, 1954), pp. 34–48. The German original is cited from *The Aphorisms of Franz Kafka*, edited, introduced, and with commentary by Reiner Stach, translated by Shelley Frisch (Princeton: Princeton University Press, 2022), p. 158.
195. Franz Kafka, *The Blue Octavo Notebooks*, edited by Max Brod, translated by Ernst Kaiser and Eithne Wilkins (Cambridge: Exact Change, 1991), p. 35.
196. This is the implication of the translation in *The Aphorisms*, p. 158: "Truth is indivisible, and so it cannot recognize itself; anyone claiming to recognize it must be a lie." And see the explanation offered on p. 159:

> The indivisibility of the truth could be taken to mean that nothing is true that is not *utterly* true, and that anything that is almost true is inescapably untrue.... It is striking, however, that Kafka chose "lie" as an antonym for truth, as opposed to a falsehood or untruth. A lie is an *intentional* negation of the truth; its assessment is a matter not of epistemology but of ethics (emphasis in original).

197. See my previous explanation of Kafka's aphorism in Elliot R. Wolfson, *Venturing Beyond: Law and Morality in Kabbalistic Mysticism* (Oxford: Oxford University Press, 2006), pp. 254–255.
198. Aphorism 58 in Kafka, *Wedding Preparations*, p. 44: "One tells as few lies as possible only by telling as few lies as possible, and not by having the least possible opportunity to do so." German original in *The Aphorisms*, p. 118: "*Man lügt möglichst wenig nur, wenn man möglichst wenig lügt, nicht wenn man möglichst wenig Gelegenheit dazu hat.*"
199. Compare Adorno, *Minima Moralia: Reflexionen*, pp. 81–82; English translation in idem, *Minima Moralia: Reflections*, p. 73:

> Did not Karl Kraus, Kafka, even Proust prejudice and falsify the image of the world in order to shake off falsehood and prejudice? The dialectic cannot stop short before the concepts of health and sickness, nor indeed before their siblings reason and unreason.... The dialectician's duty is thus to help this fool's truth to attain its own reasons, without which it will certainly succumb to the abyss of the sickness implacably dictated by the healthy common sense of the rest.

See the analysis of this passage in Rose, *Melancholy Science*, pp. 20–21, and compare her discussion of Adorno's view of Kafka, op. cit., p. 125:

> For Adorno, therefore, there is no need to choose between Franz Kafka and Thomas Mann. He scorns the interpretation of Kafka which sees in the writing a vision of "nothingness" and impotence, accomplished by means of "realistic symbolism" [Theodor W. Adorno, *Prisms*, translated by Shierry Weber Nicholsen and Samuel Weber (Cambridge, MA: MIT Press, 1983), p. 245]. Instead he pays close attention to various features of Kafka's style, emphasising how the texts are structured in ways which undermine conventional habits of reading and modes of communicating meaning. For example, he points out, with close reference to, and quotation from, Kafka's texts, how the latter frequently pits gestures against dialogue so as to undermine the intention of the words spoken [Adorno, *Prisms*, pp. 248–249], how he uses narrative form but eschews traditional progression in the narrative by substituting various forms of repetition of events, places and so on [Adorno, *Prisms*, pp. 252–253, 265–266]. He thus produces "tortuous epics" in which the "boundary between what is human and the world of things becomes blurred" [Adorno, *Prisms*, p. 262]. This style yields the contours of Kafka's subjectivity. It is an extreme and absolute subjectivity, which does not connect with the external world—"objectless inwardness"—and therefore cannot distinguish itself from the world. Thus, first, to withdraw into absolute subjectivity is, strictly speaking, impossible because words and sentences break any illusion of absolute immediacy, and Kafka's style is designed to avoid this paradox, but, secondly, such withdrawal succumbs to the very estrangement which it is attempting to escape: "The subject seeks to break the spell of reification by reifying itself" [Adorno, *Prisms*, p. 270].

200. Friedrich Nietzsche, *On Truth and Lie in an Extra-Moral Sense*, translated by Andrew Keith Malcolm Adam (Oxford: Quadriga, 2019), p. 3. Compare Friedrich Nietzsche, *Unpublished Fragments from the Period of Thus Spoke Zarathustra (Spring 1884–Winter 1884/85)*, translated and with an afterword by Paul S. Loeb and David F. Tinsley (Stanford: Stanford University Press, 2022), p. 100:

> On the origin of *art*. The ability to lie and to dissemble has been developed the longest: feeling of *security* and of intellectual superiority in the deceiver during

this.... In the case of poets, we often find self-alienation: they feel themselves "transformed." Likewise in dancers and actors, with nervous breakdowns, hallucinations etc. Artists now also still deceitful and resembling children. Inability to differentiate between "true" and "illusion" (emphasis in original).

For my previous analysis of this emphasis in Nietzsche's thought, see Elliot R. Wolfson, *The Philosophical Pathos of Susan Taubes: Between Nihilism and Hope* (Stanford: Stanford University Press, 2023), pp. 248–249.

201. Friedrich Nietzsche, *Writings from the Early Notebooks*, edited by Raymond Geuss and Alexander Nehamas, translated by Ladislaus Löb (Cambridge: Cambridge University Press, 2009), p. 136 (emphasis in original). For a sampling of Nietzsche's reflections on Buddhism, see ch. 1 n. 80.

202. Nietzsche, *Will to Power*, p. 298. For a different rendering, see Friedrich Nietzsche, *Writings from the Late Notebooks*, edited by Rüdiger Bittner, translated by Kate Sturge (Cambridge: Cambridge University Press, 2003), p. 154. See also Nietzsche, *Will to Power*, p. 300:

> The sore spot of Kant's critical philosophy has gradually become visible even to dull eyes: Kant no longer has a right to his distinction "appearance" and "thing-in-itself"—he had deprived himself of the right to go on distinguishing in this old familiar way, in so far as he rejected as impermissible making inferences from phenomena to a cause of phenomena—in accordance with his conception of causality and its purely intra-phenomenal validity—which conception, on the other hand, already anticipates this distinction, as if the "thing-in-itself" were not only inferred but *given* (emphasis in original).

203. For more elaborate discussions of the topic of the dream as the fictional truth that undermines the epistemological distinction between truth and untruth, see Elliot R. Wolfson, *A Dream Interpreted Within a Dream: Oneiropoiesis and the Prism of Imagination* (New York: Zone Books, 2011), pp. 16–17, 47–48, 55–56, 61–64, 85–86, 105–106, 110, 124, 160–161, 188–197, 202, 210, 239, 266–269.

204. Friedrich Nietzsche, *Menschliches, Allzumenschliches I–II*, edited by Giorgio Colli and Mazzini Montinari (Munich: Walter de Gruyter, 1999), p. 639; idem, *Human, All Too Human: A Book for Free Spirits*, translated by R. J. Hollingdale, with an introduction by Richard Schacht (Cambridge: Cambridge University Press, 1996), p. 358. For citation and analysis of other relevant Nietzschean material, see Wolfson, *A Dream*, pp. 44–45, 200–201, 416 n. 103.

205. Aphorism 63 in Kafka, *Wedding Preparations*, p. 45; German original in *The Aphorisms*, p. 128.

206. Kafka, *The Blue Octavo Notebooks*, p. 39.

207. With some technical modification I have followed the analysis in Agamben, *What Is an Apparatus?*, pp. 44–45.

208. Aphorism 55 in Kafka, *Wedding Preparations*, p. 44; German original in *The Aphorisms*, p. 112.

209. Rose, *Judaism and Modernity*, pp. 48–49. The text appeared with slight variation in idem, "Diremption of Spirit," p. 53.

210. See the comments of Lloyd in the introduction to "Interview," p. 203.

211. On the possible Hegelian influence on Rose's acceptance of the need to construct her speculative social theory on the basis of beginning in the middle, see Latz, *Social Philosophy*, p. 49.

212. Hans-Georg Gadamer, "Towards a Phenomenology of Ritual and Language (1992)," in *Language and Linguisticality in Gadamer's Hermeneutics*, edited by Lawrence K. Schmidt (Lanham: Lexington Books, 2000), p. 25.

213. Rose, *Broken Middle*, pp. 85, 235, 277.

214. Ibid., p. 277 (emphasis in original).

215. Even though Rose is not mentioned, it seems that her terminology was appropriated by Andrew F. Walls, "Old Athens and New Jerusalem: Some Signposts for Christian Scholarship in the Early History of Mission Studies," *International Bulletin of Missionary Research* 21 (1997): 146–153.

216. Rose, *Broken Middle*, pp. 100–101.

217. Ibid., p. 101.

218. The essay was first published in the *Archiv für Sozialwissenschaft und Sozialpolitik* (1921), and it is reprinted in Walter Benjamin, *Gesammelte Schriften*, 2.1, edited by Rolf Tiedemann and Hermann Schweppenhäuser (Frankfurt am Main: Suhrkamp, 1991), pp. 179–203. English translation in idem, *Selected Writings*, vol. 1, pp. 236–252. It would be worthwhile to compare Rose's brief but incisive comments on Benjamin's essay with the extensive analysis of Jacques Derrida, "Force of Law: The 'Mystical Foundation of Authority,'" in *Deconstruction and the Possibility of Justice*, edited by Drucilla Cornell, Michael Rosenfeld, and David Gray Carlson (New York: Routledge, 1992), pp. 29–57. The English translation together with the original French were published in Jacques Derrida, "Force de loi: Le Fondement Mystique de l'Autorité," *Cardozo Law Review* 11 (1990): 920–1046. A satisfactory discussion of Derrida's study is beyond the scope of this note, but two points are important to underscore. First, Derrida, "Force of Law," p. 29, tellingly characterized Benjamin's essay as at once "mystical" and "hypercritical," even suggesting that it could be read as an example of "neo-messianical Jewish mysticism (*mystique*) grafted onto post-Sorelian neo-Marxism (or the reverse)." Secondly, in the same context, Derrida, p. 30, pointed out that it is "impossible to miss" the

> analogies between *Zur Kritik der Gewalt* and certain turns of Heideggerian thought ... especially those surrounding the motifs of *Walten* and *Gewalt*. *Zur Kritik der Gewalt* concludes with divine violence (*göttliche Gewalt*) and in the end Walter says of divine violence that we might call it *die waltende* (*Die gött-*

liche Gewalt . . . mag die waltende heißen): "Divine violence . . . may be called sovereign violence." ". . . *die waltende heißen*" are the last words of the text.

In the continuation of his essay, Derrida chronicled in more detail some of these analogies. See ch. 3 at n. 107. And compare the analysis in "The Time of Violence: Derrida, Deconstruction, and Value" in Elizabeth Grosz, *Time Travels: Feminism, Nature, Power* (Durham: Duke University Press, 2005), pp. 55–70.

219. Rose, *Judaism and Modernity*, pp. 187–189.
220. Rose, *Broken Middle*, p. 277 (emphasis in original).
221. Ibid., p. 282 (emphasis in original).
222. For a comprehensive analysis of dualism in Rose's thought, see Lloyd, *Law and Transcendence*, pp. 33–63.
223. Rose, *Mourning*, p. 36.
224. Ibid.
225. Rose, *Paradiso*, p. 21.
226. Rose, *Mourning*, p. 34. See Anna Rowlands, "Beginning in the Middle: The Third City and the Politics of Membership," in *Misrecognitions*, pp. 29–46.
227. Rose, *Mourning*, p. 29.
228. Ibid., p. 30.
229. Ibid., pp. 30–31 (emphasis in original).
230. Schick, *Gillian Rose*, pp. 77–79.
231. Ratzman, "At the Common Altar," p. 179: "The third city is neither the perfect Athenian city of law nor the Jerusalem of love. It is the work in progress and the object of our political lives. This real city also entails actual selves in the fray of limited knowledge, imperfect activity, and broken selves. The self too is bound up with the imperfect texture of social life."
232. Rose, *Judaism and Modernity*, p. 257.
233. Ibid.
234. Rose, *Mourning*, pp. 21–22.
235. Ibid., p. 26 (emphasis in original).
236. Rose, *Paradiso*, p. 25.
237. See Rose, *Broken Middle*, pp. 117 n. 18, 119 nn. 28, 30, 31, 147 n. 164.
238. Rose, *Paradiso*, p. 27.
239. Ibid., p. 26.
240. Ibid., pp. 26–27.
241. Ibid., p. 25.
242. Ibid., p. 27.
243. See Rose, *Broken Middle*, pp. 118–122.
244. Rose, *Paradiso*, p. 27.
245. Ibid. (emphasis in original).
246. Ibid.

247. Rose, *Broken Middle*, p. 121.
248. Adorno, *Minima Moralia: Reflexionen*, p. 283; idem, *Minima Moralia: Reflections*, p. 247.
249. Adorno, *Minima Moralia: Reflexionen*, p. 283; idem, *Minima Moralia: Reflections*, p. 247.

Chapter 3

This chapter is a greatly revised and expanded version of Elliot R. Wolfson, "Death and the Infinitization of Finitude: Negation and the Ethical Crisis of Modernity in Edith Wyschogrod's Postmodern Hermeneutic." In *Modern Jewish Thought on Crisis: Interpretation, Heresy, and History*, edited by Ghilad H. Shenhav, Cedric Cohen-Skalli, and Gilad Sharvit, 241–266 (Berlin: Walter de Gruyter, 2024).

1. Edith Wyschogrod, *Spirit in Ashes: Hegel, Heidegger, and Man-Made Mass Death* (New Haven: Yale University Press, 1985), p. x (emphasis in original).
2. Ibid.
3. Ibid., pp. xii, 36–39, 46, 182, 199, 213, 215.
4. Ibid., p. 52.
5. Edith Wyschogrod, "Concentration Camps and the End of the Life-World," in *Echoes from the Holocaust: Philosophical Reflections on a Dark Time*, edited by Alan Rosenberg and Gerald E. Myers (Philadelphia: Temple University Press, 1988), p. 330.
6. Wyschogrod, *Spirit*, p. 38 (emphasis in original).
7. Ibid., p. 182.
8. See below at n. 58.
9. Wyschogrod, *Spirit*, p. 182.
10. See the discussion and citation of relevant passages in ch. 1 n. 57.
11. Georg Wilhelm Friedrich Hegel, *Wissenschaft der Logik I. Erster Teil: Die objective Logik. Erstes Buch* [Werke 5] (Frankfurt am Main: Suhrkamp, 1986), pp. 139–140; idem, *The Science of Logic*, translated by W. H. Johnston and L. G. Struthers (New York: Macmillan, 1929), p. 129 (emphasis in original). I cited the translation utilized by Wyschogrod, *Spirit*, p. 150. For a more recent translation, see Georg Wilhelm Friedrich Hegel, *The Science of Logic*, translated and edited by George di Giovanni (Cambridge: Cambridge University Press, 2010), p. 101: "They *are*, but the truth of this being is (as in Latin) their *finis*, their *end*. The finite does not just alter, as the something in general does, but *perishes*, and its perishing is not just a mere possibility, as if it might be without perishing. Rather, the being as such of finite things is to have the germ of this transgression in their in-itselfness: the hour of their birth is the hour of their death" (emphasis in original). Henceforth, all subsequent citations are from this translation of *Science of Logic*.
12. See the comment of di Giovanni in Hegel, *Science of Logic*, p. 101 n. 55.

13. Wyschogrod, *Spirit*, p. 150.

14. Ibid.

15. Hegel, *Wissenschaft der Logik I*, p. 139; idem, *Science of Logic*, p. 101.

16. Hegel, *Wissenschaft der Logik I*, p. 140; idem, *Science of Logic*, p. 102.

17. Wyschogrod, *Spirit*, pp. 150–151. Compare idem, *Crossover Queries: Dwelling with Negatives, Embodying Philosophy's Others* (New York: Fordham University Press, 2006), p. 251:

> Heidegger describes this everyday standpoint as parasitic upon a more fundamental understanding of temporality. . . . Life is lived in anticipation of death: not as something not yet present, for death will never be present to someone, but rather as not being able to be anywhere. Hegel already notices the importance of human mortality in deriving other expressions of nonbeing, for example, logical negation. But if for Hegel the negative is ultimately transcended, for Heidegger the human being is "thrown," suspended over the abyss of its own nonexistence, oriented by its own projected nonbeing.

For a different interpretation of Hegel and Heidegger on this point, see my brief remarks in Elliot R. Wolfson, *Suffering Time: Philosophical, Kabbalistic, and Ḥasidic Reflections on Temporality* (Leiden: Brill, 2021), pp. 7–9.

18. Wyschogrod, *Spirit*, pp. x–xi.

19. Ibid., p. xi.

20. Wyschogrod, "Concentration Camps," pp. 327–331.

21. Ibid.

22. Ibid., p. 328.

23. For example, see Wyschogrod, *Spirit*, p. 176, where the "last fruit" of the history of metaphysics is said to mark "our own era of nihilism and is expressed in atomic power and ecological decline."

24. Ibid., p. xi. Compare Edith Wyschogrod, "The Civilizational Perspective in Comparative Studies of Transcendence," in *Transcendence and the Sacred*, edited by Alan M. Olson and Leroy S. Rouner (Notre Dame: University of Notre Dame Press, 1981), pp. 61–62:

> The position I propose . . . rejects the view that *transcendence* is a referring term—that is, the notion that "something" transcends or that this "something" can be interpreted as having causal efficacy. Bearing the post-Nietzschean deconstruction of metaphysics in mind, I interpret the point of fixity revealed in the languages which transcendence "speaks" as constituted after the fact; transcendence becomes manifest only through this *post hoc* constitution. I shall, in accordance with the usage developed in the work of Martin Heidegger, Emmanuel Levinas, and Jacques Derrida, call this mode of manifesting a "trace." With Derrida and Levinas I see the trace not as an effect of which transcendence is the

cause; such an interpretation lies well within the sphere of natural theology. But, on the contrary, I interpret the trace as marking the disappearance of the origin through a reciprocal, back-and-forth oscillation which permits the emergence of both trace and origin.... The trace acquires its meaning from its unique relation to time. It refers to an immemorial past which can never become present, thus precluding the conformity of transcendence with the logic of presence.... Similarly, in the dialectic of trace and origin the moment of reciprocal constitution is a non-event . . . as such it can never become the object of thought (emphasis in original).

See as well Edith Wyschogrod, "Intending Transcendence: Desiring God," in *Companion to Postmodern Theology*, edited by Graham Ward (London: Blackwell, 2001), pp. 349–365, reprinted in Wyschogrod, *Crossover Queries*, pp. 13–28. For previous reference and brief discussion of these sources, see Elliot R. Wolfson, *A Dream Interpreted Within a Dream: Oneiropoiesis and the Prism of Imagination* (New York: Zone Books, 2011), pp. 32 and 295 n. 55.

25. Wyschogrod, *Spirit*, p. 46.

26. Edith Wyschogrod, "Those Weeping Eyes, Those Seeing Tears: Reading John D. Caputo's Ethics," in *Styles of Piety: Practicing Philosophy After the Death of God*, edited by S. Clark Buckner and Matthew Statler (New York: Fordham University Press, 2006), p. 215.

27. Gilles Deleuze and Félix Guattari, *What Is Philosophy?*, translated by Hugh Tomlinson and Graham Burchell (New York: Columbia University Press, 1994), p. 59. The passage is cited by Wyschogrod, "Those Weeping Eyes," p. 215, but the wrong pagination is given on p. 296 n. 7. See, however, Wyschogrod, *Crossover Queries*, pp. 46–47: "Deleuze and Guattari's antinomianism derives from an account of desiring production that conceals a metaphysical monism beneath the differential and pluralistic character of their version of the real."

28. Gilles Deleuze, *Foucault*, translated and edited by Seán Hand, foreword by Paul Bové (Minneapolis: University of Minnesota Press, 1988), p. 97. For citation of this passage and other relevant sources, see Wolfson, *Suffering Time*, p. 52 n. 160, and the reference cited there to Keith Robinson, "Thought of the Outside: The Foucault/Deleuze Conjunction," *Philosophy Today* 43 (1999): 57–72.

29. Deleuze and Guattari, *What Is Philosophy?*, p. 37.

30. Wyschogrod, "Those Weeping Eyes," p. 215.

31. Martin Heidegger, *Was Heißt Denken?* [GA 8] (Frankfurt am Main: Vittorio Klostermann, 2002), p. 82; idem, *What Is Called Thinking?*, translated by Fred W. Wieck and J. Glenn Gray, with an introduction by J. Glenn Gray (New York: Harper & Row, 1968), p. 76. See discussion in Jacques Derrida, *Of Spirit: Heidegger and the Question*, translated by Geoffrey Bennington and Rachel Bowlby (Chicago: University of Chicago Press, 1989), pp. 9–10, 13; idem, *Psyche: Inventions of the*

Other, vol. 2, edited by Peggy Kamuf and Elizabeth Rottenberg (Stanford: Stanford University Press, 2008), pp. 205, 209, 212–213; Elliot R. Wolfson, *Heidegger and Kabbalah: Hidden Gnosis and the Path of Poiēsis* (Bloomington: Indiana University Press, 2019), pp. 11, 68–75, 165–166, 311. Heidegger marks the distinction between the same (*das Selbe*) and the identical (*das Gleiche*) by noting that the former upholds the "belonging together of what differs, through a gathering by way of the difference" (*das Zusammengehören des Verschiedenen aus der Versammlung durch den Unterschied*), whereas the latter "always moves toward the absence of difference" (*verlegt sich stets auf das Unterschiedlose*). See Martin Heidegger, *Vorträge und Aufsätze* [GA 7] (Frankfurt am Main: Vittorio Klostermann, 2000), pp. 196–197; idem, *Poetry, Language, Thought*, translations and introduction by Albert Hofstadter (New York: Harper & Row, 1971), p. 218. Regarding this distinction in the Heideggerian lexicon, see Wolfson *Heidegger and Kabbalah*, pp. 11–13, 40, 55 n. 102, 265.

32. Wyschogrod, "Those Weeping Eyes," p. 215.

33. Wyschogrod, *Crossover Queries*, p. 44. Compare Edith Wyschogrod, *Emmanuel Levinas: The Problem of Ethical Metaphysics* (New York: Fordham University Press, 2000), pp. 97–102.

34. See ch. 2 n. 27.

35. Theodor W. Adorno, *Negative Dialektik* [GS 6] (Frankfurt am Main: Suhrkamp, 1966), p. 21; idem, *Negative Dialectics*, translated by E. B. Ashton (New York: Seabury Press, 1973), p. 9.

36. Wyschogrod, *Spirit*, p. 95.

37. Ibid., 96–97. See Edith Wyschogrod, *Saints and Postmodernism: Revisioning Moral Philosophy* (Chicago: University of Chicago Press, 1990), p. 121, and the analysis in Elliot R. Wolfson, *Giving Beyond the Gift: Apophasis and Overcoming Theomania* (New York: Fordham University Press, 2014), p. 224.

38. *Physics* 219^{b}13–219^{b}34, in *The Complete Works of Aristotle: The Revised Oxford Translation*, edited by Jonathan Barnes (Princeton: Princeton University Press, 1984), p. 372:

> The "now" in one sense is the same, in another it is not the same. In so far as it is in succession, it is different (which is just what its being now was supposed to mean), but its substratum is the same; for motion, as was said, goes with magnitude, and time, as we maintain, with motion. Similarly, then, there corresponds to the point the body which is carried along, and by which we are aware of the motion and of the before and after involved in it. This is an identical *substratum* (whether a point or a stone or something else of the kind), but it is different in definition—as the sophists assume that Coriscus' being in the Lyceum is a different thing from Coriscus' being in the market-place. And the body which is carried along is different, in so far as it is at one time here and at another there. But the "now" corresponds to the body that is carried along, as time corresponds to the motion. For it is by means of the body that is carried along that we become

aware of the before and after in the motion, and if we regard these as countable we get the "now". Hence in these also the "now" as substratum remains the same (for it is what is before and after in movement), but its being is different; for it is in so far as the before and after is that we get the "now". This is what is most knowable; for motion is known because of that which is moved, locomotion because of that which is carried. For what is carried is a "this", the movement is not. Thus the "now" in one sense is always the same, in another it is not the same; for this is true also of what is carried (emphasis in original).

See the analysis of this Aristotelian text in Claude Romano, *Event and Time*, translated by Stephen E. Lewis (New York: Fordham University Press, 2014), pp. 41–43. Compare the account of the "double visage" of Aristotle's understanding of the now in Martin Heidegger, *Die Grundprobleme der Phänomenologie* [GA 24] (Frankfurt am Main: Vittorio Klostermann, 1997), pp. 349–351; idem, *The Basic Problems of Phenomenology*, translation, introduction, and lexicon by Albert Hofstadter (Bloomington: Indiana University Press, 1982), pp. 247–248. The passage is cited and analyzed in Wolfson, *Heidegger and Kabbalah*, p. 262, and again in idem, *Suffering Time*, pp. 59–60.

39. Maurice Merleau-Ponty, *Le visible et l'invisible suivi de Notes de travail*, edited by Claude Lefort (Paris: Gallimard, 1964), p. 315; idem, *The Visible and the Invisible: Followed by Working Notes*, edited by Claude Lefort, translated by Alphonso Lingis (Evanston: Northwestern University Press, 1968), p. 267.

40. Wyschogrod, *Saints*, pp. 107–111.

41. Compare Wolfson, *Giving*, pp. 159–161, 169, and references to other scholars cited on p. 406 n. 31.

42. See Bettina Bergo, "The Historian and the Messianic 'Now': Reading Edith Wyschogrod's *An Ethics of Remembering*," in *Saintly Influence: Edith Wyschogrod and the Possibilities of Philosophy of Religion*, edited by Eric Boynton and Martin Kavka (New York: Fordham University Press, 2009), pp. 202–218, esp. 212–216. Bergo emphasized the similarity between Wyschogrod and Benjamin in contrast to my emphasis on Derrida, but our analyses are in basic agreement.

43. Edith Wyschogrod, *An Ethics of Remembering: History, Heterology, and the Nameless Others* (Chicago: University of Chicago Press, 1998), p. 242. Wyschogrod quotes the following passage from Jacques Derrida, *Points . . . Interviews, 1974–1994*, edited by Elisabeth Weber, translated by Peggy Kamuf and others (Stanford: Stanford University Press, 1995), p. 83: "How could the desire for presence let itself be destroyed? It is desire itself. But what gives it . . . breath and necessity—what there is and what remains thus to be thought—is that which in the presence of the present does not present itself."

44. Wyschogrod, *An Ethics*, p. 242. See the citation and analysis of this passage in Wolfson, *Giving*, p. 213.

45. Maurice Blanchot, *L'Attente l'oubli* (Paris: Gallimard, 1962), p. 27; idem,

Awaiting Oblivion, translated by John Gregg (Lincoln: University of Nebraska Press, 1997), p. 16.

46. I have repeated my formulation in Wolfson, *Suffering Time*, pp. 256–257.

47. Edith Wyschogrod, "Crossover Dreams," *Journal of the American Academy of Religion* 54 (1986): 546. For a fuller discussion, see Elliot R. Wolfson, "Apophasis and the Trace of Transcendence: Wyschogrod's Contribution to a Postmodern Jewish Immanent A/Theology," *Philosophy Today* 55 (2011): 328–347, esp. 337–339, and idem, *Giving*, pp. 224–225. I have taken the liberty to repeat some of my previous analyses here.

48. Wyschogrod, "Crossover Dreams," p. 546.

49. Ibid.

50. Wyschogrod, *Spirit*, p. 95.

51. Elliot R. Wolfson, "Coronation of the Sabbath Bride: Kabbalistic Myth and the Ritual of Androgynisation," *Journal of Jewish Thought and Philosophy* 6 (1997): 301–343. For references to primary and secondary sources, see op. cit., p. 307 n. 19.

52. Wyschogrod, "Crossover Dreams," p. 546.

53. I am here responding to the brief account of Wyschogrod's view on the cosmic Sabbath and my interpretation thereof given by Agata Bielik-Robson, "Political Theology of the Death of God: Hegel and Derrida," in *Nothing Absolute: German Idealism and the Question of Political Theology*, edited by Kirill Chepurin and Alex Dubilet (New York: Fordham University Press, 2021), pp. 205–206 n. 31, and repeated now in Agata Bielik-Robson, *Derrida's Marrano Passover: Exile, Survival, Betrayal, and the Metaphysics of Non-Identity* (New York: Bloomsbury Academic, 2023), p. 124 n. 38. In theory, I accept the validity of Bielik-Robson's contention that the positions of Wyschogrod and Derrida should be distinguished, but I would counter, firstly, that the former's reading of Hegel is indebted to the latter, which was the main point of my argument (see Wolfson, *Giving*, p. 435 n. 154), and secondly, I do not think it is accurate to say that for Wyschogrod there is a final rectification at the end of time that may be characterized as a Hegelian repetition of the original withdrawal or contraction.

54. Wyschogrod, "Crossover Dreams," p. 546.

55. Wyschogrod, *Saints*, p. 119.

56. Wyschogrod, "Crossover Dreams," pp. 546–547.

57. Ibid., p. 547. Compare the analysis of Nietzsche's "nomad thought" in Deleuze and Guattari offered by Wyschogrod, *Saints*, pp. 205–208. It is beyond the scope of this chapter to analyze the trope of nomadism in Wyschogrod's thought, but perhaps this will be a future undertaking. See my brief comments in Wolfson, *Giving*, pp. 219, 223, 225.

58. Heidegger, *Vorträge*, p. 35; idem, *The Question Concerning Technology and Other Essays*, translated and with an introduction by William Lovitt (New York: Harper & Row, 1977), p. 34: "There was a time when it was not technology alone that bore the name *technē*. Once that revealing that brings forth truth into the

splendor of radiant appearing also was called *technē*. . . . And the *poiēsis* of the fine arts also was called *technē*."

59. Wyschogrod, *Spirit*, pp. 178–179. Wyschogrod's analysis is based on Heidegger, *Question*, pp. 3–35, esp. 12–23.

60. Wyschogrod, *Spirit*, pp. 27–28.

61. Ibid., pp. 25–26.

62. Ibid., pp. 185–186. For a nuanced analysis of Wyschogrod's view, which stands in sharp contrast to Heidegger, see Virginia Burrus, "Wyschogrod's Hand: Saints, Animality, and the Labor of Love," *Philosophy Today* 55 (2011): 412–421.

63. Heidegger, *Vorträge*, p. 180, idem, *Poetry*, pp. 178–179. Compare idem, *Unterwegs zur Sprache* [GA 12] (Frankfurt am Main: Vittorio Klostermann, 1985), p. 203, where the matter is presented in terms of the essential relation between death and language: "Die Sterblichen sind jene, die den Tod als Tod erfahren können. Das Tier vermag dies nicht. Das Tier kann aber auch nicht sprechen. Das Wesensverhältnis zwischen Tod und Sprache blitzt auf, ist aber noch ungedacht." English translation in idem, *On the Way to Language*, translated by Peter D. Hertz (New York: Harper & Row, 1971), p. 107: "Mortals are they who can experience death as death. Animals cannot do so. But animals cannot speak either. The essential relation between death and language flashes up before us, but remains still unthought." Concerning Heidegger's notion of Dasein's confronting death as the sacrifice of the individual's animality, see Bruce Rosenstock, "The Flight of the Gods: A Comparative Study of Martin Heidegger and Oskar Goldberg," *New German Critique* 137 (2019): 247–248.

64. Heidegger, *Vorträge*, p. 200; idem, *Poetry*, p. 222. Regarding the anthropocentric dimension of this aspect of Heidegger's thinking, see Elliot R. Wolfson, *The Philosophical Pathos of Susan Taubes: Between Nihilism and Hope* (Stanford: Stanford University Press, 2023), pp. 235–236.

65. See Thomas J. J. Altizer, "The Impossible Possibility of Ethics," in *Saintly Influence*, pp. 31–47.

66. Heidegger, *Vorträge*, p. 184: "Erst die Menschen als die Sterblichen erlangen wohnend die Welt als Welt. Nur was aus Welt gering, wird einmal Ding." English translation in idem, *Poetry*, p. 182: "Men alone, as mortals, by dwelling attain to the world as world. Only what conjoins itself out of world becomes a thing."

67. Heidegger, *Unterwegs*, p. 220; idem, *On the Way*, p. 151, referenced in ch. 1 at n. 229. Compare Heidegger, *Unterwegs*, pp. 154–155; idem, *On the Way*, pp. 62–63:

> Only where the word for the thing has been found is the thing a thing. . . . The word alone gives being to the thing. . . . We could go further and propose this statement: something *is* only where the appropriate and therefore competent word names a thing as being, and so establishes the given being as a being (emphasis in original).

For the poet, the relationship of word and thing is akin to the relationship of world and thing in Heidegger's notion of worlding (see reference in n. 69). Consider Heidegger, *Unterwegs*, p. 159; idem, *On the Way*, p. 66. The poet is said to obtain "entrance into the relation of word to thing," but this relation is not "a connection between the thing that is on one side and the word that is on the other. The word itself is the relation which in each instance retains the thing within itself in such a manner that it 'is' a thing." On the renunciation and self-denial of the poet by which the word becomes thing, see reference cited in ch. 1 n. 228.

68. Heidegger, *Unterwegs*, p. 174; idem, *On the Way*, pp. 79–80. See Heidegger, *Unterwegs*, pp. 189, 191; idem, *On the Way*, pp. 94 and 96. Heidegger refers to the proposition "the being of language: the language of being" as the "guide-word" (*Leitwort*) that "holds the primal tidings of linguistic nature" and as that which "beckons us away from the current notions about language, to the experience of language as Saying."

69. Heidegger, *Unterwegs*, p. 19; idem, *Poetry*, pp. 199–200.

70. Wyschogrod, *Spirit*, p. 188.

71. Heidegger, *Unterwegs*, p. 19; idem, *Poetry*, p. 199. Numerous scholars have discussed Heidegger's idea of the fourfold. See, for instance, Andrew J. Mitchell, *The Fourfold: Reading the Late Heidegger* (Evanston: Northwestern University Press, 2015), and other references cited in Wolfson, *Heidegger and Kabbalah*, p. 179 n. 94.

72. Heidegger, *Unterwegs*, p. 21; idem, *Poetry*, p. 201.

73. Heidegger, *Unterwegs*, p. 22; idem, *Poetry*, pp. 202–203. See also Martin Heidegger, *Überlegungen II–VI (Schwarze Hefte 1931–1938)* [GA 94] (Frankfurt am Main: Vittorio Klostermann, 2014), pp. 209, 212; idem, *Ponderings II–VI: Black Notebooks 1931–1938*, translated by Richard Rojcewicz (Bloomington: Indiana University Press, 2016), pp. 153, 155. The first of these passages is cited and discussed in Elliot R. Wolfson, "*Gottwesen* and the De-Divinization of the Last God: Heidegger's Meditation on the Strange and Incalculable," in *Heidegger's Black Notebooks and the Future of Theology*, edited by Mårten Björk and Jayne Svenungsson (New York: Palgrave Macmillan, 2017), p. 221. Needless to say, many have opined on the Heideggerian tautology of worlding the world (*Welt-weltung*). Particularly pertinent is the study by Katherine M. Robiadek, "Worlding Versus Worldview: Heidegger's Thinking on Art as a Critique of German Historicism," *Monatshefte* 108 (2016): 383–394.

74. Heidegger, *Unterwegs*, p. 27; idem, *Poetry*, p. 207.

75. Heidegger, *Unterwegs*, p. 179; idem, *On the Way*, p. 84.

76. Wyschogrod, *Spirit*, p. 187. It is worth considering Wyschogrod's criticism of Heidegger in light of the discerning—and, in the context of recent discussions about artificial intelligence, the increasingly germane—musing of Ludwig Wittgenstein, *Remarks on the Foundations of Mathematics*, revised edition, edited by Georg Henrik von Wright, Rush Rhees, and Gertrude Elisabeth Margaret Anscombe, translated by Gertrude Elisabeth Margaret Anscombe (Cambridge, MA: MIT Press, 1978), p. 234: "If calculating looks to us like the action of a machine, it

is *the human being* doing the calculation that is the machine. In that case the calculation would be as it were a diagram drawn by a part of the machine" (emphasis in original).

77. Emmanuel Levinas, *Totalité et infini: Essai sur l'extériorité* (The Hague: Martinus Nijhoff, 1980), p. 209; idem, *Totality and Infinity: An Essay on Exteriority*, translated by Alphonso Lingis (Dordrecht: Kluwer Academic, 1969), p. 233.

78. Levinas, *Totalité et infini*, p. 154; idem, *Totality and Infinity*, p. 179 (emphasis in original).

79. Levinas, *Totalité et infini*, p. 210; idem, *Totality and Infinity*, p. 233.

80. There is a slight inaccuracy in Wyschogrod's citation of the passage from Jacques Lacan, *Écrits: A Selection*, translated by Alan Sheridan (New York: W. W. Norton, 1977), p. 317: "'I' am in the place from which a voice is heard clamouring 'the universe is a defect in the purity of Non-Being'." On some of the conceptual affinities between Heidegger and Lacan, see Wolfson, *Heidegger and Kabbalah*, pp. 45–46, and references to primary and secondary sources cited on pp. 58–59 n. 131.

81. Wyschogrod, *Saints*, p. 120.

82. Wyschogrod, *Spirit*, p. 94.

83. Wyschogrod, *Crossover Queries*, p. 2. I have taken the liberty to rework my previous analysis in Wolfson, *Giving*, pp. 205–207.

84. Wyschogrod, *Crossover Queries*, p. 1.

85. Georg Wilhelm Friedrich Hegel, *Phenomenology of Spirit*, translated by Arnold V. Miller (Oxford: Oxford University Press, 1977), p. 19, cited by Wyschogrod, *Crossover Queries*, p. 3.

86. Wyschogrod, *Crossover Queries*, pp. 3–4.

87. Wyschogrod, *Spirit*, pp. 144–145.

88. Ibid., p. 145.

89. Ibid.

90. Ibid., p. 144.

91. Ibid., p. 94.

92. On *différance* and Hegelian negation, see Marian Hobson, *Jacques Derrida: Opening Lines* (London: Routledge, 1998), pp. 154–161.

93. Wyschogrod, *Spirit*, p. 145.

94. Edith Wyschogrod, "Preface," in *Phenomenon of Death: Faces of Mortality*, edited by Edith Wyschogrod (New York: Harper & Row, 1973), p. vii.

95. Wyschogrod, "Concentration Camps," p. 334 (emphasis in original). The claim that in the world of the concentration camp, the only signified is death somewhat undermines the distinction made by Wyschogrod between the "concentration camp" and the "extermination camp" on the basis that the latter was "designed solely for the extermination of Jews and Gypsies." See op. cit., p. 338 n. 1.

96. Wyschogrod, "Preface," pp. vii–viii.

97. Wyschogrod, "Concentration Camps," p. 336.

98. Ibid., pp. 337–338. Significantly, Wyschogrod concludes her entry on "Value" in *Critical Terms for Religious Studies*, edited by Mark C. Taylor (Chicago: University of Chicago Press, 1998), p. 381, on this note:

> If value is seen as determined by power, the question of how a society's assigning of value might benefit those who are powerless inevitably arises. This worry has prompted some thinkers to propose that the other, whether construed individually or collectively, is to be understood as the ultimate source of worth. Claims of otherness bring to bear interests apart from those of the investigator who inquires into the beliefs and practices of the world's religions. Neither prizing nor holding dear disappear from contemporary accounts of value; rather, the multiple ways in which these attitudes function in a variety of contexts is brought to the fore.

99. Wyschogrod, *Spirit*, p. 163.
100. Ibid., p. 172.
101. Ibid., pp. 170–174. Compare the criticism of Heidegger's perspective in the section "Death and the Time That Is Left," supported partially by Levinas, in Wyschogrod, *Saints*, pp. 64–65, and my own discussion in the section "Death and the Surplus of Not Yet" in Wolfson, *Suffering Time*, pp. 577–592. See also Wyschogrod, "Value," pp. 376–377.
102. Reiner Schürmann, *Broken Hegemonies*, translated by Reginald Lilly (Bloomington: Indiana University Press, 2003), p. 17.
103. Martin Heidegger, *Sein und Zeit* (Tübingen: Max Niemeyer, 1993), §50, p. 250; idem, *Being and Time*, translated by Joan Stambaugh, revised and with a foreword by Dennis J. Schmidt (Albany: State University of New York Press, 2010), p. 241.
104. Wyschogrod, *Spirit*, p. 188. The example of death provides another illustration of the continuity of Heidegger's thought in spite of the obvious shift in orientation that marks the turn (*Kehre*) upon which he embarked in the 1930s. The following passage in Heidegger, *On the Way*, p. 85, can be applied to the path of his own thinking:

> We must first turn, turn back to where we are in reality already staying. The abiding turn, back to where we already are, is infinitely harder than are hasty excursions to places where we are not yet and never will be. . . . To turn back to where we are (in reality) already staying: that is how we must walk along the way of thinking which now becomes necessary.

I thus concur with the observation of Wyschogrod, *Spirit*, p. 189:

> Although extensive commentaries properly record and interpret changes in Heidegger's thought which result from the shift to Being and appropriation in his

later work, it is all too often forgotten that there is an extraordinary unity in Heidegger's thinking as well, a unity deriving from his single-minded concern with world and thing. Heidegger has not written an ontological *Bildungsroman* first of Dasein and then of Being; to the contrary, he has written a legend of the grail, a quest for the thing by way of different paths.

On the problematic nature of the chronological schematization of Heidegger's thinking, and references to others who have challenged it, see Wolfson, *Heidegger and Kabbalah*, p. 55 n. 102.

105. Elliot R. Wolfson, *The Duplicity of Philosophy's Shadow: Heidegger, Nazism, and the Jewish Other* (New York: Columbia University Press, 2018), pp. 33–34, 145–146, 199 n. 3. The flaws, moral failings, and cowardice of Heidegger are indefensible, but I do not accept the perspective of those who fail to see the more complex relationship to National Socialism and the criticisms leveled against the movement that can be extracted from his notebooks and other writings. Such a one-sided perspective is epitomized most recently in Richard Wolin, *Heidegger in Ruins: Between Philosophy and Ideology* (New Haven: Yale University, 2023). To illustrate my contention that Heidegger was circumspect about Nazi ideology and its practical ramifications, I will cite a passage that I neglected to mention in my previous work, the aphorism "Der Kern des Irrtums" in Martin Heidegger, *Zum Wesen der Sprache und Zur Frage nach der Kunst* [GA 74] (Frankfurt am Main: Vittorio Klostermann, 2010), pp. 38–39:

> Man meint, das, was "das Vaterland" angehen soll, müßte "politisch" sein. Nun aber kann "das Vaterland" nur in seinem Wesen angegangen und getroffen werden, wenn es selbst offen ist gegen seinen Wesensgrund. Reicht es zu diesem hin, dann ist es schon im Wesen ein anderes als es selbst und alles "Politische" ist die Einkerkerung des Vaterlandes in sein Unwesen. Um das Vaterland "anzugehen", muß Etwas weither seinen Gang haben und lange unterwegs gewesen und zu langer Wanderung entschlossen sein. . . . Das Unreife und Urteilslose zerbricht das Wesen; und alle Jugendlichkeit ist nur der Taumel in das Besinnungslose, vollends dann, wenn es in der Leere seiner Unwissenheit gar noch nach dem "Alten" greift und, ohne je die Reife erfahren zu haben, sich anmaßt, dieses auslegen zu dürfen. Wo das Gesetz der Wesensfülle gebrochen und gebeugt, hat der Untergang schon begonnen, und seine Bahn verwehrt jede Umkehr.

English translation in Heidegger, *On the Essence of Language and the Question of Art*, edited by Thomas Regehly, translated by Adam Knowles (Cambridge: Polity Press, 2022) p. 33:

> They believe that everything concerned with "the fatherland" must be "political." But "the fatherland" can only be approached and arrived at essentially if the fatherland itself is open to its essential ground. If the fatherland accomplishes

that, then it has already become something essentially other than itself and everything political is the confinement of the fatherland into its corrupted essence. In order to "approach" the fatherland, something must begin its journey from afar, and must have been underway for a long time, harboring the resolve for a long sojourn.... Those who are unripe and undiscriminating shatter the essence; and all youthfulness is nothing more than a way of reveling in mindlessness, especially when the youth still clings to the "old" in the emptiness of its ignorance, without ever having experienced maturity and ripeness, and it is presumptuous enough to assume that it is capable of interpreting the old. Wherever the law of the plenitude of the essence is broken and bent, there the downfall has already begun, and there is no chance of turning it back.

While I make no excuses for Heidegger's Nazi affiliation and the harmful rhetoric he espoused and injurious actions he took against German Jews, it is hard not to see in the aforecited passage a derisive censure of the political interpretation of the concept of the fatherland as a corruption of its essential meaning and a reproof of the foolhardiness of the Hitler-Jugend, who blindly and immaturely followed the ignorant mistakes of the older generation.

106. Wyschogrod, *Spirit*, p. 174.

107. Jacques Derrida, "Force of Law: The 'Mystical Foundation of Authority,'" in *Deconstruction and the Possibility of Justice*, edited by Drucilla Cornell, Michael Rosenfeld, and David Gray Carlson (New York: Routledge, 1992), pp. 62–63.

108. Wyschogrod, *Spirit*, p. 174.

109. Heidegger, *Was Heißt Denken?*, p. 174; idem, *What Is Called Thinking?*, pp. 169–170. See Heidegger, *Was Heißt Denken?*, p. 189: "Das Wort von einem Denkversuch ist keine Redensart, die bescheiden tun soll. Diese Benennung erhebt den Anspruch, daß hier ein Weg des *Fragens* begangen wird, auf dem das Fragwürdige als der einzige Aufenthaltsbereich des Denkens übernommen ist" (emphasis in original). English translation in idem, *What Is Called Thinking?*, p. 185: "To speak of an 'attempt at thinking' is not an empty phrase meant to simulate humility. The term makes the claim that we are here taking a way of *questioning*, on which the problematic alone is accepted as the unique habitat and *locus* of thinking" (emphasis in original). See Heidegger, *Unterwegs*, p. 187; idem, *On the Way*, p. 92. Heidegger explicitly mentions the role of Tao in Laotse's poetic thinking as an analogue to his notion of the way or the method as the source of our power to think. On Heidegger's engagement with Taoism, see sources cited in Wolfson, *Heidegger and Kabbalah*, pp. 82 n. 1 and 232–233 n. 10.

110. For example, compare Heidegger, *Unterwegs*, p. 165: "das Fragen nicht die eigentliche Gebärde des Denkens ist, sondern—das Hören der Zusage dessen, was in die Frage kommen soll. Nun gilt jedoch von altersher in der Geschichte unseres Denkens das Fragen als der maßgebende Zug des Denkens, und dies nicht von

ungefähr." English translation in idem, *On the Way*, p. 71: "the authentic attitude of thinking is not a putting of questions—rather, it is a listening to the grant, the promise of what is to be put in question. But in the history of our thinking, asking questions has since the early days been regarded as the characteristic procedure of thinking, and not without good cause." See Wyschogrod, *An Ethics*, p. 139. For a fuller analysis of the primacy of the question on Heidegger's path of thinking, see Wolfson, *Heidegger and Kabbalah*, pp. 77–78, 92 n. 150.

111. Heidegger, *Vorträge*, p. 36; idem, *Question*, p. 35. See the exposition of this statement in Heidegger, *Unterwegs*, p. 165; idem, *On the Way*, p. 72.

112. Wyschogrod, *An Ethics*, p. 140.

113. Ibid.

114. Wyschogrod, *Spirit*, p. 214.

115. Ibid.

116. Ibid., pp. 214–215.

117. Ibid., p. 215.

118. Wyschogrod, "Concentration Camps," p. 335 (emphasis in original).

119. Wyschogrod, *An Ethics*, p. 140.

120. Wyschogrod, *Spirit*, p. 97.

121. Ibid., p. 98.

122. Wyschogrod, *Saints*, p. 110.

123. Wyschogrod, *An Ethics*, p. 139.

124. Ibid., p. 141.

125. Ibid., pp. 146–147. See ibid., pp. 148–152, where Wyschogrod examines the task of the historian in light of the possibility of time travel entertained by contemporary physicists.

126. For discussion of the realist and antirealist positions regarding the historiographical possibility of retrieving the past, see Michael Dummett, *Truth and Other Enigmas* (Cambridge, MA: Harvard University Press, 1978), pp. 358–374, and Shigeto Nuki, "Temporality and Historicity: Phenomenology of History Beyond Narratology," in *The Many Faces of Time*, edited by John B. Brough and Lester Embree (Dordrecht: Kluwer Academic, 2000), pp. 149–165. Particularly relevant is Nuki's presentation of the Husserlian position on pp. 161–163:

> The content of the "past-in-itself," which lies beyond the clarifying process of our available remembering, is unknowable, but it can function as the "regulative Idea" of our experience, because it indicates negatively that our available remembering is always insufficient. Even if Husserl talks about the "being-in-itself" or "true-being" of the past, he does not suppose that "the past-in-itself" exists independently of our experience, much less the possibility of our experiencing it. Rather, the structure of the "presence of the absence" of the past itself in our descriptive structure of consciousness presents the meaning of the reality of the

past for us.... The division of Past-Present-Future can thus be clarified phenomenologically from the structure of our intentional experience, where something is past when it belongs to a totally different kind of time-order than the present.... The reality of the past is thus clarified phenomenologically as the limit, or Idea, indicated from within the actual structure of remembering, which contains associative indications toward the present in the objectified time-order constituted through a mechanism, the vector of which is the opposite of the normal cognitive activity.... Presence has the privilege of indefeasible validity, but it must be remembered iteratively in order to be an object, and the original content of presence cannot be perfectly revived. Similarly, the original experience of the past person—of a Roman, for example—is something absolute as an experience, but its meaning is determined only by historiography narrated by historians, and the original experience cannot be completely reproduced. This tension between the present and the past, especially the impossibility of the complete reproduction of the past, does not indicate the limit of our cognition, but rather indicates the necessary condition of our experience of the past as past.

It seems to me that Wyschogrod's view is in accord with the phenomenological insistence that the past can be present only as the presence of absence, but recovering this absence is endowed with paramount ethical import to the extent that it gives voice to the voiceless victims of violence. Also note the observation made by Nuki, p. 156, with respect to the Holocaust—through an example drawn from the movie *Shoah*—that it is impossible to narrate "because the 'meaning' of the matter concerned cannot be drawn into any familiar plot, such as Tragedy or Irony, while we cannot deny the existence of the facts concerned." Wyschogrod's position is that the historian's narration is necessitated precisely because the events themselves are beyond narration. In spite of this difference, Nuki's summation on pp. 164–165 surely can be applied to Wyschogrod: "History for phenomenologists means first of all the 'footing [*Boden*]' which motivates judgements or practical activities, including narrative acts." Many have opined on the relationship of phenomenology and history. See, for instance, David Carr, "Phenomenology of Historical Time," in *The Past's Present: Essays on the Historicity of Philosophical Thinking*, edited by Marcia Sá Cavalcante Schuback and Hans Ruin (Huddinge: Södertörn Academic Studies, 2006), pp. 7–23, and in the same volume, Marléne Zarader, "The Event—Between Phenomenology and History," pp. 25–54, esp. 37–49. The crucial difference between phenomenologist and historian is demarcated in the following way by Zarader, pp. 43–44:

> What the historian wants to do is actually to qualify the event on the basis of but also beyond the recognition of its phenomenological aspect, as he takes upon himself to define, not only what the event "is," but also what it opens up, what terminates with it, etc. This he cannot do without transcending the phenomeno-

logical attitude in the directions of *before and after.* Transcending it in this way, his real activity starts, which is that of weaving and unweaving the structure of sense.... The historian thus believes himself to have *done justice* by the phenomenon of the event, in the same process whereby he has come to *understand* it (i.e. by subjecting it to contextualization) (emphasis in original).

Zarader upholds the validity of the truths announced respectively by the phenomenologist and the historian even though their beliefs are irreconcilable. See ch. 4 n. 177. For additional references to the relation of phenomenological analysis and historical inquiry, see Elliot R. Wolfson, *Language, Eros, Being: Kabbalistic Hermeneutics and the Poetic Imagination* (New York: Fordham University Press, 2005), p. 396 n. 65.

127. Wyschogrod, *An Ethics*, pp. 147, 166. On time's duality, see the extended discussion in ibid., pp. 152–159.

128. Ibid., p. 166 (emphasis in original). Compare Wyschogrod, *Crossover Queries*, p. 253:

> The past does not give itself all at once as spectacle before an absolute subject, but is disclosed by the "not" that is imprinted, in Derrida's phrase, *sous rature*, under erasure, in what is actually imaged and told. Memory holds before itself what will take shape as the remembered past.

The point is repeated in ibid., p. 259. Lamentably, in spite of its obvious relevance, Wyschogrod's work is not cited in the analysis of memory, history, and the present in François Hartog, *Regimes of Historicity: Presentism and Experiences of Time*, translated by Saskia Brown (New York: Columbia University Press, 2015), pp. 101–148.

129. Wyschogrod, *Crossover Queries*, p. 253.

130. Wyschogrod, *An Ethics*, pp. 167–168. Compare Werner H. Kelber, "Memory and Violence, or Genealogies of Remembering," in *Saintly Influence*, pp. 175–201.

131. Wyschogrod, *Crossover Queries*, pp. 248–249.

132. Ibid., p. 250.

133. Ibid. A similar approach to the dialectical interrelation between remembering and forgetting can be elicited from Claudia Welz, "The Future of the Past: Memory, Forgetting, and Personal Identity," in *Impossible Time: Past and Future in the Philosophy of Religion,* edited by Marius Timmann Mjaaland, Ulrik Houlind Rasmussen, and Philipp Stoellger (Tübingen: Mohr Siebeck, 2013), pp. 191–212, esp. 201–204.

134. Wyschogrod, *Crossover Queries*, p. 250.

135. Ibid., p. 260.

136. Ibid., p. 252.

137. Ibid.

138. On Heidegger's notion of *Gleichursprünglichkeit*, see ch. 1 n. 172.

139. See Wolfson, *Heidegger and Kabbalah*, pp. 263–265; idem, *Suffering Time*, pp. 14–16, 359–360. And compare the reference to the study of Kouba cited in ch. 1 n. 197.

140. Heidegger, *The Concept of Time*, translated by William McNeill (Oxford: Blackwell, 1992), pp. 17–18.

141. See my previous discussion in Wolfson, *Suffering Time*, pp. 583–584.

142. Heidegger, *Concept of Time*, pp. 12–14 (emphasis in original).

143. Ibid., p. 19.

144. Ibid., p. 20 (emphasis in original).

145. Wolfson, *Suffering Time*, pp. 61–62.

146. Martin Heidegger, *Beiträge zur Philosophie (Vom Ereignis)* [GA 65] (Frankfurt am Main: Vittorio Klostermann, 1989), §33, p. 73; idem, *Contributions to Philosophy (Of the Event)*, translated by Richard Rojcewicz and Daniela Vallega-Neu (Bloomington: Indiana University Press, 2012), p. 58. This passage and others that articulate the novelty of the repetition of the unique as the replication of difference in Heidegger's thought are cited and discussed in Wolfson, *Heidegger and Kabbalah*, pp. 39–40; idem, *Suffering Time*, pp. 67–70. For additional references, see ch. 1 n. 162.

147. Eugene Gendlin, "*Befindlichkeit*: Heidegger and the Philosophy of Psychology," in *Heidegger and Psychology*, edited by Keith Hoeller, Special issue of *Review of Existential Psychology and Psychiatry* (1988): 60–61. See also Joan Stambaugh, "Existential Time in Kierkegaard and Heidegger," in *Religion and Time*, edited by Anindita Niyogi Balslev and Jitendra N. Mohanty (Leiden: Brill, 1993), pp. 54–55:

> The three modes of experience to which time is related are understanding, attunement and discourse. These three modes undercut the traditional philosophical distinction of reason and the senses.... Understanding (*Verstehen*), which is not identical with reason, is primarily related to the future, to our fundamental existential "project" with all of its concrete potentialities, and affords us our dimension of transcendence.... Attunement (*Befindlichkeit:* literally, how I find myself) is primarily related to the past, to our "thrownness", our having been thrown into the world, and imposes on us the stricture of facticity.... Finally, discourse (*Rede*) is primarily related to the present.... Now, we must distance ourselves from the Aristotelian conception of time in which the past is that which is no more, the future is that which is not yet, and the present is a sort of "knife-edged" *now* that is not even a part of time. Here Heidegger draws on the literal meaning of the German words for his purposes. The future (*die Zukunft*) is literally what is coming toward me and is already with me. The past (*die Gewesenheit*) is what has been and still is. The present (*die Gegenwart*) is what emerges from the meeting of future and having-been in the senses of those

words discussed. I project myself toward my existential potentialities and, in so doing, come back to the facticity of my having-been, what I have done and been thus far. Thus the present is engendered. Time is not conceived as a linear string of unrelated "nows"; future, having-been and present are always inseparably together. The future is not "later" than the past; the past is not "earlier" than the present (emphasis in original).

I note, finally, that the reversal of the timeline has found support in the theorizing about the indeterminacy of time in quantum physics. See, for instance, Carlo Rovelli, *The Order of Time*, translated by Erica Segre and Simon Carnell (New York: Riverhead Books, 2018), p. 88: "Even the distinction between present, past, and future thus becomes fluctuating, indeterminate. Just as a particle may be diffused in space, so, too, the differences between past and future may fluctuate: an event may be both before and after another one."

148. See Walter Benjamin, *Gesammelte Schriften*, 5.1, edited by Rolf Tiedemann (Frankfurt am Main: Suhrkamp, 1991), pp. 591–592. English translation in idem, *The Arcades Project*, translated by Howard Eiland and Kevin McLaughlin (Cambridge, MA: Harvard University Press, 1999), p. 473:

> It is the inherent tendency of dialectical experience [*dialektischen Erfahrung*] to dissipate the semblance of eternal sameness [*den Schein des Immer-Gleichen*], and event of repetition [*Wiederholung*], in history. Authentic political experience is absolutely free of this semblance. . . . The dialectical image [*dialektische Bild*] is an image that emerges suddenly, in a flash [*aufblitzendes*]. What has been is to be held fast—as an image flashing up in the now of its recognizability [*Jetzt der Erkennbarkeit*]. The rescue that is carried out by these means—and only by these—can operate solely for the sake of what in the next moment is already irretrievably lost.

See additional references cited in ch. 1 n. 144. Heidegger's affirmation of sameness similarly entails dissimilarity and his idea of repetition signifies that which occurs unexpectedly. See Wolfson, *Heidegger and Kabbalah*, pp. 10, 355; idem, *Suffering Time*, pp. 398, 512 n. 24, 608–640, and pp. 611–612 n. 129, where I discuss and cite other sources on the affinities between Benjamin and Heidegger.

149. See Slavoj Žižek, *The Fragile Absolute or, Why Is the Christian Legacy Worth Fighting For?* (London: Verso, 2000), pp. 89–90:

> This is what . . . Walter Benjamin was trying to articulate in his explicitly anti-evolutionist notion of the Messianic promise of a revolutionary Act that will retroactively redeem the Past itself: the present revolution will retroactively realize the crushed longings of all the past, failed revolutionary attempts. What this means is that, in a properly *historical* perspective as opposed to evolutionist historicism, the past is not simply past, but bears within it its proper utopian prom-

ise of a future Redemption: in order to understand a past epoch properly, it is not sufficient to take into account the historical conditions of which it grew—one has also to take into account the utopian hopes of a Future that were betrayed and crushed by it—that which was "negated", that which did not happen—so that the past historical reality was the way it was (emphasis in original).

150. Wyschogrod, *Crossover Queries*, pp. 260–261.
151. Ibid., p. 253.
152. Ibid.
153. Ibid., p. 255.
154. Ibid., p. 262. Wyschogrod's critique of a lingering ontological realism on the part of historians and her emphasis on the polysemic play of presence and absence in the attempt to retrieve the past are compatible with the orientation of Ethan Kleinberg, *Haunting History: For a Deconstructive Approach to the Past* (Stanford: Stanford University Press, 2017).
155. Wyschogrod, *An Ethics*, p. 173.
156. Ibid., p. 213:

But it is precisely the stationing of the heterological historian just as that point where she neither ignores nor is overwhelmed by the cataclysm, is neither inured to alterity nor so wounded by it that she cannot speak, that enables her to evade totalization. Can she not from the non-space of ethics transform a vat of DNA with its unheard of stockpiling potential into a memory palace, a lukasa board upon whose retained events she may draw in her depiction of the past?

157. Ibid., p. 179. For further discussion of Wyschogrod's affirmation of heterology and the role of the historian, see John D. Caputo, "Hearing the Voices of the Dead: Wyschogrod, Megill, and the Heterological Historian," in *Saintly Influence*, pp. 161–174, and in the same volume, Peter Ochs, "Saints and the Heterological Historian," pp. 219–237.
158. Wyschogrod, *Crossover Queries*, p. 314.
159. Wyschogrod, *An Ethics*, p. 213.
160. For an elaboration of this motif and the citation and analysis of the philosophical sources that have informed my view, see the chapter "Timemask and the Telling of Time in the Time of Telling" in Wolfson, *Suffering Time*, pp. 1–71.
161. Wyschogrod, *Crossover Queries*, p. 6. The text to which Wyschogrod referred is Jean-François Lyotard, *The Differend: Phrases in Dispute*, translated by Georges Van Den Abbeele (Minneapolis: University of Minnesota Press, 1988), pp. 88–89. I note, parenthetically, that the precise locution used by Lyotard is not "non-negotiable negative" but rather "non-negatable negative" (*un négatif non niable*), that is, the negative that cannot be negated and therefore cannot be denied.
162. Adorno, *Negative Dialektik*, p. 161; idem, *Negative Dialectics*, p. 158.

163. Adorno, *Negative Dialektik*, p. 162; idem, *Negative Dialectics*, pp. 159–160.
164. Adorno, *Negative Dialektik*, p. 163; idem, *Negative Dialectics*, pp. 160–161.
165. Wyschogrod, *Spirit*, p. 212.
166. Edith Wyschogrod, "Trends in Postmodern Jewish Philosophy: Contexts of a Conversation," in Steven Kepnes, Peter Ochs, and Robert Gibbs, *Reasoning After Revelation: Dialogues in Postmodern Jewish Philosophy* (Boulder: Westview Press, 1998), pp. 133–134.
167. Wyschogrod, *Spirit*, p. 209.
168. Ibid., p. 215.
169. Ibid., pp. 209–210.
170. Ibid., p. 192. Wyschogrod cites Heidegger, *Poetry*, p. 125.
171. Emmanuel Levinas, *En découvrant l'existence avec Husserl et Heidegger*, third corrected edition (Paris: Librairie Philosophique J. Vrin, 2001), p. 323; idem, *Collected Philosophical Papers*, translated by Alphonso Lingis (Dordrecht: Martinus Nijhoff. 1987), p. 122.
172. On the contrast between Heidegger's delimitation of the saying of speech as subservient to language as a monologue and Levinas's view of speech as a saying of that which is held in common between the self and the other, see Wyschogrod, *Crossover Queries*, pp. 498–499. See, however, Emmanuel Levinas, *De Dieu qui vient à l'idée*, second edition (Paris: Librairie Philosophique J. Vrin, 2004), p. 123; English translation in idem, *Of God Who Comes to Mind, translated by Bettina Bergo* (Stanford: Stanford University Press, 1998), p. 75: "The religious discourse prior to all religious discourse is not dialogue. It is the 'here I am,' said to the neighbor to whom I am given over, and in which I announce peace, that is, my responsibility for the other."
173. Emmanuel Levinas, *Autrement qu'être ou au-delà de l'essence* (Dordrecht: Kluwer Academic, 1974), p. 6 (emphasis in original); idem, *Otherwise Than Being or Beyond Essence*, translated by Alphonso Lingis (Dordrecht: Kluwer Academic, 1991), p. 5 (emphasis in original).
174. Levinas, *Autrement qu'être*, p. 9; idem, *Otherwise Than Being*, p. 8.
175. Levinas, *Autrement qu'être*, p. 9; idem, *Otherwise Than Being*, p. 8.
176. Levinas, *Autrement qu'être*, p. 17; idem, *Otherwise Than Being*, p. 14.
177. Levinas, *Autrement qu'être*, pp. 12–13; idem, *Otherwise Than Being*, pp. 10–11 (emphasis in original).
178. Levinas, *Autrement qu'être*, p. 8 n. 4; idem, *Otherwise Than Being*, p. 187 n. 5.
179. Plato, *Parmenides* 156d, in *The Collected Dialogues of Plato Including the Letters*, edited by Edith Hamilton and Huntington Cairns, with introduction and prefatory notes (Princeton: Princeton University Press, 1961), p. 947.
180. Levinas, *Autrement qu'être*, p. 138. I have slightly modified the translation in idem, *Otherwise Than Being*, p. 109.
181. Emmanuel Levinas, *Basic Philosophical Writings*, edited by Adriaan T. Peperzak, Simon Critchley, and Robert Bernasconi (Bloomington: Indiana Uni-

versity Press, 1996), p. 67. See the passage of Levinas cited below at n. 202. It is of interest to compare Levinas's description of "the trace of a beyond-being where day and night do not divide the time" to the remark of Heidegger, *Contributions*, §142, p. 207 (*Beiträge*, p. 263): "The appropriating event and its joining in the abyss of time-space form the net in which the last god is self-suspended in order to rend the net and let it end in its uniqueness, divine and rare and the strangest amid all beings. The sudden extinguishing of the great fire—this leaves behind something which is neither day nor night, which no one grasps, and in which humans, having come to the end, still bustle about so as to benumb themselves with the products of their machinations, pretending such products are made for all eternity, perhaps for that 'and so forth' which is neither day nor night." For a brief discussion of this passage, see Elliot R. Wolfson, "To Stand in Relation with Something Which Is Neither Day nor Night: Temporal Overcoming and Heidegger's Notion of Destiny," *Gatherings: The Heidegger Circle Annual* 10 (2020): 207–210.

182. Wyschogrod, *Crossover Queries*, p. 499.

183. Ibid., p. 426. On the utopian implications of this theme in Levinas, see Xin Mao, "Utopia in Lévinas: Null-Site as Reduction from Said to Saying, from Politics to Ethics," *Azimuth: Philosophical Coordinates in Modern and Contemporary Ages* 2 (2014): 123–138, and idem, "Subjectivity, Infinite Ethical Responsibility and Null-Site Exposure: A Constructive Exploration of Levinasian Subjectivity Through the Lens of the Levinasian Concept of Utopia," PhD dissertation, King's College London, 2019.

184. Levinas, *Autrement qu'être*, p. 135; idem, *Otherwise Than Being*, p. 106. Regarding this theme, see Lisa Guenther, "'Nameless Singularity': Levinas on Individuation and Ethical Singularity," *Epoché: A Journal for the History of Philosophy* 14 (2009): 168–187.

185. Levinas, *Autrement qu'être*, p. 10; idem, *Otherwise Than Being*, p. 8. See Wolfson, *Giving*, pp. 148–149.

186. Levinas, *Autrement qu'être*, pp. 103–104; idem, *Otherwise Than Being*, p. 82. I have slightly modified the translation.

187. Levinas, *Autrement qu'être*, p. 104; idem, *Otherwise Than Being*, p. 82.

188. Levinas, *Autrement qu'être*, p. 186; idem, *Otherwise Than Being*, p. 146.

189. Levinas, *Autrement qu'être*, p. 185; idem, *Otherwise Than Being*, p. 145.

190. Levinas, *Autrement qu'être*, p. 148; idem, *Otherwise Than Being*, p. 116. I have slightly modified the translation.

191. Levinas, *Autrement qu'être*, p. 180; idem, *Otherwise Than Being*, p. 141.

192. Levinas, *Autrement qu'être*, p. 107; idem, *Otherwise Than Being*, p. 85.

193. Levinas, *En découvrant*, p. 321; idem, *Collected Philosophical Papers*, p. 120.

194. Levinas, *Autrement qu'être*, p. 114; idem, *Otherwise Than Being*, p. 90.

195. Levinas, *En découvrant*, pp. 321–322; idem, *Collected Philosophical Papers*, pp. 120–121 (emphasis in original).

196. See ch. 2 n. 18. The affinity between the sense of comedy implied in Rose's idea of misrecognition and Levinas's notion of skepticism was duly noted by Martin Kavka, "Saying Kaddish for Gillian Rose, or on Levinas and *Geltungsphilosophie*," in *Secular Theology: American Radical Theological Thought*, edited by Clayton Crockett (London: Routledge, 2001), p. 125.

197. Levinas, *De Dieu*, p. 108; idem, *Collected Philosophical Papers*, p. 162.

198. Levinas, *Of God*, p. 69.

199. Levinas, *En découvrant*, p. 322; idem, *Collected Philosophical Papers*, p. 121 (emphasis in original).

200. Levinas, *Totalité et infini*, pp. xiv–xv; idem, *Totality and Infinity*, p. 26.

201. Levinas, *Totalité et infini*, pp. 3–5; idem, *Totality and Infinity*, pp. 33–35. See Wyschogrod, *Emmanuel Levinas*, pp. 123–124. For the narrowing of the gap between Heidegger and Levinas with respect to the inseparability of concealment and disclosure, absence and presence, see Wolfson, *Giving*, pp. 94–102.

202. Levinas, *Totalité et infini*, p. 4; idem, *Totality and Infinity*, p. 34.

203. Levinas, *Totalité et infini*, p. 154; idem, *Totality and Infinity*, p. 179. See Wyschogrod, *Emmanuel Levinas*, p. 89. See passage of Susan Taubes cited in ch. 1 at n. 202.

204. Levinas, *Totalité et infini*, p. 221; idem, *Totality and Infinity*, p. 243.

205. Levinas, *Totalité et infini*, pp. 221, 225; idem, *Totality and Infinity*, pp. 243–244, 247.

206. Levinas, *Totalité et infini*, p. 51; idem, *Totality and Infinity*, p. 78. For discussion of Levinas's description of the infinite as "the invisible but personal God," see Elliot R. Wolfson, "Imagination, Theolatry, and the Compulsion to Worship the Invisible," in *Religion in Reason: Metaphysics, Ethics, and Politics in Hent de Vries*, edited by Tarek R. Dika and Martin Shuster (London: Routledge, 2023), pp. 53–55.

207. Levinas, *Basic Philosophical Writings*, p. 67.

208. Levinas, *Autrement qu'être*, p. 120; idem, *Otherwise Than Being*, p. 94.

209. Wyschogrod, *Crossover Queries*, pp. 24–25. See also Wyschogrod, *Emmanuel Levinas*, pp. 90–93.

210. Wyschogrod, *Crossover Queries*, pp. 316–317.

211. Wyschogrod, *Crossover Queries*, p. 344.

212. Jacques Derrida, *The Gift of Death*, translated by David Wills (Chicago: University of Chicago Press, 1995), p. 100.

213. Jacques Derrida, *Geneses, Genealogies, Genres, and Genius: The Secrets of the Archive*, translated by Beverley Bie Brahic (New York: Columbia University Press, 2006), p. 32. For a more extended discussion of the Derridean notion of secrecy, see Wolfson, *Giving*, pp. 154–200, esp. 182–183, 191–195.

214. Wyschogrod, *Spirit*, p. 94 (emphasis in original).

215. Ibid., p. 63.

216. Ibid., pp. 15–16.

217. Wyschogrod, *Crossover Queries*, p. 77.
218. Ibid., p. 311.
219. Ibid., pp. 372–373. Wyschogrod cites the passage from Jacques Derrida, *Dissemination*, translated and with an introduction and additional notes by Barbara Johnson (Chicago: University of Chicago Press, 1981), p. 351, where the distinction between "discursive polysemy" and "textual dissemination" is made. Interestingly, in her interview with Levinas, in Wyschogrod, *Crossover Queries*, p. 294, she noted that Derrida's emphasis on writing is "perhaps a Jewish moment in thinking, Kabbalistic maybe, but Jewish nonetheless." Levinas replied incredulously, "Now for Derrida. That he knows Kabbalah!" To which Wyschogrod responded by referring to the essay in *Dissemination* on Phillipe Sollers where references were made to the kabbalah. Tellingly, Levinas did not respond to Wyschogrod's bibliographical citation. Derrida's relationship to the kabbalistic tradition has been examined by a number of scholars. For my own assessment, which includes references to a number of others who have previously discussed the topic, see Wolfson, *Giving*, pp. 154–200.
220. Edith Wyschogrod, "Religion as Life and Text: Postmodern Refigurations," in *The Craft of Religious Studies*, edited by Jon R. Stone (New York: St. Martin's Press, 1998), p. 248. Compare Edith Wyschogrod, "How to Say No in French: Derrida and Negation in Recent French Philosophy," in *Negation and Theology*, edited by Robert P. Scharlemann (Charlottesville: University Press of Virginia, 1992), pp. 46–54.
221. Edith Wyschogrod, "Hasidism, Hellenism, Holocaust: A Postmodern View," in *Interpreting Judaism in a Postmodern Age*, edited by Steven Kepnes (New York: New York University Press, 1996), p. 312.
222. Wyschogrod, "How to Say No," p. 40.
223. Levinas, *Totalité et infini*, p. 232; idem, *Totality and Infinity*, p. 254.
224. Wyschogrod, *Crossover Queries*, p. 15 (emphasis in original).
225. Levinas, *Totalité et infini*, p. 234; idem, *Totality and Infinity*, p. 256 (emphasis in original). See Elliot R. Wolfson, "Secrecy, Modesty, and the Feminine: Kabbalistic Traces in the Thought of Levinas," *Journal of Jewish Thought and Philosophy* 14 (2006): 203–205.
226. Levinas, *Totalité et infini*, p. 233; idem, *Totality and Infinity*, p. 256.
227. Levinas, *Totalité et infini*, p. 234; idem, *Totality and Infinity*, pp. 256–257.
228. Levinas, *Autrement qu'être*, p. 174; idem, *Otherwise Than Being*, p. 137.
229. Levinas, *Autrement qu'être*, p. 179; idem, *Otherwise Than Being*, p. 140.
230. Levinas, *Totalité et infini*, p. 236; idem, *Totality and Infinity*, p. 259 (emphasis in original).
231. Levinas, *Totalité et infini*, p. 242; idem, *Totality and Infinity*, p. 264.
232. Levinas, *Totalité et infini*, p. 234; idem, *Totality and Infinity*, p. 257. See Wolfson, "Secrecy," p. 208.
233. Levinas, *Autrement qu'être*, p. 137; idem, *Otherwise Than Being*, p. 108.

234. Wyschogrod, *An Ethics*, p. 240.
235. Edith Wyschogrod, "Doing Before Hearing: On the Primacy of Touch," in *Textes pour Emmanuel Lévinas*, edited by François Laruelle (Paris: Collections Surfaces, 1980), p. 187.
236. Wyschogrod, *An Ethics*, p. 14.
237. Wyschogrod, *Spirit*, p. 196.
238. Ibid.
239. Wyschogrod, *Saints*, p. 55.
240. Jean Genet, *Our Lady of the Flowers*, translated by Bernard Frechtman, with an introduction by Jean-Paul Sartre (New York: Bantam, 1964), p. 283.
241. Wyschogrod, *Crossover Queries*, p. 378.
242. Ibid., p. 390.
243. Ibid., p. 396.
244. Ibid., p. 308.
245. Ibid., p. 397. Wyschogrod contrasts this view of poetry in Blanchot and Levinas with that of Heidegger on the grounds that the latter affirmed a sanctification of language conceived as the gift, whereas the former were more skeptical about the cultic nature of language as holy. In support of her position, Wyschogrod evoked Blanchot's description of writing as a "giving withholding." No reference is given, but I assume that she had in mind the discussion in Maurice Blanchot, *The Writing of Disaster*, translated by Ann Smock (Lincoln: University of Nebraska Press, 1986), pp. 101–102, where the following words of Heidegger are cited, "There is reason to meditate upon whether being, and thus the history of being, can still be spoken of after the entry into the advent; this is the case, at least, if the history of being is understood as the history of the endowments, the gifts in which the advent (*Ereignis*) keeps withdrawn." Despite the explicit assertion that the withdrawal of what is endowed is essential to the advent of being, Blanchot commented,

> But it is doubtful whether Heidegger would recognize his own thinking in such a proposition, whose merit is its temerity and whose meaning is only too clear: the donations which are the ways in which being gives by withholding itself (*logos* in Heraclitus, *One* in Parmenides, *Idea* in Plato, *enérgeia* in Aristotle if we stay with the Greeks, and the final, modern version, *Gestell*—for which Lacoue-Labarthe proposes this equivalent: "installation") would be interrupted from the moment that the *Ereignis*, the advent, arrives, ceasing to let itself be hidden by the "donations of meaning" which it makes possible by its retreat.

In my opinion, the criticism of Heidegger is unwarranted. To the extent that he maintained that every act of bestowal is at the same time a refusal to bestow, the paradox of giving by withholding can be applied to his thinking as well. I have discussed this topic in various publications, but see especially the section "Heidegger's Venture: Giving the Gift Ungiven" in Wolfson, *Giving*, pp. 236–246.

246. Emmanuel Levinas, *Proper Names*, translated by Michael B. Smith (Stanford: Stanford University Press, 1996), p. 147.

247. Ibid. (emphasis in original). This passage and the one referenced in the following note are cited in a different translation by Wyschogrod, *Crossover Queries*, pp. 400–401.

248. On the messianic implications of the diachronic temporality of the futural awaiting without an awaited in Levinas, see Wolfson, *Giving*, pp. 113–120.

249. Levinas, *Proper Names*, p. 148.

250. Wyschogrod, *Crossover Queries*, p. 401.

251. Levinas, *Proper Names*, p. 157 (emphasis in original).

252. Theodor W. Adorno, *Prisms*, translated by Shierry Weber Nicholsen and Samuel Weber (Cambridge, MA: MIT Press, 1983), p. 34. I am taking the liberty to repeat my argument in Wolfson, *Duplicity*, pp. 163–164.

253. Adorno, *Negative Dialektik*, pp. 355–356; idem, *Negative Dialectics*, pp. 362–363.

254. On the use of the expression "metapolitics," see Matthew Feldman, "Between *Geist* and *Zeitgeist*: Martin Heidegger as Ideologue of 'Metapolitical Fascism,'" *Totalitarian Movements and Political Religions* 6 (2005): 175–198; Peter Trawny, *Heidegger and the Myth of a Jewish World Conspiracy*, translated by Andrew J. Michell (Chicago: University of Chicago University Press, 2015), p. 112 n. 12; Jeff Love and Michael Meng, "Heidegger's Metapolitics," *Cultural Critique* 99 (2018): 97–122; Charles Bambach, *Of an Alien Homecoming: Reading Heidegger's "Hölderlin"* (Albany: State University of New York Press, 2022), pp. 102–110.

255. On the classification of poetry as an act of measuring (*Vermessung*) essential to human dwelling in the ground of being, see Heidegger, *Vorträge*, pp. 199–200; idem, *Poetry*, pp. 221–222.

256. Heidegger, *Vorträge*, p. 26; idem, *Question*, p. 25.

257. Wyschogrod, *Spirit*, p. 194.

258. Ibid., p. 197.

259. Ibid., p. 173.

Chapter 4

1. The date was supplied in the version of the conversation given by Max Brod, *Franz Kafka: Eine Biographie*, third, expanded edition (Berlin: S. Fischer, 1954), p. 94. English edition: Max Brod, *Franz Kafka: A Biography*, second, expanded edition, translated by G. Humphreys and Richard Winston (New York: Schocken Books, 1960), p. 75.

2. Max Brod, "Der Dichter Franz Kafka," *Die neue Rundschau* 11 (1921): 1213. Since a copy of this journal was not available to me, I am citing the German text from the reprint of Brod's essay in *Juden in der deutschen Literatur. Essays über zeitgenössische Schriftsteller*, edited by Gustav Krojanker (Berlin: Welt, 1922), p. 58:

Notes to Chapter 4   287

> Ich erinnere mich eines Gesprächs mit Kafka, das vom heutigen Europa und dem Verfall des Menschheit ausging. "Wir sind", so sagte er, "nihilistische Gedanken, Selbstmordgedanken, die in Gottes Kopf aufsteigen". Mich erinnerte das zuerst an das Weltbild der Gnosis: Gott als böser Demiurg, die Welt sein Sündenfall. "O nein", meinte er, "unsere Welt ist nur eine schlechte Laune Gottes, ein schlechter Tag."—"So gäbe es außerhalb dieser Erscheinungsform Welt, die wir kennen, Hoffnung?"—Er lächelte: "Oh, Hoffnung genug, unendlich viel Hoffnung,—nur nicht für uns."

For discussion of this passage, see Ansgar Martins, *The Migration of Metaphysics into the Realm of the Profane*, translated by Lars Fischer (Leiden: Brill, 2020), pp. 91–92.

3. Walter Benjamin, *Selected Writings*, vol. 2: *1927–1934*, edited by Michael W. Jennings, Howard Eiland, and Gary Smith, translated by Rodney Livingstone and others (Cambridge, MA: Harvard University Press, 1999), p. 798. German original: Walter Benjamin, *Gesammelte Schriften*, 2.2, edited by Rolf Tiedemann and Herman Schweppenhäuser (Frankfurt am Main: Suhrkamp, 1991), p. 414. There is one notable difference between the text reproduced by Benjamin and the German cited in the previous note: in the first line, we find "entsinne" in place of "erinnere." The meaning is not altered by this variant.

4. Brod, *Franz Kafka: A Biography*, p. 75. Original German in Brod, *Franz Kafka: Eine Biographie*, pp. 94–95:

> Er: "Wir sind nihilistische Gedanken, die in Gottes Kopf aufsteigen." Ich stellte damit die Lehre der Gnosis vom Demiurgen, dem bösen Weltschöpfer, von der Welt als Sündenfall Gottes in Entsprechung. "Nein", sagte Kafka, "ich glaube, wir sind nicht ein so radikales Hinabsinken Gottes, nur eine seiner schlechten Launen, ein schlechter Tag." "So gäbe es außerhalb unserer Welt Hoffnung?" Er lächelte: "Viel Hoffnung—für Gott—unendlich viel Hoffnung–, nur nicht für uns."

5. This locution is found in the account in Brod, *Franz Kafka: Eine Biographie*, p. 95; idem, *Franz Kafka: A Biography*, p. 75.

6. Brod, *Franz Kafka: Eine Biographie*, p. 95; idem, *Franz Kafka: A Biography*, p. 75.

7. See ch. 2 n. 40.

8. My approach is more aligned with others who have viewed Kafka as espousing a tragic sense of human existence, accentuating predominantly self-abnegation and despair. For a different perspective, which places emphasis on Kafka's hopefulness, positivity, love of life and the earth, even a religious aspiration for fulfillment, see Brod, *Franz Kafka: Eine Biographie*, pp. 207–210; idem, *Franz Kafka: A Biography*, pp. 170–172. I might agree with Brod that it would be inaccurate to place Kafka in

line with those who promote a theology of crisis predicated on a "yawning abyss" between God and human that can never be bridged. However, it is hard not to see the dark irony of Kafka's worldview encapsulated in his retort to Brod that the only hope to be sought is in the hopelessness of our situation. Brod himself acknowledged that the more "hopeful side" of Kafka appears only intermittently (*fünkchenweise*), rendered in the translation as an "occasional flash," whereas the other passages from his work that describe the human being as powerless represent the "overwhelming majority." See Brod, *Franz Kafka: Eine Biographie*, p. 209; idem, *Franz Kafka: A Biography*, p. 171.

9. Emmanuel Levinas, *Autrement qu'être ou au-delà de l'essence* (Dordrecht: Kluwer Academic, 1974), p. 165; idem, *Otherwise Than Being or Beyond Essence*, translated by Alphonso Lingis (Dordrecht: Kluwer Academic, 1991), p. 129.

10. Ludwig Wittgenstein, *Moments of Thought: Ludwig Wittgenstein's Diary, 1930–1932 and 1936–1937*, translated by Alfred Nordmann, edited by James C. Klagge and Alfred Nordman, with an introduction by Ray Monk (Lanham: Rowman & Littlefield, 2023), p. 47:

> At the time the opposition between comedy & tragedy was always worked out as an a priori division of the dramatic concept of space. And certain remarks could then be found puzzling, for instance that comedy deals with types and tragedy with individualities. In reality comedy & tragedy are no opposition as if the one were only that part of dramatic space that was excluded by the other.

11. Gillian Rose, *The Broken Middle: Out of Our Ancient Society* (Oxford: Blackwell, 1992), p. 123.

12. Ibid., p. 121.

13. See ch. 2 at n. 208.

14. Aphorism 54 in Franz Kafka, *Wedding Preparations in the Country and Other Posthumous Prose Writings*, notes by Max Brod, translated by Ernst Kaiser and Eithne Wilkins (London: Secker and Warburg, 1973), p. 43; German original in *The Aphorisms of Franz Kafka*, edited, introduced, and with commentary by Reiner Stach, translated by Shelley Frisch (Princeton: Princeton University Press, 2022), p. 110.

15. Rose, *Broken Middle*, p. 75.

16. Brod, *Franz Kafka: Eine Biographie*, p. 95; idem, *Franz Kafka: A Biography*, p. 75.

17. Rose, *Broken Middle*, p. 75 (emphasis in original).

18. Søren Kierkegaard, *Concluding Unscientific Postscript*, translated by David F. Swenson, completed with introduction and notes by Walter Lowrie (Princeton: Princeton University Press, 1968), p. 448. I have utilized this translation as it is the one cited by Rose, but I have also consulted the more recent translation, Søren Kierkegaard, *Concluding Unscientific Postscript to Philosophical Fragments*, vol. 1:

Text, edited and translated with introduction and notes by Howard V. Hong and Edna H. Hong (Princeton: Princeton University Press, 1992). Unless otherwise noted, all references are to the older translation by Swenson.

19. Kierkegaard, *Concluding Unscientific Postscript*, p. 412.

20. Ibid., p. 446. It is noteworthy that in the more recent translation of Hong and Hong, religious suffering is rendered as a "dying to immediacy" as opposed to a "dying away from immediacy." See Kierkegaard, *Concluding Unscientific Postscript to Philosophical Fragments*, vol. 1, p. 499.

21. Kierkegaard, *Concluding Unscientific Postscript*, pp. 413, 448.

22. Ibid., pp. 446–447.

23. Ibid., p. 447.

24. Ibid., p. 452.

25. Ibid., p. 450.

26. The point is expressed succinctly in the diary fragment in Søren Kierkegaard, *Concluding Unscientific Postscript to Philosophical Fragments*, vol. 2: Historical introduction, supplement, notes, and index, edited and translated with introduction and notes by Howard V. Hong and Edna H. Hong (Princeton: Princeton University Press, 1992), p. 92: "... and the jest becomes manifest to the religious person himself when in the external world it beings to look as if he were capable of something."

27. Regarding this theme in Kierkegaard's *Works of Love*, see Nehama Verbin, "Self-Deception and the Life of Faith," *Heythrop Journal* 55 (2014): 845–859, esp. 849–858.

28. Kierkegaard, *Concluding Unscientific Postscript*, p. 413.

29. Ibid., pp. 448–449.

30. Rose, *Broken Middle*, p. 76.

31. The link between Jews and melancholy, based on the connection between melancholy and Saturn, and the further association of that planet and Saturday, the Jewish Sabbath, has roots in late antiquity. See Raymond Klibansky, Erwin Panofsky, and Fritz Saxl, *Saturn and Melancholy: Studies in the History of Natural Philosophy, Religion, and Art* (New York: Basic Books, 1964), p. 161 n. 115. On the explanation of melancholy related to the astral influences of Saturn, see also Walter Benjamin, *Ursprung des deutschen Trauerspiels*, in *Gesammelte Schriften*, 1.1, edited by Rolf Tiedemann and Herman Schweppenhäuser (Frankfurt am Main: Suhrkamp, 1991), pp. 326–329; idem, *Origin of the German Trauerspiel*, translated by Howard Eiland (Cambridge, MA: Harvard University Press, 2019). pp. 151–156. Following Panofsky and Saxl, Benjamin highlights the dialectical and antithetical nature of Saturn as the planet that confers on an individual both a sense of dejection and a spirit of delirium. See also Alina N. Feld, *Melancholy and the Otherness of God: A Study of the Hermeneutics of Depression* (Lanham: Lexington Books, 2011), pp. 50–55. For more in-depth studies on the connection between Jews and melancholy, see Ephraim Nissan and Abraham Ofir Shemesh, "Saturnine Traits,

Melancholia, and Related Conditions as Ascribed to Jews and Jewish Culture (and Jewish Responses) from Imperial Rome to High Modernity," *Quaderni di Studi Indo-Mediterranei* 3 (2010): 97–128; Ephraim Nissan and Abraham Ofir Shemesh, "Melancholia in Jewish Rabbinic and Medical Sources Through the Ages, I: From Antiquity to the Middle Ages," *Rivista di Storia della Medicina* 22 (2012): 7–33; Ephraim Nissan and Abraham Ofir Shemesh, "Melancholia and Diabetes? Clinical Description and Therapy in Nathan b. Joel Falaquera," *Rivista di Storia della Medicina* 232 (2013): 15–28; Irven M. Resnick, *Marks of Distinction: Christian Perceptions of Jews in the High Middle Ages* (Washington, DC: Catholic University of America Press, 2012), pp. 175–214. See as well the wide-ranging discussion of Saturn, Sabbath, and sorcery in Jewish sources in Moshe Idel, *Saturn's Jews: On the Witches' Sabbat and Sabbateanism* (London: Continuum, 2011), pp. 1–46.

32. See Rok Benčin, "Melancholy, or the Metaphysics of Fictional Sadness," *Filozofski Vestnik* 37 (2016): 101–117. As the author notes, his argument builds on the merging of thought and feeling in the analysis of Klibansky, Panofsky, and Saxl, *Saturn and Melancholy*.

33. Friedrich Wilhelm Joseph Schelling, *Philosophische Untersuchungen über das Wesen der menschlichen Freiheit und die damit zusammenhängenden Gegenstände*, edited by Thomas Buchheim (Hamburg: Felix Meiner, 1997), pp. 70–71; idem, *Philosophical Investigations into the Essence of Human Freedom*, translated and with an introduction by Jeff Love and Johannes Schmidt (Albany: State University of New York Press, 2006), p. 62 (emphasis in original).

34. Elliot R. Wolfson, "The Holy Cabala of Changes: Jacob Böhme and Jewish Esotericism," *Aries—Journal for the Study of Western Esotericism* 18 (2018): 44–47.

35. Friedrich Hölderlin, *Sämtliche Werke und Briefe*, edited by Michael Knaupp, 3 vols. (Munich: Carl Hanser, 1992), 2:114, cited by David Farrell Krell, "Three Ends of the Absolute: Schelling on Inhibition, Hölderlin on Separation, and Novalis on Identity," *Research in Phenomenology* 32 (2002): 69.

36. Schelling, *Philosophische Untersuchungen*, p. 71; idem, *Philosophical Investigations*, p. 63.

37. Schelling, *Philosophische Untersuchungen*, p. 31; idem, *Philosophical Investigations*, p. 28 (emphasis in original). See the comment marked for insertion after the phrase *"was in Gott selbst nicht Er Selbst ist"* in Schelling, *Philosophische Untersuchungen*, p. 31 n. 11:

> Es ist dies der einzig rechte Dualismus, nämlich der, welcher zugleich eine Einheit zuläßt. Oben war von dem modifizierten Dualismus die Rede, nach welchem das böse Prinzip dem guten nicht bei-, sondern untergeordnet ist. Kaum ist zu fürchten, daß jemand das hier aufgestellte Verhältnis mit jenem Dualismus verwechseln werde, in welchem das Untergeordnete immer ein wesentlich-böses Prinzip ist und eben darum seiner Abkunft aus Gott nach völlig unbegreiflich bleibt.

The note is translated, albeit in the wrong place, in Schelling, *Philosophical Investigations*, p. 30:

> This is the only correct dualism, namely that which at the same time permits a unity. The above discussion concerned the modified dualism, whereby the evil principle is not coordinated with, but subordinated to, the good principle. It is hardly to be feared that someone will confuse the relationship put forward here with that dualism in which the subordinate is always an essentially evil principle and, precisely for that reason, in respect of its origin in God remains completely incomprehensible.

See David Farrell Krell, "The Crisis of Reason in the Nineteenth Century: Schelling's Treatise on Human Freedom (1809)," in *The Collegium Phaenomenologicum: The First Ten Years*, edited by John C. Sallis, Giuseppina Moneta, and Jacques Taminiaux (Dordrecht: Kluwer Academic, 1988), pp. 21–22; John C. Sallis, *The Return of Nature: On the Beyond of Sense* (Bloomington: Indiana University Press, 2016), pp. 36–43; Elliot R. Wolfson, *Heidegger and Kabbalah: Hidden Gnosis and the Path of Poiēsis* (Bloomington: Indiana University Press, 2019), pp. 204–205.

38. Schelling, *Philosophische Untersuchungen*, p. 71; idem, *Philosophical Investigations*, pp. 62–63. See Martin Heidegger, *Schelling's Treatise on the Essence of Human Freedom*, translated by Joan Stambaugh (Athens: Ohio University Press, 1985), pp. 160–161; idem, *Schelling: Vom Wesen der menschlichen Freiheit (1809)* [GA 42] (Frankfurt am Main: Vittorio Klostermann, 1988), pp. 277–279; David Farrell Krell, *The Tragic Absolute: German Idealism and the Languishing of God* (Bloomington: Indiana University Press, 2005), pp. 102–103; Elliot R. Wolfson, *The Duplicity of Philosophy's Shadow: Heidegger, Nazism, and the Jewish Other* (New York: Columbia University Press, 2018), pp. 125–126; Földényi, *Melancholy*, pp. 280–282; Jason M. Wirth, *Schelling's Practice of the Wild: Time, Art, Imagination* (Albany: State University of New York Press, 2015), pp. 75–76, 104. On the suggestion that Schelling's statement about the veil of melancholy spread over all of nature is related to his despondency over the fatal illness of his wife Caroline in 1809, see Friedrich Wilhelm Joseph Schelling, *The Ages of the World (Fragment) from the Handwritten Remains, Third Version (c. 1815)*, translated and with an introduction by Jason M. Wirth (Albany: State University of New York Press, 2000), pp. ix–x. For a more general background of the melancholic view of nature embraced by Schelling, see Frederick C. Beiser, *Weltschmerz: Pessimism in German Philosophy, 1860–1900* (Oxford: Oxford University Press, 2016). See also Julian Young, *The Philosophy of Tragedy: From Plato to Žižek* (Cambridge: Cambridge University Press, 2013), pp. 68–94. Finally, it is worth comparing Schelling's statement with the comment of Paracelsus cited by Benjamin, *Origin*, p. 149:

> Joyfulness and mournfulness were born along with Adam and Eve. Joyfulness was given to Eve and mournfulness to Adam. . . . So joyful a human being as

Eve was will never be born again, and no man as mournful as Adam will ever be born. For the two matters, Adam and Eve, have been mingled, so that mournfulness has been tempered by joyfulness and joyfulness likewise by mournfulness.

39. Friedrich Wilhelm Joseph Schelling, *Sämmtliche Werke 1805–1810*, vol. 7, edited by Karl Friedrich August Schelling (Stuttgart: Cotta, 1860), pp. 465–466; idem, *Stuttgart Seminars*, in *Idealism and the Endgame of Theory: Three Essays by F. W. J. Schelling*, translated, edited, and with a critical introduction by Thomas Pfau (Albany: State University of New York Press, 1994), p. 230 (emphasis in original).

40. No pun intended, but this point is lost is the description of Schelling's view of melancholy as "mourning for a lost possession" in Reinhold Brinkman, *Late Idyll: The Second Symphony of Johannes Brahms*, translated by Peter Palmer (Cambridge, MA: Harvard University Press, 1995), p. 134. By contrast, see Teresa Fenichel, *Schelling, Freud, and the Philosophical Foundations of Psychoanalysis* (London: Routledge, 2019), pp. 84–87.

41. Jacques Derrida, "By Force of Mourning," translated by Pascale-Anne Brault and Michael Nass, *Critical Inquiry* 22 (1996): 173 (emphasis in original), reprinted in Jacques Derrida, *The Work of Mourning*, edited by Pascale-Anne Brault and Michael Nass (Chicago: University of Chicago Press, 2001), p. 144.

42. Derrida, "By Force of Mourning," p. 172 (emphasis in original); idem, *The Work of Mourning*, p. 143.

43. Schelling, *Sämmtliche Werke 1805–1810*, p. 468; idem, *Stuttgart Seminars*, p. 232 (emphasis in original). For the influence of this dimension of Schelling's thought on Heidegger, see Wolfson, *Duplicity*, pp. 141–143.

44. Emmanuel Levinas, *De l'Existence à l'existant*, second edition (Paris: Librairie Philosophique J. Vrin, 1998), p. 109; idem, *Existence and Existents*, translated by Alphonso Lingis, foreword by Robert Bernasconi (Pittsburgh: Duquesne University Press, 2001), p. 61 (emphasis in original).

45. Levinas, *De l'Existence*, p. 110; idem, *Existence*, p. 61.

46. Levinas, *De l'Existence*, p. 111; idem, *Existence*, p. 62.

47. Levinas, *De l'Existence*, p. 113; idem, *Existence*, p. 64. Levinas's account of the depersonalization of self can be profitably compared to the analysis in Thomas Fuchs, "Corporealized and Disembodied Minds: A Phenomenological View of the Body in Melancholia and Schizophrenia," *Philosophy, Psychiatry, & Psychology* 12 (2005): 95–107. See also Stefano Micali, "The Alteration of Embodiment in Melancholia," in *The Phenomenology of Embodied Subjectivity*, edited by Rasmus Thybo Jensen and Dermot Moran (Cham: Springer, 2013), pp. 203–219, especially the discussion of melancholia as the experience of the void and the transformation of temporalization and spatialization on pp. 213–218. Also beneficial is the analysis of lived-time and melancholic suffering in Martin Wyllie, *Merleau-Ponty and Melancholia* (Saarbrücken: Lambert Academic, 2010), pp. 96–132. See below, n. 200.

48. Maurice Blanchot, *L'Attente l'oubli* (Paris: Gallimard, 1962), p. 38; idem, *Awaiting Oblivion*, translated by John Gregg (Lincoln: University of Nebraska Press, 1997), p. 24. For discussion of the Levinasian nocturnal phenomenology, see Raoul Moati, *Levinas and the Night of Being: A Guide to* Totality and Infinity, translated by Daniel Wyche, with a foreword by Jocelyn Benoist (New York: Fordham University Press, 2017).

49. Emmanuel Levinas, "The Servant and Her Master," in *The Levinas Reader*, edited by Seán Hand (Oxford: Blackwell, 1989), p. 155 (emphasis in original).

50. Ibid.

51. Blanchot, *L'Attente l'oubli*, p. 27; idem, *Awaiting Oblivion*, p. 16.

52. Blanchot, *L'Attente l'oubli*, p. 24; idem, *Awaiting Oblivion*, p. 14. See the section "Waiting for the End of Waiting" in Elliot R. Wolfson, "Not Yet Now: Speaking of the End and the End of Speaking," in *Elliot R. Wolfson: Poetic Thinking*, edited by Hava Tirosh-Samuelson and Aaron W. Hughes (Leiden: Brill, 2015), 142–156, and the revised version in Elliot R. Wolfson, *Suffering Time: Philosophical, Kabbalistic, and Ḥasidic Reflections on Temporality* (Leiden: Brill, 2021), pp. 592–608. I will not repeat here the references to primary and secondary sources noted in that essay.

53. William S. Allen, "The Absolute Milieu: Blanchot's Aesthetics of Melancholy," *Research in Phenomenology* 45 (2015): 83. See idem, "To Articulate the Void by a Void: Aporetic Writing and Thinking in L'Attente l'oubli," *Word and Text: A Journal of Literary Studies and Linguistics* 5 (2015): 52–67.

54. Emmanuel Levinas, *Ethics and Infinity: Conversations with Philippe Nemo*, translated by Richard A. Cohen (Pittsburgh: Duquesne University Press, 1985), p. 49. See Elliot R. Wolfson, *Giving Beyond the Gift: Apophasis and Overcoming Theomania* (New York: Fordham University Press, 2014), pp. 108–113, 136–138, and reference to other scholars cited on p. 373 n. 171. For a broader context to understand Levinas's choice of the imagery of music in his discussion of melancholy, see Michael P. Steinberg, "Music and Melancholy," *Critical Inquiry* 40 (2014): 288–310.

55. Emmanuel Levinas, *On Escape*, translated by Bettina Bergo (Stanford: Stanford University Press, 2003), p. 67. When considering this early essay of Levinas, it is worthwhile recalling the words placed in the mouth of the "old magician" in the section "The Song of Melancholy" in Friedrich Nietzsche, *Thus Spoke Zarathustra: A Book for All and None*, edited by Adrian Del Caro and Robert B. Pippin, translated by Adrian Del Caro (Cambridge: Cambridge University Press, 2006), p. 241:

> And already, you higher men . . . already my wicked deceiving and magic spirit befalls me, my melancholy devil,—who is an adversary of Zarathustra from the ground up: forgive him! Now he *wants* to conjure before you, right now is *his* hour; I wrestle in vain with this evil spirit. All of you, whatever honors you may give yourselves with words . . . all of you who suffer from the *great nausea* like

me, for whom the old God died and no new god is lying yet in cradles and crib clothes—all of you are favored by my evil spirit and magic devil (emphasis in original).

It is significant that Zarathustra's nemesis is named the "melancholy devil"—or, alternatively, as the "spirit of melancholy" and the "twilight devil," who desires to come naked—and that the higher men, together with the old magician, are said to be suffering from great nausea. Perhaps Levinas's description of nausea as that which discovers the nakedness of being in its plenitude and in its utterly binding presence is, in part, influenced by the Nietzschean text.

56. See Michael J. Brogan, "Nausea and the Experience of the '*il y a*': Sartre and Levinas on Brute Existence," *Philosophy Today* 45 (2001): 144–153. For a meticulous analysis of the interrelated themes of anxiety, intersubjective sensibility, and melancholia in Levinas, see Bettina Bergo, *Anxiety: A Philosophical History* (Oxford: Oxford University Press, 2021), pp. 397–437.

57. Emmanuel Levinas, *Dieu, la mort et le temps*, edited and with notes and afterword by Jacques Rolland (Paris: Éditions Grasset, 1993), pp. 114–116; idem, *God, Death, and Time*, translated by Bettina Bergo (Stanford: Stanford University Press, 2000), pp. 99–101. The citation is drawn from lectures that were delivered respectively on April 30 and May 7, 1976.

58. Levinas, *Dieu*, p. 120; idem, *God*, p. 105.

59. See reference cited in ch. 3 n. 103.

60. Levinas, *Dieu*, p. 120; idem, *God*, p. 105.

61. Emmanuel Levinas, *Totalité et infini: Essai sur l'extériorité* (The Hague: Martinus Nijhoff, 1980), pp. 232–233; idem, *Totality and Infinity: An Essay on Exteriority*, translated by Alphonso Lingis (Dordrecht: Kluwer Academic, 1969), pp. 254–255.

62. Levinas, *Dieu*, pp. 120–121; idem, *God*, p. 105. Levinas's comments are a philosophical exegesis of the verse "for love is as strong as death," *ki azzah kha-mawet ahavah* (Song of Songs 8:6).

63. Timothy K. Beal, *The Book of Hiding: Gender, Ethnicity, Annihilation, and Esther* (London: Routledge, 1997), pp. 79–80.

64. Levinas, *Autrement qu'être*, p. 118; idem, *Otherwise Than Being*, p. 93.

65. Emmanuel Levinas, *De Dieu qui vient à l'idée*, second edition (Paris: Librairie Philosophique J. Vrin, 2004), pp. 98–99; idem, *Collected Philosophical Papers*, translated by Alphonso Lingis (Dordrecht: Martinus Nijhoff. 1987), pp. 155–156 (emphasis in original).

66. Robert Bernasconi, "No Exit: Levinas' Aporetic Account of Transcendence," *Research in Phenomenology* 35 (2005): 101–117. See the passage of Freud cited in the Introduction at n. 40.

67. Elliot R. Wolfson, *Venturing Beyond: Law and Morality in Kabbalistic Mysticism* (Oxford: Oxford University Press, 2006), pp. 252–253.

68. Paul Celan, *Selected Poems and Prose of Paul Celan*, translated by John Felstiner (New York: W. W. Norton, 2001), pp. 24–25.

69. Levinas, *Autrement qu'être*, p. 125; idem, *Otherwise Than Being*, p. 99. Compare Eric Kligerman, *Sites of the Uncanny: Paul Celan, Specularity and the Visual Arts* (Berlin: Walter de Gruyter, 2007), p. 66; Matthew Del Nevo, "The Kabbalistic Heart of Levinas," *Culture, Theory and Critique* 52 (2011): 185.

70. Levinas, *Autrement qu'être*, p. 125; idem, *Otherwise Than Being*, p. 99 (emphasis in original).

71. Emmanuel Levinas, *Basic Philosophical Writings*, edited by Adriaan T. Peperzak, Simon Critchley, and Robert Bernasconi (Bloomington: Indiana University Press, 1996), p. 5 (emphasis in original).

72. Ibid.

73. Parmenides, Fragment 3, in Kathleen Freeman, *Ancilla to the Pre-Socratic Philosophers* (Cambridge, MA: Harvard University Press, 1978), p. 42. See also Fragment 8.34, *tauton d'esti noein te kai houneken esti noēma*, rendered in Freeman, *Ancilla*, p. 44: "To think is the same as the thought that It Is," which is to say, as the continuation of the aphorism makes clear, without what is, that is, being, there is no thought, and hence thinking and that of which there is thinking are the same. See Néstor-Luis Cordero, *By Being, It Is: The Thesis of Parmenides* (Las Vegas: Parmenides, 2004), pp. 81 n. 339, 86–87. Concerning these Parmenidean teachings, see Martin Heidegger, *Einführung in die Metaphysik* [GA 40] (Frankfurt am Main: Vittorio Klostermann, 1983), pp. 145–155; idem, *Introduction to Metaphysics*, new translation by Gregory Fried and Richard Polt (New Haven: Yale University Press, 2000), pp. 145–155.

74. Levinas, *Basic Philosophical Writings*, p. 6. Particularly instructive is the remark in Emmanuel Levinas, *Oeuvres 1: Carnets de captivité suivi de Écrits sur la captivité et Notes philosophiques diverses*, edited and annotated by Rodolphe Calin, preface and explanatory notes by Rodolphe Calin and Catherine Chalier, general preface by Jean-Luc Marion (Paris: Éditions Grasset & Fasquelle, 2009), p. 409:

> La pensée de l'origine—c'est la <u>tradition</u>. Je ne dis pas que le contenu transmis sur l'origine est la vérité sur l'origine. La vérité sur l'origine—la <u>relation avec</u> l'origine = accueil d'un enseignement. Vérité n'est pas ici *adaequatio rei ac intellectus*—mais tradition. Vérité = simultanéité. Se débarrasser de la vérité = dévoilement.

The concluding statement—I have followed the suggestion in the accompanying note to correct *débarrasse* to *débarrasser*—that commends ridding ourselves of the sense of truth as unveiling strikes me as a critique of Heidegger's *alētheia*. For the influence of this Heideggerian theme on Levinas, see Jacques Derrida, *Writing and Difference*, translated and with an introduction and additional notes by Alan Bass (Chicago: University of Chicago Press, 1978), pp. 141–144, and discussion in Wolfson, *Giving*, pp. 100–101.

75. Levinas, *Totalité et infini*, p. 173; idem, *Totality and Infinity*, p. 199 (emphasis added).

76. Emmanuel Levinas, *En découvrant l'existence avec Husserl et Heidegger*, third corrected edition (Paris: Librairie Philosophique J. Vrin, 2001), p. 241; idem, *Collected Philosophical Papers*, p. 55.

77. Levinas, *Totalité et infini*, p. 175 ; idem, *Totality and Infinity*, p. 200.

78. Levinas, *Totalité et infini*, p. 175; idem, *Totality and Infinity*, p. 201.

79. Levinas, *Totalité et infini*, p. 175; idem, *Totality and Infinity*, p. 201. The epiphany of the face translates theologically into the phenomenon of revelation. See Emmanuel Levinas, "Revelation in the Jewish Tradition," in *The Levinas Reader*, pp. 208–209:

> The Revelation, described in terms of the ethical relation or the relation with the Other, is a mode of the relation with God and discredits both the figure of the Same and knowledge in their claim to be the only site of meaning (*signification*). . . . Should we not go beyond the consciousness which is equal to itself, seeking always to assimilate the Other (*l'Autre*), and emphasize instead the act of deference to the other in his alterity, which can only come about through the awakening of the Same—drowsy in his identity—by the Other? The form of this awakening . . . is obedience. And, surely, the way to think about the consciousness which is adequate to itself is as a mode or modification of this awakening, this disruption which can never be absorbed, of the Same by the Other, in his difference. Surely we should think of the Revelation, not in terms of received wisdom, but as this awakening?

80. On the inseparability of truth and untruth in Heidegger's idea of *alētheia*, see references in ch. 1 n. 43. See especially Wolfson, *Giving*, pp. 130–131, where I discuss Levinas's interpretation of this matter in Heidegger and Blanchot.

81. Levinas, *Autrement qu'être*, pp. 216–217; idem, *Otherwise Than Being*, p. 170.

82. Levinas, *Autrement qu'être*, p. 195; idem, *Otherwise Than Being*, p. 153.

83. Wolfson, *Giving*, p. 135 and reference cited on p. 392 n. 368.

84. Levinas, *Autrement qu'être*, p. 217; idem, *Otherwise Than Being*, pp. 170–171. The same sentiment underlies the remark in Emmanuel Levinas, *Beyond the Verse: Talmudic Readings and Lectures*, translated by Gary D. Mole (London: Athlone Press, 1994), p. 120: "Whatever our mistrust towards the letter and our thirst for the Spirit may be, monotheistic humanity is a humanity of the Book. Scriptural tradition provides the trace of a beyond of this very tradition."

85. Levinas, *De Dieu*, pp. 121–122; idem, *Collected Philosophical Papers*, p. 170.

86. Levinas, *De Dieu*, p. 122; idem, *Collected Philosophical Papers*, p. 170.

87. See Philippe Crignon, "Figuration: Emmanuel Levinas and the Image," *Yale French Studies* 104 (2004): 100–125; Hagi Kenaan, "Facing Images: After Levinas," *Angelaki* 16 (2011): 143–159; and my own comments in Wolfson, *Giving*, pp. 141–146, esp. 144–145.

88. The expression of Adorno is applied to Levinas by Bettina Bergo, "The Face in Levinas: Toward a Phenomenology of Substitution," *Angelaki* 16 (2011): 34.

89. On the phenomenology of the inapparent in Heidegger and Levinas, see Wolfson, *Giving*, pp. 94–102.

90. Levinas, *Autrement qu'être*, pp. 115, 118; idem, *Otherwise Than Being*, pp. 91, 93.

91. Levinas, *De Dieu*, p. 121; idem, *Collected Philosophical Papers*, p. 169.

92. Levinas, *De Dieu*, p. 120; idem, *Collected Philosophical Papers*, p. 168 (emphasis in original).

93. Levinas, *Autrement qu'être*, pp. 119–120; idem, *Otherwise Than Being*, p. 94.

94. On Levinas's critique of the Christian doctrine of incarnation, see Wolfson, *Giving*, pp. 135–136, and references cited on p. 392 n. 370.

95. Levinas, *Totalité et infini*, p. 175; idem, *Totality and Infinity*, p. 201.

96. Levinas, *Autrement qu'être*, p. 114; idem, *Otherwise Than Being*, p. 90 (emphasis in original).

97. Levinas, *En découvrant*, p. 241; idem, *Collected Philosophical Papers*, p. 55.

98. Levinas, *En découvrant*, p. 241; idem, *Collected Philosophical Papers*, p. 55.

99. Levinas, *En découvrant*, pp. 237–238; idem, *Collected Philosophical Papers*, p. 53.

100. Levinas, *Totalité et infini*, p. 178; idem, *Totality and Infinity*, p. 203.

101. Levinas, *De Dieu*, p. 119; idem, *Collected Philosophical Papers*, p. 168.

102. Levinas, *De l'Existence*, p. 143; idem, *Existence*, p. 84.

103. See Wolfson, *Giving*, pp. 111, 137.

104. Levinas, *Totalité et infini*, pp. 178–179; idem, *Totality and Infinity*, p. 204.

105. Gillian Rose, *Mourning Becomes the Law: Philosophy and Representation* (Cambridge: Cambridge University Press, 1996), p. 37 (emphasis in original). On the possible similarity between the Levinasian *il y a* and the Buddhist notion of the emptiness that is the fullness of being, see the brief comment in Wolfson, *Giving*, p. 136.

106. Rose, *Mourning*, p. 37 (emphasis in original).

107. Espen Hammer, "Being Bored: Heidegger on Patience and Melancholy," *British Journal for the History of Philosophy* 12 (2004): 292.

108. Levinas, *De l'Existence*, p. 110; idem, *Existence*, p. 62 (emphasis in original). The original French "*le réveil de l'*il y a *au sein de la négation*" can be rendered more literally as "the awakening of the *there is* within the negation."

109. John Drabinski, "Beginning's Abyss: On Solitude in Nietzsche and Levinas," in *Nietzsche and Levinas: "After the Death of a Certain God,"* edited by Jill Stauffer and Bettina Bergo (New York: Columbia University Press, 2009), pp. 134–149, esp. 136–137. See as well Stine Holte, *Meaning and Melancholy in the Thought of Emmanuel Levinas* (Göttingen: Vandenhoeck & Ruprecht, 2015), pp. 133–139.

110. Sigmund Freud, *The Standard Edition of the Complete Psychological Works of Sigmund Freud*, vol. 14: *On the History of the Psycho-Analytic Movement, Papers on*

Meta-Psychology and Other Works (1914–1916), translated under the general editorship of James Strachey in collaboration with Anna Freud, assisted by Alix Strachey and Alan Tyson (London: Hogarth Press, 1957), pp. 243–258. See also the studies of Melanie Klein, "A Contribution to the Psychogenesis of Manic-Depressive States" and "Mourning and Its Relation to Manic-Depressive States" in *Contributions to Psycho-Analysis, 1921–1945*, introduction by Ernest Jones (London: Hogarth Press, 1948), pp. 282–338.

111. Levinas, *Autrement qu'être*, p. 124; idem, *Otherwise Than Being*, p. 97.

112. Emmanuel Levinas, *Le Temps et l'autre* (Paris: Presses Universitaires de France, 1983), p. 10; idem, *Time and the Other*, translated by Richard A. Cohen (Pittsburgh: Duquesne University Press, 1987), p. 32 (emphasis in original). See ch. 3 n. 248.

113. Gershom Scholem, *On the Possibility of Jewish Mysticism in Our Time & Other Essays*, edited and with an introduction by Avraham Shapira, translated by Jonathan Chipman (Philadelphia: Jewish Publication Society of America, 1997), p. 216.

114. Elliot R. Wolfson, *A Dream Interpreted Within a Dream: Oneiropoiesis and the Prism of Imagination* (New York: Zone Books, 2011), p. 222. I have taken the liberty to repeat some of my language here.

115. On Scholem's melancholic and demonic orientation, see Giorgio Agamben, *Potentialities: Collected Essays in Philosophy*, edited, translated, and with an introduction by Daniel Heller-Roazen (Stanford: Stanford University Press, 1999), pp. 138–145; Moshe Idel, *Old Worlds, New Mirrors: On Jewish Mysticism and Twentieth-Century Thought* (Philadelphia: University of Pennsylvania Press, 2010), pp. 102–105; idem, *Saturn's Jews*, pp. 91–95; Vivian Liska, "Against Melancholy: On the Demonic in Gershom Scholem," in *Das Dämonische: Schicksale einer Kategorie der Zweideutigkeit nach Goethe*, edited by Lars Friedrich, Eva Geulen, and Kirk Wetters (Paderborn: Wilhelm Fink, 2014), pp. 311–324, reprinted in idem, *German-Jewish Thought and Its Afterlife: A Tenuous Legacy* (Bloomington: Indiana University Press, 2017), pp. 114–124; Enrico Lucca, "Translating, Interpreting the Bible, Fighting Satan: Rosenzweig, Scholem, and the End of Their Correspondence (with Three Unpublished Letters from Scholem to Rosenzweig)," in *"Into Life": Franz Rosenzweig on Knowledge, Aesthetics, and Politics*, edited by Antonios Kalatzis and Enrico Lucca (Leiden: Brill, 2021), pp. 11–14.

116. Gershom Scholem, *The Fullness of Time: Poems*, translated by Richard Sieburth, introduced and annotated by Steven M. Wasserstrom (Jerusalem: Ibis Editions, 2003), pp. 68–69. The influence of Benjamin's preoccupation with mourning (*Trauer*) in Scholem's poem is duly noted by Wasserstrom, op. cit., p. 146. The poem is reproduced in Gershom Scholem, *Poetica: Schriften zur Literatur, Übersetzungen, Gedichte*, edited and with commentary by Herbert Kopp-Oberstebrink, Hannah Markus, Martin Treml, and Sigrid Weigel, with the cooperation of Theresia Heuer (Berlin: Suhrkamp, 2019), p. 717.

117. Lina Barouch, "The Erasure and Endurance of Lament: Gershom Scholem's

Early Critique of Zionism and Its Language," *Jewish Studies Quarterly* 21 (2014): 13–26. It goes without saying that the bibliography of scholarly analyses of Scholem's Zionism is quite extensive. I will here mention a modest sampling of relevant studies: David Biale, *Gershom Scholem: Kabbalah and Counter-History* (Cambridge, MA: Harvard University Press, 1979), pp. 8–10, 53–72, 171–196, 207–210; idem, "Scholem und der moderne Nationalismus," in *Gershom Scholem: Zwischen den Disziplinen*, edited by Peter Schäfer and Gary Smith (Frankfurt am Main: Suhrkamp, 1995), pp. 257–274; Nathan Rotenstreich, "Gershom Scholem's Conception of Jewish Nationalism," in *Gershom Scholem: The Man and His Work*, edited by Paul Mendes-Flohr (Albany: State University of New York Press, 1994), pp. 104–119; Daniel Weidner, *Gershom Scholem: Politisches, esoterisches und historiographisches Schreiben* (Munich: Wilhelm Fink, 2003), pp. 40–54, 69–73, 91–103, 105–121; Pierre Bouretz, *Witnesses for the Future: Philosophy and Messianism*, translated by Michael B. Smith (Baltimore: Johns Hopkins University Press, 2010), pp. 224–351, esp. 231–251, 335–348; Zohar Maor, "Scholem and Rosenzweig: Redemption and (Anti-)Zionism," *Modern Judaism* 37 (2017): 1–23; Amir Engel, *Gershom Scholem: An Intellectual Biography* (Chicago: University of Chicago Press, 2017), pp. 26–61, 94–123, 168–198; Noam Zadoff, *Gershom Scholem: From Berlin to Jerusalem and Back*, translated by Jeffrey Green (Lebanon, NH: University Press of New England, 2018), pp. 3–83.

118. Scholem, *Fullness*, pp. 68–69; idem, *Poetica*, p. 717. In light of my ensuing analysis, it should be noted that Wasserstrom already remarked that "echoes of the doctrine of *tzimtzum* (self-contraction) and the shattering of the vessels are conspicuous" in the poem "Traurige Erlösung." See Scholem, *Fullness*, p. 146.

119. See the emotive beginning of the poem "W.B." in Scholem, *Fullness*, pp. 62–63: *Trauernder, nah mir und doch stets verborgen*, "Mournful one, near to me yet always in hiding." See Scholem, *Poetica*, p. 702.

120. See my application of this term to Benjamin in Wolfson, "Not Yet Now," pp. 169–170 n. 160, and the citation there of other studies that address the phenomenon of melancholy in Scholem and Benjamin. For the revised version, see Wolfson, *Suffering Time*, p. 628 n. 177. In *Origin*, p. 155, Benjamin remarked that Renaissance thinkers "reinterpreted saturnine melancholy in the sense of a theory of genius, and did so with a radicality unprecedented in the thought of antiquity."

121. Scholem, *Fullness*, pp. 88–89; idem, *Poetica*, p. 726.

122. Scholem, *Fullness*, pp. 94–95; idem, *Poetica*, p. 727.

123. Scholem, *Fullness*, pp. 98–99; idem, *Poetica*, p. 731. Regarding this statement of Scholem, see Idel, *Saturn's Jews*, p. 91.

124. Scholem, *Fullness*, pp. 96–97; idem, *Poetica*, p. 728. Mention should be made of Scholem's expression "nothingness of revelation" (*Nichts der Offenbarung*) referenced in the letter of Benjamin to Scholem from August 11, 1934, and in Scholem's response to Benjamin from September 20, 1934, in *The Correspondence*

of Walter Benjamin and Gershom Scholem 1932–1940, edited by Gershom Scholem, translated by Gary Smith and Andre Lefevere, with an introduction by Anson Rabinbach (New York: Schocken Books, 1989), pp. 135 and 142. See Wolfson, *Venturing Beyond*, p. 233, and reference to other scholars cited in n. 166, to which one might add David Kaufmann, "Imageless Refuge for All Images: Scholem in the Wake of Philosophy," *Modern Judaism* 20 (2000): 154–155; Ilit Ferber, "A Language of the Border: On Scholem's Theory of Lament," *Journal of Jewish Thought and Philosophy* 21 (2013): 169–170.

125. Elliot R. Wolfson, "Nihilating Nonground and the Temporal Sway of Becoming: Kabbalistically Envisioning Nothing Beyond Nothing," *Angelaki* 17 (2012): 31–45.

126. Dermot Moran, "*Spiritualis Incrassatio*: Eriugena's Intellectualist Immaterialism: Is It an Idealism?," in *Eriugena, Berkeley, and the Idealist Tradition*, edited by Stephen Gersh and Dermot Moran (Notre Dame: University of Notre Dame Press, 2006), p. 131.

127. Walter Benjamin, *Gesammelte Schriften*, 2.1, edited by Rolf Tiedemann and Hermann Schweppenhäuser (Frankfurt am Main: Suhrkamp, 1991), pp. 203–204; idem, *Selected Writings*, vol. 3: *1935–1938*, edited by Howard Eiland and Michael W. Jennings, translated by Edmund Jephcott, Howard Eiland, and others, (Cambridge, MA: Harvard University Press, 2002), p. 305.

128. Benjamin, *Gesammelte Schriften*, 2.1, p. 204; idem, *Selected Writings*, vol. 3, p. 306. For an analysis of this text as the framework within which to evaluate Benjamin's early thinking on history and redemption, see Eric Jacobson, *Metaphysics of the Profane: The Political Theology of Walter Benjamin and Gershom Scholem* (New York: Columbia University Press, 2003), pp. 19–51. See also the attempt of Jacob Taubes, *The Political Theology of Paul*, edited by Aleida Assmann and Jan Assmann, in conjunction with Horst Folkers, Wolf-Daniel Hartwich, and Christoph Schulte, translated by Dana Hollander (Stanford: Stanford University Press, 2004), pp. 72–74, to read Benjamin's insistence on world politics as nihilism in light of the use of the expression *hōs mē* ("as not") by Paul in his description of the *kairós* in 1 Corinthians 7:29. On Heidegger's explication of this locution, which he translated as *als ob nicht*, "as if not," see Giorgio Agamben, *The Time That Remains: A Commentary on the Letter to the Romans*, translated by Patricia Dailey (Stanford: Stanford University Press, 2005), pp. 33–34, whose reading has much affinity to the interpretation I proffered in Wolfson, *Giving*, pp. 231–232, of Heidegger's rendering of the expression *ouk edexanto*, "they received not," in 2 Thessalonians 2:10, as an "enactmental not" (*vollzugsmäßige Nicht*). For discussion of Agamben and the structure of messianic time, and Paul's exhortation for the community to love *hōs mē*, see Elizabeth A. Castelli, "The Philosophers' Paul in the Frame of the Global: Some Reflections," in *Paul and the Philosophers*, edited by Ward Blanton and Hent de Vries (New York: Fordham University Press, 2013), pp. 151–153. On *hōs mē* and

Paul's meontology according to Heidegger, see also Simon Critchley, *The Faith of the Faithless: Experiments in Political Theology* (London: Verso, 2012), pp. 177–183; idem, "You Are Not Your Own: On the Nature of Faith," in *Paul and the Philosophers*, pp. 236–240.

129. Gillian Rose, *Judaism and Modernity: Philosophical Essays* (Oxford: Blackwell, 1993), p. 189. See Rebecca Comay, "Benjamin's Endgame," in *Walter Benjamin's Philosophy: Destruction and Experience*, edited by Andrew Benjamin and Peter Osborne (Manchester: Clinamen Press, 2000), pp. 246–285.

130. Rose, *Judaism and Modernity*, p. 181 (emphasis in original). The topic of melancholia and Benjamin's thought has been explored by a number of scholars. For two exemplary studies, see Max Pensky, *Melancholy Dialectics: Walter Benjamin and the Play of Mourning* (Amherst: University of Massachusetts Press, 1993), and Ilit Ferber, *Philosophy and Melancholy: Benjamin's Early Reflections on Theater and Language* (Stanford: Stanford University Press, 2013). See also the analysis of melancholy in Benjamin, Adorno, and Bloch in Shannon Hayes, "To Write the Body: Lost Time and the Work of Melancholy," PhD dissertation, University of Oregon, 2019, pp. 121–162.

131. Walter Benjamin, *Gesammelte Schriften*, 5.1, edited by Rolf Tiedemann (Frankfurt am Main: Suhrkamp, 1991), pp. 591–592: "Das dialektische Bild ist ein aufblitzendes. So, als ein im Jetzt der Erkennbarkeit aufblitzendes Bild, ist das Gewesene festzuhalten." English translation in idem, *The Arcades Project*, translated by Howard Eiland and Kevin McLaughlin (Cambridge, MA: Harvard University Press, 1999), p. 473: "The dialectical image is an image that emerges suddenly, in a flash. What has been is to be held fast—as an image flashing up in the now of its recognizability." Compare my previous discussion of this Benjaminian theme in Wolfson, *Suffering Time*, pp. 615–616.

132. Rose, *Judaism and Modernity*, pp. 208–209 (emphasis in original).

133. The juxtaposition of melancholy (*Wehmut*) and the yearning for Paris as if it were paradise lost is found in a passage by Siegfried Kracauer cited by Benjamin, *Gesammelte Schriften*, 5.1, p. 167; idem, *Arcades Project*, p. 110.

134. Benjamin, *Gesammelte Schriften*, 5.1, p. 444; idem, *Arcades Project*, p. 351.

135. The passage is cited in Benjamin, *Gesammelte Schriften*, 5.1, p. 599; idem, *Arcades Project*, p. 478.

136. Scholem, *On the Possibility*, pp. 217–218. See Warren S. Goldstein, "Messianism and Marxism: Walter Benjamin and Ernst Bloch's Dialectical Theories of Secularization," *Critical Sociology* 27 (2001): 246–281.

137. Judith Butler, *The Psychic Life of Power: Theories in Subjection* (Stanford: Stanford University Press, 1997), pp. 167–198; Donald Capps, *Men, Religion, and Melancholia: James, Otto, Jung, and Erikson* (New Haven: Yale University Press, 1997), pp. 1–21. For comparison of Freud and Benjamin on melancholy and the commitment to the lost object, see also Ferber, *Philosophy and Melancholy*, pp.

302 *Notes to Chapter 4*

32–41. For another comparison of Freud and Benjamin, related to the depiction of Shakespeare's Hamlet as the paradigmatic melancholiac, see Steinberg, "Music and Melancholy," p. 293.

138. Butler, *Psychic Life*, p. 174.

139. Jacques Lacan, *The Seminar of Jacques Lacan. Book VIII: Transference*, edited by Jacques-Alain Miller, translated by Bruce Fink (Cambridge: Polity Press, 2015), p. 396.

140. Ibid., pp. 396–397. Compare Darian Leader, "Some Thoughts on Mourning and Melancholia," in *Lacan on Depression and Melancholia*, edited by Derek Hook and Stijn Vanheule (London: Routledge, 2023), pp. 48–75.

141. Jacques Lacan, *The Seminar of Jacques Lacan. Book XXIII: The Sinthome*, edited by Jacques-Alain Miller, translated by A. R. Price (Cambridge: Polity Press, 2016), p. 187. See also the chapter on "Melancholic Phenomenology: Merleau-Ponty and Proust on Phantoms and Involuntary Memories" in Hayes, "To Write the Body," pp. 84–120; and idem, "Merleau-Ponty's Melancholy: On Phantom Limbs and Involuntary Memory," *Epoché: A Journal for the History of Philosophy* 24 (2019): 201–219.

142. Julia Kristeva, "On the Melancholic Imaginary," *New Formations* 3 (1987): 5–18, and idem, *Black Sun: Depression and Melancholia*, translated by Leon S. Roudiez (New York: Columbia University Press, 1992). See Lawrence D. Kritzman, "Melancholia Becomes the Subject: Kristeva's Invisible 'Thing' and the Making of Culture," *Paragraph* 14 (1991): 144–150; Tsu-Chung Su, "Writing the Melancholic: The Dynamics of Melancholia in Julia Kristeva's *Black Sun*," *Concentric: Literary and Cultural Studies* 31 (2005): 163–191.

143. Kristeva, *Black Sun*, p. 3.

144. Ibid., p. 97.

145. Ibid., p. 99 (emphasis in original).

146. Ibid., pp. 101–102 (emphasis in original).

147. Ibid., pp. 100–101 (emphasis in original).

148. Butler, *Psychic Life*, p. 186. It is beyond the scope of this study to analyze Butler's view in comparison to Kristeva, but I draw the reader's attention to Kristina Marie Darling, "Mourning, Melancholia, and the Possibility of Transformation: Comparing Julia Kristeva's *Black Sun* and Judith Butler's *The Psychic Life of Power*," MA thesis, University of Missouri, St. Louis, 2011.

149. Benjamin, *Gesammelte Schriften*, 2.1, p. 154; idem, *Selected Writings*, vol. 1: *1913–1926*, edited by Marcus Bullock and Michael W. Jennings (Cambridge, MA: Harvard University Press, 1996), p. 72.

150. Benjamin, *Gesammelte Schriften*, 2.1, p. 154; idem, *Selected Writings*, vol. 1, p. 72. Benjamin revisited the Genesis narrative in the *Trauerspiel*. See Benjamin, *Gesammelte Schriften*, 1.1, p. 407; idem, *Origin*, pp. 255–256:

> The Bible introduces evil with the concept of knowledge. To become as one "knowing good and evil"—this is what the serpent promises the first human

beings. . . . Knowledge of good and evil is thus contrary to all objective knowledge. Referring as it does to the depths of the subjective, it is at bottom only knowledge of evil. . . . As the triumph of subjectivity and the inception of an arbitrary rule over things, this knowledge is origin of all allegorical vision. In the very fall of man emerges the unity of guilt and signifying before the tree of "knowledge" as abstraction. The allegorical lives in abstractions; as abstraction, as a capacity of the spirit of language itself, it is at home in the fall. For good and evil, being unnameable as they are nameless, stand outside the language of names, the language in which paradisiacal man named things and which, in the abyss opened by this question, he forsakes. The name is, for languages, only a ground in which the concrete elements are rooted. The abstract elements of language, however, are rooted in the judging word, in judgment.

151. Benjamin, *Gesammelte Schriften*, 2.1, p. 155; idem, *Selected Writings*, vol. 1, pp. 72–73.

152. Jacques Derrida, *The Animal That Therefore I Am*, edited by Marie-Louise Mallet, translated by David Wills (New York: Fordham University Press, 2008), p. 19 (emphasis in original). Derrida compares Benjamin's discussion of the muteness (*Stummheit*) or the speechlessness (*Sprachlosigkeit*) of nature to Heidegger's delineation in *Die Grundbegriffe der Metaphysik: Welt—Endlichkeit—Einsamkeit*, based on the seminar given in 1929–1930, of the essence of animality (*das Wesen der Tierheit*) as a stupor (*Benommenheit*) or the absence of language (*alogon*), which renders the animal "poor in world" (*weltarm*). The Heideggerian text is discussed at greater length by Derrida, *Animal*, pp. 141–160, and esp. pp. 142–143. See also Wolfson, *Duplicity*, pp. 70–71.

153. Derrida, *Animal*, p. 19.

154. Gershom Scholem, "Über Klage und Klagelied," in *Tagebücher nebst Aufsätzen und Entwürfen bis 1923*, vol. 2: *1917–1923*, edited by Karlfried Gründer, Herbert Kopp-Oberstebrink, and Friedrich Niewöhner, with the assistance of Karl E. Grözinger (Frankfurt am Main: Jüdischer, 2000), p. 128; idem, "On Lament and Lamentation," in *Lament in Jewish Thought: Philosophical, Theological, and Literary Perspectives*, edited by Ilit Ferber and Paula Schwebel (Berlin: Walter de Gruyter, 2014), p. 313.. See Wolfson, *Heidegger and Kabbalah*, pp. 314–315, and reference to other scholars cited on p. 327 nn. 140–141.

155. Scholem, "Über Klage," p. 130; idem, "On Lament," p. 316 (emphasis in original).

156. Gershom Scholem, *Major Trends in Jewish Mysticism* (New York: Schocken Books, 1954), pp. 260–264, 267–268, 269, 279–280, 286; idem, *Kabbalah* (Jerusalem: Keter, 1974), p. 143. See also Isaiah Tishby, "Gnostic Doctrines in Sixteenth-Century Jewish Mysticism," *Journal of Jewish Studies* 6 (1955): 146–152, and the expanded analyses in idem, *The Doctrine of Evil and the "Shell" in Lurianic Kabbalah*, translated by David Solomon (Los Angeles: Cherub Press, 2022). The Sab-

batian and Frankist heresies were also characterized by Scholem as gnostic on account of their nihilism, antinomianism, and the positing of a dualism between the hidden God and the demiurgic potency. See Scholem, *Major Trends*, pp. 297–299, 316, 322–323; idem, *The Messianic Idea in Judaism and Other Essays on Jewish Spirituality* (New York: Schocken Books, 1971), pp. 104–107; idem, *Sabbatai Ṣevi: The Mystical Messiah 1626–1676*, translated by R. J. Zwi Werblowsky (Princeton: Princeton University Press, 1973), pp. 253, 311–312, 797. On the importance of Gnosticism in Scholem's historiography of Jewish mysticism, see Moshe Idel, "Subversive Catalysts: Gnosticism and Messianism in Gershom Scholem's View of Jewish Mysticism," in *The Jewish Past Revisited: Reflections on Modern Jewish Historians*, edited by David N. Myers and David B. Ruderman (New Haven: Yale University Press, 1998), pp. 39–76. See also Michael Brenner, "Gnosis and History: Polemics of German-Jewish Identity from Graetz to Scholem," *New German Critique* 77 (1999): 45–60. For a different approach, see Agata Bielik-Robson, "The God of Luria, Hegel and Schelling: The Divine Contraction and the Modern Metaphysics of Finitude," in *Mystical Theology and Continental Philosophy: Interchange in the Wake of God*, edited by David Lewin, Simon D. Podmore, and Duane Williams (London: Routledge, 2017), pp. 40–41.

157. Scholem, *Messianic Idea*, p. 35 (emphasis in original).

158. I have taken the liberty to repeat my analysis in Wolfson, *Heidegger and Kabbalah*, pp. 319–321. Gershom Scholem, *From Berlin to Jerusalem: Memories of My Youth*, translated by Harry Zohn (New York: Schocken Books, 1980), p. 140, reports that Rosenzweig regarded him as a nihilist. This is corroborated in the description of the "evil Scholem" (*der böse Scholem*) in Rosenzweig's letter to Rudolf Hallo, dated March 27, 1922, in Franz Rosenzweig, *Der Mensch und sein Werk: Gesammelte Schriften I. Briefe und Tagebücher*, vol. 2: *1918–1929*, edited by Rachel Rosenzweig and Edith Rosenzweig-Scheinmann, with the assistance of Bernhard Casper (The Hague: Martinus Nijhoff, 1979), p. 768:

> Am wenigsten mit einem Nihilisten wie Scholem. Der Nihilist behält immer recht.... In Scholem steckt das Ressentiment des Asketen.... Wir haben nicht Nichts, wie Scholem dem zionistischen Dogma zuliebe möchte, aber auch nicht Alles, wie du, verstört von Scholems kalt dir zugeschleudertem "Nichts", es nun am liebsten bei mir fändest, sondern beide nur Etwas, wirklich und wahrhaftig nur Etwas.

The connection Rosenzweig made between nihilism, the resentment of an ascetic, and the Zionist dogma is a topic that merits a separate discussion. For a preliminary analysis, see Elliot R. Wolfson, "Rosenzweig on Human Redemption: Neither Nothing nor Everything, but Only Something," *Journal of Jewish Thought and Philosophy* 29 (2021): 121–150, esp. 122–126. On the anarchistic and nihilistic dimensions of Scholem's theological politics, see Jacobson, *Metaphysics*, pp. 52–81. For discussion of the German Jewish background of Scholem's apocalyptic pessimism and the repudiation of the world, see Anson Rabinbach, "Between Enlightenment and Apocalypse: Benjamin, Bloch and Modern German Jewish Messianism," *New German Critique* 34 (1985): 78–124, esp. 80–82, and my own reflections on messianic time and historical disjointedness in Benjamin in Wolfson, "Not Yet Now," pp. 156–180, and the revised version in idem, *Suffering Time*, pp. 608–640. See also the intriguing discussion of the Weimar paradox as it relates to understanding National Socialism as a form of Jewish heresy predicated on the annihilation of Israel and God in William H. F. Altmann, *The German Stranger: Leo Strauss and National Socialism*, foreword by Michael Zank (Lanham: Lexington Books, 2011), pp. 281–300, esp. 283–287.

159. The expression, which is the scriptural etymology for the name of the firstborn son of Moses and Zipporah, Gershom, *ger hayyiti be-ereṣ nokhriyyah* (Exodus 2:22), is appropriated from George Prochnik, *Stranger in a Strange Land: Searching for Gershom Scholem and Jerusalem* (New York: Other Press, 2016). Scholem's disappointment with Zionism and his sense of personal despair are documented by Engel, *Gershom Scholem*, pp. 109–115, and Zadoff, *Gershom Scholem*, pp. 83–94.

160. Rosenzweig, *Briefe und Tagebücher*, vol. 2, p. 704 (emphasis in original).

161. Gershom Scholem, "Abschied," *Jerubbaal, Eine Zeitschrift der jüdischen Jugend* 1 (1918–1919): 125–130, and translated in Gershom Scholem, *On Jews and Judaism in Crisis: Selected Essays*, edited by Werner J. Dannhauser (New York: Schocken Books, 1976), pp. 54–60.

162. Scholem, *On Jews*, pp. 55–57. I previously cited this passage in Wolfson, *Heidegger and Kabbalah*, p. 326 n. 126, where I noted the affinity of Scholem's view with the position adopted by Heidegger.

163. Scholem, *On Jews*, p. 55.

164. For discussion of this theme and citation of some of the appropriate sources, see Elliot R. Wolfson, "Theolatry and the Making-Present of the Nonrepresentable: Undoing (A)Theism in Eckhart and Buber," in *Martin Buber: His Intellectual and Scholarly Legacy*, edited by Sam Berrin Shonkoff (Leiden: Brill, 2018), pp. 5–9. David Biale, *Gershom Scholem: Master of the Kabbalah* (New Haven: Yale University Press, 2018), pp. 60–61, suggested that the tension between desire for community, on the one hand, and the need for solitude, on the other hand, may explain why Scholem "found it so hard to fulfill his Zionist dreams." Finally, mention should be made of the analysis offered by Nitzan Lebovic, *Zionism and Melancholy: The Short Life of Israel Zarchi* (Bloomington: Indiana University Press, 2019), of the left-wing political melancholy in the generations of Israelis in the second half of the twentieth century arising from the gap between the utopian hope of Zionist ideology and the stark reality of the realpolitik of the state.

165. See Introduction at n. 58.

166. Scholem, *From Berlin*, pp. 139–141. See Stéphane Mosès, "Langage et sécu-

larisation chez Gershom Scholem," *Archives de sciences sociales des religions* 60 (1985): 87–88; idem, *The Angel of History: Rosenzweig, Benjamin, Scholem*, translated by Barbara Harshav (Stanford: Stanford University Press, 2009), pp. 171–172. In addition to the passage from Scholem's autobiography, Mosès refers to Rosenzweig's letter to Scholem from January 5, 1922, in which he reproached the latter for positing as a "central dogma" that Judaism in the Diaspora was in a state of apparent death and that only in the land of Israel could it be restored to life (*das Judentum scheintot ist und erst "drüben" wieder lebendig werden wird*). For the original German, see Rosenzweig, *Briefe und Tagebücher*, vol. 2, p. 741. The material is discussed as well by Jacques Derrida, *Acts of Religion*, edited and with an introduction by Gil Anidjar (New York: Routledge, 2002), pp. 192–194, and see Galili Shahar, "The Sacred and the Unfamiliar: Gershom Scholem and the Anxieties of the New Hebrew," *The Germanic Review: Literature, Culture, Theory* 83 (2008): 302–308.

167. See especially the letter to Rosenzweig, "Bekenntnis über unsere Sprache," translated as "Thoughts About Our Language" in Scholem, *On the Possibility*, p. 28. A Hebrew version of the letter appeared in Gershom Scholem, *Explications and Implications: Writings on Jewish Heritage and Renaissance*, vol. 2, edited by Avraham Shapira (Tel Aviv: Am Oved, 1989), pp. 59–60 (Hebrew). The text was translated into French by Stéphane Mosès, "Une lettre inédite de Gershom Scholem à Franz Rosenzweig. A propos de notre langue. Une confession," *Archives de sciences sociales des religions* 60 (1985): 83–84, and analyzed by Mosès, "Langage et sécularisation," pp. 85–96; idem, *Angel*, pp. 168–182. See also Michael Brocke, "Franz Rosenzweig und Gerhard Gershom Scholem," in *Juden in der Weimarer Republik. Skizzen und Porträts*, edited by Walter Grab and Julius H. Schoeps (Stuttgart: Burg, 1986), pp. 127–152; Derrida, *Acts of Religion*, pp. 191–227; Shahar, "The Sacred," pp. 299–320; Annabel Herzog, "'Monolingualism' or the Language of God: Scholem and Derrida on Hebrew and Politics," *Modern Judaism* 29 (2009): 226–238; Lina Barouch, *Between German and Hebrew: The Counterlanguages of Gershom Scholem, Werner Kraft and Ludwig Strauss* (Berlin: Walter de Gruyter, 2016), pp. 47–48. According to the signature of the original German, the letter was written on 7 Tevet 5687, which corresponds to December 12, 1926. The date given in the Hebrew, English, and French versions, is December 26, 1926, which refers not to the date of composition but the date of the occasion for which the letter was written, namely, the celebration of Rosenzweig's fortieth birthday. To be precise, Rosenzweig's birthdate is December 25, but apparently it was commemorated one day after the Christmas holiday. Particularly perceptive is the conjecture of Shahar, "The Sacred," p. 303, that the letter written by Scholem in December 1926 was "a gesture of confession that displays the signature of friendship and rivalry."

168. On Rosenzweig's theo-philological view of Hebrew and his anxieties about Zionism as a mimicry of German nationalism, see Shahar, "The Sacred," p. 306:

Rosenzweig's argument on the *Unheimlichkeit* of Hebrew, its "homelessness," its "uncanniness," is bound up with the view that its theological depth and its fullness cannot be reduced to a particular historical or territorial experience, but rather should be attributed to its transcendence, its foreignness, its being like a "guest." Hebrew is like an eternal wanderer who lives *un-heimlich* in the world. This is how Hebrew reveals itself as an abyss—the gap, the absence, the wound of *Heimat*.

Shahar, op. cit., pp. 303–304, draws the reader's attention to Rosenzweig's "Neuhebräisch? Anläßlich der Übersetzung von Spinozas Ethik," a review of Jakob Klatzkin's Hebrew translation of Spinoza's *Ethics*, where he criticizes the hope of Zionism to create a genuinely national culture (*"echtnationale" Kultur*) based on a conception of the language that is indigenous (*bodenwüchsige*). The sense of newness and future-orientation is misguided as it obscures the sanctity of Hebrew connected to the past and empowers one to invent a language that is novel and unique. To speak Hebrew correctly, one must speak it as it is and not as one wants it to be: "Man kann eben nicht so Hebräisch sprechen wie man möchte, sondern man muß es schon so sprechen, wie es einmal ist." Rosenzweig agrees that the core of all national existence is language, but he insists that this is a matter of traditional inheritance and not territorial emplacement:

> Was hier allgemein gesagt ist, das gilt nun ganz und gar von dem Kern alles nationalen Daseins, von der Sprache. Sie kann nicht werden wie sie will, sondern sie wird werden wie sie muß. Und dieses Muß liegt nicht wie bei jeder natürlich-nationalen Sprache in ihr selber, sondern außerhalb ihrer Gesprochenheit, in der Erbmasse der Vergangenheit und in dem gewahrten Zusammenhang mit denen, deren Judentum notwendig wesentlich das des Erben ist.

See Franz Rosenzweig, *Der Mensch und sein Werk: Gesammelte Schriften III. Zweistromland: Kleinere Schriften zu Glauben und Denken,* edited by Reinhold and Annemarie Mayer (The Hague: Martinus Nijhoff, 1984), pp. 727–728. Rosenzweig's review is translated into English in Nahum N. Glatzer, *Franz Rosenzweig: His Life and Thought* (Philadelphia: Jewish Publication Society of America, 1953), pp. 263–271. The passages to which I alluded appear on pp. 268–270. See also Paul Mendes-Flohr, "Hebrew as a Holy Tongue: Franz Rosenzweig and the Renewal of Hebrew," in *Hebrew in Ashkenaz: A Language in Exile*, edited by Lewis Gilbert (Oxford: Oxford University Press, 1993), pp. 222–241.

169. Scholem, *On the Possibility*, p. 28.

170. Benjamin, *Gesammelte Schriften*, 2.1, p. 203; idem, *Selected Writings*, vol. 3, p. 305. Compare the detailed analysis of this text in Jacobson, *Metaphysics*, pp. 19–51, and see Bouretz, *Witnesses*, pp. 165–223, esp. 212–221.

171. Benjamin, *Gesammelte Schriften*, 2.1, p. 204; idem, *Selected Writings*, vol. 3, p. 306.

308 Notes to Chapter 4

172. Walter Benjamin, *Gesammelte Schriften*, 1.3, edited by Rolf Tiedemann and Herman Schweppenhäuser (Frankfurt am Main: Suhrkamp, 1991), p. 1246: "Die Ewigkeit der geschichtlichen Vorfälle festhalten, heißt eigentlich: sich an die Ewigkeit ihrer Vergängnis halten." English translation in idem, *Selected Writings*, vol. 4: *1938–1940*, edited by Howard Eiland and Michael W. Jennings, translated by Edmund Jephcott and others (Cambridge, MA: Harvard University Press, 2003), p. 407: "To grasp the eternity of historical events is really to appreciate the eternity of their transience."

173. For my previous discussion of this theme, see reference in ch. 2 n. 33. The paradox of time is applied by Benjamin in his description of Baudelaire's poetry as revealing the new (*das Neue*) in that which is always the same (*Immerwiedergleichen*), and that which is always the same in the new. See Walter Benjamin, *Gesammelte Schriften*, 1.2, edited by Rolf Tiedemann and Herman Schweppenhäuser (Frankfurt am Main: Suhrkamp, 1991), p. 673; idem, *Selected Writings*, vol. 4, p. 175.

174. I have discussed this aspect of Scholem's understanding of the messianic element in Lurianic kabbalah and Sabbatianism in Elliot R. Wolfson, "The Engenderment of Messianic Politics: Symbolic Significance of Sabbatai Ṣevi's Coronation," in *Toward the Millennium: Messianic Expectations from the Bible to Waco*, edited by Peter Schäfer and Mark Cohen (Leiden: Brill, 1998), pp. 204–206. From Scholem's perspective, the failure of Sabbatian messianism was the split between the political and the mystical, and the eventual privileging of the latter. Compare Gershom Scholem, *History of the Sabbatian Movement: Lectures Given at the Hebrew University of Jerusalem 1939–1940*, edited by Jonatan Meir and Shinichi Yamamoto (Jerusalem: Schocken Books, 2018), p. 81 (Hebrew).

175. Scholem, *Messianic Idea*, pp. 35–36. Significantly, in the concluding remarks offered by Scholem at a conference on "The Messianic Idea in Jewish Thought," held in honor of his eightieth birthday at the Israel Academy of Sciences and Humanities on December 4–5, 1977, he ended by quoting the final paragraphs from the essay "Toward an Understanding of the Messianic Idea in Judaism," in which he expressed his concerns about the viability of the "utopian return to Zion" and the negative impact it might have on the fate of Jewish history. Scholem emphasized, moreover, that even though the sentiment expressed in the end of that seminal study constituted his "own personal credo," it was not mentioned by the participants of the conference. See Scholem, *On the Possibility*, pp. 112–113.

176. To appreciate Scholem's position, we should note the idiosyncratic view of Jewish messianism proffered by Mircea Eliade, *The Myth of the Eternal Return*, translated by Willard R. Trask (Princeton: Bollingen Foundation, 1954), pp. 105–107. According to Eliade, the messianic idea overcomes the historical and restores Judaism to the archetypal structure of mythic time, but not absolutely, as there is still a privileging of the historical overcoming of history. In his precise words:

Yet Messianism hardly succeeds in accomplishing the eschatological valorization of time: the future will regenerate time; that is, will restore its original purity and integrity. Thus, *in illo tempore* is situated not only at the beginning of time but also at its end. In these spacious Messianic visions it is also easy to discern the very old scenario of annual regeneration of the cosmos by repetition of the Creation and by the drama of the suffering king. The Messiah—on a higher plane, of course—assumes the eschatological role of the king as god, or as representing the divinity on earth, whose chief mission was the periodical regeneration of all nature. His sufferings recalled those of the king, but, as in the ancient scenarios, the victory was always finally the king's. The only difference is that this victory over the forces of darkness and chaos no longer occurs regularly every year but is projected into a future and Messianic *illud tempus*.... When the Messiah comes, the world will be saved once and for all and history will cease to exist. In this sense we are justified in speaking not only of an eschatological granting of value to the future, to "that day," but also of the "salvation" of historical becoming. History no longer appears as a cycle that repeats itself *ad infinitum*.... Directly ordered by the will of Yahweh, history appears as a series of theophanies, negative or positive, each of which has its intrinsic value.

The viewing of historical events as a theophany became the basis for the Christological philosophy of history, but, according to Eliade, the messianic impulse in both Judaism and Christianity did not break with the archaic abolition of time as it reflects the antihistorical aspiration to put an end to history. See ibid., p. 111:

> But let us repeat: neither in Christianity nor in Judaism does the discovery of this new dimension in religious experience, faith, produce a basic modification of traditional conceptions. Faith is merely made possible for each individual Christian. The great majority of so-called Christian populations continue, down to our day, to preserve themselves from history by ignoring it and by tolerating it rather than by giving it the meaning of a negative or positive theophany. However, the acceptance and consecration of history by the Judaic elites does not mean that the traditional attitude ... is transcended. Messianic beliefs in a final regeneration of the world themselves also indicate an antihistoric attitude. Since he can no longer ignore or periodically abolish history, the Hebrew tolerates it in the hope that it will finally end, at some more or less distant future moment. The irreversibility of historical events and of time is compensated by the limitation of history to time. In the spiritual horizon of Messianism, resistance to history appears as still more determined than in the traditional horizon of archetypes and repetitions; if, here, history was refused, ignored, or abolished by the periodic repetition of the Creation and by the periodic regeneration of time, in the Messianic conception history must be tolerated because it has an

eschatological function, but it can be tolerated only because it is known that, one day or another, it will cease.

For a critical assessment of Eliade's interpretation of Jewish messianism, see Steven M. Wasserstrom, *Religion After Religion: Gershom Scholem, Mircea Eliade, and Henry Corbin at Eranos* (Princeton: Princeton University Press, 1999), pp. 328–329 n. 22.

177. Blanchot, *L'Attente l'oubli*, pp. 13, 16, 38–39; idem, *Awaiting Oblivion*, pp. 6, 8, 24. For a more contemporary articulation that parallels the understanding of the diachronic temporality of the deferred present and the impossible possibility of a religious hope predicated on waiting for a future that is already past when it arrives, see Claude Romano, "Awaiting," in *Phenomenology and Eschatology: Not Yet in the Now*, edited by Neal DeRoo and John Panteleimon Manoussakis (Burlington: Ashgate, 2009), pp. 35–52. A more technical exposition of the motifs of memory and the past, as well as the future and its availability, can be found in Claude Romano, *Event and Time*, translated by Stephen E. Lewis (New York: Fordham University Press, 2014), pp. 155–184. To assess Romano's position properly, we must start with acknowledging his unwavering commitment to the radical newness of the event as the temporalization of time. The point is reiterated often in his writings, but for the purposes of illustration, see Romano, *Event and Time*, pp. xii, 128, 137–138, 175–176. The definition of the human—designated as the advenant—as being constitutively open to the event, which is understood as pure mobility without anything that moves and therefore ungraspable within the ontic frame of the beingness of beings and unincorporable ontologically in relation to the being of beings, is explored in detail by Claude Romano, *Event and World*, translated by Shane Mackinlay (New York: Fordham University Press, 2009). See also Claude Romano, *There Is: The Event and the Finitude of Appearing*, translated by Michael B. Smith (New York: Fordham University Press, 2016), pp. 3–66, 213–236. This is not the place to interrogate Romano's evential hermeneutics, but I am skeptical about the possibility of an incomparable novelty implied by his conception of an absolute diremptive break in time, an orientation that bears affinity to Jean-Luc Marion's discussion of the event as a mode of givenness of unforeseeable contingency, the fold of the given that interrupts the world insofar as it shatters every expectation and escapes the temporal-spatial coordinates of conventional experience, and thus it is most appropriately described as a saturated phenomenon, the present without presence, the gift whose excess overpowers human subjectivity as it arises and imposes itself in its unanticipated and nonphenomenal visibility. See Jean-Luc Marion, *Being Given: Toward a Phenomenology of Givenness*, translated by Jeffrey L. Kosky (Stanford: Stanford University Press, 2002), pp. 64–66, 79–81, 111–112, 125–131, 159–178, 238–239, and note the brief comparison of the views of Marion and Romano in Marléne Zarader, "The Event—Between Phenomenology and History," in *The Past's Present: Essays on the Historicity of Philosophical Thinking*, edited by Marcia Sá Cavalcante

Schuback and Hans Ruin (Huddinge: Södertörn Academic Studies, 2006), pp. 28–30. Both Marion and Romano, whatever their differences—the most obvious being Marion's Christocentric interpretation of the event—presume that there can be a temporal rupture that has the property of being completely unprecedented. But how is one to conceive of such a notion of spontaneity that presumes a temporality outside the contours of chronological time? Is there any philosophical justification for depicting the event as an "unrepeatable and indomitable singularity" (Romano, *There Is*, p. 4) that has no distension other than itself, a present that extends neither into the past nor into the future? Even the pure immediacy of now occasions the reiteration of the new that renders the supposition of radical newness suspicious. In the temporal flow, what was before can never be retrieved except as what has not yet taken place. Hence, rather than speaking of the event occurring for the first time historically, it is more accurate to speak of the event transpiring in the present that is the reprise of what has always been what is to become. My disagreement is anticipated by Romano, *Event and Time*, p. 143, but he insists nonetheless that in contrast to the inner-temporal present subordinated to the double horizon of the past and the future as it was conceptualized in Husserlian phenomenology, the instant that he proposes

> bursts forth itself only from itself, according to its own in-stasy. Radically freed with regard to the form of "succession," it escapes inner-temporal categories that govern its economy.... The paradox of such an instant as pure initiation to itself, whose entire "adventure" consists in occurring, is that one must already be in it in order to begin to be there, but that this "already" does not refer to a past or to a present prior to that of the beginning; instead, it describes the internal drama of the present as a pure beginning, a coming from itself into itself, an *instant*—the very "process" by which the present is constituted as such in itself, *is instantiated*, without ever succeeding or proceeding from any prior time (emphasis in original).

The critical question centers on the semiotic valence we accord to the notion of newness, and this very much depends on how we assess continuity and discontinuity across the temporal divide. The assumption that something utterly new and unparalleled can appear in history for the first time—exploding, as it were, *ex nihilo*—is problematic unless we understand the paradox of what I have called in my thinking the *linear circularity of the timeswerve*: what is new is new because it is old, and what is old is old because it is new. Within the parameters of this temporal spirality, the advance to the future is naught but a reversion to the past that is a return to where one has never been. The challenge I have offered is echoed in Zarader, "Event," pp. 31–33, in her raising the question of who experiences the generalized eventicity supposedly shaped by the structure of perpetual novelty and continual virginity whereby worlds are constantly being reborn. I concur with her embrace of the phenomenological view that what is experienced by consciousness is not the spontaneous surfacing of things but rather the appearance of those things as they have already appeared in their given presence. In Heideggerian terms, she contends that

> the only means to define the event in its differences and relations to other phenomena, i.e., to phenomenality in its entirety, is to distinguish between *concealed eventicity* and *manifest eventicity*. On the basis of this very definition, the event can get to be assigned an extremely precise and also precious *function* within the phenomenological framework, where an event would then be the particular phenomenon that reveals the (usually concealed) structure of all phenomenality (emphasis in original).

The logical fallacy of generalizing the depiction of the event as radically novel and unpredictable is drawn by Zarader, "Event," pp. 34–35:

> In fact: if all phenomena are events, then the event in itself ceases to exist. And this is no return to a coarse common sense, but to an irrevocable, phenomenological demand. The event is given in the modes of excess, rupture and discontinuity, i.e. *as an exception*. Such is its proper phenomenality. But if we universalize this rule of exception, we will no longer have any means of distinguishing the specific phenomenon of the event from other phenomena. We believe that we are multiplying the event *ad infinitum*, but in reality we are annulling it, by effacing the very place where it could have existed (emphasis in original).

The critical question concerning the ontological status of the event is posed concisely by Zarader, "Event," pp. 47–48:

> is what presents itself as irreducible here *really* irreducible? Or in other words: is what consciousness lives as something absolute *really* absolute? . . . Clearly stated: the conflicting attitudes assumed in regard to the event are derived directly from the diverging responses to this unique question, even though it remains implicit within most texts on the subject. It is this question, thus, that we must unconditionally elucidate if we want to understand anything of the present debate concerning the event, i.e. if we want to identify its (real, even if implicit) *object* (emphasis in original).

Romano's confounding of the *phenomenology of the event* and the *hermeneutics of the event* implied in his affirming that the event is inseparable from its own sense is noted by Zarader, "Event," pp. 45–46. The same interplay of novelty and repetition is applied to the task of the historian by Zarader, "Event," pp. 40–42:

> But to what will history be obliged, inversely, when it is demanded of it to account for the event? The event will oblige history, on the one hand, not to limit

itself only to structures, but to let *the singularities manifested by the event* intervene; and it will oblige it, on the other hand, not to limit itself to the unrolling of a thread of continuity, but to let *the discontinuity indicated by the event* intervene. How can the historian let the event intervene? Not by denouncing processuality (which he surely cannot avoid), but by no longer identifying history as a *simple* process. And this will lead him to render his scientific discipline more complex, to admit of equally valid, coexisting histories (in the plural), and to define his field of research by its internal plurality: it will be constituted by a manifold of series open to alternative interpretations (as opposed to a unique series constituted by progress), and it will entail heterogeneous levels of reality and discourse that will be for the historian to articulate.... But the event cannot be *totally* respected by the historian, and this he knows very well. The events need to be *reduced* in some way to assume their place within history, or within *a* history, if only as that which upsets that history itself (emphasis in original).

I note finally that the criticism I am leveling against Romano is similar to my challenge to the temporal underpinnings of the thinking now occurring promulgated by David G. Leahy, a philosophical worldview that is predicated as well on the delineation of time as an absolute novum causally severed from the now that came before and the now that comes after. See Elliot R. Wolfson, "Temporal Diremption and the Novelty of Genuine Repetition," in *D. G. Leahy and the Thinking Now Occurring*, edited by Lissa McCullough and Elliot R. Wolfson (Albany: State University of New York Press, 2021), pp. 53–96. The quandary of speaking about an unqualified commencement in time was raised years ago by Gerard van der Leeuw, "Primordial Time and Final Time," in *Man and Time: Papers from the Eranos Yearbooks* (New York: Bollingen Foundation, 1957), p. 325: "The riddle of time is the riddle of the beginning. We know that there can be no true beginning. Something has always gone before. In the beginning lies the whole past. The beginning is the past. Yet we say that we begin something, that we make a new beginning. And we call the long list of such beginnings, time." See ibid., p. 336: "The circular course of time impresses itself upon us more and more. There are no new times, no moment that has not yet been attained. There is only primordial time, today as in the past and in the most distant future."

178. Wolfson, "Not Yet Now," pp. 188–193; idem, *Suffering Time*, pp. 653–658.

179. Romano, *Event and Time*, pp. 175–176 (emphasis in original). The nonteleological depiction of the future rests on Romano's view of the radical newness of the event. See above, n. 177.

180. Georg Trakl, *Poems and Prose: A Bilingual Edition*, translated by Alexander Stillmark (Evanston: Northwestern University Press, 2005), pp. 94–95.

181. Martin Heidegger, *Unterwegs zur Sprache* [GA 12] (Frankfurt am Main: Vittorio Klostermann, 1985), p. 53; idem, *On the Way to Language*, translated by Peter

D. Hertz (New York: Harper & Row, 1971), p. 177. Compare the analysis in Jacques Derrida, *Geschlecht III: Sex, Race, Nation, Humanity*, edited by Geoffrey Bennington, Katie Chenoweth, and Rodrigo Therezo, translated by Katie Chenoweth and Rodrigo Therezo (Chicago: University of Chicago Press, 2020), pp. 66–67.

182. For discussion of this term in Heidegger's interpretation of Trakl, see Ian Alexander Moore, "Heidegger's Trakl-Marginalia," *Research in Phenomenology* 51 (2021): 118–119; idem, *Dialogue on the Threshold: Heidegger and Trakl* (Albany: State University of New York Press, 2022), pp. 103–109. See also the comments of Derrida, *Geschlecht III*, pp. 28–30, 52–54, 103–104, 114–115.

183. The expression is from the poem "Gesang des Abgeschiedenen" in Trakl, *Poems*, pp. 102–103. For a partial analysis of this poem, see Heidegger, *Unterwegs*, pp. 66, 74–75; idem, *On the Way*, pp. 187–188, 194–195. Compare Moore, *Dialogue*, pp. 99–102. On the image of the ghostly twilight of the blueness of night in Trakl's poetry, see Heidegger, *Unterwegs*, pp. 43–48, 62; idem, *On the Way*, pp. 168–172, 184. The theme of the blueness of night is discussed also in Heidegger, *Unterwegs*, pp. 48, 65, 66; idem, *On the Way*, pp. 173, 187, 188. See as well the interpretation of the image of the soul speaking silence to the blue springtime from the opening line of the poem "Im Dunkel" (Trakl, *Poems*, pp. 100–101), "Es schweigt die Seele den blauen Frühling," offered by Heidegger, *Unterwegs*, p. 75: "Ihn singt die Seele, indem sie ihn schweigt.... Das Zeitwort 'schweigen' ist hier in der transitiven Bedeutung gesagt. Trakls Dichtung singt das Land des Abends." English translation in idem, *On the Way*, p. 195: "The soul sings of the blue spring by keeping it silent.... 'Keep silent' is here used transitively. Trakl's poem sings of the land of evening." See also Martin Heidegger, *Vorträge und Aufsätze* [GA 7] (Frankfurt am Main: Vittorio Klostermann, 2000), p. 205: "Das Blau der lieblichen Bläue des Himmels ist die Farbe der Tiefe. Der Glanz des Himmels ist Aufgang und Untergang der Dämmerung, die alles Verkündbare birgt. Dieser Himmel ist das Maß." English translation in Heidegger, *Poetry, Language, Thought*, translations and introduction by Albert Hofstadter (New York: Harper & Row, 1971), p. 226: "The blue of the sky's lovely blueness is the color of depth. The radiance of the sky is the dawn and dusk of the twilight, which shelters everything that can be proclaimed. This sky is the measure."

184. My language is drawn from the extended analysis of the philosophic-poetic import of the color blue in Heidegger, *Unterwegs*, pp. 38–40. Commenting on the words "Geistlich dämmert / Bläue über dem verhauenen Wald" in the poem "Frühling der Seele," rendered as "The sacred dusking / Of blue above the mutilated forest," in *The Damned: Selected Poems of Georg Trakl*, edited and translated by Daniele Pantano (Ceredigion: Broken Sleep Books, 2023), pp. 146–147, Heidegger wrote:

> "Dämmern" bedeutet zunächst das Dunkelwerden. "Bläue dämmert".... "Dämmerung" ist jedoch kein bloßes Untergehen des Tages als Verfall seiner Helle in die Finsternis. Dämmerung meint überhaupt nicht notwendig Untergang. Auch der Morgen dämmert. Mit ihm geht der Tag auf. Dämmerung ist zugleich

Aufgehen.... Die Bläue der Nacht geht auf am Abend. "Geistlich" dämmert die Bläue. Das "Geistliche" kennzeichnet die Dämmerung.... Zwar ist die Nacht dunkel. Aber das Dunkle ist nicht notwendig Finsternis.... Aus der Bläue leuchtet, aber zugleich durch ihr eigenes Dunkel sich verhüllend, das Heilige. Dieses verhält, während es sich entzieht. Es verschenkt seine Ankunft, indem es sich in den vehaltenden Entzug verwahrt. Die ins Dunkel geborgene Helle ist die Bläue.... Die Bläue hallt in ihrer Helle, indem sie läutet. In ihrer hallenden Helle leuchtet das Dunkel der Bläue.... Das Blau ist kein Bild für den Sinn des Heiligen. Die Bläue selber ist ob ihrer versammelnden, in der Verhüllung erst scheinenden Tiefe das Heilige.

English translation in *On the Way*, pp. 164–166:

"Dusk" means, first, darkness falling. "Dusk bluing."... But dusk is not a mere sinking of the day, the dissolution of its brightness in the gloom of night. Dusk, anyway, does not necessarily mean the twilight of the end. The morning, too, has its twilight. The day rises in twilight. Twilight, then, is also a rising.... The night's blueness rises, in the evening. The twilight dusk blues "ghostly." This "ghostliness" is what marks the dusk.... The night is dark, to be sure. But darkness is not necessarily gloom.... The holy shines out of the blueness, even while veiling itself in the dark of that blueness. The holy withholds in withdrawing. The holy bestows its arrival by reserving itself in its withholding withdrawal. Clarity sheltered in the dark is blueness.... Blueness resounds in its clarity, ringing. In its resounding clarity shines the blue's darkness.... Blue is not an image to indicate the sense of the holy. Blueness itself is the holy, in virtue of its gathering depth which shines forth only as it veils itself.

Mention should also be made of Heidegger's interpretation of the image of the "blue prey" (*ein blaues Wild*) found in several of Trakl's poems, for example, "Elis" (Trakl, *Poems*, pp. 44–45) and "Sommersneige" (Trakl, *Poems*, pp. 94–95). The latter is cited in Heidegger, *Unterwegs*, p. 39; idem, *On the Way*, pp. 164–165. For discussion of this motif, together with other instances of Trakl's use of the color blue to name the sacred as the slippage of the between and the indeterminacy of the blurring of oppositions, see Andrew J. Mitchell, "Heidegger's Later Thinking of Animality: The End of World Poverty," *Gatherings: The Heidegger Circle Annual* 1 (2011): 74–85, esp. 75–77. See also Derrida, *Geschlecht III*, pp. 37–39, 44, 50, 65, 159; David Farrell Krell, "Marginalia to *Geschlecht III*: Derrida on Heidegger on Trakl," *New Centennial Review* 7 (2007): 185–186.

185. The expression is based on the locution "melancholy jouissance" found in Kristeva, *Black Sun*, p. 102 (cited above at n. 146). See also Steven M. Wasserstrom, "Melancholy Jouissance and the Study of Kabbalah: A Review Essay of Elliot R. Wolfson, *Alef, Mem, Tau*," *Association for Jewish Studies Review* 32 (2008): 389–396.

186. For an analysis of *Nachträglichkeit* and the time of melancholia in Freud

and Lacan, see Hayes, "To Write the Body," pp. 44–83. See also Wolfson, *Suffering Time*, pp. 23–25; idem, *Heidegger and Kabbalah*, pp. 58–59 n. 131.

187. Scholem, *Fullness*, pp. 52–53. In the version of this poem in Scholem, *Poetica*, p. 694, the last line "In der Entfremdung werden wir befreit" is missing and in its place the transcription reads "Mich und das Tagebuch das aus dir schreit."

188. Gershom Scholem, "Bemerkungen über die Zeit im Judentum," in *Tagebücher nebst Aufsätzen und Entwürfen bis 1923*, vol. 2: *1917–1923*, edited by Karlfried Gründer, Herbert Kopp-Oberstebrink, and Friedrich Niewöhner, with the assistance of Karl E. Grözinger (Frankfurt am Main: Jüdischer, 2000), p. 236: "Die religiöse Zeit ist immer Entscheidung, d. h. aber Gegenwart. Alle andern Zeitbegriffe aber basieren auf diesem." A partial rendering is found in Gershom Scholem, *Lamentations of Youth: The Diaries of Gershom Scholem 1913–1919*, edited and translated by Anthony David Skinner (Cambridge, MA: Harvard University Press, 2007), p. 246: "Time in religion is always a decision, i.e., the present."

189. On the diremptive nature of the present, see Elliot R. Wolfson, *Alef, Men, Tau: Kabbalistic Musings on Time, Truth, and Death* (Berkeley: University of California Press, 2006), pp. 71–72. See also Wolfson, *Suffering Time*, pp. 9–11, 176, 192, 243, 381, 596.

190. Benjamin, *Arcades Project*, p. 471. For the original German, see Benjamin, *Gesammelte Schriften*, 5.1, p. 588: "Es ist die Gegenwart, die das Geschehen in Vor- und Nachgeschichte polarisiert."

191. The citation is from Hermann Cohen, *Der Begriff der Religion im System der Philosophie* (Giessen: Alfred Töpelmann, 1915), p. 22:

> Wenn dem Futurum die Bedeutung des Präsens zuerteilt wird, so wird dadurch eben auch die Differenz zwischen Gegenwart und Zukunft verringert. Das Sein wird nicht in der Gegenwart festgelegt, sondern es schwebt über sie hinaus. Gegenwart und Zukunft werden in diesem Sein Gottes verbunden.

192. Scholem has in mind the passage on negative attributes in Cohen, *Der Begriff der Religion*, pp. 46–47:

> Maimonides aber unterscheidet daher das Sein Gottes vom Leben. Dies aber bedeutet, obwohl er diese Bedeutung nicht ausdrücklich ausspricht, die Unterscheidung zwischen dem Sein Gottes und seinem Dasein..... Wir dürfen nur denken: Gott hat nicht das Dasein. Damit ist nach Maimonides gesagt: Gott ist der Ursprung des Daseins; ohne ihn gäbe es kein Dasein.

For discussion of this text, see Wolfson, *Giving*, pp. 17–18. On the distinction between the respective attributions of *Sein* and *Dasein* to God, see also Hermann Cohen, *Religion der Vernunft aus den Quellen des Judentums*, second edition (Frankfurt am Main: J. Kaufmann, 1929), p. 51; idem, *Religion of Reason Out of the Sources of Judaism*, translated and with an introduction by Simon Kaplan, introductory essay by Leo Strauss, and introductory essays for the second edition by

Steven S. Schwarzschild and Kenneth Seeskin (Atlanta: Scholars Press, 1995), p. 44, and the analysis in Wolfson, *Giving*, pp. 19–20.

193. Scholem, "Bemerkungen," pp. 235–237; idem, *Lamentations*, pp. 245–246 (emphasis in original). The translation has been slightly modified. I have here offered an abbreviated version of the more extensive analysis of Scholem's idea of messianic time in Wolfson, *Heidegger and Kabbalah*, pp. 279–281. See as well Willem Styfhals, "Predicting the Present: Gershom Scholem on Prophecy," *Journal of Jewish Thought and Philosophy* 28 (2020): 259–286, esp. 270–271.

194. Compare Gershom Scholem, "On Jonah and the Concept of Justice," translated by Eric J. Schwab, *Critical Inquiry* 25 (1999): 356–357 (idem, "Über Jona und den Begriff der Gerechtigkeit," in *Tagebücher nebst Aufsätzen und Entwürfen bis 1923*, vol. 2: *1917–1923*, edited by Karlfried Gründer, Herbert Kopp-Oberstebrink, and Friedrich Niewöhner, with the assistance of Karl E. Grözinger [Frankfurt am Main: Jüdischer, 2000], p. 526):

> The deep conflict of the Book of Jonah resides in Jonah's desire to see an identity between prophecy, which from an empirical point of view is a prediction of the future, and historiography, which is a prediction of the past. The prediction about the future should not be any different from one about the past: Nineveh *is* annihilated *in* the prophecy (precisely from a historian's standpoint) (emphasis in original).

And see ibid., pp. 359–360 (Scholem, "Über Jona," pp. 529–531):

> The historical ideas of the Bible all relate to the temporal concept of the eternal present. Messianic time as eternal present, and justice as something that is present and substantial, are corresponding notions. Were justice not present, then the messianic realm too would not only not be present but would be altogether impossible. Justice, like all Jewish concepts, is not a border concept, not liminal, not some mechanically infinite, ever-approachable regulative idea. (Whatever is liminal can be anticipated: the secret of Christianity.) "The reason for what the wise men call the world to come is not that this coming world is not already present, and that only after the demise of this world the other one would come. This is not how things are; rather, that world is continually present" (Maimonides). Prophetism is the prediction of the eternal present. . . . Seen from this standpoint, the problem of the Book of Jonah can also be grasped in this way: its conflict is based on a fundamental confusion. For why does Jonah want to identify prophetism with historiography? It is clear that he is confusing the eternal and the noneternal present. In Nineveh he is supposed to make a prediction about the eternal present, but he himself considers this prediction as bearing on the noneternal one. The times that *transform* themselves within the eternal present are supposed to be identical. But what is identical does not transform itself, and what transforms itself is not identical (emphasis in original).

195. On Scholem's use of the *waw ha-hippukh* as grammatical support for his conception of the conflation of the future and the present, see Wolfson, *Heidegger and Kabbalah*, p. 281 and references cited on p. 297 n. 217.

196. Laozi, *Daodejing*, ch. 2, in *A Source Book in Chinese Philosophy*, translated and compiled by Wing-Tsit Chan (Princeton: Princeton University Press, 1963), p. 140: "Therefore the sage manages affairs without action (*wu-wei*) and spreads doctrines without words." See ibid., ch. 3, p. 141: "By acting without action, all things will be in order." Ibid., ch. 10, p. 144: "Can you understand all and penetrate all without taking any action? . . . To act, but not to rely on one's own ability, to lead them, but not to master them—This is called profound and secret virtue (*hsüan-te*)." Ibid., ch. 16, p. 147: "Attain complete vacuity, maintain steadfast quietude." Ibid., ch. 37, p. 158: "Tao invariably takes no action, and yet there is nothing left undone. . . . Simplicity, which has no name, is free of desires. Being free of desires, it is tranquil." Ibid., ch. 43, p. 161: "Non-being penetrates that in which there is no space. Through this I know the advantage of taking no action. Few in the world can understand teaching without words and the advantage of taking no action." Ibid., ch. 48, p. 162: "The pursuit of Tao is to decrease day after day. It is to decrease and further decrease until one reaches the point of taking no action. No action is undertaken, and yet nothing is left undone." Ibid., ch. 63, p. 169: "Act without action. Do without ado. Taste without tasting." Ibid., ch. 64, p. 170: "He who takes action fails. He who grasps things loses them. For this reason the sage takes no action and therefore does not fail. He grasps nothing and therefore he does not lose anything." The paradoxical logic that is the foundation of the ethics of *wuwei* is made explicit in ch. 22, p. 151:

> To yield is to be preserved whole. To be bent is to become straight. To be empty is to be full. To be worn out is to be renewed. To have little is to possess. To have plenty is to be perplexed. Therefore the sage embraces the One and becomes the model of the world.

See ibid., ch. 36, p. 157:

> In order to contract, it is necessary first to expand. In order to weaken, it is necessary first to strengthen. In order to destroy, it is necessary first to promote. In order to grasp, it is necessary first to give. This is called subtle light.

On *wuwei* and the nonaction of the Tao, which is prior to all events, see Chung-Ying Cheng, *The Primary Way: Philosophy of Yijing*, foreword by Robert Cummings Neville (Albany: State University of New York Press, 2020), pp. 86–87.

197. Martin Heidegger, *Feldweg-Gespräche* [GA 77] (Frankfurt am Main: Vittorio Klostermann, 1995), pp. 76–79, 106, 108–109, 117–118, 121–122; idem, *Country Path Conversations*, translated by Bret W. Davis (Bloomington: Indiana University Press, 2010), pp. 48–50, 68, 70–71, 76–77, 79–80. Especially pertinent is the depiction of *Gelassenheit* as the "movement on a way" (*Be-wegung*) that "comes from rest

and remains engaged in rest" in Heidegger, *Feldweg-Gespräche,* p. 118; idem, *Country Path Conversations,* p. 77. Also noteworthy is the fact that Heidegger identified the "essence of thinking" as a form of "waiting" that is "releasement to the openregion." Compare Heidegger, *Feldweg-Gespräche,* pp. 122–123; idem, *Country Path Conversations,* pp. 79–80. See Bret W. Davis, *Heidegger and the Will: On the Way to Gelassenheit* (Evanston: Northwestern University Press, 2007), pp. 14–17; Holger Zaborowski, "Origin, Freedom, and *Gelassenheit*: On Heidegger's Second 'Country Path Conversation,'" in *Phenomenological Perspectives on Plurality,* edited by Gert-Jan van der Heiden (Leiden: Brill, 2015), pp. 137–157; Hans Ruin, "The Inversion of Mysticism—*Gelassenheit* and the Secret of the Open in Heidegger," *Religions* 10 (2019): 15, 1–9. On the attempt to distinguish his own sense of the willing of nonwilling and Eckhart's *Gelassenheit,* see Heidegger, *Feldweg-Gespräche,* p. 109; idem, *Country Path Conversations,* p. 70. Many have discussed the Eckhartian term and its influence on Heidegger. See John D. Caputo, *The Mystical Element in Heidegger's Thought* (Athens: Ohio State University Press, 1978), pp. 118–127, 173–183; Davis, *Heidegger and the Will,* pp. 18–20, 122–145, 195–197; John van Buren, *The Young Heidegger: Rumor of the Hidden King* (Bloomington: Indiana University Press, 1994), pp. 53, 55, 63, 99–102, 113–122, 297–313; Sonya Sikka, *Forms of Transcendence: Heidegger and Medieval Mystical Theology* (Albany: State University of New York Press, 1997), pp. 127–128, 131–133, 168, 184, 223; Christopher Rickey, *Revolutionary Saints: Heidegger, National Socialism, and Antinomian Politics* (University Park: Pennsylvania State University Press, 2002), pp. 81–91; Sean J. McGrath, *The Early Heidegger and Medieval Philosophy: Phenomenology for the Godforsaken* (Washington, DC: Catholic University Press, 2006), pp. 134–138, 142, 230; Barbara Dalle Pezze, *Martin Heidegger and Meister Eckhart: A Path Towards Gelassenheit,* foreword by Timothy O'Leary (Lewiston: Edwin Mellen Press, 2008), pp. 127–188; Vincent Blok, "Massive Voluntarism or Heidegger's Confrontation with the Will," *Studia Phaenomenologica* 13 (2013): 449–465; Ian Alexander Moore, *Eckhart, Heidegger, and the Imperative of Releasement* (Albany: State University of New York Press, 2019); Dermot Moran, "'Let It Be': Heidegger and Eckhart on *Gelassenheit,*" in *The Routledge Handbook of Phenomenology of Mindfulness,* edited by Susi Ferrarello and Christos Hadjioannou (London: Routledge, 2024), pp. 231–251. Particularly noteworthy is the innovative deployment of Heideggerian themes to interpret Eckhart proffered in various studies by Schürmann. See Reiner Schürmann, "Trois penseurs du délaissement: Maître Eckhart, Heidegger, Suzuki: Part One," *Journal of the History of Philosophy* 12 (1974): 455–477; idem, "Trois penseurs du délaissement: Maître Eckhart, Heidegger, Suzuki: Part Two," *Journal of the History of Philosophy* 13 (1975): 56–60; idem, *Meister Eckhart: Mystic and Philosopher* (Bloomington: Indiana University Press, 1978), pp. 192–213; idem, *Broken Hegemonies,* translated by Reginald Lilly (Bloomington: Indiana University Press, 2003), pp. 271–340, especially the discussion on the expropriation of detachment and the singularization of nonattachment, pp. 320–324, 335–339; idem, "Heidegger and the Mystical Tradition," *Journal of Continental Philosophy* 1 (2020): 284–303. Also relevant is the comparative study of Holger Helting, *Heidegger und Meister Eckehart: Vorbereitende Überlegungen zu ihrem Gottesdenken* (Berlin: Duncker & Humblot, 1997).

198. Heidegger, *Feldweg-Gespräche*, p. 106; idem, *Country Path Conversations*, p. 69.

199. See the discussion of this well-known motif in the Introduction and references cited in n. 38. See also Leon S. Brenner, "Excessive Creativity in Melancholia," in *Lacan on Depression and Melancholia*, pp. 137–156.

200. Wyllie, *Merleau-Ponty*, p. 99.

201. Bob Dylan, *The Lyrics*, edited by Christopher Ricks, Lisa Nemrow, and Julie Nemrow (New York: Simon & Schuster, 2014), p. 734. For a more elaborate discussion of the gnostic dimension of Dylan's creativity, see Elliot R. Wolfson, "Saturnine Melancholy and Dylan's Jewish Gnosis," in *World of Bob Dylan*, edited by Sean Latham and Brian Hosmer (Cambridge: Cambridge University Press, 2021), pp. 214–225.

202. Leonard Cohen, *The Flame: Poems, Notebooks, Lyrics, Drawings*, edited by Robert Faggen and Alexandra Pleshoyano (New York: Farrar, Straus and Giroux, 2018), p. 143.

203. Olivier Clément, *Transfiguring Time: Understanding Time in the Light of the Orthodox Tradition*, translated by Jeremy N. Ingpen (Hyde Park: New City Press, 2019), p. 81.

204. Cohen, *The Flame*, p. 144.

205. Ibid. (emphasis in original).

206. Butler, *Psychic Life*, p. 186.

207. Werner Hamacher, "Messianic Not," in *Messianic Thought Outside Theology*, edited by Anna Glazova and Paul North (New York: Fordham University Press, 2014), pp. 224–225 (emphasis in original). For my previous citation and brief analysis of this passage, see Wolfson, *Heidegger and Kabbalah*, p. 176 n. 47.

Bibliography

Abrams, Daniel. *Kabbalistic Manuscripts and Textual Theory: Methodologies of Textual Scholarship and Editorial Practice in the Study of Jewish Mysticism.* Foreword by David Greetham. Los Angeles: Cherub Press, 2010.

Adorno, Theodor W. *Kierkegaard: Construction of the Aesthetic.* Translated, edited, and with a foreword by Robert Hullot-Kentor. Minneapolis: University of Minnesota Press, 1989.

———. *Kierkegaard: Konstruktion des Ästhetischen* [GS 2]. Frankfurt am Main: Suhrkamp, 1962.

———. *Minima Moralia: Reflections from a Damaged Life.* Translated by E. F. N. Jephcott. London: Verso, 1974.

———. *Minima Moralia: Reflexionen aus dem beschädigten Leben* [GS 4]. Frankfurt am Main: Suhrkamp, 1951.

———. *Negative Dialectics.* Translated by E. B. Ashton. New York: Seabury Press, 1973.

———. *Negative Dialektik* [GS 6]. Frankfurt am Main: Suhrkamp, 1966.

———. *Prisms.* Translated by Shierry Weber Nicholsen and Samuel Weber. Cambridge, MA: MIT Press, 1983.

Agamben, Giorgio. "Philosophical Anthropology." *Law and Critique* 20 (2009): 211–231.

———. *Potentialities: Collected Essays in Philosophy.* Edited, translated, and with an introduction by Daniel Heller-Roazen. Stanford: Stanford University Press, 1999.

———. *The Signature of All Things: On Method.* Translated by Luca D'Isanto with Kevin Attell. New York: Zone Books, 2009.

———. *The Time That Remains: A Commentary on the Letter to the Romans.* Translated by Patricia Dailey. Stanford: Stanford University Press, 2005.

———. *The Use of Bodies*. Translated by Adam Kotsko. Stanford: Stanford University Press, 2016.

———. *What Is an Apparatus? and Other Essays*. Translated by David Kishik and Stefan Pedatella. Stanford: Stanford University Press, 2009.

Alexander, Philip S. "The Talmudic Concept of Conjuring (*'Aḥizat 'Einayim*) and the Problem of the Definition of Magic (*Kishuf*)." In *Creation and Re-Creation in Jewish Thought: Festschrift in Honor of Joseph Dan*, edited by Rachel Elior and Peter Schäfer, 7–26. Tübingen: Mohr Siebeck, 2005.

Allen, William S. "The Absolute Milieu: Blanchot's Aesthetics of Melancholy." *Research in Phenomenology* 45 (2015): 53–86.

———. "To Articulate the Void by a Void: Aporetic Writing and Thinking in L'Attente l'oubli." *Word and Text: A Journal of Literary Studies and Linguistics* 5 (2015): 52–67.

Altizer, Thomas J. J. "The Impossible Possibility of Ethics." In *Saintly Influence: Edith Wyschogrod and the Possibilities of Philosophy of Religion*, edited by Eric Boynton and Martin Kavka, 31–47. New York: Fordham University Press, 2009.

Altmann, Alexander. "Symbol and Myth." *Philosophy* 20 (1945): 162–171.

Altmann, William H. F. *The German Stranger: Leo Strauss and National Socialism*. Foreword by Michael Zank. Lanham: Lexington Books, 2011.

Amoroso, Leonardo. "Heidegger's *Lichtung* as *lucus a (non) lucendo*." In *Weak Thought*, edited by Gianni Vattimo and Pier Aldo Rovatti. Translated and with an introduction by Peter Carravetta, 155–179. Albany: State University of New York Press, 2012.

Angermann, Asaf. "The Diremption of Love: Gillian Rose on Agency, Mortality, and Hegelian Feminism." *Hypatia* 34 (2019): 309–328.

Arendt, Hannah. *The Human Condition*, second edition. Introduction by Margaret Canovan. Chicago: University of Chicago Press, 1996.

———. "Introduction—Walter Benjamin: 1892–1940." In Walter Benjamin, *Illuminations*, edited and with an introduction by Hannah Arendt. Translated by Harry Zohn, 1–55. New York: Schocken Books, 1969.

———. "Martin Heidegger at Eighty." In *Heidegger and Modern Philosophy: Critical Essays*, edited by Michael Murray, 293–303. New Haven: Yale University Press, 1978.

Aristotle. *The Complete Works of Aristotle: The Revised Oxford Translation*. Edited by Jonathan Barnes. Princeton: Princeton University Press, 1984.

Armstrong, Isobel. "Writing from the Broken Middle: The Post-Aesthetic." *Women: A Cultural Review* 9 (1998): 62–96.

Ashton, Paul. "The Beginning Before the Beginning: Hegel and the Activation of Philosophy." *Cosmos and History: The Journal of Natural and Social Philosophy* 3 (2007): 328–356.

Auweele, Dennis Vanden. *The Kantian Foundation of Schopenhauer's Pessimism.* London: Routledge, 2017.

Avrahami, Einat. "'Keep Your Mind in Hell and Despair Not': Illness as Life Affair in Gillian Rose's *Love's Work.*" *Narrative* 9 (2001): 305–321.

Bacharach, Naftali. *Emeq ha-Melekh.* Jerusalem: Yerid ha-Sefarim, 2003.

Backman, Jussi. *Complicated Presence: Heidegger and the Postmetaphysical Unity of Being.* Albany: State University of New York Press, 2015.

Bambach, Charles. *Of an Alien Homecoming: Reading Heidegger's "Hölderlin."* Albany: State University of New York Press, 2022.

Barouch, Lina. *Between German and Hebrew: The Counterlanguages of Gershom Scholem, Werner Kraft and Ludwig Strauss.* Berlin: Walter de Gruyter, 2016.

———. "The Erasure and Endurance of Lament: Gershom Scholem's Early Critique of Zionism and Its Language." *Jewish Studies Quarterly* 21 (2014): 13–26.

Beal, Timothy K. *The Book of Hiding: Gender, Ethnicity, Annihilation, and Esther.* London: Routledge, 1997.

Beiser, Frederick C. "Schiller and Pessimism." In *Aesthetic Reason and Imaginative Freedom: Friedrich Schiller and Philosophy,* edited by María del Rosario Acosta López and Jeffrey L. Powell, 83–97. Albany: State University of New York Press, 2018.

———. *Weltschmerz: Pessimism in German Philosophy, 1860–1900.* Oxford: Oxford University Press, 2016.

Benčin, Rok. "Melancholy, or the Metaphysics of Fictional Sadness." *Filozofski Vestnik* 37 (2016): 101–117.

Benjamin, Walter. *The Arcades Project.* Translated by Howard Eiland and Kevin McLaughlin. Cambridge, MA: Harvard University Press, 1999.

———. *Gesammelte Schriften,* 1.1. Edited by Rolf Tiedemann and Herman Schweppenhäuser. Frankfurt am Main: Suhrkamp, 1991.

———. *Gesammelte Schriften,* 1.2. Edited by Rolf Tiedemann and Herman Schweppenhäuser. Frankfurt am Main: Suhrkamp, 1991.

———. *Gesammelte Schriften,* 1.3. Edited by Rolf Tiedemann and Herman Schweppenhäuser. Frankfurt am Main: Suhrkamp, 1991.

———. *Gesammelte Schriften,* 2.1. Edited by Rolf Tiedemann and Hermann Schweppenhäuser. Frankfurt am Main: Suhrkamp, 1991.

———. *Gesammelte Schriften,* 2.2. Edited by Rolf Tiedemann and Herman Schweppenhäuser. Frankfurt am Main: Suhrkamp, 1991.

———. *Gesammelte Schriften,* 5.1. Edited by Rolf Tiedemann. Frankfurt am Main: Suhrkamp, 1991.

———. *Illuminations.* Edited and with an introduction by Hannah Arendt. Translated by Harry Zohn. New York: Schocken Books, 1969.

———. *Origin of the German Trauerspiel.* Translated by Howard Eiland. Cambridge, MA: Harvard University Press, 2019.

———. *Selected Writings*. Vol. 1: *1913–1926*. Edited by Marcus Bullock and Michael W. Jennings. Cambridge, MA: Harvard University Press, 1996.

———. *Selected Writings*. Vol. 2: *1927–1934*. Edited by Michael W. Jennings, Howard Eiland, and Gary Smith. Translated by Rodney Livingstone and others. Cambridge, MA: Harvard University Press, 1999.

———. *Selected Writings*. Vol. 3: *1935–1938*. Edited by Howard Eiland and Michael W. Jennings. Translated by Edmund Jephcott, Howard Eiland, and others. Cambridge, MA: Harvard University Press, 2002.

———. *Selected Writings*. Vol. 4: *1938–1940*. Edited by Howard Eiland and Michael W. Jennings. Translated by Edmund Jephcott and others. Cambridge, MA: Harvard University Press, 2003.

Bergo, Bettina. *Anxiety: A Philosophical History*. Oxford: Oxford University Press, 2021.

———. "The Face in Levinas: Toward a Phenomenology of Substitution." *Angelaki* 16 (2011): 17–39.

———. "The Historian and the Messianic 'Now': Reading Edith Wyschogrod's *An Ethics of Remembering*." In *Saintly Influence: Edith Wyschogrod and the Possibilities of Philosophy of Religion*, edited by Eric Boynton and Martin Kavka, 202–218. New York: Fordham University Press, 2009.

Bernasconi, Robert. "No Exit: Levinas' Aporetic Account of Transcendence." *Research in Phenomenology* 35 (2005): 101–117.

Bernet, Rudolf. "Phenomenological Concepts of Untruth in Husserl and Heidegger." In *Husserl: German Perspectives*, edited by John J. Drummond and Otfried Höffe. Translated by Hayden Kee, Patrick Eldridge, and Robin Litscher Wilkins, 239–262. New York: Fordham University Press, 2019.

———. "The Limits of Conceptual Thinking." *Journal of Speculative Philosophy* 28 (2014): 219–241.

Bernstein, Sara. "Ontological Pluralism About Non-Being." In *Non-Being: New Essays on the Metaphysics of Non-Existence*, edited by Sara Bernstein and Tyron Goldschmidt, 1–16. Oxford: Oxford University Press, 2021.

Biale, David. *Gershom Scholem: Kabbalah and Counter-History*. Cambridge, MA: Harvard University Press, 1979.

———. *Gershom Scholem: Master of the Kabbalah*. New Haven: Yale University Press, 2018.

———. "Scholem und der moderne Nationalismus." In *Gershom Scholem: Zwischen den Disziplinen*, edited by Peter Schäfer and Gary Smith, 257–274. Frankfurt am Main: Suhrkamp, 1995.

Bielik-Robson, Agata. *Derrida's Marrano Passover: Exile, Survival, Betrayal, and the Metaphysics of Non-Identity*. New York: Bloomsbury Academic, 2023.

———. "The God of Luria, Hegel and Schelling: The Divine Contraction and the

Modern Metaphysics of Finitude." In *Mystical Theology and Continental Philosophy: Interchange in the Wake of God*, edited by David Lewin, Simon D. Podmore, and Duane Williams, 32–50. London: Routledge, 2017.

———. "Political Theology of the Death of God: Hegel and Derrida." In *Nothing Absolute: German Idealism and the Question of Political Theology*, edited by Kirill Chepurin and Alex Dubilet, 188–206. New York: Fordham University Press, 2021.

Blanchot, Maurice. *L'Attente l'oubli*. Paris: Gallimard, 1962.

———. *Awaiting Oblivion*. Translated by John Gregg. Lincoln: University of Nebraska Press, 1997.

———. *The Writing of Disaster*. Translated by Ann Smock. Lincoln: University of Nebraska Press, 1986.

Blok, Vincent. "Massive Voluntarism or Heidegger's Confrontation with the Will." *Studia Phaenomenologica* 13 (2013): 449–465.

Bourdieu, Pierre. *Pascalian Meditations*. Translated by Richard Nice. Stanford: Stanford University Press, 2000.

Bouretz, Pierre. *Witnesses for the Future: Philosophy and Messianism*. Translated by Michael B. Smith. Baltimore: Johns Hopkins University Press, 2010.

Brann, Eva. *What, Then, Is Time?* Lanham: Rowman & Littlefield, 1999.

Brencio, Francesca. "'The Nocturnal Point of the Contraction': Hegel and Melancholia." In *Melancholia: The Disease of the Soul*, edited by Dariusz Skórczewski and Andrzej Wierciński, 149–167. Lublin: Wydawnictwo KUL, 2014.

Brenner, Leon S. "Excessive Creativity in Melancholia." In *Lacan on Depression and Melancholia*, edited by Derek Hook and Stijn Vanheule, 137–156. London: Routledge, 2023.

Brenner, Michael. "Gnosis and History: Polemics of German-Jewish Identity from Graetz to Scholem." *New German Critique* 77 (1999): 45–60.

Brinkman, Reinhold. *Late Idyll: The Second Symphony of Johannes Brahms*. Translated by Peter Palmer. Cambridge, MA: Harvard University Press, 1995.

Brocke, Michael. "Franz Rosenzweig und Gerhard Gershom Scholem." In *Juden in der Weimarer Republik. Skizzen und Porträts*, edited by Walter Grab and Julius H. Schoeps, 127–152. Stuttgart: Burg, 1986.

Brod, Max. "Der Dichter Franz Kafka." *Die neue Rundschau* 11 (1921): 1210–1216. Reprinted in *Juden in der deutschen Literatur. Essays über zeitgenössische Schriftsteller*, edited by Gustav Krojanker, 55–63. Berlin: Welt, 1922.

———. *Franz Kafka: A Biography*, second, expanded edition. Translated by G. Humphreys and Richard Winston. New York: Schocken Books, 1960.

———. *Franz Kafka: Eine Biographie*, third, expanded edition. Berlin: S. Fischer, 1954.

Brogan, Michael J. "Nausea and the Experience of the '*il y a*': Sartre and Levinas on Brute Existence." *Philosophy Today* 45 (2001): 144–153.

Burrus, Virginia. "Wyschogrod's Hand: Saints, Animality, and the Labor of Love." *Philosophy Today* 55 (2011): 412–421.
Butler, Judith. *The Psychic Life of Power: Theories in Subjection*. Stanford: Stanford University Press, 1997.
Camus, Albert. *The Myth of Sisyphus*. Translated by Justin O'Brien. New York: Alfred A. Knopf, 1955.
Capps, Donald. *Men, Religion, and Melancholia: James, Otto, Jung, and Erikson*. New Haven: Yale University Press, 1997.
Caputo, John D. "Hearing the Voices of the Dead: Wyschogrod, Megill, and the Heterological Historian." In *Saintly Influence: Edith Wyschogrod and the Possibilities of Philosophy of Religion*, edited by Eric Boynton and Martin Kavka, 161–174. New York: Fordham University Press, 2009.
———. *The Mystical Element in Heidegger's Thought*. Athens: Ohio State University Press, 1978.
Carew, Joseph. *Ontological Catastrophe: Žižek and the Paradoxical Metaphysics of German Idealism*. Ann Arbor: Open Humanities Press, 2014.
Carr, David. "Phenomenology of Historical Time." In *The Past's Present: Essays on the Historicity of Philosophical Thinking*, edited by Marcia Sá Cavalcante Schuback and Hans Ruin, 7–23. Huddinge: Södertörn Academic Studies, 2006.
Cassin, Barbara. *Nostalgia: When Are We Ever at Home?* Translated by Pascale-Anne Brault. New York: Fordham University Press, 2016.
Castelli, Elizabeth A. "The Philosophers' Paul in the Frame of the Global: Some Reflections." In *Paul and the Philosophers*, edited by Ward Blanton and Hent de Vries, 143–158. New York: Fordham University Press, 2013.
Caygill, Howard. "The Broken Hegel: Gillian Rose's Retrieval of Speculative Philosophy." *Women: A Cultural Review* 9 (1998): 19–27.
Celan, Paul. *Selected Poems and Prose of Paul Celan*. Translated by John Felstiner. New York: W. W. Norton, 2001.
Cheng, Chung-Ying. *The Primary Way: Philosophy of Yijing*. Foreword by Robert Cummings Neville. Albany: State University of New York Press, 2020.
Clément, Olivier. *The Roots of Christian Mysticism: Text and Commentary*. Translated by Theodore Berkeley and Jeremy Hummerstone. Hyde Park, NY: New City Press, 1995.
———. *Transfiguring Time: Understanding Time in the Light of the Orthodox Tradition*. Translated by Jeremy N. Ingpen. Hyde Park, NY: New City Press, 2019.
Cohen, Hermann. *Der Begriff der Religion im System der Philosophie*. Giessen: Alfred Töpelmann, 1915.
———. *Religion of Reason Out of the Sources of Judaism*. Translated and with an introduction by Simon Kaplan. Introductory essay by Leo Strauss, and intro-

ductory essays for the second edition by Steven S. Schwarzschild and Kenneth Seeskin. Atlanta: Scholars Press, 1995.

———. *Religion der Vernunft aus den Quellen des Judentums*, second edition. Frankfurt am Main: J. Kaufmann, 1929.

Cohen, Leonard. *The Flame: Poems, Notebooks, Lyrics, Drawings*. Edited by Robert Faggen and Alexandra Pleshoyano. New York: Farrar, Straus and Giroux, 2018.

Comay, Rebecca. "Benjamin's Endgame." In *Walter Benjamin's Philosophy: Destruction and Experience*, edited by Andrew Benjamin and Peter Osborne, 246–285. Manchester: Clinamen Press, 2000.

Cooper, Andrew. *The Tragedy of Philosophy: Kant's Critique of Judgment and the Project of Aesthetics*. Albany: State University of New York Press, 2016.

Cordero, Néstor-Luis. *By Being, It Is: The Thesis of Parmenides*. Las Vegas: Parmenides, 2004.

The Correspondence of Walter Benjamin and Gershom Scholem 1932–1940. Edited by Gershom Scholem. Translated by Gary Smith and Andre Lefevere, with an introduction by Anson Rabinbach. New York: Schocken Books, 1989.

Cowper, William. *The Poetical Works of William Cowper: Complete Edition*. New York: John Wurtele Lovell, 1881.

Crignon, Philippe. "Figuration: Emmanuel Levinas and the Image." *Yale French Studies* 104 (2004): 100–125.

Critchley, Simon. *The Faith of the Faithless: Experiments in Political Theology*. London: Verso, 2012.

———. "You Are Not Your Own: On the Nature of Faith." In *Paul and the Philosophers*, edited by Ward Blanton and Hent de Vries, 224–255. New York: Fordham University Press, 2013.

Crowe, Benjamin D. *Heidegger's Phenomenology of Religion: Realism and Cultural Criticism*. Bloomington: Indiana University Press, 2008.

———. *Heidegger's Religious Origins: Destruction and Authenticity*. Bloomington: Indiana University Press, 2006.

Daoist Resonances in Heidegger: Exploring a Forgotten Debt. Edited by David Chai. London: Bloomsbury Academic, 2022.

Darling, Kristina Marie. "Mourning, Melancholia, and the Possibility of Transformation: Comparing Julia Kristeva's *Black Sun* and Judith Butler's *The Psychic Life of Power*." MA thesis, University of Missouri, St. Louis, 2011.

Davey, Nicholas. "Towards a Community of the Plural: Philosophical Pluralism, Hermeneutics, and Practice." In *Phenomenological Perspectives on Plurality*, edited by Gert-Jan van der Heiden, 88–102. Leiden: Brill, 2015.

Davis, Bret W. *Heidegger and the Will: On the Way to Gelassenheit*. Evanston: Northwestern University Press, 2007.

Davis, Joshua B. "Introduction: By Way of the Valley of Roses." In *Misrecognitions:*

Gillian Rose and the Task of Political Theology, edited by Joshua B. Davis, 1–25. Eugene: Cascade Books, 2018.

Deleuze, Gilles. *Foucault*. Translated and edited by Seán Hand. Foreword by Paul Bové. Minneapolis: University of Minnesota Press, 1988.

Deleuze, Gilles, and Félix Guattari. *What Is Philosophy?* Translated by Hugh Tomlinson and Graham Burchell. New York: Columbia University Press, 1994.

Del Nevo, Matthew. "The Kabbalistic Heart of Levinas." *Culture, Theory and Critique* 52 (2011): 183–198.

Derrida, Jacques. *Acts of Religion*. Edited and with an introduction by Gil Anidjar. New York: Routledge, 2002.

———. *The Animal That Therefore I Am*. Edited by Marie-Louise Mallet. Translated by David Wills. New York: Fordham University Press, 2008.

———. *The Beast & the Sovereign*. Vol. 2. Edited by Michel Lisse, Marie-Louise Mallet, and Ginette Michaud. Translated by Geoffrey Bennington. Chicago: University of Chicago Press, 2011.

———. "By Force of Mourning." Translated by Pascale-Anne Brault and Michael Nass. *Critical Inquiry* 22 (1996): 171–192.

———. *Dissemination*. Translated and with an introduction and additional notes by Barbara Johnson. Chicago: University of Chicago Press, 1981.

———. "Force de loi: Le Fondement Mystique de l'Autorité." *Cardozo Law Review* 11 (1990): 920–1046.

———. "Force of Law: The 'Mystical Foundation of Authority.'" In *Deconstruction and the Possibility of Justice*, edited by Drucilla Cornell, Michael Rosenfeld, and David Gray Carlson, 3–67. New York: Routledge, 1992.

———. *Geneses, Genealogies, Genres, and Genius: The Secrets of the Archive*. Translated by Beverley Bie Brahic. New York: Columbia University Press, 2006.

———. *Geschlecht III: Sex, Race, Nation, Humanity*. Edited by Geoffrey Bennington, Katie Chenoweth, and Rodrigo Therezo. Translated by Katie Chenoweth and Rodrigo Therezo. Chicago: University of Chicago Press, 2020.

———. *The Gift of Death*. Translated by David Wills. Chicago: University of Chicago Press, 1995.

———. *Of Spirit: Heidegger and the Question*. Translated by Geoffrey Bennington and Rachel Bowlby. Chicago: University of Chicago Press, 1989.

———. *On the Name*. Edited by Thomas Dutoit. Stanford: Stanford University Press, 1995.

———. *Points . . . Interviews, 1974–1994*. Edited by Elisabeth Weber. Translated by Peggy Kamuf and others. Stanford: Stanford University Press, 1995.

———. *Psyche: Inventions of the Other*. Vol. 2. Edited by Peggy Kamuf and Elizabeth Rottenberg. Stanford: Stanford University Press, 2008.

———. *The Work of Mourning*. Edited by Pascale-Anne Brault and Michael Nass. Chicago: University of Chicago Press, 2001.

———. *Writing and Difference*. Translated and with an introduction and additional notes by Alan Bass. Chicago: University of Chicago Press, 1978.

Drabinski, John. "Beginning's Abyss: On Solitude in Nietzsche and Levinas." In *Nietzsche and Levinas: "After the Death of a Certain God,"* edited by Jill Stauffer and Bettina Bergo, 134–149. New York: Columbia University Press, 2009.

Dummett, Michael. *Truth and Other Enigmas*. Cambridge, MA: Harvard University Press, 1978.

Dylan, Bob. *The Lyrics*. Edited by Christopher Ricks, Lisa Nemrow, and Julie Nemrow. New York: Simon & Schuster, 2014.

Dynner, Glenn. "The Hasidic Tale as a Historical Source: Historiography and Methodology." *Religion Compass* 3–4 (2009): 655–675.

Eliade, Mircea. *The Myth of the Eternal Return*. Translated by Willard R. Trask. Princeton: Bollingen Foundation, 1954.

Elior, Rachel. *Israel Ba'al Shem Tov and His Contemporaries: Kabbalists, Sabbatians, Hasidim and Mitnaggedim*. Vol. 1. Jerusalem: Karmel, 2014 (Hebrew).

Elman, Benjamin A. "Nietzsche and Buddhism." *Journal of the History of Ideas* 44 (1983): 671–686.

Engel, Amir. *Gershom Scholem: An Intellectual Biography*. Chicago: University of Chicago Press, 2017.

Feld, Alina N. *Melancholy and the Otherness of God: A Study of the Hermeneutics of Depression*. Lanham: Lexington Books, 2011.

Feldman, Matthew. "Between *Geist* and *Zeitgeist*: Martin Heidegger as Ideologue of 'Metapolitical Fascism.'" *Totalitarian Movements and Political Religions* 6 (2005): 175–198.

Fenichel, Teresa. *Schelling, Freud, and the Philosophical Foundations of Psychoanalysis*. London: Routledge, 2019.

Ferber, Ilit. "A Language of the Border: On Scholem's Theory of Lament." *Journal of Jewish Thought and Philosophy* 21 (2013): 161–186.

———. *Philosophy and Melancholy: Benjamin's Early Reflections on Theater and Language*. Stanford: Stanford University Press, 2013.

Fernández, Jordi. "Schopenhauer's Pessimism." *Philosophy and Phenomenological Research* 73 (2006): 646–694.

Ferraris, Maurizio. "The Aging of the 'School of Suspicion.'" In *Weak Thought*, edited by Gianni Vattimo and Pier Aldo Rovatti. Translated and with an introduction by Peter Carravetta, 139–153. Albany: State University of New York Press, 2012.

Ficino, Marsilio. *Three Books on Life: A Critical Edition and Translation*. Introduction and notes by Carol V. Kaske and John R. Clark. Tempe: Renaissance Society of America, 1998.

Fišerová, Michaela. *Event of Signature: Jacques Derrida and Repeating the Unrepeatable*. Albany: State University of New York Press, 2022.

Földényi, László F. *Melancholy = Melankólia*. Translated by Tim Wilkinson, with a foreword by Alberto Manguel. New Haven: Yale University Press, 2016.

Fortenbaugh, William W. "On *Problemata* 3: Wine-Drinking and Drunkenness." In *The Aristotelian Problemata Physica: Philosophical and Scientific Investigations*, edited by Robert Mayhew, 100–123. Leiden: Brill, 2015.

Foucault, Michel. "Nietzsche, Freud, Marx." In *Essential Works of Foucault, 1954–1984*. Vol. 2: *Aesthetics, Method, and Epistemology*, edited by James D. Faubion, 269–278. New York: New Press, 1998.

Freeman, Kathleen. *Ancilla to the Pre-Socratic Philosophers*. Cambridge, MA: Harvard University Press, 1978.

Freud, Sigmund. *The Standard Edition of the Complete Psychological Works of Sigmund Freud*. Vol. 14: *On the History of the Psycho-Analytic Movement, Papers on Meta-Psychology and Other Works (1914–1916)*. Translated under the general editorship of James Strachey in collaboration with Anna Freud, assisted by Alix Strachey and Alan Tyson. London: Hogarth Press, 1957.

Fuchs, Thomas. "Corporealized and Disembodied Minds: A Phenomenological View of the Body in Melancholia and Schizophrenia." *Philosophy, Psychiatry, & Psychology* 12 (2005): 95–107.

Gabriel, Markus, and Slavoj Žižek. *Mythology, Madness and Laughter: Subjectivity in German Idealism*. London: Continuum, 2009.

Gadamer, Hans-Georg. "Towards a Phenomenology of Ritual and Language (1992)." In *Language and Linguisticality in Gadamer's Hermeneutics*, edited by Lawrence K. Schmidt, 19–50. Lanham: Lexington Books, 2000.

Gall, Robert S. *Beyond Theism and Atheism: Heidegger's Significance for Religious Thinking*. Dordrecht: Kluwer Academic, 1987.

Gendlin, Eugene. "*Befindlichkeit*: Heidegger and the Philosophy of Psychology." In *Heidegger and Psychology*, edited by Keith Hoeller. Special issue of *Review of Existential Psychology and Psychiatry* (1988): 43–71.

Genet, Jean. *Our Lady of the Flowers*. Translated by Bernard Frechtman, with an introduction by Jean-Paul Sartre. New York: Bantam, 1964.

Glatzer, Nahum N. *Franz Rosenzweig: His Life and Thought*. Philadelphia: Jewish Publication Society of America, 1953.

Goldstein, Warren S. "Messianism and Marxism: Walter Benjamin and Ernst Bloch's Dialectical Theories of Secularization." *Critical Sociology* 27 (2001): 246–281.

Goodstein, Elizabeth S. *Experience Without Qualities: Boredom and Modernity*. Stanford: Stanford University Press, 2005.

Gorman, Anthony. "Gillian Rose's Critique of Violence." *Radical Philosophy* 197 (2016): 25–35.

———. "Whither the Broken Middle? Rose and Fackenheim on Mourning, Modernity and the Holocaust." In *Social Theory After the Holocaust*, edited by Robert Fine and Charles Turner, 47–70. Liverpool: Liverpool University Press, 2000.

Gorman, Tony. "Gillian Rose and the Project of a Critical Marxism." *Radical Philosophy* 105 (2001): 25–42.
———. "Nihilism and Faith: Rose, Bernstein and the Future of Critical Theory." *Radical Philosophy* 134 (2005): 18–30.
Govrin, Ido. *Philosophical Archaeology: With and Beyond Agamben on Philosophy, History, and Art*. Albany: State University of New York Press, 2023.
Guenther, Lisa. "'Nameless Singularity': Levinas on Individuation and Ethical Singularity." *Epoché: A Journal for the History of Philosophy* 14 (2009): 168–187.
Greer, Clare. "A Critical Conversation Between Gillian Rose and John Milbank and Its Implications for an Aporetic Political Theology." PhD dissertation, University of Manchester, 2011.
Gregory, Wanda Torres. *Speaking of Silence in Heidegger*. Lanham: Lexington Books, 2021.
Grillmayr, Julia, and Christine Hentschel. "World Without Humans, Humans Without World: Apocalyptic Passions in the Anthropocene." In *Worlds Ending, Ending Worlds: Understanding Apocalyptic Transformation*, edited by Jenny Stümer, Michael Dunn, and David Eisler, 209–225. Berlin: Walter de Gruyter, 2024.
Grosz, Elizabeth. *Time Travels: Feminism, Nature, Power*. Durham: Duke University Press, 2005.
Hamacher, Werner. "Messianic Not." In *Messianic Thought Outside Theology*, edited by Anna Glazova and Paul North, 221–234. New York: Fordham University Press, 2014.
Hammer, Espen. "Being Bored: Heidegger on Patience and Melancholy." *British Journal for the History of Philosophy* 12 (2004): 277–295.
Hartog, François. *Regimes of Historicity: Presentism and Experiences of Time*. Translated by Saskia Brown. New York: Columbia University Press, 2015.
Hayes, Shannon. "Merleau-Ponty's Melancholy: On Phantom Limbs and Involuntary Memory." *Epoché: A Journal for the History of Philosophy* 24 (2019): 201–219.
———. "To Write the Body: Lost Time and the Work of Melancholy." PhD dissertation, University of Oregon, 2019.
Hegel, Georg Wilhelm Friedrich. *Aesthetics: Lectures on Fine Art*. Vols. 1–2. Translated by Thomas Malcom Knox. Oxford: Oxford University Press, 1975.
———. *Hegel: The Letters*. Translated by Clark Butler and Christiane Seiler, with a commentary by Clark Butler. Bloomington: Indiana University Press, 1984.
———. *Phenomenology of Spirit*. Translated by Arnold V. Miller. Oxford: Oxford University Press, 1977.
———. *The Science of Logic*. Translated by W. H. Johnston and L. G. Struthers. New York: Macmillan, 1929.
———. *The Science of Logic*. Translated and edited by George di Giovanni. Cambridge: Cambridge University Press, 2010.

———. *Wissenschaft der Logik I. Erster Teil: Die objective Logik. Erstes Buch* [Werke 5]. Frankfurt am Main: Suhrkamp, 1986.

Heidegger, Martin. *Aus der Erfahrung des Denkens 1910–1976* [GA 13]. Frankfurt am Main: Vittorio Klostermann, 2002.

———. *The Basic Problems of Phenomenology*. Translation, introduction, and lexicon by Albert Hofstadter. Bloomington: Indiana University Press, 1982.

———. *Being and Time*. Translated by Joan Stambaugh. Revised and with a foreword by Dennis J. Schmidt. Albany: State University of New York Press, 2010.

———. *Being and Truth*. Translated by Gregory Fried and Richard Polt. Bloomington: Indiana University Press, 2001.

———. *Beiträge zur Philosophie (Vom Ereignis)* [GA 65]. Frankfurt am Main: Vittorio Klostermann, 1989.

———. *The Concept of Time*. Translated by William McNeill. Oxford: Blackwell, 1992.

———. *Contributions to Philosophy (Of the Event)*. Translated by Richard Rojcewicz and Daniela Vallega-Neu. Bloomington: Indiana University Press, 2012.

———. *Country Path Conversations*. Translated by Bret W. Davis. Bloomington: Indiana University Press, 2010.

———. *Einführung in die Metaphysik* [GA 40]. Frankfurt am Main: Vittorio Klostermann, 1983.

———. *Elucidation of Hölderlin's Poetry*. Translated by Keith Hoeller. Amherst, NY: Humanity Books, 2000.

———. *Erläuterungen zu Hölderlins Dichtung* [GA 4]. Frankfurt am Main: Vittorio Klostermann, 1981.

———. *The Essence of Truth: On Plato's Cave Allegory and Theaetetus*. Translated by Ted Sadler. New York: Continuum, 2002.

———. *Feldweg-Gespräche* [GA 77]. Frankfurt am Main: Vittorio Klostermann, 1995.

———. *Four Seminars: Le Thor 1966, 1968, 1969, Zähringen 1973*. Translated by Andrew Mitchell and François Raffoul. Bloomington: Indiana University Press, 2003.

———. *The Fundamental Concepts of Metaphysics: World, Finitude, Solitude*. Translated by William McNeill and Nicholas Walker. Bloomington: Indiana University Press, 1995.

———. *Die Grundbegriffe der Metaphysik: Welt—Endlichkeit—Einsamkeit* [GA 29/30]. Frankfurt am main: Vittorio Klostermann, 1983.

———. *Die Grundprobleme der Phänomenologie* [GA 24]. Frankfurt am Main: Vittorio Klostermann, 1997.

———. *Hölderlin's Hymn "Remembrance."* Translated by William McNeill and Julia Ireland. Bloomington: Indiana University Press, 2018.

———. *Hölderlins Hymne "Andenken"* [GA 52]. Frankfurt am Main: Vittorio Klostermann, 1992.
———. *Hölderlins Hymnen "Germanien" und "Der Rhein"* [GA 39]. Frankfurt am Main: Vittorio Klostermann, 1999.
———. *Hölderlin's Hymns "Germania" and "The Rhine."* Translated by William McNeill and Julia Ireland. Bloomington: Indiana University Press, 2014.
———. *Holzwege* [GA 5]. Frankfurt am Main: Vittorio Klostermann, 2003.
———. *Identity and Difference*. Translated and with an introduction by Joan Stambaugh. New York: Harper & Row, 1969.
———. *Introduction to Metaphysics*. New translation by Gregory Fried and Richard Polt. New Haven: Yale University Press, 2000.
———. *Metaphysics and Nihilism: 1. The Overcoming of Metaphysics 2. The Essence of Nihilism*. Edited by Hans-Joachim Friedrich. Translated by Arun Iyer. Cambridge: Polity Press, 2022.
———. *Metaphysik und Nihilismus: 1. Die Überwindung der Metaphysik 2. Das Wesen der Nihilismus* [GA 67]. Frankfurt am Main: Vittorio Klostermann, 1999.
———. *Off the Beaten Track*. Edited and translated by Julian Young and Kenneth Haynes. Cambridge: Cambridge University Press, 2002.
———. *On Inception*. Translated by Peter Hanly. Bloomington: Indiana University Press, 2023.
———. *On the Essence of Language and the Question of Art*. Edited by Thomas Regehly. Translated by Adam Knowles. Cambridge: Polity Press, 2022.
———. *On the Way to Language*. Translated by Peter D. Hertz. New York: Harper & Row, 1971.
———. *Pathmarks*. Edited by William McNeill. Cambridge: Cambridge University Press, 1998.
———. *Poetry, Language, Thought*. Translation and introduction by Albert Hofstadter. New York: Harper & Row, 1971.
———. *Ponderings II–VI: Black Notebooks 1931–1938*. Translated by Richard Rojcewicz. Bloomington: Indiana University Press, 2016.
———. *Ponderings VII–XI: Black Notebooks 1938–1939*. Translated by Richard Rojcewicz. Bloomington: Indiana University Press, 2017.
———. *The Question Concerning Technology and Other Essays*. Translated and with an introduction by William Lovitt. New York: Harper & Row, 1977.
———. *Schelling: Vom Wesen der menschlichen Freiheit (1809)* [GA 42]. Frankfurt am Main: Vittorio Klostermann, 1988.
———. *Schelling's Treatise on the Essence of Human Freedom*. Translated by Joan Stambaugh. Athens: Ohio University Press, 1985.
———. *Sein und Wahrheit* [GA 36/37]. Frankfurt am Main: Vittorio Klostermann, 2001.

———. *Sein und Zeit*. Tübingen: Max Niemeyer, 1993.
———. *Seminare* [GA 15]. Frankfurt am Main: Vittorio Klostermann, 2005.
———. *Über den Anfang* [GA 70]. Frankfurt am Main: Vittorio Klostermann, 2005.
———. *Überlegungen II–VI (Schwarze Hefte 1931–1938)* [GA 94]. Frankfurt am Main: Vittorio Klostermann, 2014.
———. *Überlegungen VII–XI (Schwarze Hefte 1938/39)* [GA 95]. Frankfurt am Main: Vittorio Klostermann, 2014.
———. *Unterwegs zur Sprache* [GA 12]. Frankfurt am Main: Vittorio Klostermann, 1985.
———. *Vom Wesen der Wahrheit: Zu Platons Höhlengleichnis und Theätet* [GA 34]. Frankfurt am Main: Vittorio Klostermann, 1988.
———. *Vorträge und Aufsätze* [GA 7]. Frankfurt am Main: Vittorio Klostermann, 2000.
———. *Was Heißt Denken?* [GA 8]. Frankfurt am Main: Vittorio Klostermann, 2002.
———. *Wegmarken* [GA 9]. Frankfurt am Main: Vittorio Klostermann, 1996.
———. *What Is Called Thinking?* Translated by Fred W. Wieck and J. Glenn Gray, with an introduction by J. Glenn Gray. New York: Harper & Row, 1968.
———. *Zum Wesen der Sprache und Zur Frage nach der Kunst* [GA 74]. Frankfurt am Main: Vittorio Klostermann, 2010.
Helting, Holger. *Heidegger und Meister Eckehart: Vorbereitende Überlegungen zu ihrem Gottesdenken*. Berlin: Duncker & Humblot, 1997.
Hemming, Laurence Paul. *Heidegger's Atheism: The Refusal of a Theological Voice*. Notre Dame: University of Notre Dame Press, 2002.
Herskowitz, Daniel M. *Heidegger and His Jewish Reception*. Cambridge: Cambridge University Press, 2021.
———. "Reading Heidegger Against the Grain: Hans Jonas on Existentialism, Gnosticism, and Modern Science." *Modern Intellectual History* 19 (2022): 527–550.
Herzog, Annabel. "'Monolingualism' or the Language of God: Scholem and Derrida on Hebrew and Politics." *Modern Judaism* 29 (2009): 226–238.
Hobson, Marian. *Jacques Derrida: Opening Lines*. London: Routledge, 1998.
Hölderlin, Friedrich. *Poems and Fragments*. Translated by Michael Hamburger. Cambridge: Cambridge University Press, 1980.
———. *Sämtliche Werke und Briefe*. Edited by Michael Knaupp. 3 vols. Munich: Carl Hanser, 1992.
Holte, Stine. *Meaning and Melancholy in the Thought of Emmanuel Levinas*. Göttingen: Vandenhoeck & Ruprecht, 2015.
Hotam, Yotam. *Critiques of Theology: German-Jewish Intellectuals and the Religious Sources of Secular Thought*. Albany: State University of New York Press, 2023.

Hugh-Donovan, Stefanie. "Olivier Clément: French Thinker and Theologian of the Eastern Orthodox Church in Dialogue with Western Catholic Thought on Ecclesiology, Theology and the Identity of Europe." PhD dissertation, Heythrop College, University of London, 2015.

Idel, Moshe. *Hasidim: Between Ecstasy and Magic*. Albany: State University of New York Press, 1995.

———. *Old Worlds, New Mirrors: On Jewish Mysticism and Twentieth-Century Thought*. Philadelphia: University of Pennsylvania Press, 2010.

———. "Prayer, Ecstasy, and 'Alien Thoughts' in the Religious Experience of the Besht." In *Let the Old Make Way for the New: Studies in the Social and Cultural History of Eastern European Jewry Presented to Immanuel Etkes*. Vol. 1: *Hasidism and the Musar Movement*, edited by David Assaf and Ada Rapoport-Albert, 57–120. Jerusalem: Zalman Shazar Center, 2009 (Hebrew).

———. *Saturn's Jews: On the Witches' Sabbat and Sabbateanism*. London: Continuum, 2011.

———. "Subversive Catalysts: Gnosticism and Messianism in Gershom Scholem's View of Jewish Mysticism." In *The Jewish Past Revisited: Reflections on Modern Jewish Historians*, edited by David N. Myers and David B. Ruderman, 39–76. New Haven: Yale University Press, 1998.

Jacob Joseph of Polonnoye. *Ben Porat Yosef*. Korzec: Avraham Dov of Melnyk, 1781.

Jacobs, Louis. *Hasidic Prayer*. New York: Schocken Books, 1973.

Jacobson, Eric. *Metaphysics of the Profane: The Political Theology of Walter Benjamin and Gershom Scholem*. New York: Columbia University Press, 2003.

Jay, Martin. "The Conversion of the Rose." *Salmagundi* 113 (1997): 41–52.

Jung, Carl G. *Psychological Types*. A revision by R. F. C. Hull of the translation by H. G. Baynes [CW 6]. Princeton: Princeton University Press, 1971.

———. *The Symbolic Life: Miscellaneous Writings*. Translated by R. F. C. Hull [CW 18]. Princeton: Princeton University Press, 1950.

Kafka, Franz. *The Aphorisms of Franz Kafka*. Edited, introduced, and with commentary by Reiner Stach. Translated by Shelley Frisch. Princeton: Princeton University Press, 2022.

———. *The Blue Octavo Notebooks*. Edited by Max Brod. Translated by Ernst Kaiser and Eithne Wilkins. Cambridge: Exact Change, 1991.

———. *Dearest Father: Stories and Other Writings*. Translated by Ernst Kaiser and Eithne Wilkins. New York: Schocken Books, 1954.

———. *Wedding Preparations in the Country and Other Posthumous Prose Writings*. Notes by Max Brod. Translated by Ernst Kaiser and Eithne Wilkins. London: Secker and Warburg, 1973.

Kaufman, Tsippi. *In All Your Ways Know Him: The Concept of God and Avodah be-Gashmiyut in the Early Stages of Hasidism*. Ramat-Gan: Bar-Ilan University Press, 2009 (Hebrew).

Kaufmann, David. "Imageless Refuge for All Images: Scholem in the Wake of Philosophy." *Modern Judaism* 20 (2000): 147–158.

Kavka, Martin. "Saying Kaddish for Gillian Rose, or on Levinas and *Geltungsphilosophie*." In *Secular Theology: American Radical Theological Thought*, edited by Clayton Crockett, 104–129. London: Routledge, 2001.

Keane, Niall. "The Silence of the Origin: Philosophy in Transition and the Essence of Thinking." *Research in Phenomenology* 43 (2013): 27–48.

Kelber, Werner H. "Memory and Violence, or Genealogies of Remembering." In *Saintly Influence: Edith Wyschogrod and the Possibilities of Philosophy of Religion*, edited by Eric Boynton and Martin Kavka, 175–201. New York: Fordham University Press, 2009.

Kenaan, Hagi. "Facing Images: After Levinas." *Angelaki* 16 (2011): 143–159.

Kierkegaard, Søren. *Concluding Unscientific Postscript*. Translated by David F. Swenson. Completed with introduction and notes by Walter Lowrie. Princeton: Princeton University Press, 1968.

———. *Concluding Unscientific Postscript to Philosophical Fragments*. Vol. 1: Text. Edited and translated with introduction and notes by Howard V. Hong and Edna H. Hong. Princeton: Princeton University Press, 1992.

———. *Concluding Unscientific Postscript to Philosophical Fragments*. Vol. 2: Historical introduction, supplement, notes, and index. Edited and translated with introduction and notes by Howard V. Hong and Edna H. Hong. Princeton: Princeton University Press, 1992.

Klein, Melanie. *Contributions to Psycho-Analysis, 1921–1945*. Introduction by Ernest Jones. London: Hogarth Press, 1948.

Kleinberg. Ethan. *Haunting History: For a Deconstructive Approach to the Past*. Stanford: Stanford University Press, 2017.

Kleinberg-Levin, David Michael. *Critical Studies on Heidegger: The Emerging Body of Understanding*. Albany: State University of New York Press, 2023.

Klibansky, Raymond, Erwin Panofsky, and Fritz Saxl. *Saturn and Melancholy: Studies in the History of Natural Philosophy, Religion, and Art*. New York: Basic Books, 1964.

Kligerman, Eric. *Sites of the Uncanny: Paul Celan, Specularity and the Visual Arts*. Berlin: Walter de Gruyter, 2007.

Kouba, Petr. *The Phenomenon of Mental Disorder: Perspectives of Heidegger's Thought in Psychopathology*. Cham: Springer, 2006.

Kovacs, George. *The Question of God in Heidegger's Phenomenology*. Evanston: Northwestern University Press, 1990.

Krell, David Farrell. "The Crisis of Reason in the Nineteenth Century: Schelling's Treatise on Human Freedom (1809)." In *The Collegium Phaenomenologicum: The First Ten Years*, edited by John C. Sallis, Giuseppina Moneta, and Jacques Taminiaux, 13–32. Dordrecht: Kluwer Academic, 1988.

———. "Marginalia to *Geschlecht III*: Derrida on Heidegger on Trakl." *New Centennial Review* 7 (2007): 175–199.

———. "Three Ends of the Absolute: Schelling on Inhibition, Hölderlin on Separation, and Novalis on Identity." *Research in Phenomenology* 32 (2002): 60–85.

———. *The Tragic Absolute: German Idealism and the Languishing of God*. Bloomington: Indiana University Press, 2005.

Kristeva, Julia. *Black Sun: Depression and Melancholia*. Translated by Leon S. Roudiez. New York: Columbia University Press, 1992.

———. *Dostoyevsky in the Face of Death or Language Haunted by Sex*. Translated by Armine Kotin Mortimer. New York: Columbia University Press, 2024.

———. "On the Melancholic Imaginary." *New Formations* 3 (1987): 5–18.

Kritzman, Lawrence D. "Melancholia Becomes the Subject: Kristeva's Invisible 'Thing' and the Making of Culture." *Paragraph* 14 (1991): 144–150.

Lacan, Jacques. *Écrits: A Selection*. Translated by Alan Sheridan. New York: W. W. Norton, 1977.

———. *The Seminar of Jacques Lacan. Book VIII: Transference*. Edited by Jacques-Alain Miller. Translated by Bruce Fink. Cambridge: Polity Press, 2015.

———. *The Seminar of Jacques Lacan. Book XXIII: The Sinthome*. Edited by Jacques-Alain Miller. Translated by A. R. Price. Cambridge: Polity Press, 2016.

Landsberg, Paul-Louis. *Essai sur l'expérience de la mort suivi de le problème moral du suicide*. Paris: Éditions du Seuil, 1951.

———. *The Experience of Death: The Moral Problem of Suicide*. Translated by Cynthia Rowland. New York: Philosophical Library, 1953.

Larrabee, Mary Jeanne. "There's No Time Like the Present: How to Mind the Now." In *The Many Faces of Time*, edited by John B. Brough and Lester Embree, 85–111. Dordrecht: Kluwer Academic, 2000.

Latz, Andrew Brower. *The Social Philosophy of Gillian Rose*. Eugene: Cascade Books, 2018.

Leader, Darian. "Some Thoughts on Mourning and Melancholia." In *Lacan on Depression and Melancholia*, edited by Derek Hook and Stijn Vanheule, 48–75. London: Routledge, 2023.

Lebovic, Nitzan. *Zionism and Melancholy: The Short Life of Israel Zarchi*. Bloomington: Indiana University Press, 2019.

Leerink, Herbert. *Das dunkle Licht: Gnosis, Irrsinn und Genialität im Werk Friedrich Hölderlins*. Varik: De Betuwsche Morgen, 2019.

Lefebve, Maurice-Jean. "The Nude as Symbol." In *Facets of Eros: Phenomenological Essays*, edited by F. Joseph Smith and Erling Eng, 101–115. The Hague: Martinus Nijhoff, 1972.

Lepenies, Wolf. *Melancholy and Society*. Translated by Jeremy Gaines and Doris Jones, with a foreword by Judith N. Shklar. Cambridge, MA: Harvard University Press, 1992.

Levin, David Michael. *The Opening of Vision: Nihilism and the Postmodern Situation.* New York: Routledge, 1988.

Levinas, Emmanuel. *Autrement qu'être ou au-delà de l'essence.* Dordrecht: Kluwer Academic, 1974.

———. *Basic Philosophical Writings.* Edited by Adriaan T. Peperzak, Simon Critchley, and Robert Bernasconi. Bloomington: Indiana University Press, 1996.

———. *Beyond the Verse: Talmudic Readings and Lectures.* Translated by Gary D. Mole. London: Athlone Press, 1994.

———. *Collected Philosophical Papers.* Translated by Alphonso Lingis. Dordrecht: Martinus Nijhoff. 1987.

———. *De Dieu qui vient à l'idée*, second edition. Paris: Librairie Philosophique J. Vrin, 2004.

———. *De l'Existence à l'existant*, second edition. Paris: Librairie Philosophique J. Vrin, 1998.

———. *Dieu, la mort et le temps.* Edited and with notes and afterword by Jacques Rolland. Paris: Éditions Grasset, 1993.

———. *En découvrant l'existence avec Husserl et Heidegger*, third corrected edition. Paris: Librairie Philosophique J. Vrin, 2001.

———. *Ethics and Infinity: Conversations with Philippe Nemo.* Translated by Richard A. Cohen. Pittsburgh: Duquesne University Press, 1985.

———. *Existence and Existents.* Translated by Alphonso Lingis. Foreword by Robert Bernasconi. Pittsburgh: Duquesne University Press, 2001.

———. *God, Death, and Time.* Translated by Bettina Bergo. Stanford: Stanford University Press, 2000.

———. *Oeuvres 1: Carnets de captivité suivi de Écrits sur la captivité et Notes philosophiques diverses.* Edited and annotated by Rodolphe Calin. Preface and explanatory notes by Rodolphe Calin and Catherine Chalier. General preface by Jean-Luc Marion. Paris: Éditions Grasset & Fasquelle, 2009.

———. *Of God Who Comes to Mind.* Translated by Bettina Bergo. Stanford: Stanford University Press, 1998.

———. *On Escape.* Translated by Bettina Bergo. Stanford: Stanford University Press, 2003.

———. *Otherwise Than Being or Beyond Essence.* Translated by Alphonso Lingis. Dordrecht: Kluwer Academic, 1991.

———. *Proper Names.* Translated by Michael B. Smith. Stanford: Stanford University Press, 1996.

———. "Revelation in the Jewish Tradition." In *The Levinas Reader*, edited by Seán Hand, 190–210. Oxford: Blackwell, 1989.

———. "The Servant and Her Master." In *The Levinas Reader*, edited by Seán Hand, 150–159. Oxford: Blackwell, 1989.

———. *Le Temps et l'autre*. Paris: Presses Universitaires de France, 1983.
———. *Time and the Other*. Translated by Richard A. Cohen. Pittsburgh: Duquesne University Press, 1987.
———. *Totalité et infini: Essai sur l'extériorité*. The Hague: Martinus Nijhoff, 1980.
———. *Totality and Infinity: An Essay on Exteriority*. Translated by Alphonso Lingis. Dordrecht: Kluwer Academic, 1969.
Liska, Vivian. "Against Melancholy: On the Demonic in Gershom Scholem." In *Das Dämonische: Schicksale einer Kategorie der Zweideutigkeit nach Goethe*, edited by Lars Friedrich, Eva Geulen, and Kirk Wetters, 311–324. Paderborn: Wilhelm Fink, 2014.
———. *German-Jewish Thought and Its Afterlife: A Tenuous Legacy*. Bloomington: Indiana University Press, 2017.
Lloyd, Vincent. "Gillian Rose, Race, and Identity." *Telos* 173 (2015): 104–124.
———. "Interview with Gillian Rose." *Theory, Culture & Society* 25, 7–8 (2008): 201–218.
———. "Law All the Way Down: Gillian Rose and Robert Cover as Jewish Philosophers." In *Misrecognitions: Gillian Rose and the Task of Political Theology*, edited by Joshua B. Davis, 202–226. Eugene: Cascade Books, 2018.
———. *Law and Transcendence: On the Unfinished Project of Gillian Rose*. Hampshire: Palgrave Macmillan, 2009.
———. "The Secular Faith of Gillian Rose." *Journal of Religious Ethics* 36 (2008): 683–705.
Love, Jeff, and Michael Meng. "Heidegger's Metapolitics." *Cultural Critique* 99 (2018): 97–122.
Lucca, Enrico. "Translating, Interpreting the Bible, Fighting Satan: Rosenzweig, Scholem, and the End of Their Correspondence (with Three Unpublished Letters from Scholem to Rosenzweig)." In *"Into Life": Franz Rosenzweig on Knowledge, Aesthetics, and Politics*, edited by Antonios Kalatzis and Enrico Lucca, 9–38. Leiden: Brill, 2021.
Lyotard, Jean-François. *The Differend: Phrases in Dispute*. Translated by Georges Van Den Abbeele. Minneapolis: University of Minnesota Press, 1988.
Mao, Xin. "Subjectivity, Infinite Ethical Responsibility and Null-Site Exposure: A Constructive Exploration of Levinasian Subjectivity Through the Lens of the Levinasian Concept of Utopia." PhD dissertation, King's College London, 2019.
———. "Utopia in Lévinas: Null-Site as Reduction from Said to Saying, from Politics to Ethics." *Azimuth: Philosophical Coordinates in Modern and Contemporary Ages* 2 (2014): 123–138.
Maor, Zohar. "Scholem and Rosenzweig: Redemption and (Anti-)Zionism." *Modern Judaism* 37 (2017): 1–23.
Moati, Raoul. *Levinas and the Night of Being: A Guide to* Totality and Infinity.

Translated by Daniel Wyche, with a foreword by Jocelyn Benoist. New York: Fordham University Press, 2017.

Marion, Jean-Luc. *Being Given: Toward a Phenomenology of Givenness*. Translated by Jeffrey L. Kosky. Stanford: Stanford University Press, 2002.

Martins, Ansgar. *The Migration of Metaphysics into the Realm of the Profane*. Translated by Lars Fischer. Leiden: Brill, 2020.

Matějčková, Tereza. "Eternity's Death in Modernity: A Case of Murder? Of Resurrection?" *International Journal of Philosophical Studies* 28 (2020): 452–469.

Mayse, Ariel Evan. *Speaking Infinities: God and Language in the Teachings of Rabbi Dov Ber of Mezritsh*. Philadelphia: University of Pennsylvania Press, 2020.

McCullough, Lissa. *The Religious Philosophy of Simone Weil: An Introduction*. London: I. B. Tauris, 2014.

McGrath, Sean J. *The Early Heidegger and Medieval Philosophy: Phenomenology for the Godforsaken*. Washington, DC: Catholic University of America Press, 2006.

Mendes-Flohr, Paul. "Hebrew as a Holy Tongue: Franz Rosenzweig and the Renewal of Hebrew." In *Hebrew in Ashkenaz: A Language in Exile*, edited by Lewis Gilbert, 222– 241. Oxford: Oxford University Press, 1993.

Merleau-Ponty, Maurice. *Le visible et l'invisible suivi de Notes de travail*. Edited by Claude Lefort. Paris: Gallimard, 1964.

———. *The Visible and the Invisible: Followed by Working Notes*. Edited by Claude Lefort. Translated by Alphonso Lingis. Evanston: Northwestern University Press, 1968.

Micali, Stefano. "The Alteration of Embodiment in Melancholia." In *The Phenomenology of Embodied Subjectivity*, edited by Rasmus Thybo Jensen and Dermot Moran, 203–219. Cham: Springer, 2013.

Milton, John. *Complete Poems and Major Prose*. Edited and with notes and introduction by Merritt Y. Hughes. Indianapolis: Hackett, 2003.

Mitchell, Andrew J. *The Fourfold: Reading the Late Heidegger*. Evanston: Northwestern University Press, 2015.

———. "Heidegger's Later Thinking of Animality: The End of World Poverty." *Gatherings: The Heidegger Circle Annual* 1 (2011): 74–85.

Moore, Ian Alexander. *Dialogue on the Threshold: Heidegger and Trakl*. Albany: State University of New York Press, 2022.

———. *Eckhart, Heidegger, and the Imperative of Releasement*. Albany: State University of New York Press, 2019.

———. "Heidegger's Trakl-Marginalia." *Research in Phenomenology* 51 (2021): 99–122.

Moran, Dermot. "'Let It Be': Heidegger and Eckhart on *Gelassenheit*." In *The Routledge Handbook of Phenomenology of Mindfulness*, edited by Susi Ferrarello and Christos Hadjioannou, 231–251. London: Routledge, 2024.

———. "*Spiritualis Incrassatio*: Eriugena's Intellectualist Immaterialism: Is It an Idealism?" In *Eriugena, Berkeley, and the Idealist Tradition*, edited by Stephen Gersh and Dermot Moran, 123–150. Notre Dame: University of Notre Dame Press, 2006.

Morrison, Robert G. *Nietzsche and Buddhism: A Study in Nihilism and Ironic Affinities*. Oxford: Oxford University Press, 1997.

Mosès, Stéphane. *The Angel of History: Rosenzweig, Benjamin, Scholem*. Translated by Barbara Harshav. Stanford: Stanford University Press, 2009.

———. "Langage et sécularisation chez Gershom Scholem." *Archives de sciences sociales des religions* 60 (1985): 85–96.

———. "Une lettre inédite de Gershom Scholem à Franz Rosenzweig. A propos de notre langue. Une confession." *Archives de sciences sociales des religions* 60 (1985): 83–84.

Mozersky, M. Joshua. "Presentism." In *The Oxford Handbook of Philosophy of Time*, edited by Craig Callender, 122–144. Oxford: Oxford University Press, 2011.

Muller, Jerry Z. *Professor of Apocalypse: The Many Lives of Jacob Taubes*. Princeton: Princeton University Press, 2022.

Nelson, Eric S. *Heidegger and Dao: Things, Nothingness, Freedom*. London: Bloomsbury Academic, 2024.

Nietzsche, Friedrich. *Also Sprach Zarathustra I–IV*. Edited by Giorgio Colli and Mazzino Montinari. Berlin: Walter de Gruyter, 1999.

———. *Human, All Too Human: A Book for Free Spirits*. Translated by R. J. Hollingdale, with an introduction by Richard Schacht. Cambridge: Cambridge University Press, 1996.

———. *The Joyful Science, Idylls from Messina, Unpublished Fragments from the Period of* The Joyful Science *(Spring 1881-Summer 1882)*. Translated and with an afterword by Adrian Del Caro. Stanford: Stanford University Press, 2023.

———. *Menschliches, Allzumenschliches I–II*. Edited by Giorgio Colli and Mazzini Montinari. Munich: Walter de Gruyter, 1999.

———. *Morgenröte, Idyllen aus Messina, Die fröhliche Wissenschaft*. Edited by Giorgio Colli and Mazzino Montinari. Munich: Walter de Gruyter, 1999.

———. *On Truth and Lie in an Extra-Moral Sense*. Translated by Andrew Keith Malcolm Adam. Oxford: Quadriga, 2019.

———. *Thus Spoke Zarathustra: A Book for All and None*. Edited by Adrian Del Caro and Robert B. Pippin. Translated by Adrian del Caro. Cambridge: Cambridge University Press, 2006.

———. *Unpublished Fragments from the Period of* Thus Spoke Zarathustra *(Spring 1884–Winter 1884/85)*. Translated and with an afterword by Paul S. Loeb and David F. Tinsley. Stanford: Stanford University Press, 2022.

———. *The Will to Power*. Translated by Walter Kaufmann and R. J. Hollingdale. Edited and with commentary by Walter Kaufmann. New York: Random House, 1967.

———. *Writings from the Early Notebooks*. Edited by Raymond Geuss and Alexander Nehamas. Translated by Ladislaus Löb. Cambridge: Cambridge University Press, 2009.

———. *Writings from the Late Notebooks*. Edited by Rüdiger Bittner. Translated by Kate Sturge. Cambridge: Cambridge University Press, 2003.

Nissan, Ephraim, and Abraham Ofir Shemesh. "Melancholia and Diabetes? Clinical Description and Therapy in Nathan b. Joel Falaquera." *Rivista di Storia della Medicina* 232 (2013): 15–28.

———. "Melancholia in Jewish Rabbinic and Medical Sources Through the Ages, I: From Antiquity to the Middle Ages." *Rivista di Storia della Medicina* 22 (2012): 7–33.

———. "Saturnine Traits, Melancholia, and Related Conditions as Ascribed to Jews and Jewish Culture (and Jewish Responses) from Imperial Rome to High Modernity." *Quaderni di Studi Indo-Mediterranei* 3 (2010): 97–128.

Novalis. *Hymns to the Night,* third edition. Translated by Dick Higgins. Kingston: McPherson & Company, 1988.

———. *Novalis: Philosophical Writings*. Translated by Margaret Mahony Stoljar. Albany: State University of New York Press, 1997.

Nuki, Shigeto. "Temporality and Historicity: Phenomenology of History Beyond Narratology." In *The Many Faces of Time*, edited by John B. Brough and Lester Embree, 149–165. Dordrecht: Kluwer Academic, 2000.

Ochs, Peter. "Saints and the Heterological Historian." In *Saintly Influence: Edith Wyschogrod and the Possibilities of Philosophy of Religion*, edited by Eric Boynton and Martin Kavka, 219–237. New York: Fordham University Press, 2009.

Panaïoti, Antoine. *Nietzsche and Buddhist Philosophy*. Cambridge: Cambridge University Press, 2013.

Pareigis, Christina. "The Connecting Paths of Nomads, Wanderers, Exiles. Stationen Einer Korrespondenz." In *Die Korrespondenz mit Jacob Taubes 1950–1951*, edited by Christina Pareigis, 259–288. Munich: Fink, 2011.

———. *Susan Taubes: Eine intellektuelle Biographie*. Göttingen: Wallstein, 2020.

Parry, Gregory David. "The 'Void' in Simone Weil and the 'Broken Middle' in Gillian Rose: The Genesis of the Search for Salvation." PhD dissertation, University of Durham, 2006.

Pensky, Max. *Melancholy Dialectics: Walter Benjamin and the Play of Mourning*. Amherst: University of Massachusetts Press, 1993.

Pezze, Barbara Dalle. *Martin Heidegger and Meister Eckhart: A Path Towards Gelassenheit*. Foreword by Timothy O'Leary. Lewiston: Edwin Mellen Press, 2008.

Plato. *The Collected Dialogues of Plato Including the Letters*. Edited by Edith Hamilton and Huntington Cairns, with introduction and prefatory notes. Princeton: Princeton University Press, 1961.

Polt, Richard. "The Secret Homeland of Speech: Heidegger on Language, 1933–1934." In *Heidegger and Language*, edited by Jeffrey Powell, 63–85. Bloomington: Indiana University Press, 2013.

———. *Time and Trauma: Thinking Through Heidegger in the Thirties*. London: Rowman & Littlefield, 2019.

Pound, Marcus. "Political Theology and Comedy: Žižek Through Rose Tinted Glasses." *Crisis and Critique* 2 (2015): 179–191.

———. "Rose *Contra* Girard: Kenotic Comedy and Social Theory (Or, Žižek as a Reader of Rose)." In *Misrecognitions: Gillian Rose and the Task of Political Theology*, edited by Joshua B. Davis, 67–86. Eugene: Cascade Books, 2018.

Prochnik, George. *Stranger in a Strange Land: Searching for Gershom Scholem and Jerusalem*. New York: Other Press, 2016.

Puech, Henri-Charles. "Gnosis and Time." In *Man and Time: Papers from the Eranos Yearbooks*, 38–84. New York: Bollingen Foundation, 1957.

Rabinbach, Anson. "Between Enlightenment and Apocalypse: Benjamin, Bloch and Modern German Jewish Messianism." *New German Critique* 34 (1985): 78–124.

Raffoul, François. *Thinking the Event*. Bloomington: Indiana University Press, 2020.

Ratzman, Elliot Ashley. "At the Common Altar: Political Messianism, Practical Ethics and Post-War Jewish Thought." PhD dissertation, Princeton University, 2009.

Resnick, Irven M. *Marks of Distinction: Christian Perceptions of Jews in the High Middle Ages*. Washington, DC: Catholic University of America Press, 2012.

Rickey, Christopher. *Revolutionary Saints: Heidegger, National Socialism, and Antinomian Politics*. University Park: Pennsylvania State University Press, 2002.

Robiadek, Katherine M. "Worlding Versus Worldview: Heidegger's Thinking on Art as a Critique of German Historicism." *Monatshefte* 108 (2016): 383–394.

Robinson, Keith. "Thought of the Outside: The Foucault/Deleuze Conjunction." *Philosophy Today* 43 (1999): 57–72.

Romano, Claude. *At the Heart of Reason*. Translated by Michael B. Smith and Claude Romano. Evanston: Northwestern University Press, 2015.

———. "Awaiting." In *Phenomenology and Eschatology: Not Yet in the Now*, edited by Neal DeRoo and John Panteleimon Manoussakis, 35–52. Burlington: Ashgate, 2009.

———. *Event and Time*. Translated by Stephen E. Lewis. New York: Fordham University Press, 2014.

———. *Event and World*. Translated by Shane Mackinlay. New York: Fordham University Press, 2009.

———. *There Is: The Event and the Finitude of Appearing*. Translated by Michael B. Smith. New York: Fordham University Press, 2016.

Rose, Gillian. *The Broken Middle: Out of Our Ancient Society*. Oxford: Blackwell, 1992.

———. *Dialectic of Nihilism: Post-Structuralism and Law*. Oxford: Basil Blackwell, 1984.

———. "Diremption of Spirit." In *Shadow of Spirit: Postmodernism and Religion*, edited by Philippa Berry and Andrew Wernick, 45–56. London: Routledge, 1992.

———. *Hegel Contra Sociology*. London: Verso, 2009.

———. *Judaism and Modernity: Philosophical Essays*. Oxford: Blackwell, 1993.

———. *Love's Work: A Reckoning with Life*. Introduction by Michael Wood. New York: New York Review of Books, 2011.

———. *The Melancholy Science: An Introduction to the Thought of Theodor W. Adorno*. London: Macmillan, 1978.

———. *Mourning Becomes the Law: Philosophy and Representation*. Cambridge: Cambridge University Press, 1996.

———. *Paradiso*. Bristol: Shearsman Books, 2015.

Rose, Jacqueline. *Women in Dark Times*. London: Bloomsbury, 2014.

Rosenstock, Bruce. "The Flight of the Gods: A Comparative Study of Martin Heidegger and Oskar Goldberg." *New German Critique* 137 (2019): 221–252.

Rosenzweig, Franz. *Der Mensch und sein Werk: Gesammelte Schriften I. Briefe und Tagebücher*. Vol. 2: *1918–1929*. Edited by Rachel Rosenzweig and Edith Rosenzweig-Scheinmann, with the assistance of Bernhard Casper. The Hague: Martinus Nijhoff, 1979.

———. *Der Mensch und sein Werk: Gesammelte Schriften III. Zweistromland: Kleinere Schriften zu Glauben und Denken*. Edited by Reinhold and Annemarie Mayer. The Hague: Martinus Nijhoff, 1984.

———. *The Star of Redemption*. Translated by Barbara Galli. Madison: University of Wisconsin Press, 2005.

Ross, Nathan. *Walter Benjamin's First Philosophy: Experience, Ephemerality and Truth*. New York: Routledge, 2021.

Rotenstreich, Nathan. "Gershom Scholem's Conception of Jewish Nationalism." In *Gershom Scholem: The Man and His Work*, edited by Paul Mendes-Flohr, 104–119. Albany: State University of New York Press, 1994.

Rovelli, Carlo. *The Order of Time*. Translated by Erica Segre and Simon Carnell. New York: Riverhead Books, 2018.

Rowlands, Anna. "Beginning in the Middle: The Third City and the Politics of Membership." In *Misrecognitions: Gillian Rose and the Task of Political Theology*, edited by Joshua B. Davis, 29–46. Eugene: Cascade Books, 2018.

Ruin, Hans. "The Inversion of Mysticism—*Gelassenheit* and the Secret of the Open in Heidegger." *Religions* 10 (2019): 15, 1–9.

Sallis, John C. *The Return of Nature: On the Beyond of Sense*. Bloomington: Indiana University Press, 2016.

Sandbothe, Mike. *The Temporalization of Time: Basic Tendencies in Modern Debate on Time in Philosophy and Science*. Translated by Andrew Inkpin. Lanham: Rowman & Littlefield, 2001.

Sax, Benjamin E. *Winged Words: Benjamin, Rosenzweig, and the Life of Quotation*. Leiden: Brill, 2023.

Schelling, Friedrich Wilhelm Joseph. *The Ages of the World (Fragment) from the Handwritten Remains, Third Version (c. 1815)*. Translated and with an introduction by Jason M. Wirth. Albany: State University of New York Press, 2000.

———. *Philosophical Investigations into the Essence of Human Freedom*. Translated and with an introduction by Jeff Love and Johannes Schmidt. Albany: State University of New York Press, 2006.

———. *Philosophische Untersuchungen über das Wesen der menschlichen Freiheit und die damit zusammenhängenden Gegenstände*. Edited by Thomas Buchheim. Hamburg: Felix Meiner, 1997.

———. *Sämmtliche Werke 1805–1810*. Vol. 7. Edited by Karl Friedrich August Schelling. Stuttgart: Cotta, 1860.

———. *Stuttgart Seminars*, in *Idealism and the Endgame of Theory: Three Essays by F. W. J. Schelling*. Translated, edited, and with a critical introduction by Thomas Pfau. Albany: State University of New York Press, 1994.

Schick, Kate. *Gillian Rose: A Good Enough Justice*. Edinburgh: Edinburgh University Press, 2012.

———. "Gillian Rose and Vulnerable Judgement." In *The Vulnerable Subject: Beyond Rationalism in International Relations*, edited by Amanda Russell Beattie and Kate Schick, 43–61. Hampshire: Palgrave Macmillan, 2013.

Schlosser, Joel Alden. "'Hope, Danger's Comforter': Thucydides, Hope, Politics." *Journal of Politics* 75 (2013): 169–182.

Scholem, Gershom. "Bemerkungen über die Zeit im Judentum." In *Tagebücher nebst Aufsätzen und Entwürfen bis 1923*, vol. 2: *1917–1923*. Edited by Karlfried Gründer, Herbert Kopp-Oberstebrink, and Friedrich Niewöhner, with the assistance of Karl E. Grözinger, 235–240. Frankfurt am Main: Jüdischer, 2000.

———. *Erlösung durch Sünde*. Edited by Jonatan Meir. Jerusalem: Blima Books, 2023.

———. *Explications and Implications: Writings on Jewish Heritage and Renaissance*. Vol. 2. Edited by Avraham Shapira. Tel Aviv: Am Oved, 1989 (Hebrew).

———. *From Berlin to Jerusalem: Memories of My Youth*. Translated by Harry Zohn. New York: Schocken Books, 1980.

———. *The Fullness of Time: Poems*. Translated by Richard Sieburth. Introduced and annotated by Steven M. Wasserstrom. Jerusalem: Ibis Editions, 2003.

———. *History of the Sabbatian Movement: Lectures Given at the Hebrew University of Jerusalem 1939–1940*. Edited by Jonatan Meir and Shinichi Yamamoto. Jerusalem: Schocken Books, 2018 (Hebrew).

———. *Kabbalah*. Jerusalem: Keter, 1974.

———. *Lamentations of Youth: The Diaries of Gershom Scholem 1913–1919*. Edited and translated by Anthony David Skinner. Cambridge, MA: Harvard University Press, 2007.

———. *Major Trends in Jewish Mysticism*. New York: Schocken Books, 1954.

———. *The Messianic Idea in Judaism and Other Essays on Jewish Spirituality*. New York: Schocken Books, 1971.

———. *On Jews and Judaism in Crisis: Selected Essays*. Edited by Werner J. Dannhauser. New York: Schocken Books, 1976.

———. "On Jonah and the Concept of Justice." Translated by Eric J. Schwab. *Critical Inquiry* 25 (1999): 353–361.

———. "On Lament and Lamentation." In *Lament in Jewish Thought: Philosophical, Theological, and Literary Perspectives*, edited by Ilit Ferber and Paula Schwebel, 313– 319. Berlin: Walter de Gruyter, 2014.

———. *On the Possibility of Jewish Mysticism in Our Time & Other Essays*. Edited and with an introduction by Avraham Shapira. Translated by Jonathan Chipman. Philadelphia: Jewish Publication Society of America, 1997.

———. *Poetica: Schriften zur Literatur, Übersetzungen, Gedichte*. Edited and with commentary by Herbert Kopp-Oberstebrink, Hannah Markus, Martin Treml, and Sigrid Weigel, with the cooperation of Theresia Heuer. Berlin: Suhrkamp, 2019.

———. *Sabbatai Ṣevi: The Mystical Messiah 1626–1676*. Translated by R. J. Zwi Werblowsky. Princeton: Princeton University Press, 1973.

———. *Studies and Texts Concerning the History of Sabbetianism and Its Metamorphoses*. Jerusalem: Bialik Institute, 1982 (Hebrew).

———. "Über Jona und den Begriff der Gerechtigkeit." In *Tagebücher nebst Aufsätzen und Entwürfen bis 1923*, vol. 2: *1917–1923*. Edited by Karlfried Gründer, Herbert Kopp-Oberstebrink, and Friedrich Niewöhner, with the assistance of Karl E. Grözinger, 522–532. Frankfurt am Main: Jüdischer, 2000.

———. "Über Klage und Klagelied." In *Tagebücher nebst Aufsätzen und Entwürfen bis 1923*. Vol. 2: *1917–1923*. Edited by Karlfried Gründer, Herbert Kopp-Oberstebrink, and Friedrich Niewöhner, with the assistance of Karl E. Grözinger, 128–133. Frankfurt am Main: Jüdischer, 2000.

Schopenhauer, Arthur. *Parerga and Paralipomena: Short Philosophical Essays*. Vol. 2. Translated and edited by Adrian del Caro and Christopher Janaway, with an

introduction by Christopher Janaway. Cambridge: Cambridge University Press, 2015.
Schroeder, Brian. "Dancing Through Nothing: Nietzsche, the Kyoto School, and Transcendence." *Journal of Nietzsche Studies* 37 (2009): 44–65.
Schürmann, Reiner. *Broken Hegemonies*. Translated by Reginald Lilly. Bloomington: Indiana University Press, 2003.
———. "Heidegger and the Mystical Tradition." *Journal of Continental Philosophy* 1 (2020): 284–303.
———. *Meister Eckhart: Mystic and Philosopher*. Bloomington: Indiana University Press, 1978.
———. "Trois penseurs du délaissement: Maître Eckhart, Heidegger, Suzuki: Part One." *Journal of the History of Philosophy* 12 (1974): 455–477.
———. "Trois penseurs du délaissement: Maître Eckhart, Heidegger, Suzuki: Part Two." *Journal of the History of Philosophy* 13 (1975): 56–60.
Schütrumpf, Eckart. "Black Bile as the Cause of Human Accomplishments and Behaviors in *Pr.* 30.1: Is the Concept Aristotelian?" In *The Aristotelian Problemata Physica: Philosophical and Scientific Investigations*, edited by Robert Mayhew, 357–380. Leiden: Brill, 2015.
Schwarzschild, Steven S. *The Tragedy of Optimism: Writings on Hermann Cohen*. Edited by George Y. Kohler. Albany: State University of New York Press, 2018.
Segall, Matthew David. *Crossing the Threshold: Etheric Imagination in the Post-Kantian Process Philosophy of Schelling and Whitehead*. Olympia: Integral Imprint, 2023.
Shahar, Galili. "The Sacred and the Unfamiliar: Gershom Scholem and the Anxieties of the New Hebrew." *The Germanic Review: Literature, Culture, Theory* 83 (2008): 299–320.
Shanks, Andrew. *Against Innocence: Gillian Rose's Reception and Gift of Faith*. Foreword by Giles Fraser. London: SCM Press, 2008.
Shapira, Kalonymus Kalman. *Hakhsharat ha-Avrekhim—Mevo ha-She'arim*. Jerusalem: Ḥasidei Piaseczno, 2001.
Sikka, Sonya. *Forms of Transcendence: Heidegger and Medieval Mystical Theology*. Albany: State University of New York Press, 1997.
Simmons, Byron. "Ontological Pluralism and the Generic Conception of Being." *Erkenntnis* 87 (2022): 1275–1293.
Smith, Quentin. "The Uncaused Beginning of the Universe." In *Theism, Atheism, and Big Bang Cosmology*, edited by William Lane Craig and Quentin Smith, 108–140. Oxford: Clarendon Press, 1993.
Soloveitchik, Joseph B. "Lectures of Rabbi Dr. Joseph B. Soloveitchik: The Relationship Between Halakhah, Aggadah, and Kabbalah." Transcribed by Robert Blau.

Edited and footnotes by Eliyahu Krakowski, Heshey Zelcer, and Mark Zelcer. *Ḥakirah: The Flatbush Journal of Jewish Law and Thought* 33 (2023): 19–82.

———. "Rabbi Joseph B. Soloveitchik's Lectures on 'Concepts in Halakha as Elaborated Upon by the Aggada and Kabbala.'" Transcribed and edited by Yaakov Homnick, with contributions by Daniel Rynhold, Jeffrey Saks, and Shlomo Zuckier. *Tradition: Special Digital Issue* (2023): 4–53.

Snoek, Anke. "Agamben's Foucault: An Overview." *Foucault Studies* 10 (2010): 44–67.

A Source Book in Chinese Philosophy. Translated and compiled by Wing-Tsit Chan. Princeton: Princeton University Press, 1963.

Stambaugh, Joan. "Existential Time in Kierkegaard and Heidegger." In *Religion and Time*, edited by Anindita Niyogi Balslev and Jitendra N. Mohanty, 46–60. Leiden: Brill, 1993.

Stanley, Liz. "Mourning Becomes . . . : The Work of Feminism in the Spaces Between Lives Lived and Lives Written." *Women's Studies International Forum* 25 (2002): 1–17.

States, Bert O. *Seeing in the Dark: Reflections on Dreams and Dreaming*. New Haven: Yale University Press, 1997.

Steinberg, Michael P. "Music and Melancholy." *Critical Inquiry* 40 (2014): 288–310.

Styfhals, Willem. "Predicting the Present: Gershom Scholem on Prophecy." *Journal of Jewish Thought and Philosophy* 28 (2020): 259–286.

Su, Tsu-Chung. "Writing the Melancholic: The Dynamics of Melancholia in Julia Kristeva's *Black Sun*." *Concentric: Literary and Cultural Studies* 31 (2005): 163–191.

Tanna de-vei Eliyahu im ha-Perush Ramatayim Ṣofim. Jerusalem: Meqor ha-Sefarim, 2012.

Taubes, Jacob. *The Political Theology of Paul*. Edited by Aleida Assmann and Jan Assmann, in conjunction with Horst Folkers, Wolf-Daniel Hartwich, and Christoph Schulte. Translated by Dana Hollander. Stanford: Stanford University Press, 2004.

Taubes, Susan. "The Absent God: A Study of Simone Weil." PhD dissertation, Radcliffe College, 1956.

———. *Die Korrespondenz mit Jacob Taubes 1950–1951*. Edited by Christina Pareigis. Munich: Fink, 2011.

———. *Die Korrespondenz mit Jacob Taubes 1952*. Edited by Christina Pareigis. Munich: Fink, 2014.

———. *Divorcing*. Introduction by David Rieff. New York: New York Review of Books, 2020.

———. *Lament for Julia*. Introduction by Francesca Wade. New York: New York Review of Books, 2023.

———. "The Nature of Tragedy." *Review of Metaphysics* 7 (1953): 193–206.
———. "Review of *Tragedy and the Paradox of the Fortunate* by Herbert Weisinger." *Ethics* 64 (1954): 321–325.
Taubes, Susan Anima. "The Absent God." *Journal of Religion* 35 (1955): 6–16.
———. "The Gnostic Foundations of Heidegger's Nihilism." *Journal of Religion* 34 (1954): 155–172.
Tenzin Gyatso and Thubten Chodron. *The Foundation of Buddhist Practice*. Somerville: Wisdom Publications, 2018.
The Texts of Early Greek Philosophy: The Complete Fragments and Selected Testimonies of the Major Presocratics. Part 1. Edited and translated by Daniel W. Graham. Cambridge: Cambridge University Press, 2010.
Tiqqunei Zohar. Edited by Reuven Margaliot. Jerusalem: Mosad ha-Rav Kook, 1978.
Tishby, Isaiah. *The Doctrine of Evil and the "Shell" in Lurianic Kabbalah*. Translated by David Solomon. Los Angeles: Cherub Press, 2022.
———. "Gnostic Doctrines in Sixteenth-Century Jewish Mysticism." *Journal of Jewish Studies* 6 (1955): 146–152.
Trakl, Georg. *The Damned: Selected Poems of Georg Trakl*. Edited and translated by Daniele Pantano. Ceredigion: Broken Sleep Books, 2023.
———. *Poems and Prose: A Bilingual Edition*. Translated by Alexander Stillmark. Evanston: Northwestern University Press, 2005.
Trawny, Peter. *Freedom to Fail: Heidegger's Anarchy*. Translated by Ian Alexander Moore and Christopher Turner. Cambridge: Polity Press, 2015.
———. *Heidegger and the Myth of a Jewish World Conspiracy*. Translated by Andrew J. Michell. Chicago: University of Chicago Press, 2015.
Treanor, Brian. *Melancholic Joy: On Life Worth Living*. London: Bloomsbury Academic, 2021.
Tsongkhapa. *The Middle-Length Treatise on the Stages of the Path to Enlightenment*. Translated by Philip Quarcoo. Somerville: Wisdom Publications, 2021.
Tsoumpra, Natalia. "The Politics of Hopelessness: Thucydides and Aristophanes' *Knights*." In *Hope in Ancient Literature, History, and Art*, edited by George Kazantzidis and Dimos Spatharas, 111–129. Berlin: Walter de Gruyter, 2018.
Turner, Jason. "Logic and Ontological Pluralism." *Journal of Philosophical Logic* 41 (2012): 419–448.
———. "Ontological Pluralism." *Journal of Philosophy* 107 (2010): 5–34.
Van Buren, John. *The Young Heidegger: Rumor of the Hidden King*. Bloomington: Indiana University Press, 1994.
Van der Leeuw, Gerard. "Primordial Time and Final Time." In *Man and Time: Papers from the Eranos Yearbooks*, 324–350. New York: Bollingen Foundation, 1957.

Van der Lugt, Mara. *Dark Matters: Pessimism and the Problem of Suffering.* Princeton: Princeton University Press, 2021.

Vattimo, Gianni. *Beyond the Subject: Nietzsche, Heidegger, and Hermeneutics.* Translated, edited, and with an introduction by Peter Carravetta. Albany: State University of New York Press, 2019.

———. *The End of Modernity: Nihilism and Hermeneutics in Postmodern Culture.* Translated and with an introduction by Jon R. Snyder. Baltimore: Johns Hopkins University Press, 1991.

Vedder, Ben. *Heidegger's Philosophy of Religion: From God to the Gods.* Pittsburgh: Duquesne University Press, 2007.

Verbin, Nehama. "Self-Deception and the Life of Faith." *Heythrop Journal* 55 (2014): 845–859.

Vinzent, Markus. *The Art of Detachment.* Leuven: Peeters, 2011.

Von Balthasar, Hans Urs. *Apokalypse der deutschen Seele. Studien zu einer Lehre von letzten Haltungen. I: Der deutsche Idealismus.* Salzburg-Leipzig, Pustet, 1937.

Walls, Andrew F. "Old Athens and New Jerusalem: Some Signposts for Christian Scholarship in the Early History of Mission Studies." *International Bulletin of Missionary Research* 21 (1997): 146–153.

Wasserstrom, Steven M. "Defeating Evil from Within: Comparative Perspectives on 'Redemption Through Sin.'" *Journal of Jewish Thought and Philosophy* 6 (1997): 37–57.

———. "Melancholy Jouissance and the Study of Kabbalah: A Review Essay of Elliot R. Wolfson, *Alef, Mem, Tau.*" *Association for Jewish Studies Review* 32 (2008): 389–396.

———. *Religion After Religion: Gershom Scholem, Mircea Eliade, and Henry Corbin at Eranos.* Princeton: Princeton University Press, 1999.

Weatherall, James Owen. *Void: The Strange Physics of Nothing.* New Haven: Yale University Press, 2016.

Weidner, Daniel. *Gershom Scholem: Politisches, esoterisches und historiographisches Schreiben.* Munich: Wilhelm Fink, 2003.

Weiss, Joseph. "Beginnings of Hasidim." *Zion* 16 (1951): 46–105 (Hebrew).

Welz, Claudia. "The Future of the Past: Memory, Forgetting, and Personal Identity." In *Impossible Time: Past and Future in the Philosophy of Religion*, edited by Marius Timmann Mjaaland, Ulrik Houlind Rasmussen, and Philipp Stoellger, 199–212. Tübingen: Mohr Siebeck, 2013.

Wildmann, Yiṣḥaq Eizik Ḥaver. *Beit Olamim.* Warsaw: Meir Yeḥiel Halter, 1889.

Williams, Rowan D. "Between Politics and Metaphysics: Reflections in the Wake of Gillian Rose." *Modern Theology* 11 (1995): 3–22.

Wirth, Jason M. *Schelling's Practice of the Wild: Time, Art, Imagination.* Albany: State University of New York Press, 2015.

Withy, Katherine. "Concealing and Concealment in Heidegger." *European Journal of Philosophy* 25 (2017): 1496–1513.
———. *Heidegger on Being Self-Concealing*. Oxford: Oxford University Press, 2022.
———. *Heidegger on Being Uncanny*. Cambridge, MA: Harvard University Press, 2015.
Wittgenstein, Ludwig. *Moments of Thought: Ludwig Wittgenstein's Diary, 1930–1932 and 1936–1937*. Translated by Alfred Nordmann. Edited by James C. Klagge and Alfred Nordman, with an introduction by Ray Monk. Lanham: Rowman & Littlefield, 2023.
———. *Remarks on the Foundations of Mathematics*, revised edition. Edited by Georg Henrik von Wright, Rush Rhees, and Gertrude Elisabeth Margaret Anscombe. Translated by Gertrude Elisabeth Margaret Anscombe. Cambridge, MA: MIT Press, 1978.
———. *Tractatus Logico-Philosophicus*. Translated by Charles K. Ogden, with an introduction by Bertrand Russell. London: Routledge, 1995.
Wolfson, Elliot R. *Alef, Men, Tau: Kabbalistic Musings on Time, Truth, and Death*. Berkeley: University of California Press, 2006.
———. "Apophasis and the Trace of Transcendence: Wyschogrod's Contribution to a Postmodern Jewish Immanent A/Theology." *Philosophy Today* 55 (2011): 328–347.
———. "Becoming Invisible: Rending the Veil and the Hermeneutic of Secrecy in the *Gospel of Philip*." In *Practicing Gnosis: Ritual, Magic, Theurgy and Liturgy in Nag Hammadi, Manichean and Other Ancient Literature: Essays in Honor of Birger A. Pearson*, edited by April D. DeConick, Gregory Shaw, and John D. Turner, 113–135. Leiden: Brill, 2013.
———. *Circle in the Square: Studies in the Use of Gender in Kabbalistic Symbolism*. Albany: State University of New York Press, 1995.
———. "Coronation of the Sabbath Bride: Kabbalistic Myth and the Ritual of Androgynisation." *Journal of Jewish Thought and Philosophy* 6 (1997): 301–343.
———. "Death and the Infinitization of Finitude: Negation and the Ethical Crisis of Modernity in Edith Wyschogrod's Postmodern Hermeneutic." In *Modern Jewish Thought on Crisis: Interpretation, Heresy, and History*, edited by Ghilad H. Shenhav, Cedric Cohen-Skalli, and Gilad Sharvit, 241–266. Berlin: Walter de Gruyter, 2024.
———. "Do Not Wake or Arouse Love: Erotics of Time and the Dream of Messianic Waiting." In *The Song of Songs Through the Ages: Studies on the Song's Reception History in Different Epochs, Contexts, and Genres*, edited by Annette Schellenberg, 129–144. Berlin: Walter de Gruyter, 2023.
———. *A Dream Interpreted Within a Dream: Oneiropoiesis and the Prism of Imagination*. New York: Zone Books, 2011.

———. *The Duplicity of Philosophy's Shadow: Heidegger, Nazism, and the Jewish Other*. New York: Columbia University Press, 2018.

———. "The Engenderment of Messianic Politics: Symbolic Significance of Sabbatai Ṣevi's Coronation." In *Toward the Millennium: Messianic Expectations from the Bible to Waco*, edited by Peter Schäfer and Mark Cohen, 203–258. Leiden: Brill, 1998.

———. *Giving Beyond the Gift: Apophasis and Overcoming Theomania*. New York: Fordham University Press, 2014.

———. "Gnosis and the Covert Theology of Antitheology: Heidegger, Apocalypticism, and Gnosticism in Susan and Jacob Taubes." In *Depeche Mode: Jacob Taubes Between Politics, Philosophy, and Religion*, edited by Herbert Kopp-Oberstebrink and Hartmut von Sass, 151–202. Leiden: Brill, 2022.

———. "*Gottwesen* and the De-Divinization of the Last God: Heidegger's Meditation on the Strange and Incalculable." In *Heidegger's Black Notebooks and the Future of Theology*, edited by Mårten Björk and Jayne Svenungsson, 211–255. New York: Palgrave Macmillan, 2017.

———. "Heeding the Law Beyond the Law: Transgendering Alterity and the Hypernomian Perimeter of the Ethical." *European Journal of Jewish Studies* 14 (2020): 215–263.

———. *Heidegger and Kabbalah: Hidden Gnosis and the Path of Poiēsis*. Bloomington: Indiana University Press, 2019.

———. "Heidegger's Apophaticism: Unsaying the Said and the Silence of the Last God." In *Contemporary Debates in Negative Theology and Philosophy*, edited by Nahum Brown and J. Aaron Simmons, 185–216. New York: Palgrave, 2017.

———. "The Holy Cabala of Changes: Jacob Böhme and Jewish Esotericism." *Aries—Journal for the Study of Western Esotericism* 18 (2018): 21–53.

———. "Imagination, Theolatry, and the Compulsion to Worship the Invisible." In *Religion in Reason: Metaphysics, Ethics, and Politics in Hent de Vries*, edited by Tarek R. Dika and Martin Shuster, 50–79. London: Routledge, 2023.

———. *Language, Eros, Being: Kabbalistic Hermeneutics and the Poetic Imagination*. New York: Fordham University Press, 2005.

———. "Light Through Darkness: The Ideal of Human Perfection in the Zohar." *Harvard Theological Review* 81 (1988): 73–95.

———. "Nihilating Nonground and the Temporal Sway of Becoming: Kabbalistically Envisioning Nothing Beyond Nothing." *Angelaki* 17 (2012): 31–45.

———. "Not Yet Now: Speaking of the End and the End of Speaking." In *Elliot R. Wolfson: Poetic Thinking*, edited by Hava Tirosh-Samuelson and Aaron W. Hughes, 127–193. Leiden: Brill, 2015.

———. *Open Secret: Postmessianic Messianism and the Mystical Revision of Menaḥem Mendel Schneerson*. New York: Columbia University Press, 2009.

———. "Patriarchy and the Motherhood of God in Zoharic Kabbalah and Meister Eckhart." In *Envisioning Judaism: Studies in Honor of Peter Schäfer on the Occasion of His Seventieth Birthday,* edited by Ra'anan S. Boustan, Klaus Hermann, Reimund Leicht, Annette Yoshiko Reed, and Giuseppe Veltri, with the collaboration of Alex Ramos, 1049–1088. Tübingen: Mohr Siebeck, 2013.

———. "Phenomenology, Theosophic Topography and the Structures of Being: Unveiling the Seventh of Scholem's Ten Unhistorical Aphorisms on the Kabbalah." *Kabbalah: Journal for the Study of Jewish Mystical Texts* 55 (2023): 7–71.

———. *The Philosophical Pathos of Susan Taubes: Between Nihilism and Hope.* Stanford: Stanford University Press, 2023.

———. "Rosenzweig on Human Redemption: Neither Nothing nor Everything, but Only Something." *Journal of Jewish Thought and Philosophy* 29 (2021): 121–150.

———. "Saturnine Melancholy and Dylan's Jewish Gnosis." In *World of Bob Dylan,* edited by Sean Latham and Brian Hosmer, 214–225. Cambridge: Cambridge University Press, 2021.

———. "Secrecy, Modesty, and the Feminine: Kabbalistic Traces in the Thought of Levinas." *Journal of Jewish Thought and Philosophy* 14 (2006): 195–224.

———. *Suffering Time: Philosophic, Kabbalistic, and Ḥasidic Reflections on Temporality.* Leiden: Brill, 2021.

———. "Temporal Diremption and the Novelty of Genuine Repetition." In *D. G. Leahy and the Thinking Now Occurring,* edited by Lissa McCullough and Elliot R. Wolfson, 53–96. Albany: State University of New York Press, 2021.

———. "Theolatry and the Making-Present of the Nonrepresentable: Undoing (A)Theism in Eckhart and Buber." In *Martin Buber: His Intellectual and Scholarly Legacy,* edited by Sam Berrin Shonkoff, 3–32. Leiden: Brill, 2018.

———. *Through a Speculum That Shines: Vision and Imagination in Medieval Jewish Mysticism.* Princeton: Princeton University Press, 1994.

———. "To Stand in Relation with Something Which Is Neither Day nor Night: Temporal Overcoming and Heidegger's Notion of Destiny." *Gatherings: The Heidegger Circle Annual* 10 (2020): 207–210.

———. *Venturing Beyond: Law and Morality in Kabbalistic Mysticism.* Oxford: Oxford University Press, 2006.

Wolin, Richard. *Heidegger in Ruins: Between Philosophy and Ideology.* New Haven: Yale University, 2023.

Woolf, Virginia. *To the Lighthouse.* New York: Harcourt, Brace & Company, 1927.

Wyllie, Martin. *Merleau-Ponty and Melancholia.* Saarbrücken: Lambert Academic, 2010.

Wyschogrod, Edith. "The Civilizational Perspective in Comparative Studies of

Transcendence." In *Transcendence and the Sacred*, edited by Alan M. Olson and Leroy S. Rouner, 58–79. Notre Dame: University of Notre Dame Press, 1981.

———. "Concentration Camps and the End of the Life-World." In *Echoes from the Holocaust: Philosophical Reflections on a Dark Time*, edited by Alan Rosenberg and Gerald E. Myers, 327–340. Philadelphia: Temple University Press, 1988.

———. "Crossover Dreams." *Journal of the American Academy of Religion* 54 (1986): 543–547.

———. *Crossover Queries: Dwelling with Negatives, Embodying Philosophy's Others*. New York: Fordham University Press, 2006.

———. "Doing Before Hearing: On the Primacy of Touch." In *Textes pour Emmanuel Lévinas*, edited by François Laruelle, 179–203. Paris: Collections Surfaces, 1980.

———. *Emmanuel Levinas: The Problem of Ethical Metaphysics*. New York: Fordham University Press, 2000.

———. *An Ethics of Remembering: History, Heterology, and the Nameless Others*. Chicago: University of Chicago Press, 1998.

———. "Hasidism, Hellenism, Holocaust: A Postmodern View." In *Interpreting Judaism in a Postmodern Age*, edited by Steven Kepnes, 301–321. New York: New York University Press, 1996.

———. "How to Say No in French: Derrida and Negation in Recent French Philosophy." In *Negation and Theology*, edited by Robert P. Scharlemann, 39–55. Charlottesville: University Press of Virginia, 1992.

———. "Intending Transcendence: Desiring God." In *Companion to Postmodern Theology*, edited by Graham Ward, 349–365. London: Blackwell, 2001.

———. "Preface." In *Phenomenon of Death: Faces of Mortality*, edited by Edith Wyschogrod, vii–xii. New York: Harper & Row, 1973.

———. "Religion as Life and Text: Postmodern Re-Figurations." In *The Craft of Religious Studies*, edited by Jon R. Stone, 240–257. New York: St. Martin's Press, 1998.

———. *Saints and Postmodernism: Revisioning Moral Philosophy*. Chicago: University of Chicago Press, 1990.

———. *Spirit in Ashes: Hegel, Heidegger, and Man-Made Mass Death*. New Haven: Yale University Press, 1985.

———. "Those Weeping Eyes, Those Seeing Tears: Reading John D. Caputo's Ethics." In *Styles of Piety: Practicing Philosophy After the Death of God*, edited by S. Clark Buckner and Matthew Statler, 212–221. New York: Fordham University Press, 2006.

———. "Trends in Postmodern Jewish Philosophy: Contexts of a Conversation." In Steven Kepnes, Peter Ochs, and Robert Gibbs, *Reasoning After Revelation: Dialogues in Postmodern Jewish Philosophy*, 123–136. Boulder: Westview Press, 1998.

———. "Value." In *Critical Terms for Religious Studies*, edited by Mark C. Taylor, 365–382. Chicago: University of Chicago Press, 1998.

Yazicioğlu, Sanem. "Identity or Identities? The In-Between of 'No Longer and Not Yet.'" In *Phenomenological Perspectives on Plurality*, edited by Gert-Jan van der Heiden, 75–87. Leiden: Brill, 2015.

Yifrach, Yehuda. "The Elevation of Foreign Thoughts in the Traditions of Israel Baal Shem Tov as Transmitted in the Works of His Students." MA thesis, Bar-Ilan University, 2008 (Hebrew).

Young, Julian. *The Philosophy of Tragedy: From Plato to Žižek*. Cambridge: Cambridge University Press, 2013.

Zaborowski, Holger. "Origin, Freedom, and *Gelassenheit*: On Heidegger's Second 'Country Path Conversation.'" In *Phenomenological Perspectives on Plurality*, edited by Gert-Jan van der Heiden, 137–157. Leiden: Brill, 2015.

Zadoff, Noam. *Gershom Scholem: From Berlin to Jerusalem and Back*. Translated by Jeffrey Green. Lebanon, NH: University Press of New England, 2018.

Zarader, Marléne. "The Event—Between Phenomenology and History." In *The Past's Present: Essays on the Historicity of Philosophical Thinking*, edited by Marcia Sá Cavalcante Schuback and Hans Ruin, 25–54. Huddinge: Södertörn Academic Studies, 2006.

Zimmerman, Dean. "Presentism and the Space-Time Manifold." In *The Oxford Handbook of Philosophy of Time*, edited by Craig Callender, 163–244. Oxford: Oxford University Press, 2011.

Žižek, Slavoj. *The Fragile Absolute or, Why Is the Christian Legacy Worth Fighting For?* London: Verso, 2000.

Index

Abgeschiedenheit, 63, 192, 238n243. *See also* detachment
Abgrund, 130
absence, of God, 23–24, 48
absence, presence of, 17, 45, 52
Absolute, 26, 120, 130; movement of, 70; separation from, 26, 66
abyss, of nothingness, 177–183
ad infinitum, cycles of history, 309n176; process of interpretation, 173; speaking of the secret, 150
Adorno, Theodor, 68; Benjamin and, 75, 97, 254n161; on Christianity, 251n121; critical method of, 80; on gnostic heresy, 95–96; Hegel and, 141–142; Heidegger and, 156–157; on humanity, 114–115; on Kafka, 258n199; on Kierkegaard, 84; metaphysics and, 91, 252n124; Nietzsche and, 254n159; Rose and, 75–77, 247n54, 253n156, 254n162; system and, 73; understanding of philosophy as critical intervention, 76
Advaita school of Vedānta, 35
aesthetic experience, 154
aesthetic representation, 72
Agamben, Giorgio, 74, 244n36, 248–249 n71, 300n128
agapē, 91, 102, 108
agapeic love, 108
agnosia, 65
agnosticism: agnostic middle, 99–100; of gnosis, 76–80; Gnosticism and, 23; Rose and, 78; Weil and, 93

alētheia, 26, 173, 295n74. *See also* truth
alienation, 21, 23, 193; double concealment and, 112; of the divine, 124; of the poets, 259–260n200
allegory, 65; aesthetic production of, 184; contrasted to parable, 65, 240 n256; symbol and, 65
Allen, William S., 168
aloneness, 14, 15–16, 56–57, 189
ambivalence, 101, 109, 247n55; ambiguity and, 137; of identity, 86
anarchy, 84, 176; of theopolitical resignation, 177–183
Anaximander, 27–28
"Anaximander's Saying" (Heidegger), 26–27
androcentrism, 44
angels, and demons, 83
Angelus Dubiosus, 88–90, 251n109
Angelus Novus, 89
aniconism, 148, 152
animality, essence of, 303n152; melancholy of, 186–187
animals, 269n63; death and, 127, 228 n140, 269 n63; language and, 269 n63, 303 n152; suffering and, 14
annihilation, 33, 54, 96, 116, 128, 130–131, 142; of Christ, 251n121; of the Holocaust, 151; of Israel and God, 305n158
antinomian/antinomianism, 70, 81, 100, 190–191, 222n98, 265n27, 304n156
antinomy/antinomies: being and nonbeing, 142; of doubt, 35; existence and

antinomy/antinomies (*cont.*)
nonexistence, 31; identification of, 38; of modernity, 97; of monistic uniformity, 99; ontic experience of the world, 35; of realization, 97; sameness of, 9; uncertainty of truth and certainty of untruth, 80
antirealism, 275n126
antisystem, 74
Antonov, Simeon Ivanovich, 91–92. *See also* Silouan, Staretz
anxiety: ambivalence and, 109; beginning of, 68, 90, 107; of beginning, 68, 90, 92, 106–107; of death, 169–170; Hegel on, 248n67; Heidegger's view of, 13, 33, 132, 170, 203n38, 233–234n197; Judaism and, 107–108; melancholia and, 294n56; of middle, 83; Rose and, 68–69, 248n67; test of salvation and, 96
apeiron (infinity), 99
aphasic naming, 183–187
apocalypse, 190–191, 192–193, 228n144
apocalyptic hope, 7, 58
apocalyptic pessimism, 305n158
apophasis, 150
apophatic disavowal, 187
apophatic discourse, 64, 143
apophatic gesture, 60
apophaticism, 60
apophatics of denial, 152
apophatic theology, 152
aporia, 67, 84, 94, 99, 167; of death, 16, 157; of universal, 102
appearance, 35, 63, 95, 104; and disappearance, 112; image of, 114; of inapparent, 174; of nonappearance, 153, 204n41; reality and, 30, 104, 221n90, 260n202; of truth, 11
appearing, by not-appearing, 28; of nonappearing, 97, 167–177, 204 n41
appropriation (*Ereignis*), 145, 256 n170, 285n245; of death, 127; and disappropriation, 99; of ethical life, 114; event of, 98; and the nothing, 241n261
Arendt, Hannah, 45, 209n73, 229n146
Aristotle, 80, 94, 122, 236n229, 239n245, 266–267n38, 285n245
art: aesthetic representation, 72; ethics and, 154–155; Nietzsche on, 259n200; truth and, 105

ascetic renunciation, 153
aṣmut (essence), 225n114
assimilation, 97
atheism, 23–25; purification of theism, 78
Athens and Jerusalem, 89, 101–102, 105, 110–111
atheology, 25, 48, 108, 228n144, 230n150
attunement, 12–14, 29–30, 62, 105, 278n147; of the errant, 217n64
Augustine, 28, 95–96; conversion of, 96
Auschwitz, 91, 110–111, 141, 156, 252n124
authentic time (*eigentliche Zeit*), 138–139
authorial irony, 90
authority, 103; of system, 67
authorship, double competition of, 102–103
Awaiting Oblivion (Blanchot), 168
axiology, 119, 134–135, 245n42

Bataille, George, 41–42
Baudelaire, Charles, 182, 203n37
Befindlichkeit, 278 n147
"Before the Law" (Kafka), 171
beginning: anxiety of, 68, 90, 92, 107; of anxiety, 68, 90, 107; before the beginning, 68; difficulty of, 67; of disclosure of the messianic, 39; and end, 106, 193, 239n245; Greek quest for, 106; making apparent the inapparent, 28; palindromic retrieval of the end, 57; self-alienation of the divine, 124; withholding of, 168
being, forgetfulness of, 5, 30; oblivion of, 11, 27. *See also* Seinsvergessenheit
being-alone (*Alleinsein*), 15
Being and Time (Heidegger), 13–15, 26, 35–36, 60, 118–119, 132, 170
being-at-home (*Zuhause-sein*), 13
being-in-the-world (*In-der-Welt-sein*), 15, 23, 171, 207–208n67
being-toward-death (*Sein zum Tode*), 14, 32–33, 55–58, 133, 170–171, 206–207n64
being-with (*Mitsein*), 15, 207n64, 207–208n67
being-within-self (*Insichsein*), 118
being-with-one-another, 60
Belaval, Yvon, 55
Benjamin, Walter: Adorno and, 75, 97, 254n161; Arendt on, 229n146; Baudelaire and, 203n37; Bloch and, 182–183; Butler on, 183; Derrida on, 186, 261n218;

on Goethe, 75, 159–160; Heidegger and, 42–45, 133–134; on history, 140, 300n128; on Kafka, 158; on language, 185–186; on linearity, 44–45; on melancholic disposition, 8, 182; on messianism, 189–190, 228n144, 279n149; political agenda of, 181–182; Proust's influence on, 228n144; Scholem and, 180–181, 192–193, 299n124; taxonomist of sadness,181; on violence, 108;
Bergmann, Hugo, 51, 211n11
Bernard of Clairvaux, 96
Bernfeld, Siegfried, 188
Beshṭian Ḥasidism, 38–39
bethinging (*Bedingnis*), 62, 127
binary: attainment and nonattainment, 220n80; Buddhist overcoming of, 220n80; invisible Father and visible Son, 95; life and death, 126; logic, 10; messianic consciousness and breakdown of, 39; metaphysical conceit, 108; oppositions, 84; reality and appearance, 30. *See also* opposites
black sun, 10
Blanchot, Maurice, 123, 134–135, 155, 168, 191, 285n245, 310n177
blemish (*pegam*), 37–38
Bloch, Ernst, 169–170, 177, 182–183
blue/blueness, 192, 314n183, 314–315n184
Böhme, Jacob, 164–165
Book of Jonah, 317n194
Brod, Max, 83, 158–161, 286n2, 287n8
brokenheartedness, 151–157
The Broken Middle (Rose): authority of system and, 67–68; grayness of night and, 74–75; idea of singularity and, 84; opposition between comprehension and revelation, 87; Owl of Minerva and, 69; paradox and, 74–75, 102–111; puzzle of beginning and, 67; recognition and misrecognition, 81–88
broken middle, 6, 8, 76, 81–82, 88, 101–102, 246n48; chasm of, 115; triune structure of, 83; void of, 85
brokenness, breaking of, 7, 31, 53–59; of broken middle, 8, 76, 84, 93, 106, 110, 113; of disequilibrium, 31
Buber, Martin, 37, 189
Buddhism: Buddhist Judaism in Levinas, 176; doctrine of anātman, 55;
doctrine of conditioned phenomena, 209n75; doctrine of emptiness, 62, 104, 297n105; Hegel and, 209n75; Hinduism and, 136; Kant and, 104; logic of middle way and, 223n104; Nietzsche's views on, 219–220n80; nihilism and, 31–32, 219–220n80; nonduality and, 230n148
Butler, Judith, 183, 185, 196–197

caesura, 244n36
Campbell, Joseph, 50
Camus, Albert, 25, 51, 221n88
capitalism, 156, 247n54
carnal sexuality, spiritual eros and, 86, 250n88
Celan, Paul, 171, 175
challenging-forth (*Herausforderung*), 126
change, constancy of, 123; hope for, 168; possibility of, 191, 194–195, 206n64
chaos, 20, 22, 54, 58–59, 111, 309n176
childhood, 44
Christ, 78, 87, 90–91, 196, 251–252n121. *See also* Jesus
Christianity: Adorno on, 251n121; apocalypse and, 107, 228n144; authority and, 55; eternity and, 53; evil and, 302n150; faith and, 85; gnosis and, 34–35; Gnosticism and, 34–35; God and, 47–48, 196; Hegel and, 120–121; Heidegger and, 46–48; inherent sinfulness of human agency, 36; Judaism and, 86–88, 107–108, 113, 136, 181–182, 308n176; Kierkegaard and, 90–91; law and, 36–37; melancholia and, 184–185; myth of, 175; revelation and, 87, 107, 296n79; Rose and, 86–87; salvation and, 24; secret of, 317n194; Taubes, S. and, 36, 46, 53, 223n102; theology and Heidegger, 230n154; transgression in Garden of Eden, 185–186; Weil and, 24, 51
circular linearity, 52
clearing, 30–31, 217n59, 218n71; twofold concealment of, 30; vacuity of, 62. *See also* Lichtung
clock time (*Uhrzeit*), 42, 139; punctiform homogeneity of, 122
Cohen, Hermann, 200n9, 316n191, 316–317n192
Cohen, Leonard, 195–196

comedy: divine, 147; euporia, 94; irony and, 70–72; Rose on, 161; tragedy and, 101–102, 288n10; tragicomedy, 3, 69–76. *See also* tragicomedy
communication, 143–150, 154
concealment, of concealment, 225n114; of disclosure, 63, 218n70; of *Ein Sof*, 180; through exposure, 97; of errancy, 26; of the given, 148; of infinity, 148; of manifestation, 26; twofold nature of, 30; of the unconcealed, 156; unconcealment of, 29–30, 173; of untruth, 63, 98–99, 218n70; of the world, 225n114
conjuncture (*Fuge*), 30
consciousness: disjunction of, 82; function of, 167–168; humanity and, 44–45; identity and, 73; of the Other, 170–171; of self, 176
contemporary philosophy, 81–82
contraction, 124, 217n59; nocturnal point of, 8; of self, 168. *See also* şimşum
contraries, 81–82
Contributions to Philosophy (Heidegger), 61
creativity, 16; and melancholia, 194
"Critique of Violence" (Benjamin), 108, 133–134
"Cultural Criticism and Society" (Adorno), 156
culture, 24, 85, 155, 250n96

darkness: dark luminosity, 182; dark night, 34–41, 55; dark void, 105; dusk, 314n184; Hegel on, 76–77; Heidegger on, 132–133; light and, 4–5, 9, 37–38, 105, 110–111; luminescent, 164–167; middle and, 114–115; Novalis on, 17; Rose and, 6, 69–76
Dasein, 13–15, 171–172, 207n67; animals and, 269n63; death and, 14, 132–133; definitions of, 255n170; the future and, 138–139; Heidegger on, 15–16, 22–23, 234n198; historicity of, 139–140; memory and, 63; mortality and, 127; poetry and, 55; psychology of, 56–57, 189; Rilke and, 156–157; silence and, 60–61; theology and, 46; time and, 44; and untruth, 26
Davis, Joshua B., 100
death: anguish of, 220n84; anxiety of, 169–170; birth and, 17; camps, 131–132, 271n95; Dasein and, 132–133; death-world, 126–127, 157; emptiness of, 109–110; events, 116–117, 119–126, 127–128, 134–135, 156–157; Hegel on, 17; Heidegger on, 118–119, 272n104; hope and, 33–34; love as strong as, 57, 294n62; man-made mass, 120–121; melancholia and, 169–170; negation and, 169; philosophical inquiry of, 16–17, 52–53; sacrifice and, 251n121; source of all myths, 128; survivors of, 141; Taubes, S., and, 31–33; time and, 45, 56–59; tragedy and, 41–42; truth of, 55; Wyschogrod's explication of, 116–119
decadence, in humanity, 3
deconstruction, 133–134, 152
dehumanization, 2, 127
De Laudibus Virginis Matris (Bernard of Clairvaux), 96
Deleuze, Gilles, 11–12, 121, 265n27, 265n59, 268n57
Derrida, Jacques, 4–5, 17, 133–134, 151–152; on Benjamin, 186, 261n218; Hegel and, 130–131, 151; kabbalah and, 284n219; law of mourning, 166–167; messianicity and, 99, 122; on nostalgia, 202n19; secrecy and, 150; Taylor and, 149–150; textual dissemination and, 151; time in thought of, 137; trace and, 264n24; writing and, 64; Wyschogrod and, 268n53, 277n128, 284n219
Descartes, René, 35–36, 77, 226n126
desire, 84–86, 147–148, 152–153, 267n43
despair, 92
despondency, 4
destruction, 133–134; of being and nihilism, 257n186; of knowledge, 79; of truth and metaphysics, 29; powers of, 54; time and, 93, 116, 252n124
Destruktion (Heidegger), 133–134
detachment, 63–64, 185, 192, 238n243, 319–320n197. *See also* Abgeschiedenheit
deus ex machina, 54
diachrony, 144, 153, 168, 177
diachronicity: dark, 122; diachronic temporality, 310n177; diachronic transcendence, 143–150; time and, 177
Dialect of Enlightenment (Adorno), 80
Dialect of Nihilism (Rose), 79

dialectic, 34, 79; contrasted with dialetheic, 9, 59; embraced by Adorno, 142, 252n124, 259n199; equivocation and, 77; Hegelian, 83–84, 101, 118, 121, 129–130, 141, 241n261, 254n162; of hopelessness of hope, 90; of humanism, 80; of mercifulness and mercilessness, 86; negation of negation, 97, 142; overcoming, 130; of the Passion, 96; sublation of, 111, 124; of the trace, 265n24
dialectical experience, 279n148
dialectical image, 140, 182, 279n148, 301n131
dialetheic logic, 97
dialetheic paradox, 66, 84
dialetheic truth, 163
diary, and the writing of the book of time, 42–43
Diels, Hermann Alexander, 27
différance, 130, 151; and Hegelian negation, 271n92; heterological nonspace of, 154
difference: absolute, 130; age of, 2; between the said and the saying, 143; eternal cycle of recurring, 123; henological, 49; of identity, 40, 125; interval of, 146; nondifferential, 147; ontological, 11, 27–29, 97, 216n58; polyontological, 16; replication of, 48; sameness of, 9, 38–39, 66; thinking of, 97
diremption, 76, 81–82, 100, 103; of Judaism, 87; of law and ethics, 100; of spirit, 99
diremptive temporality, 7, 193
discernment, of blemish as aspect of rectification, 38; of disillusionment, 100; of surface, 5; of truth of illusion, 35;
dishomogeneity, 244n36
divine comedy, 71, 94, 147
divine emanation, as self-exile, 124
double-disclosiveness, of memory, 137
Dov Ber of Mezhirech, 38
dream, 74, 104, 177; as fictional truth, 260n203; seeing in the night, 4
dualism, 101, 290–291n37; between hidden God and demiurgic potency, 304n156; and Gnosticism, 36, 112; Kantian, 109; Manichean, 95; of modernity, 113; ontological, 39, 165
duplexity, 72
duplicitous truth, 159–163

duplicity, 72, 160
duration, 53, 122
dusk, 144, 314–315n184; ghostliness of, 192; of twilight, 314n183
Dylan, Bob, 195
demythologizing, 119–126
dys-chrony, 74

Eckhart, Meister, 63, 238n243, 319n197
Einzigkeit (singularity, oneness), 16, 50
Elective Affinities (Goethe), 75
Eliade, Mircea, 308n176
emptiness (*śūnyatā*), 62, 104, 230n148, 297n105
"Encounter with Zion and the World" (Scholem), 179
endtime, 124, 141, 157
Enlightenment, 111–112
epistemology: of Descartes, 77; of Rose, 245n42; of tragedy and comedy, 71
equiprimordiality, 255n168
equivocation, 68–69, 102
Eriugena, John Scotus, 181
erotics, of transcendence, 152–153
errancy, 29–31, 41; of metaphysics, 214–215n57; nonessence of truth, 26; of untruth, 213n39
error, placelessness of, 30
es gibt (it gives), 98
essence, above essence, 181; of being, 30, 104; counteressence and, 26; extraction from, 144; in Ḥabad-Lubavitch, 225n114; of Hebrew, 189; of human freedom, 166; of language, 61, 143, 172; of nature, 186–187; of nonessence, 153; subversion of, 173; of technology, 126–127; of thinking, 319n197; of truth, 26, 29, 218n70; withdrawal from, 145
estrangement, 3, 192, 259n199; from the world, 20–25, 95, 112
eternal sameness, 279n148
eternity, 33, 93, 141; absolute timelessness of, 122; and death-world, 135; finitude of time and, 91; Heideggerian view of, 53; of historical events, 308n172; of love, 58; ocean of, 123; phenomenology of, 52; Rosenzweig on, 243–244n33; structure of time and, 253n136; temporalization of, 123; timeliness of time, 53

ethics: aesthetics and, 155, 161, 163; art and, 154–155; apophatic materialization and, 156; culture and, 85; equivocation and, 102; gestures and, 145–146; language of, 174–175; law and, 7, 100, 102; Levinas and, 152; life of, 114–115; nonspace of, 141, 280n156; politics and, 1–2; of social criticism, 76–77; resistance and, 172
ethnocentrism, 126
euporia, 94, 99
everydayness (*Alltäglichkeit*), 15, 139
evil: aspect of the good, 35; in Christianity, 302n150; death as, 132; demiurge and, 158–159; Gnostic view of world and, 21–22, 32, 36, 112–113; good and, 251–252n121; in Hegel, 46; Manichean dualism and, 95; nature of the world and, 161; necessity of, 165; Schelling's view of, 164–167, 290–291n37; spiritual world and, 160–161; transmuted into good, 37–38; Tree of Knowledge and, 186, 302–303n150; within God, 164–165
excluded middle, 143–150, 223n104
experience, structure of, 119–120

face, 204n42; defacement of, 149; depersonalization of, 176; epiphany of, 296n79; facelessness of, 59, 149, 234n209; invisibility of, 149–150; mask of, 11, 204n42; of neighbor, 147; of the other, 170, 172, 174, 175; of the stranger, 174; thematization of, 149, 174; trace of, 174, 175; unveiling of, 59
facetious irony, 88–94
facetiousness, beyond facetiousness, 89; of dubious angel, 89; fiction and, 102–103; of irony, 70; of myth, 90; of reason, 89
facetious reason, 89
faith, 35, 78, 84–85, 87, 213n33, 309n176; knight of, 87, 96, 163; leap of, 87; messianic, 192; passion of, 74, 85; skeptical, 25, 53
"Farewell" (Scholem), 188–189
Feldman, Sándor, 4
feminism, 78, 247n55
Ficino, Marsilio, 10–11
fiction, 102–104
finitude, 116–119, 147, 157, 166
"Force of Law" (Derrida), 133–134, 261–262n218

formlessness, 65, 154–155
Foucault, Michel, 5, 244–245n36
The Fragments of the Presocratics (Diels), 27
freedom, 81, 175, 192–193; Dasein's sense of, 30; of interpretation, 73; nomadic, 81; repetition and, 248n67; in Schelling's philosophy, 164–166, 217n59; of solitude, 234n208; subjective, 81, 84, 87; unfreedom and, 81, 84, 87, 107, 108
Freud, Sigmund: on anxiety, 68, 92; Benjamin and, 301–302n137; Butler on, 185; Kierkegaard and, 68; Lacan and, 183; melancholia and, 11, 86, 176–177, 183
fundamental attunement (*Grundstimmung*), 12–13, 62
"The Fundamental Concepts of Metaphysics" (Heidegger), 12–13
future, 138–139, 191–194, 196–197, 275n126, 278n147
futural remembering, 140, 228n144

Gadamer, Hans-Georg, 106
Garden of Eden, 185–186
Gelassenheit, 61, 194, 318–319n197. *See also* releasement
Genet, Jean, 154
Gestell, 97–98, 126, 285n245
gift, 62, 92; bestowed by thinking, 121; of knight of faith, 87; of language, 285n245; of nothingness, 165; of the present, 27; of saturated phenomenon, 310n177; of truth, 29
giving: of being, 29; of the law, 98; passivity of, 173–174; of the ungiven, 98, 148; withholding of, 285n245
gnosis: agnosticism of, 76–80; bound to agnosia, 65; Christianity and, 34–35; ethical life and, 114; Heidegger and, 23, 28; heretical, 222n98; as judgment on reality, 21; Kafka and, 287n4; melancholic, 90; mystical, 37; radical intellectualization of experience, 22; Taubes, S., and, 21–23, 34; visionary nature of, 21; Weil and, 212–213n30
"The Gnostic Foundations of Heidegger's Nihilism" (Taubes, S.), 23, 28–29
gnostic heresy, 95–96
Gnosticism: agnosticism and, 23; Augustinian, 28; Christianity and, 34–35; as counterhistory, 112; dualism of, 36, 112; gnostic

nihilism, 32; Gnostic remnant, 95;
  God in, 158–159; Heidegger and, 30, 41;
  Judaism and, 187–188; Kierkegaard and,
  253n151; myth of, 112–113; Rose and, 95,
  112–115; spiritual world in, 161; Taubes, J.
  and, 211n18; Taubes, S. and, 20–21; Weil
  and, 23–24; as world-denial, 6
gnostic myth, 11, 36, 112
God: in Christianity, 47–48, 196; desire of,
  152–153; evil and, 164–167; Gnosticism,
  158–159; idolatry and, 50; in in Judaism,
  98; in Kafka, 159–160, 287n8; in Kierkegaard on, 161–162; in Levinas, 148–149,
  178–179; in literature, 41; love of, 38–39,
  164; nature and, 225n114; the Other
  and, 296n79; prophecies and, 194; in
  quantum physics, 229–230n148; reality
  and, 23–24; time and, 49; trust in, 34;
  truth and, 58; in Weil, 24–25, 45–46
Goethe, Johann Wolfgang von, 75, 159–160
"Goethe's Elective Affinities" (Benjamin),
  159–160, 245n40
Gospel of Philip, 65
grammatical hermeneutics, 98–99
Gramsci, Antonio, 200n9
grayness, of night, 69, 75
Guattari, Félix, 265n27, 268n57
guilt, 156–157; and the fall of man, 303n150;
  and innocence, 100; and the law, 36–37

habitus, 232n173
halakhah, 87–88, 99, 108, 211n11, 223n104
Hallo, Rudolf, 188, 304n158
Hamacher, Werner, 196–197
Ḥasidism, 38–40
Hebrew language, 189, 194
Hegel, Georg Wilhelm Friedrich: Adorno
  and, 141–142; on anxiety, 248n67;
  Buddhism and, 209n75; Christianity
  and, 120–121; on darkness, 76–77; on
  death, 17; Derrida and, 130–131, 151; on
  finitude, 118, 263n11; on history, 141–
  142, 254n162; on human mortality, 119,
  264n17; on humanity, 118; on hypochondria, 8; on irony, 71–72; idea of
  Spirit, 120, 129–130, 141–142; Kant and,
  83; Kierkegaard and, 82; knowledge
  and, 75–76; philosophical wit and, 68;
  on relation of philosophy and freedom,
  241n4; Rose and, 83–84, 94, 242n16;
  253n136; speculation on relation of
  time to space, 124; on suffering, 70–71;
  system in, 46, 70; Taubes, S., criticism
  of, 59; on truth, 122, 129–130, 136; Wyschogrod and, 124–125, 268n53
Heidegger, Martin, 1, 5, 35–36, 60–61, 194–
  195, 206n64, 281n181; Adorno and, 156–
  157; affinity with kabbalists, 65; Arendt
  and, 209n73; Benjamin and, 42–45,
  133–134, 261n218; Bloch and, 169–170;
  Christianity and, 46–48, 230n154;
  confrontation of Jewish thinkers with,
  201n17; criticism of, 55–59; on darkness,
  132–133; on Dasein, 15–16, 22–23,
  234n198; on death, 118–119, 272n104;
  on errancy, 29–31, 41; eternity and, 53;
  gnosis and, 28; on Gnosticism, 30, 41;
  grammatical hermeneutics and, 98–99;
  on historicism, 218n71; on history,
  97–98; on humanity, 98–99; idea of
  singularity in the thought of, 208n71;
  Landsberg's criticism of, 33; language
  and, 61–63, 80, 127–128, 237n235,
  278n147; Levinas and, 128–129, 143, 145,
  171–172, 264n24, 281n172, 285n245,
  295n74; metaphysics of, 204n43,
  214n57; on myth, 20–21; National
  Socialism and, 273n105; Nazism and,
  70, 117–118, 133; Nietzsche and, 12, 27;
  nothingness and, 136, 229n148; on
  nihilism, 257n186; Novalis and, 12–14;
  ontological difference and, 11, 27–29,
  97, 216n58; ontology of, 11, 25, 211n18;
  phenomenology and, 310n177; poetry
  and, 238n240, 269n67; radical finitude
  of, 54–55; reflections on time and temporality, 99, 139–140, 232n173, 233n197,
  264n17; repetition of the same, 48, 99,
  139–140, 279n148; Rilke and, 143; Rose
  and, 255n168, 255n170; on sadness, 158;
  Schelling and, 203n38, 206n56, 217n59,
  240n256; on silence, 62–63; Taoism
  and, 274n109; Taubes, S., on, 14–15, 19–
  20, 28–29, 54–55; on truth and untruth,
  11–12, 26–30, 53, 61, 63, 98–99, 172–173,
  213–214n43, 218n70; *Unterwegs*, 13,
  134; Weil and, 46, 48–49; worlding
  (*Welten*), 128; Wyschogrod and, 118–119,
  126–128, 135, 138–140, 270n76
hell, 3, 5, 91–92

364 Index

Heraclitus, 28, 215n57, 285n245
hermeneutics: cutting of timeline, 123; first principle of, 139; grammatical, 98; hermeneutical circularity, 57; modern, 5–6; rabbinic, 173; of suspicion, 17; ontological, 21
The Hero with a Thousand Faces (Campbell), 50
Heschel, Abraham Joshua, 123
heterodox diversity, 2–3
heterogeneity, 74, 122
heterological epiphany, 135–142
heterology, 141, 149, 280n157
Hinduism, 34–35, 49–50, 136
historicism, 139, 218n71
historicity (*Geschichtlichkeit*), 138–140
history: act of recollecting, 45; apophatics of, 149; of being, 26, 54, 97, 238n240, 285n245; Benjamin's view of, 182–183, 189–190, 228n144, 229n145, 300n128; casting out of beings, 27–28; disavowal of, 60; Eliade's view of, 308–310n175; emerging nature of, 51; exterminations of, 133; forgetfulness of being and, 30; Hegel's view of, 46, 129–130, 141–142, 254–255n162; Heidegger's conception of, 5, 28, 30, 97–98, 139; of metaphysics, 28; phenomenology and, 275–277n126, 310–313n177; salvation in, 24; sameness and repetition in, 140; teleological view of, 85, 101; writing of, 89, 123, 137, 229n145
Hölderlin, Friedrich, 42, 46–48, 56, 164–165, 204n41
Holocaust: Auschwitz, 91, 110–111, 141, 156, 201n17, 252n124; language of, 141–142; Nazism and, 131–132; philosophy after, 91; Polish Commission on the Future of Auschwitz, 110–111; survivors of, 141; time and, 135–136; totalitarianism and, 4
Holy Spirit, 95, 130
homeostasis, 10
homelessness, 12, 21, 23; of Hebrew, 307n168; of the Jew, 126. *See also* uncanniness
homesickness, 12–14
homogeneity, 74, 122; hermeneutical, 131
hope: apocalyptic, 7–8, 58; death and, 33–34; of hopelessness, 25–34, 158–159; in humanity, 3–4; infinity of, 159–160, 163; in Israel, 41; Kafka on, 159–163, 167, 180; melancholia and, 194–195; memory and, 144–145; messianic, 193–194; nihilism and, 41; poetry and, 195–196; possibility in the impossibility of, 16–17, 123
horizon, 43, 115; of being, 172; of Dasein's being, 57; death and, 128; of experience, 119; of past and future, 311n177; temporality and, 44; of thinking, 237n235
Horkheimer, Max, 228n144, 253n156
Human, All Too Human (Nietzsche), 4, 104–105
humanity: Adorno on, 114–115; chaos of, 22; Christianity and, 21; consciousness and, 44–45; death events in, 116–117, 127–128; decadence in, 3; eternity and, 92–93; Hegel on, 118; Heidegger on, 98–99; hell and, 5; hope in, 3–4; human affliction, 24; human subjectivity, 142; immortality and, 57–58; Judaism and, 125–126; Kafka on, 158–163, 287–288n8; love and, 34, 172–173; Nietzsche on, 137–138; selfhood in, 165–166; suffering in, 7
humor, boundary between ethical and religious, 161, 163; in Kierkegaard's idea of religiosity, 162. *See also* comedy
Husserl, Edmund, 99, 145, 147, 151, 171–172, 275n126, 310n177
hypernomian, 37, 54, 223n103
hypochondria, 8

iconoclasm, 50, 151–152
ideality, 59, 72, 173; of Dasein, 46; of space, 122, 124
identity: aloneness and, 15–16; consciousness and, 73; of difference, 40, 125; of ego, 145; Hegel's idea of Spirit and, 120; in-difference, 123, 125–126; of ipseity, 145; Kristeva and, 184–185; lost, 184; nomadic, 125; nonidentity and, 9, 73, 80, 83, 125, 225n114; of opposites, 37; poetry and, 155–156; principle of, 9–10; of the same, 142
idolatry, 50, 78
illumination, dark night of, 34–41
immanence, 91, 121, 152, 153, 155, 225n114, 252n124; of the said, 173
immortality, 57–58, 68; of death, 41–53

Index   365

impermanence, 17, 58, 120, 181, 209n75
impossibility: of Dasein, 133; of escape, 169–170; of getting hold of the present, 123; of interpretation, 6; of the possible, 16; of the possibility of the ethical, 127; of the possibility of the question, 134; of thinking, 121; of waiting, 191
indifference, 89, 252n124
infinity: abyssal, 91; anarchic, 113; *apeiron*, 99; expanse of, 124; exterior of, 121; finitude and, 59, 74, 116–119, 147, 157; of hope, 159–160, 163; infinite transcendence, 140; infinitesimal point of singularity and, 124; infinition of, 147; light of, 39, 178; madness and, 6; movement of, 121; nothingness of, 230n148; presence of, 147, 172; simultaneous revelation and concealment of, 148; time and, 122–123, 176; trace of, 174; transcendence of, 225n114
insomnia, 168–171
insufficiency, 13, 48, 148, 194–195, 276–277
interpretation, 5–6, 202n19; of Dasein, 139; excess and deficiency of, 17; in rabbinic tradition, 51, 151, 173
intertexuality, 151
invisibility, 5, 48, 97, 147–148
irony: authorial, 90; comedy and, 70–72; facetious, 88–94; Hegel on, 71–72; Kierkegaard on, 162–163; lack of, 95–101; mask of, 112; Rose on, 160, 254n159
Islam, 136
Israel, land of, 189; state of, 41, 50–51, 190
Israel ben Eliezer (Ba'al Shem Tov), 38–39
"Is There a Jewish Philosophy" (Rose), 88

Jacob Joseph of Polonnoye, 38
Janus-faced, 68, 90, 103
Jesus, 24, 91, 223n102. *See also* Christ
Jonas, Hans, 22, 112, 211–212n18
Joseph and His Brothers (Mann), 113
joyfulness, 291–292n38
Judaism: apocalypse in, 192–193; Buddhist, 176; Christianity and, 86–88, 107–108, 113, 136, 181–182, 308n176; culture of, 250n96; giving of the law at Sinai, 98; Gnosticism and, 187–188; humanity and, 125–126; law and, 107–108; Levinas and, 284n219; melancholia and, 164, 289n31; messianism, 7–8, 176–177, 190–191, 194–195, 197; middle and, 108; philosophy and, 85; psychology of, 151–152; revelation in, 25, 39, 51–52, 296n79; Rose and, 86, 102, 250n95; Sabbath in, 124–126; Scholem and, 304n158, 305n166, 308n175; sources of, 189–190; technical lexicon of, 99; tradition and the tensiveness of time, 52
Judaism and Modernity (Rose), 85
judgment, 21–22

kabbalah, 37–38, 65, 99, 178, 188, 190, 223n104; Derrida and, 284n219; influence on Schelling, 218n70
Kafka, Franz: Adorno and, 258n199; Brod and, 158–159, 161; hopelessness of hope and, 159–163, 167, 180; interpretation of Kierkegaard, 83; Nietzsche and, 104–105; Rose and, 163; selfhood and, 171; tragic sense of humanity and, 287n8; truth and, 103–105, 160, 258n196; Zürau aphorisms, 103, 160
Kant, Immanuel, 34–35, 83, 104, 109, 260n202
Kavka, Martin, 94
Keats, John, 56
Kierkegaard, Søren: Adorno and, 84; Christianity and, 90–91; on contradiction between immortality and mortality, 68; faith and, 84; Gnosticism and, 253n151; God and, 161–162; Hegel and, 82; hopelessness of hope and, 90; irony and, 162–163; Rose and, 72, 83, 90, 96
King Arthur, tales of, 93–94, 253n140
Klee, Paul, 89–90, 251n109
knowledge, 106, 109–111, 113–115, 248n67, 262n231
Kristeva, Julia, 3, 10, 184–185, 199n4

Lacan, Jacques, 125, 129, 183, 271n80
lack: desire and, 85–86; God's, 47–48; of identity, 83, 88; of irony, 95–101; nonplace, 125; of system, 70; signifier of barred other, 125
Lament for Julia (Taubes, S.), 4, 41, 55, 226–227n126
Landauer, Gustav, 189
Landsberg, Paul-Louis, 33, 206–207n64, 220n84

language: about the past, 140; action and, 318n196; analytic functions of, 142; Benjamin on, 185–186; of being, 240n256; of border, 187; communication with, 143–150, 154; correlation with being in Western philosophy and, 173–174; ethical, 174–175; Hebrew, 189, 194; of Hegel, 118, 121; Heidegger on, 61–63, 80, 127–128, 237n235, 278n147; of Holocaust, 141–142; of lament, 187; melancholia and, 183–184; for mourning, 167; noncoincidence of, 168; poetic, 155, 236n229; poetry and, 180–181; polysemic, 151–157; silence and, 61–62

Laozi, 237n236, 318n196

law: Christianity and, 36–37; ethics and, 7, 100, 102; 223n104; of excluded middle, 143–150; Judaism and, 99, 108; metaphysics and, 79–80; modernity and, 108–109; of mourning, 166–167; Pauline concern with, 36, 108

Leahy, David G., 208n70, 313n177

Levin, David Michael, 257n186

Levinas, Emmanuel: Bloch and, 170; Deleuze and, 121; desire and, 147–148; divine comedy and, 147; ethics of, 152; God in the thought of, 148–149, 178–179; Heidegger and, 15, 128–129, 145, 171–172, 264n24, 281n172, 285n245, 295n74; insomnia and phenomenology, 168–169; Jewish messianism and, 177, 286n248; Nietzsche and, 293n55; nocturnal time, 168; *non-lieu*, 143–147; the Other, 171–177; philosophy and skepticism, 94; rabbinic hermeneutic and, 173; Rose's view of, 176; on selfhood, 292n47; on time, 170, 177, 282n181, 286n248; on Tolstoy, 160; Weil and, 89

liberalism, and illiberalism, 2

Lichtung (clearing), 30–31, 217n59, 218n71

life-world, 119–126

light, darkness and, 4–5, 9, 37–38, 105, 110–111; luminescent darkness, 164–167; luminosity, 171; truth and, 77; vessels and, 39–40

linear circularity, 63–64, 68, 192, 311n177

linearity, 52, 57; Benjamin's explication of, 44–45; of mundane time, 43; overcoming of, 42–43

listening, 63, 275n110

lived time, diremptive heterogeneity of, 122

Lloyd, Vincent, 78, 242n23

loneliness, contrasted with solitariness, 209n73; detachment and, 185; introversion and, 12

Lotze, Hermann, 182

love: agapeic, 108; capacity to, 176–177; community and, 102; death and, 53, 56–58, 234n208; desire and, 85–86; ecclesiological, 6; erotic exuberance and, 48; eternal possibility of, 59; of God, 38–39, 164; humanity and, 34, 172–173; loveful polity, 107; New Jerusalem and, 111; of neighbor, 112; nighttime and, 49, 74; of the Other, 170–171; polarity of law and, 85; present of the infinity of its finitude, 59; salvation and, 58–59; sympathy and, 172; transience of, 66; triumph over law, 86; vibrancy of, 48; violence of New Jerusalem masquerading as, 109

Love's Work (Rose), 3, 74–77, 91–92, 96–97

lucus a non lucendo, 30, 218n71

Lukács, György, 42

luminescent darkness, 164–167

luminosity, 96, 171, 182

Luria, Isaac, 39, 178

madhyamaka, 223n104

madness, 6, 19, 27–28, 56–57

magic, 34, 39, 50; of the threshold, 203n30

malevolence, 3

man-made mass death, 120–121

Mann, Thomas, 113, 160, 258n199

marginalization, 2

Marion, Jean-Luc, 310n177

Marrano identity, 86

Marx, Kitty, 180–181

Marxism, 70, 77–78, 82, 182–183, 200n9

mask/masking, 5, 11–12, 67–69, 102, 112, 204n42

"Media in Vita" (Scholem), 179–181

melancholia/melancholy: Butler on, 196–197; Christianity, and, 184–185; death and, 169–170; Freud and, 11, 176–177; Gnosticism and, 112–115; hope and, 194–195; Judaism and, 164, 289–290n31; language and, 183–184; melancholic messianism, 181–182; melancholic rap-

ture, 167–168; melancholic redemption, 158–159; melancholic spectrality, 196–197; melancholic temperament, 182–183; mourning and, 183, 186–187; nostalgia and, 166–167; psychology of, 21–22; repudiation of the law of noncontradiction, 9–10; Saturn and, 289–290n31; speaking the unspeakable, 185; spirit of, 294n55; surplus of time and, 8; tragicomedy of being and, 3; treatment of, 203n38; veil of, 206 n56; wellspring of creativity, 194
melancholy devil, 293–294n55
melancholy jouissance, 7, 185, 192, 315n185
"Melancholy Redemption" (Scholem), 178
The Melancholy Science (Rose), 76–77
memory: collapse of gulf separating past and present, 53; Dasein and, 63; double-disclosiveness of, 137; forgetting and, 277n133; hope and, 144–145; retrieval and, 140
meontology, 29, 145, 301n128
mercy, 86, 124
Merleau-Ponty, Maurice, 122, 244n33
messianism: Benjamin on, 189–190, 279n149; Eliade on, 308n176; Jewish, 7–8, 176–177, 190–191, 194–195, 197; Marxism and, 182–183; melancholic, 181–182; messianic deferment, 187–197; messianic hope, 193–194; politics of, 308n174; pseudo-messianism, 190–191
metanoia, 3
metaphysics: after Auschwitz, 91, 252n124; aporia and, 94; Aristotle's understanding of, 94; creativity and, 16; deconstruction of, 79, 264n24; errancy of, 214–215n57; Heidegger and, 204–205n43, 214–215n57; history of, 28; law and, 79–80; of melancholy, 164; nihilism and, 28, 264n23; overcoming of, 23; philosophical eros and, 33; postmodern dismissal of, 89–90; truth and, 29; Western, 82–83, 214n57
"The Metaphysics of Youth" (Benjamin), 42–45, 192
Mevo ha-She'arim (Shapira), 39–40
middle, agnostic, 99–100; anxiety of, 83; between and, 128; commencement and termination of philosophy in, 105–106;

darkness and, 114–115; elusiveness of, 68; equivocation of, 68–69; excluded, 105, 143–150, 223n104; Judaism and, 108; neglected by Kant, 109; Rose on, 110–111; singularity of, 81–88
Mikrokosmos (Lotze), 182
Milbank, John, 108
Milton, John, 5
Minima Moralia (Adorno), 68, 114–115
modernity: antinomies of, 97; broken promises of, 85; collapse of, 110; crisis of, 116, 130; dualisms of, 113; in Jewish philosophy and theology, 87–88; law in, 108–109. *See also* postmodernism
Moré, Marcel, 212n30
mortality: Dasein and, 127; psychology of, 131–132; resurrection and, 43–44
mourning: joyfulness and, 291n38; law of, 166–167; melancholia and, 183, 186–187; prayer in, 195–196; presence and, 176–177
"Mourning and Melancholia" (Freud), 11, 176–177
Mourning Becomes the Law (Rose), 79
Muller, Jerry Z., 21, 211n11, 213n33
mundus, 128
muteness, 131; of nature, 183–187, 303n152; of not speaking, 62; reticence of, 154. *See also* Stummheit
mystery, and death, 16, 51; of being, 127; of hiddenness of disclosure, 97; and the invisible, 148; of origin, 40; of originary silence, 62; of the past, 192; and the periphery of hopelessness, 134; repudiation of, 134; and silence, 130; of the unsaid, 237n235; and the unspoken, 62–63, 237n236
mystical atheism, 23, 46
mysticism, 31, 37, 41–42, 78–79
myth, 19–20, 22; of death event, 116, 120; facetiousness of, 90; of fallen self, 11; gnostic, 11, 36, 112; of Gnosticism, 112–113; lie in, 31; and Lurianic kabbalah, 178; and Sabbatian theology, 188; of ṣimṣum, 217n59

Nachträglichkeit, 137–138, 192–193, 315–316n186
Naḥman of Bratslav, 24

naked truth, 11, 65, 166
nameless singularity, 145
naming, 183–187
National Socialism, 120, 126–129, 273n105; as a form of Jewish heresy, 305n158
nature, 164–167, 183–187, 225n114
Nausea (Sartre), 3
Nazism: dehumanization in, 127, 132; ethnocentrism in, 126; Heidegger and, 70, 117–118, 133; the Holocaust and, 131–132; *non-lieu* and, 149; politics of, 273n105; victims of, 135. See also National Socialism
negation/negativity: of Absolute, 130; of ceasing, 209n75; dialectic negation of negation, 97; dialetheic negation of negation of negation, 97; at ground of reason, 73; in Hegel, 130–131; negation of, 129–135, 141–142; of time, 190–191; of the tragic, 24
negative epiphany, 154
negative theology, 23, 84, 142, 152
New Jerusalem, 11, 106–111
Nietzsche, Friedrich: Adorno and, 254n159; on art, 259n200; chaos and, 20; Foucault and, 5; gnostic nihilism of, 32; Heidegger and, 12, 27; Kafka and, 104–105; Kant and, 260n202; Levinas and, 293n55; reflections on Buddhism, 219–220n80; slaying of God, 131; times of darkness, 4; to be rid of what comes after, 137–138; truth and the errors of humanity, 7; on writing, 103–104; Wyschogrod and, 268n57
night, 192; womb of revelations, 17
nihilation, 176; pleromatic, 45
nihilism: Buddhism and, 219n80; Buddhist, 31–32; gnostic, 32; God in, 45–46; Heidegger on, 257n186; hope and, 41; psychology of, 159; Rose and, 79, 100–101; Taubes, S., and, 21–23, 30; Zionism and, 304n158
nirvāṇa, 55; identified with saṃsāra, 220n80
nocturnal figuration, 69, 74, 115
nocturnality, 74; and oblivion of self, 168
nocturnal luminosity, 4
nocturnal seeing, 4–6
nocturnal time, 168
nomad, 125–126, 268n57

nonappearance, appearance of, 153
nonappearing, 167–177
nonattachment, singularization of, 320n197
nonattainment, 55, 220n80
noncontradiction, law of, 9; principle of, 66
nondualism, 40
nonidentity, 9, 73
nonphenomenal/nonphenomenalizable, 5, 29, 154
nonplace (*non-lieu*), of the death-world, 139; of diachronic transcendence, 143–150; place of, 125. See also nullsite
nonshowing, showing of, 48, 148
nostalgia, 50–51, 166–167, 183, 202n19
nothingness: abyss of, 177–183; awaiting, 167–177; Heidegger on, 229n148; presence and, 167–168; Taubes, S., on, 48–49; time and, 46–47; unreality and, 153
Novalis, 12–14, 17
now-time (*Jetztzeit*), 45, 97, 228n145
nudity, 66, 146, 153
Nuki, Shigeto, 275–276n126
nullsite, 143–147, 149. See also nonplace
nunc stans, 74

oblivion, 28, 58–59, 142; of being, 11, 27; to being, 29; of self, 168
Old Athens, 107–111
O'Mahony, Andy, 78, 85, 92
"On Escape" (Levinas), 169
"One-Way Street" (Benjamin), 180
"On Lament and Lamentation" (Scholem), 187
"On Language as Such and on the Language of Man" (Benjamin), 185–186
"The Only One" (Heidegger), 46–47
"On the Essence of Truth" (Heidegger), 26, 61
On the Way to Language (Heidegger), 62–63
ontology: Heidegger and, 11, 25, 211n18; metaphysics and, 27–28; of not-yet, 191; ontological dyad of something and nothing, 145; ontological monism, 40; ontological realism, 280n154; ontological untruth, 31, 53–59, 66; pluralism and, 16, 208n69

opposites: dialetheic coalescence of, 9; in Kristeva, 10; opposition subverted by Jewish mystical gnosis, 38–40; in postmodernism, 106–107; psychology of, 9–10; same in virtue of their difference, 223n104; similar in virtue of their dissimilarity, 97
optimism, 75, 110, 177; pessimistic, 4; tragic, 4, 200–201n9
optimistic pessimism, 4
order, and disorder, 54
orthodox uniformity, 2–3
the Other: being and, 155; consciousness of, 170–171; death and, 128–129, 170; God and, 296n79; in Lacan, 125; in Levinas, 128–129, 145, 152, 175; love of, 170; plurality of, 89
Otherwise Than Being or Beyond Essence (Levinas), 171–177
Owl of Minerva, 69

parable, contrasted with allegory, 65
parabolic dissimulation, 60–66
Paradise Lost (Milton), 5
Paradiso (Rose), 95, 109–110
paradox: α and ¬α, 9; the beginning before the beginning, 68; concurrent concealment and disclosure, 218n70; confluence of manifest and unmanifest, 48; desire not to desire, 152; dialetheic, 66, 84; the distance that is proximate, 177; and the excluded middle, 37; giving by withholding, 285n245; the hope of hopelessness, 191; and Kafka, 159, 161; and Kierkegaardian irony, 95–96, 163; knot of, 97; liar's, 105; of novel repetition, 244n33; of the present, 190; repetition as iteration of the same, 139; the saying not-saying, 60; simultaneity of the nonsimultaneous, 137; the success of failure, 167; of the trace, 147, 150; of Zeno, 117
"Paraphrase of the Prose of 'The Diary'" (Scholem), 192–193
Parmenides, 215n57, 285n245, 295n73
parousia, time of, 244n36
Pascal, 131
passion, 4, 58, 72, 96, 162; apocalyptic, 192; and eros, 74; ethical, 161, 163; of faith, 74, 85; sacramental, 84;

the Passion, 96
past, 136–137, 140, 193–194, 275n126, 278n147
patience, 191–192
Paul, 223n102, 244n36
permanence, 17, 58, 120, 181, 214n57
pessimism, 75, 159, 177, 200n6, 202n26, 305n158
pessimistic utopianism, 188
phenomenology: of consciousness, 99; of eternity, 52; of the event, 312n177; Heidegger and, 310n177; and history, 276n126; of Husserl, 145, 147, 171; of the inapparent, 297n88; Levinas and, 149, 171–172; nocturnal, 293n48; nonintentional, 149; of Romano, 191, 311n177
Phenomenology of Mind (Hegel), 77
Phenomenology of Spirit (Hegel), 68
philology, 214n57, 255n170
"Les Philosophes et leur Langage" (Belaval), 55
philosophical inquiry, 16–17, 52–53
Philosophical Investigations into the Essence of Human Freedom (Schelling), 164–167
philosophy: end of the end of, 105; positioned between potentiality and actuality of the world, 75–76; unsayable and incommunicable element of thought, 209n73
Philosophy in the Tragic Age of the Greeks (Nietzsche), 27
physics, deliverance from the laws of, 49
piety, impiety of, 34–41; of hopelessness, 180; of thought, 134
Plaskow, Judith, 78
Plato, 16, 144, 209n73, 285n245
pluralism, 16
plurivocality, heteromorphic sense of, 120; of the rabbinic hermeneutic, 173; of the singular, 72
poetry: of Celan, 171, 175; Heidegger and, 60, 63, 238n240, 269–270n67; hope and, 195–196; language in, 180–181; Levinas and, 155–156; poetic language, 155, 236n229; poetic speech, 60–66; poetic stuttering, 151–157; religion and, 56; saying the unsayable, 60–61, 155; writing of after Auschwitz, 156
"Poet's Calling" (Hölderlin), 47

poiēsis, 63, 154, 156, 269n58
Polish Commission on the Future of Auschwitz, 110–111
politics: of capitalism, 247n54; ethics and, 1–2; knowledge and, 113; of messianism, 308n174; of National Socialism, 126–129; of Nazism, 273n105; theopolitical discourse, 7; theopolitical resignation, 177–183; *Weltpolitik*, 190; world, 181
polyontological difference, 16
polysemic language, 151–157
positivity, 209n75
possibility: beyond apocalypse, 190–191; of change, 206n64; hope and, 16–17, 123; imageless image of, 174; impossibility of, 16
postmodernism/postmodernity: antinomianism of, 70; contemporary philosophy and, 81–82; contrasted with broken middle, 83; in culture, 155; and deconstructionism, 80, 90; and deconstruction of language, 152; epistemological skepticism of, 100; ethos of, 151; false promise of, 69; metaphysics in, 89–90; new ethics of, 89; opposites in, 80; postmodern sensibility, 151; post-theological theology, 110; theology in, 108–109; thought in, 69–70; utopianism of, 101; Western metaphysics in, 82–83, 214n57
poverty, 14
power, 106, 109–111, 272n98
"Praise of Distance" (Celan), 171
prayer, 49, 74, 96, 110; and mourning, 195–196; and Torah study, 38
prejudice, 258n199
presence, 17, 167–168, 176–177
primitive myths, 19–20
Problemata (pseudo-Aristotle), 10–11, 238n245
prophecies, 194
pseudo-messianism, 190–191
psychology: axiology and, 135; of childhood, 44–45; of Dasein, 56–57, 189; despondency, 4; diaries, 42–43; from Freud, 86, 91; guilt, 156–157; of Judaism, 151–152; of melancholia, 21–22; of mortality, 131–132; of nihilism, 159; of opposites, 9–10; the Other and, 120–122, 125–126, 129, 145; resignation, 177–183; separation, 66; solitude, 14; tautology and, 175–176; writing, 64
punctiformity, of space, 122, 124

qaddish, 195–196

Ramatayim Ṣofim (Samuel of Sieniawa), 40
Raschke, Carl, 149
rationalism, 76–80
realism, 275n126, 280n154
reality: in Beshṭian Ḥasidism, 38–39; in Buddhism, 62; finitude of, 166; gnosis and, 21; God and, 23–24; linearity and, 42–43; memory and, 53; ontological untruth of, 53–59; opposites in, 11–12; truth and, 30–31, 252n124; and unreality, 153
reason, 76–80; of Athens, 85; and unreason, 82, 249n76, 259n199
recollection/remembrance (*Eingedenken*), 45, 228n144
rectification (*tiqqun*), 37–38, 40–41, 124–125
redemption, 25, 36, 49, 58, 98, 114, 181, 190, 195; flash of, 97; from the need to be redeemed, 113; and melancholy, 168, 179; through sin, 36, 222n98
reductionism, 76
reification, 78
reiteration, 136; of the again, 99; of the new, 311; of the novel, 7
releasement, 61; to the open-region, 319n197; of time, 125
religiosity, 161–163
renunciation (*Verzicht*), 61–62, 269n67
repetition, of again as altogether otherwise, 48, 139–140; freedom and, 248n67; inducement of, 68; movement of, 90; novel, 244n33; novelty and, 312–313n177; replication of difference, 278n146; of the same, 79; sameness and, 140, 279n148
representation: aesthetic, 72; and configural misrepresentation, 114; imagistic, 66, 150; pictorial, 41; role of language, 236n229; rule of the word, 62; secular, 128; subjectivity beyond, 145
resignation, 177–183
responsibility, 146–147

restlessness, 13, 145, 146–147
resurrection, 43–44, 191; hope of, 24; promise of, 58
revelation, 25, 51–52, 87, 98, 107, 138, 296n79; and concealment, 148; and the epiphany of the face, 296n79; of the eventual, 191; of Ḥasdisim, 39–40; and the infinition of infinity, 147; of the infinite, 148; and the metaphysical desire for infinity, 147; of mourning's self-overturning, 187; of nothing to be revealed, 130; nothingness of, 299–300n124; in the Other, 94; of the *Zohar*, 39
"Review of *Tragedy and the Paradox of the Fortunate* by Herbert Weisinger" (Taubes, S.), 36
Rickert, Heinrich, 245–246n42
Rilke, Rainer Maria, 143, 156–157
Rimbaud, Arthur, 56
Romano, Claude, 191, 310–311n177
Rose, Gillian: Adorno and, 75–77, 247n54, 253n156, 254n162m 258n199; anxiety, 68–69; beholding darkness, 6; on Benjamin and Derrida, 261n218; on comedy, 161; conversion to Christianity, 86–87, 250n95; critique of postmodernism, 69–70, 80–83, 89–90, 100–103, 108–109; epistemology of, 245n42; ethical character of *agapē*, 91; facetious irony, 88–94; on feminism, 247n55; on freedom, 81; Gnosticism, 95, 112–115; Hegel, 83–84, 242n16, 253n136; Heidegger, 255n168, 255n170; illness of, 3; irony, 160; Judaism, 102; Kafka, 163; Kierkegaard, 72, 83, 90, 96–97; Levinas and, 147, 176; melancholia, 8–11; on modernity, 248n71; nihilism, 79, 100–101; notion of the middle, 110–111; on rationalism, 76–80; on suffering, 3, 93–94; seeing the dark, 69–76; Taubes, J., and, 181–182; Taubes, S., and, 99; transcendence, 252n125; truth, 11–12
Rosenzweig, Franz, 188, 243n33, 306nn167–168
Russia, 91–92

Sabbath, 40, 123–125, 223n102, 268n53, 289n31

salvation, 58–59
sameness, of antinomies, 9; of being, 207n67; of difference, 38–39, 66; and repetition, 140, 279n148
Samuel of Sieniawa, 40
Sartre, Jean-Paul, 3
Saturn, and melancholia, 289–290n31
saturnine distrust, 179
saturnine melancholy, 299n120
saying, 61, 63, 122, 127, 143, 145, 155–156, 173–175; differentiated from the said, 143, 173–174; not-saying, 60; as showing, 63; and the trace of infinity, 174; and the unsaid, 136; the unsayable, 155; unspoken, 63
saying-after (*Nachsagen*), 63
Schelling, Friedrich Wilhelm Joseph, 164–167, 203n38, 206n56, 217n59, 240n256, 290n37
Schneerson, Menaḥem Mendel, 225n114
Scholem, Gershom, 36, 65, 177–183, 187–194; Benjamin and, 180–181, 192–193, 298n116, 299–300n124; Bloch and, 177; on book of Jonah, 317n194; distinction between symbol and allegory, 65; Gnosticism, 304n156; interpretation of Jewish messianism, 190, 193–194, 222n98, 308nn174, 175; Judaism, 306n166; melancholy and, 180, 298n115; Rosenzweig's view of, 304n158; on sanctity of Hebrew language, 306n167; Taubes, S., and, 36, 37, 65, 222n98; Zionism and, 177–180, 206n58, 299n117, 305n159, 305n164
Schopenhauer, Arthur, 3–4
Schürmann, Reiner, 49, 132–133
secrecy, double bind of, 150; double structure of, 192
secret, apocalyptic, 191; of Christianity, 317n194; enunciated by kabbalists, 38; hidden through exposure, 150, 153, 156, of secrecy, 150; of subjectivity, 147; uttered nakedly, 64
secular: atheology, 25; order, 190; religion, 7; state of limbo, 51; world, 181
secularization, of holy language, 189
Seinsdenken, 19–20, 66
Seinsvergessenheit, 28, 30
self-denial, 269n67

372 Index

self-destruction, 4, 71
self-esteem, 120
self-exile, 124
selfhood, 162, 165–166, 171, 174–175, 292n47
self-negation, 176
self-revelation, 95
separation, from the absolute, 26, 41, 66
setting-upon (*Stellen*), 126
sexuality, 86, 250n88
Shanks, Andrew, 87
Shapira, Kalonymus Kalman, 39–40
Shelley, Percy Bysshe, 56
signification, 20, 143, 152–153, 175; beyond being, 175; beyond essence, 144; of death, 132
silence: Dasein and, 60–61; death and, 131; disappearance of time and, 43; of grace, 96; guarding of truth and, 64; Heidegger's view of, 62–63; kataphatic avowal of apophatic disavowal, 187; language and, 60–62; as mystery, 130; and nothingness of God, 23; of not speaking, 60–61; restraint of speaking-not, 62; sacramental passion and, 84; of the sceptic, 172; spoken through the hyperbolic passivity of giving, 173–174; of temporal interval, 43; truth and, 64
Silouan, Staretz, 3, 91–92
Simḥah Bunem of Przysucha, 40
ṣimṣum, 124, 217n59
simultaneity, nonintentional, 172; of the clandestine and the exposed, 153; of disclosure and concealing, 26; of past, present, and future, 52; of the nonsimultaneous, 137; of three tenses in the instant, 53; of time, 50
sin, 36–37
singular, *agapē* of, 102; aporetic universalism and, 103; infiltration of, 6; plurivocality of, 72; truth of beyng, 215n57; and the universal and the particular, 83–84
singularity: Heidegger's view of, 208n71, 215–216n57; infinitesimal point of, 124; of the middle, 81–88; of the moment, 49; nameless, 145; of the subject, 148; temporality of the event, 311n177; truth of beyng and, 215n57; uniqueness and, 16
Sittlichkeit (ethical life), 114–115
skeptical faith, 20–25, 53–54

skepticism, 94–95, 283n196
slave labor camps, 133
social criticism, 76–77
Socialism, 304n158
social theory, 90, 113, 146–147
social world, 232n173
Socrates, 16, 78
solitude (*Einsamkeit*), 12, 14, 16, 206n62, 208n72; and philosophical life, 209n73
Sollers, Phillipe, 284n219
Soloveitchik, Joseph B., 223n104
Song of Songs, 85–86, 250n88
soul, 166; dark night of, 55, 95
space, 39, 43, 122–124; of the broken middle, 76; and death event, 132, 154; of différance, 154; of divergence, 128; discursive, 154; homogenization into now-points, 138; intersubjective, 135; nonspatiality of, 125; of the opening, 62; of the present, 49; punctiformity of, 122, 124; temporalization of, 57, 124; of time, 190; and Zeno's paradoxes, 117
spacetime, vacuum of, 181
speaking-not, 60, 62, 84, 143
spectrality, 196–197
speech: cessation of, 6; of death-world, 131; infinite fecundity of, 143; in Levinas contrasted with Heidegger, 281n172; melancholic, 185; poetic, 60–66; unavowable, 150; without speech, 186
speechlessness (*Sprachlosigkeit*), 186, 303n152; of nature, 187
Spinoza, 225n114, 307n168
spirit, 32–33, 68–69, 82–88, 120, 130–131, 142, 166
spiritual eros, 86, 250n88
spiritual world, 160–161
Stearns, Isabel, 20
Steinschneider, Karl, 180–181
stillness, 61; peal of, 128; of silence, 235n224
Stummheit, 186, 303n152
stutter/stutterer, 152, 154
suchness (*tathātā*), 104; constituted by emptiness, 62
suicide, 3, 22, 34, 58, 134, 183, 185, 221n88
suffering: acceptance of, 92–93; Hegel on, 70–71, 142; in humanity, 7; Rose's view of, 3, 93–94
śūnyatā. *See* emptiness
sympathy, and ethical resistance, 172

system, 70–76, 254n159; Adorno on, 73; and antisystem, 74; authority of, 67; and fragment, 67, 73; Hegel and, 46, 70; hypersystem, 72; lack of, 70; open, 72; of signs, 140, 143; totalizing nature of, 70; of traces, 150

taciturnity, 60, 132
Taoism, 237n236, 274n109
tathātā. See suchness
Taubes, Jacob, 32, 40–41, 54; correspondence with, 19–22, 25–26, 31–32, 49–50, 54–55, 58, 64–65; Hans Jonas and, 211n18; heresy versus paganism of Susan, 211n11; interpretation of Benjamin, 300n128; Rose and, 181–182
Taubes, Susan: Camus and, 25, 51, 221n88; on Campbell, 50; Christianity and, 46, 223n102; criticism of Hegel, 59; criticism of Heidegger, 14–15, 19–20, 28–29, 32–33; Descartes and, 35–36, 226n126; family of, 233n184; Gnosticism and, 20–21; kabbalah and, 37, 65, 217n59; Kant and, 34–35; madness and, 27–28; melancholia and, 8–11; More and, 212–213n30; mysticism and, 41–42; Nietzsche and, 219n80; nihilism and, 22–23, 30; on nothingness, 48–49; on perfection and imperfection, 6, 25, 31; poetic speech, 60–66; reflections on death, 31–33; Rose and, 99; Scholem and, 222n98; sin, 36–37; suicide, 3–4; on tautology, 240n256; on temporarily, 210n5; time in the philosophy of, 51–53; truth and, 11–12; on Weil, 23–24, 45, 213n33; on wholeness, 40–41
tautology, 175–176, 240n256
Taylor, Mark, 108, 149, 239n246
technology, 126–129, 268n58
temperament: demeanor of, 166; melancholic, 9, 182–183; mystical, 39; philosophical, 94
temporality: anticipation of death, 264n17; authentic, 57, 234n198; Dasein and, 44, 57; diachronic, 286n248, 310n177; diremptive, 7, 193; and eternal ideas, 252n124; eternalization of, 123; finitude of, 36; horizon of, 44; nonlinear conception of, 210n5; outside the contours of chronological time, 311n177; redeemed, 124; shudder of, 44; suspension of, 187–197; temporalization of, 57; of this-worldliness, 42
temporalization, of eternity, 123; of space, 57, 124
temporal path, 63–64
tertium quid, 88, 105–106, 110
testimony, 174
Tetragrammaton, 98, 255n168
"Theological-Political Fragment" (Benjamin), 189–190
theology: apophatic, 152; atheistic, 21; Christian, 46; Dasein and, 46; Heidegger and, 230n154; Kierkegaardian, 96; mystical, 85; negative, 23, 84, 142, 152; political, 100; postmodern, 108; post-theological, 110; Sabbatian, 188; and the trace, 150, 264–265n24; theological discourse, 150
theopolitical discourse, 7
theopolitical resignation, 177–183
third city, 110–111, 262n231
Thucydides, 3
Thus Spoke Zarathustra (Nietzsche), 12–13
time: Aristotle on, 266n38; authentic, 139; beginning of, 310n177; circuitous in its linearity, 57; clock, 139; dark diachronicity of, 122; Dasein and, 44; death and, 45, 56–59; and Derrida, 137; diachronicity and, 177; dys-chrony and, 74; evanescence of, 17; experience of, 278n147; future and, 193–194; God and, 49; Heidegger and, 232n173, 233n197; Holocaust and, 135–136; ideality of space, 122; infinity of, 122–123; Jewish messianic speculation and, 7–8; Levinas and, 153, 168, 177, 282n181; linear circle of, 106; monstrosity of, 53; negative infinity of, 122; negativity of, 190–191; nocturnal, 168; nontemporality of, 125; nothingness and, 46–47; now-time, 45, 97, 228n145; paradox of, 68–69, 73–74; soteriology of Sabbath, 124–125; spatialization of, 57; structure of, 136; subjectivity of, 44–45; system and, 72; Taubes, S., and, 51–53; and timelessness in Benjamin, 42–43; timeliness of, 53; time-space, 122–124; timeswerve, 52, 68, 238n245, 311n177; tradition and, 52
time-space, 128, 140, 282n181

374 Index

Tolstoy, Leo, 160
Torah, 38, 50, 98, 108, 250n88, 255n167
totalitarianism, 4
"Toward an Understanding of the Messianic Idea in Judaism" (Scholem), 190–191
trace, of an abandon, 174; apophatic nature of, 150; of beyond-being, 144, 282n181; of departure, 147; and the face, 174–175; of illeity, 149; of infinity, 174; mark of the sacred, 150; origin and, 265n24; paradox of, 147, 150; of the past, 75, 149, 265n24; signifier of absent presence, 150, 175–176; of silence, 131; and time, 264–265n24; visible invisibility of, 147; of withdrawal, 146, 153
tragedy: comedy and, 101–102, 288n10; culture and, 24; death and, 41–42; epistemology of, 71
Tragedy and the Paradox of the Fortunate (Weisinger), 36
tragicomedy, 3, 69–76
Trakl, Georg, 191–192
transcendence: axiology of, 245n42; deconstruction and, 152; diachronic, 143–150; erotics of, 152–153; immanence and, 91, 152, 153, 252n124; infinite, 140; Levinas and, 143–149; Rose and, 252n125; Wyschogrod and, 124, 140, 152–153, 264–265n24
Trauerspiel (Benjamin), 184, 289n31, 302–303n150
trust, in God, 34
truth: Adorno's critique of the immutability of, 252n124; appearance of, 11; appropriative event of, 30–31; art and, 105; distortion of, 11–12; duplicitous, 159–163; God and, 58; Hegel on, 122, 129–130, 136; Heidegger's view of, 26–27, 61, 172–173; hope of hopelessness and, 25–34; inseparability of light and darkness, 77; Kafka's view of, 103–105, 160, 258n196; knowledge and, 114–115; metaphysics as destruction of, 29; naked, 11, 65, 166; Nietzsche's view of, 7; silence and, 64; singularity and, 215n57; of space, 124; truthful duplicity, 159–163; untruth and, 101–110; veil of, 11–12, 65–66, 156

uncanniness (*Unheimlichkeit*), 13, 189; of Hebrew, 307n168
understanding, 101
underway (*Unterwegs*), 13, 134
uniqueness, 16
universal history, 254n162
unmasking, 5, 102, 151, 154, 159–163, 190
unnameable, 45, 183–187
unreality, of the present, 193–194; threshold of the real, 153
unreason, of Jerusalem, 85; and reason, 82, 249n76, 259n199
unsaid (*Ungesagte*), 61–62, 237n235
unsayable (*Unsägliche*), 61, 130, 155
unsaying, 145, 154
unspoken (*Ungesprochene*), dimension of language, 61, 63; and poetic discourse, 63, 238n240; preserved by the spoken, 237n236; source of the spoken, 61; and the unsaid, 62–63, 237n235
unthought, 121, 237n235
untruth, 80; error of, 59; ontological, 31, 53, 66; stems from double negation, 30; in theopolitical discourse, 7; truth and, 11–12, 26, 30, 53, 63, 98–99, 101–110, 173, 213n39, 213–214n43, 218n70; veil of, 65, 104; veiling of the Being, 28
untruthfulness, 29
unveiling, 17, 26, 30, 39–40, 59, 65–66, 172
utopia, 183, 193–194

value, 272n98
Vedānta, 35
veil, appearing as what veils, 156; lifting of, 97; of melancholy, 206n156; of nature, 164–167; of night, 192; of truth, 11–12, 65–66, 156; of untruth, 65, 104; unveiling, 17, 26, 30, 39–40, 59, 65–66, 172; veiling of being, 11, 28–29
Vergehen, 118
via negativa, 64
void, 45, 48–49, 62, 105, 129–130, 154, 176

Wahl, Jean, 56
waiting/awaiting: anxiety of death, 170; for the future, 50; impossibility of waiting, 191; nothing awaited, 155; nothing more to await, 167–177; for the redeemer, 7; refusal to wait, 191; solitary, 168; wait

for waiting, 168; without an awaited, 177, 286n248
Weil, Simone, 23–25, 45–46, 48–49; agnosticism, 93; Christianity, 51; Gnosticism, 23–24; Levinas and, 89; mystical piety, 45–46; on mysticism, 78–79; Taubes, S., and, 23–24, 45, 213n33
Weisinger, Herbert, 36
Weltpolitik, 181, 190
Western metaphysics, 27, 82, 108
wholeness, 40–41
Wildmann, Yiṣḥaq Eizik Ḥaver, 38
Windischmann, Karl Joseph Hieronymus, 8
Wittgenstein, Ludwig, 239n251, 288n10
Wordsworth, William, 56
world-picture (*Welt-bild*), 156
world politics, 181
World-Spirit, 129–130
World War I, 201n17
World War II, 190–191, 201n17. *See also* Holocaust
Woolf, Virginia, 206n57
writing, 64, 123, 228n145
The Writing of Disaster (Blanchot), 134–135
Wyllie, Martin, 195
Wyschogrod, Edith: absence of noumenal truth, 154; brokenheartedness and, 151–157; death, 116–119; demythologizing, 119–126; Derrida and, 268n53, 277n128, 284n219; diachronic transcendence, 143–150; distinction between concentration camp and extermination camp, 271n95; Hegel and, 124–125, 136; Heidegger and, 138, 270n76, 272n104; heterological epiphany and seeing nothing to be seen, 135–142; heterology and, 149, 280n157; on negation, 129–135; Nietzsche and, 268n57; on poetry, 154–157; reflections on the Holocaust, 131–132, 142, 151, 276n126; task of the historian, 6, 123, 136–141, 149, 280n156; on transcendence, 264n24; technology, 126–129

"Year" (Trakl), 191–192

Zarader, Marléne, 276–277n126, 310–313n177
Zellman, Christian Gotthold, 16
Zeno, 117
Zerstörung, 133–134
Zionism, 51, 177–180, 188–191, 206n58, 304n158, 305n164
Zohar, 37–38
Zukünftigkeit (futuricity), 138–139
Zürau aphorisms, 103, 160

Cultural Memory in the *Present*

Severo Sarduy, *Barroco and Other Writings*

David D. Kim, *Arendt's Solidarity: Anti-Semitism and Racism in the Atlantic World*

Hans Joas, *Why the Church?: Self-Optimization or Community of Faith*

Jean-Luc Marion, *Revelation Comes from Elsewhere*

Peter Sloterdijk, *Out of the World*

Christopher J. Wild, *Descartes' Meditative Turn: The Practice of Thought*

Eli Friedlander, *Walter Benjamin and the Idea of Natural History*

Helmut Puff, *The Antechamber: Toward a History of Waiting*

Raúl E. Zegarra, *A Revolutionary Faith: Liberation Theology Between Public Religion and Public Reason*

David Simpson, *Engaging Violence: Civility and the Reach of Literature*

Michael Steinberg, *The Afterlife of Moses: Exile, Democracy, Renewal*

Alain Badiou, *Badiou by Badiou*, translated by Bruno Bosteels

Eric Song, *Love against Substitution: Seventeenth-Century English Literature and the Meaning of Marriage*

Niklaus Largier, *Figures of Possibility: Aesthetic Experience, Mysticism, and the Play of the Senses*

Mihaela Mihai, *Political Memory and the Aesthetics of Care: The Art of Complicity and Resistance*

Ethan Kleinberg, *Emmanuel Levinas's Talmudic Turn: Philosophy and Jewish Thought*

Willemien Otten, *Thinking Nature and the Nature of Thinking: From Eriugena to Emerson*

Michael Rothberg, *The Implicated Subject: Beyond Victims and Perpetrators*

Hans Ruin, *Being with the Dead: Burial, Ancestral Politics, and the Roots of Historical Consciousness*

Eric Oberle, *Theodor Adorno and the Century of Negative Identity*

David Marriott, *Whither Fanon? Studies in the Blackness of Being*

Reinhart Koselleck, *Sediments of Time: On Possible Histories*, translated and edited by Sean Franzel and Stefan-Ludwig Hoffmann

Devin Singh, *Divine Currency: The Theological Power of Money in the West*

Stefanos Geroulanos, *Transparency in Postwar France: A Critical History of the Present*

Sari Nusseibeh, *The Story of Reason in Islam*

Olivia C. Harrison, *Transcolonial Maghreb: Imagining Palestine in the Era of Decolonization*

Barbara Vinken, *Flaubert Postsecular: Modernity Crossed Out*

Aishwary Kumar, *Radical Equality: Ambedkar, Gandhi, and the Problem of Democracy*

Simona Forti, *New Demons: Rethinking Power and Evil Today*

Joseph Vogl, *The Specter of Capital*

Hans Joas, *Faith as an Option*

Michael Gubser, *The Far Reaches: Ethics, Phenomenology, and the Call for Social Renewal in Twentieth-Century Central Europe*

Françoise Davoine, *Mother Folly: A Tale*

Knox Peden, *Spinoza Contra Phenomenology: French Rationalism from Cavaillès to Deleuze*

Elizabeth A. Pritchard, *Locke's Political Theology: Public Religion and Sacred Rights*

Ankhi Mukherjee, *What Is a Classic? Postcolonial Rewriting and Invention of the Canon*

Jean-Pierre Dupuy, *The Mark of the Sacred*

Henri Atlan, *Fraud: The World of Ona'ah*

Niklas Luhmann, *Theory of Society, Volume 2*

Ilit Ferber, *Philosophy and Melancholy: Benjamin's Early Reflections on Theater and Language*

Alexandre Lefebvre, *Human Rights as a Way of Life: On Bergson's Political Philosophy*

Theodore W. Jennings, Jr., *Outlaw Justice: The Messianic Politics of Paul*

Alexander Etkind, *Warped Mourning: Stories of the Undead in the Land of the Unburied*

Denis Guénoun, *About Europe: Philosophical Hypotheses*

Maria Boletsi, *Barbarism and Its Discontents*

Sigrid Weigel, *Walter Benjamin: Images, the Creaturely, and the Holy*

Roberto Esposito, *Living Thought: The Origins and Actuality of Italian Philosophy*

Henri Atlan, *The Sparks of Randomness, Volume 2: The Atheism of Scripture*

Rüdiger Campe, *The Game of Probability: Literature and Calculation from Pascal to Kleist*

Niklas Luhmann, *A Systems Theory of Religion*

Jean-Luc Marion, *In the Self's Place: The Approach of Saint Augustine*

Rodolphe Gasché, *Georges Bataille: Phenomenology and Phantasmatology*

Niklas Luhmann, *Theory of Society, Volume 1*

Alessia Ricciardi, *After La Dolce Vita: A Cultural Prehistory of Berlusconi's Italy*

Daniel Innerarity, *The Future and Its Enemies: In Defense of Political Hope*

Patricia Pisters, *The Neuro-Image: A Deleuzian Film-Philosophy of Digital Screen Culture*

François-David Sebbah, *Testing the Limit: Derrida, Henry, Levinas, and the Phenomenological Tradition*

Erik Peterson, *Theological Tractates*, edited by Michael J. Hollerich

Feisal G. Mohamed, *Milton and the Post-Secular Present: Ethics, Politics, Terrorism*

Pierre Hadot, *The Present Alone Is Our Happiness, Second Edition: Conversations with Jeannie Carlier and Arnold I. Davidson*

Yasco Horsman, *Theaters of Justice: Judging, Staging, and Working Through in Arendt, Brecht, and Delbo*

Jacques Derrida, *Parages*, edited by John P. Leavey

For a complete listing of titles in this series, visit the Stanford University Press website, www.sup.org.

The authorized representative in the EU for product safety and compliance is:
Mare Nostrum Group
B.V Doelen 72
4831 GR Breda
The Netherlands

www.ingramcontent.com/pod-product-compliance
Lightning Source LLC
Chambersburg PA
CBHW030602230426
43661CB00053B/1813